JOSEPH BANKS

in Newfoundland and Labrador, 1766

JOSEPH BANKS

in Newfoundland
and Labrador, 1766

His Diary, Manuscripts

and Collections

★

A. M. LYSAGHT

WITH A FOREWORD BY
the Hon. Joseph Smallwood

UNIVERSITY OF CALIFORNIA PRESS

Berkeley and Los Angeles

University of California Press
Berkeley and Los Angeles

First published in 1971
by Faber and Faber Limited
3 Queen Square London WC1
Printed in Great Britain by
W. & J. Mackay & Co Ltd Chatham
Colour plates and charts printed by
W. S. Cowell Ltd Ipswich

ISBN 0 520 01780 3
LCCC No. 70–81800

To my Mother
and in grateful memory of
Harry Borrer Kirk
✝ 1948
from 1903 to 1944
Professor of Biology
at Victoria College, Wellington
New Zealand

Foreword

by the Hon. Joseph Smallwood
Premier of Newfoundland

DOCTOR Lysaght has written a book that will take its place at once with the dozen greatest works written about Newfoundland or anything connected with Newfoundland. When the reader remembers that Sir Richard Whitbourne wrote his book about Newfoundland in 1622, and that Sir William Vaughan wrote three books about this island, my statement may appear to be somewhat extravagant. W. E. Cormack's 'Account of a Journey Across the Island of Newfoundland', 1824, is one of our Newfoundland classics. Philip Henry Gosse did a very notable book on one aspect of this island's life. Daniel Woodley Prowse in 1895 published what has ever since been regarded as the classic history of the island. Cartwright's Journal ranks high in our Newfoundland literature. Harold A. Innis and Ralph Greenlee Lounsbury wrote the two great books on the cod fisheries of this island. In 1915 James P. Howley produced 'The Beothuks or Red Indians', and that is the finest thing of its kind yet written. As late as 1944, V. Tanner did his great work, 'Outlines of the Geography, Life and Customs of Newfoundland-Labrador'.

Doctor Lysaght's book opens a rich new vein in our Newfoundland and Labrador story, and she mines it with great skill, efficiency, tidiness, and a never-ending interest. Scholarship is written all over it. The book is quite evidently a work of love as well as scholarship on the author's part. It is obvious that she enjoyed doing it, as we enjoy reading it.

No one will read this book with such profound interest as Newfoundlanders will do, for they take unending delight in any good writing about their island story or anything connected with it. The sad thing about that story is the fact that most of the writing has been done, not by Newfoundlanders themselves, but by others who fell in love with Newfoundland or with some part of it. We have gained immeasurably by the calibre of many of those writers; it is not every small island that has a Philip Henry Gosse or an Averil Lysaght.

Of course we cannot claim Joseph Banks merely because he visited Newfoundland and did some of his work here: but we do claim him as one of the procession of great Englishmen, Scots, Welsh and Irish explorers, seamen, artists, hunters, scientists, writers, who have come to see us through the centuries since we became Britain's first colony, 'the first of Britain overseas'. We cannot even claim Cartwright himself as a Newfoundlander, though he spent all those years in the Labrador part of the

7

FOREWORD

colony. (It was at Cartwright, the Labrador seaport named after that remarkable man, that another remarkable man, Clarence Birdseye, the American, noticed the way that fish caught through the ice, when laid on the ice, froze as hard as a plank and, though kept for months in that frozen state, were just as fresh when thawed out as when they came out of the water, and thereby discovered a fact that enabled him to lay the foundation of the remarkable quick-freeze industry.)

This is a delightful book in many different ways, and it will be added to the library of every real reader everywhere; or if not, shame on them!

Joseph R. Smallwood,
Premier's Office,
St. John's,
Newfoundland.

Preface and acknowledgements

THIS publication of Banks's Newfoundland-Labrador diary, with the associated MSS and plates, was undertaken for three reasons: to record the first extensive and properly documented scientific collections from that region; to show the outstanding ability and accomplishment of Joseph Banks at the age of twenty three, working alone on a new fauna and flora under the strenuous conditions of the eighteenth century, and to give some personal details about Banks and his friend George Cartwright, usually regarded as the father of ornithology in Labrador.

Banks arrived at St. John's on 11 May 1766, spent the spring, summer and autumn on that coast, sailing north to Labrador, and left St. John's for Lisbon on 28 October. He was ill most of July, yet in four and a half months he had collected or recorded 340 species of plants, 91 species of birds, and a number of fishes and invertebrates. It would be a creditable achievement for one man today; how much more so under the cramped and rigorous conditions of 1766. The difficulties he successfully overcame in Newfoundland and Labrador gave him the experience and confidence to organize so superbly the scientific staff and equipment of Captain Cook's great voyages round the world. His own achievements have been underrated because the results of his work were not published under his name, and because on his voyage in the *Endeavour* (1768–71) with Captain Cook he was accompanied by one of Linnaeus's brightest pupils, Daniel Solander, and by three skilled draughtsmen, Parkinson, Spöring and Buchan. It has been believed that Banks featured as their wealthy employer rather than as the experienced and highly qualified leader of an able and industrious group of young men. His wealth too has helped in the current view of his abilities since he had an assured position and clearly was driven by no great urge to publish his own records; moreover he was always exceedingly generous in lending other scientists his material and MSS, and many of his discoveries have been published by other men. For these reasons he has been dubbed the Gentleman Amateur of Science. If we take our definitions from the sporting pages of the Press and make clear that such is our standard, this is acceptable. Banks certainly did not make his living from practising science. Darwin too can equally well be regarded as a Gentleman Amateur; he died worth £100,000, not through his sales of the *Origin of Species*, nor from his books on earthworms or on orchids, but because each morning of the week he brought his large intelligence to bear on the columns of the *Financial Times*, and was an expert on the Stock Exchange. If we abandon the sporting Press and turn to the *Shorter Oxford*

English Dictionary (1945) we find amateur defined as 'one who loves, or has a taste for, or is fond of anything', and amateurish as 'having the faults of a. work'. There is a slightly derogatory flavour about the entries. But Banks was well trained, fundamentally serious and extremely industrious in all his scientific undertakings.

The publication of this book would have been impossible if a large number of busy people had not co-operated with me in trying to cover some part of the great range of Banks's interests; it is difficult to thank them all adequately for the time and scholarship which they have given in the search for and the identification of Banks's various specimens and manuscripts.

The final stages of the work have been helped by a grant from the British Museum (Natural History) for work on Banks's plants, and by grants from the American Philosophical Society and from the Chapman Memorial Fund, which have enabled me to visit Newfoundland, McGill University, Montreal, and libraries and museums in New York and Pittsburgh. I wish to express my best thanks to the Trustees of these funds for their help, and I am deeply grateful to Dr. Dean Amadon, Dr. R. C. Murphy, Dr. Erwin Stresemann and Dr. Charles Vaurie for their practical aid and encouragement in connection with these visits and the completion of this research.

The publication of the natural history drawings and maps would have been impossible had not the Council of the Library of New South Wales advanced a generous subsidy towards publication costs.

Banks's Newfoundland and Labrador MSS are scattered. The botanical drawings are in the British Museum (Natural History), where are also Banks's catalogue of the plants he collected, his sister's transcript of his diary, and other relevant MSS. The zoological drawings are in the Print Room of the British Museum. I wish to express my thanks to the Trustees of both institutions for the abundant facilities I have been given in studying these papers, and for permission to publish them.

Banks's holograph diary is in the possession of the South Australian branch of the Royal Geographical Society in Adelaide. I am very grateful to the President and Council of that body for granting me the privilege of publishing the diary.

Banks's long-lost zoological notebook is in McGill University Library. It is a pleasure to acknowledge my debt to Miss Margaret Hibbard, formerly of the Blacker Library, McGill, who in 1956 drew my attention to that manuscript which had been acquired by McGill from a dealer shortly before the Second World War. The Newfoundland and Labrador bird paintings had been found in the Print Room only two or three years earlier and I had been looking for the notebook ever since. Its discovery made the publication of the 1766 diary possible.

It is difficult to make adequate acknowledgement of what I owe to Miss Phyllis Mander Jones, former Mitchell Librarian of the Library of New South Wales where there are very large holdings of Banks papers. It was indeed fortunate for me that she has been working in London in recent years and that I have been able to ask for her help and advice in all sorts of matters connected with the progress of this book.

PREFACE AND ACKNOWLEDGEMENTS

I owe a special debt to the late Sir Norman Kinnear and to Dr. John Beaglehole, who first interested me in the zoological collections made on Cook's voyages and gave me the chance to work on them.

Many past and present members of the staff of the British Museum (Natural History) have assisted me to identify Banks's specimens. In the following list their names appear against the groups with which they were concerned; my thanks are due to them for their help given over many years:

CRUSTACEA	Dr. J. P. Harding	MOLLUSCA	Mr. S. P. Dance
	Dr. Isabella Gordon	ECHINODERMATA	Miss A. M. Clark
INSECTA	Dr. W. E. China	FISHES	Dr. E. Trewavas
	Mr. N. D. Riley		Dr. N. B. Marshall
	Mr. E. G. Brittain		Mr. A. C. Wheeler
	Mr. P. Freeman	MAMMALIA	Dr. P. Crowcroft
	Miss C. M. F. von Hayek		Dr. G. B. Corbet
	Mr. D. E. Kimmins		Miss Jean Ellis
	Mr. H. Oldroyd		Mr. R. W. Hayman
	Dr. Richard Thompson		Miss Judith King
	Dr. I. H. Yarrow	MINERALS	Mr. Peter Embry

The identification of Banks's birds is my responsibility but Mr. Derek Goodwin, of the British Museum, gave me much assistance with problems in this group. In the United States, Dr. Alexander Wetmore and Dr. Kenneth Parkes were also generous with their help, and the late Mr. Todd, with a lifelong knowledge of the birds of Labrador, very kindly read and criticized all the ornithological material.

The *Niger* and the *Endeavour* both sailed from Plymouth; it was therefore a particular pleasure to ask Sir Frederick Russell, former Director of the Marine Laboratory there, for help in identifying the 'polypes' Banks noted in rock pools in Plymouth Sound.

Most of the work on Banks's plants was carried out in the Botany Department of the British Museum (Natural History). I am greatly indebted to Mr. J. E. Dandy and Mr. R. Ross, past and present Keepers of Botany, for giving me every facility during the years I have spent in the department, and in particular I wish to express my thanks to Dr. W. T. Stearn. My thanks are also due to my colleagues named below who helped me to solve the many problems that arose in connection with Banks's plant collection:

Mr. J. F. M. Cannon	Mr. P. W. James	Dr. A. Melderis
Mr. J. A. Crabbe	Mr. A. C. Jermy	Mr. A. H. Norkett
Mr. A. Eddy	Mr. J. C. Laundon	Mr. J. H. Price
Miss M. B. Gerrans	Mr. J. Lewis	Dr. N. K. B. Robson
Mr. E. W. Groves	Mr. F. Ludlow	Miss C. Whitefoord
Miss D. Hillcoat	Mr. J. B. Marshall	Mr. L. H. J. Williams
Mr. J. O. Hillman	Mr. G. A. Matthews	

PREFACE AND ACKNOWLEDGEMENTS

It is my particular pleasure to acknowledge the unselfish and generous assistance of Professor Ernest Rouleau of the Institut Botanique, Université de Montréal. He has been working on a flora of Newfoundland and Labrador for more than sixteen years, and had, unknown to me, spent some months in the British Museum in 1949 searching for Banks's plants from those countries with the intention of publishing an annotated edition of Banks's diary. When he found that I had completed the zoological work on the diary and was also working on the plants he most generously handed over to me all his lists and determinations; furthermore he has helped identify other Banksian specimens that have turned up more recently, and when I obtained a grant to visit Canada he provided transport for me in Newfoundland so that we could together visit some of Banks's collecting grounds and check some doubtful localities. It was he who made arrangements for me to meet so many kind and helpful people in Newfoundland; of these I should in the first place like to thank the Premier, Dr. Joseph Smallwood, who has written a foreword to this volume; secondly, my thanks are due to Mr. Harry Walters who introduced Professor Rouleau and myself to the Grenfell Memorial Hospital at St. Anthony's where we stayed, and to the staff, particularly the matron, Miss Peggy Dunk, and Dr. Gordon Thomas who arranged for the Grenfell seaplane to take us to Croque. There we were made welcome by Mr. and Mrs. Edward Johnson who, with Mr. Maurice Reardon, took us by boat to some of the places visited by Banks, enabling us to check many of the species recorded by him. At St. John's, Dr. Leslie Tuck read through much of my MS and made useful emendations regarding my identifications of mammals as well as birds; Dr. H. J. Squires of the Fisheries Research Board of Canada checked the determinations of crabs, molluscs and fishes, and Mr. Ray Morris helped me with the insects which were particularly difficult. I also thank Mr. A. W. H. Damman of the Department of Forestry of the Government of Canada for his interest and help with some of Banks's plants. Acknowledgement is also due to Professor Joseph Ewan for drawing my attention to Fernald's annotation of Banks's plant catalogue, now in the Gray Herbarium.

The staff of the libraries in both British Museums have helped me continuously over the past years. In the British Museum (Natural History) I am much indebted to the late Mr. A. C. Townsend, who translated de Loureiro's letter from the Portuguese for me, checked some of my Latin translations, and assisted me in various other ways. I am pleased to have this opportunity of expressing my thanks to the present Librarian, Mr. M. J. Rowlands, and to past and present members of his staff, particularly Mr. Halliday, and past and present departmental librarians, Miss P. I. Edwards, Mr. F. C. Sawyer and Mr. G. D. R. Bridson. Mr. R. Desmond, Librarian, Royal Botanic Gardens, Kew, has given me kind help on many occasions.

My best thanks are due to Mr. Richard Pennington and Mrs. Elizabeth Lewis lately of the Redpath Library, McGill University, for assistance with the Banks MSS and related paintings and books in that collection. Other libraries from which

12

PREFACE AND ACKNOWLEDGEMENTS

various MSS have been copied and used are the following; the Morgan Library, New York; the William Clements Library, Ann Arbor; the Mitchell Library of the Library of New South Wales; the National Library, Canberra; the Alexander Turnbull Library, Wellington, New Zealand; the Royal Society; the Linnean Society; the Royal Botanic Gardens, Kew; the Royal Geographical Society; the Public Record Office; the Naval Library of the Ministry of Defence, and the Chelsea Public Library, all of London. I am most grateful to the Directors of these various libraries and institutions for permission to use the documents in their collections. I am also happy to acknowledge the assistance of Miss Agnes O'Dea, Centre of Newfoundland Studies, Memorial University of Newfoundland.

I have drawn freely on the late Mr. Warren Dawson's great calendar of Banks papers in Great Britain and he personally helped me with a number of difficulties.

The maps reproduced in this volume have come from various sources: official material from the Hydrographic Department, Ministry of Defence, Taunton, is reproduced by kind permission of the Comptroller of H.M. Stationery Office; I am pleased to express my indebtedness to Dr. Helen Wallis and Mr. T. A. Corfe of the Map Room, British Museum, for advice and help in connection with this aspect of the work; to the late Mr. R. A. Skelton, of the Map Room, who kindly lent the photograph of the map of Newfoundland on which the dates of the surveys by Cook and Lane are marked; to Mr. G. P. B. Naish of the National Maritime Museum who assisted me with references and various nautical matters; and to Mr. Bathe of the Science Museum who gave me technical information about the ships and was very helpful about eighteenth-century records. Lord Cadogan has kindly allowed me to use Richardson's map of Chelsea in 1769; the Chelsea Public Library has provided a print of Maurer's engraving of the Chelsea waterfront in 1750—and here I must take the opportunity of thanking Miss M. P. Baldwin who traced the exact position of Banks's Chelsea house for me and drew my attention to Thorowgood's engraving of it when it was Rothery's school. The Moravian maps of Newfoundland and Labrador in 1765 are reproduced by the kind courtesy of the British Province of the Moravian Church, and I should particularly like to thank Mr. Schooling, their librarian, who traced these maps and the original diaries kept by the missionaries at that time. The Hon. R. S. Furlong, Chief Justice of Newfoundland, owns the watercolour of St. John's, painted by an unknown artist about 1770, and had it photographed for me to use in this book. It gives me much pleasure to acknowledge his kindness.

Most of the portraits reproduced here come from private collections and I am much indebted to their owners for permission to publish them. Lord Brabourne owns the portraits by Russell of Banks, his mother and his wife, and one by Angelica Kauffmann of Sarah Sophia Banks; the delightful drawings of the Eskimos, Caubvick and Attuiock, by Nathaniel Dance are also in his collection; the portraits of Phipps by Gainsborough and by an unknown artist belong to Lord Normanby; the miniature

PREFACE AND ACKNOWLEDGEMENTS

of Captain Cook formerly in the possession of Banks is now owned by Mrs. Daphne Foskett. Miss Sandra Raphael, former Librarian of the Linnean Society, found the watercolour of Banks and Solander in Iceland amongst some miscellaneous MSS there and I am most grateful to the Society for allowing me to reproduce it. Edridge's drawing of Banks is reproduced by kind permission of the Art Gallery of New South Wales; Nathaniel Hone's miniature of Sarah Sophia Banks by courtesy of the National Gallery of Ireland.

The extracts from *Augustus Hervey's Journal*, edited by David Erskine, are reproduced by permission of Messrs. William Kimber; that from Robin Hallett's *The Penetration of Africa to 1815* by permission of Messrs. Routledge and Kegan Paul Ltd., and Frederick Praeger, Inc.

Particularly, I wish to thank Mr. Richard Stuart whose encouragement throughout the writing of this book has sustained me through many difficulties; and Mrs. Nicolette Devas, Mr. James Fisher and Mr. Charles Gibbs-Smith, without whose timely aid in the final stages of parturition this book might indeed have been stillborn.

Several of my friends have read the MS in various stages and my special thanks are due to them for helpful discussions and for assistance with proof-reading; in particular, I should like to express my gratitude to the late Mrs. Denston-Fenelle, Mrs. Margaret 'Espinasse, Mr. John Cannon, Mr. Leonard Forman, Mr. Owen Hickey, Mr. Paul Hulton, Mr. and Mrs. David Mackay, Miss Sandra Raphael, Mr. Rolf du Rietz, Miss Miranda Robinson and Mr. Julian Robinson.

Mrs. Margaret 'Espinasse and Mr. John Carter have read the whole of the manuscript, which has been greatly improved by their thoughtful criticism. Paul Cannon, when eight years old, read a typescript of Banks's journal with interest and enjoyment and is partly responsible for its being printed with all the original irregularities of punctuation and spelling that the editors of other Banksian MSS have sought to amend. Mrs. Truda Satchell kindly checked the typescript of Banks's diary, made from an enlarged microfilm, against the holograph MS in Adelaide before I was able to visit that city myself.

Many plates, particularly the natural history drawings in the Print Room, British Museum, and the portraits of Phipps, would not have been so good had not Axel Poignant taken great care in photographing the originals. Dennis Frone, too, has made careful copies of some of the MSS.

I am indebted to various people who helped to type this complex manuscript, but most of all to Mrs. Alice Allen, who undertook the most difficult technical sections and showed a craftsman's attitude to her work. Finally, I must thank Mr. Brian Rooney who designed the book, and Messrs. Faber and Faber for the trouble they have taken with it. I know it has many gaps and faults but, I hope it does some belated justice to Joseph Banks and his achievements on the first scientific expedition to Newfoundland and Labrador.

Contents

CONTENTS

PART THREE: Supplementary papers

PART FOUR: Banks's scientific collection and manuscripts

CONTENTS

PART FIVE

Illustrations

THE illustrations in this volume come from many sources. Most of the portraits are privately owned and formal acknowledgement is made of the source of these, and of those in public collections, in the lists that follow this note. Both private and public owners have been very generous in allowing me to reproduce these paintings and drawings.

The natural history drawings by Sydney Parkinson and Peter Paillou are in the Print Room, British Museum. Most of the invertebrates figured by Parkinson are in water colour on vellum, in a volume with the press mark 199 a 8; many notes on locality (sometimes only Newfoundland) are on the back of these drawings. They are not always signed and throughout the natural history paintings it is important to distinguish a signature on the right from any name on the left, the latter being usually in the hand of Dryander, for many years Banks's librarian. Dryander catalogued many of the natural history drawings and often added the artist's name. The folio number of the British Museum drawings is given in the lists below.

Parkinson's drawings of fishes from Plymouth, Newfoundland and Labrador are bound in volume 199* B 1, at the end of his series of Newfoundland birds. Detailed notes on the bird paintings were published by the author in 1959 and are not repeated here.

Paillou's bird paintings are in another Print Room volume, 199* B 4. They were also discussed in 1959.

Ehret's paintings of Banks's plants are in two volumes in the Botany Library, British Museum (Natural History); notes on locality are often on the versos of the plates, just as in the case of the zoological drawings; they are not all quoted in these lists since some are obviously inaccurate.

A certain number of the natural history drawings are scattered throughout the text but most of them are in series according to subject, and are arranged in systematic order.

The maps and charts come from various sources. Most of Cook's charts, and MS versions of them by other hands, are reproduced by kind permission of the Navy Department, Ministry of Defence, and come from the Naval Library at Earl's Court, and the Hydrographic Department at Taunton. Two, however, which

ILLUSTRATIONS

belong to the William Clements Library at Ann Arbor, have special relevance to the voyage of the *Niger* in 1766, and I am pleased to be able to include them in this book. These may have been copies made for the Earl of Shelburne, to which Palliser refers in a letter to Philip Stephens, January 1767 (P.R.O. Adm. 1/2300). The Moravian facsimiles are reproduced by kind permission of the Moravian Church in London and have a special value in that only one of the formal copies made by the missionaries for Palliser appears to have survived; it is now in the Naval Library, Ministry of Defence, and is reproduced with the Moravian diaries.

The measurements throughout the lists are given in centimetres; they include the signature. All the drawings have been considerably reduced for reproduction.

COLOUR PLATES

20

ILLUSTRATIONS

MORAVIAN FACSIMILES

Charts and sketches made from the *Lark* when stationed in Croque Harbour, and from the *Hope* on the coast of Labrador, 1765. Courtesy of the Moravian Church, Muswell Hill, London.

a. Croque Harbour, showing ships at anchor and hamlets. 23·3 × 34·2 cm.

facing page 192

b. Hare Bay and the adjacent coast from St. Anthony's to Groais, now Grey, Island. 37·5 × 46·5 cm.   193

c. Prince Edward's Harbour, Hare Bay, with soundings. 23 × 34·2 cm.   208

d. The *Hope* at anchor in Davis's Inlet. The legend in the corner is barely decipherable—'Prospect von dem Schiff B vom Ende Davis Inlet. Berg a ist in der Passage durch . . . See nur 3 Mln. lang u.2 breit

    Wir lagen daselbst vom 8 August . . . Aug. 65. Es lagen uns gegen SW.' (Prospect from the ship B to the end of Davis Inlet. Hill *a* is in the entrance . . . sea only 3 miles long and 2 broad. We lay here from 8 August to . . . August, '65. It lay to the SW from us.) 22·5 × 37 cm.   209

e. Croque Harbour and the adjacent coast. 24 × 15·2 cm.   216

f. Sketch of a rowing boat in Croque harbour. 'Prospect der Erde gegen Westen des Hafens Croque von dem Schiff, Die Lerche aus genommen 1765.' (Prospect of the land towards the west in Croque harbour from the ship called the *Lark*, 1765.) 16·2 × 10·5 cm.   216

g. Davis's Inlet and the adjacent coast, with the route of the *Hope* shown by the dotted line. 36 × 28 cm.   *between pages* 216–217

h. The *Hope* in Comfort Harbour. 'Prospect in Cofforts Harb. in Davis' Inlet, auf der Nord Sud'.' 19 × 12 cm.   *facing page* 217

i. Profiles showing the entrance to Davis's Inlet. The two views in each pair of sketches fit end to end; the sketch with the legend beginning 'Prospect in Davis's Inlet . . .' is a small version of sketch f. 15·5 × 15·2 cm.   217

Some of the charts bear little relationship to the current Admiralty charts of the area; nevertheless, as Gosling wrote in 1910 (p. 266), 'The history of the Moravian ships and their captains is one of the most remarkable in the records of navigation. For 137 years they have made an annual trip to this stormy, ice-beset, and still uncharted coast, but have not yet lost a vessel!'

    The charts published here are a selection from a series of eighteen sketches and maps in the Moravian library. Most of the others relate to the voyage of 1765, but there is one of 1796, showing the entrance to Hudson's Bay, with a long legend in German script.

    These Moravian charts and those of Chateau Bay published in this book have a particular significance for the study of the manuscript charts of the Labrador coast. Cook's charts of 1763, one published by Blewitt (1957), another in this book, pl. 16, were made when Smart was his assistant. Pl. 40, based on Cook's original chart, must have been copied and embellished by Michael Lane or Lieutenant Lucas in 1765 (see the note on p. 25). Palliser's copy showing the correct position of the blockhouse, with his

ILLUSTRATIONS

notes (I have not checked his writing), was certainly made in 1766, when Michael Lane was still in the *Guernsey*. Lieutenant Lucas was in the *Hope* in 1765 for the purpose of making charts of the coast north of Chateau Bay, so he may have had a hand in the little coastal profiles of Davis's Inlet. I have not seen any work ascribed to him in the Hydrographic Department, Ministry of Defence, or any other collection. Plate 91 is the work of Michael Lane. It would appear that a careful study of the techniques and writing on these charts should enable their authorship to be accurately determined, and thus help in the identification of the other eighteenth century charts of Newfoundland and Labrador.

MONOCHROME PLATES AND MAPS

ILLUSTRATIONS

ILLUSTRATIONS

ILLUSTRATIONS

25

ILLUSTRATIONS

ILLUSTRATIONS

ILLUSTRATIONS

TEXT FIGURES

PART ONE
General introduction

'Ithaka gave you the splendid journey'
CAVAFY

1
A note on the eighteenth-century background

JOSEPH BANKS was born in 1743, in the middle of a century of profound social, economic and scientific change. This century is remarkable not so much for fertility of invention in the many fields of human endeavour where change was apparent but rather for the application and consolidation of methods and ideas which had been formulated in the seventeenth century and even earlier. Of the complex contributing factors three deserve special consideration: first, an increase in agricultural production necessitating improvements in transport; second, social mobility in two senses, i.e. the less rigid separation of classes in Britain than on the continent of Europe and the greater facility for getting about the countryside resulting from the building of canals and the extension of roads; and, third, an astonishing rise in population for reasons not yet clearly understood; all these factors stimulated ideas and facilitated their application. It was in this century that daily newspapers first appeared in England (well in advance of any continental countries), and periodicals combined amusement and instruction in a way that astonishes us today.

Since the Second World War intensive research into demography and agricultural economics has noticeably altered our ideas of the eighteenth-century background.[1] In the second half of that century educated people formed but a small minority of the rapidly increasing population and the upper and middle classes were closely connected. The groups to which Banks and his friends belonged, the scientists, the writers and the painters of the period, were widely linked by marriage (for instance Banks's friend Arthur Young, the writer on agriculture, was married to a sister of Fanny Burney's stepmother); often the men belonged to clubs which brought them together. Samuel Johnson, Boswell, Joshua Reynolds, Thomas Pennant, Joseph Banks, Lord Sandwich, the Hunters, Sir John Pringle and Garrick all knew each other; they endlessly discussed ideas and it was possible to try them out, often with relative success, in a way that had never before been so practicable.

The eighteenth-century agriculturalists are widely known today: Townshend, popularly believed to have been responsible for the introduction of turnips, important in the winter feeding of stock; Tull, generally credited with the introduction of

[1] I am indebted to Mr. Julian Robinson for assistance with this part of the introduction.

principles of crop cultivation based on sound soil physics; Bakewell, famous for his success in breeding sheep and cattle; and Arthur Young, so persuasive a writer and popularizer of the methods advocated by these other men; but in fact we now know that they all had their predecessors in the seventeenth century and many of the procedures attributed to them were advocated by Blith and Weston in Cromwellian times.

In his book *The English Improver Improved* (1652), Walter Blith advocated water meadows, field drainage, enclosure, the use of grass leys in worn-out arable land and the general use of manures. Sir Richard Weston, famous for his use of water meadows, studied agricultural methods in the Low Countries and in his *Discourse of Husbandrie used in Brabant and Flanders* (1650) discussed the value of convertible husbandry (the alternation of grass and arable) which had been practised there since the Middle Ages. In the seventeenth century the Dutch were sowing clover to replace grass; although they knew nothing of its nitrogen-fixing properties they had observed the increase of fertility resulting from its use. They also knew the importance of animal manures. The dung from their stall-fed cattle was added to town sewage and transported by barge to the farms where it was needed. In England in the early part of the eighteenth century economic difficulties forced the farmers to use their land as intensively as possible and therefore encouraged initiative and experiment; in the second half, when conditions were more favourable, the writings of Arthur Young and William Marshall widened the knowledge of new methods and created an atmosphere of enterprise so that experiments were undertaken on a much larger scale.

Eighteenth-century poets played their part; James Granger, M.D. (1721–67), entranced Boswell (21 March, 1776) with verses (declaimed in the house of Sir Joshua Reynolds) beginning, 'Now Muse, Let's sing of rats', and enriched our heritage with these lines:

> Of composts shall the Muse disdain to sing?
> Nor soil her heavenly plumes? The sacred Muse
> Nought sordid deems, but what is base; nought fair,
> Unless true Virtue stamp it with her seal.
> Then, planter, wouldst thou double thine estate?
> Never, ah! never, be asham'd to tread
> Thy dung-heaps.

In Cromwellian times the barriers between the upper, middle and working classes, much less rigid in England since the Black Death than on the continent of Europe, were further weakened and this social mobility helped the spread of ideas. The drainage of the fens begun by Vermuyden in the reigns of James I and Charles I brought some 380,000 acres of good land into use; both drainage and enclosure were greatly accelerated in the eighteenth century. The improvement of agricultural methods and the increase in farm produce necessitated the improvement of transport; the *Gentleman's Magazine* for 1772 contains five folding plans of proposed canals; this was the year in which Brindley died, a man without education but a mechanical genius.

> So with strong arm immortal BRINDLEY leads
> His long canals, and parts the velvet meads;
> Winding the lucid lines, the watery mass
> Mines the firm rock, or loads the deep morass,
> With rising locks a thousand hills alarms,
> Flings o'er a thousand streams its silver arms,
> Feeds the long vale, the nodding woodland laves,
> And Plenty, Arts, and Commerce freight the waves.

So wrote that indefatigable scientist and versifier, Erasmus Darwin, grandfather of Charles.

With the encouragement and patronage of the Duke of Bridgwater, Brindley was wonderfully successful in the planning and construction of canals[1] and their importance in that period can still be gauged from the surviving beautiful merchants' buildings in old inland ports such as Wisbech, Bedford and St. Neots.

Not only the waterways but also the roads were considerably extended and improved, and these helped the movements of population and, inevitably, of ideas.

Throughout the eighteenth century there was a noticeable rise in the population of the British Isles; estimated at $5\frac{1}{2}$ millions in 1695, it was stated by Rickman to have reached 9,168,000 in 1801; and a similar rise occurred in other European countries. Economists still disagree about the causes of this increase in numbers; Habbakuk, in Glass & Eversley's *Population in History* (1965), sets out to show that it was primarily the result of specifically economic changes, and probably the result of a higher birth rate rather than a fall in the death rate; others in the same collection of essays think that the fall in the death rate was likely to have been the chief factor.

The physiological factors involved in the rise of the birth rate are not fully understood; in the seventeenth century there was great prejudice against the drinking of coffee which was thought to reduce the fertility of the male; a league of women was formed petitioning men to reject a poison which would make them 'as unfruitful as those Desarts whence that unhappy Berry is said to be brought' (Wilson 1965:307). In the eighteenth century gin was believed to have a similar effect and even today we still do not know much about the basic factors which affect fertility in man; it is of interest that the enormous bulk of work by zoologists on other animal populations is scarcely referred to in the formidable collection of essays edited by Glass & Eversley and referred to above.

[1] Banks saw the 'Staffordshire navigation' under construction and described it in the journal of his tour to Wales in the winter of 1767–8.

THE EIGHTEENTH-CENTURY BACKGROUND

The death rate in the eighteenth century is not easy to assess, partly because of emigration to North America and other countries, the numbers of men at sea and in the army, and partly because of the imperfections of the methods used in rural registers. It seems quite certain that infant mortality decreased during the century and it is a common generalization even by recent historians that this noticeable fall in the death rate was due to advances in medical knowledge. That there were great increases in knowledge is indisputable, but their immediate effects on the sick and ailing were very often disastrous.

The persisting international character of medical education was one of the reasons for the medical advances of the eighteenth century. Students moved from British universities to Leyden where they studied with Albinus and Boerhaave, or they went to Paris or Orange; or, later, to Göttingen to learn from Haller. The movement was in both directions: Dutch and other European students worked at the medical schools in Glasgow and Edinburgh. Such travelling was a notable stimulus to thought and doctors began to explore the association between environment and disease. In England the major advances were primarily due to four Scotsmen: Sir John Pringle, William Smellie, John Hunter and his brother William. Pringle was responsible for extensive reforms in military hygiene which gradually spread throughout the civilian population; a graduate of Leyden, he also studied at Paris and later had charge of the British military hospital in Flanders, remaining abroad until 1749. The following year he made a name for himself in London by dealing satisfactorily (he used ammonia as an antiseptic) with an outbreak of 'jail fever' (typhus) in Newgate Prison which had caused the deaths of the Lord Mayor, two judges, an alderman and forty other persons who had appeared at sessions of the Old Bailey. William Smellie, a brilliant teacher, brought revolutionary methods into midwifery; the Hunter brothers are still famous for their work on comparative anatomy and in surgery, and for their museums.

During this century hospitals were widely established, both for maternity cases and for illness in general; the first children's orphanage, the Foundling Hospital, was built largely by the efforts of the kind-hearted sailor Thomas Coram with the help of Taylor White whose name recurs in the later part of this volume. But the immediate results of hospital treatment did nothing to reduce the death rate. Ignorance of asepsis led to a high mortality rate in hospitals, the patients commonly dying not from the disease for which they were admitted but from the prevalent infection in the building since not even cholera patients were isolated. The results of surgical operations were equally deplorable; even in the last quarter of the nineteenth century the mortality rate following amputations at one famous London hospital varied from 35 to 50 per cent. It was Florence Nightingale who in the middle of that century asserted vigorously that the first requirement of a hospital was that it should do the patient no harm.

The efforts for improvement of hygiene and the introduction of sewage systems

34

led first of all to the discharge of sewage into streams used for drinking water and thus to the spread of typhoid and other fevers. Apparently the sixteenth-century work of Girolamo Frascatoro of Verona, *De Contagione*, on ways by which infection was spread was largely forgotten.

Some doctors of high intelligence, however, worked empirically and C. White in 1773 wrote a book on the care of pregnant women, and on the technique of delivery, in which he claimed that he had never lost a patient from puerperal fever, simply through observing elementary rules of hygiene and ventilation. But his work was largely ignored and maternal mortality remained shockingly high until well into the next century.[1]

Still there were considerable advances in other branches of medicine: Bougainville and Cook kept their crews almost free from scurvy; Lady Mary Wortley Montagu, who had lost a brother from smallpox, introduced inoculation against smallpox from Turkey into England in 1718, established an inoculation hospital in London and, although only the upper and middle classes used the treatment widely, she created a background of opinion which must have greatly facilitated the acceptance of Jenner's discovery of vaccination at the end of the century.

There was also a noticeable improvement in infant health, though whether this was due to better economic conditions or medical care is not easily ascertainable. In London in 1715 a committee set up by the Commons to investigate infant mortality found that out of 1,200 babies born in one year in the Parish of St. Martin-in-the-Fields only 300 survived. These figures improved noticeably in the second half of the century though in 1835 T. R. Edmonds showed that in the period 1770 to 1789, 51·5 per cent of the infants baptized in London died before they reached the age of five. Elsewhere in England improvements in housing, food and clothing reduced infant and other mortality but improvements in medical care had no great effect until the nineteenth century.

Concern for the poor and unemployed in the latter part of the seventeenth century had led to the founding of the Charity Schools and Wilson, in his *England's Apprenticeship* (1965:348), reminds us that in the eighteenth century large numbers of private donors combined to set up thousands of schools where hundreds of thousands of children, for whom no other possibility of education existed, received elementary but valuable instruction and this contributed immeasurably to the social betterment of Britain. At the end of the century these schools declined in numbers and degenerated in quality and left a gap in the educational system which was not filled until late Victorian times.

---

[1] Some seventy years after White's publication, Semmelweiss in Vienna, troubled at the incidence of puerperal fever and the resulting deaths in his hospital, insisted on the doctors washing their hands in a weak disinfectant before attending the labour wards; the number of deaths fell spectacularly but his methods were opposed, then forgotten, and twenty years later it fell to Lister and Pasteur to make their own discoveries.

THE EIGHTEENTH-CENTURY BACKGROUND

In Scotland in the eighteenth century teaching at the Universities of Glasgow and Edinburgh, particularly in medicine, was of a high standard but the role of English universities was very different; there was very little teaching and the colleges at best functioned largely as centres of intellectual discussion, sometimes scarcely reaching even that level. But this stagnation was limited. Thus some dissenting academies founded in the seventeenth century expanded in the eighteenth, introducing new methods and highly qualified teachers; amongst them one of the most remarkable was Warrington Academy where Priestley the chemist taught in the early 1760s; he was succeeded by J. R. Forster, a polyglot (with seventeen languages) and biologist who was the first to publish a brief record of some of Banks's Newfoundland collections.

In Sweden the famous systematist Linnaeus had tidied up the whole world of biology by producing his classification of the plant and animal kingdoms; this gave a great stimulus to exploration and the investigation of living organisms. In France Réaumur expanded the detailed methods of observation of invertebrate structures propounded by Swammerdam in Leyden in the seventeenth century;[1] he published a monumental work on insect biology in six volumes, the last of which appeared in the year of Banks's birth; he also invented the temperature scale bearing his name, which is still widely used. Another French naturalist, Buffon, produced the first comprehensive scientific work on natural history, and showed the fundamental similarity between all living organisms, both plant and animal. He regarded life not as a metaphysical characteristic of living creatures, but as a physical quality of matter. In the purely theoretical sphere he was the foremost biologist of the eighteenth century and one whose ideas had perhaps the greatest influence on the next generation of scientists. Thomas Pennant, the most able British zoologist between Ray and Darwin, published the first major work on zoogeography in his *Arctic Zoology* (1784–7). In other fields too there were scientists of great ability.

To an intelligent and imaginative boy such as Joseph Banks, who had an assured social position and an aptitude for biology dating from his schooldays, science must have seemed to hold limitless possibilities; scientific knowledge properly applied could show men how to map the unknown parts of the world, and make proper use of vast natural resources; science would bring the millennium. It was no wonder that Banks should have decided to study botany and zoology at Oxford, and that influenced by his Moravian neighbours' tales of Greenland, he should when opportunity arose have visited Newfoundland and Labrador, a region almost unknown to the scientists of that day.

Observations and collections had been made in other parts of North America from the time of Raleigh when John White had painted the people, other animals

---

[1] Swammerdam would have accomplished more but 'by intense application he became a hypochondriac and wholly unfit for society', then fell under the influence of the mystic Antoinette Bourignon, 'a fanatical female', left his scientific pursuits and died at the early age of forty-three.

and plants (Hulton & Quinn 1963). In 1635 Cornut published an illustrated book on Canadian plants growing in Parisian gardens. They were followed by others, notably by Mark Catesby who early in the eighteenth century collected extensively in Florida and elsewhere and wrote a natural history of the region; by Clayton who supplied Catesby, R. F. G. Gronovius and Linnaeus with North American plants, and whose catalogue of these plants was published by Gronovius as the *Flora Virginica*, the first American flora, in Leyden in 1739 and 1743; and by John Bartram who, particularly from 1735 to 1760, sent seeds and newly discovered plants from Pennsylvania and surrounding districts to Peter Collinson, Philip Miller (Stearn 1961: LXXX ff.) and a group of English collectors who formed a syndicate for their commercial distribution; other early eighteenth-century collectors have been reviewed by Rendle (1929). The Swedish naturalist Peter Kalm botanised in Pennsylvania, New Jersey and southern Canada from 1748 to 1751 and published an account of his journey; many of his plants were described by Linnaeus. Northern plants and animals were sent to England by employees of the Hudson's Bay Company; those of Greenland were collected by the Danish and German missionaries who lived and worked among the Eskimos in that fearful climate. But Banks's collections were more comprehensive and better documented than any earlier ones from northern North America or from Greenland.

At the time of Kalm's journey, some sixteen years before Banks's, Canada was still a French possession, but in 1759 Quebec was captured by Wolfe; four years later Canada was formally ceded to England by the Treaty of Paris. Newfoundland had come under British jurisdiction much earlier, through the Treaty of Utrecht in 1713 which allowed the French to retain certain fishing rights and to dry their nets on the northern shores; in 1763 the islands of St. Pierre and Miquelon were returned to them. The French had indeed been fishing Newfoundland waters since 1534; huge sums of money were made from selling cod, which was enormously abundant, to Roman Catholic countries as far away as the Mediterranean. The French naturally resented the curtailment of their fisheries and were inclined to infringe the regulations by which they were supposed to be bound. The English therefore patrolled the coast with fishery protection vessels, and established small permanent stations for garrisons.

Banks and Constantine Phipps arranged to visit Newfoundland and Labrador as passengers in one of these fishery protection vessels, H.M.S. *Niger*, a 32-gun frigate of 679 tons built in 1759, and under the command of their friend Sir Thomas Adams. The *Niger* was under orders to take a party of marines to Chateau Bay in Labrador to build a fort where a small permanent garrison could winter; in addition Adams was to continue his work of strengthening good relations with the Indians and Eskimos who had been treated with horrifying barbarity by both French and English fishermen; and there was also surveying to be carried out along the coast of the Northern Peninsula of Newfoundland, in Hare Bay and elsewhere.

Banks had made ample preparations for the voyage. He had excellent opportunities for collecting plants and animals along the coast, and made the most of them. Many of the species he brought back to England were unknown and undescribed, and some remained so for another fifty years since he published no account of his voyage and specimens but allowed other scientists full use of his collection and manuscripts. Like the mediaeval scholars he was uninterested in having his name attached to his researches; his great and lifelong passion was to investigate and extend all scientific knowledge, especially in the field of biology.

Some of his specimens are of great historic and systematic value and hence it is important that even now, two hundred years later, they should be listed together with all the available information about the place and date of collection. They are valuable for another reason. Many plants in the North American flora belong to European species and their exact status is not yet known. Lindroth in 1957 published a careful survey of the plants and animals carried from England to North America in the ballast of the old sailing ships; he searched the areas in southern England from which the fishing vessels loaded ballast and compared his lists of plants and insects from them with those he found in Newfoundland and in the Maritime Provinces of North America. Banks's records provide valuable comparative material, especially since he made a point of collecting even those plants which were apparently identical with British forms for, as he remarked, one cannot be certain of this without a very careful comparison of these forms. His specimens therefore include a number of 'weeds' from the shores of the fishing harbours visited by the *Niger*, many of which are common both to Europe and America. It may be that some of these weeds originated not from British ports but from those of the French coasts used by the Basque and other French fishermen for some hundred and fifty years before their British competitors began to exploit the vast cod fisheries of the Newfoundland Banks. It may even be the case that some were carried to the shores of Newfoundland by the much earlier Viking explorers whose settlement of northern Newfoundland is now being investigated. No analysis of these naturalized species has been attempted in the following pages, but in the systematic lists, species considered to be naturalized have been noted; it should be mentioned here that Lindroth (1957:146) believes that Fernald (1950) underestimates the number of introduced species in North America.

Although Banks published no formal account of his expedition, his MS descriptions of many of the plants appear to have been copied in due course by Daniel Solander and Jonas Dryander who worked as his secretaries and librarians. Solander, a favourite pupil of Linnaeus, was appointed to the British Museum when he first arrived in England, but he sailed in the *Endeavour*, 1768–71, as a member of Banks's staff; after the voyage he and Banks planned to prepare an edition of the *Systema Naturae*, the comprehensive work in which Linnaeus had published a classification of all the plants and animals known to him. Solander and Dryander compiled their descriptions of new species from Banks's Newfoundland material, from the collections made in the course of Cook's great circumnavigations, from specimens obtained in other parts of the world by other collectors working for Banks and his friends and from material acquired in exchange or purchased by Banks from foreign scientists such as Pallas. The descriptions, which are beautifully accurate, were written on slips of paper now bound into many volumes preserved in the Botany and Zoology Libraries of the British Museum (Natural History). They appear to have been composed as soon as the specimens were obtained; in 1772 the Rev. William Sheffield, Keeper of the Ashmolean Museum in Oxford, wrote to Gilbert White giving a vivid account of his visit (pp. 253–5) to Banks's collection, describing his herbarium, Parkinson's drawings, etc., and ended thus: 'And what is more extraordinary still, all the new genera and species contained in this vast collection are accurately described, the descriptions fairly transcribed and fit to be put to the press'.

Descriptions of the Newfoundland plants successfully grown in the Royal Botanic Gardens at Kew appeared indeed in the *Hortus Kewensis* (1789) under Aiton's name although he had little to do with the writing of that book; in his letters the younger Linnaeus stated (Uggla 1959:90) that throughout the summer of 1781 he worked from ten to four o'clock for four days every week with Banks, Solander and Dryander in studies for that publication in which some of the descriptions are exact copies of the Solander MSS now in the British Museum. Some of the pages of these MSS are missing, not surprisingly when one considers how many people had access to them and to Banks's herbarium. They were used by Georg and Reinhold Forster who published some of them; by Pursh who visited England before publishing his *Flora Americae Septentrionalis* (1814), sometimes copying them and citing 'Banks's MSS'; by Sneyd of Bishton, Rugeley, Staff., who borrowed the herbarium while Banks was on the *Endeavour* voyage, in order to use it for reference when he was working with the Botanical Society of Lichfield on the translation of the *Genera Plantarum* (p. 294); Sneyd's friend William Withering also saw Banks's herbarium at Bishton and used it as a basis for his *Botanical Arrangement* of 1776 (D.T.C. 5:269).

Duplicate specimens also were generously distributed. Thus Samuel Törner[1] (1762–1822), a later librarian of Banks, and a botanist, sent much material to his compatriots Swartz and Wahlenberg who published notes on it. The great flower painter, Georg Dionysius Ehret, who came via Nuremberg to England and worked for Banks, also sent specimens and drawings back to his friend and patron, Dr. Trew of that city. The Leyden-born Jacquin, who brought botanical fame to Vienna, also used the collections, as did most of the European botanists of any note

[1] Samuel Törner, the son of Daniel Törner, a snuff maker, should not be confused with Erik Törner, author of *Centuria II Plantarum*, no. 21, in the Linnaean Dissertations of 1756 (du Rietz *in lit* 1970).

who visited London in Banks's lifetime, and it is probable that searches of the major European herbaria today would bring to light many more examples of Banksian material than have yet been recorded.

The same kind of thing happened with Banks's birds and fishes, and some of his invertebrate collections; Pennant borrowed the Newfoundland birds and MSS; the lists of species he prepared were published by J. R. Forster (p. 397) in 1771; the detailed descriptions based on Banks's MSS and specimens appeared in the *Arctic Zoology*, 1784–7. John Latham used the descriptions of birds, sometimes relying on Pennant, sometimes working directly from Banks's material, and published notes on many species in the *General Synopsis of Birds*, 1781–1802. Finally in 1788–9 Gmelin gave them scientific binomials, referring to Pennant, Latham and Forster. Details of the published work based on Banks's material are given elsewhere in this volume; here it is only necessary to establish that, although Banks himself published nothing about his Newfoundland voyage, many of his specimens and drawings became types of the new species published by others. They are thus of considerable value to specialists today. For this reason an attempt has here been made to publish in one volume all the known material relating to Banks's collections from Newfoundland and Labrador, and to give all the available information about localities where type specimens were collected. This information is contained in the lists of species at the end of this book.

2

Biographical sketches

BANKS'S voyage to Newfoundland and Labrador is of peculiar interest to us today. On that journey, in 1766, he set a standard of biological exploration which was to be maintained throughout his voyage round the world with Captain Cook in the *Endeavour*, 1768–71. Cook's experience in surveying the coasts of Newfoundland and Labrador from 1762 to 1767 enabled him to make superb use of his voyages round the world; Banks's experience in collecting and describing the plants and animals taught him to work with careful accuracy in the confined space and under the arduous conditions prevailing in the small ships suitable for exploration at that time. His collections and manuscripts provided a pattern for the great scientific voyages of the later eighteenth century, and led ultimately to the establishment of such research ships as the *Challenger*, the precursor of the marine biological research ships and stations of this century. It was appropriate that Cook and Banks should meet briefly at St. John's, Newfoundland, through their mutual friend Sir Thomas Adams, and in that bleak and tiny fishing port should lay the foundations of their splendid partnership in the *Endeavour*.

It helps us to understand the significance of Banks's diary and the related MSS if we know something of the lives and personalities of the men who figure most prominently in them. These men might never have become friends nor have been so closely associated had it not chanced that in 1766 Joseph Banks, Constantine Phipps, Sir Thomas Adams, William Brougham Munkhouse, Hugh Palliser, James Cook and the Cartwright brothers were all in ships that spent the summer patrolling and surveying the Newfoundland coasts. The following biographical notes are intended to explain in some degree how this came about, and to indicate the range of interests which was to bind these men throughout the rest of their lives.

The movements of the tiny fleet of naval vessels in Newfoundland waters, the names of the officers and crews, their ages and birth places, their transfers from one ship to another, the dangers and disasters of the voyages—all of these can be found in the stained and battered muster rolls and logs now in the Public Record Office. They are the bare bones of a remarkable narrative of the companionship and courage of the men in the tiny ships of that day, with imperfect methods of navigation, dependent on sail in storm and fog, and often in danger from French or American privateers. With such a common background of hazard, endurance and resourcefulness these men must have known each other's strengths and weaknesses to an uncommon degree.

Nearly nineteen months after their return in the *Niger* from Newfoundland, Banks and Munkhouse sailed with Cook in the *Endeavour*. Beaglehole has stated that Banks proposed to 'plant himself, a train of dependants and a mass of impedimenta on a small and overcrowded vessel commanded by a man he did not know. . . . He simply, we may say, walked on board the *Endeavour*, elbowed her officers out of the way, and was made welcome' (1962, *1*:23–4). Now that we know something of the Newfoundland background, these and similar comments appear groundless, and totally at variance with Banks's character as it is revealed in the diary and manuscripts published in this volume.

Joseph Banks

THERE is no definitive life of Sir Joseph Banks. Such a work was indeed planned by Edward Smith who completed a manuscript of some 200,000 words early this century (Lysaght, 1964). This was submitted to and rejected by twelve publishers. Finally the Bodley Head accepted it on condition that Smith should shorten it, add a chapter on caricature and make it a book for the general reader instead of a serious study. It appeared in 1911, having been reduced to 116,000 words; it is still the most comprehensive life available. There is a possibility that some of the original, unabridged manuscript may turn up in some dusty cupboard in a London suburb; it is clear that Smith had access to papers which have long since been lost and if only he had had some other name a search for his MSS would long ago have been initiated.[1] Cameron's life (1952) is short but carefully documented and contains valuable material.

Other books deal with Banks in some particular role or other. De Beer's study (1952) surveys some of his work for international co-operation in science, a matter with which he was deeply concerned; Beaglehole's introduction to the 1962 edition of Banks's *Endeavour* journal deals especially with him as a young man, and with the fate of his papers, the sales of which, in 1886, 1887, 1918 and 1928, resulted in their being dispersed all over the world; the late Warren Dawson's great calendar (1958) of Banksian correspondence in English collections, together with his introduction, gives an astonishing picture of the range of Banks's interests; the late S. Rydén in a

---

[1] His family has now been found, but no papers.

delightful and scholarly study (1963) has written of Banks's friendship with the Alströmer family in Sweden; Carter has given an exhaustively detailed account (1964) of Banks's part in introducing merino sheep to the royal flock at Windsor and later Australia; Arber (1945) has outlined Banks's special contribution to botany and noted some of his detailed editorial work on other people's publications; as Cuvier did in his *Eloge* of 1821, she has also discussed with judgement and knowledge the reasons for his failure to publish his own work (and see p. 271); Hallett and Bovill have investigated Banks's activities in initiating exploration in Africa; there are also surveys of Banks and the Royal Society, and of Banks as the father of Australia but studies of him in depth are almost non-existent. Hallett's work on the African Association—Banks was a founder member—is a beginning, and Mackay is now studying Banks's political influence on the development of imperial economic botany and botanical exploration—a remarkable story. Currey's edition (1967) of the Caley-Banks correspondence, a well-documented and most interesting piece of scholarship, makes strange reading about one of Banks's most difficult and enthusiastic collectors, and reveals Banks's astonishing tolerance and his ability to balance the strengths and weaknesses of a man's character, and induce him to give his best. Further studies in depth are essential before it will be possible to make adequate assessment of a man so varied, so intelligent and so influential.

In this book I have made no attempt to survey the many fields of Banks's interests and accomplishments but only to show his professional ability and achievements when he was young and working alone. I have also tried to give some idea of his intelligence and powers of application, his warmth of feeling for other people whatever the colour of their skin, the riches or poverty of their background; these are important in attempting to understand why he was so singularly happy in his personal relationships with Eskimos and Polynesians as well as with European scientists and his immediate family. Most of the brief notes given below concern his life before he became President of the Royal Society; I have also tried to indicate something of the continuity of his interest in Newfoundland and other northern lands throughout his life.

Joseph Banks was born in February 1743, heir to the great estates of Revesby Abbey, near Boston in Lincolnshire, bought by his great-grandfather in 1714 (p. 105) for £14,000. His only sister, Sarah Sophia, was born the following year; his parents had no other children. He started his schooling at Harrow when he was nine years old but learnt so little that in 1755 he was moved to Eton. His father was better pleased with his progress there but not so his form master, Edward Young, who in February 1757 wrote to William Banks deploring his late return to school after the Christmas holidays, his deficiencies in Greek and Latin, his inattention and his immoderate love of play (he was just fourteen), finally softening his asperities with 'I really think him a very good-tempered and well disposed boy'.

It was at Eton that Banks first developed an interest in natural history, which his mother encouraged and stimulated. She owned a copy of Gerard's *Herball* in which he delighted, and she taught him about animals as well as plants; she appears as a shadowy but formidable figure. In a letter to an unknown correspondent quoted by Bowdler Sharpe (1900, 1:69), Banks wrote: 'I have from my childhood, in conformity with the precepts of a mother void of all imaginary fear, been in the constant habit of taking toads in my hand, and applying them to my nose and face as it may happen. My motive for doing this very frequently is to inculcate the opinion I have held, since I was told by my mother, that the toad is actually a harmless animal; and to whose manner of life man is certainly under some obligation as its food is chiefly those insects which devour his crops and annoy him in various ways.'

Long after this, in 1830, George Colman the Younger, who was a boy in the party when Banks and Phipps visited Mulgrave Castle, Phipps's Yorkshire home, in 1775, wrote:

'Our progress, under all its cumbrous circumstances, was still further retarded by Sir Joseph's indefatigable botany: we never saw a tree with an unusual branch, or a strange weed, or anything singular in the vegetable world but a halt was immediately ordered—out jumped Sir Joseph; out jumped the two boys (Augustus and myself) after him; and out jumped Omai,[1] after us all . . ., among all our jumpings, the most amusing to me was the jump of a frog down the throat of the said Sir Joseph; he held it in the palm of his hand (having picked it up in the grass) till it perform'd this gutteral somerset [*sic*] to convince his three followers that there is nothing poisonous in this animal.'

In December 1760 Banks matriculated at Oxford and became an undergraduate of Christ Church. Here, in due course, finding that the Professor of Botany, Humphrey Sibthorp,[2] did no teaching, Banks made his own arrangements; he went off to Cambridge and brought back as his tutor Israel Lyons, son of a Jewish watchmaker, a young man noted for his abilities in astronomy as well as in botany. Lyons must have given Banks much formal instruction, as the Newfoundland manuscripts show, but, during the vacations, Banks undoubtedly learnt a great deal about practical and theoretical botany from Philip Miller (1691–1771), who was in charge of the Chelsea Physic Garden from 1722 until a year before his death.

Founded in 1673 by the Society of the Art and Mistery of Apothecaries of the City of London, the garden was purchased in 1712 by Hans Sloane who, ten years later, settled it upon the Society by a deed of conveyance. Through Sloane's

[1] Omai was the Tahitian brought back to England by Captain Furneaux of the *Adventure*, companion ship to the *Resolution* on Captain Cook's second voyage round the world.

[2] Sibthorp was professor at Oxford from 1747 to 1783; during this period of thirty-six years he is said to have delivered only one lecture (Stearn 1967: 168).

influence, Miller was appointed gardener there (Stearn 1961; Wall and Cameron 1963). Miller had had a sound education and was thoroughly versed in botanical method. The first edition of his famous *Gardeners Dictionary* appeared in 1731, and during his lifetime twenty-four further editions appeared, including translations and abridgements. He was a friend of Linnaeus who said of him that he was not only a prince of gardeners but a prince of botanists. During his time at Chelsea he increased the numbers of species grown in the garden from about one to five thousand.

Banks's father died in 1761 and his mother then took for her London home Turret House, 24 Paradise Row (Blunt 1906:175), adjacent to the Swan Inn and just east of the Chelsea Physic Garden. Turret House was a Queen Anne building, formerly Rothery's School, which fortunately was engraved for the prospectus (pl. 7), a copy of which still exists in the British Museum. Maurer's engraving (pl. 4) of the Chelsea waterfront shows the turret from which the house derived its name, and its proximity to the Chelsea Physic Garden. Turret House was pulled down in 1816. Haynes's plan of the garden (pl. 5) shows better than any description can how extensive and elaborate the facilities for growing plants had become in Miller's day.

Miller had collectors and friends all over the known world; it would have been from him that Banks learnt the best methods of collecting exotic plants, and the most successful means of transporting and propagating them, matters which were to be so important to him when he directed the development of the Royal Botanic Gardens at Kew. It is said that Solander met Miller soon after his arrival in London in 1760 (Rauschenberg 1968:16) and it may have been through Miller that, in or about 1764, Banks and Solander first became acquainted (Danielsson 1969:16). It is more certain that, through Miller, Banks got to know Ehret, the great flower painter, who married Miller's sister-in-law. As we shall see, he painted some of Banks's plants from Newfoundland and Labrador.

Mrs. Banks was deeply religious and she may have been further influenced in her choice of Turret House by the presence of the Moravian headquarters in Lindsey House near by in Cheyne Walk (pl. 6). Banks was certainly in touch with the missionaries before his voyage to Newfoundland; his herbarium contains several sheets of plants labelled 'Labrador 1765, Soc. Unit. Frat.'—the Moravian brethren were also known as the United Brethren or *Unitas Fratrum*. It may well have been the Moravians' accounts of life in Greenland and their plans for settling and working with the Eskimos in Labrador, together with the Canadian plants in the Chelsea Physic Garden, as well as in the Fulham Nursery of Christopher Gray, with which Catesby had been so closely associated, that stimulated Banks's interest in north-eastern America and led him to make his Newfoundland journey.

Banks's voyage in the *Niger*, one of the naval vessels patrolling the Newfoundland fisheries at that time, was probably facilitated by the fact that one of his

Chelsea neighbours was John Montagu, 4th Earl of Sandwich (1718–92), First Lord of the Admiralty at various times, a musician and a passionate fisherman.[1]

Sandwich had estates in Lincolnshire and Banks, when a boy, had fished with him. When they were both living in Chelsea, they had many fishing expeditions on the Thames. Night fishing was best. They had a large and comfortable punt, their rods, each with a little bell, sticking out all round it. With plenty to eat and drink, they often fished from dusk to dawn and thus were laid the foundations of a friendship which probably was of considerable help to Banks, not only regarding his passage in the *Niger* but also in his being given facilities for his voyage in the *Endeavour*. Sandwich was also a close friend of Phipps's uncle, Augustus Hervey, whose sister Mary was believed to have been his mistress at one time.

The young men must have planned their journey in detail during the winter of 1765–6. With Solander's help and advice (Danielsson 1969:16), Banks equipped himself for making extensive botanical and zoological collections. He had a small library which included works of Linnaeus, Edwards and Catesby; he took plant presses, notebooks, fishing gear including nets and trawls, butterfly nets and other entomological equipment, and a keg of spirits for preserving the animals that he wished to take back to England to be stuffed and painted. Just before he left he was nominated as a Fellow of the Royal Society. Smith (1911:10) lists his supporters who included Dr. Charles Lyttelton, the Bishop of Carlisle and a noted antiquary, the librarian of the British Museum, Dr. Morton and a Dr. William Watson, who was a year younger than Banks and became a noted physicist and astronomer.

Banks and Phipps arrived in Plymouth *en route* for Newfoundland on 11 April 1766. Here they spent nearly a fortnight looking at the sights, collecting plants and intertidal animals in an area now internationally famous through the Marine Biological Station. Most of Banks's British plants have vanished so that I have been unable thoroughly to check his records from Plymouth but there are some drawings and notes on fishes and other animals which are listed later. The *Niger* sailed from Plymouth Sound on 22 April, the first of a long line of scientifically equipped ships to leave that harbour.

The *Niger* arrived at St. John's on 11 May. Snow still lay on the ground, but Banks collected vigorously, noting when the thaw set in that plants found only at considerable heights in England occurred at sea level there. A month later the

---

[1] No truly scholarly assessment of Sandwich has yet been published. His association with Wilkes, the condition of the Navy at one time when he was First Lord of the Admiralty, his association with the rakes of Medmenham, these and other matters have given him a poor reputation. No one, however, who has read the Admiralty minutes of the period can doubt that there is another very different side to his character. He supported Anson in many naval reforms; did a great deal to further Cook's voyages, was a close friend of Banks, and was devotedly attached to the singer Martha Ray, with whom he lived for many years and who was, to Fanny Burney's surprise, a modest and charming woman.

ship left for Croque on the east coast of the Northern Peninsula. This harbour with its deep inlets was an excellent base for collecting and for expeditions to neighbouring islands and harbours; but unfortunately both Banks and Adams were very ill from some kind of fever for most of July and they sailed for Chateau Bay on the Labrador coast on 6 August, sooner than Banks had expected, so that he lamented the fact that many of the plants he had collected were not properly dried and were bound to suffer. Banks's description of Croque and the fishing settlement there is still valid today in many respects. The tiny hamlet is peopled by vigorous independent Newfoundlanders whose only access to other settlements is by rough tracks through the unspoilt tangled woods, or by open boat along the coast, although in the summer months a coastal vessel calls, and a seaplane is able to land in an emergency. Cod is still gutted on the waterfront and the guts still lie in decomposing piles until cleaned up to some extent by spring tides or storms.

Banks preferred the life at Chateau Bay where the surrounding country was more open and it was easier to get about on foot, but unfortunately he failed to keep a regular journal there. However he made many observations on the birds and kept records of his plant collections; his detailed descriptions and notes on plants are nearly all missing, but many of his specimens remain and are reviewed in the last section of this book. In Labrador Banks again noticed that plants regarded as alpines in Europe grew at sea level in the vicinity of Chateau Bay, and that in general it was much colder on the coast than further inland.

The building of the blockhouse in Chateau Bay, which was the main object of the *Niger's* voyage, was completed in record time, by 4 September, but the ship remained in harbour until 3 October when she sailed for Croque. Barely a week was spent at Croque before they sailed south again, to St. John's where they remained for two weeks before leaving for Lisbon. The Saturday before they left, Palliser, the Governor of Newfoundland and Commodore of the Fleet there, gave a party in honour of the anniversary of the coronation of George III. On the Monday morning Cook, who had surveyed Chateau Bay in 1763, arrived in the *Grenville*; he states in his log that the *Niger* sailed on Wednesday afternoon whereas Banks states that they left on Tuesday. Which day it actually was does not matter much; the stay of the *Niger* and the *Grenville* overlapped for at least thirty hours and I cannot believe that Palliser, Cook, Adams and Banks did not meet to discuss their activities during the summer and the successful building of the blockhouse with which they had all been concerned in one way or another.

The *Niger* arrived in Lisbon on 17 November and after a stay of six weeks left for England; Banks returned to London on 30 January. Within a short time he and his sister moved from their mother's house in Chelsea to one in New Burlington Street where there was more room for his expanding collections and library. He planned to visit Linnaeus and see Lapland in 1768 but abandoned this on hearing of Cook's projected voyage to the Pacific; the Royal Society, with great discernment, used its influence with the Admiralty to procure accommodation for him and a small scientific staff on board the *Endeavour*, under Cook's command.

So, on 25 August 1768, Banks again sailed from Plymouth, this time on one of the most famous of all voyages. Owing to Cook's superb seamanship, and to Banks's experience in Newfoundland and Labrador, his careful planning and his ability even at that comparatively early age to choose the right men for the work in hand, the biological results of the voyage were magnificent. Three years later Banks and Solander arrived back with splendid collections of hitherto unknown plants and animals, MS notes and hundreds of drawings executed during their passage across the Atlantic, along the coast of South America, across the Pacific via the Society Islands, New Zealand and the east coast of Australia, through Torres Straits, and on to Batavia, Cape Town, St. Helena and home. In London they were greatly acclaimed though Cook was rather overshadowed. With no father or brother to criticize or to stem the adulation of friends and acquaintances, the overflowing pride of his mother and sister, Banks lost his head. When a second voyage round the world was arranged he tried to get Cook's ship, the *Resolution*, altered to his requirements so as to accommodate a larger staff. The superstructure necessary would have endangered the vessel; Sandwich and the Admiralty objected, and Banks withdrew after a heated exchange.

Instead of sailing with Cook, Banks took his staff and equipment to Iceland, leaving in July 1772 and returning via the Orkneys in November. It was his moment of truth and a turning point in his life. Intelligent enough to see that he had behaved most foolishly, he must have been overcome with vexation and chagrin. But it is pleasant to be able to record that, although he had made such a mistake, his friendship with Cook and the other officers remained unimpaired and he took an active part in dealing with the natural history collections and the publication of the accounts of this voyage as well as of the third and last, with its tragic ending.

Besides Banks's voyage to Iceland in 1772 he entered upon another commitment later that year which was to be of far-reaching importance. There had been notable gardens at Kew since the time of Sir Henry Capel, who took Kew House soon after the restoration of Charles II. In 1730 Frederick, Prince of Wales, obtained the lease from the Capel family; after his death his widow, together with the Earl of Bute, set about the restoration of the gardens and inaugurated the scientific study of botany there. William Aiton, who had been trained by Philip Miller of the Chelsea Physic Gardens, was appointed to Kew in 1759; thirteen years later the Dowager Princess died and George III took charge of Kew Gardens.

The king selected Joseph Banks as his unofficial scientific adviser and through Banks's vision and great practical ability, to be implemented later by William and Joseph Hooker, Kew became a great open-air herbarium for exotic plants from all over the world. Botanical exploration and the study of economic plants were vigorously promoted. Kew Gardens today are primarily the result of Banks's

1. Joseph Banks as a boy.
Artist unknown

2. Mrs. William Banks, 'A mother void of all imaginary fear'.
John Russell

3. Joseph and Sophia Banks? Engraved by C. Grignion after the painting by S. Wale, 1759.

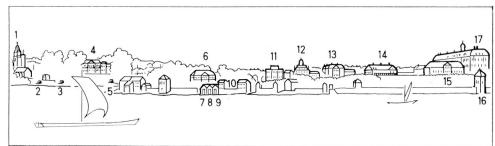

4. View of Chelsea by J. Maurer, 1744. 1, Chelsea Church. 4, Cheyne Walk. 6, Greenhouse of the Physic Garden. 7–9, Barge Houses. 10, Old Swan Tavern. 11, Houses in Paradise Row. 12, Turret House, formerly Rothery's School, where Banks lived from 1761–1767. 14, Greenhouse of Sir Robert Walpole. 15, 17, Parts of Chelsea Hospital. 16, Octagon Summer House of Sir Robert Walpole.

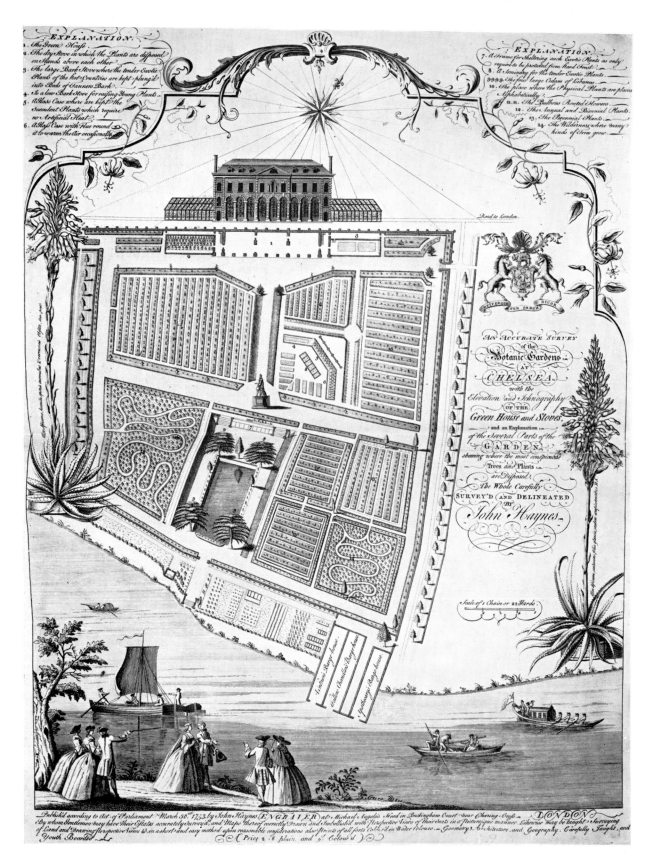

5. Plan of Chelsea Physic Garden.
John Haynes, 1763

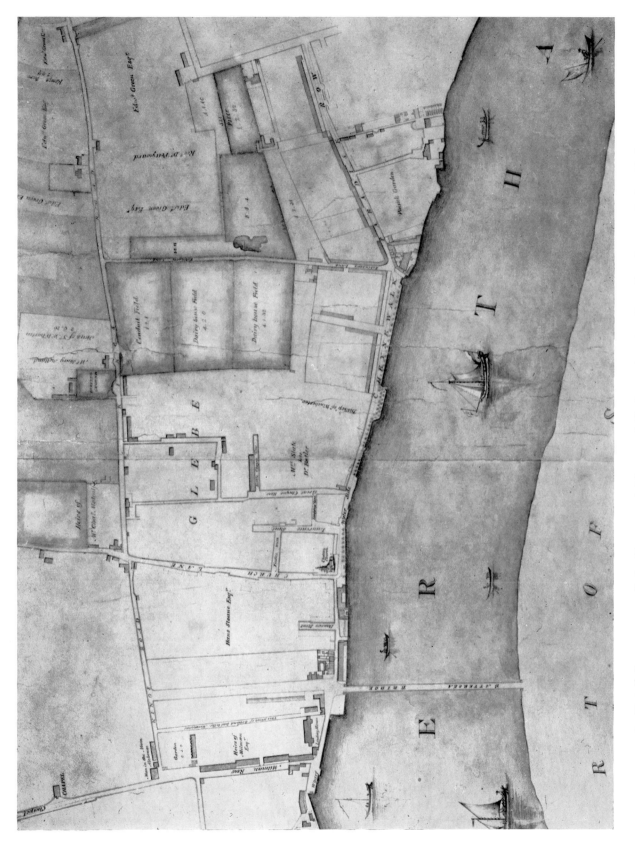

6. Detail from a map of the Estate and Manor of Chelsea, showing Paradise Row and the Chelsea Physic Garden on the right, and Lindsey House on the waterfront, left of Battersea Bridge.
T. Richardson, 1769

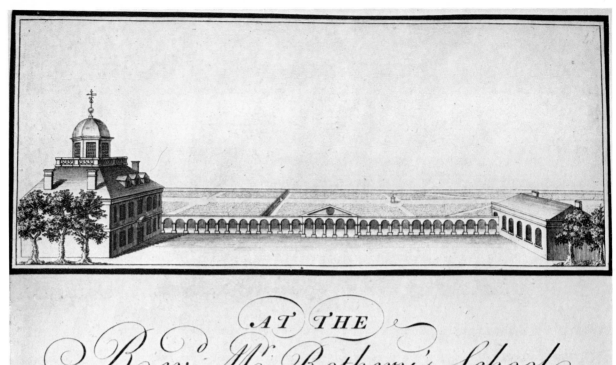

At the Rev.ᵈ Mr. Rothery's School, the Turret House Paradise Row, Chelsea, Young Gentlemen are Boarded and Qualified for the University or Business, on the following Terms, Viz.

Board Learning included, £25 — *Guineas* *5*

Day Boarders — £15 *per Ann.* & *3* *Entrance*

Day Scholars 6 Guineas *2*

Dancing, Drawing, & Fencing, at reasonable Rates.

Single Bed, if required, £5 per Annum.

Gadesby scrip.ᵗ

Thorowgood sculp.ᵗ

7. Rothery's School or Turret House; the engraved prospectus by Thorowgood

labours and his persistent interest. In 1772 Banks and Sir John Pringle, President of the Royal Society, suggested to the king that Francis Masson, an able under-gardener at Kew, should be sent to the Cape of Good Hope to make botanical collections; he was the first of a notable line of Kew collectors that included David Nelson, who went on Cook's third voyage, Robert Brown and Ferdinand Bauer in Australia, and many others.

The winter of 1772–3 was memorable for Banks not only on account of his developing interest in Kew Gardens but also because he was at last able to meet some Eskimos, which must have compensated to some extent for his failing to see them in their native land in 1766. Just before Christmas George Cartwright arrived from Labrador with a family of five and settled them in London for some weeks before taking them to his country home in Nottinghamshire. Banks and Solander paid them frequent visits and must have learnt a good deal about Eskimo life and customs, although there do not seem to be any surviving written records among the Banksian papers. Some portraits of them commissioned by Banks have, however, been found, are are discussed later (pls. 21a, 21b). One result of these meetings was that Cartwright undertook to make observations and collections for Banks.

Here it seems appropriate to go back some years and to touch very briefly on Banks's love affairs. They have been the subject of endless trivial gossip from his youth to the present day but the writers have not shed much light on the women he cared for and who enriched his life.

Joseph Banks, gay, intelligent, wealthy and good-looking, would have been a subject for hopeful speculation on the part of ambitious mothers and daughters in any age. His 'engagement' to Harriet Blosset, a ward of James Lee of the Vineyard Nursery, Hammersmith (p. 102), appears to have been a carefully calculated affair on her part (Cameron 1952:285) from which the Blosset family was rumoured to have withdrawn with a substantial sum of money from Banks (Lee 1810) to console her for all the knitted waistcoats with which she had sought to enmesh him. But there seems no doubt that on his return from the voyage of the *Endeavour* he fell deeply in love with a girl he had known as a child. 'Her person was remarkably genteel, and her countenance particularly engaging. All the elegant accomplish-ments were united in her, and were only surpassed by her mental improvements.' During Banks's absence in the *Endeavour* her father died, having lost a fortune through gambling, and left her penniless. Joseph found her living as companion to an old lady and placed her in the home of a respectable family where she had com-panions of her own age, and where he visited her frequently. She became his mistress, and he then installed her in a house in Orchard Street, probably the street of that name off Portman Square which was then fashionable and inhabited by such people as Sheridan and his wife. A highly-coloured account of the relationship was published in September 1773, in *The Town and Country Magazine*, a periodical specializing in scandals of a kind which could scarcely appear in the gutter press of today without the law of libel being invoked. But the article contains the above description and is illustrated with an engraving (pl. 12) which gives an impression of a girl of charm and intelligence. Some of Banks's champions have been so anxious to present their own views of him that his surviving correspondence appears to have been censored and there exists no adequate account of why he did not marry until he was thirty-six.

The tone of the article mentioned above, one of a series entitled 'Histories of the Tête à Tête annexed', is such that I would have discounted it had it not been for a letter from the Danish entomologist, J. C. Fabricius, a pupil of Linnaeus's, which I found many years ago in Banks's correspondence; it too might have been destroyed had not the first part been devoted to botanical affairs. Fabricius visited Edinburgh in 1767 to see a brother who was studying medicine there; they toured the Highlands on horseback and then rode south to London where they met Banks and Solander. Fabricius took a great interest in the preparations for the voyage of the *Endeavour*, and in later years made many visits to London in order to see Banks and work on his collections from which he named some 500 species. In November 1773, Fabricius wrote thus:

Dear Sir,

Here I am happy and merry at Coppenhagen thinking about all the happy houres I spend in Engelland with my friends, and recollecting all the fine things I saw in your house from the human down to the little Mosses Dr. Muselius was tired with. . . .

My best compliments and wishes in Orchard Street, what has shee brought you? Well, it is all the same, if a Boy, he will be clever and strong like his father, if a girl, she will be pretty and genteel like her mother. . . .

Life well, dear Banks, remember sometimes you have a friend in Coppenhagen, for really if You think their is a man in the world who is more your friend than I You certainly wrong

Your
most obed. humb. servant
J. C. Fabricius
Professor of Oeconomy.

Fabricius's wife Cecilia wrote a gay postscript to his letter; it is possible that Banks's reply has been preserved in some Danish library. *The Town and Country Magazine* noted that 'The circumnavigator and Miss B——n' had become even more devoted through the birth of their child. Why Banks failed to marry this girl can only be guessed at. It is probable that his mother objected, but there is no evidence for this. Banks may have felt happy enough as it was; both his mother and sister were strong characters and it might have been difficult for the girl to become a member of their household; moreover, as Currey (1967:37) points out, Banks later held the view that marriage and a life of scientific research were incompatible. Quite apart from this there is the fact of the high rate of infant and maternal mortality in London in the 1770s, and the possibility that Miss B——n died at the birth of a second child.

In the spring of 1773 Banks went abroad for the last time; he made a brief visit to Holland to see various collections, and at The Hague he consulted a group of Greenland captains in order to gain information which would be useful in furthering Phipps's projected voyage towards the North Pole. Later that year he went on a plant-hunting expedition to Wales with Lightfoot the botanist, Solander and Paul Sandby, the artist. At home he worked with Solander on his growing herbarium. Miller of the Chelsea Physic Garden had died shortly after the return of the *Endeavour*, and Banks had bought his collection; he and Solander were busy with the classification of the *Endeavour* plants, the preparation of the drawings and MSS for publication, and with the engraving of the copperplates intended to illustrate their account of the rarities they had discovered.

The Royal Society had elected Banks as a Fellow just after he sailed for Newfoundland, and in 1774, eight years later, he began to serve on the Council. He was already a corresponding member of the French Academy of Sciences and was beginning to extend his circle of European scientific friends. His meticulous feeling for order and method enabled him to manage his private and public affairs with extraordinary ability; his zest for life and people, his charm and his great wealth all helped but even so his capacity and his actual accomplishment are astonishing. In 1776 he and his sister moved house again, this time to a mansion large enough for his collections and ever-expanding library—No. 32 Soho Square, which was to remain his London headquarters for the rest of his life, and to become an international centre for visiting scientists.

Banks succeeded Sir John Pringle as President of the Royal Society in 1778, holding this post until his death more than forty years later. By virtue of this office he wielded enormous power both scientifically and politically, and the respect in which the President was held enabled him to promote scientific exploration and international co-operation, fields in which the Royal Society is active today. Banks's friendship with George III, due to their common interest in agriculture and in the Royal Botanic Gardens at Kew, his excellent relationships with French, German, Russian and Italian scientists, the range of his knowledge: he could appreciate his friend Herschel's astronomical discoveries as well as those in the more familiar field of biology—all these set him above most intrigues and the temptation to use his great power unworthily. Of necessity his vision sometimes failed and he made mistakes, but on the whole he was wonderfully perceptive in his choice of the ways in which scientific work in biology could best be promoted and in his selection of the right men for such work. This can be seen in the late eighteenth- and early nineteenth-century records of the history of Australia and Africa, and particularly in the unfolding of the latter continent to European eyes.

Another aspect of his presidency was that he became *ex officio* one of the Trustees of the British Museum where he had long owned a reader's ticket. He attended his first meeting in December 1778, his last in February 1820, the year of his death. He bequeathed his library to the Museum and his bookplate is on many of its treasures; his collection of plants is the basis of the Herbarium in the British Museum (Natural History); his MS notes may still be seen on many sheets of exotic plants collected by himself or his friends and other botanists of the time; his own interleaved copies of the works of Linnaeus, heavily annotated by Solander and Dryander, are still in constant use.

In 1777 Banks introduced Johan Alströmer to another mistress, a Miss Walls, at whose house they dined, together with Solander, on more than one occasion (Rydén 1963:28–29); she may have been Ann, baptized in 1740, or Mary, baptized in 1742, daughters of Joseph and Mary Walls of East Kirkby, a parish adjoining Revesby. I am much indebted to Miss Joan Gibbons for searching the county records and giving me these facts about the Walls family. It would be interesting to know whether there are any direct descendants of Miss B——n and Miss Walls since there was no surviving child of Banks's marriage with Dorothea Hugessen in 1779.

Dorothea Hugessen was fifteen years younger than her husband. She and her sister Mary were co-heirs to the family estate at Norton in Kent; and had an annual income of some £1,000 each from rents. Mary married Edward Knatchbull of Provender, Kent, shortly after her sister's marriage with Joseph Banks. Many personal records including some of Banks's letters to his brother-in-law as well as more formal papers are lodged with the Brabourne papers in the Kent County Archives, and it is from these as well as from Sir Hughe Knatchbull-Hugessen's book *A Kentish Family* that I have compiled these notes on Dorothea Banks.

John Russell's portrait of her (pl. 13) does not reveal much; she looks cheerful and confident but not particularly intelligent or sensitive though this may have been due to the artist's lack of perception. A letter from Banks written from Revesby in October 1780, to Edward Knatchbull tells us a little about her:

My Dear Brother,

I received your Obliging Favor on my return home from a Long Journey which business obliged me to take into Staffordshire in which my Wife and Sister accompanied me Travelling stew [*sic*] through cross countrey roads in a mountanous countrey & sleeping at miserable ale houses without even a maid to Assist at their Toilets all which Hardship they voluntarily subjected to & chearfully endurd without a complaint I think they deserve a little eulogy for it.

The year has been (much to my dissatisfaction) most remarkable for publick meetings & dancing assemblys the races were no sooner finished than the interest I have in the neighboring burrough of Boston Call'd me there to exert myself in an opposition which ending in a victory produced a ball for the Freemen at which it was necessary that Mrs B should be present thank god she escaped pretty well as only one pot of Porter was thrown over her gown tho she dancd between more Pots & porter & Bowls of Negus than Couples in the Countrey dance.

From Boston in three days we were hurried to Lincoln in fear of an opposition in the countrey this ended in two Balls *don't you pity me.*

Shooting has gone but ill what with business & Journey I have not for three weeks handled my Fire Lock but now I am returned the Pheasants must look sharp I walkd out yesterday & shot at but one who fell to the aim so at least I have not Miss'd a Pheasant this year.

I rejoice to hear of your being at Provender & shall always be happy to hear that you keep the old house warm . . . shall you be there at Christmas we would if you like it spend our Holidays with you I have three excellent spaniels Mab Tiney & Juno I do not think we should cut a bad figure in Put wood

> Adieu my dear Brother
> give my affect Cmpts to my sister & believe me
> your affect. Brother
> Jos. Banks.

One of Dorothea Banks's account books remains; it dates from 1797 to 1817 and in it she faithfully records her expenses for laundry (£15 8s 8½d for 1797); losses, and very few gains, at cards; regular weekly payments to Dr. Burney for music lessons until his death in 1814 (she had four from Mrs. Burney in 1817), and odd sums to various performers at her own concerts. She collected old china, an interest which her husband shared; amongst her good works are payments to schools and for the education of certain children; she was a subscriber to the lying-in-hospital, and to the eye hospital (Banks complained of failing sight as early as 1808); and then there were presents from Banks, to her godchildren, and so on. Many of the entries are regrettably brief stating simply, 'Mr. Smith's bill, Mr. Tomlinson's bill,' etc. All the papers concerned with her suggest that she was a kind and agreeable woman, beloved by her nephews and nieces as well as by the elder members of the family.

After their marriage, in 1779, Banks bought a house at Spring Grove, Heston, where they spent much of their time. The garden there was an old-established one in which he grew many exotic plants and fruits. He was the first successfully to cultivate American cranberries, and he was particularly interested in methods of improving fruits such as apples, peaches, figs and grapes. In the late summer they briefly visited Overton in Derbyshire, an estate which had come to Banks through one of his grandmothers, Anne Hodgkinson (p. 105). From Overton they travelled to Revesby Abbey, the family home. The management of the Revesby Estate, the general agricultural problems of the county of Lincolnshire, the draining of the fens (see pl. 43) and other country matters had Banks's most careful attention. His friend Arthur Young (1799:20) has described his office of two rooms, altogether thirty by sixteen feet, with a fireproof partition, in which he kept an elaborate series of files so that information on any aspect of the estates and on all the men employed on them was instantly available.

Banks and his wife usually remained at Revesby until October, returning to Soho Square for the winter. They seem to have enjoyed a happy stable marriage; this is implicit in many surviving letters from their visitors.

Sarah Sophia Banks continued to live with them. She was a vigorous woman, tall and with a booming voice like her brother's. She drew, fished, drove a four-in-hand and kept numbers of scrap books which show the range of her interests; many of them are in the British Museum. One is devoted to newspaper cuttings and illustrations of balloons of the period; another to the funeral of Nelson, another to heraldry; she collected visiting cards, tradesmen's cards, medals and so on. She probably kept another collection of cuttings about her brother but I have not found any reference to this and since she died two years before him he might have destroyed it.

Dorothea Banks and Sarah Sophia loyally supported Joseph in many of his activities; they wore dresses woven entirely of wool when he was busy popularizing merino sheep. His sister had three such garments, Hightum, Tightum and Scrub, suitable for social occasions of varying grandeur; Joseph himself wore woollen suits. Visiting botanists brought them fashion books from Paris as well as specimens and books; the ladies sent the latest London hats to Cecilia Fabricius in Copenhagen (not much use when they moved to Kiel, Fabricius wrote). Such a household made an agreeable background for the meetings of scientists who came to Soho Square from all over Europe and North America to see Banks's great herbarium and library, his extensive ethnographical and other collections.

Banks's great library, which was made available to many other scientists, was catalogued by Dryander in five volumes, published 1796–1800. Dryander used an interleaved set in which he noted additions; after his death this set was kept up to date by his successor until Banks's death in 1820. These volumes are now in both parts of the British Museum. Beaglehole in his long and careful introduction to the published version of Banks's *Endeavour* diary is rather hard on Banks's intellectual ability (1962, 1:123). He suggests that if education entails real discipline of the mind, Banks was not truly educated. Certainly Banks preferred biology to the classics, although he was able to write and read Latin, and probably also to speak that language.

That Banks enjoyed scholarship for its own sake is however apparent from his interleaved and heavily annotated copy of Tusser's long poem on agricultural husbandry, first published in 1557, now with the Brabourne papers in the Kent Archives. Reginald Blunt possessed a copy of Elizabeth Blackwell's *Curious Herbal*

(1737) which he said was enriched with Banks's annotations on every page. Miss Mander Jones tells me that in about 1948 Messrs. Quaritch sold a kind of Commonplace Book of Banks, with the same type of scholarly annotation. These and other personal copies of Banks's books were perhaps retained by Lady Banks and dispersed at some later period. This may account for the absence from the British Museum libraries of the reference books he took with him both in the *Niger* and in the *Endeavour*.

Banks's warmth and generosity to other scholars is exemplified in a letter written about him by Johan Alströmer in 1777 (Rydén 1963:29): 'I have,' he says, 'completely won Banks's friendship. He has not only introduced me among all Scholars but also promised me in the Way of Learning to accomplish everything he can. . . . No week passes but he receives huge *Paquets* of Naturalia from all parts of the world, for he has friends in all places and all extend themselves to show him courtesy.

'Banks and Solander are inseparable. They are esteemed by all Classes of People from the King himself down, and with his Yeomen, Dukes, Lords, Ladies, Baronets, Gentlemen, etc., all speak with respect of Them and all are content when they can have their Company. They must consequently against their will often frequent most high Society, which they detest, but the rest of their time they devote to Natural History and all the noble sciences . . .'.

One of Banks's closest friends was the Frenchman, P. M. Auguste Broussonet (1761–1807), whose letters give a wonderfully vivid picture of the life of an energetic and scholarly man in scientific circles in Paris and in the countryside of the Midi at that time. In them we read of current botanical and zoological research, of Montgolfier's aeronautical experiments, of arrangements for sending Banks a special umbrella, wine, and merino sheep with their shepherd from Broussonet's estates near Montpellier. There is gossip of Marie Antoinette and her diamond necklace, of Count Cagliostro, that king of quacks, and his discharge; of Broussonet's own political troubles when he had to flee from Paris in the aftermath of the Revolution and make his way in winter across the Pyrenees into Spain. Unfortunately I have not found Banks's replies but we deduce from Broussonet that Banks wrote frequently and sent him much of interest, including books (the account of Cook's first voyage for one), fishes, kangaroos (which they thought might run wild and become a favourite target for French hunters), plants such as New Zealand flax, *Phormium tenax*, and many other things. He also regaled Broussonet with details of his battles with the dissidents in the Royal Society, and he feasted and entertained Broussonet's friends when they visited London. How important this friendship was to Banks can be gauged from the unusual speed with which he answered the letters (the date is scribbled on the back of many of them), and from the money and introductions he sent to Broussonet in Spain where, refugee though he was, he continued assiduously to collect any scientific specimens he thought Banks might like.

55

Less is known of Banks's kindness to the aged and obscure such as the widowed sister of his friend, Daniel Solander. In 1792, ten years after Solander's death, we find Banks arranging an annuity for her in Pitea, Sweden, asking Aron Mathesius to see to the details which were to be kept secret, and furthermore to arrange that after her death the income should go to augment the salary of Olof Swartz, Professor of Botany in Stockholm.

A few years later, 1799, Banks was helping Magnus Behm who had arrived impoverished in London. As Governor of Kamchatka, twenty years earlier, Behm had used his own money to supply Cook's ships, and had refused reimbursement from the English Admiralty who had then presented him with some handsome silver plate. Prince Potemkin had taken it from him and placed it in a museum in St. Petersburg on the grounds that it was a gift to the Russian people. Banks managed to get Behm a pension from the Russian Government. Then in 1818, when Banks was an old man, Behm's daughter and son-in-law were discovered to be nearly destitute. Banks wrote vigorously to Nicholas Vansittart, then Chancellor of the Exchequer, to try to get help for them: 'Allow me to implore your attention', he wrote, 'to a Case in which the honor of the nation we belong to is in my opinion called in question.' The whole story is summed up in the letters printed in the supplementary papers (pp. 278, 283) and is typical of Banks, I believe, throughout his life.

A few years earlier, Banks tried to find adequate lodgings for Domingo Vandelli, an eminent Portuguese botanist whom he had met in Lisbon on the return journey from Newfoundland (pp. 177, 282). Vandelli, Keeper of the Royal Museum and Exotic Gardens (which Banks had helped to found) in Lisbon, had been exiled to the Azores for political reasons. Banks used his influence to procure his release and a pension. In the course of negotiating for the pension Banks wrote: 'He [Vandelli] is soon expected to arrive and I am sorry to say that it appears by his Letter to me that he is wholly destitute of Property. . . . Well aware of the Liberality and Generosity of the Marquis's Character I can have no doubt of his Intention to assign to this Ancient Philosopher who is represented to be at least 80 years of age a proper and Competent maintenance such as will give comfort to the Latter End of a well spent Life now almost exhausted, what I wish you to obtain for me is a knowledge of the sum that is intended to be applied to the old man's use, in order that I may be enabled to Look out for some proper house in which he may be boarded and Lodged with people who will be Kind and Civil to him and these are not easy to Obtain but which I shall seek for with diligence as soon as I am acquainted with the amount of the offer that it will be in my power to make for the accommodation.'

However, Vandelli was accompanied by his son, unknown to Banks, and a letter, apparently written by the son although signed by Vandelli, came to Banks asking him for £27 monthly; this was a large sum when we remember that Miller when

8. Sarah Sophia Banks.
Angelica Kauffman

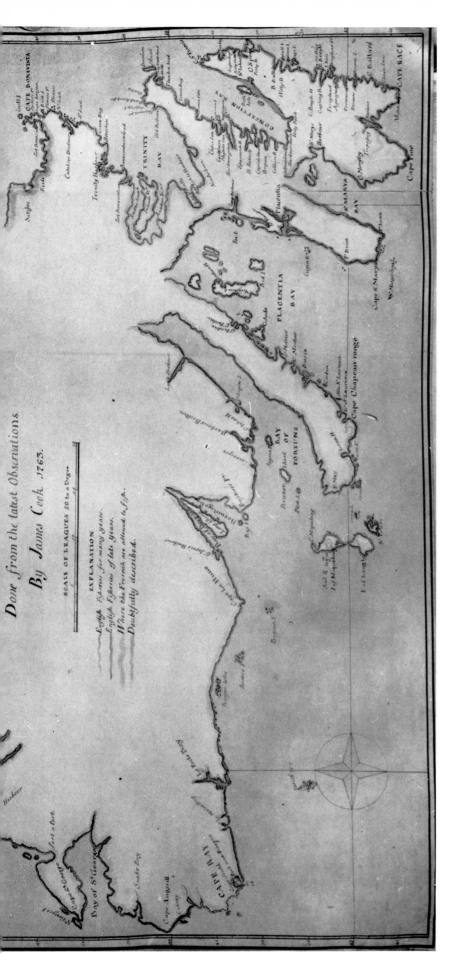

9. Map of Newfoundland, 1763.
Ascribed to James Cook

10*a*. Sarah Sophia Banks.
Nathaniel Hone

10*b*. Miniature of James Cook,
owned by Joseph Banks.
Margaret Bingham, after
Nathaniel Dance

superintendent of the Chelsea Physic Garden had had a salary of £50 p.a., and that Mungo Park in European settlements on his way to Gambia in 1794 was allowed 7s. 6d. daily, this sum to be doubled on the way from Gambia to the Niger. Banks was vexed and wrote back sharply, asking him to send his son home but repeating that he himself would give him the standard rate of subsistence for the many foreigners who had taken refuge in England.

Banks even assisted the distressed relatives of persons who had often been insolent and troublesome to him such as Georg and Reinhold Forster, the naturalists on Cook's second voyage. There is a letter (p. 278) from Reinhold Forster's married daughter, Wilhelmina Sprengel, dated June 1799, thanking Banks for cancelling the debt owed him by her recently deceased father, a generous action which had greatly eased her mother's troubles. One is reminded of Cartwright's kindness to the family of John Baskem who had broken into and robbed one of his Labrador trading posts; Cartwright wrote: 'He not being at home, and observing that neither his wife nor children had a shoe to their feet, and were in the utmost poverty and distress, my resentment was turned into pity, and I accordingly made him a present, by a written deed of gift, of my houses and all my interest in that place.'

Banks heard of the death of Dryander (du Rietz 1964:83) from Sir Everard Home, the surgeon who had been attending him. 'I was so stunned by the unlooked for Blow I received from the Perusal of your Letter that I was utterly unable to answer by return of Post. I have lost my right hand & can never hope to provide any thing as a substitute that can at all make amends to me . . . For me I console myself in Feeling that my departure cannot be long delayed . . . My Pen almost refuses its office.' It was October 1810; they had been friends since 1777 when Dryander had come to England.

There is a parallel in Cartwright's affection for his old servant Charles Atkinson who attended him during his army service and then obtained his discharge to accompany him to Labrador. On 13 January 1772, Cartwright wrote, 'I thought Charles would have died every minute of this day; which kept me at home. I read prayers to him for he retains his senses, notwithstanding he is so bad that he can take nothing.' And finally on 6 February, 'During our absence, my faithful old servant Charles breathed his last.'

Neither Banks nor Cartwright expressed their deeper feelings easily but both had a great respect for truth, a respect stated by Banks, implicit in much of Cartwright's journal. Banks wrote in a letter (1784) to Brissot de Warville, 'My disposition is not of a nature to wish for the control of any man's sentiments: we should all speak or print what we think is true; for we shall certainly be esteemed by the world in proportion to the truth or justice of what we speak or print'. And this is borne out by the practical honesty of his life.

In his vivid account of the near disasters to the *Endeavour* on the Australian coast in June and August 1770 (Beaglehole 1962, 2:81, 107), Banks never once mentioned

Providence—'The Fear of Death is Bitter,' he wrote, 'the prospect we now had of saving our lives at the expense of everything we had made my heart set much lighter on its throne, and I suppose there were none but felt the same sensations.' And that was all.

His lack of orthodox beliefs is also suggested in his sister's 'Memorandums' (p. 264) where she expresses her thankfulness to the 'Merciful God who has not only daily preserv'd my Dear Brother from the perils & very great ones of the Sea' and ends with her hope that those 'who are not enlightened with the Bright Sunshine of the Gospel, or who differ in points of faith; but who (according to their Faith) use their best Endeavours, as far as in their power they can, to do the Will of the SUPREME BEING: will be accepted at the THRONE OF GRACE'. Long afterwards Banks echoed her words; in a letter to one of the founders of the London Missionary Society, the Reverend Thomas Haweis, he wrote: 'Tho you and I certainly differ in opinion respecting the things we both deem necessary for salvation, yet under a firm belief in the boundless mercy of God I have no doubt that all men who strive according to their Consciences to do what they think good in his sight, will find favour in his Judgments . . .' (Strauss 1963–5:251; Gunson 1963–5:513–4).

After Banks became President of the Royal Society he lived an extremely busy life and little original work came from his own hand although his vast correspondence and his editing of other people's publications show that he astonishingly maintained his meticulous care for detail, and his awareness of current research in many fields other than botany. Thus, thanks to his great gifts and early training, he became one of the most intelligent and generous patrons of science ever known to the western world. It is good to remember him when we enjoy the glories of the Royal Botanic Gardens at Kew; when the Chinese tree peonies in our own gardens open in early summer; when we buy Australian wine and wool, use a humble india-rubber, and in many ordinary everyday matters.

I think that he was greatly influenced by the teachings of his Chelsea neighbours, the Moravians; from them he learnt to practise goodness rather than to preach it, and he had no desire for public recognition of his achievements. A man of enormous distinction, he asked that he should have no public funeral and no tombstone; his grave at Heston church is still, like Keats's, without his name, but on Keats's grave there is at least a stone engraved with the famous line 'Here lies one whose name is writ in water', which could better serve as Banks's memorial.

I believe that this lack of public recognition would in fact give him some satisfaction. Amongst the family papers in the Kent Archives is this note in his own hand:

'I have taken the Lizard, an Animal said to be Endow'd by nature with an instinctive Love of Mankind, as my Device, & have Caus'd it to be Engrav'd as my Seal, as a Perpetual Remembrance that a man is never so well Employ'd, as when he is laboring for the advantage of the Public; without the Expectation, the Hope or Even a wish to derive advantage of any Kind from the Result of his exertions.

Jos: Banks'

Constantine John Phipps

BANKS'S closest friend in the *Niger* was Constantine John Phipps (1744–92), who later became the second Lord Mulgrave. Phipps came from a distinguished family; his maternal grandfather was John, Lord Hervey (1696–1743), an M.A. of Clare, and author of *Some Materials Towards Memoirs of the Reign of George II*.[1] He married Mary Lepell (1700–68), an Irish beauty famous for her wit and the range of her scholarship. Pope and Gay sang her praises and Voltaire wrote verses to her in English, beginning,

> 'Hervey, would you know the passion
> You have kindled in my breast?'

Hervey himself, delicate in health (he was heavily rouged and painted to disguise his pallor), was a brilliant and courageous swordsman, a polished poet and a bitter enemy of Pope who satirized him as Sporus. The charm, sparkling intelligence and eccentricity of the family led to Lady Mary Wortley Montagu's famous saying that mankind was composed of men, women and Herveys. Constantine Phipps, the first Lord Mulgrave, married the Herveys' eldest daughter, Lepell. The gaiety and scholarship which characterized her own home appear to have illuminated her marriage which was a very happy one. Her brother Augustus John Hervey, who became the third Lord Bristol and was a highly competent naval officer, visited her in 1751 and commented in his journal: 'For my part I left Mulgrave with regret, as they were the most pleasing and obliging people to live with that were possible, and did everything for their company with an ease and exactness that left no one unwatched, whilst they appeared without the least care upon them' (Erskine 1954: 116). Their small son, Constantine John Phipps, made his first public appearance at the age of ten when he played Cupid in a masque written for his father's birthday by

---

[1] He directed that this was not to be published until long after his death, on account of its frankness about members of the royal family. It first appeared in 1848, edited and slightly bowdlerized by B. M. Croker, and was not published, unabridged, until Romney Sedgwick's edition of 1931.

a 'happy, grateful and most tenderly attached wife'; the earliest portrait I have found of him, painted when he was about nineteen, suggests a most sensitive intelligence (pl. 14).

Constantine John Phipps was at Eton with Banks but left in the winter of 1758–9, and in January joined his uncle, Augustus John Hervey, as a cadet in the *Monmouth*, 60 guns. Hervey, rash and impetuous in his personal affairs, had a most distinguished naval career. He was noted for loyalty to his friends. One of Byng's lieutenants, he opposed the Admiralty (and particularly Anson) in its verdict and condemnation of the unfortunate admiral and was one of the three officers who supported Byng throughout the period of his 'disgrace' which in fact reflected far more dishonour on the court that condemned him than on himself. Hervey's journal, first published in 1953, is a wonderful document of the life of a naval officer at that time, with its abundant commentary on the officers, ships and engagements of his day, his defence of Byng and the brilliant strategy he brought to bear not only on naval engagements but also on his innumerable love affairs, some of which are very funny indeed.[1]

Hervey's account of Lisbon in the years before the earthquake is interesting to compare with Banks's visit in the winter of 1766–7, when Pombal's reforms had taken effect. Hervey's journal ends in June 1759, six months after Phipps had joined the *Monmouth*, and just at the beginning of his most famous exploit. He was ordered to take a squadron to harass the French fleet in the Brest Road so as to prevent the projected invasion of Ireland. His editor writes: 'Between the 19th June and 5th November the *Monmouth* never once entered a friendly harbour. Throughout those twenty one weeks, even when the westerly gales forced Hawke's main squadron to take shelter in Plymouth Sound, or Torbay, Hervey kept the *Monmouth* at sea, maintaining constant watch and ward upon the motions of the French fleet in Brest Road.' Admiral Hawke wrote 'Through the whole he has given such proofs of diligence, activity, intrepidity and judgement that it would be doing injustice to his merit as an officer not to acknowledge that I part with him

---

[1] As a young man Hervey acquired brief but unhappy fame as the first husband of the notorious Miss Chudleigh. Among her escapades was her appearance at a ball given by the Turkish Ambassador, as Iphigenia ready for the sacrifice, a role which she transfigured by wearing a robe of gauze so fine that, as Lady Mary Wortley Montagu remarked, the entrails of the victim could clearly be discerned. It was probably she to whom Erasmus Darwin referred as 'a Turkish lady in an undress' (1791:196) in describing the flowers of *Hedysarum gyrans*, as a single female attracting ten bashful suitors:

> 'Loose wave her locks, disclosing as they break,
> The rising bosom and averted cheek;
> Clasp'd round her ivory neck with studs of gold
> Flows her thin vest in many a gauzy fold;
> O'er her light limbs the dim transparence plays,
> And the fair form, it seems to hide, betrays.'

with the greatest regret' (Erskine 1954:304). Hervey, worn out with fatigue, had to take the *Monmouth* into harbour before the victory at Quiberon Bay. His valour was publicly acclaimed and verses from the London *Evening Post* were quoted to him by his mother:

> 'Britons exult! all Gallia trembling stands,
> While *Hervey* executes and *Hawke* commands.'

What a beginning to the naval career of his young nephew! When Hervey was appointed to the *Dragon* in 1761, Phipps, now a midshipman, remained with him, and was present at the siege of Havannah in which his uncle played a most important part. The capture of that city broke Spanish power in America and was one of the victories that led to the end of the Seven Years' War. Hervey had no further active service. He died in 1779, at the age of fifty-five, leaving all his naval papers to Phipps.

Phipps became a lieutenant in 1762, and the following year left the *Dragon* to command the sloop *Diligence*, 12 guns; in 1765 he was appointed to the *Terpsichore*, 26 guns, and in 1767 became commander of the *Boreas*, 28 guns.

It seems that in 1766 he obtained leave of absence to visit Newfoundland with Banks since, although it is frequently stated that he was one of the lieutenants in the *Niger*, this is not so. His name appears nowhere on the muster rolls nor is he mentioned in the ship's log; the first and second lieutenants were, respectively, the Right Hon. David Rutherford and John Gurling. Banks refers to Phipps's building a house at Croque and to their garden there, which suggests that he may have had some official duties on the voyage but what these were and whether he sailed in the *Niger* on the return voyage I do not know. In 1768 he became Member for Lincoln but continued with his naval career, in which he proved courageous and competent although he failed to attain the high distinction of his uncle. His only voyage of discovery, the attempt to find a passage to the North Pole, in 1773, was unsuccessful and is chiefly remembered because Nelson was a midshipman in one of the two ships under his command. Zoologically it was more memorable; Banks had given him a long list of desiderata (p. 256); an autograph letter from Phipps written when he was near Spitzbergen was recently found in a grangerized volume of Smith's *Life of Sir Joseph Banks*:

My dear Banks,

I am in 79° 30' & have not seen a single bit of ice & have been these three days without any fire and have no one day had a fire all day—I have got you two small Blubbers—a Seal's Bill of Fare out of his Belly containing sundry non-descript: Crabs & other things several Birds stuffed amongst them non descripts particularly a *Larus rissa* [Kittiwake, *Rissa tridactyla* L.] with only 8 Remiges Primores tho' Linnaeus attributes 10 you know to all Birds a *Larus Niveus* [Ivory Gull *Pagophila eburnea* (Phipps)⌉ a Beautiful Bird etc. etc. Remember me to Solander & believe me most sincerely

Yours C. J. Phipps

Irvine is well & would probably have said something had he been up it is now 4 o'clock in the morning & the wind fair—

Racehorse off Spitsbergen
Lat. 79° 30′ July 4th

Phipps had a great knowledge of the higher branches of astronomy and mathematics which together with his unsparing wit and the polar voyage led to his being known as the Polar Bear or Ursa Major (Burney ed. Ellis 1907, 1:88), a name he shared with Dr. Johnson.[1]

In 1777 Phipps became Member for Huntingdon and a Lord of the Admiralty; the following year he was commissioned to the *Courageux*, a French prize, and fought in Palliser's squadron. In 1781 he captured the *Minerva* after a remarkable engagement in difficult conditions. When peace was declared the *Courageux* was paid off and he had no further active service. In the case between Palliser and Keppel, Phipps was a warm supporter of his former commodore.

Between his periods of active service Phipps actively pursued the arts of peace. His library of nautical books was famous and considered to be the best in England; he was a Fellow of the Royal Society and also of the Society of Antiquaries of London. He and Banks were close friends of George Colman, the playwright. He enjoyed society much more than Banks did, and one of the three Gainsborough portraits, with his book on the voyage towards the North Pole on a chair beside him, shows him most assured and confident (pl. 15).

His enchanting flirtation with Fanny Burney in 1780 is noted in a number of entries in her diary for that year; in April at Bath she wrote: 'Lord Mulgrave was delightful; his wit is of so gay, so forcible, so splendid a kind that when he is disposed to exert it he not only engrosses attention from all the rest of the company, but demands the full use of all one's faculties to keep pace in understanding the speeches, allusions and sarcasms which he sports . . . .' Poor Fanny—in 1787 there is an entry, 'Miss Cholmley was to be married to Lord Mulgrave on Wednesday: she is most amiable, he must be happy.' She was seventeen, he forty-three. The following January, Fanny wrote again, 'At present Lord Mulgrave is perhaps the most felicitous of men; but I fear that cannot last . . . for their mental endowments are as dissimilar as their personal . . . how precarious a foundation for permanent

---

[1] Phipps had more claim to it in a literal sense than Dr. Johnson since he was the first to give an adequate description of and a scientific binomial to the Polar Bear, *Thalarctos maritimus* (Phipps). Polar bears had long been known in England (p. 91); Banks considered that they were probably specifically and generically distinct from the Grizzly Bears with which Linnaeus had placed them, and he asked Phipps to bring one back so that this could be determined.

welfare.' Four months later, on 17 May, 'The amiable and lovely Lady Mulgrave gave a child to her lord, and died, in her first dawn of youthful beauty and sweetness, and exactly a year after she became his wife—it was all our wonder that Lord Mulgrave kept his senses.'

Two years after this tragedy Phipps wrote to Banks: 'If there is to be the comfort of honourable Peace, I hope to spend much of my time in your Society; we are, I believe, the oldest friends to each other, and I can with great truth assure you that the length has only added to the value of such a friendship in my estimation' (D.T.C. 7:169). But he died only two years later.

Thomas Adams

THOMAS ADAMS, son of a London solicitor, Sir Robert Adams, and his wife Diana, is a nebulous character about whom most of the facts hitherto recorded have been contradictory. Even the date of his birth is uncertain but he was baptized in St. Pancras Church, London, on 17 February (O.S.) 1738. His younger brother was born in Wandsworth, the borough in which his parents died. He was commissioned captain of the ketch *Happy* in 1759, and after several transfers appointed to the command of the *Niger* in 1763; that year and the next he cruised in English and Irish waters which gives some support to the statement that he married the Hon. Frances Warter-Wilson in Dublin in 1764, although when his will was proved in November 1770, after his death on the Virginia Station, he was said to have been a bachelor.

What is certain and can be confirmed through the muster rolls and other documents in the Public Record Office is that William Brougham Munkhouse[1] (1732–70) was appointed surgeon to the *Niger* in 1763, at the same time as Adams, and remained with her until early in 1767 when Adams was transferred to another

[1] Munkhouse used this form of his name when he signed his will. He sailed in the *Endeavour* with Banks and Cook; when she struck a reef off the Australian coast in 1770 it was the prompt action of his younger brother Jonathan in showing Cook how to fother the ship that saved her from total disaster; both brothers died at sea after leaving Batavia where so much illness was contracted. Another name on the muster roll of the *Niger* for 1763 is that of James Burney (1750–1821), Fanny's brother, who had already been at sea for three years. He was Adams's 'servant', a nominal post in which he would have been trained as a cadet. He sailed on the second and third of Cook's voyages, and as first lieutenant of the *Discovery* commanded her in the last stages of the third voyage, after King had left to go overland with the ship's papers from Stromness in the Orkneys to London.

command. Munkhouse must have got to know Adams and Banks very well on the Newfoundland voyage, especially since he would have treated them when they were both so ill with fever at Croque. One can only regret that Banks makes no reference to him in his diary for that period.

To go back in time a little, on Adams's first voyage to Newfoundland, in June 1765, he met Cook and Palliser in Great St. Lawrence Harbour, Placentia Bay, then sailed north to Croque Harbour in the Northern Peninsula, where the four Moravian missionaries, Haven, Schloezer, Drachardt and Hill, embarked; the *Niger* then proceeded north to Chateau Bay on the Labrador coast. The missionaries were critical of Adams since he insisted on separating them, sending two of them north in the schooner *Hope* and retaining Hill and Drachardt at Chateau Bay to act as interpreters between the Eskimos and Palliser who arrived shortly in the *Guernsey*. The diaries of the missionaries at Chateau Bay throw many sidelights on Adams and Palliser, and record the courage with which Munkhouse acted in an emergency; the diary and log of the voyage of the *Hope* give a dreary picture of the weather that may be encountered even in summer off the Labrador coast. Icebergs glistening in brilliant July sunshine in the Straits of Belle Isle are a beautiful and romantic sight viewed from the land when there are sheets of wild irises and gentians in bloom, but fogs and floe ice are frequent in some summers and in the eighteenth century such conditions were hazardous in the extreme for small sailing vessels.

The meetings with the Eskimos at Chateau Bay in 1765 were so satisfactory that Adams must have felt confident of further meetings in 1766, but, as Banks noted in his diary, although every effort was made to find them, none was successful. The blockhouse was however built, completed and manned.

Adams left the *Niger* after his voyage with Banks; he and Banks went off with friends on a visit to Kent shortly after their return and then he seems to disappear from Banksian papers. It is possible that there is some account of him amongst the Burney papers in New York, which I have not examined; he must have made a considerable impression on James Burney who was with him for three years, until he was sixteen years old.

It may be worth noting that Phipps's uncle, Augustus Hervey, the extremely sagacious naval officer who was in command of the *Monmouth* in 1758 and 1759, had a large number of cadets on board; Phipps joined them in January 1759, and the previous summer there was a Thomas Adams amongst their number. It is possible that he was the man who later commanded the *Niger*, and that it was in the *Monmouth* he got to know Constantine Phipps, and later his schoolfriend, Joseph Banks.

11. Joseph Banks and Daniel Solander in Iceland, 1772.
Probably by J. F. Miller

Miſs B——n.

12. Miss B——n. From an engraving in *The Town and Country Magazine*, 1773. Artist unknown

13. Dorothea Banks.
John Russell

14. Constantine John Phipps as a young man.
Artist unknown

15. Constantine John Phipps, 1785 or 1786.
Gainsborough

16. MS chart of Chateau Bay (York Harbour), Labrador; believed to be Cook's original chart of 1763.

harbour which lyeth N:st west by compass 2½ leagues from Cape de Grat in Newfoundland, and N:W:¾:W: leagues from the W_____
_e easily known by two very remarkable Rocks on Castle and Henley Islands, which are flat at top and something the resemblance
_d likewise by five or six small Islands to the eastward, nothing appearing to the Westward but an iron bold shore. To sail into it, you
ncit either open or shut with the point of Henley Island, giving the Shag rocks a proper birth and steer into the Harbour between the shal
_rance and Black reck off the Point of Henley Island, keeping within half a Cables length of the reck, this Passage is recommended only to the
unacquainted because the Black Reck is a good mark to sail in by. But as the two points before mentiond cannot be easily distinguished by stran
_mar best leave ⅔ of the Bay on the Starboard side untill Seal Islands are brought behind Henley Island, than Edge over toward
_ler Island and observe the foregoing directions, There is exceeding good anchoring ground in all the different Branches of this harbour
_ly in Pits harbour which must be recommended as the best for Kings Ships as having the most room and being the most convenient for wooding &
_shermen would certainly find their account in setting this place as Cod and Seals are here in great plenty, and Temple Bay and pitts harbour
_d Timber for building such as fir, Spruce, Juniper & Birch, Henly harbour seems to be the most convenient place for curing of Fish and Seal Islands
_y of Seals, where there appears to have been a considerable Seal Fishery:

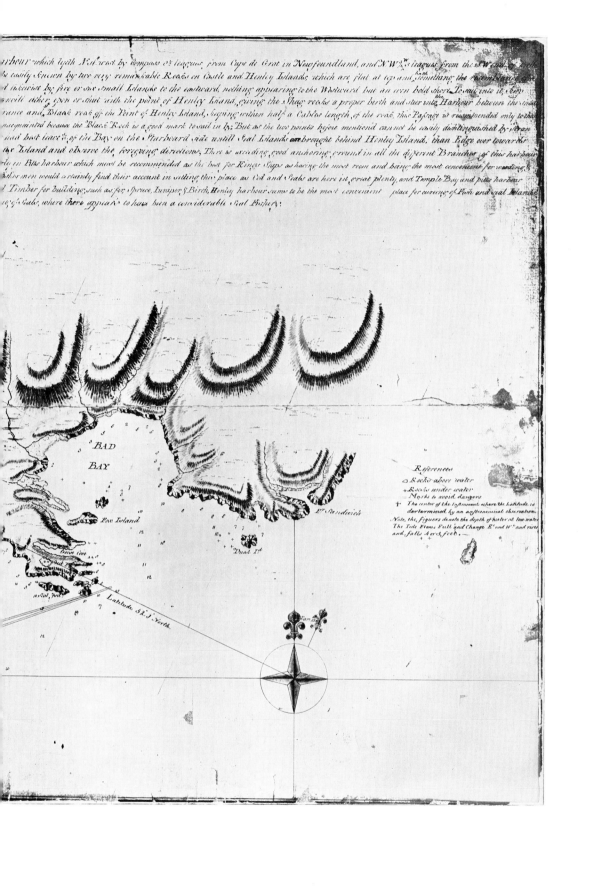

BAD
BAY

Fox Island

Goose Isles

Seal Ford

Latitude 51.J. North

Duck I:t

E:t Sandwich

References
Rocks above water
Rocks under water
Marks to avoid dangers
The center of the Instrument where the Latitude is
determined by an astronomical observation.
Note, the figures denote the depth of water at low water
The Tide Flows Full and Change E:t and W:t and rises
and falls 4 or 5 feet.

Var 2____

A CHART

of the

SEA-COAST, BAYS, HARBOURS and ISLANDS,

in

NEWFOUNDLAND.

between the

BAY of DESPAIR; and the HARBOURS of St. LAURENCE.

Survey'd By Order of Hugh Pallifer Efqr. Commodore &c: &c?.

by James Cook, 1765.

REFERENCES.

- ▬ *Stages for splitting and salting Fish.*
- ▬ *Convenient places for building of Stages, and Landing and drying of Fish.*
- *Rocks above Water.*
- *Rocks under Water.*
- ⚓ *Anchorage for Shipping.*
- ⚓ *Anchorage for small Vessels.*
- ⊙ *Denotes the depth of Water in Fathoms exceeding the inclosed Figures.*
- *Note! The Figures denote the depth of Water in Fathoms at low Water.*
- → *Shew upon what point of ye Compass the Current in general sets.*

A PLAN

of the

HARBOURS OF GREAT and LITTLE St LAURENCE.

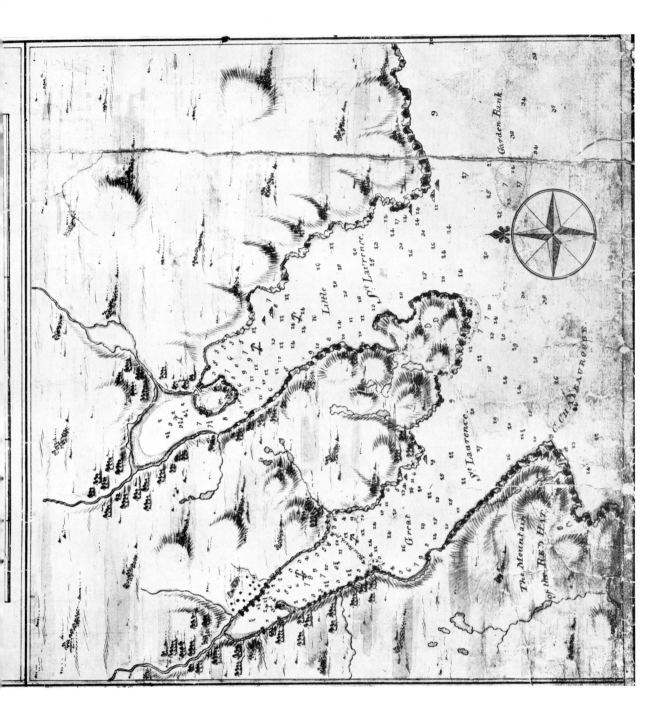

17. A plan of the harbours of the Great and Little St. Lawrence, Southern Newfoundland. A detail from Cook's chart of the south coast, 1765.

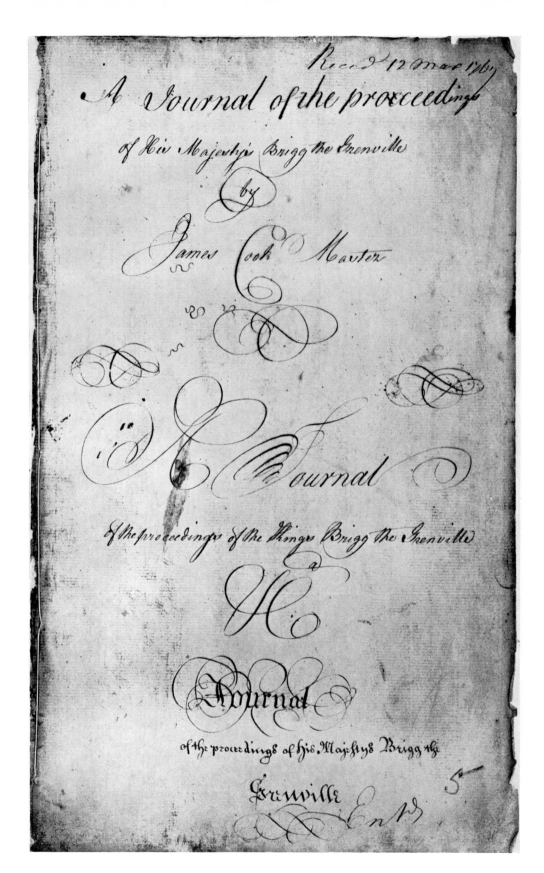

18. Title page of Cook's log of the *Grenville*, 1766.

19*a*. A vignette from an MS chart of the northern coast of Newfoundland by Cook.

19*b*. The vignette, 'improved' by Larken who engraved the chart for publication.

20. Thomas Pennant.
Gainsborough

Hugh Palliser

PALLISER is a controversial figure who still awaits full biographical treatment. The only life so far published (Hunt, 1844) is largely concerned in vindicating his part in the trial of Keppel and its aftermath. He has been much criticized for an overpaternalistic attitude when he was Governor of Newfoundland but in the limited number of his letters and reports that I have read he appears essentially a humanitarian. He was one of the first to perceive Cook's abilities and potentialities. His work in promoting exploration was recognized in 1773 when he was made a baronet.

Like Cook he was a Yorkshireman but from the West Riding. He was born at Kirk Deighton in 1723, and at the age of twelve entered the navy in the *Aldborough*, 20 guns, commanded by his mother's brother. His promotions were steady; the most interesting to us today is his posting in October 1755, to the command of the *Eagle*, 60 guns, the ship in which Cook, as an able seaman, had started his naval career some four months earlier. In 1758 Palliser commanded the *Shrewsbury*, 74 guns, in Anson's squadron, and the following year he was with the squadron operating in the St. Lawrence, where, as noted elsewhere, Cook was learning to survey, and helping to chart the river in preparation for Wolfe's assault on Quebec. In 1760 Palliser was in Sir Charles Saunders's squadron in the Mediterranean (Saunders had been with Anson in the *Centurion*) but in 1762 he was again in Newfoundland waters having been dispatched with a small squadron to capture St. John's which had been taken by the French earlier that year. However, when he arrived he found that it had just been retaken by Amherst and men, including Cook, from Lord Colville's squadron.

Palliser became Governor of Newfoundland and Commodore of the fleet there in 1764. Amongst the men in the *Guernsey* during his command were Joseph Gilbert, master, from Boston, Lincs., who later became master of the *Resolution* on Cook's third voyage; John Cartwright, appointed first lieutenant in 1766; and James King, then an A.B., who afterwards had special training in astronomy and mathematics; King sailed on Cook's third voyage, taking over the command of the *Discovery* in 1779. He and John Cartwright were lifelong friends. It was in 1764 that Cook was given his own survey ship, the *Grenville*; that summer, too, Palliser actively encouraged Jens Haven, the Moravian missionary, to try to meet the Eskimos in the Northern Peninsula of Newfoundland where Cook was surveying, and it is Palliser's transcript of Haven's diary with its references to Cook that is printed in another section of this book. In 1765 Palliser met Sir Thomas Adams and Cook in the south of Newfoundland, and shortly afterwards sailed north to rejoin Adams and the Moravian missionaries at Chateau Bay on the coast of Labrador. Here the meetings with the Eskimos were so successful—Palliser reported that about five hundred arrived—that the plans for building a blockhouse there were completed and the Moravians were encouraged and assisted to apply for grants of land where they could establish the permanent settlements which were to be so important in the history of that coast. Palliser's long dispatches about this project may be seen in the files of the Public Record Office; it was in furtherance of his plans that the following year the *Niger* carried a party of marines with her to Newfoundland and thence to Chateau Bay for the building of the blockhouse which Banks comments on in his diary; the detailed expenses were inscribed on Palliser's copy of the plan of the blockhouse, reproduced in pl. 31. Palliser's concern with the Eskimos was part of his plan to develop the great wealth of the Newfoundland and Labrador fisheries. A carefully documented assessment of this side of his work was published by Whiteley in 1969, too late for discussion here.

Palliser was appointed Comptroller of the Navy in 1770 and one of the Lords of the Admiralty in 1775. In 1778 he was commander of a ship in a squadron commanded by Keppel who reported unfavourably on Palliser's action in an abortive action with the French fleet off Ushant. Palliser asked for a court martial on Keppel who was acquitted. The mob turned on Palliser—the court had pronounced his charges malicious and ill-founded—and gutted his house in Pall Mall. Palliser, determined to clear himself, asked for a court martial on himself; Sandwich and the Admiralty supported him and he was acquitted. He asked for full reinstatement but Sandwich was unwilling to comply with this and instead made him Governor of Greenwich Hospital. In 1787 he became an admiral; he died nine years later. From the age of twenty-five years he had suffered much pain and ill health as the result of wounds from the explosion of an arms-chest when he was in the *Sutherland*. A staunch friend and admirer of Cook, Palliser erected a memorial to him in the grounds of his house at Vache in Buckinghamshire, with a lengthy inscription by Admiral Forbes, one of the very few brave men who had stood out against the sentence passed on Admiral Byng. The inscription is reproduced on p. 231. The memorial, now rather dilapidated, stands in grounds belonging unromantically to the Coal Board. Cook did better by his old friend: Palliser Bay, backed by bush-clad mountains, stands splendidly open to the great seas and storms that sweep from the South Pacific to surge against the coast of New Zealand.

James Cook

So MUCH has been written and spoken about Captain James Cook in recent years that here I shall give only some few notes, chiefly about his service in Canadian waters since this period has been recently documented with care by R. A. Skelton from whose account (1965) most of my information has been taken.

Cook was born on 27 October 1728, at Marton-in-Cleveland, Yorkshire. He learnt the elements of seamanship in colliers plying from Whitby in the North Sea trade. In June 1755, at the age of twenty-six, he enlisted as an able seaman in H.M.S. *Eagle*, 60 guns; within a month he was promoted to a master's mate. In October of that year Hugh Palliser became her commander; he was one of the first men in authority to perceive and encourage Cook's remarkable abilities. Two years later Cook received his master's warrant, having passed the necessary Trinity House examination at Deptford, and in October 1757, he was appointed master of the *Pembroke*, 60 guns, Captain John Simcoe.

Under Admiralty regulations at that time the master was charged with the care of navigating the ship, maintaining her in seaworthy condition, and of keeping the ship's log book. He was also required to take soundings near anchorages, to observe the appearance of coasts and to carry out survey work.

In July 1758 the *Pembroke* was in the St. Lawrence and here Cook received his first formal instruction in the use of the plane table, and in other trigonometrical methods, from Major Samuel Holland, a military engineer and cartographer of great competence. Years later, in 1792, Holland wrote to John Simcoe, Lieutenant Governor of Upper Canada and son of Cook's captain in the *Pembroke*, describing Cook's interest in surveying techniques and how hard he had worked to learn the necessary skills, so that they had been able together to compile the materials for a chart of the St. Lawrence, and thus to prepare the way for the taking of Quebec.

In 1759 Cook was drafted to H.M.S. *Northumberland*, 70 guns, Captain Lord Colville, Commander-in-Chief, North American Station. During the next two summers the *Northumberland* operated in the river and gulf of the St. Lawrence, and in 1762 on the south and east coasts of Newfoundland; she returned to England in the late autumn of 1762, and Cook and the rest of the ship's company were then paid off. In December Lord Colville wrote to the Admiralty of Cook's genius and ability which were based as much on his infinite capacity for taking pains as on his high intelligence. His surveys had come to the notice of Sir Thomas Graves, Governor of Newfoundland before Palliser, who was at Placentia Bay with Lord Colville's squadron in August that year. The following March Graves asked for the appointment of an official surveyor to make draughts of the coasts and harbours of Newfoundland. Cook was selected and chose as his assistant Edward Smart, a military draughtsman from the headquarters of the Board of Ordnance then in the Tower of London. These military draughtsmen not only compiled and drew maps in the Drawing Room at the Tower but were also employed in the instrumental field work of trigonometrical and topographical survey (Skelton 1965:11).

Cook sailed to Newfoundland in Graves's ship, the *Antelope*, arriving at Trepassey in June 1763, where he transferred to H.M.S. *Tweed* and with Smart went to survey the islands of St. Pierre and Miquelon. Meanwhile Graves had purchased the *Sally*, 67 tons (p. 222) for the surveys; she was renamed the *Grenville* and in her Cook sailed north to survey the eastern end of the Straits of Belle Isle, including Chateau Bay on the Labrador coast. Still officially on the complement of the *Tweed*, Cook rejoined her in order to return to England in November. That winter the Navy Board authorized a proper complement for the *Grenville*, and in May 1764, Cook and his crew sailed in H.M.S. *Lark* for St. John's, arriving in June to take over the *Grenville*. (It was Captain Thompson of the *Lark* who was so warmly thanked by the Moravians the next year for his kindness to them on the voyage to Croque, before they transferred to the *Niger*.)

The *Grenville* sailed north to Pistolet Bay; Cook's pleasure in his command is reflected in the joyful title pages to his log books, one of which is reproduced here (pl. 18). He surveyed west to Cape Norman, then transferred to the ship's cutter to continue inshore observations, and here had the accident that marked him for life: a large powder-horn exploded in his hand, they had to sail to Noddy Harbour before Cook and another injured man could get medical attention from a surgeon on a French fishing vessel. Ten days later Jens Haven, a Moravian missionary, arrived at Quirpon and went on board the *Grenville* (p. 185).

We have seen that in 1762 Cook, then master of the *Northumberland*, visited Placentia Bay in the south of Newfoundland. In 1765 he was there again, now in command of the *Grenville*, and here he met Sir Thomas Adams in the *Niger*. A little later they were joined by Hugh Palliser in the *Guernsey*. I have not found the relevant written orders from Palliser to Adams but since Cook had already made the survey of Chateau Bay, Labrador, not published until 1766, pl. 16, and Adams was to proceed there to make contact with the Eskimos, and to build a wharf, they must all three have met to discuss soundings and anchorages and make plans for the most suitable site for the wharf, and probably for the blockhouse which was to be built by marines carried in the *Niger* the following summer.

Adams then sailed north, picking up some Moravian missionaries at Croque in north east Newfoundland before proceeding to Chateau Bay where he was joined by Palliser. At the end of the season the *Guernsey* and the *Niger* arrived back in St. John's where they were joined by Cook in the *Grenville* on 21 October. On 5 November all three ships sailed for England, together with the *Spy* and the *Pearl*.

Joseph Gilbert, then master of the *Guernsey*, carried out survey work in the Straits of Belle Isle in 1767; he transferred to the *Pearl* in 1769 and remained in her complement until 1772 when he was appointed master of the *Resolution*, Cook's ship on his second circumnavigation.

While working on the Newfoundland survey Cook spent his winters at home in London, completing his charts for publication and enjoying a quiet domestic life— he had married Elizabeth Batts in December 1762. In the early summer of 1766 he sailed directly to the south coast of Newfoundland and was busy there until late October when he took the *Grenville* to St. John's, arriving there on a Monday morning, 27 October, to find both the *Guernsey* and the *Niger* at anchor in the harbour. The *Niger* sailed for Lisbon on Tuesday or Wednesday afternoon; the *Grenville* left on 4 November.

During the winter of 1766–7 Michael Lane, schoolmaster in the *Guernsey*, was transferred to the *Grenville* as assistant to Cook. Palliser had recommended another man for the post but Cook protested and it is an agreeable commentary on both men that Palliser in December 1766, sent Cook with a letter to Philip Stephens, Secretary to the Admiralty 1763–95, asking for the appointment of Cook's friend, Michael Lane, whose name appears on many of the early Newfoundland charts. The summer of 1767 was Cook's last season on the Newfoundland surveys, and he spent it working on the west coast. In December 1767 Wilkinson, who had succeeded Adams as Captain of the *Niger*, wrote to Banks suggesting that he should get in touch with Cook about an Indian canoe which, together with various fishes and plants, had been sent to England for him in the *Grenville*, but had been washed or thrown overboard when she went aground in foul weather at Deptford in the estuary of the Thames. It is a comforting thought that one of the world's greatest navigators of all time should have had a near disaster in such familiar waters. Cook's own account is given later, see page 230. It was in the summer of 1767 that he surveyed the Bay of Islands; amongst Banks's Newfoundland specimens there is a *Vaccinium* (p. 341) marked 'Bay of Isles' which may be one of the plants referred to by Wilkinson, but I think it more probable that Banks collected it himself in Great Islet Harbour, near Hare Bay where a survey party from the *Niger* did a certain amount of work in 1766.

The Newfoundland survey completed Cook's apprenticeship. He had become known for the quality of his work, his extreme competence and perseverance. In 1768 he was given command of the *Endeavour* to sail to the south Pacific, to observe the transit of Venus, in connection with the testing of chronometers for the determination of longitude; he was also to search for land in the Pacific. His discoveries on this, on his second and on the third tragic voyage were unequalled by any other navigator in historic times. The logs and muster books of the little ships of the eighteenth century, now in the Public Record Office, are a remarkable guide to his formative years in the icy waters of Newfoundland and Labrador, those romantically beautiful lands so remote in every way from the exotic shores of Hawaii where, twelve years after he had left Newfoundland, his judgement failed and he was murdered by the people who, at his first landing, had hailed him as a god.

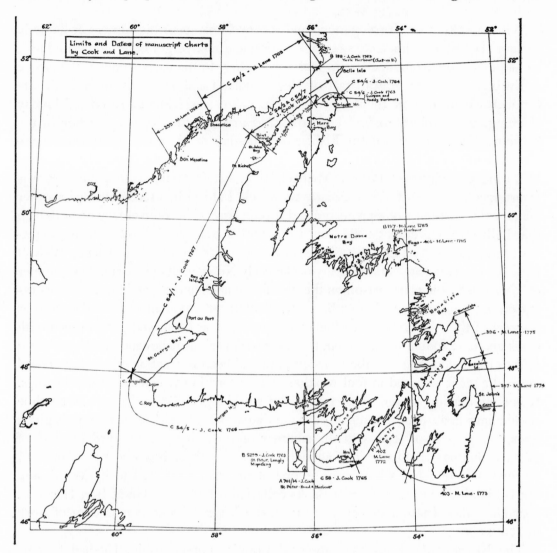

1. Map of Newfoundland showing surveys made by James Cook and Michael Lane

COOK'S NEWFOUNDLAND CHARTS

Skelton has written at length on Cook's published charts of Newfoundland and Labrador but, as far as I know, there is no detailed description of Cook's unpublished charts compiled during his time as master of the *Northumberland* as well as when he was official surveyor in the *Grenville*. Some of the charts ascribed to him appear to

70

be copies of his work, some so-called copies may be his own early draughts. His own vignettes were considerably altered by the engraver, as we can see from his sketch of almost naked Indians, altered by Larken to one of fully clothed Eskimos (pl. 19a, b). I have tried to use the MS charts that are certainly Cook's own work but may well have made some mistakes. In the absence of a detailed study showing the characteristics of unpublished work by Cook, Smart and Lane, and a complete catalogue of the Newfoundland charts of 1760–70, it is only too easy to make erroneous ascriptions.

Any study of these historic charts should be undertaken without delay since those in the Hydrographic Department of the Ministry of Defence have deteriorated considerably in recent years owing to the fact that they are kept rolled up, and that direct tracing is permitted without protective polythene sheets. Methods of storing historic charts flat or permanently suspended in racks are used successfully in many countries. One hopes that they will be adopted here before it is too late. Constant unrolling, especially in a dry atmosphere, is inevitably destructive.

One of the earliest charts of Chateau Bay ascribed to Cook, now on permanent loan to H.M.S. *Dryad*, is B 188, part of which was reproduced by Blewitt in 1957. Another chart, B 193, still in the Hydrographic Department, is regarded as a clerk's copy. I have not seen the original of B 188 but careful comparison of photographs of both charts suggests to me that the reverse may be the case, and that B 193 is Cook's own work, though the sailing directions may be in a clerk's hand. The number of trivial errors in B 193 which have been corrected in B 188 indicate that this was a second version prepared by Cook for publication. It seems improbable, for instance, that the differences in the arrangement of the references would have been made by any clerk responsible for making a copy. See pl. 16.

Major George Cartwright

GEORGE CARTWRIGHT, soldier and sportsman, moved before 1766 in a very different world from Joseph Banks but they met on the *Guernsey* at St. John's in Newfoundland at the end of the summer that year, and later became closely connected through their common interest in Labrador and its peoples.

They were exceptional men, and unlike many of their time they fought against racial prejudice and for the establishment of international goodwill. Their struggles, their love of truth and their scientific work make them significant in the history not only of Newfoundland but of human thought. In these matters Joseph Banks played a major role, and Cartwright a minor one. Banks was not only an able and dedicated scientist but a promoter of exploration and discovery in all continents, the father of Australia, a great innovator in agriculture and horticulture. Cartwright is relatively unknown save for his Labrador journal published in 1792. But for several years both men were closely associated in their interest in the far north and I have therefore devoted perhaps disproportionate space to Cartwright, about whom almost nothing has been written save in the introduction to the rare abridged reprint of his journal (1911).

Cartwright reveals much of himself in his introduction to his journal. The poet Southey in an account of him (*Commonplace Book*, 1851) says: 'I met Major Cartwright (the sportsman, not the patriot) in 1791. . . This man had strength and perseverance charactered in every muscle . . . I read his book in 1793. The annals of his campaigns among the foxes and beavers interested me far more than ever did the exploits of Marlbro' or Frederic; besides, I saw plain truth and the heart in Cartwright's book—and in what history could I look for this? Coleridge took up a volume one day and was delighted with its strange simplicity.'

George Cartwright lacked formal scientific training, nevertheless he was a careful and observant naturalist with a remarkable gift for writing. He was a delightful character, intrepid, honest and warm. What other man would have recorded that he taught the Eskimos to play leapfrog, as well as describing his feelings when he imagined that they were preparing to burn him alive? He had great vitality and large enjoyment in many activities, even in midwinter picnics in Labrador. Banks helped him financially, introduced him to some of the most notable scientists in London, and altogether showed that he had a high regard for him. The list of subscribers to his Labrador journal shows that Banks's opinion of him was shared by many other persons of distinction.

Cartwright's background was very different from Banks's, although they both came from well-connected families with substantial estates. His life in Labrador is of special interest since he was there for sixteen years and many of his notes on the habits of the birds and animals supplement Banks's formal descriptions.

George Cartwright was born in 1739, four years before Banks, at Marnham, Nottinghamshire, where his father lived in rather impoverished circumstances, his Jacobite forebears having lost much of the family fortune. There were nine other children, including his sister Catherine who became devoted to the Eskimo girl, Caubvick, whom he brought to England in the winter of 1772–3. Two of his brothers, John and Edmund, were men of outstanding ability; John, the first lieutenant of the *Guernsey*, was a year younger than George and not only a brave man—he saved people from drowning at the risk of his own life on four different occasions—and an excellent administrator, but also a high-principled politician. In

1766 Palliser appointed him his deputy or surrogate in the district of Conception or Trinity Bay, Newfoundland; the next year he became Deputy Commissar to the Vice-Admiralty Court in that country, where he served with great efficiency for five years. He and Palliser worked together to expose the outrages perpetrated by British and other fishermen against the Eskimos and Indians, and to obtain proper recognition of their rights as human beings. Later, John Cartwright resigned his commission since he would not bear arms against the American colonists, and went so far as to publish a pamphlet defending them, entitled 'American Independence the Glory and Interest of England'.

Edmund Cartwright, George's youngest brother, was a man with very different gifts. He was ordained, was a friend of Crabbe the Aldeburgh poet, and wrote poetry himself. He was also very practical, the inventor of the power loom, and the first manager of the experimental farm at Woburn established by the Duke of Bedford, now associated with the world-famous agricultural research station at Rothamsted. Probably it was he who persuaded George to pay so much attention to the use of humus and organic manures in improving Labrador soils, and to keep the meteorological records published at the end of his journal (not reprinted in the 1911 edition). The brothers' interests in agricultural improvements must have provided a further link with Banks whose work for agriculture is only now beginning to be appreciated.

Cartwright gives a note on his own formal education in the introduction to his journal. 'I received part of my education at Newark, and during a few of the last years attended the Latin School. . . . On the first of February 1753, I was appointed a Gentleman Cadet, in the Cadet Company at Woolwich, where I had the opportunity of improving myself at the Royal Academy in that place for one year. But, sorry am I to say, that either the want of genius or of application, rendered of little use to me, the instructions of these excellent masters with which that institution was then furnished.' At the age of fifteen he was sent to India in the 39th Regiment and the following year became an ensign. Later he served in Ireland and in Germany, was promoted to lieutenant when twenty years old, and shortly afterwards became aide-de-camp to John Manners, Marquis of Granby, who was a strong influence in the shaping of his character.

This Marquis of Granby, born in 1721, eldest son of the third Duke of Rutland, was a highly intelligent, brave and generous soldier. He looked after his soldiers most tenderly, provided them with necessities out of his own pocket in times of shortage, was a constant friend to the sick and wounded of all ranks, and a man of notable moral as well as physical courage. One of his most famous deeds, towards the end of the war with Germany, was to leave a sick-bed on a most inclement night to head a cavalry charge and seize a position essential to the security of our army but declared by the other generals to be impregnable. His popularity was unbounded; Fox asked for his political support and on his return to England at the end of the campaign special messengers waited at all the principal ports to offer him a choice of the Ordnance or the Horse Guards. He is still commemorated in England, nearly two hundred years after his most gallant feats, by over a hundred public houses that bear his name.

Cartwright's commendation of Captain Reynolds at St. John's in 1786 would serve as a tribute to his former commanding officer, the Marquis, as well as to the captain: 'The two last days,' he wrote 'I spent on board the *Echo* Sloop of War; the first with the officers; the second with Captan Reynolds, who appears to be in every sense of the word, a Gentleman; and, in my opinion, nothing can be a stronger proof of it, than the universal terms of attachment and approbation in which his officers constantly spoke of him. When a captain of a Man of War unites the gentleman with the officer, he will always advance to the utmost both the honour and interest of his king and country; for he not only attaches every man under his command to the service, but also to himself; consequently he is never deserted in time of action, or in other service of danger. Such men are seldom known to want courage, and are never above hearing the opinions of their officers on all points of consequence; but those who behave in a tyrannical and ungentleman-like manner, are sure to disgust every man with the service, who is unfortunate enough to be under their command, and to drive those of spirit and independence out of it. And as they are obeyed with fear and hatred only, they are often deserted, when in most need of support.'

George Cartwright remained in the service of the Marquis until the end of the war and then, on his advice, went on half-pay, for reasons concerned with regimental promotions that had taken place during his absence in Germany. He says 'In the spring of 1765 I made an excursion to Scotland, to indulge my insatiable propensity for shooting: but I soon found that two shillings and fourpence a day was too small an income to enable me to live in a Baronet's country seat, and to keep a female companion, two servants, a couple of horses and three brace of dogs. As my pocket would not permit me to have any dealings with the butcher, myself and family were compelled to fast when neither my gun nor fishing rod would supply us with provisions. No sooner did my resources fail, by the scarcity of fish and game at the approach of winter, than I made an auction of all my furniture, and returned to London by sea with the lady and dogs.'

'London being no place for a man of my scanty circumstances to remain in, I soon went down to Plymouth, where my brother John commanded the *Sherborne* Cutter, and cruised with him against the smugglers, until he was discharged from that vessel, and appointed first lieutenant of the *Guernsey*, of fifty guns, then lying at Spit Head and bound for Newfoundland; on board which ship the present Sir Hugh Palliser, who was then Governor of that Island, had his Broad-pennant. . . . On our arrival at St. John's [23 July 1766] the command of a small schooner was conferred on my brother, and he was sent on some service to one of the Northern harbours, where I accompanied him; and it was then that I obtained my first knowledge of the Red, or wild Indians.'[1]

The *Guernsey*, with the Cartwrights on board, left St. John's for England on 4 November, a week after Banks had sailed in the *Niger*. George rejoined his regiment and had a period of service at Minorca where he caught malaria and was desperately ill. Returning to England at the end of April 1768, he found the *Guernsey* again under sailing orders for Newfoundland; with Lord Granby's permission he joined her for a second voyage, by which means, he says, his health was perfectly restored. 'During the *Guernsey's* stay at St. John's, I went upon an expedition against the Wild Indians; and it was that which first gave rise to the voyages which I afterwards made to Labrador. My design, being laid before the King, his Majesty was graciously pleased to permit me to retire on half-pay, early in the year 1770, in order that I might put it in execution, and I soon after sailed for that country.'

'The reader may naturally conclude, from the life I have led since my leaving the Academy at Woolwich, that it was not probable that I should have improved the slight education which I received in my youth; and indeed such a conclusion is very just, as I had seldom, during that time, attempted to read anything but a newspaper. On my arrival in LABRADOR, being secluded from society, I had time to gain acquaintance with myself: and I could not help blushing when I perceived, how shamefully I had misemployed my time. The little improvement I have since made, has been owing entirely to my writing my Journal, and to reading a small collection of books which I took out with me; but it was too late in life for me to receive much benefits from these helps. . . . The only merit to which I have any pretentions, is that of a faithful Journalist, who prefers the simplicity of plain language and downright truth, to all the specious ornaments of modern style and description.'

Although Cartwright had so much less formal education than Banks he was an accomplished writer. With the greatest economy of phrase he gives us a wonderful self-portrait and, further, makes us see so vividly the life he lived that we almost come to believe that we are ourselves in Labrador. We see its ice and stars and storms, love the Eskimos, and love Cartwright for teaching them to play leapfrog; rejoice when the box of mustard and cress over the kitchen stove produces a midwinter salad, and share his unhappiness when he discovers treachery amongst those nearest him.

Banks, on the other hand, indulges in too didactic a style in some of his lesser journals, and the absence of personalities makes them rather dry. In the diary of his visit to Wales and the Midlands in 1767–8, there is an extraordinary lack of description of the people with whom he travelled and stayed. Even his account of his visit to the eminent zoologist and traveller, Thomas Pennant, at Downing, Flint-

---

[1] John Cartwright's account of this expedition was reprinted by Howley (1915:29–45); it contains much interesting information on the Beothuks, the original inhabitants of Newfoundland.

shire, which lasted from 21 November to 3 December 1767, gives no indication of how Pennant lived, or of what his household consisted. This is tantalizing in the extreme since we know that Peter Paillou was then working for him, painting Banks's Newfoundland birds and, amongst other subjects, four allegorical pictures of the climates, which remained in the hall at Downing until 1920 (I have been unable to trace their subsequent history). One whole week of Banks's visit is disposed of thus 'Having spent time from the last date almost intirely at home, in reviewing a Collection of English Shells, and Crabs, we rode out this day towards the Vale of Cluid.'[1]

Except in his *Endeavour* diary, and sometimes in his Newfoundland journal, Banks seldom has the faculty, so often shown by Cartwright, of making us share his experience. It is in his innumerable personal letters that he expands and shows the qualities that won him so many friends, and enabled him to make such good use of men of varying abilities. Thus, in a letter written from Chateau Bay, Labrador, on 11 August 1766, to his sister Sarah Sophia (p. 236) we read of his having foresworn the flute and learnt to play the guitar; the only reference to music in his diary is to the singing of the French officers when they are superintending the gutting and drying of cod at St. John's. Unfortunately there is no collected edition of these letters, which are widely scattered in England, America, Australia and elsewhere; only a few are sufficiently relevant to be printed in this volume, but they illustrate in some small degree his development in stature and humanity throughout his life.

The circumstances of Cartwright's life in Labrador led him to develop one skill of which Banks had only a theoretical knowledge; this was the practice of physic and surgery. He was forced into it in 1771 when his maid, Nanny, the wife of his blacksmith, gave birth to a child. The young surgeon, Mr. Jones, who had set off from Chateau Bay to attend her, had lost his way; it was February and he was later found frozen to death, less than an hour's walk from Cartwright's house.

'At six o'clock this evening', Cartwright records, 'my maid was taken in labour; and for want of better assistance, I was obliged to officiate as midwife myself. She had a severe time, but at half after eleven I delivered her of a stout boy; and she did me the honour to say, that although she had been under the hands of three male, and two female practitioners, before she left England, she never met with a person who performed his part better. Fortunately for her, Brooke's *Practice of Physic*, which was found in Mr. Jones's pocket, gave me some idea of an art, which never till then did I expect to be called upon to practise. Having taken proper care of the mother, I was next obliged to act as nurse, and take the child to bed with me; neither of which offices do I ever wish to resume.'

Cartwright must have been more highly strung than a cursory reading of his diary would lead one to imagine, since he says that he was very ill next day, which

---

[1] Pennant's relation Mrs. Thrale lived there in her youth, and again towards the end of her life.

he attributed to having been up so late the night before. In spite of what he says, he developed a considerable interest in medicine, and on many occasions acted as doctor for his family and Eskimo friends. So, five years later there is the following entry: 'At three o'clock this morning Nooquashock, the eldest Indian woman, was taken in labour: my skill was now fairly put to the test, for she had both a cross birth and twins, but at two in the afternoon I delivered her of a brace of daughters. I then visited my traps and had a marten.' He used Eskimo herbal remedies with good effect on some occasions, and was infinitely patient and usually successful in dealing with frostbite and snowblindness.

His understanding of the human heart was similar to Cook's—a small community in a Labrador settlement in the winter in those days was almost as isolated as the crew on one of Cook's or Bougainville's ships in the Southern Ocean. At the end of August 1778, towards the close of what appears to have been his only really successful trading season, he was robbed of almost all he possessed by a shipload of privateers from Boston. Such a disaster at that time left him and his dependants at the settlement in danger of starving to death since no ships were due there until the following summer. On 11 October he wrote 'Winter now begins to appear; the Mealy Mountains have put on their new liveries, and every downfall whitens the heads of the high hills. The deer are beating out to the barren headlands on the sea coast; the eider and king-ducks are hastening to the southward; and grouse are chattering in great flocks upon the hills; I am afraid that it will overtake me before I am ready for it . . . .'

'Under these distresses and inquietudes would any man believe, that my people have been ready to mutiny, because I would give them no salted pork along with their two pounds of fat venison each day for dinner? yet it is a fact: nor could I quiet them until I peremptorily declared, that I could not possibly suffer any salt meat to be expended, whilst any fresh meat remained in the house; and that if they were not content, I would give them, what I verily believed they much deserved, a hearty drubbing.' On 1 June, the following summer, he found that 'Owing to the success of our traps, slips, and guns together with good economy, I have now enough left to last until the end of September. I was under the greatest apprehension all winter, of falling short of provisions, before any vessel could arrive with a supply . . . .'

'Unfortunately the foxes went out of season much sooner than usual, and by the month of March, they smelled so rank, that I could not insist on their eating them. I then hit upon an expedient which was of singular help to me; for on catching the first white fox, I skinned him with great care and ate him myself, telling my people, that a white fox was superior to a hare. This set them a-longing; and then, by way of indulgence, I gave them all we caught afterwards; but the fact was, they were no better than those of other colours; they however satisfied the cravings of appetite, and kept us from famishing. Before they went off this morning I had the satisfaction to receive their voluntary thanks for not giving way to their unreasonable demands; they being now convinced that we must all have perished if I had.'

The parallel with Cook's attitude towards his sailors is striking. On 13 April 1769, Cook wrote 'The Sour Krout the Men at first would not eate untill I put in practice a Method I never once knew to fail with seamen, and this was to have some of it dress'd every Day for the Cabbin Table, and permitted all the Officers without exception to make use of it and left it to the option of the Men either to take as much as they pleased or none at all; . . . the Moment they see their Superiors set a Value upon it, it becomes the finest stuff in the World and the inventer an honest fellow.' (*Journals of Captain James Cook*, ed. Beaglehole 1955:74.) This passage does not appear in the Hawkesworth edition of 1775 but Cartwright may have heard his friends Banks and Solander discussing Cook's methods on one of his visits to London.

In contrast to Banks, whose dairies are pervaded by cheerful rationalism, Cartwright was a religious man and he seems to have retained his faith in spite of many misfortunes and near disasters. In 1783 he had a very successful season, but at the end of it the ship carrying all his furs and whalebone was lost at sea before the insurance papers were signed, and he very nearly lost his life in another ship. He describes their plight in a dense fog with a high wind when at two o'clock 'a most dreadful hurricane came on from the northward, such as none of us had ever seen and which beggars all description, suffice it to say that it was dreadful and terrible to the greatest degree . . . It is easier to imagine than to describe the anxiety of our minds, expecting every minute, from ten o'clock on the Saturday morning to eight on Sunday night, to discover ragged rocks under our lee, and soon afterwards to be driven upon them in a most violent gale of wind. We then, most devoutly went to prayers; I officiated as chaplain, and no sooner had we done, than, to the admiration and astonishment of every man on board, the wind became perfectly moderate; it shifted four points in our favour, the sky cleared, and miraculous to relate, the sea which but the moment before ran as high and dangerous as it could well do, in an instant became as smooth as if we had shot under the lea of Scilly at five or six leagues distance! We could attribute all these things, to nothing but the immediate intervention of the DIVINITY, who had been graciously pleased to hear our prayers, and grant our petitions; and I hope, I shall never be of a contrary way of thinking. . . . At eleven at night, on Saturday the seventh, we let go an anchor in Studland Bay, to the no small joy and satisfaction of every man on board. I then had the mortification to hear that the ship, *John*, foundered at sea . . . consequently all my furs and whalebone went to the bottom . . . not one penny had been insured on them. Early the next morning, Mr. Stone and I, together with three other passengers got into the pilot boat and went up to Poole. . . . We immediately dressed ourselves, and went to church to return God thanks for the mercies which we had so lately received at his hands; and through the minister, offered our public thanks also.' But it was the loss of the *John* that led to his bankruptcy in 1784. He made one last attempt to retrieve his fortunes in Labrador but was unsuccessful.

In 1786 he finally returned to England after an adventurous voyage, ending in one of his several escapes from shipwreck, this time off Berry Head, near Brixham. Most of the rest of his life was spent as barrack-master at Nottingham where he was known as 'Old Labrador'. He was able to enjoy falconry there, and seems to have lived happily; he died at Mansfield in 1817 at the age of eighty-one. Many of the names he gave to the harbours and islands of Labrador are still in use, and there is a memorial to him and his brother John at Cartwright, a township at the entrance to Sandwich Bay.

His published journal concluded with a long poem; the following lines about his Eskimo friends are a reflection of his own character as well as a tribute to them:

> Thrice Happy Race! Strong Drink nor gold they know;
> What in their Hearts they think, their Faces show.
> Of manners gentle, in their dealings just,
> Their plighted promise, safely you may trust.

Cartwright and the problem of colour change in northern animals

CARTWRIGHT met Banks not only in 1766 at St. John's but also on many occasions in the winter of 1772–3 in London; after 1773 he collected for him and, at Banks's request, made observations on colour change in birds and hares.

That he collected both plants and animals for Banks is clear from a letter he wrote from Sandwich Bay, Labrador, dated 12 October 1775:

Dear Sir,

I herewith send you a few Bird skins, Plants, a Frog, and a long-tailed Mouse . . . If you have an inclination for another voyage I think you would be pleas'd with this place and dare say you'd meet with some curiosities, for I've seen many birds that are entirely new to me, some of a beautiful plumage . . . Next summer I shall be very busy . . . but the Summer afterwards, if you and Dr. Solander will faver me with a visit you'll make me happier than I can express . . . Let me know next summer how many your family will consist of, and their qualities, that I may add a room or two to my house if it is not big enough to accommodate you . . . The white Grouse and Hare, you'll find in the Bag were kill'd in Spring . . .

The problem of colour change in northern animals was a subject of much interest to Banks and other naturalists in the Royal Society. More than 2,000 years earlier Aristotle had some idea that low temperature might bring about such an effect: 'Again owing to special climatic influences,' he says 'as when unusual frost prevails, a change is sometimes observed to take place in birds whose plumage is of one uniform colour; thus, birds that have dusky or downright black plumage turn white or grey, as the raven, the sparrow, and the swallow . . .' (ed. Smith & Ross 1910, 3:519a).

At a later date Pliny remarked on the difference between the summer and winter coats of the Alpine Hare: 'Of Hares there be many sorts. Upon the Alpes and such high mountaines, they bee of colour white, so long as the snow lieth; and it is verily thought, that all winter long they live with eating of snow; for surely when it is thawed and melted, all the year after they be brownish and reddish as before' (Trans. Philemon Holland, 1634, 1:232). Pliny also speaks of an Alpine *Lagopus* (*op. cit.* 1:296) 'The *Pyrrhocorax* . . . was supposed to breed only among the Alpes; and with it the *Lagopus*, a daintie bird and most pleasant in the dish. And this name it took in Greek, because it is rough-footed and haired like the Hare's foot: otherwise all over white . . .'

Aristotle wrote more than three centuries before the birth of Christ; Pliny had not quite finished his magnificent *Historia Naturalis* when he died in A.D. 79. Ray, in a discourse to the Royal Society in 1674 (Birch 1756, 3:171), gives a summary of the knowledge that had been acquired in the intervening centuries: 'What influence diversity of climate, place, or temperature of the air may have as to the alteration of these qualities, appears in many animals, which on the Alps and other high mountains, as also in those cold and northern countries, where the earth for more than half the year is continually covered with snow, are not rarely found white, though naturally of different colours: as for example bears, foxes, hares, ravens, blackbirds.'

Four years later, in the translation into English of the joint work on birds by Willughby and himself (1678:176) Ray discusses ptarmigan: 'There is another sort of *Lagopus* found on the Mountains of Switzerland . . . I am of the opinion that this Bird is not only generically, but even specifically, the same with the former or first *Lagopus* of *Pliny*: For except some marks and spots on the upper side of the body, it agrees perfectly therewith: But those are not sufficient to infer a difference in kind: seeing that the first *Species* also is said to change colour in Summer, and become dusky: Yea, those which ascend not up the Mountains are reported not to be white, no not in Winter. But I dare not pronounce anything rashly; referring the matter to the learned and curious, that live in those Countries, or have opportunity of travelling and sojourning there.'

In 1747–8 two British ships, the *Dobbs* and the *California*, sailed to Hudson's Bay; two accounts of the voyage were published immediately afterwards, a single volume in 1748 by Henry Ellis of the *Dobbs*, two volumes in 1748–9 by the clerk of the *California*. Natural history observations by the clerk of the *California* were attributed by Pennant (1785:310) and Samuel Hearne (1795:415–16) to T. S. Drage [Theodorus Swaine Drage], but others have considered that Charles Swaine was responsible. Eavenson (1950) believed that Swaine and Drage were different men but Adams (1965) has documented evidence showing that one man used both names; he does not suggest reasons for this but regards Drage as a man of integrity who used Swaine for fifteen years from 1750 and then reverted to his original name. Both Ellis and Drage wrote brief and inaccurate notes on colour change in ptarmigan. (For further biographical notes see Drage, C., 1970.)

Ptarmigan in Greenland were more carefully observed and briefly discussed by Crantz in 1767; he realized that the change in colour was brought about by moulting and not by a change of colour in full grown feathers. Then in 1772 the great French naturalist Buffon discussed species of ptarmigan (2:272), making brief observations on colour change. His references to earlier European writers who had noted this are interesting and were added to by subsequent editors of his works, such as Flourens in 1812.

In 1773 Buffon's classification of ptarmigan was attacked by Daines Barrington in a discourse to the Royal Society (*Journal Book of the Royal Society* 1771–4, 27:400–3), most of which was published in the *Philosophical Transactions* (63:224–30). He mentions the large number of ptarmigan in both summer and winter plumage sent to the Royal Society by the Hudson's Bay Company, but makes no clear statement of the nature of colour change; it may have been he who published in the *Gentleman's Magazine* (1772, 42:74) an illustration of Willow Ptarmigan from Hudson's Bay, showing winter and summer plumage; the unsigned note accompanying the engraving is inaccurate. Daines Barrington was a close friend of Banks's and it was in September, 1773, that Cartwright wrote in his diary (1:278) 'When I was in England [winter, 1772–3] Mr. Banks, Dr. Solander, and several other naturalists having enquired of me, respecting the manner of these birds changing colour, I took particular note of those I killed, and can aver for a fact, that they get at this time of the year a very large addition of feathers, all of which are white; and that the coloured feathers at the same time change to white [this is not so]. In spring, most of the white feathers drop off, and are succeeded by coloured ones: or, I rather believe, all the white ones drop off, and that they get an entire new set. At the two seasons they change very differently; in the spring beginning at the neck, and spreading from thence; now, they begin on the belly, and end on the neck.' Cartwright's account is incomplete but he was the first to draw attention to

81

the differences in spring and autumn moults. The moulting process is, in fact, very complicated, and a fully authoritative account of the various stages in both sexes of ptarmigan did not appear until 1939 when Finn Salomonsen published a monograph on the subject, and at the same time reviewed modern work on colour change in other animals including hares.

Cartwright made observations on hares as well as on ptarmigan. The entry in his diary for 1 March 1776, contains the following passage: 'Jack went to one of his traps on Earl Island and brought a rabbit:[1] on examining it, I find the white coat is an additional one which is got in autumn, and will lose it again in spring, it is composed of long coarse king-hairs; the summer fur-coat remaining underneath, and retaining its colour.' Pennant gave a very similar account in the first volume of the *Arctic Zoology* (p. 96) some nine years later, which may have been based on Cartwright's observations which he must have discussed with Banks.[2]

Cartwright's notes on colour change appear to have been generally overlooked. The slightly later notes by Samuel Hearne (1795:415–16), who was very critical of Drage (Swaine) have been brought to light recently by Mrs. Allen (1951:523).

Cartwright's other observations on natural history cover a wide variety of subjects. Among the more interesting are his notes on the weights of birds' eggs, the structure of eider down, the behaviour of bears and beavers, the nature of soils and their enrichment by the use of humus. He mentions between sixty and seventy species of birds (see 1911 reprint of his journal). His pets were various, and his account of his young caribou calf shows him at his best. 'This deer of mine has had its full liberty ever since the fourth day after it was caught . . . It will often go up to a dog and smell to him: it is well acquainted with all mine, and will lie down by the fire amongst them. I believe they scarce ever sleep, for as much as I have watched this, I could never observe, that it was ever asleep, or kept its eyes closed for more than two seconds at a time; and if I have moved ever so little, it would start up. When I have lain down on the bed, at a time when it was lying on the floor, it would start up every four or five minutes, and come to see that I was not gone; and having licked my face, or sucked my neck handkerchief a little, it would quietly lie down again . . . When at any time it lost me, it would run about grunting somewhat like a hog, and never rest until it had found me, when it would run up to me in full speed. Sometimes I have diverted myself, with stooping and running, both after and from it, which pleased it much; and it would do the same, and frisk about in the same manner, as I have seen the wild calves one among another.' And then he proceeds to give many other details of the food and behaviour of caribou in general.

---

[1] There are no true rabbits in Labrador. This must have been a Varying Hare or Snowshoe Rabbit, *Lepus americanus americanus* Erxleben. The other hare found there is Miller's Polar Hare or the Labrador Hare, *Lepus arcticus labradorius* Miller; this remains white throughout the year.

[2] A copy of Pennant's *Arctic Zoology*, annotated by Cartwright now belongs to Lord Cranbrook, who has kindly allowed me to publish Cartwright's notes as an appendix to this book.

21a. Attuiock.
Nathaniel Dance, 1773.

21b. Caubvick.
Nathaniel Dance, 1773.

Captain Cartwright setting a Fox-trap.

22. George Cartwright. 'His jacket (which is made of Indian-dressed deerskin, and painted),
sash, and rackets are Mountaineer; and his shoes Esquimaux'.
Engraving by T. Medland after the portrait by W. Hilton, from *Cartwright's* Journal, 1792.

He delighted too in his birds. 'The two jays which I caught on the fifth instant, I have hitherto kept confined in a cage; but they now [two days later] have the liberty of the room; and I was greatly surprised to see them fly to me for food, and familiarly perch upon my hand: they even suffered me to stroke them with one hand, while they were eating pork fat out of the other.'

There is only one instance in his diary where he seems to have been carried away by the desire to kill; this seems remarkable in a man who tried to make his living by trapping and shooting.

Banks, Cartwright and the Eskimos

Eskimos and Europeans had known each other long before the eighteenth century. Perhaps the first contacts were made in Greenland where waves of migrating Canadian Eskimos are believed to have arrived from prehistoric times onwards. The early Norwegian colonists in Greenland left accounts of having met some little people, whom they called Skraelings, in the far north of that country when they went on their summer hunting expeditions in the twelfth century (Ingstad 1966:25).

The first Eskimos to be brought from Labrador to England were those captured by Sebastian Cabot who took them to the court of Henry VII in 1501 or 1502—the chronicles differ (Gosling 1910:39). In the sixteenth century the Newfoundland and Labrador fisheries were frequented by fishermen from Normandy and Brittany, and in 1512 Henri Estienne published in *The Chronicles of Eusebius* a story of seven 'savages' taken from Terre Neuve to Rouen.

According to Hulton (1961) the earliest portrait of an Eskimo is one painted by Jan van Heere, about 1576, of a man captured by Frobisher and taken to Bristol. On a later voyage Frobisher brought both a man and woman from Baffin Island to England; they were painted by John White who may indeed have accompanied Frobisher on that voyage.

The history of the contacts between Eskimos and Europeans in Labrador is one of bloodshed and treachery on both sides until the coming of the Moravian missionaries; some of the Hudson's Bay settlers, however, spoke warmly of the Eskimos but it seems that once the latter people had been betrayed they determined to revenge themselves on every occasion.

BIOGRAPHICAL SKETCHES

The establishment of the Moravian settlements is briefly discussed in the introduction to their diaries (pp. 181–3). In these diaries the Moravians describe in detail their meetings with the Eskimos at Chateau Bay in 1765, with some terse comments on Adams who had taken them there in the *Niger*. Adams and Banks made every effort to get in touch with them the following year but their attempts were unsuccessful. Banks wrote flippantly about it to his sister: 'We are here in daily expectation of the Esquimaux ladies here I wish with all my heart they were Come as I might have sent you a sealskin gown and Petticoat perfumed with train oil which to them is as Sweet as Lavender water.'

In 1767 Lieutenant Lucas of the *Guernsey* was stationed at York Fort; after a skirmish caused by some of the fishermen attacking an Eskimo encampment (Gosling, 1910:201), the Eskimos retaliated. In the ensuing battle some were captured and brought to St. John's by Lucas who was then charged with taking three of them to England. These three were an intelligent woman Mykok, her small child Tootac, and a thirteen-year-old boy, Carpik. Palliser intended them to learn English and return to act as interpreters. Carpik was placed in the care of Jens Haven, who was befriended by Cook at Quirpon in 1764, but unfortunately the boy died from smallpox. Mykok was a great success in London society. She appears to have arrived after Banks had left on the *Endeavour* but he owned a portrait of her by John Russell, which he sent to his close friend J. F. Blumenbach[1] (1752–1841), the great anatomist and anthropologist. It still hangs in the Ethnographical Museum in Göttingen (Plischke 1960).

After some time in England, Mykok returned to Labrador but the rest of her life was chequered and unhappy. Lucas also returned to Labrador where he went into partnership with Nicolas Darby (Gosling, *loc. cit.*), father of the lovely and much painted Perdita.[2] Lucas did not remain long with Darby and in 1770 went into partnership with George Cartwright. They established their first trading post on the banks of the Charles River, slightly north of Chateau Bay. In the course of the next sixteen years Cartwright established other posts between Cape Charles and Hamilton Inlet. The Moravian settlements were further north, as we shall see.

To befriend the Eskimos had been Cartwright's driving ambition. If we turn to the opening pages of his journal we find his clear statement that his reasons for settling in Labrador were 'for the purpose of carrying on various branches of

[1] Blumenbach was convinced that there was only one species of *Homo sapiens*. He had a library of books by Africans which he showed to Coleridge in 1799. 'There is no so-called savage nation known under the sun,' he wrote, 'which has so much distinguished itself by such perfectibility and original capacity for scientific culture and thereby attached itself so closely to the most civilised nations of the earth as the negro.' (Hallett 1965: 190.)

[2] Darby's failure in Labrador led to her going on the stage for which she was trained by Garrick and where she attracted the attentions of the Prince of Wales. She was crippled by rheumatic fever when twenty-four years old.

business upon the coast of Labrador; and particularly, of endeavouring to cultivate a friendly intercourse with the Esquimaux Indians, who have always been accounted the most savage race of people upon the whole continent of America.'

'That our people might easily have established a friendly intercourse, and beneficial traffic with these Indians, the circumstance which I have related renders highly probable: but vile murder first produced a spirit of revenge in them and that has been a pretext for unheard of cruelties on the part of our fishermen. I could relate several instances, some of which I had from the perpetrators themselves; but they are so diabolically shocking, that I will spare the reader the pain of perusing, and myself that of writing, an account of acts which would disgrace the greatest savages.'

When Cook fired on the Maoris in Poverty Bay, New Zealand, October 1769, Banks's reaction paralleled Cartwright's. 'Thus ended the most disagreeable day My life has yet seen', he wrote, 'black be the mark for it and heaven send that such may never return to embitter future reflection.'

Cartwright's understanding of human nature, and the courage, honesty and resolution with which he behaved towards the Eskimos, resulted in his building up the happiest relationships with them. He first made friends with one named Attuiock, and then with his family who got into the way of coming to see him and sharing his meals. During his second summer in Labrador, Shuglawina, chief of Attuiock's tribe, visited him with a party of thirty-two Eskimos of both sexes and all ages. Cartwright tells us that he had nine salmon averaging nine pounds in weight boiled for them and that they ate the lot in one meal. 'I can eat pretty well myself,' he remarks 'but my performances [which had held Southey and his brother spellbound when schoolboys] are not worth recording in the history of men of such superior talents.'

The day after this feast Cartwright went alone amongst the Eskimos, setting up a trading tent and instructing his people not to approach until sent for. Trade went briskly until two o'clock in the afternoon. Shuglawina then came in. 'Taking me by the shoulder and speaking sternly, he made signs for me to go along with him. As these people have hitherto plundered and murdered Europeans whenever they had opportunity, I must confess, that I expected that was to be my fate now. . . . However I put the best face possible on this unpleasant affair, locked up my goods and followed him out. He led me to the top of an eminence, at the back of my tent, and we were followed by all the men and boys. On observing a collection of brush wood and other dry fuel, I naturally concluded, that I was to be sacrificed; but whether they intended to roast me alive or dead I could not determine. I did not, however, long remain in suspense, for Shuglawina soon dispelled my fears by saying that we had done enough business for one day, and therefore he had brought me to look for vessels at sea (that station commanding a view quite across the straits of Belle Isle as far as Quirpon . . .) adding, that the wood was to make signals to them.' Trust was established and thereafter Cartwright maintained an excellent relationship with this group of Eskimos.

At the end of 1772 he decided to take Attuiock, his brother Tooklavinia, their wives and one of their children to England with him. On Christmas Eve, 1772, *The Morning Chronicle and London Advertiser* published part of a letter from Falmouth; 'Last Monday Commander Shuldham arrived here from Newfoundland, by whom came an Esquimaux Indian and his Squaw, to wait upon his Majesty . . . This Indian seems very sagacious, is well made, and has good features; he has a great desire to see his good former friend, Capt. Palliser. . . . I think it strange to see this Savage, who but a few months past eat all flesh raw, sit at table to dine in a decent manner and handle his knife and fork much better than many foreigners I have seen.'

When Cartwright had settled his Eskimo friends in London people of all kinds flocked to see them, and he was obliged to move from lodgings to a furnished house (ten guineas a month) in Little Castle Street, near Oxford Circus, then known as Oxford Market. Here the number of visitors (including Boswell and many other celebrities as well as the merely curious) created an intense traffic problem. The Eskimos found it rather much; Southey noted (1851:516): 'There are some curious anecdotes of the Esquimaux. When they entered London with him (Cartwright), one of them cried, putting up his hand to his head "Too much noise, too much people, too much house—Oh for Labrador", an interesting fact for the history of the human mind.'

John Cartwright joined his brother in London, and in a letter quoted by their niece, F. D. Cartwright (1826, 1:48), wrote 'Tomorrow, my brother, the Esquimaux, and myself, are to dine with a select company of the Royal Society, among whom is to be Solander. We have had him frequently. My brother is in greater spirits with regard to his Labrador schemes than at first setting off; although he has experienced every loss and disappointment that could befall man.'

Banks must have been particularly pleased to hear that Cartwright had brought an Eskimo family to London. In the six years that had elapsed since his journey to Newfoundland and Labrador he had visited the Pacific with Captain Cook and his experience with the Maoris and other peoples of the Pacific had given him confidence and tact in dealing with men who had been brought up with standards very different from those of Europe.

Lloyds Evening Post for Monday to Wednesday, 4–6 January 1773, described his visits to Cartwright's friends: 'Mr. Banks and Mr. Solander have paid frequent visits to the Esquimaux Indians, under the care of Captain Cartwright, and express themselves extremely satisfied with the observations and behaviour of those people; who, in return, shew great pleasure in the visits of these Gentlemen, as they generally carry with them some presents of beads, knives, iron tools or other things, on which they set a value, behave to them with politeness and respect, and ask them such questions only, concerning their country and nation, as serve to gratify in them that natural pride of our own nation, without which it loses all its dignity. These ingenious Gentlemen, who are inquisitive to mark the discriminations of the human character in every part of the world, could not help taking notice of the intelligent countenance of the Priest, and of the easy carriage and civility of manners of the whole family; while by too many of their numerous visitors they are held in contempt as Savages, because their heads have not undergone the operations of the Friseur, and gaped at as monsters, because their dress is not according to the Bon-Ton.'

The Eskimos also dined with the great surgeon and anatomist, John Hunter (after seeing his museum they were terrified that he was going to pickle them), were presented at Court, saw and were delighted with *Cymbeline* at Covent Garden. In the early spring Cartwright took them to his family home at Marham, Notts., where they stayed for six weeks. Here the men proved to be excellent riders and distinguished themselves on the hunting field, while the women enjoyed visiting and dancing, especially Caubvick, the younger, who 'attained great perfection in that graceful accomplishment'.

The visit ended in tragedy. As they were journeying to Plymouth on the first stage of their return voyage to Labrador, Caubvick fell ill with a mild attack of smallpox; she recovered but the other members of her family died in Plymouth. Cartwright looked after her most tenderly; he kept the news of the deaths of the others from her, and while she was convalescent engaged the regimental band of the Buffs to play outside her lodgings. Eventually she was well enough to complete the voyage but worse was to come; it appears that she may have carried the infection with her (she had refused to burn her hair which had been shaved during her illness) and a year or so later a fur trader found the encampment of her tribe strewn with dead bodies; they were identified through the box of tools given by Banks to Attuiock, which was lying in one of their shelters.

Caubvick and George Cartwright's sister Catherine had become close friends and the diary kept by the latter girl was shown in 1904 in an exhibition in Bradford commemorating the work of her uncle Edmund Cartwright, the inventor of the power loom; I have been unable to trace its present whereabouts, but it is bound in red morocco with silver clasps and is unlikely to have been destroyed. 'My affection for Caubvick,' she wrote, 'is such that neither time nor distance will ever efface it.'

It appears that a family portrait of the Eskimos was painted while they were in London, and that Banks owned it. George Cartwright wrote to him many years later asking whether he had had an engraving made of it (p. 275), but none was available; I have not been successful in tracing either the painter or the present whereabouts of the painting, but Lord Brabourne has in his possession two drawings of Caubvick and Attuiock by Nathaniel Dance (best known for his portrait of Captain Cook) and has kindly allowed them to be reproduced here. In addition to these portraits Banks owned one of Caubvick now in the possession of the Royal College of Surgeons; he had copies made of the pastel drawings and sent them to J. F. Blumenbach; they are still in Göttingen with the portrait of Mykok referred to above.

Europeans had become greatly interested in primitive peoples. In 1769 Bougainville had taken Ahutoru from Tahiti to Paris where he became a devotee of opera, was presented at Court and enjoyed the same degree of social success as the Eskimos were soon to do in London. In 1775 Phipps, Banks, their great friend George Colman, the playwright, with his son and Phipps's young brother, visited Phipps's Yorkshire home, Mulgrave Castle near Whitby, taking with them Omai, the Tahitian brought to England by Furneaux, commander of the *Discovery*, sister ship to the *Resolution* on Cook's second voyage round the world. Omai appears to have enjoyed all their activities except for Banks's lectures on the Linnean system. He and Banks equally shared culinary honours on their botanical and archaeological excursions, Banks making palatable stews in a mysterious tin contraption, and Omai using a traditional Polynesian earth oven with excellent results save when he tried to roast a seagull. Omai adapted himself to European ways with such facility and developed such a sense of style that he even reproved the young Duchess of Devonshire (known to us from a wonderful portrait by Gainsborough) for the untidiness of her appearance in Hyde Park.

In the years to come even some forlorn Indians from the south of South America were to be brought to London though the visit of these three Terra del Fuegians, York Minster, Fuegia Basket and Jimmy Button, passengers in H.M.S. *Beagle*, was less successful than those of the Tahitians and Eskimos since their inadequate knowledge of the English language led many people to believe that they were cannibals and enjoyed other inhuman practices. Like many other peoples they appear to have tried to answer questions in the way they thought their interrogators desired rather than with any idea of the truth. Of course sometimes the truth was too odd for Europeans to believe. Even as Attuiock and Tooklavinia thought St. Paul's Cathedral to be a natural growth until they were shown some of the actual construction, so in Australia, in the late eighteenth and early nineteenth centuries, the English settlers refused to believe the aborigines when they told them that the huge mounds of leaf mould and sand, sometimes fifty feet in diameter and fifteen to twenty feet high, were built by those industrious birds, the megapodes, to incubate their eggs. The settlers, remembering the barrows of their native land, pronounced them to be funeral mounds. It was not until 1840 that the naturalist John Gilbert actually dug into the mounds and found that the aborigines were right after all. It is reminiscent of the mediaeval argument over the number of teeth in a horse's mouth, and how long it was before anyone thought of counting them *in situ*.

That the impact of Europeans might be disastrous for the native people of the Pacific and elsewhere was feared even in the eighteenth century. In 'Hints offered to the consideration of Captain Cooke, Mr. Bankes, Dr. Solander, and other Gentlemen who go upon the Expedition on Board the *Endeavour*' James Douglas, 14th Earl of Morton, Commissioner of Longitude, and one of the most active promoters of the expedition, asked them 'to exercise the utmost patience and for-bearance with respect to the Natives of the several Lands where the Ship may touch . . . To have it still in view that sheding the blood of those people is a crime of the highest nature :- They are human creatures, the work of the same omnipotent Author, equally under his care with the most polished Europeans; perhaps being less offensive, more entitled to his favor.' (p. 250). And after the voyage Horace Walpole wrote: 'Who is secure against Jack Straw and a whirlwind? How I abominate Mr. Banks and Dr. Solander, who routed the poor Otaheitians out of the centre of the ocean and carried our abominable passions amongst them! Not even that poor little speck could escape European restlessness.' (*Letters*, ed. Paget Toynbee, 1904, XI, 1779–1801).

3

Banks's birds

SOME EARLIER WORK ON NORTH AMERICAN BIRDS

A NUMBER of books by residents and explorers of north-eastern America appeared before 1766, several of which contained observations on natural history, with lists of birds and mammals. Banks would have read about Frobisher's journeys in Hakluyt's *Voyages*, and may have seen John White's drawings, *c.* 1577, of Eskimos from Baffin Land (Hulton, 1961). He would certainly have known of Newfoundland timbers, of the fisheries of the Newfoundland Banks, and he may have read of the birds of the fishing grounds in the writings of Nicolas Denys who in 1654 was made governor of the coast and islands of the Gulf of St. Lawrence, including Newfoundland. Another governor of Newfoundland, Baron Armand Louis de Lahontan (1667–1715), listed the birds of northern Canada in a book, much of it spurious (Adams 1962), which was published in London in 1703. Details of these men and their observations are given by Mrs. Allen in her *History of American Ornithology before Audubon* (1951).

Banks's own collections and descriptions were clearly influenced by Mark Catesby, usually regarded as the father of American ornithology, although he was by birth an Englishman, and a native of Castle Hedingham, Essex. He visited America twice, from 1712 to 1719, and from 1722 to 1726. His *Natural History of Carolina* (1731–43) is the first scientific account of the North American fauna and flora; it contains descriptions of more than one hundred species of birds. Although his travels were confined to the southern states and the Bahamas some of the birds described by him occur in Newfoundland as well as in the south. He collected for Sir Hans Sloane, William Sherard and other English scientists, and was a friend of Eleazar Albin's and George Edwards's, whose works are discussed below. Much has been written of him in recent years (Allen 1951; Frick & Stearns 1961).

It was suggested by Gosling that some Newfoundland birds were taken to England in the seventeenth century. This may be so but the earliest definite record I have found is Albin's plate and description of the Great Sea Loon (Great Northern Diver) in his *Natural History of Birds* (1738); 'It feeds altogether on fish,' says Albin, 'and was brought from Newfoundland and presented to the Right Honourable Lord Islay who was pleased to lend it to me to draw its picture.' Banks probably owned Albin's book, and he tells us that he had the more important *Natural History of Uncommon Birds* (4 parts, 1743–51) by George Edwards who also produced a revision of Catesby's book in 1754. In several places in his own book Edwards refers to a collection of Newfoundland birds preserved in the Tower of London; Banks may have known them since he was probably familiar with the menagerie there.

The Tower had become important as a repository for state documents which at the time of Queen Anne had accumulated without adequate classification or arrangement. In 1704 Lord Halifax tried to remedy this, and on his advice William Petyt was appointed Keeper of Records with four clerks to assist him, one of whom was George Holmes (1662–1749) who for many years acted as deputy-keeper. He was a Fellow of the Society of Antiquaries of London, and a member of the Spalding Gentlemen's Society, the second oldest scientific society in England, numbering among its members Ray, Pope, Addison and Newton. Late in life Holmes also became a Fellow of the Royal Society, but he contributed nothing to the *Philosophical Transactions*, his chief interests being in numismatics and Anglo-Saxon. He owned, however, a collection of Newfoundland birds which he lent to his friend George Edwards.

The menagerie at the Tower dated from the thirteenth century when a polar bear and an elephant were kept there. The bear belonged to Henry III who, in 1253 or thereabouts, issued an order providing for its welfare.

'The King to the Sheriffs of *London*, Greetings: We command you, that for the Keeper of our White Bear, lately sent us from Norway, and which is in our Tower of *London*, ye cause to be had one muzzle and one Iron Chain, to hold that Bear without the Water, and one long and strong Cord, to hold the same Bear fishing (or washing himself) in the River of *Thames*.

Witness the King at Windsor. October the 30th.'

Strype's edition of Stow (1754) contains two lists of the animals in the menagerie, including a number of foreign birds. There were also some stuffed lions but I have found no details of the collection belonging to George Holmes except for the Newfoundland birds described by Edwards. It was the custom for naval officers to bring specimens back from various parts of the world for the royal collections at the Tower, and gifts from foreign kings were usually sent there too. But it seems that the Newfoundland birds were Holmes's personal property. Edwards's careful descriptions and illustrations of them appear to be the first, apart from that of Albin's Diver mentioned above, to appear in English scientific literature.

Holmes's friend George Edwards was one of the most accomplished British naturalists and writers of the eighteenth century. Not only an accurate observer, a competent artist and linguist, he was also deeply intelligent. 'Man', he says 'ought to set before his intellectual mind the ideas of truth and falsehood, and endeavour to find out, in the most strict and absolute sense what they are; and when he hath found them he ought to govern all his actions by the former, and avoid the latter

91

but it is exceedingly hard to discover what truth is in a world of falsehood and controversy, where all of us suck in error with our mother's milk . . . it is a firm and fixed article of my private faith, that God hath given us our senses as a touchstone of truth.'

Edwards was a close friend of Sir Hans Sloane who helped to get him appointed librarian to the Royal College of Physicians, a post that gave him an adequate salary and sufficient leisure to write and illustrate his books. His introductions and appended essays are remarkable; his observations for instance on the 'salacious habits of grouse' are followed by a discussion of the prevalence of homosexuality at that time, which he ascribes to lack of co-education and the strict segregation of adolescents from those of the opposite sex. His ideas (1751–7, pt. 2:115–19), on the migration of birds were, like those of Adanson and Thomas Pennant, much in advance of his contemporaries, some of whom believed with Johnson that 'swallows certainly sleep all winter. A number of them conglobulate together by flying round and round, and then all in a heap throw themselves under water, and lye in the bed of a river'. A year before Edwards's death in 1773, one of his opponents, Daines Barrington, who was incidentally a close friend of Banks's, wrote a paper, accepted for the *Philosophical Transactions*, on the almost instantaneous revival of some swallows obtained from mud at the bottom of a pond drained in midwinter, and put forward the theory that such instances of hibernation were rarely recorded only because draining ponds at that season was such a disagreeable business.

Luckily Edwards tells us something of the history and whereabouts of each specimen he illustrates, and thus presents a fascinating picture of the pleasure given by birds throughout all ranks of society in eighteenth-century England.

It is obvious that Banks's major scientific interest throughout his life was botanical, but he was a good zoologist and his extensive collection of bird paintings and skins, his meetings with Gilbert White and Thomas Pennant at the Horace's Head for 'ornithological converse', and his careful and perceptive descriptions of the Newfoundland birds published elsewhere in this volume show that he had a considerable knowledge of ornithology. It would indeed have been eccentric for an English naturalist of that time with Banks's opportunities to have lacked this interest. Even with limited facilities for obtaining exotic foods, and in the absence of simple means for regulating heat and light, a wide variety of birds were kept as pets. It is remarkable that a bird as specialized as the flamingo should have lived for some time in the kitchen of Sir Robert Walpole's house, as Albin states. Edwards notes a White-Tailed Eagle from Hudson's Bay which for many years was the occupant of an aviary owned by Dr. R. M. Massey at Stepney, and a Great Horned Owl, also from Hudson's Bay, which was a pet at the Mourning Bush Tavern at Aldersgate.

Seafaring men of all kinds kept exotic birds as pets on their ships and brought some of them successfully back to England—everyone knows that stock figure in

English stories, the sailor, or the pirate, with his parrot; Edwards records a cage of Yellow-headed Linnets taken from a Spanish prize by an English ship in the West Indies, which eventually came to Sir Charles Wager's aviary where Edwards saw and drew them. Even earlier that excellent naturalist Dampier, a wonderfully perceptive observer with a remarkable feeling for words, made his way round the world on ships often of dubious character, and brought back various birds, and also plants some of which are still to be seen in Oxford (Clokie 1964:153).

This was all a matter of general interest but it is to Gilbert White that we owe the detailed observations and descriptions of British birds and mammals contained in one of the most famous books of the eighteenth century. White was a friend of Thomas Pennant's and of Daines Barrington's; most of his observations of natural history were made in a series of letters to them, later edited and published as the *Natural History of Selborne*, a book written with rare lucidity and truth, which still gives pleasure to many readers.

Pennant introduced Banks to White, who reveals much of himself and Banks in a letter to Pennant written on 8 October 1768, soon after the departure of the *Endeavour*. 'When I reflect on the youth and affluence of this enterprising Gent: I am filled with wonder to see how conspicuously the contempt of danger, & the love of excelling in his favourite studies stand forth in his character. And yet tho' I admire his resolution which scorns to stoop to any difficulties: I cannot divest myself of some degree of solicitude for his person.' And on 19 July 1771, 'Yesterday I had a letter from town which mentions the return of Mr. Banks; and adds that he looks as well as ever he did in his life. So agreeable an event calls for my warm congratulations; for if we rejoice at the arrival of a friend who has been absent but a few months, perhaps in a neighbouring kingdom, how shall we express ourselves when we see one restored, as it were from the other world, after having undergone the astonishing hazards and dangers that must attend the circumnavigation of the world itself! ! !' It is in Gilbert White's correspondence that we have the only detailed description (pp. 253–6) of the extent of Banks's collections as they appeared in 1772, after being arranged by the skilful hand of Edward Jenner.

THE USE OF BANKS'S COLLECTIONS
BY HIS CONTEMPORARIES

Thomas Pennant, F.R.S., 1726–98

The first person to make extensive use of Banks's zoological collections after his return in the late winter of 1766–7 was Thomas Pennant, perhaps the most able British zoologist between John Ray and Charles Darwin. He himself recorded that his interest in natural history arose when he was twelve years old through being given a copy of Willughby's *Ornithology* (1676) by a relation, John Salusbury, father of the celebrated Mrs. Thrale, Dr. Johnson's friend. Not only a good scientist but also an enthusiastic traveller and prolific writer, Pennant was friendly with the most eminent biologists of the day, including Linnaeus, Buffon, Haller and Pallas, as well as with other celebrities such as Voltaire, the Duchess of Portland, the Anson family (his notes on the authorship of Anson's *Voyage* are of considerable interest) and with Dr. Johnson who thought highly of his abilities (Boswell's *Life of Johnson*, Everyman Edition, 1949, 2:197).

He had a great range of interests, and the introduction to his *Arctic Zoology*, the first major work on zoogeography, shows much of his quality, not only his knowledge of history but also his perspicacity of vision. Here he surveys the then current theory of the discovery of America by the Welsh Madoc which he dismisses with some scorn for the linguistic theory—still attractive to a body of believers today. He also discusses the voyages of the Vikings who he believed might well have reached Labrador; this discussion makes quite extraordinary reading in the light of the present archaeological excavations in Newfoundland. At the end of his second volume he discusses the Arctic birds and suggests that many birds known in Kamschatka may migrate to the American continent; he adds: 'It is also likely, that numbers may seek a more southern retreat, and stock Japan and China with their periodical flocks. I have done as much as the lights of my days have furnished me with.

In some remote age, when the British offspring will have pervaded the whole of their vast continent, or the descendants of the hardy Russians colonized the western parts from their distant Kamschatka, the road in future time to fresh conquests: after, perhaps, bloody conquests between the progeny of Britons and Russians, about countries to which neither have any right; after the deaths of thousands of clamants, and the extirpation of the poor natives by the sword, and new-imported diseases, a quiet settlement may take place, civilization ensue, and the arts of peace be cultivated: learning, the luxury of the soul, diffuse itself through the nation, and some naturalist arise, who, with spirit and abilities, may explore each boundary of the ocean which separates the Asiatic and American continents; may render certain what I can only suspect, and by his observations on the feathered tribes, their flights and migrations, give utility to mankind, in naval and economical operations, by auguries which the antients knew well to apply to the benefits of their fellow-creatures.'

Today however, Pennant is less remembered for his major zoological writings than for his close friendship with Gilbert White and his part in the *Natural History of Selborne*.

Banks first sought Pennant out in 1766, shortly before leaving for Newfoundland; calling on him in his lodgings in St. James's Street he presented him with William Turner's book (1544) on the birds mentioned by Pliny and Aristotle. He wrote to him from Labrador and from Lisbon but these letters have not been traced. In May 1767, Pennant visited Revesby Abbey, Banks's Lincolnshire home, and from then until a disastrous quarrel in 1783 the two men were close friends. There is even a letter, August 1767, in which Pennant writes that he will shortly be visiting London and will Banks kindly see that there is a fire for him in the library.

It is clear from surviving letters (pp. 246–9) that in 1768 Banks lent Pennant his Newfoundland diary, many bird skins, and probably most of his zoological notes, as well as the paintings of his Newfoundland specimens already executed by Sydney Parkinson. At this time Peter Paillou was working for Pennant, and painted more of the birds, sometimes making additional copies for Banks to give to friends such as Taylor White (p. 104).

Pennant used the work of both artists to illustrate his *Arctic Zoology* which did not appear for another sixteen years. Much of his information about northern Canada was derived from Alexander Graham, who worked for the Hudson's Bay Company, and from Samuel Hearne, one of the searchers for a north-west passage. But his material on Newfoundland seems to have come almost entirely from Banks, and he printed the whole of Banks's description of the Newfoundland fisheries. Pennant retained copies of Parkinson's drawings and many years later some were used by Mercatti to illustrate an interleaved set of the second edition of the *Arctic Zoology*; this set, now in McGill University Library, contains copious unpublished marginal illustrations and additional watercolours; it was probably intended for a further edition in full colour. This unique and beautiful work was harshly trimmed by a Victorian bookbinder, resulting in damage to some of the watercolours.

Pennant's acknowledgement to Banks for the use of his material was extremely cursory, 'Sir Joseph Banks, Baronet, will I hope accept my thanks for the free admittance to those parts of his cabinet which more immediately related to the subject of the following sheets' (*Arctic Zoology*, 1784: 5th p.), and there are brief references to Banks in some of the notes on Newfoundland birds, but that is all. Pennant made some amends in his *Literary Life* (1793:29), but considering his strictures on others, including Buffon, who did not admit their indebtedness to him his own thanks seem more than meagre. It is largely because of this omission that Banks's contribution to the zoology of Newfoundland has so long been overlooked.

It is curious that in 1877 Thomas Bell in a Memoir prefacing his edition of the *Natural History of Selborne* should have written: 'If there be one author to whom, more than all others, Pennant is indebted for whatever is reliable or interesting in his book [*British Zoology*], particularly that portion which relates to the birds and to some of the rarer quadrupeds, that man is Gilbert White . . . But there is no acknowledgement of his help, no recognition of the debt.'

According to Bell, Pennant's attitude to other people's work was widely known; it was probably this that led to his quarrel with Banks over the illustrations he wished to use in the *Arctic Zoology*.

In 1772, at the time when Cartwright was making arrangements to bring a family of his Eskimo friends to London, Banks and Solander visited Iceland (pl. 11), taking amongst their draughtsmen John Frederick Miller, one of the twenty-seven children of Johann Sebastian Müller, a Nuremberg engraver who had come to live in England in 1744. In 1776 Miller fell into disgrace with Banks for engraving and exhibiting plates made from the Iceland drawings without having asked permission. Banks then found that Pennant had purchased some of Miller's plates to illustrate the *Arctic Zoology*; Banks felt that the plates had been stolen from him and refused to help Pennant borrow drawings made on Cook's third voyage which were in the possession of the Admiralty, and they exchanged heated letters (Smith, 1911:181–5). Pennant wrote to Banks years afterwards, in 1794, trying to patch up their friendship but it was not until 1798 when he again asked for some tangible proof that they were good friends that Banks replied with the warm generosity that characterized most of his doings. The exact form of his letter is not known to me but there is an acknowledgement from Pennant (Morgan Library, New York) dated 26 July 1798, beginning: 'Thanks over and over again for your charming letter. I wish you and I were a little more locomotive . . .' Banks was then severely incapacitated by gout.

Johann Reinhold Forster, F.R.S., 1727–98

Although it was so long after Banks's voyage that Pennant's work on his Newfoundland collections appeared in the *Arctic Zoology*, 1784–7, a list of the Newfoundland birds and fishes actually compiled by Pennant appeared in 1771 under the name of J. R. Forster, a friend and colleague of Pennant's. This German scientist was a difficult man but a most able scientist and a polyglot with seventeen languages at his command. He is best known for his work as a naturalist on Cook's second voyage round the world (1772–5) and for brilliant monographs on penguins and albatrosses; his son Georg accompanied him in the *Resolution* and it was largely Georg who inspired his friend, the young Alexander von Humboldt, with that passion for visiting tropical lands which led to his celebrated American travels and their far-reaching effects on research in botany, geology, meteorology and physics (cf. Stearn, 1960, 1968).

J. R. Forster came to England in 1766, when Banks was in Newfoundland, and the following year began teaching at Warrington Academy, a dissenting school with high academic standards, where the chemist Joseph Priestley had been employed shortly before. Forster had no aptitude for dealing with boys, 'Young monkeys' he called them 'who are quite licentious and under no discipline and tease me with their tricks to death'. The unhappy man had little financial sense, and his family—he had seven children—was in a permanent state of penury. While in Warrington he was befriended by Pennant who recognized his ability, introduced him to other scientists, helped him financially, and collaborated with him in various ways, particularly in connection with the *Indian Zoology*.[1] Forster even spent Christmas at Downing, Pennant's Flintshire home, and wrote these thanks 'I am very much obliged to You for all the kindness and Liberalities bestowed upon me during my stay at your Seat of Downing. All my Happiness is over as a Dream, and was it not for the endearing love of my Wife and Children, I would wish to live all the days of my short remaining Life with so generous a Friend. All my way from Holywell to Chester was excruciating for me, I had pains in my bowels and sorrow in my heart; the first made me one time in a violent fit faint away; but at last went off; the latter never left me, *et Post equitem sedet atra Cura*'. In April of the same year J. Lyon wrote to Pennant 'Though I was well acquainted with your Philanthropy of Disposition before, yet your Beneficence to poor Forster in his distrest Situation of Affairs is very extraordinary. The poor Man read the Intelligence with Tears of Gratitude.'

It was about this time that Pennant gave Forster access to some of the material on which he was basing his *Arctic Zoology*, originally intended to be the *Zoology of North America* (see his introduction). In 1771 Forster published the *Catalogue of the Animals of North America* (pp. 397–400) with references to some specimens brought back from Newfoundland by 'Mr. B.' No hint is given of the identity of this collector, and P. L. Sclater, the editor of the Willughby reprint (1882) of Forster's *Catalogue* quotes the suggestion by Alfred Newton, author of the enduringly interesting *Dictionary of Birds* (1893–6), that this was perhaps a Mr. Bolton of Halifax mentioned by other ornithologists of Forster's day.

Neither Newton nor Sclater knew of Banks's Newfoundland bird paintings since they were bound up with other natural history paintings which remained in the Manuscript Room at the British Museum when in 1880 the greater part of the botanical and zoological drawings was transferred to the new Natural History Departments at South Kensington. And curiously enough Pennant's autobiography, the *Literary Life* of 1793, has not been widely read so that his statement (p. 14) about his own share in Forster's publication appears to have escaped notice: 'In this year doctor *Forster* published a catalogue of the animals of *North America*. I had begun the work, by a list of the quadrupeds, birds [including Banks's] and fishes. Doctor Forster added all the rest . . . My part in this work is of so little merit that it need not be boasted of. I only lay clame to my proper right.' On pp. 28–9 he acknowledges that the *Arctic Zoology* benefited considerably from Banks's visit to Newfoundland: 'He added greatly to the ornithology by the communication of several [*sic*] new species of birds, and several other subjects.' Detailed notes on Forster's *Catalogue* are given on pp. 397–400 of this volume.

---

[1] From letters in the possession of the late Mr. Sinelnikoff who kindly gave me permission to quote from them.

BANKS'S BIRDS

John Latham, F.R.S., 1740–1837

Notes based on Banks's own descriptions of his Newfoundland collections, and on the paintings by Parkinson and Paillou, appeared not only in the writings of Forster and Pennant but also in the *General Synopsis of Birds* by John Latham, a remarkably successful doctor of medicine, who had been taught anatomy by William Hunter. Latham was immensely industrious and so successful financially that he was able to retire from medical practice in 1796 and devote the rest of his unusually long life to natural history, a subject in which he had been interested since his early youth. By 1773 he had amassed a collection that gained the admiration of Sir Ashton Lever, the founder of the Leverian Museum. Latham sent him some exhibits about which Sir Ashton wrote with enthusiasm, in the style so detested by Cartwright, 'The Manakins are the most elegant birds I ever saw, and your taste in the disposition of them is the most exquisitely beautiful. You have set us on our mettal, as I tell you honestly I have not among my cases any so attractive to my visitors as this . . . I never received so generous a present from anyone, since I began to collect' (Mathews, *Ibis*, 1931:467).

Latham became a Fellow of the Royal Society in 1775. Two years later Pennant went on a riding tour of Kent and met him in Dartford, from which time they were good friends. They collaborated to revise the second edition of the *Indian Zoology* (1792) in which Latham did most of the work on insects, as Pennant acknowledged (1793:40). An obituary of Latham in *The Analyst* (VI) for 1837 stated that 'In addition to his correspondence with eminent naturalists and friends on the subject of his favourite pursuits, the inspection of museums, and taking drawings of specimens lent to him for the purpose; he etched every copper plate in his original work, stuffed and set up every animal in his extensive museum, and put together with his own hands, a great many of the cases in which they were disposed; it is difficult to conceive how he could have been, as he most certainly was, one not only of the most punctual of men of business, but of the most attentive to all the duties and courtesies of life.'

It was a time when, unencumbered by the many labour-saving devices that clutter our paths today, people devoted themselves to their pursuits, either serious or frivolous, with tremendous singleness of purpose, achieving results that are breathtaking. There was a fashion for exhibitions large and small which led to some remarkable absurdities as well as a great advance in knowledge. Mrs. Delany's paper flowers inspired Erasmus Darwin to some extraordinary lines in the *Loves of the Plants*: many volumes of her paper cut-outs of plants may be seen in the Print Room, British Museum, but nothing is known of the fate of the botanical constructions (from fishbones) of her contemporary, Mrs. Dards:

> With bones, scales and eyes, from the prawn to the porpoise,
> Fruit, flies, birds and flowers! O! strange metamorphose!

98

'No one can imagine the trouble I had in collecting the bones for that bunch of lilies of the valley; each cup consists of the bones which contain the brains of the turbot; and from the difficulty of matching the sizes, I should never have completed my task had it not been for the kindness of the proprietors of the London Free Masons and Crown and Anchor Taverns, who desired their waiters to save all the fish-bones for me.'

How Latham met Banks I do not know but they were certainly friends and he appears to have had access to the whole of Banks's collections; a number of his plates are indeed copied from drawings by Banks's artists, although he usually signed them with his initial L. As far as the Newfoundland birds are concerned he seems to have worked largely from Pennant's notes and MSS; in many cases the observations made by both men are very similar but Pennant records a larger number of species.

2. Labrador Duck, Camptorhynchus labradorium (Gmelin)

Special interest attaches to Latham's notes (1785:497–8) on the now extinct Labrador Duck (*Camptorhynchus labradorium*) since there are few if any reliable records of the species from the country after which it was named (Todd 1963: 176–7). Latham notes: 'It inhabits the coast of Labrador; from whence a pair in the collection of Sir Joseph Banks came. That described in the *Arctic Zoology* was sent from Connecticut in New England.' This pair is listed in the catalogue of Banks's bird skins but no drawing of them by Parkinson or Paillou appears to be known. Parkinson worked for Banks from 1767 until his death in the *Endeavour* in 1771; his paintings of the Newfoundland birds must have therefore been executed in 1767 or 1768 before he set out on the voyage. There is no evidence that Paillou ever worked directly for Banks; his two chief patrons were Taylor White and Pennant; his un-dated and unsigned paintings of the Newfoundland birds must have been made when Pennant borrowed the skins of 1768 (p. 247). This indicates that Banks's pair of Labrador Ducks was acquired *after* the return of the *Endeavour* in 1771 when he had a great wealth of material from that voyage to determine and arrange, and when the collection from Newfoundland and Labrador would no longer have been of major importance to him. For various reasons it is probable that these particular birds were sent to him by George Cartwright.

Johann Friedrich Gmelin, 1748–1804

J. F. Gmelin was a member of a Tübingen family noted for intellectual achievements in botany, chemistry, medicine and related sciences, and continuously eminent enough to hold professorial chairs almost as it were by hereditary principle. Less distinguished academically than most of his relations, he is chiefly remembered today for having edited the thirteenth edition of the *Systema Naturae* of 1788–93, and the *Systema Vegetabilium* of 1796. His edition of the former work included the Newfoundland and Labrador birds mentioned by Forster, Pennant and Latham; he gave them scientific binomials and described them briefly in Latin, with reference to the earlier publications in which few or none of the names given had any scientific validity. Unfortunately he had no access to Banks's material and some descriptions were inadequate for the determination of the northern species by later workers; furthermore he followed Pennant and others in describing some immature forms as specifically distinct from adults. Inevitably some of his names had eventually to be discarded, and a few of the Newfoundland birds are now known by other names given by scientists of the next century. Able systematists such as Hellmayr and Bowdler Sharpe did their best to trace the basis of Gmelin's names but since they knew nothing of Banks's collections and MSS their task was hopeless.

4

The natural history
paintings and painters

BANKS's specimens from Newfoundland and Labrador were painted by three men; some of his plants by Georg Ehret, some invertebrates and fishes by Sydney (Sidney) Parkinson, some birds by Parkinson, others by Peter Paillou. Of these men the best known is Georg Dionysius Ehret (1708–70), the dominant figure in botanical illustration for much of the eighteenth century. He was born in Heidelberg where his family owned a smallholding and sold garden produce. His father taught him gardening and gave him his first drawing lessons, then apprenticed him to an uncle at Bessungen where he worked as gardener's assistant for three years. After his father's death his mother married a man named Kesselbach who was responsible for the gardens of the Elector of Heidelberg and gave his stepson part charge of one of them. Here Ehret was noticed by the Margrave of Baden who took him on to his staff and encouraged him to paint flowers. How he first worked for and then in 1732, met Dr. Trew, the wealthy Nuremberg physician to whom, much later, he sent some of Banks's plants (p. 343) is set out in detail in Blunt and Stearn's *Art of Botanical Illustration* (1950) from which these notes are taken. Trew was to be Ehret's lifelong friend, and it was with his encouragement and financial help that the younger man set out to travel.

Ehret first visited Switzerland and France, and then, after a short time in London, where he met Sir Hans Sloane and Philip Miller, the greatest gardener of the day, he proceeded to Leyden and then to nearby Hartecamp where Linnaeus was staying with George Clifford, cataloguing his botanical collections. The three men met and became friends, and Ehret made drawings for Clifford. In 1736 he returned to England, where he lived for the rest of his life. He became a Fellow of the Royal Society, but he enjoyed other society too and was a great favourite with London hostesses; as well as making splendid illustrations for botanists, and for collectors such as Taylor White, he gave drawing lessons to the great ladies of the day. He died when only sixty-two years old. His work never failed in quality. It is surprising that he appears to have painted only twenty-three of the plants brought back by Banks from Newfoundland and Labrador. Although Banks collected many more plants than animals the number of drawings of animals greatly exceeds that of plants; it is probable that Banks's detailed botanical notes and a further folio of plant paintings still await discovery.

Ehret's paintings of Banks's Newfoundland plants are on vellum; they are remarkable for their delicacy and vitality, and the fact that they are all based on dried specimens is nowhere apparent save in one case: the flowers of *Dryas integrifolia* are shown as yellow instead of pure white simply because herbarium specimens rapidly fade to that colour. For this reason it, pl. 53, has been reproduced here only in black and white although the original is one of the most delightful in the whole series. Some plates have notes on localities in Banks's own hand; the versos have not all been examined, owing to the way in which they are mounted.

The paintings of the animals from Newfoundland and Labrador were executed by two young men, Sydney Parkinson (1745–71) and Peter Paillou whose dates are unknown. Parkinson's self-portrait (pl. 23), which now hangs in the Zoology Library of the British Museum (Natural History), suggests an aloof and melancholy young man with considerable strength of character. A very different portrait of him reproduced by Beaglehole (1962, 1:52) probably represents him as a schoolboy. Some two thousand of his drawings, largely botanical, survive in the various departments of the British Museum; these include about 1,300 from Cook's first voyage round the world on the *Endeavour*, the ship in which Parkinson died. Others are in Australia. The warm and lively interest in his work which is still felt today is probably the kind of memorial he would best have liked had he been able to choose one.

Sydney Parkinson's father, a Quaker, was an unsuccessful Edinburgh brewer who died leaving his family with very little money. There was another son, Stanfield, an upholsterer, and a daughter named Britannia ('Rule Britannia' was written in 1740). Sydney was 'put to the business of' a woollen draper in Edinburgh but, 'taking a particular delight in drawing flowers, fruits and other objects of natural history he became soon as proficient in that stile of painting as to attract the notice of the most celebrated botanists and connoisseurs in that study'. When he was about twenty his widowed mother moved to London (he exhibited flower paintings in the Free Society in 1765 and 1766), and not long afterwards he was introduced to Banks by James Lee who ran the famous Vineyard Nursery at Hammersmith.

Lee came from Selkirk near Edinburgh and the Parkinsons may have known him before they came to London. He engaged Sydney to give painting lessons to his favourite daughter Ann, then about thirteen years old. She was fifteen when Sydney sailed in the *Endeavour*, leaving a will in which he bequeathed to her his 'utensils' and some botanical paintings which remained until 1968 in the possession of the Lee family; they are now in the National Library, Canberra. Ann Lee was considered by Fabricius (p. 50) to be the best natural history painter in England but none of her work (which has a lovely quality) was ever published. She died at the age of thirty-seven. Many of her paintings have recently been presented to Kew Gardens by descendants of James Lee.

Lee introduced Parkinson to Banks early in 1767, and between then and the sailing of the *Endeavour* in August 1768 Parkinson worked extensively on Banks's collections. He seems first to have executed the plates of the Loten collection from Ceylon, with which both Banks and Pennant were concerned; the originals, signed and dated, are in the Zoology Library of the British Museum. In the Print Room there are many of his drawings of birds and insects, a large number of which have not yet been individually identified. Parkinson's drawings of Banks's birds from Newfoundland and Labrador are of high quality, both accurate and lively, which is astonishing when one considers the state that the skins must have been in after months in a tub of spirits. Too young to have found a formula, Parkinson painted even the insects with loving care and never with the mechanical symmetry which was to overtake so much entomological illustration. He died on the ghastly return voyage of the *Endeavour*, between Batavia and the Cape of Good Hope, when so many of Cook's men succumbed to dysentery and malaria—'On our arrival at the Cape we were in great distress not having more than six men capable of duty'.

Banks wrote of him: 'Now as S. Parkinson certainly behaved to me, during the whole of the long voyage, uncommonly well, and with unbounded industry made for me a much larger number of drawings than I ever expected, I always did and still do intend to show to his relations the same gratitude for his good services as I should have done to himself.' Anyone interested in one of Newfoundland's earliest artists will find more about him in his posthumously published journal of 1773, and in the writings of Beaglehole and Sawyer. The notes on the Lee family are taken from E. J. Willson's book on James Lee.

About Peter Paillou we know very little. I have not found any portrait of him, nor any precise information about his dates; in the reference books on eighteenth-century painters he is confused with another man of the same name, probably his son, who is said to have lived in Islington and Glasgow and worked as a miniaturist. Most of the older man's work was executed for Taylor White (1701–72) of Wallingwells, Notts., and later, for Thomas Pennant at Downing. Taylor White's son who, confusingly, had the same name as his father, was a few months younger than Joseph Banks, but it would appear that Taylor White senior was undoubtedly the man to whom Banks gave some of his Newfoundland birds, and also some paintings of them executed by Paillou senior who was then working for Pennant.

As the general picture is rather confused it will perhaps be simpler to state first what is known of Peter Paillou, and then to outline the life and achievements of Taylor White; it is probable that further details about Paillou will eventually be found amongst the surviving papers of the White and Pennant families since it is unlikely that they have been destroyed but I have been unable to make a thorough search for them.

Taylor White's collection of natural history paintings was executed by several artists working for him between 1730 and 1760; most of the animal paintings from that collection were acquired by McGill University Library in Montreal about 1926, and a summary of the folios in which they were arranged (which was not their original sequence) was published by Casey Wood in his *Literature of Vertebrate Zoology* of 1931. The earliest paintings signed by Paillou in that collection are dated 1744; one represents a Bird of Paradise, the other an owl. About 1760 or 1761 Peter Paillou began to work for Pennant who in his *Literary Life* of 1793 wrote: 'About 1761 I began my *British Zoology*, which, when completed, consisted of cxxxii plates on imperial paper . . . The painter was Mr. Peter Pallou [*sic*], an excellent artist, but too fond of giving gaudy colours to his subjects. He painted, for my hall at *Downing*, several pictures of birds and animals, attended with suitable landscapes . . . all have their merit, but occasion me to lament his conviviality, which affected his circumstances and abridged his days.' In 1778 a picture by Peter Paillou entitled 'A Horned Owl (from Peru) in Feathers' was shown in an exhibition by members of the Society of Artists (Graves 1907:186); Paillou was stated to be living at Paradise Row, Islington, but this may have been his son's address. Taylor White's wife and daughter both acquired the technique of 'feather painting'; there are some references to this in *Memoirs of the House of White of Wallingwells* by M. H. Towry White. The famous feather book executed in 1618 by Dionisio Minaggio, an official of the court of Milan, was amongst Taylor White's treasures; it contained 156 pictures, including one of the Dodo, all made from feathers. It seems probable that Peter Paillou would have learnt the technique of feather painting from this book and that the picture of the Horned Owl was his work and not that of his son who, as far as I know, made no natural history paintings. It seems that Peter Paillou senior was still working for Pennant in the 1780s since the splendid frontispiece to the *Arctic Zoology*, 1784–7, was his work. If we assume that he was at least twenty years old when he began working for Taylor White in 1744 he would have been sixty in 1784, and he must have died soon after or Pennant could scarcely have lamented the abridgement of his days. There were paintings by him hanging in Pennant's old home in Flintshire until 1920 but the contents were sold and the auctioneers have long since disposed of the relevant catalogues; I have been unsuccessful in tracing the fate of the paintings. The Courtauld Institute has a note on some works by him belonging to other collectors.

Paillou worked in water colour with a great deal of body colour; his paintings of birds of prey and game birds are fine and richly coloured. When working for Pennant, and indirectly for Banks, he used often to make a pencil sketch on the verso, giving the actual measurements of the bird he was portraying. Taylor White is one of the first people to have asked his artists to portray their birds life size.

How it came about that some paintings by Paillou of Banks's Newfoundland birds are now in the Taylor White collection at McGill can best be explained by reference to Banks's immediate forebears, and to the history of the Taylor White collection.

Joseph Banks's great-grandfather, Joseph Banks I, 1665–1727, made a fortune practising as an attorney and land agent in Sheffield, and at the age of thirty-seven was able to retire to Scofton, near Worksop, Notts. Taylor White's family seat was at Wallingwells in the vicinity of Worksop, and since both families were well to do they would almost certainly have known each other. After his retirement Banks continued to work as an agent for various county families, including Lady Mary Wortley Montagu, a friend of his daughter Mary's and a cousin of Taylor White's. In 1714 Joseph Banks's son, another Joseph (1695–1741), married Anne, only daughter of William Hodgkinson of Overton in the parish of Ashover, Derby. Overton came into the Banksian inheritance conditionally upon the owner taking the name of Hodgkinson. In the same year Joseph Banks I bought Revesby Abbey for his son for the sum of £14,000. The first son of Anne and Joseph Banks II, born in 1715, was Joseph Banks III; he died without issue. The second son, William, 1719–62, was the father of Joseph Banks IV, the subject of this volume. Another son, Robert, 1722–92, came into the possession of Overton by a decree of Chancery. In other words, William Banks had inherited Overton and the name of Hodgkinson, but on the death of his eldest brother, Joseph Banks III, he became heir apparent of Revesby and so in 1743 Overton was conveyed by the aforesaid decree of Chancery to his brother Robert; William Banks Hodgkinson became William Banks once more, Robert Banks became Robert Banks Hodgkinson. Of course this change of names was very confusing, especially to later workers on Banksian papers. More so because contemporaries of William and Robert referred sometimes to Banks Hodgkinson, sometimes to Hodgkinson Banks. I believe that this confusion occurred even in the eighteenth century. There is a note in the Taylor White MSS at McGill to the effect that White had obtained an Eskimo Curlew and many other birds from North America from his 'learned friend Hodgkinson Banks'. I have not found any other reference to Joseph Banks's uncle Robert Hodgkinson Banks having been in America. In view of the fact that some of the paintings of Newfoundland birds in the White collection are copies of Paillou's work for Banks and Pennant it can only be assumed that this is a slip and that White meant Joseph Banks. White probably knew the older Banks through family connections and sought out the young nephew Joseph, on account of their mutual interest in natural history; it was almost certainly Joseph to whom White was referring when, in his notes on *Buteo lagopus sancti-johannis*, he wrote: 'This bird and the next which I take to differ in sex only were given me by Mr. Banks together with the *Lagopus* and many other birds which he brought from Canada and Labrador.' I was troubled about this exchange between Banks and White for a long time on account of the distance between London and Wallingwells, but Professor Chambers of Nottingham University kindly gave me the reference to M. H. T. White's account of the Wallingwells family and I then found that although Taylor White senior had spent his childhood at Wallingwells he did not succeed to the family seat until 1768; before that he had lived for many years in New Square, Lincoln's Inn.

According to Miss White, Taylor White senior was born 21 December 1701. There are some amusing letters written by Lady Mary Wortley Montagu from Wallingwells when he was twelve years old but they refer to his parents and sisters and the general family atmosphere, and not to him. He entered the legal profession and later became Judge of North Wales and of the Chester County Palatinate where he would certainly have known Pennant. In London he was busy with the affairs of his own district and took an active part with his friend Thomas Coram in establishing the Foundling Hospital (close to Lincoln's Inn) of which he was treasurer for twenty-seven years; he became treasurer of Lincoln's Inn in 1764.[1] Miss White says that he was known as a 'Patron of the arts. I found in the minutes of the trustees of the British Museum one to the effect that Taylor White, Esq., of Wallingwells, be allowed to borrow certain animals, shells, etc. I imagine this would be for the use of his artists, for he kept several in his employment from 1730–60. The results may be seen at Wallingwells, where there are 29 volumes containing 987 body colour drawings, atlas size, of birds, flowers, fruit, monkeys etc., by Ehrret [sic], Van Huysen [sic], Peter Paillou, Collins, etc. Their paintings were drawn from life.'

In an abridgement of her book published in the journal of the Thoroton Society for 1907 Miss White makes no mention of any disposal of this collection which seems to have been entire when sold at Sotheby's in 1926. It was bought by Messrs. Quaritch, split up and re-arranged before its dispatch to McGill a year or so later. This was unfortunate since Taylor White's notes are no longer complete and moreover do not always coincide with the numbered plates. In Sotheby's 1926 sale catalogue the plates of the Newfoundland birds 'collected by Sir Joseph Banks' were a separate item, but when the collection was re-arranged they were incorporated with the other paintings and only a few of them can now be distinguished with certainty.

The plates reproduced in this volume include all the drawings of Banks's material from Newfoundland and Labrador now in the British Museum; none of the plates in the Taylor White collection has been published here but some have been discussed in the notes on the McGill MS and elsewhere when it is obvious that they derive from Banks.

The actual location of the Newfoundland and Labrador plates in the British Museum is as follows:

The paintings of flowers by Georg Ehret came to the Botany Library apparently

[1] Taylor White's son was for many years a treasurer of the Foundling Hospital which his father had helped to found, and was so liberal a benefactor that he was buried in the chapel there, and his descendants given the right of interment there *in perpetuo*. The Hospital was established in Hatton Garden in 1741 and transferred to Bloomsbury four years later.

at the same time as the plant catalogue (q.v.). Most of them are bound in a folio volume but five, which were used as a basis for engravings to illustrate Aiton's *Hortus Kewensis*, are bound with the other original drawings that were reproduced in that publication.

Parkinson's paintings of the Newfoundland insects and an echinoderm are bound with his paintings of other insects in a volume in the Print Room; the press mark is 199 a 8. These are water colour paintings on vellum. His paintings of the birds and of a salamander from Lisbon are similarly on vellum; they are in another volume in the Print Room; the press mark is 199* B 1. At the end of that volume are the pen and wash drawings on cartridge paper of fishes and a caprellid.

Paillou's paintings of birds from Newfoundland and Labrador are bound in a volume in the Print Room, with the press mark 199* B 4. The works of several other artists are included in the same volume, together with paintings of other birds by Paillou. The Newfoundland birds do not form a continuous series. Details of MS notes on his and Parkinson's plates were given in a previous publication (Lysaght, 1959) and have not been repeated in this volume. All Paillou's plates are in water colour with much body colour; they are on cartridge paper, not vellum.

PART TWO
Banks's diary

5

Introductory note

THE chief Banksian manuscripts dealt with in this volume are the following:

The diary, now in the library of the South Australian Branch, Adelaide, of the Royal Geographical Society of Australia;
The detailed descriptions of animals and a few plants comprising the McGill MS, now in McGill University Library;
The catalogue of the names and localities of many of the plants collected in Newfoundland and Labrador, now in the Botany Library of the British Museum.

The history of Banks's Newfoundland diary is a short one; after his death it remained in the possession of his relatives until it was sold by Lord Brabourne at Sotheby's sale on 14 April 1886. It was catalogued as Item 177, *Journal of a Voyage to Newfoundland from April 7 to Nov 17, 1766*, in the autograph of Banks, 2 vols., rough calf; and was bought by Petherick for three guineas.[1] E. A. Petherick (1847–1917) was acting for S. W. Silver, a man who made his fortune dealing in rubber, and was very much interested in colonial history. His magnificent collection of books comprising the York Gate Library was bought in 1905 by the South Australian Branch of the Royal Geographical Society; Banks's diary is still in their library at Adelaide.

The diary consists of two volumes bound in rough calf with gilt clasps; the crest of the York Gate Library is stamped on the cover of each volume. The pages are 23 × 15·4 cm., watermarked with a lion rampant and the name Vriheyt. In the first volume the numbers of the pages, written on the rectos by Banks, run from 1 to 55, then jump to 60 and run on to 124; Banks numbered another twelve pages but did not use them. His note on St. John's was written on another sheet of paper which was pasted on to the verso of the flyleaf; in the present publication it is printed at the end of the diary. The second volume is exactly similar to the first but Banks numbered thirty-four rectos and used only nineteen of them, devoting this section

[1] Petherick, a young Melbourne bookseller, came to London in 1870, and worked here for thirty years, much of the time as cataloguer for Francis Edwards; in this capacity he catalogued Silver's library. Petherick himself, who boasted that he never gave more than ten shillings for a book, built up a very valuable library which he eventually gave to the Commonwealth of Australia. He became the first Government Archivist there.

to his notes on Portugal and the Portuguese. The rest of the volume consists of blank pages.

There is a contemporary copy of the diary by Sarah Sophia Banks, purchased by the British Museum in 1895. It is written on smooth Baskerville paper with chain lines 2·75 cm. apart, and no watermark; Banks used a similar type of paper for the McGill MS (p. 349) but the chain lines were less widely spaced. His sister's transcript in the British Museum lacks the Portuguese section which is in the Mitchell Library, Sydney (Miscellaneous MSS 743/3). In a marginal note she states that she has omitted the scientific names, and that some of her brother's notes refer to a catalogue which she has not seen. A so-called transcript by her in the Hawley collection is a much later copy in another hand on paper watermarked H. Mills, 1832. She died in 1818.

In Sotheby's sale of 14 April 1886, referred to above, Banks's descriptions of Newfoundland birds and plants (i.e. the McGill MS) were sold to Stanhope for *3s*. This purchaser seems to have been the Right Hon. Edward Stanhope, a collateral descendant of Banks's. The MS remained in the family until it was sold by the widow of another Stanhope, Lady Beryl Gilbert, at Sotheby's sale of 17–18 October 1918. In the catalogue of this sale Banks's *Notes on Newfoundland Birds and Plants* were listed with various other Banksian MSS, including the journal of his tour to Holland, under Item 394, which was purchased by Messrs. Quaritch for £40. At some stage or other it was bought back by Sotheby's and finally reappeared in the catalogue of their sale on 22 July 1929 under Item 658 'as an autograph MS of Sir Joseph Banks, *Notes concerning the Plants, Birds and Insects of Newfoundland made during his travels there in 1766 on about 86 pp., 8vo, a parcel'*. This lot went for £21 to Michelmore who finally sold it to McGill in 1939 for £15; this seems rather odd, and I am inclined to think that Michelmore may have sold most of Banks's descriptive notes on plants to another customer. Michelmore was a reputable London dealer who retired some years ago. Some of the sheets relating to mammals had been separated many years before and filed with Solander's scientific MSS which came to the British Museum after Banks's death. The McGill MS was not included in Dryander's catalogue of Banks's library.

Banks's catalogue of his plant collections in Labrador and Newfoundland lists only names and localities with an occasional note on habitats. It was inventoried when the major part of his library was given to the British Museum where he had for so long been a distinguished trustee, and was placed in the Botany Library when the scientific collections were moved from Bloomsbury to South Kensington.

PAGINATION OF BANKS'S DIARY

Since Banks used the pagination of his diary as a key (p. 350) to his field notes (the McGill MS), and to some of his specimens, his numbers have been retained here although his pages do not coincide with those of this volume. His page numbers have therefore been inserted on the outer margin of the text, and extra spacing between the lines shows where his pages begin and end. His dates and notes have been printed as hanging heads, as in his own text.

CROSS REFERENCES

Throughout this volume references to Banks's diary and his other manuscripts usually give the page numbers of his original text, on account of their significance for his keys.

NOTES

Banks wrote his diary on the rectos of his daybook; he used the versos for lists and determinations, and for an occasional note. It was his practice to leave blanks for determinations which had to be confirmed; there are many of these and they have been omitted in the following pages. His own notes and determinations have now been inserted in the text of his diary, between commas; determinations by the editor have been inserted within square brackets.

Notes by the editor are printed at the end of the diary; they are numbered consecutively, save where there is need to refer back, or forwards.

ASTERISKS AND DAGGERS

Asterisks throughout the systematic lists indicate the existence of herbarium material. When they precede the name of a *flowering plant* in the text of Banks's diary they show the existence of a specimen from that particular locality; in the case of *non-flowering plants* there are few or no localities other than Newfoundland on the herbarium sheets, and asterisks here show only the existence of specimens.

A dagger indicates that there is a drawing or painting of the species mentioned.

ABBREVIATIONS

Cat.   = Banks's *Catalogue of Plants*, which precedes the editor's systematic lists of the plants he collected or recorded.

N. or n. = the notes printed at the end of the diary.

Hb.   = herbarium material in the British Museum (Natural History).

Sol. MSS   or Solander MSS = the 23 bound volumes of slips prepared by Solander, with the assistance of Dryander and some others for a further edition of Linnaeus's *Species Plantarum*.
There are many other Solander MSS; details of these are given in the text where they occur.

Ph. in brackets after Fernald denotes the photostat of his annotated copy of Banks's catalogue of plants.

INTRODUCTORY NOTE

Banks's own erratic punctuation and spelling have been retained throughout his diary except that scientific names have been italicised. In his other MSS lower case is used for the initial letter of zoological and botanical specific epithets. It has not always been easy to determine whether Banks was using a capital letter or not; I have done my best to be consistent but may not have always succeeded. Banks nearly always omitted the final e in the verb ending -ed but occasionally he retained it. He favoured ampersands but also used 'and' in full. The spelling of his Latin text is not always clear, especially where Banks has corrected himself. When the meaning is doubtful the correct spelling has been used.

23. Sydney Parkinson.
Believed to be a self-portrait.

Blennius scopulorum.
D.31. P.13. V.2. A.22. C.13

Sydney Parkinson pinx. 1768

B. pholis L.

24a. Common Blenny or Shanny, Plymouth.
Sydney Parkinson

Sydney Parkinson pinx. 1768

24b. Five-bearded Rockling, Plymouth.
Sydney Parkinson

6

small Puddles of Water Left by the tide were others (1) . . . Polypes of a different sort [*Anemonia* sp.] of a light yellow with Larger Feelers which had not the Power of Contracting themselves so much as the Purple ones always did when disturbd

At seven this Morn we were call'd up by the winds being fair to get the Ship out of Hammoaze accordingly at half Past 8 we broke Lose & in about an hour came to Moorings between Drakes Island & the Land on Saturday next god willing we Sail for Nflnd

17

We went to Plymouth to Enquire about a Manufacture of China invented by a Mr Cookworthy[5] of that Place but did not see him by what We could Learn from the People in his Shop it

18

Mr Cook-
worthys
China

7

did not seem a very Eligible one as the[y] told us that a manufactary had been set up at Bristol for the Convenience of fewel but had sunk to the Partners (for several were Engag'd in it) about 600 lb merely as they told us on account of their not being able to burn the ware without Smoaking it they gave us specimens of three of the Principal ingredients[6] used in the Composition (1) More Stone (a Kind of Granate) with white specks for that with black will by no means answer the Purpose (2) a Kind of Marl of a very Saponaceous quality Comeing near to the soapie rock in appearance but Much softer & (3) a stone that has much the appearance of chalk With some few metallick grains interspersed in its substance they were all raisd in a mine

8

Calld Addy Vein near St Austel in Cornwal

We had too from Mr Cookworthy a very (1) Shewy Ore of Antimony found near Wade Bridge[7] 6 Miles Westward of Bodman in Cornwal he had 2 or three Large Lumps Possibly 3 Or 4 Pounds Each Dug out of a stratum of Clay but not in quantities enough to make it worth while to work it

Cornish
Antimony

This being a very fine Day we took our Last Leave of Mount Edgecombe we saw there some Exotick trees in very high Perfection (2) Corke trees [*Quercus suber* L.][8] & (3) the Portugal Laurel [*Prunus lusitanica* L.] of a remarkably Large size (4) Arbutus, *A. unedo*, (5) Laurustinus, *Viburnum Tinus*, in the Highest Perfection growing among the Furze in as great Perfection as they could Do in their Natural soil

20

9

(1) Tulip trees [*Liriodendron tulipifera* L.] to we saw of a size inferior to none we had seen Except that in Mr Phipps's Garden at Stoneham[9]

At ¼ past 1 P.M. Weighd Anchor from Plymouth Sound Wind E N E

22

Course Continues Perfectly good about 12 today we judged ourselves 12 Leagues from the Nearest Land which was the westermost of the Scilly Islands a little before that I found on board the insect which the Fishermen call the (2)

23

Black Caterpillar, *Tipula Nigra* [unident.],[10] about 2 spoke with a french ship Bound for N of Land we saw a good deal of Sea weed today we caught only 2 sorts upon a hook hove out for that (3) the first Knotted Sea weed, *Fucus nodosus* [*Ascophyllum nodosum* (L.) Le Jolis][11] the other the (4) Podded Fucus, *Fucus Siliquosus* [*Halidrys siliquosa* (L.) Lyngb.][12]

10

25
Shark
This day Latit: observd 48:00: Lon: Meas^d from the Lizzard 10:7 we are becalmd about 2 we observe a young (1) shark Playing about our stern which Leaves us immediately not staying for a hook to be brought up

Porpusses
This Even Take a species of (2) sea weed we had not before observd

26
This Even shoals of (3) Porpusses pass the Ship swimming by with great swiftness

29
These two Last days we have had hard Gales I have been too sick to write this Even the wind much abated

30
Wind Pretty Fresh this morn at 6 O'Clock and for some hours after great Numbers of Birds but none [of] them Near Enough the ship to determine for certain of what sort guessd them to be the bird calld

11

Birds in the
Lat: of
Rodneys
Island
in Lincolnshire a (1) tearn, *Sterna Nigra* [*Chlidonias niger* (L.)][13] our distance from the Lizzard is 240 Leagues we are not without hopes that an Island said to be discoverd in the Last Peace & calld Rodneys Island[14] but which has never since been heard of is near us send a man to mast head to Look out by 11 the Birds disapear & we give over all hopes of Rodneys Island

MAY

3
Today a calm fish'd with a landing net out of the Quarter Gallery window Caught (2) sea weed, *Fucus acinarius*,[15] with fruit Like Currants on slight Footstalks & (3) Common Knotted Fucus, *Fucus Nodusus* [*Ascophyllum nodosum* (L.) Je Jolis] also 2 species of what the seamen call Blubbers[16] (4) the one roundish & Transparent with his Edges a little Fringed the inside is hollow adornd with 4 little Clusters of Red spots within the Transparent

12

substance Possibly Eggs from the Center Proceeds 4 feelers spotted from their Bases with Longish Red Spotts & each Edgd on the upper side with 2 thin Membranes the (1) other is Conical & hollow the outer Part Transparent the inner coverd by a thin Coat of Reddish Purple which Runs up beyond the top of the Hollow Part in a line not unlike the footstalk of some Fruit the Bottom Edge seems to be broke by some accident

today being also very fine the business of fishing is Continued we now took   4
What we hope will Prove a compleat Specimen of No (1) it has a large Crenated
Fringe round the Lower Edges we also took another Fragment much like that
taken yesterday within each of the Broken ones

13

was an appearance which we supposd to be of an Insect[17] devouring it

one Part of this morn the sea was Coverd with small Transparent Bubbles (1)
which we supposed to be the spawn of some insect or fish as they were full of small
Black specks

we took also another (2) insect[18] of a very Peculiar appearance his Case is
Triangular with a very Sharp Point of a Transparent substance not unlike very thin
Glass the insect within is of a Colour not unlike New Copper

Yesterday & today hard Gale of wind with Frequent & some heavy Squalls   6
Carried away Main top Mast Myself far too sick to write[105a]

this Morn Weather much more moderate a number of Birds are about the ship   7
which the seamen call Penguins[19] [auks] Gulls Shearwaters one species of them
with sharpe tails [unident.] Puffins &

14

Sea Pigeons [*Cepphus grylle atlantis* Salomonsen] we could not get any of them tho
we took Pains we Comforted ourselves however being told that we should meet
with them all upon the Coast at Present they are a sign that we are upon the Banks

Birds Continue today in great abundance especialy Puffins & Sea Pidgeons at   8
twelve Sound & find 75 fathoms Birds Continue at 6 sound again 50 fathoms Let   Soundings upon
Down our fishing Lines but Caught nothing at ten tonight for the first time we see   the Banks
an Island of Ice the night is Hazy but the Sky clear no moon the Ice itself appears
like a body of whitish light the Waves Dashing against it appear much more   Island of Ice
Luminous the Whole is not quite unlike the Gleaming of the *Aurora Borealis*
When first it was seen it was about half a

15

Mile ahead it drives within $\frac{1}{4}$ of a mile of us it is accompanied by several small flat
Pieces of Ice which the seamen call field Ice which drives very near us & is Easily
seen by its white appearance not unlike the Breaking of a wave into foam

This Morn Seven Islands of Ice in sight one Very Large but not high about a   9
League from us we steer very near a small one which from its Transparency & the
Greenish Cast in it makes a very Beautifull appearance two very Large Cracks
Intersect it Leng[t]hways & Look Very Like mineral Veins in Rocks from its
Rough appearance the Seamen Judge that it is old Ice that is what was formd the
Winter before Last In the Course of the Day we steer still nearer to another Island

16

which Appears as if Layd Strat: Super Stratum one of White another of Greenish
at $\frac{1}{2}$ Past five this afternoon we made NFLand a quantity of (1) sea weed floated

Past of which I fish'd up 3 or 4 Species with my Landing Net tonight we stand of with too little wind to Carry us in

10   this Morn a Mist accompanied with Frost which hung our Rigging Full of Ice Continues till about twelve when we see Land again but so little wind that we cannot make it tonight This Even Fish with Landing net take 9 specimens of a singular Kind of (2) Blubber[20] which abounds here tis transparent with 2 or three Reddish lines in the middle tis octangular Each angle being adrond with an undulated red line which serves for the Basis of a fin Longitudinaly Stretchd upon it

17

which it moves with a quick undulatory Motion it is so tender I have little hopes of Preserving it as it Floats in the sea it at Pleasure Puts out two Antennae sometimes to the distance of a foot or more, but upon being taken they Constantly draw them up & do not shew the Least appearance of them

11
Arrive at
St. Johns
    this Morn quite Calm took a Large Float of (1) Long stalkd sea Belts[21] in the Roots of which were a Small sort of (2) Star fish about 3 got into St Johns on the 20th day of our Voyage

12   this morn went on shore found the Spring very Little advancd but hope its approaches will be quick as it is warmer than I Ever felt it at this time in England the Countrey is Coverd with wood fir is the only Tree which can yet be distinguishd

18

of which I observd 3 sorts (1) Black Spruce [*Picea mariana* (Mill.) B.S.P.] of which they Make a liquor Calld Spruce Beer [see p. 84] (2) white Spruce [*Picea glauca* (Moench) Voss.] & (3) weymouth Pine [*Pinus strobus* L.] no large trees
Neighbourhood
of St Johns
of any Species Possibly so near the Town they are Constantly cut down on the Trees & Rocks were (4) 3 or 4 species of Lichens,[22] *Lichen Pascalis* [*Stereocaulon paschale* (L.) Hoffm.], *Lanatus* [either *Ephebe lanata* (L.) Vainio or *Alectoria bicolor* (Ehrh.) Nyl.]? *Hirtus* [*Usnea hirta* (L.) Weber], & under them the Leaves of many rare northern Plants of the Club Mosses 3 (5) sorts,* *Lycopodium Clavatum Annotinum* ?,[23] a small Plant whose (6) blossoms have 5 stamina [*Mitella nuda* L.] Mosses (7) 3 sorts *Bryum Hornum* [**Mnium hornum* Hedwig], or *Purpureum* [*B. bicolor* Dicks.], one of which is quite new to me—too sorts of Bird were taken today one (8) the Black Cap *Parus ater* [*Parus atricapillus bartletti* (Aldrich & Nutt)],[24] the other an american thrush with a ferrugineous Breast [*Turdus migratorius nigrideus* Aldrich & Nutt][25] Possibly Describd by Catesby insects were few (10) *Cimex lineatus*[26] water Bugs in abundance one (11) *Carabus granulatus*[27]

13   Walkd out Fishing this Morn

19

Took great Plenty of small (1) Trouts, Salmo [*Salvelinus fontinalis* Mitchill][28] saw a small Fish in the Brooks Very like English (2) Stiklebacks, *Gasterosteus Aculeatus*,[29] in the way took a small (3) Bird [*Passerculus sandwichensis* (Gmelin)][30] something Between a yellow hammer & a Linnet

25. A 32-gun frigate, probably the *Southampton* of 1757, comparable to the *Niger*.
Detail from a painting by C. Brooking

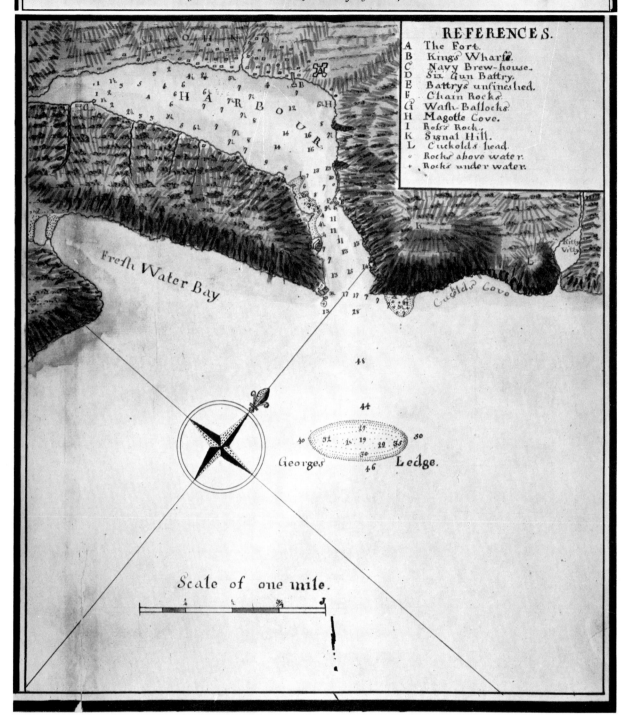

26. MS chart of the harbour of St. John's, Newfoundland, *c.* 1762.
James Cook

27. *Epilobium latifolium*, Belle Isle de Groais.
G. D. Ehret

28. *Mitella nuda*, a plant that Banks collected at St. John's, Croque and Chateau Bay. G. D. Ehret

Walkd this day to a Small Lake north of the Town found in the way (4) another species of Club moss, *Lycopodium complanatum*, (5) a Shrub with ten Stamina, *Andromeda Calyculata* [*Cassandra calyculata* (L.) D.Don],[31] which grew by the side of the Lake—upon a stoney Soil in great abundance a Kind of (6) Moss, *Bryum*, with Pendant heads in our way home we Killd a musk Rat, *Fiber Moscatus* [*Ondatra obscurus* Bangs] in Kitty Vitty Pond — 15

This day wind very high NW went into the Harbour with the Traul Took (8) Lobsters, *Cancer gammarus* [*Homarus americanus* (M. Edw.)] (9) Common Crab, *Cancer* [*Cancer irroratus* Say],[32] (10) Spider Do:, *Cancer Araneus* [*Hyas araneus* (L.)], (11) Sculpen[33] [? *Myoxocephalus scorpius* (L.)], (12) another Sort of Do: (13) Cat fish [*Anarichas* sp.], (14) a Shell of the Scallop Kind [*Chlamys islandicus* (O. F. Müller)][34] (15) One of the Muscles — 16

20

(1) Sea Urchin, *Echinus*, [? *Strongylocentrotus droebachiensis* (O. F. Müller)],[35] (2) another Kind of the *Spatagus* tribe, *Echinus* [*Echinarachnius parma* (Lam.)],† (3) Starfish, *Asterias* [unident.], (4) a . . . (5) two sort of Sea weed (10) [*sic*] Soldier Crab, *Cancer diogenes* [unident.][36]

Set out on foot to get as far into the Countrey as Possible Soon after We set out began to snow Continued all the day but did not Cover the Ground deep Enough to hinder our Observing Several Plants (6) a Kind of Bilberry in full Blossom [*Vaccinium angustifolium* Ait.] (7) a kind of Juniper with white Berries [**Juniperus communis* L. var. *depressa* Pursh, or **J. horizontalis* Moench], (8) The Larch, *Pinus Larix* [*Larix laricina* (DuRoi) Koch], which is here Calld Juniper & which is said to make better timber for shipping especialy masts than any tree this Countrey affords (9) & a species of Moss with Bending heads & fine Golden footstalks, *Bryum* No: 19:6[37] — 19

Continues to Snow all this day Which Confines us within doors — 20

21

at a small Town Calld Petty Harbour the Snow so incessant that we have not an opportunity to Stir out to make the Least Observation — Petty Harbour 21

Snow Lies now four & five feet deep upon the Ground & the Air looks so Hazey that we think it Prudent to Return upon the Rocks & Barrens (for so they Call the Places where Wood does not Grow) we find that the wind had drifted the Snow Very thin Here we observe Some few Plants (1) Fir Moss, **Lycopodium Selago*, (2) Rhein Deer Moss, *Lichen Rangiferinus* [*Cladonia* sp.], (3) A Kind of Horned Liverwort, *Lichen*, (4) a Plant that has very much the Appearance of Crow Berries, *Empetrum* [**Empetrum nigrum* L.][38] of which I have only got the female which has 10 Stigmata

22

Snow Very near gone Walk out to day gather (1) the Male Blossoms of a Plant [**Myrica gale* L.] resembling du[t]ch myrtle which like it grows in Bogs & — 25

121

watery Places also (2) a sort of *Cyperus*[39] which grew upon the same flat but not in so wet a situation & a Kind of Black (3) Liverwort [*Umbilicaria* sp.] growing upon dry tops of the Barrens the weather grows very mild many Plants are in Bud

26   this day Cap[n]: Williams sent me a (4) small Bird described N[o]: 4 [*Melospiza georgiana ericrypta* Oberholser][40]

This morn Thick Fog shot a sort of (5) Gull From the ship N[o]: 5 [?*Rissa tridactyla tridactyla* L.][41] differing But little from the Common went out with gun Shot a small Bird (6) N[o]: 3 [*Passerella iliaca iliaca* (Merrem)]†[42] Gatherd (7) Dogs violets, *Viola canina*, both Blew & White [probably *Viola cucullata* Ait. and *V. adunca* Sm. var. *minor* (Hook.) Fern.][43] also (8) a Plant growing among the moss under Bushes in great abundance of the Polyandria Class [*Coptis groenlandica* (Oeder) Fern.][44] its nectaria & Pistilla Vary much between the numbers of three & five a Kind of Cup moss [a lichen, *Cladonia* sp.] which Seems no more than

23

a variety of the English Sort

(1) a Kind of Golden Maidenhair, *Polytrichum Alpinum*?[45], Very little if at all Differing from the English Sort the heads are angulated on two sides much more remarkably than the other two & the Stalks sometimes Branch & (2) another Kind of Moss, *Mnium aquatrium*, not unlike our water *Mnium* [*? *M. punctatum* Hedwig]

27   Walkd out this day Found (3) a Species of Cotton Grass [*Scirpus hudsonianus* (Michx.) Fern.][46] (4) Prickley Fern, *Polypodium aculeatum* [*Dryopteris carthusiana* (Vill.) H. P. Fuchs][47] (5) a species of Lichen (6) a moss of the *Bryum* Kind

28   This day Very wet in the morn in the Evening went out of the Harbours mouth Kill (7) Sea Pigeon, *Colymbus Grylle* [*Cepphus grylle atlantis* Salomonsen][48] described N[o]: 6:

30   This Even sent out the boat to Trawl they Brought home a species of (8) *Fucus* we had not seen before [?*Fucus distichus* L.][49] (9) a Kind of *ulva* [*Ulva lactuca* L.] (10) a Kind of *Sertularia*,

24

Coralline (1) a Kind of worms a Kind of (2) Eel, *Blennius Gatturigine* [unident.][50] who instead of being Round is Compressed on the sides

31   today tolerably clear the first since the Bad weather set in went with gun Killd (3) a small Bird, *Tringa Hippoleucos* [*Actitis macularia* L.],[51] Calld here Beach Bird & a red (4) Bird, *Loxia Enucleator* [*Pinicola enucleator* (L.)][52] said to be very scarce here gatherd in very shady Places the (5) Plant from the Berries of which Syrup of Capillare is made [*Gaultheria hispidula* (L.) Bigel.]†[53] it is Calld here Maidinhair [sic] & drank by way of substitute for tea (6) a Kind of Juniper with white Berries, *Juniperus* [see May 19], in great abundance & upon a high Rock hanging over the sea one Plant only of (7) Rose root, *Rhodiola Rosea* [*Sedum rosea* (L.) Scop.]

JUNE 1766

This Even very Fine walk'd out Gatherd (8) Currants, *Ribes* [*Ribes glandulosum* **1st**
Grauer],[54] some Lichens which seemd to be only Varieties of English species &
abundance of (9) Water Mnium, *Mnium aquaticum* [see May 26]

25

the Female of which has Stellate Heads I have not seen any with dusty ones as they
are in England the men of the ship brought me some Large Specimens of a Kind of
(1) Stone Coral which is found Fossil in Many Parts of England by the Name of
Honeycombstone [*Favosites*][55] another man brought me the shell of a (2) tortoise
which he told me he got in the Archipelago and that it was found there in fresh water
a ship Came into harbour from which I Procurd specimens of a shell fish calld here
(3) Glams [*Cyrtodaria siliqua* (Spengler)][56] of Peculiar use in the fishery as the
fishermen depend upon them for their Baitts in their first Voyage to the Banks at
that time of the Year the fish feed upon them & Every fish they take has a number

26

of them in his Stomach which the Fishermen take out & with them Bait for others
the fish itself is Remarkable as it is far too large for the shell which is so little
adapted to Cover its inhabitants that Even when the fish is taken out the sides will
not Close together a boy brought me two (1) shells

Went this day Shooting Killd (2) a very small but beautifull bird Calld here a **2**
Gold bird describd Nº 9: [*Wilsonia pusilla pusilla* (Wilson)][57] a small (3) bird
remarkable for his shrill note which might be Easily mistaken for a man whistling
describd Nº 10 [? *W. pusilla pusilla* (Wilson), female][58] & (4) a Sort of Swallow
who differs from the English sort only in that his Breast is red instead of being
white [*Hirundo rustica erythrogaster* Boddaert][59] today saw the Pass of Kitty Vitty **Kitty Vitty**
where the English Landed

27

their Cannon when they recoverd this Place from the French the Bite for it is no
more is Extreemly Small subject to a Prodigious swell as it has no shelter from
the Ocean & commanded on all sides by very high & steep hills in short a Place very
ill calculated for such an attempt as the Least change of Weather or molestation
from the Enemy must have destroyd them intirely on the Beach here Pickd up a
Kind of (1) stone which has the appearance of chalk at Least in its whiteness &
softness it is but little rubd by the sea consequently could not have come from far tho
we could not discover any appearance of it in the rock

Walkd out this day gatherd (2) a species of *Carex* [unident.][60] (3) Horsetail, **3ᵈ**
Equisetum,[61]

28

not much differing from the English sort (1) & a Kind of *Bryum, Bryum Hornum*
[*Mnium hornum* Hedwig] common in England

123

4 Went today to see the workmen who are Leveling for a fortification on the south head Collected upon the Beach a number of the starfish 29:3 dryd by the sun on the top of the head where the miners are at work collected two Kinds of Stone the only sorts that I have yet found in Strata (2) one is a Very Coarse Grit full of Pebbles of different Shapes which Lays the undermost the other is (3) Grit also but of a much Clearer Kind which Lays over the Last forming the tops of all the Hills I have seen tho sometimes thin Beds of it are found between the interstices of the former

29

6th Walkd out to day gatherd some of the Northern English Plants which grow here Every where not Coveting high Land tho indeed we have seen no high Land here (1) the Little dwarf Honeysuckle, *Cornus Herbacea* [**Cornus suecica* L. syn. *Chamae-periclymenum suecicum* (L.) Aschers. & Graebn.], said to grow upon the cheviot hills which Part Scotland from England (2) alsinanthemos, *Trientalis Europaea* [**T. borealis* Raf.],[62] & (3) the stone Bramble, *Rubus Saxatilis* [**R. pubescens* Raf.],[63] also some Common English Plants as (4) (5) sorts of Rush grass, *Juncus Campestris* [**Luzula multiflora* (Retz.) Lejeune],[64] *Juncus Pilosus* [*?Luzula acuminata* Raf.][65] (6) Black Carex, *Carex atrata* [*C. atratiformis* Britton],[66] (7) vernal grass, *Anthoxanthum odoratum*, (8) Black headed Bog rush, *Scirpus Caespitosus*,[67] (9) sundew with round Leaves, *Drosera rotundifolia*, & several more which I mention in my Catalogue—of English Plants Some Plants also of this Country a (10) Kind of alder, *Betula* [*Alnus crispa* (Ait.) Pursh],[68] differing very little if at all from the English sort a beautiful Kind of (11) Medlar, *Mespilus Canadensis* ? [**Amelanchier bartramiana* (Tausch) Roemer], a Kind of cherry, *Prunus* [**P. pensylvanica* L.], which however is so Scarce here that I have got very few Specimens. I have not seen above 2 Plants of it neither in Blossom but at a few Extremities

30

it differs very little if at all from our English garden cherry

5 [*sic*] Today Gatherd (1) a species of Honeysuckle, *Lonicera* [*L. villosa* (Michx.) Roem. & Sch.], (2) a small Plant which Covers all the ground here, *Andromeda* [*?A. glaucophylla* Link],[69]—upon some hill sides (3) Strawberries, *Fragaria Pratensis*? [**F. virginiana* Duch.],[70] which appear exactly Like those calld scarlets by the English Gardiners which I take to be what Linnaeus calls a Variety by the name of *Pratensis* here however I have seen none but that sort (4) Ivy Leavd Crowfoot, *Ranunculus Hederaceus*,[71] growing on a bog

6 Today found (5) a sort of Everlasting, *Gnaphalium Alpinum* [**Antennaria neodioica* Green], a (6) Kind of dogberry, *Viburnum Acerifolium* [**V. edule* (Michx.) Raf.], (7) Wild millet Grass, *Millium Effusum*?

7 Today shooting Killd (8) 3 small Birds Probably varieties of the Gold Bird as there is but little difference between them cheifly the want of a black spot on the head, Foemina? Nº 10 [*Wilsonia pusilla pusilla* (Wilson)],[72] (9) & a small Bird, Nº: 11 [*Dendroica striata* (Forster)][73]

which seems to be scarce here as I have seen it only this once

Walkd out this day Gatherd a Species of (1) Solomons Seal, *Convallaria Racemosa* [*Smilacina stellata* (L.) Desf.]   8

this day at 12 set sail for Croque [see Moravian maps]   11

this Morn at 7 anchor in Croque harbour after a very favourable Passage Walk   13
out gather (2) a species of Bilberry, *Vaccinium mucronatum* [*Nemopanthus mucronatus*   Croque
(L.) Baillon],[74] (3) a species of Orchis, *Ophrys* [*?*Corallorhiza trifida* Chat.],[75] a
(4) Beautifull Plant describd Nᵒ: 5, *Uvularia Amplexifolia* [*Streptopus roseus*
Michx.], (5) another of the Hexandria Class Nᵒ: 6 [*?*Triantha glutinosa* (Michx)
Baker] another (6) Nᵒ: 7 which is of the Pentandria Class tho both Calyx &
Corolla are divided into 6 Laciniae [either *Halenia deflexa* (Sm.) Griseb. or
Parnassia parviflora DC.] (7) Water Ranunculus [unident.] (8) several sorts of
Lichens (9) two sorts of Mosses This morn Experiencd a Very Extraordinary
Transition from Cold to Heat The air at 5 in the morning while we were at sea
being so Cold that with great Coat buttond I was forcd

32

Every moment to Come down to the Fire at seven we came into harbour in ½ of an
hour were set on shore where the weather was as hot or hotter than Ever I knew it
in England I Lament much not having noted the Difference by Thermometer but
hope for future opportunities

This day still Extreemly Hot spend most of our time in working in the garden   14
go out however in the Evening Find (1) a Kind of Bramble, *Rubus Arcticus* [?*R.
pubescens* Raf.],[76] (2) a Kind of Meadow Rue, *Thalictrum alpinum*, (3) Dwarf Birch,
Betula Nana [*B. pumila* L.][76a] (4) 2 Varieties of a Beautifull Plant Possibly our
English Birds Eye [*Primula farinosa* L.] one of which had flowers of a Clear white
[*Primula mistassinica* Michx. forma *leucantha* Fern.] the other Blueish [*P.
laurentiana* Fern.][77] (5) in the woods found one tree only of Takamahaka [*Populus
balsamifera* L.] in the Evening went out Fishing had no sport at all at the harbours
mouth tho there seemd to be abundance of Small Trout saw no signs of Large ones
Killd

today a Kind of (1) Mouse, *Mus Terrestris*, [*Microtus pennsylvanicus terraenovae*
(Bangs)],[78] which Differs scarce at all From the English Sort but is Rather Larger
& his Ears Extreemly Broad

Weather today Extreemly Hot walk out in the Evening find (2) a Kind of   15
Butter Bur, *Petasites* [*P. palmatus* (Ait.) A. Gray],[79] with Palmated Leaves
Broad Leavd (3) *Kalmia, Kalmia Latifolia* [*K. angustifolia* Wang.][80] in prodigious
abundance scattered without distinction over Bogs & hills wherever it is not shaded
by trees but rather affecting dry soil (4) a kind of Rush, *Juncus trifidus*,[81] upon the
Highest and Dryest tops of hills (5) one Blade, *Convallaria unifolium* [*Maianthemum*

canadense Desf.], every where in great abundance most commonly with 3 Leaves on each stalk from the Luxuriancy with which it grows (6) a Kind of Very small *Carex* [?*C. pauciflora* Lightf.][82] a Kind of (7) *Andromeda* [*Vaccinium oxycoccus* L.] whose Calyx & Corolla are both 4 fid growing always upon Bogs (8) a Kind of Bilberry [*Vaccinium uliginosum* L.] growing on the most exposd sides of Rocks Today shot (9) a beautiful Kind of Kingfisher *Alcedo Alcyon* [*Megaceryle alcyon* (L.)],[83] figurd both

34

by Catesby & Edwards Linnaeus's Description of it seemd Faulty in many Parts N°: 12 I took great Pains to make as Particular as Possible (1) a Kind of Bird which seems to belong to the Butcher Bird tribe, *Lanius?* [?*Lanius excubitor borealis* Vieillot][84] but I cannot find that he is described N°: 13 also another Small Bird (2), *Motacilla* [*Hylocichla ustulata clarescens* Burleigh & Peters],[85] N°: 14 who sings agreably Enough

16   Walkd today from the watering Place to Crusoe hall Mr Phipps's Habitation of which more when it is Finishd at Present give him his due he works night & day & Lets the Mosquetos eat more of him than he does of any Kind of food all through Eagerness in the way to him I found (3) Moon wort, *Osmunda Lunaria* [*Botrychium lunaria* (L.) Swartz], (4) a Kind of Grass (5) a Plant which seems of the *Carex* kind dioecious but found only males [*Carex gynocrates* Wormsk.],[86] (6) a Kind of Cuckow flower [*Cardamine pratensis* L.]

17   Walkd out found a sort of (7) Currants, *Ribes* [*Ribes triste* Pallas] which seem different from any I have seen tho Possibly not Specificaly

35

the Leaves are Less Sinuated than the Common sort & the flowers Red also (1) gooseberries, *Ribes Grossulariata* [*R. hirtellum* Michx.], & another (2) sort of them, *Ribes* [*R. lacustre* (Pers.) Poir.][87] with Leaves very deeply Cut which I should have taken for the *Oxacanthofolia* of Linnaeus if he had not described that set thick with thorns which this is very near without at Least the few there are are very small (3) a Kind of Rush, *Juncus* [?*J. balticus* Willd.],[88] growing upon Rocks near the Head of the Harbour

18   Walkd out shooting today Killd nothing but found (4) a Plant which I thought had been Peculiar to Lapland, *Diapensia Lapponica*, it grew however but in one spot & there was only a single Plant of it (5) Wooly Mouse Ear, *Cerastium alpinum tomentosum* [*C. alpinum* L.], (6) a small Flower Like a daizy, ?*Erigeron* ?*Philadelphicum* [*E. philadelphicus* L.],[89] (7) a species of Moss, *Bryum*, (8) a small nest *Nidus*, was brought to me by the Master Carpenter who Declard he saw a bee fly out of it When he took it

36

(1) a Species of stone which appears white from a great distance (2) Mr Ankille[132] brought me in a species of (2) Owl, *Strix* ?*Ulula* [*Surnia ulula caparoch* (Müller)],†[90]

126

he had shot (3) My Servant shot a bird quite Black [?*Euphagus carolinus nigrans* Burleigh and Peters][91] Neither of which I can find Describd

This Morn we had intelligence that a white Bear [*Thalarctos maritimus*(Phipps)][92]   19 with two cubbs had been seen on a hill above St Julians a Party was raisd to go in search of her of which I was one but we returnd without success Just as we returnd a shallop with the master on board was Setting Sail to Examine some of the Harbours to the southward I got on board in hopes of some opportunity of Gathering Plants or Collecting insects that night we arriv'd at Inglie [Englée] in the   Inglie Mouth of Canada Bay 11 Leagues to the southward of Croque but so Late that I had not an opportunity of Collecting any thing the next morn Wind blew to hard   20 for our Vessel to

37

Attempt getting out which gave me an opportunity of Examining a small Island above the Harbour which I found Loaded with Plants I had not seen before in a Wonderful manner (1) a Kind of Cinquefoil, *Potentilla* [*P. norvegica* L.],[93] upright & rough (2) a shrub with small flowers without Petals of the Dioecia octandra Class [*Shepherdia canadensis* (L.) Nutt.] it had Rough Leaves & Lay on the ground (3) Takamahaca [**Populus balsamifera* L.] with Plenty of Fruit but the flowers were gone a species of (4) Grass, *Poa ?Trivialis* [*P. pratensis* L.][94] which I take to be the Common Poa grass of England (5) a Podded Plant, **Arabis Alpina* ?, growing on Rocks near the sea side (6) Plenty of the *Uva ursi, Arbutus Uva ursi* [*Arctostaphylos uva-ursi* (L.) Spreng.], Alpine Mouse Ear, **Cerastium alpinum*, (8) a Shrub for it no where was so Large as a Small Tree, *Acer ? Pseudoplatanus* [*Acer spicatum* Lam.], which Very much resembled Scycamore a Kind of Willow with silky Leaves [unident.][95] (9) a Plant That appeared to be a species of Whitlow grass [*Draba incana* L.][96] (10) a Plant with a

38

beautifull Yellow Flower growing on the tops of dry hills [*Potentilla nivea* L.]†[97] (1) a Kind of Anemone in Company with it [?**Anemone parviflora* Michx.]†[98] (2) Mossy Campion, *Cucubalus Acaulis* [*Silene acaulis* L.], (3) a Kind of Chickweed [?*Minuartia rubella* (Wahl.) Hiern],[99] (4) a species of sedum, *Saxifraga* [**S. cespitosa* L.] on the barrenest Hills (5) another growing near the sea side [*S. oppositifolia* L.],[100] (6) a Kind of Willow with smooth Leaves [unident.] the Harbour of Inglie is formed by the Island Not very Commodious as the Vessels we   21 [*sic*] saw were moord head & stern there were about 6 English Vessels fishing there &   Inglie near twice that number of french the French indeed have almost the Sole Possession of the Fishery in this Part of the Island Many Harbours here (St Julians for instance) not having so much as one Englishman in them they seem to Value & Encourage the trade more than

39

we do sending out infinitely Larger ships & Employing more hands in the Trade

127

21
Wild Cove

This Morn Proving Clear we Ran Across Canada bay to a small Harbour calld Wild Cove Where Lay two French Ships it seemd Perfectly Commodious for Large ships & shelterd from seas & winds but the ground very Foul as the Frenchmen had boyd up their anchors with Barrels it Raind the whole time we stayd here which made it impossible for me to Collect any thing indeed the Country bore much the appearance of Inglie from hence we went to Canada harbour where were several french Ships but the Harbour more Exposd & the ground as foul as in the Last the Reason of their Chusing this

40

Rather than Wild Cove is its situation nearer the mouth of the Bay which Saves much time to their Batteaux when the fish are on the outside of the bay from hence

Hiliards arm

we went to Hiliards arm a very Exposd harbour where some French fishd walking out above the Harbour I found a most Elegant Plant with red Flowers [?*Epilobium angustifolium* L.]101

22

Here we slept tonight the next morn Early set out for Conche102 with the wind Directly in our teeth here we found a bad harbour Exposd to both sea & wind only one Englishman & 3 or 4 french were fishing here the Englishman complained grieviously of the french hindering him from taking bait by denying him his Proper turn with the Seine while they were fishing & mooring bait boats on the ground where the fish were

41

usualy Caught he told us that if Proper Precautions were not taken mischeif would certainly Ensue as the french sent out arms allowing two Musquets to Each Bait boat we had intelligence during this Voyage that the French Carreid on an illicit trade with the Esquimaux indians tho Probably not Countenancd by Government as one ship only had been seen Engagd in it Precautions will be taken this fall to find what ship it is if she ventures to attempt it again this night at 3 o'clock came to the ship very Compleatly tired as we had not Pulld off our Cloaths since we came out nor lodgd any where but in the aft Cuddy of our boat

JULY

[There are no entries for this month. Banks's pagination runs on without any break; he states (p. 42) that he laid the diary aside on account of his illness which lasted for most of July].

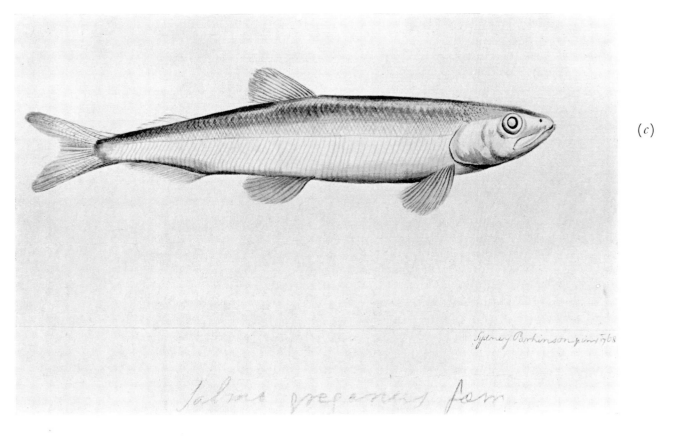

29. Capelin; *a* and *b*, lateral and ventral views of a male, *c*, a female.
Sydney Parkinson

in assisting in the building of a
Block house — in which a Leiutenants
& 20 men are to be left in the winter
to defend the winterers & Protect
the fishery for the future from the
Indians

The Country about this Place
tho much more Barren is far more
agreable then Croque — here you
may walk for miles over Barren
Rocks without being interupted by
a Bush or a tree — when there you
Could not go as many yards without
being Entangled in the Brushwood
it abounds also in game Partridges
of 2 sorts Ducks teal — in great abundance
But Particularly at this season
with a Bird of Passage Calld here a
Curlew from his great Likeness
to the smaller sort of that Bird found
in England their Cheif food is Berries

Curlews
came here
august 9

32. Page 46 of Banks's diary; from the holograph manuscript.

AUGUST

Interrupted by Very frequent Expeditions of this Sort In which as I could not   2, 3
Carry my Book without submitting it to the Inspection of Every Petty

42

officer who chose to Peruse it I was Contented with notes taken on small Peices of
Paper which as I was Pretty sufficiently Employd in Examining By Books what I
had got in my Expeditions whenever I was aboard the ship I never Copied into
this Book. I Laid it aside till July when I was Compleatly hindered from making
use of it By a fever which to my great misfortune Confined me the greatest Part of
that month to the ship incapable of Collecting Plants at the Very season of the Year
when they are the most Plentifull Some few indeed I got by the Diligence of my
servant who I sent often Out to bring home any thing he thought I had not got
He also shot several birds for me But My situation far too weak and dispirited by
my Illness to

43

Examine Systematically any thing that was brought has made my Bird tub a Chaos
of which I Cannot Give so good an account as I could wish & has Left many Blanks
in my Plants which I fear I must trouble my good freinds in England to fill up

As soon as my health was sufficiently Establishd to be allowd to go on shore I
employd my time in Collecting insects[103] & the remainder of the Plants which ought
to have been Collected through the month of July and Insects tho I was Baffled by
Every Butterfly who chose to fly away for some time till my strengh returned &
which it did in an uncommonly short time & I thought myself able to take another
Boat Expedition to the Island of Bellisle de Grois for

44

which Place I set out about the 1st or 2nd of this month & was repayd for my
Trouble by the acquisition of several Valuable Plants[104] & the sight of a wild
Bear who was seen about 4 Miles above Conche[105] into which harbour we were
forc'd by Contrary winds

But Successfull as This Expedition was in itself in its Consequences it was much
the Contrary as Several Plants were Left at Croque some not in Perfect order for
Drying others which as I could every day Procure were Left For the Present Least
they should take up time Better Employd in Visiting Places I had not seen since my
Illness upon my arrival at Croque I found the Ship under orders to Sail without
Delay for Chatteaux Bay which the Next morning august 6th She did & met   August 6

45

with as Strong a gale of Wind as She Could have feard had she saild at the worst
time of the Year which however She weatherd it out Extreemly well & on the 9th
arrivd at Chatteaux where she Found the Zephyr Cap^tn Omyny & the Wells Cutter
Cap^tn Lawson which Last She had sent from Croque before her

In this Trip I for the first time Experiencd the happiness of Escaping intirely the seasickness which had so much harrassd me always before in the Least Degree of Rough Weather [105a] which I attributed in Great measure to my having been so much at sea in Boats which by being much more uneasy than the Ship made me Less Sensible of her motion

Here we have remaind Ever since the Ships Company Employd

46

in Assisting in the Building of a Block house in which a Leuftenant & 20 men are to be Left in the winter to Defend the winterers & Protect the fishery for the Future from the Indians

The Country about this Place tho much more Barren is far more agreeable than Croque here you may walk for miles over Barren Rocks without being interupted by a Bush or a tree—when there you Could not go as many Yards without being Entangled in the Brushwood it abounds also in Game Partridges of 2 sorts Ducks teal[106] in great abundance But Particularly at this season with a Bird of Passage Calld here a Curlew [Eskimo Curlew, *Numenius borealis* (Forster)]†[107] from his Great Likeness to the smaller sort of that Bird found in England their Chief food is Berries

Curlews came here August 9

47

which are here in Great abundance of Several Sorts with which they make themselves very near as fat & I think tho Prejudicd almost as good as our Lincolnshire Ruff & Reve

[verso of 46]
about a week after the Curlew The Green Plover [Golden Plover, *Pluvialis dominica dominica* (Müller)] made its appearance tho not in near so great abundance feeding like him upon Berries!

Charadrias Pluvialis

I have not Yet been able to trace their Source but Find that by the Latter End of September they arrive at Trinity Bay after having Coasted so far along the Island of Nfland in Vast abundance where they Proceed to from thence or when they return I cannot Learn I have heard but not from any Certain Authority that they go to the Vast Lakes at the head of the River St Laurence this is all the account I have yet been able to Learn of them Probably in the Southern Parts of the Island more may be Learnt if it is it shall be inserted by & by

48

Chatteaux Bay where we now Lie was Calld so by the french when they were in Possession of this Coast from two Remarkable rocks both situated on Islands in the mouth of the Harbour which at a distance as you come into the Harbour appear not unlike Castles I have yet been upon only one of them The Largest tho I believe not the highest of the two it is Situated in the Middle of an Island Calld Castle Island out of which it at once rises Perpendicular in Some Places to the hight (as I

Chatteaux on Castle Island

130

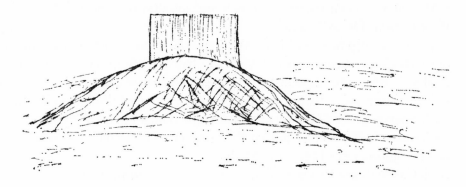

3. Banks's sketch of Castle Island, facing page 48 of his diary

guesd by my Eye) of 100 feet in some Places indeed there are Ascents to it by Climbing among Lose stones the top is Pretty near a Plain Coverd in many Parts with Loose stones & those small seldom Larger than two fists its lengh may be about a furlong or rather more its breadth not quite

49

Half as much in Walking upon the Side of it next to the Sea I Pickd up the Horn of one of the Country Deer[108] Shed Probably on the Spot as they are remarkable for swimming from the main to Islands sometimes to those that are far out at sea

Just opposite to Henley Island and very near it is a small Flat Island Calld Esquimaux Island where Last Year in digging an Extraordinary discovery was made of a quantity of Whalebone[109] Carefully & regularly buried upon tiles & so large that I have been told by those who saw it that at one time as much was dug as had it been sound would have been worth 20000 lb it is by age so totaly Decayd that it is scarce distinguishable from Birch Bark which indeed it has much more the appearance of than of whalebone

Whalebone on
Esquimaux
Island

50

Dividing itself Easily into Laminae as thin almost as you split it with the Edge of a Knife & the outside Parts being Exactly of the Colour of Decayd Birch Bark it is supposd to be Left here by the Danes who in their Return from Groenland South about touchd upon this Coast & Left several Whaling Crews tempted no doubt by the Large quantity of Whales which Pass Every Year through the Straights of Bellisle into the Gulph of St Laurence here we are to suppose that the fortunate Crew who had taken this immence quantity of Bone fixd their habitation upon this Island till the Ships should return as usual where upon an attack of the Inland Indians they Buried their Bone for greater security & most Probably were cut of to

Danes on the
Coast of
Labrador

131

a Man so that their treasures remaining unfound till Chance Directed us to them in their Present Decayd state

Since the ship has Layd here We have made 2 or three Boat Expeditions but not of much Consequence as we never Laid from the Ship one night in one of them we landed on the outermost of the St Peters Islands in hopes of Young Birds or Eggs in both which indeed we were disapointed but found the Island in a manner Coverd with Scurvy grass [*Cochlearia tridactylites* Banks ex DC.][110] which may be worth notice as it is Extreemly Scarce Every where Else upon the Coast where I have yet been in another we Landed in St Peters Bay where we found the Wreck of a Birch Bark Canoe a sign Probably that some of the Inland Indians Live not

St Peters
Islands

St Peters Bay

52

Very far from thence tho as Yet we Know nothing of them

This Subject Leads me to say Something (tho I have as yet been able to Learn Very little about them) of the Indians that inhabit the interior Parts of Newfoundland and are supposed to be the orinatal inhabitants of that Countrey[111] they are in general thought to be very few as I have been told not Exceeding 500 in number but why that should be imagind I cannot tell as we Know nothing at all of the Interior Parts of the Island nor Ever had the Least Connextion with them tho the french we are told had

The only Part of the Island that I have heard of their inhabiting is in the neighbourhood of Fogo where they are said to be as near the coast as 4 miles

Nfland
Indians

53

Our People who fish in those Parts Live in a continual State of warfare with them firing at them whenever they meet with them & if they chance to find their houses or wigwams as they call them Plundering them immediately tho a Bow & arrows & what they call their Pudding is generaly the whole of their furniture.

They in return Look upon us in exactly the same Light as we Do them Killing our people whenever they get the advantage of them & Stealing or Destroying their nets wheresoever they find them

The Pudding which I mentiond in the Last Paragraph is our People say always found in their hutts made of Eggs & Dears hair to make it hang together as we put hair into our mortar and Bakd

in the Sun our People beleive it to be Part of their food—but do not seem Certain whether it is intended for that or any other use They are said to fetch Eggs for this Composition as far as fung [Funk] or Penguin Island ten Leagues from the nearest Land[112]

They are Extreemly Dextrous in the use of their Bows & arrows & will when Pressd by an Enemy take 4 arrows 3 between the Fingers of their Left hand with which they hold the Bow & the fourth notchd in the string & Discharge them as quick as they Can draw the bow & with great Certainty

Their Canoes by the Gentlemans account from whom I have all this are made like the Canadians of Birch Bark sewd together with

55

Deers sinews or some other material but Differ from the Canadians Essentialy in that they are made to shut up by the sides Closing together for the Convenient Carriage of them through the woods which they are obligd to do on account of the many Lakes that abound all over the Island

Their Method of Scalping to is very Different from the Canadian they not being content with the Hair but skinning the whole face at Least as far as the upper Lip

I have a scalp of this Kind which was taken from one Sam Frye a fisherman who they shot in the water as he attempted to swim off to his ship from them they Kept this Scalp a year but the features

60 [*sic*]

were so well Preservd that when upon a Party of them being Pursued the next summer they Dropd it it was immediately Known to be the scalp of the Identical Sam Frye who was Killd the year before

So much for the Indians if half of what I have wrote about them is true it is more than I expect tho I have not the Least reason to think But that the man who told it to me beleivd it & had heard it all from his own people & those of the neighbouring Planters & fishermen

It is time that I should give Some account of the Fishery[113] both French & English as they Differ much in their methods of Fishing and have Each their Different merits the Englishman indeed has the advantage as he catches considerably

61

a larger quantity of Fish & his Fish fetch more money at Foreign markets being better Cured

First then of the English method they use boats almost twice as large as the French Some of them being 40 feet in the Keel they are Calld here Shallops Riggd with a main mast & foremast & Lugsail & furnishd also with 4 oars 3 of which row on one side & the other which is twice as long as any of the rest Belays as they Call it the other three by being rowd sideways over the stern by a man who stands up for that Purpose with his face towards the Rowers Counteracting them & Steering at the same time as he gives way to the Boat

62

Each of the men in this Boat is furnishd with two Lines one at Each side of the boat Each of which Lines are furnishd with two hooks so here are 16 hooks Constantly Employd which are thought to make a tolerably good Days work if they bring in from 5 to ten Quintals of fish tho they have Stowage for & sometimes bring

Sam frye

English Fishery

English Fishery

133

in as far as 30 : 200 Quintals a boat is Calld a saving Voyage but not under Their Bait are small Fish of all Kinds when they Can gett them Herring Capelin† Lance† Tom Cod or young Cod†[114] the first of which they salt & Keep for some time in case of a scarcity of the rest but they are not near so well taken by the Fish when Salted

63

as when they are fresh when Small Fish is not to be got as in some situations it cannot they use sea birds [*Oceanodroma leucorhoa leucorhoa* (Vieillot)][115] which are Easily taken in vast numbers by Laying nets over the holes in the Rocks where they make their nests & roost in the night when neither small fish or birds are to be Come at they are forcd to use the maws of the fish they catch which tho the worst bait of any they will make a shift to take fish with

When the Fish are Catchd they are Carried to the Stage which is built with one End Hanging over the water for the Sake of throwing away the offals into the sea & of their boats being able to Come close to them & Discharge their fish with as little [trouble]

64

as Possible as soon as they come upon the stage they are handed by a Boy to the header who stands on the side of the table nearest to the water End whose business it is to gut the Fish & cut of its head which he does by Pressing the Back of the head with Both hands against the side of the table made sharp for the Purpose when both head and Guts fall through a hole in the Floor into the water he then Shoves the fish to the Splitter who Stands opposite to him his business is to split the fish beginning at the head & opening it Down to the tail at the next cut he takes out the Larger Part of the Back Bone which falls through the Floor into the water He then

65

Shoves the Fish off the table which fall into a Kind of hand barrow set there to receive it which as soon as it full is wheeld off to the Salt Pile by another hand (I had almost forgot a part of the Headers business which is to seperate the Liver which he throws into a seperate Basket for the making of train oyl[115a] which is the Oyl usd by Curriers & bears a much higher Price than whale oyle) In the Salt Pile the fish are Placd spread open one upon another & between Each Layer of fish a layer of salt is thrown here they remain an uncertain time till they have taken salt they are then Carried From thence & the Salt washd out of them in sea water by towing them off from shore in a

66

Kind of float made for that Purpose calld by them a Pound as soon as this is Completed they are Carried to the Last operation of Drying them which the English Do upon Standing flakes made by a slight Wattle Just strong enough to support the men who Lay on the fish supported upon Poles in some Places as high as twenty feet from the ground here they are Exposd with the open side to the sun &

134

every night or when it is bad weather Piled up five or 6 on a heap with a large one his back or skinny Part uppermost to be a Shelter to the rest from rain which hardly damages him throught his Skin as he rests Slanting Each way to Shoot off the Rain when it is dry which it is in about a weeks time in Good weather It is done with*

*[Verso of p. 65]
I had almost Forgot that when the Fish are tolerably dry they Put them in Round Piles of 8 or ten Quintals Each Covering them on the top with bark in these Piles they remain 3 or 4 days or a week to sweat after which they are again Spread & when dry Put up in Larger heaps Coverd with Canvass & Left till they are put on board

& ready for the Mediterranean trade where it fetches a good

67

Price But is not Esteemd in England for which Place they Prepare another Kind of fish Cured wet & calld by them mud Fish which instead of Being split quite open as their Dry Fish are are only opend Down to the navel They are salted & Lie in salt & the Salt is washd out of them in the Same manner as the others but instead of Being Laid out to Dry they are Barrelld up in a Pickle of Salt Boild in water

Lastly Let us remember their Train Oyl for by that name they distinguish it from Whale or Seal oyle which they Call Fat Oyle Which is sold at a Lower Price being only usd for the Lighting of Lamps than the train oyl which is usd by the Curriers They make it thus they Take a half tub & boring a hole

68

Through the Bottom Press hard Down into it a Layer of Spruce boughs upon which they Lay the Livers & place the whole apparatus in as sunny a Place as Possible as the Livers Corrupt the Oyl runs from them & straing itself clear through the Spruce Boughs is caught by a Vessel set under the hole in the tubs bottom

So much For the English Fishery I shall now mention the methods of the French which are Different from ours in some of which as I said before they Excell us but more in their neatness & manner of Carrying on Business among their People than in any Superiority in Point of Curing

Their Boats are not much more than half as Large as ours much more Clumsily Built & Less

French Fishery

69

adapted for sailing Each of them are workd by three men who Each Fish with two Lines in the Same manner & with the same Bait as Our People this when the fish will take Bait but they who in General Come Earlier upon the Coast than we do begin also to fish before us by a method Calld here Jigging Done by 2 Large hooks Each of them twice as Large as those usd for bait these hooks are fastend together back to back and a heavy Lead Plac'd upon their shanks which the french whither

Jigging

135

out of whim or from any use they find in it I do not Know Cast in the Shape of a fish these Jiggs are fastend to the Ends of their Lines & Let Down to the bottom from

70

whence they are raisd Every half minute or their abouts by a strong Jerk of the Fishermans arm in hopes of striking them into the fish who are accidentaly swimming by. the Jerk of the arms nesscessary in this Fishing makes it so Laborious that we can seldom or ever get any of our Country men to do it

Their Method of washing their Fish out of the Salt is very Different & much worse then ours they do it in a square trought the sides of which are securd with Lattice work this is set between 4 poles raisd up in the water always where I have seen it close by the side of the stages on the tops of these poles are blocks by which the Trough is easily hoisted up or Let

71

Down into the water into this they Put their Fish & Letting it down into the water Poke them about with Sticks till they are Sufficiently washd some of the People also getting into the trough & moving them about with their hands & feet

The cheif inconvenience of this method is this the water by the washing of 3 or 4 troughsfull of fish becomes Exceedingly muddy so much so that I have seen it Discolourd for 20 or 30 yards round the trough its situation too so near the stage makes the water round it subject to be corrupted & stink in a manner not to be describd from the Quantities of Cods heads & guts thrown in by the Splitters

72

In these very Essential Particulars we Excell them but in the neatness of their Stages & manner of working they are much our superiors

Their Stages are much Broader then ours Coverd with the Sails of their Ships which makes them much Lighter as well as sweeter or rather Less Stinking for either theirs or ours would turn an Englishmans Stomach who had not been inurd to them by degrees as we were ours are built with spruce boughs & Coverd with the same Material which makes them Disagreeably Dark in the middle of theirs is a Salt Pile as long as the Stage almost by which means the Salt is always at hand in ours the Salt is heapd up in a corner & run about the Stage where ever it is

73

wanted in handbarrows over the Salt pile in the French stage is a little Scaffolding on which the People Lay their trunks & to which they swing their Hammocks while our People are Lying about the Stage in little Cabbins which in England would be thought far too bad for hogsties

The Seconde or mate of the French ships the Major or surgeon occasionaly the Captain are the People who split the Fish by which means it is never Carelessly or ill Done as is too often the Case among our People where splitting is done by the Common People the too first of these officers are not qualified for their office unless they can sing which they Do to amuse the People

Pl. I Fox Sparrow, *Passerella iliaca iliaca*
Sydney Parkinson

who occasionly all join the chorus the whole time of their Splitting I remember Coming into a french Stage & hearing Voi amante[116] as agreably sung as Ever I heard it by the Major & seconde the first of whoom had a remarkably good voice

These Officers being of some Consequence among the People & commonly going Pretty well Dressd have an Ingenious way of Keeping themselves Clean in the dirty operation of Splitting they have a Case made of Bark to Cover them from their chins to their heels which Constantly stands over their Stools in the splitting table into this they Creep & Putting on sleeves & Large woolen gloves split the fish in a manner without touching

it

Their Oyl they also make in a much neater manner than we do if neatness is an excellence in so nasty a thing they certainly excell us much theirs is all straind through a thin Cloth not unlike the Canvas that Ladies work Carpeting upon strechd on the upper side of a Vessel made with Poles Placd in the shape of a Pyramid Reversd under which is Placd a trough for the receiving it as it strains out

After having said so much about Fishing it will not be improper to say a little about the Fish that they catch & of the Dish they make of it Calld Chowder which I believe is Peculiar to this Country tho here it is the Cheif food of the Poorer & when well made a

76

Luxury that the rich Even in England at Least in my opinion might be fond of It is a Soup made with a small quantity of salt Pork cut into Small Slices a good deal of fish and Biscuit Boyled for about an hour unlikely as this mixture appears to be Palatable I have Scarce met with any Body in this Country Who is not fond of it[116a] whatever it may be in England Here it is Certainly the Best method of Dressing the Cod which is not near so firm here as in London whether or not that is owing to the art of the fishmongers I cannot Pretend to say Salmon & herrings we also have in Plenty but neither of them near so rich & fat as they are in England Halibuts are the only fish common

Chowder

Fish

To both places in which this Country Excells Lance too is Very Good here but that is a fish I never Eat in England but their greatest Delicacy in the fish way is a small Fish calld here Capelin[114] in appearance not unlike a smelt tho scarce half as Large they Come in Very Large Shoals From the southward to Deposite their spawn they were at Croque this year but are not Yet Come here as it is but seldom they Come so far norward tis Probable that they will not come at all this Year there are also Tolerable Plenty of Flounder[117] but as soon as the Fishery begins they become so strong by feeding upon the stinking heads etc. of fish thrown from the stages that they are by no means fit to Eat

Capelin

Sept[r] 1st [*sic*]

Trout

So much for Salt water fish the Fresh here are in great Plenty tho but of 2 sorts Trout[118] & Eels[119] the First of which afford good Diversion to an angler biting Very well at the artificial Particularly if it has gold about it with this Peculiarity in the rivers that they are to be caught in abundance no where but in tide & at no time but from about two hours before highwater till Ebb In Pools indeed they always bite but best in sunshiny weather I have seen no large ones none I believe above half a Pound weight but am told that in some Parts of Nfland they are Very Large

SEPTEMBER

Birds

Birds here are many sorts of which as well as Every other natural Production I shall Subjoin a Cataloge mentioning in this Place only those good for Food or some other

way remarkable among the best of the First Sort is the Curlew who was mentiond before here are also 2 more species[120] of it both very good Eating tho not so delicate as the first the golden Plover[121] too is here & feeds with the Curlew upon Crowberries Ducks & Teal many sorts all the fresh water ones very good but

Sept[r] 1st those who inhabit Salt water the most fishy Birds I Ever met with the wild geese[122] here are Just now Comeing in very Fat and Larger I think than Tame geese in England here are Partrides also of two Kinds[123] brown & white for so they Call those Distinguished by a white spot upon their wings they are like our heath fowl but near as Large as the Black game

these are all good to Eat but Some birds there are that I must mention tho they have not that Excellence Particularly one Known here by the name of Whobby [*Gavia stellata* Pontoppidan][124] he is of the Loon Kind & an Excellent Diver but Very often amuses himself especialy in the night by flying high in the air and makeing a very Loud & alarming noise at least to those who do not Know the Cause of it as the following circumstance will shew

In August 1765 as Commodore Paliser in the Guernsey a 50 gun ship Lay in this Harbour Expecting the Indians one Dark night in a thick fog the Ships Company were alarmed by a noise they had not before heard Every one awoke Conjecturd what it could Possibly be it came nearer & nearer grew louder & louder the first Lieuftenant was calld up he was the only man in

the Ship Who had Ever seen the Esquimaux immediately as he heard the noise he declard he rememberd it well it was the war whoop of the Esquimaux who were certainly Coming in their Canoes to board the Ship & Cut all their throats the Commodore was aquainted up he Bundled upon Deck orderd ship to be cleard for Engaging all hands to Great Guns arms in the Tops Every thing in as good order as if a french man of war of Equal Force was within half a mile Bearing down upon them The Niger which Lay at some Distance from them was haild & told the indians were Coming when the Enemy appeared in the shape of a Troop of these Whobbys swimming & flying about the Harbour which From the Darkness of the

82

night they had not before seen all hands were then sent down to Sleep & no more though[t] of the indians till the Nigers People came on board next morning who will Probably never Forget that their Companion Cleard Ship & turnd up all hands to a flock of Whobbies

The People here tell a remarkable Fact if it is a true one of a Kind of duck Cald here Lords & Ladies [*Histrionicus histrionicus* (L.)][125] who they say at times Pursue the Gulls whom they Persecute till they make them Dung which they catch with great dexterity before it reaches the water & immediately Leave off the Chace

Lords & Ladies

This day a Halibut was brought aboard so large that his dimensions I fear will appear incredible in England the first I took with my own hands therefore I can venture to affirm

Sept[r] 2nd Halibut

83

them Exact They are as follows

	ft		inch
From the Tip of his nose to the end of his Tail	6	:	11
Breadth from fin to fin	3	:	10
Thickness of his solid Flesh By running a priming wyer through	0	:	$8\frac{1}{4}$
Breadth of his Tail	2	:	$0\frac{1}{2}$
Lengh of the Fin next his Gills	0	:	10
he weighd			284 lb

which was only 14 lb Less than an Ox Killd for the ships Company the Day he was weighd which was not till near 24 hours after he was Caught so he may fairly be said to have weighd as much as the Ox had he not been wasted as all fish do considerably by Keeping

When Chowder was mentiond Something was hinted about Spruce Beer the Common Liquor of the Country The receipt for making it take as follows as Perfectly as I can get it

84

Take a copper that Contains 12 Gallons fill it as full of the Boughs of Black spruce as it will hold Pressing them down pretty tight Fill it up with water Boil it till the Rind will strip off the Spruce Boughs which will waste it about one third take them out & add to the water one Gallon of Melasses Let the whole Boil till the Melasses

Spruce Beer

are disolvd take a half hogshead & Put in nineteen Gallons of water & fill it up with the Essence. work it with Barm or Beergrounds & in Less than a week it is fit to Drink from this Liquor in itself Very Weak are made three Kinds of Flip Cald here

Callibogus Callibogus, Egg Calli & King Calli the first

85

Simply By adding Rum Brandy or Gin If you cannot get Either of the First as much as is agreable The second by heating the first with the Addition of an Egg & Some Sugar the third King Calli By adding spirit to the Contents of the Copper as soon as it is ready to Put into the Cask & Drinking it hot

Sep[tr] 6 The Curlews are quite Gone none being Left behind but a few wounded ones

Curlews gone Near to Castle Island is situated Henley Island which like the other is Crownd with a rock considerably Higher & more Beautifull in Many Parts at Least 150 feet

About the Middle of this Month an Extrordinary animal[126] was seen by Mr Phipps on the

86

Main Opposite the Seal Islands the Same Was Seen By Mr Ankille[132] who was with the Survey in Hare bay the two Gentlemens accounts of their Shape etc agreing I set them Down The whole animal of a shining Black Bigger than a Fox tho not much in Make & shape nearest to be compard to an Italian Grayhound Legs Long tail Long & tapering as in that animal that that Mr Phipps Saw Came up from the Sea & Crossd a morass to the Hills not at a very Quick Pace Mr Ankille had a much Better opportunity of Examining his He says there were five together Setting upon the Rocks at the Mouth of a fresh water river with young ones by them that he saw them Leap into the water & Diving

87

bring up trouts which they Gave to their Young ones who sat Still upon the Rocks that upon his shewing himself they all Leapd into the water & swimming a little way from shore Put out their heads from the water & observd him that he Might Easily have shot one or more of them had he not seen that the Stream would have Carried the Dead one into the Sea without his having a chance of Recovering it The French say they Every now & then See these animals in hare bay & an old Furrier we spoke with told us he rememberd a skin sold for five Guineas which was taken somewhere in Canada bay & he beleivd was of the same animal

In the Course of this Month we made an Excursion to the top of Temple Bay but without the[127]

88

We were told by the Old Salmoneer that there were Owls there as big as Turkies[128] he indeed gave us the Claws of one which I take to be the *Strix Bubo* of Linnaeus tho I was never Lucky Enough to See one of them the whole time of our Stay nor any of the Shipps Company tho they were Eternaly Employd in Cutting wood for the Fort in temple Bay

140

As An Excuse for my not Stirring More from home while at this Place I mention an escape I had on the Second of this month when mere accident[129] Preservd my Life I set out with the Master of our Ship on a Cruise to the northward meaning to Cruise along shore for a week or ten days where no vessel that we Knew of had Ever been we

89

were Both Extreemly fond of the Plan & Pushd out of Chatteaux with a foul wind in an open Shallop by way of putting ourselves in a fair winds way we with dificulty Turnd the Lengh of Castle Island when the wind Coming right ahead we agreed it was impossible to go any farther & we Put back into Esquimaux harbour to stay till the next morn in hope of change of wind we had Scarcely made our Boat fast along side of a snow there when it began to Blow Very hard and that night Came on a most severe Gale of Wind which Destroyd an infinite number of boats Everywhere the French Particularly whose boats are smaller than ours are said to have Lost an hundred men & three of their Ships Drove on shore a brig of Captain Derbys[130]

90

at Isle Bois a little down the Streights was Beat all to Peices this totaly Destroyd our scheme to the northward Sr Thomas being after that very Careful of Letting the boats go out & indeed as the blowing Season was Come in I was Easily Persuaded that I was Safer on board the Niger than in any Boat in the Country

Events now began to be very scarce hardly any thing more happening worth the Relation on an Excursion to St Peters bay we found many remains of the wreck of a Canoe made of Birch Bark such as the Canadian Indians make use of this at first sight appeard to me a Plain Proof that those Indians at Certain Seasons at Least visited this Coast but I was afterwards told that the Whale Fishers many of which Come here

91

Every winter from new England etc often make use of them as Boats About the Latter End of this month Partridges[131] Became much more Plenty then they were before Possibly they came from the Norward Mr Ankille[132] while Shooting in the neighbourhood of St Peters Bay saw by his account at Least 100 in one Company while he was making up to them to have shot at them an Eagle made a Stoop among them & Carried of one the rest immediately took wing & went off I should mention here that tho I have not been able to Procure an Eagle from their Scarcity here are two sorts one of which we had a young one who got away is the *Chrysaetos* of Linnae [*Aquila chrysaëtos canadensis* (L.)][133] the other I apprehend to be the *Canadensis*[134] but I never could

92

see him but upon the Wing

Just before we Left this Place the Sergeant of marines belonging to York fort brought me a Porcupine alive [*Erethizon dorsatum* (L.)][135] it is quite Black except

141

the Quills which are Black & white alternately about the size of an English hare but shorter made after sulking for three or four Days he begins to Eat & I have great hopes of Carrying him home alive

Sept^r: $\frac{C}{4}$ Last York fort [see map] was finishd which Every Body agrees is a surprizing Peice of Work to have been finishd in the time as it was almost intirely Done by the Ships Company Leutenant Walters has taken up his Residence in the fort I have Spard him the only Thermometer I have Left He promises to give me an account of the weather next year

OCTOBER

93

Octr 1st This Day We meant to have saild for Croque but were hinderd by a Gale of Wind & a terrible Sea without the heads However on the 3^d we sail for Croque & arrive there on the 4th after a tolerably lucky Passage Now Chatteaux is Left for Good I can but say of it that it is far the Pleasantest harbour we have been in the Countrey about it is tolerably Clear of Wood so that you are always sure of a good walk & Plenty of Shooting Ducks Curlew geese etc: on the Marsh between Bad Bay & York fort Partrides on the Hills between Pitts harbour & St Peters bay & tolerable trout fishing at the top of Pitts harbour I forgot to mention before that in all the Harbours hereabouts are quantities of Offal bone of Whales some very

94

Large a sure Sign that a Considerable Whale Fishery has sometime or Other been Carried on here[109]

There is Far Less Variety of Vegetables here[136] than at Croque & the Whole Soil Bears the appearance of a much more inclement Climate tho at so little a distance how far the Difference may be formd by its being on the Continent I can not say or whether that is at all the Reason one Observation I have made all along this Coast which seems to Contradict this Opinion that Contrary to what we see in England the Snow lies Longest upon the Lands immediately Contiguous to the Sea and the Cold in all appearance is there infinitely more intense Probably owing to the Islands of Ice almost Constantly Floating Past this is nowhere

95

more remarkable than at Chatteaux Where the Masters of ships all agree that there is at all times the difference of a Coat between Pitt & Esquimaux harbour another Observation I have Constantly made Here & more Particularly in Newfoundland is that the alpine Plants are not Found here as in England upon the Tops of Hills but very near the Edge of the Sea indeed here are no hills of any Consequence between Six and seven hundred feet is the Greatest hight I have heard of being measured Chappeau Rouge indeed is said to be higher but it is in a Part of the Island which we did not Visit

Islands of ice we saw Very few of Comparatively Speaking & no Large ones according to the accounts we have heard Mr. Palliser

96

Himself Measurd one Last year by the going of his Ship which gave him 600 feet when the Largest we saw I do not suppose Could be one third of that hight

Whilst we stayd at Croque I Employd myself in searching for the Remains of Plants I had Left by our Sudden Departure some I found Particularly a species of Assorabacca [*Pyrola asarifolia* Michx.][137] as I Judged from its Leaves I also Went up the River at the Head of the harbour to Explore the Countrey Which I found Pleasanter than any Part of the Island I had seen tho the Thickness of the wood made it almost inaccessible in the Spot I mean the River Runs in the space of about a mile & a half through Six or Seven

97

Distinct Pools some Very Large all Quite to the waters Edge ornamented with wood in some Islands Coverd also with Tall Firrs the most of them winding among the hills So that You never could Command the Whole at one view but had a part Left for the Imagination to Supply the Water in Every one as Clear as Tis Possible to Conceive in Short not one of them but was Well worth a place in the First improvements I have seen in England but what better repayd my walk Even than the Sight of these Beautifull Prospects was the Finding appearances of a Large & well Furnishd stratum of Statuary Marble such at Least

98

Who had no opportunity of Examining more than Exterior Surface which was Perfectly white & Clear treating it however Merely as Lime stone which upon Experiment it has Proved to be it is not to be neglected in this Island where that substance has not before been discoverd I therefore Give a very Particular Direction by which any Body who wishes to find it may do it with Certainty

I would advise a Person unaquainted with the Countrey to follow the Course of the Salmon River[138] till he comes to the Pools I have Just mentiond then turning to the Right hand to search Carefully Between them & a Large tract of Burnt wood above them I say search Carefully

99

as I did nowhere observe it bedding above the surface of the Earth The Place where I most Particularly observ'd it and got my specimen was a gully through which winter water Passes but which in Summer is dry in such Places & rivulets it is most Probably to be found in abundance as my first hint was from a Pebble of it I pickd up in the River a Careful search is however renderd very nescessary by the Thickness of the wood which will never Let you see more than the ground under your feet

The Soil about here is very different from & much superior to that at Chatteaux that being Light Sand Very unfit for Gardening

143

100

This is a very Strong Vegetable mould which with the Quickness of Vegetation in this Climate had such an Effect on many of our English Seeds that the[y] Run themselves out in stalk Producing little or no fruit Pea haulm we had 11 feet high & as thick as my finger which Producd scarce anything Beans ran till they could not support their own weight & fell without Producing a Pod Probably from the Ignorance of the gardener we Left behind who did not Know the Common Practise Even in England of Cutting of their tops Cabbage & Lettuce Throve surprizingly as did our Radishes & small Sallet carrots & Turnips which especialy the Last were remarkably

101

Sweet The Coldness of our nights made it nescessary to Cover our Onions with Hammocks we left them also till the Very Last but when we got them tho they were very small they were very good Spinage ran to Seed before it had well got its Leaves an inch broad so was of no manner of Service

I should not omit to give Some account of an Enemy we had here who gave us great Trouble I mean Feild mice[78] of which there are Wonderfull abundance all over this Countrey they attackd all our Vegetables without distinction Eating the Leaves Especialy our Peas the stalk of which they Cut off Close to the Ground Even after they were in Blossom nothing preservd our gardens from

being Totaly Destroyd but a Very good Look out and the noise of Cherry Clacks two of which we Set up which for some time had Very good Effect

Our Poultrey here throve Very well & would have bred much had not they been Disturbd by the Weasels[139] of which there are also Great Plenty so bold that they would take away their Eggs almost before our faces our only Defence was Gins in which we took a great number turkeys were Particularly lucky after they were hatchd for out of 11 the whole number we did not Lose one till the Hawks[140] at the Latter End of the Year Destroyd only one

Croque tho tolerably Pleasant now was intolerable in the Summer

on account of its heat & the Closeness of its situation confind on all sides by woods & no place But the Ship Free From mosketos and Gadflies in Prodigious abundance we had only one Clear walk on a morass a little above the Gardens but there you could not Long walk dry shod Sr Thomas & I were both Very Ill here Especialy me who at one time they did not Expect to recover I know not whether that gave a disgust but we both Joind in Pronouncing the Place the Least agreable of any we had Seen in the Countrey

The Seal Fishery is Carried on all over this Countrey as I have not before mentiond it I will give a short account of the manner in

33. St. John's, Newfoundland, c. 1770. From a watercolour.
Artist unknown

36. *Vaccinium macrocarpon*, a commercial cranberry. See p. 341.
G. D. Ehret

STRIX funerea Linné Syst. nat.

Pl. II Hawk Owl, *Surnia ulula caparoch*
Sydney Parkinson

which it is Carried on

[Verso of p. 103]

The Kinds of Seals Taken I can give a Very Imperfect account of having it only from the Fishermen as the most of them are only seen in winter they divide them into five sorts[141] which they Call Square Phipper Hooded Seal Heart or houke Bedlamer & harbour seal which Last stays in the Countrey all the year & is the Common in Europe the *Phoca Vitulina* of Linnaeus their Descriptions of the others are as follows square Phipper they say is the Largest sometimes weighing 500 weight as they tell you rough like an English Water Dog the hooded Seal differs from the rest by a white hood or peice of Moveable Skin upon his head which he can at Pleasure throw over his nose & with it defend himself from the Blows of the Fishermen who cannot Kill him till they remove it—the Heart or Possibly Harp Seal is markd over the Shoulders with a brown figure rudely resembling a harp which they Call the Saddle the Bedlamer Quite dusky without any mark they themselves tell you that the Bedlamer is the young harp they have also another sort which they say [verso of p. 104] never Exceeds two feet or two & a half in Lengh

what is Extrordinary is that tho there is Great quantities of Seals taken here Every winter the time of Doing it never exceeds seven or Eight Days at most the Seals at Some uncertain time in the winter sometime about Christmas Coming from the northward in Shoals which are never more than that time in Passing any Particular Place this Time is Carefully watch'd for by the Sealers who are Prepard according to their Situation to secure as many of them as the Shortness of their Stay will Permit

If they have a narrow Streight between two Islands or an Island & the main which is much the most Convenient

105

Situation it is Crossd by a number of nets the Last of which only is Drawn tight the rest remaining Close to the Bottom of the Water the Seals who Come in Shoals finding themselves Stopd by the tight net Crowd to it trying to find some way of getting on in the mean time the fishermen Draw tight the second net by which they are inclosd in a pound the Second Shoal of Seals are stopd by the second net & securd by the third & so they Proceed till they have filld all their nets or taken all the Seals that Come through that Passage which are Easily Drawn ashore from the Pounds by a little Seine made for the

106

Purpose this is much the most Certain as well as the Easiest method of Taking them but Few Places are furnishd with a streight Proper for this method those who Lie in open harbours are obligd to Content themselves with setting a number of netts up & down in the harbour both the Upper & under Lines of which are moord with Graplins these the Seals swim into & intangling themselves in the Meshes are Drownd

For the Prosecuting of this Fishery many hands are Left every year in the different Harbours who by this & furring give a very good account of their time to their Employers the Furrs taken here are Black Patch[142]

107

and Red Fox Beaver Otter & Martin in tolerable Plenty these Emoluments the English Enjoy without any molestation the French not being allowd to Leave a man here in the winter or to benefit themselves in any Degree by the Produce of the Countrey Except merely the Codfish notwithstanding which we have reason to beleive that some of the French this Year (who in general made very bad fishing Voyages) made up their freights by Carrying home timber tho had they been discoverd it would have been a sufficient cause to Seize & Condemn their Vessels

I observd Particularly in the neighbourhood of Croque & Hare bay Great abundance of the Eider[143] making their nests no doubt a quantity of their Valuable

108

Down might be Collected if Our People were Put into the way of gathering it

The Whale Fishery here is Carried on by the North Americans upon the Same Principle as the Seal Fishery the Whales like them Comeing to the Southward in winter time are met by the Fishermen in the Streights of Bellisle where they take numbers of them

After this Short Stay at Croque intended only for filling Water & getting on board the Produce of the Gardens & Poultry we Saild for St Johns on the 10th & arriv'd there on the 13th without any Particular Transaction During our Passage Here we found the Greater Part of the Squadron under the Command of Mr. Palliser in the Guernsey whose Civilities

Oct.r 10th

109

We ought to acknowledge as he Shewd us all we could Expect we all Felt great Pleasure in Returning to Society which we had so long been depriv'd of St Johns tho the Most Disagreeable Town I Ever met with was For some time Perfectly agreable to us I should not omit to mention the Ceremonies with which we Celebrated The Coronation[144] which happened whilst we were there the Guernsey was Dressd upon the Occasion & if I may Compare Great things with small Lookd Like a Pedlars Basket at a Horse race where ribbons of divers Colours fly in the wind fastend to yard wands stuck around it after this we were all invited to a Ball Given By Mr Governor where the want of Ladies was so great that My Washerwoman & her sister were there by formal Invitation but what surprizd me the most was that

146

110

after Dancing we were Conducted to a realy Elegant Supper Set out with all Kinds of Wines & Italian Liqueurs To the Great Emolument of the Ladies who Eat & Drank to some Purpose Dancing it seems agreed with them By its getting them such Excellent stomachs

It is very difficult to Compare one town with another tho that Probably is the Best way of Conveying the Idea St Johns however Cannot be Compard to any I have seen it is Built upon the side of a hill facing the Harbour Containing two or three hundred houses & near as many fish Flakes interspersed which in summer time must Cause a stench scarce to be supported thank heaven we were only there spring & fall before the fish were come to the Ground & after they were gone off

For dirt & filth of all

111

Kinds St Johns may in my opinion Reign unrivald as it Far Exceeds any Fishing town I Ever saw in England here is no regular Street the houses being built in rows immediately adjoining to the Flakes Consequently no Pavement offals of Fish of all Kinds are strewd about The remains of The Irish mens chowder who you see making it skinning and gutting fish in Every Corner

As Every thing here smells of fish so You cannot get any thing that does not Taste of it hogs Can scarce be Kept from it by any Care and When they have got it are by Faar the Filthyest meat I Ever Met with Poultry of all Kinds Ducks geese Fowls & Turkies infinitely more Fishy than the Worst tame Duck That Ever was sold For a wild one in Lincolnshire The Very Cows Eat the Fish offal & thus milk is Fishy This Last Particular indeed I have

112

not met with myself but have been assurd it is often the Case

On a little hill Just at the Entrance of the Town the Fort is situated Defended by a ditch & Pallisades it seems to be as indefensible a building as Ever was Calld by that name being Commanded by Hights Immediately above it it was Taken Last war by the French who strenghtend as much as they could by out works of Picketting but notwithstanding all they could do was retaken in a very small time by Colonel Amherst While we were there I went upon the Hills on purpose to See the Progress of his attack Which was Extreemly spirited the French having Possession not only of the Hights which there was an absolute nesscessity of his Gaining but of a situation which Greatly molested the Landing of his Cannon from the first he immediately dislodged them fording the River Soon after he attackd them in their hights & drove them

113

From thence also without any Material Loss Tis difficult for any but those who are accquainted with the Countrey to Conceive the Advantages of their Situation which was on the tops of hills almost Perpendicular the ascent of which was thick grown

147

with shrubbs here they kept their fire till our people were within a few yards of them but immediately on our peoples returning it quitted their ground scarce any of our wounded recoverd being torn not only with the Shot but by the Explosion of the Peice fird almost at their breasts this advantage being gaind they retird to the Fort where they Capitulated as soon as our Cannon were brought up

It is remarkable that During the whole Attack our people did not receive the Least Intelligence from the People of St Johns nor Countenance not Even Seeing one of them till they were marching down to take Possession of the Fort that & the Behaviour of the Irish & fishermen who almost one & all joind the French

114

as soon as Ever they saw them give a pretty good Idea of the Loyalty of the Inhabitants

While we remaind here I got an account From the Gentleman who had the Gulph Station of the Sea Cow[145] fishery which is Carried on upon the Magdalen Islands it is Carried on by two people whose names are Brindley If I mistake not by a patent Great Profit is made every Year of their Oil & teeth which are Very fine Ivory

For the Easy method they have of taking them the people are intirely indebted to the Excessive Laziness of the Animal they Land on Particular Parts of the Islands well Known to the People there being most Commonly some few on shore tho at Particular times they Land in surprizing numbers as Soon as one is Landed & has found sufficient Space for his body to remain dry he lies Still nor does he move till the next drives him on by beating

115

him with his Teeth Thus they Continue Landing for some time Tumbling one over the other & the hinder ones still driving forward those that are before them till a quantity sufficient for a Cut as they call it are Drove far Enough from the water the People then Begin with Clubs to beat the hindermost of those they chuse to take who imagining the Blows to Proceed from the teeth of those who come after still continue to drive those who lie before them till the whole are drove so far into the Country that they have not a Possibility of retreating to the sea they then begin to Kill them which they are obligd to do by shooting Every one Singly into a Particular Part of the head which is said to be the only Part about them Penetrable by a musquet Ball

The Danger of Doing this is far greater than it appears to be the People who do it must Chuse a time when the wind blows off the Land

116

that they may come under the wind upon those they mean to take the rest who have the wind of them immediately throwing themselves headlong into the Sea it is remarkable that the animal who has so little Dread of man at least the Sight of him Should so readily Fly from his Smell if the wind should Change while they are

148

Driving them or the animals by any other accident (as has Sometimes been Known to happen) should take it into their heads to return to the sea not a man who drives them can Escape the animals rolling themselves with great alertness when they are frightned Either crush the men to death or Carry them with them into the water

Their Long teeth Projecting from their Mouths 12 or 15 inches seem to be calculated only for inconvenience but the People there [say] that the animal living upon a shell fish who buries himself under the Sand makes them nesscessary to dig for them they also tell you that they

117

Climb Rocks in landing by hooking these teeth in Crevises & by that means hauling up their Enormous Bodies

While we remaind here I Employd some of my Time in searching for Plants but the Season was so far advancd that I could find none in Blossom by the Leaves & remains indeed I discoverd that there were several here different from any I had seen to the northward the Leaves of Some I Collected but many were so far destroyd by the Cold that Even that was Impossible so that here remains a feild for any body who will Examine this And the more southern Part of the Island but I have Vanity Enough to beleive that to the northward not many will be found to have Escapd my observation

I take this opportunity of setting down the dimensions of a schooner Boat we had with us for a tender as it appears to me the most rational Plan of a

118

Pleasure Boat I have met with our People all agreeing that when her hatches were shut down it was scarcely in the Power of wind or water to sink she swimming upon the surface like a corkd bottle her schooner sails also allowing her to be workd by fewer hands than any other Kind she had 42 feet Keel 12 feet Beam & was $5\frac{1}{2}$ feet Deep Pink stern deckd flush fore & aft our People who went in her agreed that had they allowd her 14 feet Beam she would then have born 6 feet Depth which would have made her a better boat as well as made her cabbin more convenient She Carried mainsail Foresail Fore stay sail & Gib with a square sail to go before the wind

Almost Every Body has heard of the Newfoundland Dogs I myself was desird to Procure some of them & when I set out for the Countrey firmley beleivd

119

that I should meet with a sort of Dogs different from any I had Seen whose Peculiar Excellence was taking the water Freely I was therefore the more surprizd when told that there was here no distinct Breed[146] those I met with were mostly Curs with a Cross of the Mastiff in them Some took the water well others not at all the thing they are valued for here is strenght as they are employd in winter time to Draw in Sledges whatever is wanted from the woods I was told indeed that at

149

trepassy Livd a man who had a distinct breed which he calld the original Newfoundland Dogs but I had not an opportunity of Seeing any of them

I should not omit saying something of the Intended Fortification which if it is Carried into Execution according to the Present Plan will be the Strongest in all America the Situation is fixd upon & the Expence Calculated but the whole is in the first instance so liable to Objections that it does not seem likely that the Government should Consent to it

120

They have however began a small work upon the South head which with a Boom over the Narrow Entrance of the Harbour will Probably be a Very efficient Defence

Newfoundland has always been Defended by a Squadron of Ships the Commodore of which for the Time being is Governor & administers Civil Justice Returning home in the winter & Leaving to a Deputy whose title is no more than Justice the Power of Regulating small disputes in his absence. the Captains of the different ships are sent Each to his Particular Station with the title of Leutenant governor & in Every harbour the First arriving Ship is admiral of the harbour her Captain administering Justice tho with Frequent Appeals to the Leutenant Governor to whom both French & English are Equaly subject tho they have Each their Seperate admiral in Every Port where they meet

121

This Countrey is of Infinite Consequence from the quantity of Fish which it Every Year sends Cheifly to the Mediterranean & from the number of hands Employd in it who must of Consequence be good Seamen

The french are Extreemly Sensible of this last advantage Restricted as they are to a small Part of the Island & that the worst fishing ground about it they Encourage their People By Premiums & Every method in their Power ten thousand men is the Least number they Employ every one of whom is obligd by us to return to Old France Every winter while we who Employ three times that number do not see so many return the rest staying to Prosecute the Sealing & furring marying & Setling in the Countrey or what is most frequent & worst of all having spent their wages in ale which their masters supply them with at an extravagant rate they are not able to Pay their Passage home & are obligd to Stay the winter starvd to Death if they Cannot find somebody to [employ]

122

them for their Victuals which is the most they ever think of getting

Mr Palliser who has taken more Pains & Enterd more into the true Interests of the Countrey than I beleive any Governor it Ever had has been Labouring by Every method in his Power to make it as much as Possible a returning Fishery as the French is In this he has all along been oppos'd by Every body of any Interest in the Countrey who found his plan as much against their Private advantages as it was for the Publick

150

Notwithstanding all their opposition he has in great measure Gaind his Point & if he is Continued in the Government which Seems likely in a few years more will Probably Compleat it

He has already abridgd the Property extreemly Even about St Johns & allows of no such thing to the northward of Cape Bonavista suffers nobody there to stay the winter without his express leave which in time of war may at any time be refusd & will Probably in a very short time put an End to the

123

tricks by which the People are Kept here such as Paying in Bills which they discount greatly or they are not Changd at all and masters supplying their Servants with Liquor which regulation the French Have been under time out of mind

Octr 28

On the 28th of Octr we Left St Johns in our Passage to Lisbon where we Arrived on the 17th on the fifth of Novr we had a very hard Gale of Wind of the Western Islands which has almost ruind me in the Course of it we shipp'd a Sea which Stove in our Quarter & almost Filld the Cabbin with water in an instant where it washd backward & forward with such rapidity that it Broke in Peices Every chair & table in the Place among other things that Sufferd my Poor Box of Seeds was one which was intirely demolish'd as was my Box of

124

Earth with Plants in it which Stood upon deck

[Note on sheet of paper pasted on to the fly leaf.]

St Johns Contains about 300 houses in winter 1765:66 its inhabitants were 1100 viz 750 men 350 women & children in some Years the number of returning fishermen have increasd the number of inhabitants of this Place only to the number of 10000 the number of Irish in this Place are recorded in winter to double the number of English tho in summer they are nearly Equal tho in other Parts of the Island they are reccond to Exceed the English ten times of the Irish in general $\frac{1}{18}$ are imagind to be catholicks mostly disafected as was seen in the year 1762 when the french took this Place 700 irish immediately enterd into their service the number of winterers in the whole island are recond at 10000 the Harbour here is remarkably fine Capable of Containing 200 Sail of Vessels Secure from Every wind that can blow at the Entrance of it stand 2 opposite Rocks calld the chain rocks which are only 90 fathoms asunder between them is water for the Largest men of war the tide does not rise above 6 feet in any Part of this Harbour

VOLUME 2 : LISBON

1

1766
Nov^{br} 17

Arrivd from Newfoundland in the River Tagus the Larboard Shore seems to be Lind with small Batteries the Whole way From the Rock of Lisbon up St. Julians

151

Castle mounts a great many Guns but the People must be dreadfully Exposd to the shot of any Ship that attemted it Bogri[147] is a round Fort also stuck full of Guns Built upon a sand always Surrounded by the Tide in the Mouth of the Tagus in this their State Prisoners are Kept we Came to an Anchor under Belam Castle[148] which is likewise Surrounded by the Water it is more Like a church than a fort and in its Situation appearing rather to float than Be built in a solid foundation it makes a pretty appearance

Tho we came to an Anchor by 11 oclock we were obligd to wait

2

Till 6 before we Could get Product* which hinderd our Going up to the

[Verso of p. 1]
* Pratica or Liberty of Going Ashore after being inspected in the usual manner by the officers of Health

Town that Evening On the Top of a hill On our Larboard hand appears the Pallace which on account of the Earthquakes this Place is Liable to is only one Story high it makes a Very singular appearance being Extended into an immensely Long front is not unlike Barracks in England

I have now been here Long Enough to make some Judgement of the Countrey About Lisbon it is Composd of a number of Small Hills Covered to the Top with very good Soil in which Corn & Vines grow in Great Abundance but Cheifly the Former the Divisions are Either Stone walls or Aloe hedges Encompassing Large Spaces every here & there a row of olive trees is Planted along the Fence which are the only trees

3

you see in the Countrey Want of Wood is its Great Fault the Various Risings and fallings of the Hills afford a thousand Vales and banks which would be very Pleasing Were they not so totaly destitute of it

Population in this Part of the Countrey is very thick I have been told that half the inhabitants of Portugall Live within ten miles Compass round the city of Lisbon that Calculation Probably is Infinitely too Great but the Countrey Every where Else is Certainly Very thinly Inhabited

The Portugese have no Idea of Improving Ground tho they have a climate in which wood Grows wonderfully fast

4

& a Countrey Especialy in the Neighbourhood of Lisbon which abonds in Situations Commanding Delightfull Views of the River there is Scarce an Instance of a Portugese having Ever Planted any tree but an Olive which by its Oyl brings them in a yearly revenue but what is more Extrordinary tho almost Every Body has his Kinta or Countrey house in the neighbourhood of the City their Taste in Gardening

37. *Davallaria canariensis*, from the Rock of Lisbon.
G. D. Ehret

38. *Salamandra salamandra*, a salamander from Portugal.
Sydney Parkinson

is more trifling than Can be Conceivd a Pond Scarce Large Enough for a frog to swim in the Sides of Which are lind with Glaz'd tiles and which has two or three fountains in it about

5

as thick as a quill is their Greatest Ornament this with a few Close Walks of Myrtle and Vines & a Statue or two Placed on awkard Pedestals at the Entrance of the Walks make a Place that People are Carried to See

At the Gardens of Keylas[149] belonging to the Infant Don Pedro you are told that 150,000 has been Layd out you Come in & see nothing but Parterres of Box ornamented with Yew trees cut into Shapes at Proper Distances & Avenues of Lime trees which Point to nothing here & there indeed are Little Rooms for Drinking tea ornamented with a Vast Deal of Glass and Gilding

6

but how that Money Could be Expended Does not appear the Ponds & fountains indeed & Lind with white marble & the walks are Every where Stuck full of Statues & busts of that material

The House indeed is Elegant Many of the Rooms are Very Magnificent tho an English man is rather disgusted at their being Pav'd with Brick the Furniture Consists of Silk hangings and french Tapistry with a Large number of Looking Glasses which are much Esteemd here The State Room Painted al Fresco & on Each Side of it a row of Very Large China

7

Jars at Each End is a platform of Deal with a Canopy over it but so little are the People here usd to Clean the Boards that they are Staind & dirtyd with Every Kind of nastiness that Can be Conceivd & Look literaly as if they had not been Washd Since they were Layd down

The Portugese tho Very Complaisant to Strangers are nevertheless Shy of Entertaining them which Proceeds as we were told from the Badness of their Living their first People Living in a Style much inferior even to Our Merchants who reside among them Whether it Proceeds from that or any other

8

Cause I shall not take upon me to Determine but Content myself with Saying that in Six months [weeks] stay I never had a opportunity of Seeing the inside of a Portugese Gentlemans house tho several of their Noblesse were Very Civil when they met us they never offerd more than the Civility of the present moment as a place in their Box at the Opera etc.

They are said to be Extreemly Proud & as ignorant & from the very little I saw of them I am much inclind to beleive not unjustly Learning is almost totaly Confind to their Convents where indeed it an inferior Style for as one of our Poets tell us
Where none admire how useless to Excell

153

as for their People of fashion they have no opportunity from their method of Education of Ever acquiring any as Soon as a boy is able to Walk alone he is Dressd in a fine Coat Visits with his father & is as much a man as in any Part of his Life he is indeed attended by a preist who teaches him what he pleases to Learn if he Compasses writing & reading he is thought to be sufficiently learned the rest of his time must be given up to his Exercises in Which indeed they are in General very clever & in Riding Particularly in which they are said to Equal at Least any other nation

10

Traveling is forbid here under the Severest Penalties Which is Doubtless the reason why they are so much behind the rest of Europe in improvements of all Kinds & taste which they are in Every particular remarkably Deficient in the Whole City of Lisbon will not Produce one hansome building of any Kind nor did I see one Good Picture I was told indeed that there were some but Extreemly dificult to be seen as the People who they Belongd to would not Even give themselves the trouble of Shewing them But Put you of as not being Capable of Conceiving that any body could have a Curiosity to

See them 11

In their Churches they have an Idea of Magnificence far beyond what you see any where else among them but that without taste their Splendores as they Call the Box which Contains the host are ornamented with a Clumsey heap of immensely Valuable Diamonds as are the mitres of their Patriarch and archbishops but with as little taste as Brass nails upon a Coffin in England

Massey Gold & Silver you also find in Every corner & Chapple in their Churches in Vast abundance forming Every Kind of Ornament one Chapple in St Roylues however Deserves to be taken Particular notice of from its immense

12

Riches which indeed are Disposd with more taste than any thing Else of the Kind tho that is Paying them no great Compliment here are three Pictures in Mosaick Work said by the Portugese to be first things of there Kind in the World the Pillars which are 16 or 18 inches in diameter are inlayd with Lapis Lazuli & Every other ornament is Massy Silver Gilt the whole was made at Rome

These peices of Expence Serve to Shew how much they were attach'd to their Religion a few years ago they were the Greatest bigots in the world but now the Case is very materialy alterd since

The Expulsion of the Jesuits in Consequence of an attempt to assassinate the Present King it has been Daily Loosing Ground the Present Prime minister Conde Oyares Governs the Church Just as absolutely as the State Subjecting the Inquisition Even to his Power who dare no more make use of their Secret Processes but are reduced nearly to the same footing as other Courts of Judicature[150]

In the Case of the Prime minister the government of Portugal is most Particular the King here is as absolute as man can be the Lives & fortunes of his Subjects depending intirely upon his will

14

without any controul which Power he exercises I may say wantonly imprisoning for life & without any reason given almost without Process giving the Portugese Frequent opportunities of making use of their favourite word Patientia a Virtue which they Possess to a surprising degree as the King is absolute over all so the Prime minister is next to him in absoluteness Governing Every body Else and so tenaciosis is he of that Priviledge that he will not suffer any body to govern but himself he himself manages Every Material Department which makes publick business here more tedious than any where

15

Else all the inferior offices he himself fills up with his Creatures who he turns out upon the Least offence given by them if a Judge who he orders to give a particular Sentence should refuse he would be Changd the next day of which instances are frequent & yet the Portugese bear Even this without a murmur except shrugging up their Shoulders & crying Patientia may be Calld one

Patientia in Cases of Government at Least may truly be said to be the motto of these people who certainly shew the most abject submission to their Governors of any people in the world tho in Cases of receiving Private Injuries their Behaviour

16

nothing Less than the Blood of the Person offending will satisfie them & that at the distance of years if they cannot sooner get an opportunity Poison or the Knife are the methods they make use of a Duel is a thing that hardly happens once in an age so Carefull are they of Putting themselves upon an Equal footing with an Enemy that they will follow him for months & years nay Even from Countrey to Countrey till they have him in their Power they Esteem an affront as a stain which nothing but the Blood of the Party offending can Wash out and are therefore never Easy till they have murtherd him which when they have done they

17

return home Easy and happy

These kind of Murthers are Renderd Easy by their Cloaks which are a Part of the Dress I may say of Every man in Portugal from the highest to the Lowest they Consist of a Large peice of Cloth Gatherd at one End which Goes over their Shoulders whilst the other falls down to their feet their method of Wearing them is to take the Right hand flap & throw it over the Left Shoulder raising it with their right hand as high over their faces as they Please often as high as their noses by which means they are Easily Disguisd beyond a Possibility of being known especialy in the night when as there are no Lamps in the City dark places

18

are Very Frequent, in this way they attack bringing their hands under the Skirt of the Cloak if they should miss their Blow & the Person attackd attempt to Defend himself with his sword they immediately with the Right hand bring the Cloak under the Right arm & throw it over the Left hand where it Lies in a fold impenetrable from its thickness upon this they receive their adversaries Point & Passing it on one side immediately Close in & Strike him with the Knife

Murthers of this Kind formerly happend every night but of Late are much Less frequent on account of an Edick Lately Passd which

19

makes the Penalty very severe upon those who are found with any Sharp instrument even a pen knife in their Possession Except swords which are to be Carried openly & not Conceald the Police also has been new modeld & is now I beleive one of the Strictest in Europe from the number of Soldiers Constantly Passing about the City throughout the whole night

7

Notes on the diary

1. Mrs. B. Harrington, former Librarian, Royal Astronomical Society, considers that this was probably Comet 1766 (II) which was first observed at Dillingen on 1 April, and at Paris on 8 April of that year. See J. G. Galle, *Verzeichniss der Elemente der bisher berechneten Cometenbahnen, nebst Anmerkungen und Literatur-Nachweisen.* . . . Leipzig, 1894. See also *Nature*, 22 April 1875: 489, where notes on its orbit are given. Banks's joke about comets was omitted by his sister Sophia when she transcribed his diary.

2. There are many amusing references to Lord and Lady Edgcumbe in Fanny Burney's early diary.

2a. Protuberant eyes are not always obvious in young goldfish and may not appear for several years. These and other varietal characteristics are aberrations which have only persisted in goldfish on account of their protection by man. Shisan Chen records that their domestication in China began in the Sung Dynasty A.D. 960–1278. They were introduced into England about 1691. For an interesting account of their cultivation and history see G. F. Hervey and J. Hems, *The Goldfish*, 1948 (2nd edition, 1967).

3. This was probably a dark red *Actinia*. Banks refers to it on p. 6 as purple.

4. The Five-bearded Rockling *Ciliata mustela* (L.) resembles a Stone Loach. It is common under stones and weed between the tidemarks in the Plymouth area where the Common Blenny *Blennius pholis* L. lives in the rock pools. There are drawings of both species by Sydney Parkinson (pl. 24a, b) and Plymouth is written on the verso of that of the Blenny.

5. William Cookworthy (1705–80), important in the early development of English china. He discovered kaolin, and porcelain granite or fine china clay in Cornwall. A collection of his china ware is in the city museum at Plymouth. (Prideaux 1847 and D.N.B.)

6. These ingredients are granites in varying stages of kaolinization. The metallic grains could be löllingite but are more probably biotite.

7. There is a stibnite from Wadebridge at the British Museum (Natural History) but it seems more likely that this was jamesonite which has been found nearby with other alteration products.

8. Only three of Banks's botanical specimens from Plymouth have been located. It seems certain, however, that this was *Quercus suber* and not a *Phellodendron* since the former species is supposed to have been introduced into England in the late seventeenth century and flourishes in the south western counties, whereas the latter was not brought here until the nineteenth century and is less suited to this climate. The whereabouts of Banks's British herbarium is unknown.

9. Stoneham is on the outskirts of Reading. It was a large house which has been converted into flats. There is no tulip tree in the garden now.

10. *Tipula nigra* L. is a valid species of cranefly but its larvae live in marshy ground and are unlikely to have been found on shipboard unless taken there in ballast.

11. There are three specimens of *Ascophyllum nodosum* collected by Banks in the British Museum. Two are mounted on small sheets, one is unlocalized and may have been the specimen taken here; the other is marked 'Newfoundland'. This is probably one recorded in the diary on 3 May. The third specimen is marked '*nodosus* young sp^m' in Banks's MS; no locality is given on the sheet.

12. There are also two similar sheets of *Halidrys siliquosa*, one is marked 'Newfoundland' although Taylor (1957:189) stated that this species was not currently known from that coast. The Newfoundland specimen was seen in the Banksian herbarium by Turner who recorded it in 1811 (3:57–8).

13. *Chlidonias niger*, the Black Tern, frequents marshes and lagoons but at this time of the year migrating flocks may be seen at sea.

14. Rodney's Island, non-existent now as then.

15. *Fucus acinarius* is now *Sargassum acinarium* (L.) C. Ag. which has not been recorded from this region; the limits of range of *Sargassum* spp. are not yet clearly defined.

16. Blubber is a common nautical term for jellyfish; the first of these may have been a species of *Pelagia*; the second description applies to several genera.

17. An amphipod, *Hyperia galba* (Montagu), occasionally taken on *Rhizostoma*, *Chrysaora*, etc.

18. The word insect was generally used in Banks's time for any small invertebrate. The description suggests a species of *Muggiaea*, a siphonophore.

19. There are no true penguins in the northern hemisphere but this name was originally (1536) applied to the Great Auk in the vicinity of Newfoundland (Newton 1893–6:703–4), and sometimes to its smaller relatives. The French still use the word 'pingouin' for an auk and 'manchot' for a penguin.

20. Possibly a species of ctenophore. These animals are very difficult to preserve, as Banks implies.

21. This may have been *Laminaria longicruris*, described by La Pylaie in 1825 (p. 177). He says 'Il est rare que l'on approche de Terre-Neuve, ou des îles des Saint-Pierre et Miclon, sans rencontrer, à la surface de la mer, cette grande plante marine: elle ressemble à un large baudrier.' There is a much branched holdfast.

22. There are three Banksian sheets of *Alectoria* spp. from Newfoundland in the British Museum, and a few other lichens but none of the species noted here. *Lichen lanatus* Huds. is now *Alectoria bicolor* (Ehrh.) Nyl.; *L. lanatus* L. is now *Ephebe lanata* (L.) Vainio, a much smaller species and likely to have been overlooked by Banks. According to La Pylaie (1826:505) the abundant growth of *Alectoria sarmentosa* (Ach. ex Libjebl.) Ach. and *A. trichodes* (now *Usnea trichoidea* Ach.) on old fir trees in Newfoundland forests had led to the sailors telling him that bears were so common there that their hair was to be found hanging from the branches of almost every tree.

23. Banks's specimens of *Lycopodium annotinum* L., *L. dendroideum* Michx. and *L. sabini-folium* Willd. var. *sitchense* (Rupr.) Fern., as well as some other *Lycopodium* spp. mentioned later in the diary, are still in the British Museum but no specimen of *L. clavatum* L. collected by him has been found, although it occurs in Newfoundland.

24. *Parus ater* L., the Coal Tit, does not occur in North America, and it seems that Banks had a specimen of the Black-capped Chickadee *Parus atricapillus bartletti* (Aldrich & Nutt), a common resident in Newfoundland. It was probably the specimen listed without a key number in his keg contents as *Parus palustris*, the Marsh Tit. This entry in Banks's diary is almost certainly the basis of Pennant's statement (1785:424) that a 'Colemouse' had been shot during the summer in Newfoundland.

25. Linnaeus based his description of the nominate race of *Turdus migratorius* on Catesby's account. Banks gave further details in the McGill MS, pp. 75–6. He had at least four skins in his keg, and one of a female in his London collection.

26. *Cimex lineatus* L. is a common Mediterranean species of Shield Bug (Pentatomidae) which does not occur in America. It is just possible that Banks had a specimen of *Poecilo-capsus lineatus* (Fabr.), a common bug (Miridae) in Quebec, Ontario and New England. Although this species was not described by Fabricius until 1798 (in the genus *Lygaeus*) it would have been regarded by Banks as a *Cimex*. It is yellow with four black longitudinal lines whereas *C. lineatus* is terra cotta with black lines. I am indebted to Dr. W. E. China for this information.

27. Dr. Carl Lindroth considers that this beetle may have been *Carabus maeander* Fisch.–W. a rather similar species. *C. granulatus* L., which has been introduced from Europe, has been recorded only from the maritime provinces further south (see also Lindroth 1957).

28. *Salvelinus fontinalis* is common in these waters. See *Newfld. Fish Res. Com.* 1932:107.

29. *Gasterosteus aculeatus* L., the Stickleback, is a widespread Palaearctic species.

30. Banks gave an account of this Savannah Sparrow *Passerculus sandwichensis* (Gmelin) in the McGill MS, p. 88, as *Fringilla* sp., 19:3, no. 2. There were five skins in his keg. He was actually the discoverer of the species but twenty-three years elapsed before it was described by Gmelin from a specimen taken on the west coast of North America during Cook's third voyage. Gmelin was mistaken in thinking that it came from Hawaii, then named one of the Sandwich Islands by Cook after Lord Sandwich, First Lord of the Admiralty, a great friend of Banks and a warm supporter of Cook.

31. This could have been *Cassandra calyculata* var. *angustifolia* (Aiton) Rehder but was more probably var. *latifolia* (Aiton) Fern. since Aiton says that this is a native of Newfoundland (1789, 2:70).

32. Banks wrote *arrosus* after *Cancer*, but deleted it and in fact that species, now *Dardanus arrosus* (Herbst), does not occur in Newfoundland waters. Forster (1771:33) lists the 'Common Crabfish *Cancer maenas*' from Newfoundland in the collection of Mr. B. (i.e. Banks, see p. 400) which is very likely a reference to this specimen. *Carcinus maenas* (Pennant) although a widely distributed species has not been recorded from Newfoundland and it is probable that Banks collected *Cancer irroratus* Say which does occur there; in its young stages it is not easily distinguished from *C. maenas*. Dr. H. J. Squires tells me that there has been a population explosion of *C. maenas* on the east coast of North America in recent years but that it has not been recorded north of Nova Scotia.

33. Sculpin is a name often applied to Bullheads of the family Cottidae. Pennant (1787:118) described *Myoxocephalus scorpius* (L.), very probably from one of Banks's specimens, and said that it was common off the coast of Newfoundland. Other species currently known as sculpin are mentioned in the reports of the Newfoundland Fishery Research Commission (1932:108, etc.). See also p. 407.

34. This was probably the Newfoundland shell of *Chlamys islandicus* (Müller) which still exists in Banks's shell collection at the British Museum (Wilkins 1955:108). Solander states that Banks took it from a cod's maw but this is probably an error; *Cyrtodaria siliqua* (Spengler) is typically taken from cod for bait and Banks had that bivalve also. See diary 25, n. 56.

35. There are very few echinoids known from Newfoundland. This was probably *Strongylocentrotus droebachiensis* (O. F. Müller).

36. *Cancer diogenes* is now *Diogenes diogenes* (Herbst), but this hermit crab does not occur in Newfoundland waters and some other crab must be intended.

37. The unidentified moss collected on 15 May.

38. Banks's specimens unfortunately now lack flowers but have glandular young leaves and correspond to *Empetrum nigrum* L. as accepted by Fernald. According to A. Löve and D. Löve (1959:36) Newfoundland and other North American specimens referred to *E. nigrum* belong to *E. hermaphroditum* (Lange) Hagerup, but see p. 333.

39. The genus *Cyperus* is not represented in Newfoundland; Banks may have collected *Dulichium arundinaceum* (L.) Britt. which occurs there and at that time was included in *Cyperus*. He is not likely to have mistaken an immature *Eriophorum* for *Cyperus* since he was familiar with European *Eriophorum* spp.

40. Banks's account of the Swamp Sparrow *Melospiza georgiana ericrypta* Oberholser in the McGill MS, pp. 89–90, bears the index number 22:4, no. 4, which corresponds with this entry.

41. Probably a young Kittiwake, *Rissa tridactyla tridactyla* (L.). Banks's short account of this particular specimen, McGill MS, p. 90, 22:5, no. 5, is inadequate but he made detailed descriptions of other specimens, McGill MS, pp. 27–30; there were two skins of the species in his keg, and see Parkinson's plate 80.

42. Banks wrote two accounts of this Fox Sparrow, *Passerella iliaca iliaca* (Merrem); first as *Fringilla* sp., from St. John's, McGill MS, pp. 88–9, 22:6, no. 3; then as *Fringilla betula* from Croque, McGill MS, pp. 81–2, 27:28, the latter specimen was taken on 7 October. Parkinson's specimen pl. 1, was labelled *F. betula* and probably represents the Croque bird. Merrem's description published in 1786 was based on a specimen brought to Europe by a German officer from North America without precise locality.

43. Banks's specimen of the purple *Viola adunca* Smith var. *minor* (Hook.) Fern. comes from St. John's. He also collected *V. cucullata* Ait. but there is no locality other than Newfoundland on the herbarium sheet. There are blue and white forms of this species but the specimens are too faded to show any indication of their original colour. There are other *Viola* spp. in Newfoundland.

44. Banks's specimens of *Coptis groenlandica* (Oeder) Fern. are marked 'Newfoundland dampish and shady places'. There is no locality against his catalogue entry, p. 9a.

45. *Polytrichum alpinum* Hedwig occurs in Newfoundland but there are no Banksian specimens in the British Museum.

46. Banks's sheet of *Scirpus hudsonianus* (Michx.) Fern. was determined by him as *Eriophorum alpinum*; the name is written on his sheet of specimens from St. John's and Croque, and appears also in his catalogue, p. 5. Since this is the only 'Cotton Grass' he recorded from St. John's it was almost certainly this *Scirpus*. Cotton Grass is the common name for *Eriophorum* spp.; there are a number of species on the Avalon Peninsula.

47. *Polypodium aculeatum* is now *Polystichum aculeatum* (L.) Roth but this fern does not occur in Newfoundland; Banks may well be referring to *Dryopteris carthusiana* (Vill.) H. P. Fuchs which is still among his Newfoundland specimens.

48. For the description of this Black Guillemot see the McGill MS, pp. 23, 91, 23:7, no. 6.

49. This was probably the specimen of *Fucus distichus* L. brought back by Banks from Newfoundland. It is of considerable interest since it was also recorded by La Pylaie (1829:9) but according to Taylor (1957:189) is not currently known from these coasts.

50. *Blennius gattorugina* Bloch does not occur in Newfoundland; Banks decided that in fact this was an eel and in his keg list it is placed in the genus *Muraena* with the number corresponding to this entry. There are no notes or drawings known at present by which it can be identified.

51. Banks understandably confused this Spotted Sandpiper, *Actitis macularia* (L.), with the European Common Sandpiper, *Actitis hypoleucos* (L.); they are indistinguishable save in breeding plumage but *A. hypoleucos* does not occur in North America. See his description, McGill MS, p. 91, 24:3, no. 7, and his keg list.

52. The Pine Grosbeak. See McGill MS, p. 91, 24:3, no. 7, and Banks's keg list.

53. Banks's specimens of *Gaultheria hispidula* (L.) Bigel. are marked 'Newfoundland shady places everywhere'; one of them, pl. 58, was drawn by Ehret and Banks has written 'St. John's' on the back of the plate.

54. *Ribes glandulosum* was described by Grauer in 1784 from material collected in Labrador by Brassen, a surgeon working with the Moravians who was drowned in a boating accident in 1774. L'Héritier published a description of the same species as *Ribes prostratum* in 1785, giving the locality as Terra Nova. A sheet of his cultivated material from Paris dated 1784, probably derived from Banks, is in the British Museum with Banks's own specimens from St. John's dated June 1766.

55. Honeycombstone is the common name for *Favosites*, a fossil coral found in Silurian rocks in England and elsewhere, including Newfoundland.

56. *Cyrtodaria siliqua* (Spengler), a bivalve still taken from cod's stomachs for bait; these molluscs are known by the French name of 'pitot' and the areas where they live are called 'pitot banks'. See also fn. 34.

57. Banks's account of Wilson's Warbler, *Wilsonia pusilla*, in the McGill MS, p. 92, has the appropriate number for this entry, 26:2, no. 9. He appears to have used the name Gold Bird for two different warblers, *W. pusilla*, and the Yellow Warbler *Dendroica petechia amnicola* Batchelder. A descriptive note below Parkinson's painting, pl. 83, of the Yellow Warbler

is a quotation from Linnaeus. (See Systematic List, p. 419). There were four skins of 'gold birds' in Banks's keg. See also n. 58.

58. This bird is rather puzzling. In the keg list there is an entry '26:3 *Fringilla* species' but no description of a finch with such a number. In the McGill MS, p. 92, however, after the notes on *Wilsonia pusilla*, numbered 26:2, no. 9, there is an entry 30:8, no. 10, which may relate to this bird with a shrill note since although it concerns a warbler and not a finch the number 30:8 has been written over 24:3, a correction of an obvious slip as that number refers to *Actitis macularia*, n. 51. Did Banks first mean to write 26:3, no. 10? If so, this note on p. 26 probably refers to the same species as his note 30:8, no. 10 on p. 30; the descriptive note in the McGill MS, p. 93, shows that this was a female or immature Wilson's Warbler.

59. This was the *Hirundinis* recorded in the keg list.

60. Banks collected many species of *Carex* but there is nothing to link any of his notes or specimens with this entry.

61. Banks collected both *Equisetum palustre* L. and *E. sylvaticum* L. but these are both labelled Newfoundland only; other species are found there.

62. *Alsinanthemos* was a pre-Linnaean name given by John Ray to the European member of the genus *Trientalis*.

63. Banks's only specimen of *Rubus* from St. John's now in the British Museum is *R. pubescens* Raf. which was labelled by him 'shady woods Croque St. John's'.

64. *Juncus campestris* is a synonym of *Luzula campestris* (L.) DC. *L. multiflora* was formerly regarded as a variety of *campestris* but is now accepted as having specific rank. Banks's specimens bear his determination of *Juncus campestris*, but no locality save Newfoundland. Since, however, there is no other mention of the species in any of his papers it would seem that St. John's can be taken as the locality where his specimens were collected.

65. *Juncus pilosus* L. was transferred to *Luzula* by Willdenow. In 1840 Rafinesque separated the American species *L. acuminata* from *L. vernalis* DC. which is synonymous with *L. pilosa* (L.) Willd. (see Fernald, *Rhodora* 1944, 46:4, 5). There is no Banksian material of *Luzula acuminata* Raf. and in the absence of any other records of this species from the Avalon Peninsula Banks's determination must be regarded as doubtful.

66. There are in the British Museum three sheets of *Carex atratiformis* Britton collected by Banks. K. K. Mackenzie (1935:371–2) states that *Carex atrata* L. occurs in alpine and arctic North America but Raymond (1950) in his study of *Carex* and *Kobresia* from Anticosti Island shows that in eastern North America *C. atrata* is an arctic species found in northern Labrador, which is replaced in southern Labrador and Newfoundland by *C. atratiformis*. Thus Banks's statement that he collected *C. atrata* at St. John's must refer to his specimens of *C. atratiformis* Britton. For full notes on this *Carex* see the systematic list, p. 319.

67. There is no reason to doubt Banks's determination of *Scirpus cespitosus* L. His only surviving material in the British Museum, however, came from Croque.

68. Banks's two sheets of *Alnus crispa* (Ait.) Pursh are both marked Newfoundland without further locality but one sheet shows ripe catkins and may be assumed to be the specimen referred to here. Aiton's diagnosis (1789, 3:339) of *Betula crispa* is identical with that in

Solander MS 19:45. Both give the distribution as Newfoundland (on the authority of Banks's material according to Solander's MS) and Hudson's Bay whence it was sent to Kew Gardens in 1782.

69. This may have been *Andromeda glaucophylla* Link, but there is no material nor an entry in Banks's catalogue to support this. His specimens of *Kalmia polifolia* Wangenheim are labelled *Kalmia glauca*, a synonym published by Aiton a year after Wangenheim's description; all the notes on both species refer to their having been collected at Croque, and in the case of *A. glaucophylla* also at Chateau Bay. Banks clearly distinguished between the genera *Andromeda* and *Kalmia* in his catalogue.

70. Banks's specimens of *Fragaria virginiana* Duch. from St. John's were determined by G. Staudt in 1958. Banks noted that he found no specimens at Croque but the date on the herbarium sheet is wrong since he gave it as May instead of June.

71. Banks's specimens of this *Ranunculus* come from Croque, but Lyman Benson (1948:230) records it from the vicinity of Quiddy Viddy, i.e. Kitty Vitty, Lake. Other plants collected at St. John's were:

Eleocharis acicularis (L.) R. & S.	*Streptopus roseus* Michx.
Eriocaulon septangulare With.	*Thalictrum polygamum* Muhl.
Juncus trifidus L.	*Vaccinium macrocarpon* Ait.
Polygonum sagittatum L.	*Veronica serpyllifolia* L.
Sisyrinchium angustifolium Mill.	

72. This seems to be the entry 30:8 superimposed upon 26:3 in the McGill MS and discussed in n. 58 above.

73. Banks's detailed description, McGill MS 30:9, no. 11, shows that this was a female Black-polled Warbler, *Dendroica striata* (Forster).

74. *Vaccinium mucronatum* L. is now *Nemopanthus mucronatus* (L.) Baillon, a species commonly found in the south of Newfoundland but rare and localized in the Northern Peninsula. Full notes on Banks's determination and on the authorship of the name of the species are given in the systematic list of plants (p. 333).

75. According to his catalogue Banks collected four species of orchids at Croque which he referred to the genus *Ophrys*. His specimen of *Corallorhiza trifida* Chat. from Croque was labelled by him *Ophrys corallorhiza* and may well have been this specimen.

76. This bramble was probably *Rubus pubescens* Raf. since when Banks was at Croque he collected this species which is close to *R. arcticus* L.; it should be noted however that material of *Rubus acaulis* Michaux which he collected at St. Julian's Isle and Hare Bay was determined by him as *R. arcticus*.

76a. One of the specimens of *Betula pumila* collected by Banks at Croque has very small leaves and is probably his *B. nana*. His writing on the herbarium sheet is no longer legible.

77. Banks catalogued these primulas as 'Primula farinosa, bogs, Croque' but in fact he had both *P. mistassinica* Michx. forma *leucantha* Fern. and *P. laurentiana* Fern. and his specimens are labelled 'Bogs Croque'. He made further notes about them in the McGill MS (p. 341).

78. Banks left a detailed description of this vole (see p. 394) and it is in any case the only endemic microtine known from Newfoundland. See his p. 101.

79. This plant of *Petasites palmatus* (Ait.) A. Gray from Croque is the type of Aiton's species, and Ehret's painting, reproduced in *Hortus Kewensis* 3: facing p. 188, is a representation of this very plant. See pl. IX.

80. *Kalmia latifolia* L. does not occur in Newfoundland, and it is probable that Banks is here referring to *K. angustifolia* since his specimens of this are marked 'Hillsides, Croque' whereas his plants of *K. polifolia* Wang. are labelled 'Damp places, Croque'.

81. Banks's determination is acceptable although his surviving specimens are from 'Dry tops of hills, St. John's'.

82. Banks's specimens of *Carex pauciflora* Lightf. are marked 'Newfoundland' only; he may have given some material to Lightfoot who refers to Banks's Labrador material (1777, 2:544).

83. Banks identified this Belted Kingfisher correctly, and gave a clear description of it in the McGill MS, pp. 47, 48. The plates to which he refers are in Catesby, 1731: pl. 69, and Edwards, 1750, 3: pl. 115.

84. The Northern Shrike *Lanius excubitor borealis* Vieillot is the only shrike that occurs regularly in Newfoundland. Banks's description is missing but since he had a skin labelled *Lanius excubitor* from Labrador in his London collection (p. 402) he is unlikely to have made a mistake in his determination here. Cartwright had a pair nesting close to his house in Labrador in May 1779, and he shot and stuffed both birds. It is possible that it was one of these which came into Banks's collection.

85. Banks's description of Swainson's Thrush, *Hylocichla ustulata clarescens* Burleigh & Peters, in the McGill MS, pp. 77, 78, is amplified by notes in Pennant's *Arctic Zoology* (1785:338), and it is on this basis that I have identified this bird.

86. Banks's specimens of *Carex gynocrates* Wormsk. were determined by him as *Carex dioica* and since he catalogued this species from 'Bogs Croque' it seems that this entry in his diary refers to those specimens although the only locality marked on the sheet is 'Newfoundland'.

87. Poiret, who saw Michaux's material, described *Ribes lacustre* (1811:856) quoting his account (1803, 1:111) of a plant from the borders of Lake Mistassini which he, Michaux, queried as *R. oxyacanthoides*, a European species referred to by Poiret as *R. grossularoides* (*lapsus calami*). No Newfoundland material collected by Banks has been found but there is a sheet marked by him 'Hort. Fothergill 1781, *Ribes armatum* MSS' which was, perhaps, grown from seed brought back from Newfoundland. *Ribes armatum* is an unpublished name of Solander's (6:611) given to material apparently from North America. It seems clear that there was some confusion about its origin since in Banks's annotated copy of the *Species Plantarum* (1762, 1: facing p. 291) Solander has left a blank after 'Hab.', and this is also the case in the annotated copy of Reichard's edition of the *Systema Plantarum* (1799, 1: facing p. 566).

88. Banks collected *Juncus balticus* Willd. from Croque but whether this entry in the diary refers to that species or not is uncertain since the herbarium sheet is marked '*Juncus effusus* Bogs near the sea Croque' while the catalogue entry for that species is 'Bogs and near the sea'.

89. *Erigeron philadelphicus* L. occurs in Newfoundland but there is no material to support Banks's determination and the only confirmation of it is his catalogue entry in which he has omitted the marks of interrogation.

90. This owl appears to have been the Hawk Owl *Surnia ulula caparoch* (Müller) noted by Banks both at Croque and Chateau Bay, McGill MS, p. 39, 10:11; the number of the description does not correspond with this entry in his diary. See Parkinson's pl. II.

91. In Banks's list of skins in his London collection there is an entry '148 *unicolor Turdus* corpore toto atro caerulescente 1 Labrador', which is an adequate description of a male Rusty Blackbird, *Euphagus carolinus* (Müller). This record is confirmed by Pennant (1785: 340) who describes a male in breeding plumage from Labrador. Latham (1783:46) gives further details and states that a specimen from Labrador was in Banks's collection. None of the skins in Banks's list of his London collection is referred to Newfoundland; some of the Labrador entries may include birds shot in Newfoundland. See p. 402.

92. Polar bears were recorded on Funk Island in May 1534 by Cartier, who wrote 'Notwithstanding that the island lies fourteen leagues from shore, bears swim out to it from the mainland in order to feed on these birds; and our men found one as big as a calf and as white as a swan that sprang into the sea in front of them' (*The Voyages of Jacques Cartier*, ed. H. P. Biggar 1924:9). Polar bears still come as far south as St. John's from time to time. Seven years after Banks and Phipps were in Newfoundland Phipps led an expedition towards the North Pole in search of a north-east passage to the East Indies. He collected several animals for Banks, including a polar bear which was described and given a scientific binomial for the first time in his published account of the voyage (1774).

The only plants recorded by Banks from St. Julian's were *Alchemilla filicaulis* Buser and *Rubus acaulis* Michx.

93. Banks's specimens of this *Potentilla* are marked Croque, not Inglie.

94. There is one sheet of *Poa pratensis* L. marked by Banks 'Grassy places Croque', and a second of *Poa* cf. *pratensis*, too damaged for precise determination, labelled by him *Poa trivialis* (almost illegible) from the same location.

95. Banks catalogued a willow from Inglie as *Salix repens*, a name used by Pursh (1814: 610) for a willow from Newfoundland and Nova Scotia, which he saw in Banks's herbarium. Pursh's use of the name is now regarded as applying to *Salix argyrocarpa* Anderss. but this species has not been recorded from Newfoundland. Many species of willow are prostrate in Newfoundland and since no Banksian specimens marked *S. repens* have been located recently it is impossible to decide which one he collected here on what is now known as Englée Island.

96. Banks's Newfoundland specimens of *Draba incana* L. come from Croque not Inglie.

97. The specimens and painting (pl. 50) of *Potentilla nivea* L. are labelled Conche and Croque, respectively.

98. *Anemone parviflora* Michx. grows in both wet and dry situations. Banks's specimens are labelled 'Newfoundland Croque Inglie Rocks near the waters edge'; Ehret's painting (pl. 48) appears to be a composite representation of this material and is marked 'Croque'.

99. The locality on Banks's specimens of *Minuartia rubella* (Wahlenb.) Hiern is 'Newfoundland Croque etc. dry hillsides', and he determined it as *Arenaria saxatilis*, a synonym of the closely allied *M. verna*. Saxatilis has been crossed out and *juniperina* written over it. *A. juniperina* Pursh was based partly on Willdenow's *A. juniperina* from Armenia and partly on Banks's material from Newfoundland and Labrador which is therefore part of the type collection.

100. Pursh (1814:311) stated that Banks collected *Saxifraga oppositifolia* L. from both Newfoundland and Labrador but the only material I have found is this specimen from Inglie.

Other species collected at Inglie were *Dryas integrifolia* Vahl, *Oxytropis terrae-novae* Fern., and *Rhododendron canadense* (L.) Torrey.

101. Banks's specimen of *Epilobium angustifolium* is marked 'Newfoundland' only.

102. Banks collected several plants from Conche which he visited again in early August. See fn. 105.

103. It is clear that Banks collected a larger number of insects than I have been able to trace. It is possible that some of his Newfoundland species are amongst the uncatalogued paintings by Sydney Parkinson, and there may be unrecognized specimens in his insect collection at the British Museum, since this has never been completely worked out. An experienced Newfoundland entomologist might find riches there, but the scarcity of locality labels makes it a very difficult collection to deal with.

104. The species collected at Belle Isle de Groais, now Bell Island, were *Aralia nudicaulis* L., *Epilobium latifolium* L., *Lomatogonium rotatum* (L.) Fries, *Luzula parviflora* (Ehrh.) Desv., *Lychnis dioica* L., *Nemopanthus mucronatus* (L.) Baillon, *Oxyria digyna* (L.) Hill, *Saxifraga aizoides* L. and *S. paniculata* Miller (= *S. aizoön* Jacq.). Notes on these plants are given in the systematic list, pp. 311–48. Bell Island was probably well wooded at the time of Banks's visit (cf. map, p. 334). The name Belle Isle is now used for the island in the strait between the Northern Peninsula and Labrador. Banks did not visit it.

105. The note on the bear suggests that it was on this occasion that Banks landed at Conche and collected the following species: *Agrostis hyemalis* (Walt.) B.S.P., *A. tenuis* Sibth., *Calamagrostis canadensis* (Michx.) Nutt., *Gymnocarpium dryopteris* (L.) Newm. *Lobelia dortmanna* L., *Lychnis dioica* L., *Monotropa uniflora* L., *Osmunda claytoniana* L., *Potentilla nivea* L., *P. tridentata* Ait., *Ranunculus flammula* L. var. *filiformis* (Michx.) Hook., *Sparganium angustifolium* Michx. *Thlaspi arvense* L. and *Veronica serpyllifolia* (L.). For details see list, pp. 311–48.

105a. Banks makes only the briefest references to seasickness in his diaries, but Sir Everard Home, one of the closest friends of his later years, told this story of him in the Hunterian Oration of 1822: 'Early in the voyage [to Newfoundland] it blew a gale which made him dreadfully seasick, and unable to keep his legs upon deck: determined not to go below he made himself fast to a gun, by means of ropes knotted and twisted in all the different ways he could contrive. In this situation he was making the most solemn vows, that nothing should ever again tempt him to go to sea; these were interrupted by the mizen-topmast coming rattling down in the shrouds, immediately over his head; this sudden alarm put a stop to the sea-sickness, his mind being wholly occupied in disengaging himself, and trying to escape from the impending danger.'

106. Amongst the birds collected by Banks at Chateau Bay were Rock and Willow Ptarmigan, Spruce Grouse, Harlequin Duck, Pintail, Surf Scoter, Common Scoter, Green- and Blue-Winged Teal, all of which are discussed in the notes on the McGill MS.

107. Banks's note on the Eskimo Curlew appears to be the first account of the great flocks of this species on the Labrador coast. Nearly twenty years later Pennant (1785:461) published the dates of the arrival and departure of these birds, obviously from Banks's papers: 'Seen in flocks innumerable, on the hills about Chateaux Bay, on the Labrador

Coast, from August 9th to September 6th.' Banks's informant was of course wrong in suggesting that the birds wintered in the region of the Great Lakes. They used to migrate over the Atlantic to the eastern areas of South America, and most of them wintered on the campos of Argentina (J. C. Greenway 1958:264; Swenk 1916:325–40). These birds have been regarded as extinct for many years but recently they have been reported regularly, although in very small numbers. The illustration of the Eskimo Curlew in Pennant's *Arctic Zoology* (1785:463, pl. 19) is based on Parkinson's painting which is reproduced in this volume, pl. III.

108. Caribou, *Rangifer tarandus* (L.), were the only deer found in Newfoundland–Labrador. According to Taylor White a pair of living caribou were captured and taken alive to England *en route* for Holland in 1769. Paintings of them by Charles Collins are in the Blacker-Wood Library at McGill University.

109. Basque whalers operated off the Labrador coast as early as the sixteenth century. Gosling (1910:131–5) speaks of the enormous quantity of old whalebone found at Bradore by Courtemanche when he established a settlement there in 1704; he estimated that there were remains of two to three thousand whales. See also the Moravians' diary for 18 July 1765.

110. Solander (MSS 14:67) gave this Scurvy Grass the MS name of *Cochlearia tridactylites*; it was ultimately published by DeCandolle (1821, 2:367). The syntype material consists of specimens from Whale Island in Chateau Bay and from St. Peter's Islands (now a Federal Bird Sanctuary); there is a third specimen from the Moravians without locality other than Labrador.

111. When Banks was in Newfoundland the Beothuk Indians still lived in the interior of the island but he did not meet them for by that time they had been so harshly treated by the white fishermen (Howley 1915: 29–45; 233 ff.) that they avoided contact with them as far as possible. Howley pointed out that Cormack, who in 1822 walked across Newfoundland in an attempt to cultivate better relations with the Indians, 'did not credit the bloodthirsty stories of the fierce relentless disposition of the Indians current among the fisherfolk. He knew that in most instances their ferocity was grossly exaggerated for the purpose of forming an excuse for their own inhuman conduct.' Their condition in Banks's time was made worse by attacks from the Micmac Indians of Cape Breton and Nova Scotia who had procured firearms from the French settlers of Acadia and invaded Newfoundland. The Beothuks had only bows and arrows and were no match for them; none has survived.

The Eskimos of Labrador occupied coastal tundra and the neighbouring islands, fiords, shores and strips of woodland; the Indians lived in the forest lands and on the inland mountains and tundra. But the boundaries between the two were uncertain, and bitter disputes resulted when either people attempted to hunt in areas claimed by the other. Tanner (1944:440–700) surveys the characteristics and origins of both peoples at considerable length, and gives maps showing their distribution. Banks did not discriminate between them at all in 1766 and uses the word Indians for both races. See also pp. 83–9 of the introduction to this volume.

112. Cartwright (1792, 1:10) gives a more detailed account of Eskimo pudding, which he calls their sausages: 'They consisted of the flesh and fat of seals, eggs and a variety of other rich matter, stuffed into the gut of seals; for want of salt and spices, the composition had the *haut gout* to perfection. . . . It is a remarkable and almost incredible fact, that these people

should visit Funk Island, which lies forty miles from Cape Freels, and sixty from the Island of Fogo. The island being small and low they cannot see it from either of these places, nor is it possible to conceive, how they could get information from any other nation. The Indians repair thither once or twice every year, and return with their canoes laden with birds and eggs; for the number of sea-fowl which resort to this island to breed, are far beyond credibility.'

When Cape *Mutton* bears NE. about five Leagues off, it appears thus, with the Land to the Eastward of it.

Some Directions which ought to be taken Notice of by those who sail to Newfoundland.

THE Bank of *Newfoundland* would be of very great Service to those that are bound to that Coast, was the said Bank exactly laid down; therefore I inform you that are bound to that Coast that you may not be deceived, as I myself was like to have been in going to St. *John's*, on the 29th of *June*, 1715, at 8 a Clock in the Morning, and then in the Lat. of 48d. 44m. having been just a Month that very Day from *Plymouth* Sound, bound to St. *John's* was brought too, and founded, where we had 92 Fathom Water, fine white Sand, which I suppose to be the outward edge of the Bank: For after we had sailed From thence W. 26d. 30m. S. about 18 Miles, (don't mistake me, or rather don't *mistake yourselves by sailing* W. 26d. 30m. S. *for you must understand I made my Course good so, my Compass at that time having 19 deg. West Variation, understand the same of the other Courses,* &c.) we founded again, and had but 72 fath. fine Sand as before; and this I reckon'd the middle of the said Bank, or at least the shoalest part of it; for having sailed from this about 34 Miles upon a W. 28d. 00m. South Course, and then founded the third time, we

had 84 Fath. still very fine white Sand, but some pieces of flaty sort of Stones mix'd therewith; which is a great Sign you are going off the said Bank, that is between it and the Shore, &c. for after we had run 26 Miles more upon a W. by S. half S. Course, we had 100 fathom oazy Ground, and Slate Stones, as beforesaid; which may be taken for a certain Rule, that one is between the Bank and the Shore, having this quality of Ground and quantity of Water. Here I find a very great Error in those Charts that have been hitherto published, in laying down this Bank so far off the Shore as they do: For, by the aforesaid Observations, I made no more than 35 Leagues, from the first Sounding 92 fathom; which as I told you before, was the outer Edge of the Bank of St. *John's*, and from the said outer Edge, to the inward Edge between 16 and 17 Leagues, which is the Breadth of the Bank between the Lat. of 48d. 44m. and of 48d. 20m. &c. and from this inward Edge, 48d. 20m. to St. *John's*, which lies in the Lat. 47d. 50m. it is not above 18 Leag. between which is all very deep Water; for you have 60 and 50 Fath. to

Note, These Fowls never fly, for their Wings are very short, most like the Fins of a Fish, having nothing upon them but a sort of Down and short Feathers.

the very Rocks Nose, and the above-mentioned Charts make it above 40 Leag. from St. *John's* to the said inward Edge of the Bank, which is about 22 Leag. out of the way, (I suppose they look'd upon it 22 Leag. as nothing, where Water is so deep, or rather indeed, that they keep a very bad Account) and I think a very great Error in so small a Dist. and consequently very dangerous, if a Man should depend upon such a Chart; for very often you'll hear the Sea break upon the Shore, before you can see it, by reason of the constant Fog, especially from the Month of *May* to the Month of *July*, and most part of *August*, which is the time that all Ships bound to this Country generally come, and therefore ought to keep a very good look-out, lest they be deceived, &c.

There is also another thing to be taken Notice of by which you may know when you are upon the Bank, I have read an Author that says, in treating of this Coast, that you may know this

by the great quantities of Fowls upon the Bank, *viz. Sheer-waters, Willocks, Noddies, Gulls* and *Penguins,* &c. without making any Exceptions; which is a mistake, for I have seen all those Fowls 100 Leag. off this Bank, the *Penguins* excepted. It's true that all their Fowls are seen there in great quantities, but none are to be minded so much as the *Penguins,* for these never go without the Bank as the others do, for they are always on it, or within it, several of them together, sometimes more, other times less, but never less than 2 together; they are large Fowls about the bigness of a Goose, a cole black Head and Back, with a white Belly, and a Milk white Spot under one of their Eyes, which nature has ordered to be under the right Eye, and extraordinary remarkable: For my part I never saw any with such a Spot under their left Eye, the Figure of which I have here set down to facilitate the Knowledge of them, &c.

4. Page 19 from *The English Pilot. The fourth Book. Describing the West India Navigation, from Hudson's Bay to the River Amazones.* London, 1767

Funk Island was of course one of the chief breeding grounds of the Great Auk whose extinction was foreseen by Cartwright. In the third volume of his diary (p. 55) he records the depredations of the white fishermen on the island: 'When the water is smooth, they make their shallop fast to the shore, lay their gang-boards from the gunwale of the boat to the rocks, and then drive as many penguins [Great Auks] on board as she will hold; for, the wings of those birds being remarkably short, they cannot fly. But it has been customary of late years, for several crews of men to live all the summer on that island, for the whole purpose of killing birds for the sake of their feathers, the destruction which they have made is incredible. If a stop is not soon put to that practice, the whole breed will be diminished to almost nothing, particularly the penguins: for this is now the only island they have left to breed upon: all the others lying so near to the shores of Newfoundland, they are continually robbed. The birds which the people bring from thence, they salt and eat, in lieu of salted pork.' There is a useful account of this extinct species, and of the extensive literature on it, in Greenway (1958:271–91). Banks's Great Auk was taken in Chateau Bay (McGill MS,

168

p. 17). Its ultimate fate is unknown but it was too greasy to last long as a stuffed specimen; little was known at that time about preserving birds efficiently. Great Auks were so abundant on the Newfoundland Banks that they were illustrated in the *English Pilot* and used as an indicator in navigating Newfoundland waters (fig. 4, opposite).

113. Much of what Banks said about the fisheries was published by Pennant (1784: cxcvi–cxcviii). The most important commercial fish on the Newfoundland Banks was and is the cod *Gadus morhua* L. Today Newfoundlanders make an irreverent pun on 'Cod's country', and 'fish' unspecified always means cod.

114. Capelin, *Mallotus villosus* (Müller), spawns along the Newfoundland coast in June and July. The male is distinguished by the anal fin's being on a hump, and the pectoral fin's being relatively longer than in the female. Pennant (1787:141) mentions the swarms off Newfoundland. See the drawings by Parkinson, pl. 29a, b, c. The adjoining plate in Parkinson's drawings in the British Museum folio, 199* B 1, is of a Launce or Sand Eel, *Ammodytes* sp., and probably represents the American Sand Eel *Ammodytes americanus* De Kay. Someone has written *A. tobianus* on the drawing (pl. 89a). Pennant (1787:113) stated that the European Sand Eel *Ammodytes tobianus* L. was common off Newfoundland. The distinctions (if any) between the American and European species are now being investigated. Parkinson also made a drawing (pl. 89b) of a young cod, *Gadus morhua* L., from a specimen taken by Banks at St. John's. Newfoundland fishermen still call young cod 'Tomcod' but true Tomcod, *Microgadus tomcod* (Walbaum) is found only on the south and west coasts of Newfoundland.

115. Dr. Tuck tells me that Leach's Petrel, *Oceanodroma leucorhoa leucorhoa* (Vieillot), is still the most abundant sea bird in the Newfoundland area. Several million pairs breed on the islands off the Newfoundland coast. These birds make their nests at the end of a burrow one to three feet long in turf, not in rocks. Fishermen also netted murres and kittiwakes on Baccalieu Island.

115a. Train oil was an old term dating from the fifteenth century for any oil obtained by extraction or exudation; in Banks's time cod liver oil was largely used for dressing leather; whale and seal oil were used for lamps.

116. Mrs. Espinasse tells me that this is a song (ca. 1760) by Felice Giardini, eminent violinist and composer. He lived in London for a time, and was very friendly with Dr. Burney. A woodcut in Gesner (1558:138) shows a piper playing on a similar occasion in the Faroe Islands.

116a. This traditional meal is still in favour, under the name of 'fish and brewis'.

117. There are various flatfishes called flounders in Newfoundland waters, and there is nothing to indicate which species these were.

118. The common sea and brook trout in Newfoundland is *Salvelinus fontinalis* Mitchill, but the Arctic Char *Salvelinus alpinus* (L.) (pl. 87a, b), occurs in the Northern Peninsula and in Labrador. These vary in colour, the sea-run fish being silvery while the basic coloration of the fresh-water fish is red.

119. The American Eel is *Anguilla rostrata* (Lesueur).

120. It is most interesting that Banks should have recorded three species of curlew for Labrador; clearly, he has not made a slip in writing since he goes on to say 'both very good eating tho not so good as the first'. The Eskimo Curlew *Numenius borealis* (Forster) used

to be the commonest of these waders in Newfoundland-Labrador during the autumn migration, and we know that Banks collected it (n. 107) since we still have Parkinson's painting of one of his specimens and a description in the McGill MS 55–6. The second species was probably the Hudsonian Whimbrel *Numenius phaeopus hudsonicus* Latham. It migrates along that coast in the autumn, and Banks appears to have given Taylor White a specimen (p. 413). The third species is a mystery since all that Banks says about it is that it is not such good eating as the Eskimo Curlew. And if there is anyone in these days of bird protection who can discriminate between the species of North American curlews on a gustatory basis he or she is not likely to boast about such an accomplishment. Cartwright's notes seem to apply only to the Hudsonian Whimbrel and the Eskimo Curlew (ed. 1911: 207). Townsend and Allen (1907:353) state that Coues was assured that the Long-billed Curlew *Numenius americanus* Bechstein occurred in Labrador. They give reasons for doubting this but they thought it worth recording. Todd (1963:304–5) has seen it in the James Bay area.

121. The Golden Plover *Pluvialis dominica dominica* (Müller) was first recorded by Banks at Chateau Bay about 16 August, a week after the curlews had arrived but, as he said, 'not in near so great abundance'. Todd (1963: 293–6) discusses the migratory route of this plover. See also McGill MS, p. 25.

122. Banks left no detailed notes on these geese. They were probably the Canada Goose *Branta canadensis canadensis* (L.) which is the common breeding species in Newfoundland and Labrador.

123. Amongst the game birds from that region Banks described the Rock Ptarmigan *Lagopus mutus rupestris* (Gmelin) from Chateau Bay (McGill MS, p. 73). At the end of his notes on this species he gave a few particulars of some larger birds which were probably Willow Ptarmigan, *Lagopus lagopus albus* (Gmelin). Both Rock and Willow Ptarmigan have white wings in summer. Banks was much interested in seasonal colour changes in fur and feathers (see introduction pp. 79–82). By Heath Fowl he appears to have meant Red Grouse, *Lagopus scoticus scoticus* (Latham), males of which are 14–15½ inches in length, females 13–14 inches. Heath Cock and Heath Hen are old names for Black Game *Lyrurus tetrix britannicus* With. & Lönnb., used in the eighteenth century. Males of Black Game are 20–22 inches in length, females 16–17 inches; Spruce Grouse, *Canachites canadensis* (L.), is 15–17 inches; and Ruffed Grouse, *Bonasa umbellus* (L.) 16–19 inches. Banks's remarks here suggest that he may have had Ruffed Grouse but there is no other reference to that species. We know, however, that he had Spruce Grouse since he described it (McGill MS, p. 71) and Parkinson painted a pair, pl. V.

124. Banks described this loon in the McGill MS, p. 21.

125. Lords and Ladies is a popular name for the male and female Harlequin Ducks, *Histrionicus histrionicus* (L.). Ducks do not behave in this way. Banks has here confused them with skuas which typically chase gulls making them drop their catch (not their dung) which the skuas then seize. Alfred Newton (1893–6: 868) says that popular misconception has led to skuas being sometimes known as 'dunghunters'.

Banks gave this species the key number of 20:21 (McGill MS, pp. 9–10), whereas the loon of the last note was numbered 1:2. It is clear that the numbers in this part of his diary do not refer to his pages, unless he rewrote the whole of this section and forgot to alter the pagination.

126. Although Banks says that the two accounts of the animals seen in Labrador and Hare Bay agree, his further remarks suggest that two distinct species were involved. The behaviour of the group of animals in Hare Bay is typically that of otter or mink but these have not long legs and in any case they were familiar animals to the people concerned. The Labrador animal seen by Phipps to leave the sea and cross a morass to the hills may have been a Fisher Cat. Phipps would have seen the legs clearly and was probably responsible for saying that they were long; they are certainly longer than those of mink and otter. There are no records of the Eastern Fisher Cat in this region but it was reported in Prince Edward Island in the winter of 1948–9 (Austin Cameron 1958:51) and may occur in localized areas further north on the north-eastern seaboard. The animals described by Ankille could not have been Fisher Cats since these do not dive in to fish but scoop their prey from the edge of the water. The whole of Ankille's account, and the rarity of the skins mentioned by the furrier, show clearly that the Hare Bay animals were not any of the common fur-bearers of the region, but the fact that they were behaving exactly as otter and mink do is very suggestive. Pennant published Banks's account almost verbatim without suggesting what these animals were but he placed it immediately after his account of 'Terrier Beavers' (1784:103). Matthiessen (1964:85), quoting Pennant, considers that this is a record of the large extinct Sea Mink, an animal so fiercely hunted for its skin along the coast from New England to New Brunswick that it was exterminated many years before being recognized as a species. Manville more recently (1966) gives no Newfoundland record. Now that there is so much interest in possible Viking sites along the north-eastern seaboard it is to be hoped that further archaeological investigations of ancient settlements may produce evidence of skeletal remains to support Matthiessen's suggestion. I am much indebted to Dr. Max Dunbar of McGill University, and Drs. Goodwin and Van der Gelder of the American Museum of Natural History, New York, for their helpful guidance with this problem.

127. Something is missing here, as Sarah Sophia Banks noted in her transcript.

128. These owls were probably the Great Horned Owl *Bubo virginianus heterocnemis* (Oberholser) which breeds both in Newfoundland and Labrador and is the commonest large owl in those regions. Occasionally the Arctic or Snowy Owl *Nyctea scandiaca* (L.) comes south to Newfoundland in large numbers but only when food is scarce in the northern barren lands.

129. Sarah Sophia Banks amended this to Providence in her transcript.

130. Captain Darby was one of the early traders of the region. He was the father of the lovely 'Perdita' made famous by Sir Joshua Reynolds (see also p. 84).

131. Banks collected both Rock and Willow Ptarmigan at Chateau Bay (McGill MS, p. 73). In winter both species tend to move from the higher and more northerly districts to the coastal regions.

132. Mr. Ankille appears on the muster roll of the *Niger* as Frederick Anchele, the surgeon's second mate. Mr. W. R. Le Fanu of the Royal College of Surgeons of England tells me that a Frederick Anckele appears in the records of the Court of Examiners of the Company of Surgeons on two occasions: on 2 June 1763, when he should have been at least twenty-one years old, and qualified as 2nd Mate for a 1st Rate Ship; and on 19 January 1770 when he qualified as Ship's Surgeon. I have found no other information about him. The surgeon on the *Niger* was W. B. Munkhouse, referred to earlier (pp. 41–2, 63–4).

133. The Golden Eagle *Aquila chrysaëtos canadensis* (L.) is not common in Labrador (Todd 1963:229–30) but it breeds there. Banks's determination can be regarded as sound since he had a bird in captivity, and it makes an interesting addition to the history of the subspecies in view of Todd's statement that he does not know of any reliable record of its occurrence on the Atlantic coast of Labrador.

134. This second eagle may have been the Bald Eagle *Haliaeëtus leucocephalus alascanus* Townsend which breeds both in Newfoundland and Labrador. Pennant (1785:194) refers to *Falco ossifragus* (now *Haliaeëtus albicilla* (L.)) in Newfoundland but this was probably a mistake (Peters & Burleigh 1951:403). The specific name [*Falco*] *canadensis* to which Banks refers is taken from the 1758 edition of the *Systema Naturae*, p. 88, and has long been regarded as applying to the Canadian form of the Golden Eagle. Linnaeus states '*Aquila cauda alba*' and immature Golden Eagles have a considerable amount of white in their tails. But mature Bald Eagles also have largely white tails so that if Banks was unfamiliar with the other characteristics of these birds he might have confused them. To add to the confusion the Osprey *Pandion haliaetus* (L.) also occurs in Labrador and O. L. Austin, writing in 1932, stated that the natives of Sandwich Bay called it eagle then.

135. Banks took this porcupine back to England where Pennant (1784:109) saw it but it is not clear whether it was alive or dead.

136. Banks collected the following species at Chateau Bay (for abbreviations see p. 113); they are discussed in the systematic lists: *Andromeda glaucophylla* Link, *Angelica lucida L., *Arenaria see *Honckenya*, **Calamagrostis labradorica* Kearney, *Carex pauciflora* Lightf., **Castilleja septentrionalis* Lindl., *Draba incana L. var. *confusa* (Ehrh.) Lilj., **Eleocharis palustris* (L.) R. & S., **Eleocharis kamtschatica* (C. A. Meyer) Kom., *Elymus arenarius L. var. *villosus* E. Meyer, *Festuca rubra L., *Geum rivale L., **Hippuris tetraphylla* L., **Honckenya peploides* (L.) Ehrh., *Juncus balticus Willd., **Juncus filiformis* L., *Juncus trifidus L., **Ledum groenlandicum* Oeder, *Linnaea borealis L., **Lomatogonium rotatum* (L.) Fries, *Lonicera villosa* (Michx.) Roem. & Sch., **Mertensia maritima* (L.) S. F. Gray, **Minuartia groenlandica* (Retz.) Ostenf., ✝*Mitella nuda* L., *Moneses uniflora (L.) A. Gray, **Montia lamprosperma* Cham., *Myrica gale* L., **Plantago juncoides* Lam. var. *decipiens* (Barnéoud) Fern., *Poa glauca Vahl, *Poa eminens C. B. Presl, *Poa nemoralis L., **Puccinellia paupercula* (Holm) Fern. & Weath., *Pyrola minor L., **Ranunculus hyperboreus* Rottb., *Rhinanthus minor L. (= *R. crista-galli* L. *pro parte*), **Rubus chamaemorus* L., *Salix reticulata* L. var. *semicalva* Fern., *Saxifraga aizoides* L., *Saxifraga oppositifolia* L., **Saxifraga rivularis* L., ✝**Senecio pseudo-arnica* Less., ✝*Shepherdia canadensis* (L.) Nutt., **Stellaria humifusa* Rottb., **Streptopus roseus* Michx., **Vaccinium angustifolium* Ait., **Vaccinium cespitosum* Michx., *Vaccinium myrtilloides* Michx., *Viola palustris* L.

Other Labrador specimens in Banks's herbarium collected before, during or after his own visit included the following species. The names of the collectors are in brackets after the name of the plant: **Geum macrophyllum* Willd. (collector unknown, 1763), *Linnaea borealis L. var. *americana* (Forbes) Rehd. (Richard Molesworth), **Oxytropis johannensis* Fern. (Richard Molesworth), **Pedicularis labradorica* Wirsing (Moravians), **Petasites frigidus* (L.) Fries (Moravians, 1765), ✝**Petasites palmatus* (Ait.) A. Gray (collector unknown), **Potentilla crantzii* (Crantz) G. Beck (La Trobe 1778, George Cartwright), *Ranunculus pedatifidus* Smith. (collector unknown, 1763), *Rubus acaulis Michx. (Richard Molesworth), *Salix vestita Pursh (Moravians), **Senecio pseudo-arnica* Less. (John Williams, Moravians 1766), **Solidago multiradiata* Ait. (collector unknown, 1765),

Vaccinium vitis-idaea L. (Richard Molesworth), *Viola macloskeyi* Lloyd subsp. *pallens* (Gingins ex Banks in DC.) M. S. Baker (John Williams).

Banks collected over 120 species of plants at Croque. Since they comprise so large a proportion of his total collections they are not listed separately but are all noted in the systematic section, pp. 311–48.

137. Asarabacca is an English and French name for *Asarum europaeum*. No species of *Asarum* occurs in Newfoundland, and Banks almost certainly refers here to *Pyrola asarifolia* Michx. He recorded *Asarum* leaves in a final list in his plant catalogue but no specimen has been located.

138. It is clear from Banks's note on his p. 96 about this river's being at the head of Croque Harbour that he is speaking of the Freshwater River.

139. *Mustela erminea richardsonii* Bonaparte.

140. This was the Goshawk *Accipiter gentilis atricapillus* (Wilson) as we know from Banks's description (McGill MS, 12:13, p. 33) of this bird in which he says 'Habitat in Sylvis Gallinis nostris infestissimus. Croque Oct. 5th 1766.' It is still notorious for its occasional attacks on poultry which have given it the name of hen hawk. Paillou's painting pl. VI, of Banks's specimen was the basis of Latham's account of the American race. Gmelin based his *Falco novae-terrae* on Latham's description, thus Paillou's painting becomes the type of Gmelin's species.

141. Miss Judith King has kindly given me the following notes on these seals: the Square Phipper, now called Square Flipper locally, is the Bearded Seal *Erignathus barbatus barbatus* (Erxleben); the Hooded Seal is *Cystophora cristata* (Erxleben); the Heart Seal, a corruption of Harp Seal, is *Phoca groenlandica* Erxleben; the Bedlamer is a young Harp Seal, about two years old; the Harbour Seal is *Phoca vitulina concolor* (de Kay); the small species 'never exceeding two feet or two and a half in length' is probably the Ringed Seal *Phoca hispida hispida* Schreber, of the coasts of Greenland and Labrador.

142. Black Patch is a colour phase of the Red Fox *Vulpes fulva deletrix* Bangs. The endemic Newfoundland forms of the other mammals mentioned by Banks are the Beaver *Castor canadensis caecator* Bangs; the River Otter *Lutra canadensis degener* Bangs; the Marten *Martes americana atrata* (Bangs), now extremely rare in Newfoundland.

143. This is of course a reference to Banks's observations in the spring. The American Common Eider *Somateria mollissima dresseri* Sharpe is the breeding form of eider in Newfoundland; Dr. Tuck tells me that it still nests on small islands in Hare Bay but is not very common. Townsend and Allen writing in 1907 (pp. 333–6) stressed the need for protection of these birds so that a reasonable industry could be established for utilising the down, and this has been emphasized by Peters and Burleigh; see the notes on this species in the McGill MS, p. 11. There is a painting by Parkinson, pl. 65, of a pair of eider-duck collected by Banks which appear to be Northern Common Eider, *Somateria mollissima borealis* (Brehm). Todd (1963:177–83) discusses the status of these birds at length.

144. The anniversary of the accession of George III to the throne, 25 October 1760.

145. Sea Cow today is the common name for the Manatee and other sirenians; none occurs in the North Atlantic. Here Banks is referring to the Walrus *Odobenus rosmarus rosmarus* (L.). It feeds largely on clams.

146. Banks was correct. The Newfoundland is a strain of mastiff, a variety of the domestic dog *Canis familiaris* L. According to Harold MacPherson (1937:133–40) it is a descendant of the white or cream-coloured Pyrenean sheep dog taken to Newfoundland by Basque fishermen and crossed with mastiffs and other sporting dogs taken there by the English, and with other large dogs imported by the French, Spanish and Portuguese.

147. The Bugio lighthouse and the S. Julião de Barra are two seventeenth-century towers that formerly defended the Tagus estuary.

148. The Torré de Belem was built 1515–21 by Francisco Arruda; it is a delightful example of Manuelian architecture.

149. This was the Queluz National Palace, the Portuguese equivalent of Versailles, still famous for its beautiful gardens. They were not properly established at the time of Banks's visit since the palace was built only in 1758 by the architect Mateus Vincente de Oliveira for the second son of D. Joao V.

150. See next section for a note on the political state of Lisbon at this time.

8

Banks in Lisbon: an amplification

BANKS arrived in Portugal just eleven years after the great earthquake of 1755. The Tagus had overflowed its banks, causing widespread flooding, which was followed by a terrible fire in the centre of the city. Altogether about 15,000 people had been killed.

The crisis was admirably handled by King José and his able and active Secretary of State, Sebastião José de Carvalho e Mello, who in 1759 was made Conde de Oeiras (Banks spelt it Oyares), and later, in 1770, Marquês de Pombal, the name by which he is most widely known. Englishmen were profoundly affected by the news; on 15 December 1755, Samuel Richardson wrote: 'What dreadful news we have from Lisbon. The only city in the world, out of the British dominions, by which so tremendous a shock could have so much affected us. When the Almighty's judgements are abroad, may we be warned.' Two months later, Horace Walpole commented to Henry Seymour: 'Between the French and the Earthquake you have no idea how good we are grown; nobody makes a suit now but of sackcloth turned up with ashes.'

Pombal's efficiency in handling the crisis gave him tremendous power. (He is reported to have answered a despairing cry from the King: 'Whatever shall we do?' with 'Bury the dead, feed the living'.)

In 1757 he began to attack the Jesuits who by that time had become an international corporation of immense financial and political strength. The Papacy was as jealous of the Jesuits as it had been of the Inquisition, and in 1758 Benedict XIV forbade them to trade. At this stage in the proceedings the king was wounded in the 'Tavora' plot (in which the beautiful Marchioness of Tavora was implicated), and this enabled Pombal not only to attack and execute some of the most powerful nobles who were jealous of him, but also to discredit the Jesuits. In 1759 the estates of the order were confiscated and its members expelled, the good with the bad. Pombal then attacked the Inquisition and in another ten years had reduced it to a mere ecclesiastical tribunal, conducting its proceedings with some judicial procedure, and confining its sentences for the most part to imprisonment. The root of clericalism was then destroyed by the secularization of education. The national university

175

of Coimbra was freed from the control of the priests, and the colleges for higher education founded by the Jesuits and other orders were taken over as Government institutions. Furthermore, when Pombal died he left behind him a body of civil servants trained in his tradition of honest and efficient public service.

Banks was in Lisbon, therefore, in a period of active change, and it was no wonder that many people were shy of entertaining strangers, as he complains.

Some surviving letters show, however, that he had a more interesting and entertaining time than his diary suggests. Amongst these is one from Pennant (p. 237) written from Chester on 30 January 1767, the day Banks arrived back in London from Lisbon, in which he thanks Banks for two obliging letters, one from Chateau Bay, and one from Lisbon concerning a visit to an aviary belonging to a Portuguese sea captain. 'How should I have revelled,' he writes, 'amidst that Brasilian aviary. What multitude of singular birds does that southern continent afford! of which we know only the parts, and fragments; but those so very eccentric as makes me wild to be acquainted with the whole.' But it is the letters from de Visme that gives us the most detailed picture of both the social and scientific events of Banks's visit.

According to a note in the Solander MSS (11:443) on the genus *Vismia*, Gerard de Visme was a well known English merchant living in Lisbon. He had a wide interest in birds, botany, gardens and girls and although he was seventeen years older than Banks they became firm friends. He was on sufficiently intimate terms with the Royal family for them to drop in for unexpected morning visits, and he exercised considerable political power. Banks says that he had 'an ample botanick garden', and after his return to England he sent over some American plants for it, perhaps from his Newfoundland collections. De Visme at the same time presented Banks with part of a collection from Pernambuco; after the return of the *Endeavour* it seems that Banks sent him some living plants from collections made on the voyage (p. 252).

The English colony in Lisbon had formed a Natural History Society to which Banks was of course admitted (Primatt, p. 248); de Visme writes in one letter about lectures on botany and natural history given by Mr. Auriol to various mutual acquaintances at the Quinta, and teases Banks about his popularity; there is to be a bust or statue of him—'We consulted on the choice of a worthy to place in the cobham stile in a nich of Ivy Jasmine, the majority of votes was yours, the ladies are to give the resemblance, and Auriol asserts he will manage the execution in a manner quite new and masterly; the truth is that you are a great Patron to Bemfique, and much regretted there, as well as by all your Lisbon acquaintances. The Venus of Lisbon still retains a crowd of Amorine round about her and is as beautiful as ever . . .' The king, impressed by the re-arrangement of de Visme's grounds and buildings, planned a *Relogio de Sol* for the palace at Belem, to which, says de Visme, 'my care shall be to add J.B. finxit.'

De Visme even offered to obtain introductions for Banks to all the Portuguese

G. D. Ehret pinxit
1758

Pl. IV *Senecio pseudo-arnica*
G. D. Ehret

governors of settlements he was likely to visit on Cook's second circumnavigation, and also ordered some cloaks and sheets for the voyage—'Two Portuguese Capotes, made of Irish Camblet, one of them lined with Bayze, the other still warmer lined with Portuguese manufact. and cutt of Portuguese Saragossa Cloth, which is warm, pliable, and light . . . Two pair of Sheets, made and marked; of Port^{ue} Panno and Linha, which is cottony and very snug, especially at Sea, in your state of Celibacy.' (See pp. 252–3, for these letters.)

Ten years later, November, 1782, Banks wrote to Brudenell (p. 272) to try to get permission for Masson (1741–1805), one of the earliest and most famous plant collectors for the Royal Botanic Gardens at Kew, to visit de Visme in Lisbon to assist in arranging and naming his plants, and also to obtain fresh stocks for Kew. A letter from Pigou and Duncan (p. 271) that same year makes it clear that Banks and de Visme were sharing collectors and collections from Brazil and probably China.

Amongst the botanists Banks met in Lisbon were João de Loureiro (1710–91) who later worked in the Far East, and Domingo Vandelli (1735–1816). Seven of Loureiro's letters to Banks are in the British Museum (abstracts in Warren Dawson, 1958:556), and there is another intended for Banks but actually written to de Visme. Two of these reproduced in this volume (pp. 270, 276–7) show how much trouble Banks himself took in helping Loureiro to write and publish the *Flora Cochinchinensis* (1790) although he was so uninterested in publishing his own work.

Vandelli was nearer Banks in age and was enthusiastic over the Newfoundland plants. He enlisted Banks's help in the establishment of a botanic garden in Lisbon, and obtained a rich collection of seeds from him. The garden and a museum were founded and Vandelli became keeper of both. Many years later when he fell into political difficulties and was exiled to the Azores, Banks used his influence to procure his release and permission to come to England.

The aged botanist arrived in London in July 1811, entirely without resources and accompanied by his son; Banks wrote to him referring to the kindness he had received from him in Lisbon forty-five years earlier, and assured him that he would look after him; but the son was sent off to Portugal. In fact Banks succeeded in obtaining a pardon and a pension for Vandelli and he too was able to go home (see also pp. 279–82).

Banks's six weeks in Lisbon reveal another side of him—his gaiety, warmth and enthusiasm for people are reflected in letters he afterwards received from his Lisbon friends although not in the rather gloomy picture painted in his diary.

PART THREE
Supplementary papers

9

The diaries of the Moravians in Newfoundland and Labrador, 1764, 1765

ELSEWHERE in this volume I have suggested that the Moravians exerted a profound influence on Banks; the quality of some of the men in that order is revealed in the three short diaries printed below. These records have a special interest in that the missionaries' successful survey of part of the Labrador coast in 1765 led to the establishment of the Moravian settlements (Gosling 1910, Whiteley 1964) which were to be a dominant force on that coast for the next two centuries.

The Moravians made their first attempt to establish a settlement in Labrador in 1752. Four brethren were sent there in the *Hope*, a small trading vessel commanded by Erhardt, a Moravian sailor who had worked in whalers in the Greenland trade, and had some knowledge of the Eskimo language. The *Hope* arrived on the coast, *c.* latitude 55° 10', at the end of July. The ship's company and the missionaries built a house in a sheltered harbour and the *Hope* then sailed north to seek opportunities for further trading. At the request of some Eskimos, Erhardt and some of the crew went off, unarmed, in the ship's boat with goods for trading. They failed to return. After three days the weather became stormy and Goff, mate of the *Hope*, decided to wait for them no longer. He sailed back to the harbour where the house had been built and, since he was shorthanded, took the four missionaries on board, leaving the key of the house and a letter in a hollow tree near by in case Erhardt should return.

A year later Goff revisited the harbour and there met Drage (Swaine), captain of the *Argo*, who was exploring the coast. They found the house in ruins, the cask of provisions broken. There was no trace of Erhardt, but later the body of one of his men was found on one of the near-by islands (Drage 1768:131–53; Gosling 1910: 151–3). What had happened is not precisely known but the fragment of Jens Haven's diary printed below shows that the Eskimos undoubtedly had murdered some of the men.

Haven's diary gives details of his meetings with Eskimos at Quirpon in northern Newfoundland in 1764, the success of which largely depended on the help given him by Palliser and Cook. Schloezer's account of the missionaries' voyage in the *Niger* to Chateau Bay in 1765 is valuable not only for the descriptions of Eskimos but also for the light it throws on Palliser, Adams, Munkhouse, Darby and Lucas, all of whom figure in other contemporary records. The short account of the voyage of the *Hope* up the Labrador coast, also in 1765, is chiefly of geographical interest. It gives a picture of the harsh conditions prevailing in August, although the *Hope* did not sail beyond 56° 30' N—that is, not quite as far north as the latitude in which Dundee lies.

Haven's historic meeting with the Eskimos and Cook at Quirpon is of exceptional interest today not only because he was able to speak with the Eskimos in their own language, and because of Cook's charts and descriptions of that coast, but also because more than 200 years earlier Quirpon had been visited and described by Jacques Cartier. Earlier still this peninsula must have been known to European fishermen from France, Portugal and England since, at the beginning of his voyage, Cartier stated that he intended to visit Chateau Bay, just across the strait. Now, excavations at L'Anse aux Meadows some five miles west of Quirpon have revealed evidence suggesting that there may have been Viking settlements along the coast, some 400 years before the voyage of Columbus.

Jens Haven was a remarkable man. Trained as a carpenter, he felt that his vocation was to work with the Eskimos and convert them to Christianity. With this in mind he went to Greenland to learn about them and master their language. His meeting with the tribe at Quirpon was dramatically successful. As a result, with Palliser's support, it was arranged that he, with some other brethren, should visit Labrador the following year. So, in May 1765, Jens Haven, Christian Drachardt, C. F. Hill and Christian Andrew Schloezer sailed in the *Lark* from Spithead to Croque where they embarked in the *Niger* commanded by Sir Thomas Adams. They sailed north to Chateau Bay where, protesting, the missionaries were separated into two pairs; Drachardt and Hill remained in the *Niger* at Chateau Bay, Haven and Schloezer went north in the *Hope* commanded by Lieutenant Candler (not Chandler as the Moravians spelt it). Lieutenant Lucas, who later joined Cartwright as his partner, and who took an Eskimo girl, Mykok, to London in 1768 (p. 84), accompanied them in order to make charts but only those executed by the missionaries have been traced; one of Esquimaux Bay (Hamilton Inlet) with the names both in English and Eskimo is in the Admiralty Library, the others are in the Moravian Library. The original diaries in German script, of the voyages in the *Lark*, the *Niger* and the *Hope* are also in that library. Somewhat abbreviated translations of these diaries, signed by the missionaries, were sent to the Lords Commissioners of Trade and Plantations and are reproduced below. The natural history observations in these versions are not at all detailed, although one man was a sufficiently good botanist to collect plants for Banks; there is an interesting record of wigeon in Davis's Inlet on 8 August.

THE DIARIES OF THE MORAVIANS

The Moravians planned their later settlements most carefully. In 1770 they chose a site on the west coast of Hancock's Inlet for their first house and the next year began building it. The men selected to found this settlement, Nain, which was to be of lasting importance in the lives of the Labrador Eskimos were: Jens Haven and his newly married English wife; Christian Drachardt, an old Greenland missionary; Christian Brassen or Braassen, physician and surgeon, who was to lose his life in a boating accident, and his wife; John Schneider and his wife, and six unmarried men. Brassen figures elsewhere in this volume as a plant collector. The settlement of Nain in Hancock's Inlet was followed by two others in Banks's lifetime, Okkak in 1775 and Hopedale in 1781. Labrador plants in Banks's herbarium include material from all three settlements but they are not listed here since all were collected far north of the localities he visited in the vicinity of Chateau Bay. A Moravian, Kohlmeister, sometimes spelled Colmaster, who went to Labrador somewhat later and worked there for thirty-four years, also sent plants to Europeans. It was he who, with Kmoch and a redoubtable Eskimo, went north by boat to Ungava Bay in 1811 and made a report on the stone houses on Amitok Island in 59° 30′. They were familiar with similar ruins on the islands near Nain; there were remains of walls, graves within stone enclosures and with a covering slab, totally unlike those of the Eskimos known to them.

The history of the early Labrador explorers was discussed by Gosling who as early as 1910 thought that the early Norse voyages to North America presented one of the most interesting geographical problems of his time; by Nansen whose two-volume work on early Arctic exploration was published in an English translation in 1911; by Tanner (1944) who gives a long list of biographical references; by Whiteley (1964) and others.

39. Vaccinium ovalifolium.
G. D. Ehret

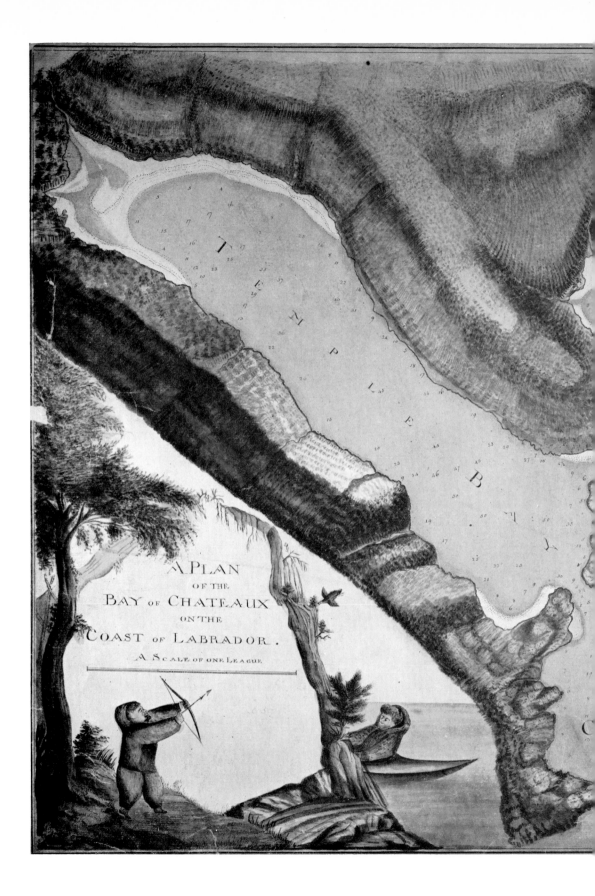

A PLAN
OF THE
BAY OF CHATEAUX
ON THE
COAST OF LABRADOR.

A SCALE OF ONE LEAGUE.

POINT SANDWICH.

DUCK I.

BAD BAY

Fox I.
GOOSE COVE

SEAL ISLANDS

HARBOUR

GULL I.

HENLEY I.

FLAT I.

WHALE I.

CASTLE ISLAND

A Y

O F

T E A U X

CHATEAU

40. MS chart of Chateau Bay, showing Eskimo kayaks approaching the *Niger* (?), and the outline of the proposed blockhouse, in Pitt's Harbour, just north of the *Guernsey* (?); a more open site was eventually selected (pl. 30).

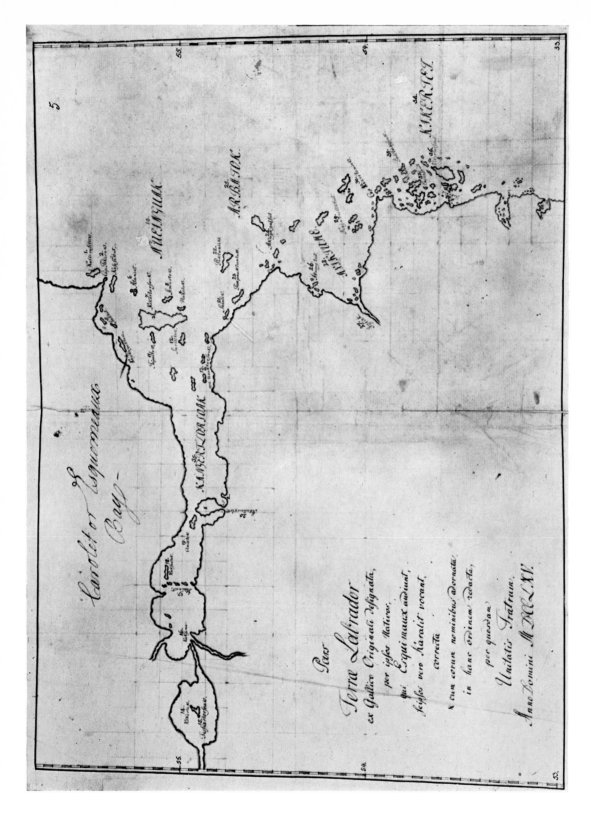

41. MS chart of Eskimo Bay, now Hamilton Inlet, by one of the Moravian missionaries in the *Hope*, 1765. The English equivalents of the numbered Eskimo names are printed on p. 185.

An explanation of the Indian Names in the Chart of that part of the Coast of Labrador where the Caralit Indians inhabit

1.	Thunder Island	Kallerusillik
2.	Cape Vissit	Tikerak
3.	Drift-Wood Island	Kesesekut
4.	White Island	Kagikaguktuk
5.	The 3 Star Islands	Siaktut (the 3 contiguous Islands)

     The Indians call these Islands by the same name they give the 3 stars in Orion's Lyre.

6.	The Flat-Island	Ataniut
7.	The Great-Island	Kikertarsoak
8.	The Carrying-Island	Amartok

     (i.e.) where the Women are forced to carry their children on their backs

9.	The Uneven-Island	Manetok
10.	The Pleasant Lands	Nueinguoak
11.	Place of Recreation	Tapeitok
12.	Stream-Island	Sariktok (Stream or Current Islands)
13.	Acquiring-Island	Unaktorsoak (where something is to be got)
14.	The Island	Kikertak
15.	The Large Fresh-Water-Lake	Tessiortorsoak
16.	The Point between the Rivers	Koksoak
17.	Shallow-water-Place	Itieikut
18.	Wedge Island	Kuksautak
19.	The Small-Island	Amiktok
20.	The Middle-Land	Akuliariktok
21.	Stinking-Island	Suialik
22.	The High-Island	Puktualik
23.	The Stoney-Island	Tuapauktualik
24.	Passage-Islands	Akugugutsut
25.	Whale Place	Arbatok
26.	Haste (or make Haste) Island	Akunigtut
27.	Throat-Sound	Iygak (or Igiak-map)
28.	Parting-Place	Aviktume
29.	Seal-Islands	Karaluliktut
30.	Cape-Islands	Kikertauiak
31.	Mountain-Island	Puktuksoak
32.	The Narrow-Passage	Ekeresauit
33.	Shadow-Island	Takanut
34.	The Many or Thousand Islands	Kikertet
35.	The Great-Bay	Kangertlorsoak
36.	The Great-Islands	Kikertarsoak

The Eskimo equivalents in the above list are taken not from the map but from the list attached to the English versions of the Moravians' diaries in the Public Record Office f. 245 of CO. 194/16. It is probable that the map of pl. 41 is in fact the chart which was formerly attached to these papers in the Public Record Office.

JENS HAVEN'S DIARY, 1764

from the transcript by Palliser

AN ACCOUNT OF AN INTERVIEW BETWEEN MR. HANS HAVEN, A MORAVIAN, AND THE ESQUIMEAUX SAVAGES.

I will according to your Ex^s Command, deliver my own Journall.

Aug. 17th. I went out with three shallops which were going to the Coast of Labradore to Fish and our mate went with us, and took some Traffick with him if he should meet with any of the Indians.

As we came to Carpoune [Quirpon], four Shallops that came from Labradore with a report that there came to York Harbour a great number of Indians, and made such terrible outcries, that surpris'd the English, who fired upon the Indians, on which the Indians retreated, and took the sails from the English people and distroyed every thing that was on Shore. Every one of our people was affrighted and would go no farther. There met about ten Shallops together, and I persuaded them there was no danger and Insinuated

20   so far that we went out from Carpoune. we were scarcely out of the Harbour, when the Shallops began to scatter from each other, so that I was left alone, some went back again, some went to the Island of Belisle but our boat carried me on board Capt. Cook because they dare not go any further by themselves. Capt Cook receiv'd me very kindly.

21   The French Capt. La Fouse sent me word that he would carry me with one of his boats to the Coast of Labradore. I sent him answer I could not go without an order from Capt. Cook, and I must have an English man with me which could speak French then I would be willing to go if it was only with two men but Capt. Cook would not Consent to it.

23   Eight English Shallops was at Carpoune which was going to fish on the Coast of Labradore. I went overland about three milles [sic] to come to them, one of them took me in, but when he heard that my design was to speak with the Indians, then said he, I have no order to go there and put me back again on board Capt. Cook and

187

return'd to St. Julian's, there was five Irish Shallops, to which Capt. Cook did speak that they should take me along with them, upon which they agreed if the Indians would come to them, but would not go to the Indians.

24   We landed at Labradore and lay there until the 29th without seeing anybody. I found here some Indian graves and Tools which gave me great hopes as well as what I heard from the French Interpreters; that it would be the same nation which I expected to see. same day we left this place and it was night before we could reach Carpoune so that we could not go into the Harbour where I wish'd to be on shore & upon much intreaty they put me ashore at Camilea [? Cramaillier].

31   We went out from Camilea but conterary winds oblig'd us back again.

Spr. 1   We had fair wind and came to Carpoune, here I found the Captains Thompson & Darby [pp. 68, 84] who were very glad to see me but was sorry that I was not there the day before. They inform'd me the Indians had been there, but did not know if they would return again.

2d   Captain Thompson left me to the care of the French Captⁿ who took care of me accordingly.

4th   Was the happy day I long wish'd for. one of the Indians came into the Harbour for to see if Captain Galliot was there. in the mean time I was prepairing to go to him he was ready to return again for to acquaint his Country men which lay in the Harbours mouth, that Captain Galliot was gone. I call'd to him to come to me, that I had some words to speak with him, and that I was his very good friend, but he was mightily surpris'd and answer'd me in some broken French but I desir'd he might speak in his own language that I understood him very well further I acquainted him that Captain Galliot was gone yesterday, but it was no matter whilst I was here and that I understood his language but Captain Galliot did not I desired he would make haste and bring some of his people, that I had something to say to them, he then went away making a great outcry that our friend is come. I therefore put on my Indian dress, and directly there did come five of them in their own Canoes. I went to meet them and said to them, I have long desired for to see you, and should be very glad if you are all in good health, he answer'd me that I was realy one of their Country men, the Joy was great on both sides and they requested of me to come over and see their Family which I promis'd to do. I then gott our Mate and an Sailor to go with me and they put me on Shore but they still continued in the Boat and put off from the Shore and waited to see what wou'd become of me then the Indians all surrounded me and every one of them would shew me his family I had a long discourse wt them for the space of two hours and I gave to every boy two fish hooks, and to every woman two or three sewing needles, and a piece of money which Captain Thompson had given me I gave to Seculia's wife (p. 209) in return

She presented me with a purse made of a Bird's skin, which I have to return to Capt. Thompson. I recommended Capt. Thompson to them well, assureing them they might be well satisfied he was a Good Man I then shew'd them a place where they might erect their Tents, then I went away telling them I would soon return again.

At 5 o'Clock in the afternoon I went with our mate to them again to endeavour if possible to trade with them, they all made answer they had Nothing at present to trade upon, and that all was gone. I then advised them to Stay all night upon this ground, and to take care they did not steale anything from our people at which they all laugh'd. I then told them the danger of so doing in good earnest which surpris'd them very much and answer'd me that it would be better for them to leave the place. I made answer there was no occasion for so doing, that no man of ours would do them any harm. I ask'd them how they wou'd like it if we should steall anything from them, one of them was so Impudent as to say the Europeans do Steal. I made answer the Europeans did not understand you, if for the future any of our people should steal any things from you let me know it and they shall be punished for so doing. I desir'd they would Come and see me which they did.

There came eighteen Indians in their Canoes the French captain was very much afraid of them he desir'd they might not come ashore all together—this was a very hard case for me who had invited them. I went down to the waterside and made themselves [? torn] And took six of the Civilest with me on Shore telling the next they might go on Shore in any other place, that nobody would do them any harm. I took these six men by themselves alone and did read to them the authority your Excellence gave me and told them the good intent of the Government towards them and wished they wou'd be partakers of such great Benefits. At which they wer very attentive. I asked them if they understood the difference between the two nations—namely the English and French they answerd they knew of no other difference but that of their Colours. I told them the English hoisted red Colours and were masters of this Country, and that I belong'd to them and am come to tell you that they love you, and will do you no harm if you behave to them like Civil and good people, at the same time I offer'd to give them that Writing given me by your Excellency. They was afraid to take it they thought it was alive because of my reading it and I was not able to persuade them to take it from me. I got a Boat and went over again to their Family and every one of them ask'd me if it was true that I would come back again the next year. When I had asured them that I would come again They were very glad, One Shallop that brought me here return'd from Labradore and our Mate went back in her to Cammila and left me alone with the French at Carpoune towards night there came three French Boats, and an English Shallop full of Indians and made up their Tents among the rest. The men came very soon to see me and beg'd of me to Visit them which I promis'd to do.

6th   Came in twenty six men in their Canoes the French Captain begg'd of me to bring these people away from the Harbour I told him it was not in my power. I promised him I would try what I could do in a Friendly manner upon which I told the Indians that these people were not of my Nation, that they belong'd to the White Colours (namely French) and I myself a stranger amonst them, and if the wind would serve I would return to my own people (to them—red Colours) namly the English; they reply'd if you go away we will stay no longer here. I answerd them they might do as they thought proper. In a Short time there arriv'd more of the Indians, and begg'd of me that I would come once more, their Wifes & Children desir'd to see me before I went away I begg'd the French captain to lend me his Boat. He said he had a mind to go wt me himselfe I answer'd he might if he pleas'd and he and his Mate and Doctor & six men with arms went with me in great fear. He put on his best apparel but none of the Indians regarded him which displeased him very much. The Indians asked me if it was realy true that I would return next year. I answer'd yes, but I believe you will kill me as you have done some of my countrymen a few years ago. Then they was very much frightned and were all Silenced and look'd down to the grownd. Then I said to them I believe you have done such things in Ignorance, but now whilst I can speak with you I hope you won't do such things any more. They Promis'd me all together that none of them would do us any harm. I said then if I come again I will tell you things of very great consequence—namly of our Lord and Creator, how dearly he loves you, and what he has done for you, and if you will belive in him then we shall live happy together one of the Indians did ask me if he did Lodge in the Sun. I told him he had created the Sun & him & I and all things, one of them asked me if I belived on him would I be more happy in my business than I am at present. I told him there was no doubt if he would be diligent in his doings, and that the life to come was far more happier than this present life which they have only to hope for who put their trust in him and walk in his Commandments. When I was return'd to my Quarters there did come all the men to take leave of me. I wished I could keep them longer with me but I could not and they would have been nothing the better for it in this place.

7th   They went away, as soon as they were out of the harbour they began to steal again [? . . . torn]

The French [? . . .] angry and said they would go and kill all the Indians men women & children. I said to the French if the Christians Steal who can take it amiss of the Heathens you must be upon your guard. all this would not prevail I was oblig'd to shew them your Excellˢ Orders and I told them it would stand them dear enough if they did them people any harm. Moreover I told them if they would give me a Boat and four men I would go to the Indians once more and earnestly tell them if they would not leave off stealing they wou'd all be killed and I could not help them but there would nobody go with me altho' the Indians were but two leagues to the westward of Carpoune.

190

27   Arrivd at St. John's in good health where I had the pleasure to see and speak with your Excell^y, that I had the good fortune to see and speak with the Indians of Labradore and that I understand their language much better than I imagin'd before and that the difference between their language and them in Davies Streights is very little. They call themselves Carrolets the very same as those in Davis Streights. I could have wished that your Excell^y had seen them and me together, the Joy was very great on both Sides for them to see one that they could speak with and for me that I understood them. I love them with all my heart because I know that they are Created and Bought with a dear price, as well as I am, and for this reason I wish that they may come to the knowledge of God and our Saviour Jesus Christ, because I know it is an unspeakable happiness to know him and to walk before him in his way.

Only I find here three Articles which are a hindrance for accomplishing this great design amongst this Nation which I must lay down before my Brethern [*sic*] or the Bishop and Elders of the Church. If the Lord wou'd point out the way to remove these difficultys so that his blessed word may be brought among These Indians it is Verily a great work. 'tis not only to Convert them to Christianity but to make almost a new people of these poor Ignorant Savages. The articles above mention'd are these.

1st   I could not have the opertunity for to find out a place to make a Settlement, that is to say where the people most resort or where they mostly inhabit.

2d   When these people have lost their former way of living as to making their own Boats and own Tools by their own Industry And the Ill practices they have taken up of Stealing Boats, Sails nay anything from the Europeans which they are not able to pay for, and at present think upon nothing else but to Steal and rob, and if they cannot get it by policy and they see that it lyes in their Power they will use Violence and Venture their life partly out of Stupidity & partly out of despairation to get what they Stand in need of. This is now a Very hard case to bring them [out] of these ill practices and to bring them of their former way of living again. from this arrives the third Article.

3d   Namely it is not sufficient to build a weak house that every one who will come to rob us if they take a likeing to any Part of our goods but we must build a Strong house which may cost more than my Brethern may think of. I do not mean a Fort or any Fortification because we are not warriors. The Trade with them is for presents of Small consequence what they have is a little Whalebone a few fox and Servail [lynx] skin it may be if they were a little encouraged and provided with some necessary tools they woud endeavour to provide us more Traffick & I believe the Fishery will be the main thing and perhaps some Whale and Swael oil. The things they are in most need of & to give them in Exch^a are namly those Viz. Some Ads's, Hatchets, Saws, drawing knives, other knives, gimbles, hammers, Files, Fishing hooks, lead, sowing needles, thimbles, Rings, Blankets, they like cooking kettles, They enquire very much after Boats, Ropes, Sails & Graplings, they enquire very much after such things, but they are not able to pay for them, because they are exceeding poor I believe their poverty proceeds very much from their Laziness and partly from their want of tools.

This is all the Inteligence I can give your Excell^y it is true that the first of our Brethern which may go to settle there they Venture thier life and they must think so, if they are Killed 'tis as the Lord pleaseth but if the Lord should grant us grace then his name will be glorified among the Wild Ignorant Savage people, I praise the Lord for his deliverance unto this present time.

I Humbly Acknowledge your Excellency's most kind assistance and Succour, without which I should not have been able to do anything—I promise myself through the good Inclination I have experienc'd in your Excell^y In forwarding this Expedition that If my Brethern will proceed farther in this work that we will find in your Excell^y a kind assistance the most gracious favour I have receiv'd from your Excell^y in regard to my own person Gives me great Confidence that your Excell^y will not think amiss of my simple performance and since I can do nothing farther this year, I hope that your Excell^y will kindly assist me in my Passage Home with the first oppertunity either in a man of war or a merchantman. I shall always and at all times remain Your Excellencys

Most Humble & most obed^t Servant

The above is a Coppy of a Journal I receivd from Mr. Hans Haven

Hugh Palliser
7 Oct. 1764

Moravian Hq
Lindsey House,
Chelsea.

Public Record Office
CO 194/16, ff.59–62.

THE VISIT OF THE MORAVIANS
TO CHATEAU BAY IN THE *NIGER*
IN 1765; THE VOYAGE OF JENS HAVEN
AND CHRISTIAN ANDREW SCHLOEZER[1]
IN THE *HOPE* TO HANCOCK'S INLET
IN 1765

To The Right Honourable The Lords
for Trade & Plantations

Your Lordships will be pleased to remember, that on the Report of our Bro[r]. Jens Haven having been able in the year 1764 to converse with the Eskimaux in their own Language, the R[t]. Hon[ble] the Lords for Trade & Plantation desired to speak with him, & having heard from his own mouth divers Particulars which seem'd to them to make it a matter worthy of their very great attention, desired that our Brethren of the Unitas Fratrum would go & settle there, which being reported to our Brethren abroad, they in consequence thereof desired & engaged the four underwritten Brethren & Members of the Church of the Unitas Fratrum to offer their service accordingly in order to reconnoitre the Coast of Labradore, & chuse such tracts of land as might be agreeable to the Esquimaux & suitable for them to make a Settlement on, & live together; in order, if possible in time, thro' the preaching of the Gospel to make them real Christians, & consequently good & quiet Neighbours, which was look'd upon to be of very great Benefit to the Trade of these Nations.

We have herewith the Honour to present to your Lordships the account of the Voyage, by which your Lordships will be able to judge whether the Design of it undertaken by us in order to look out for proper Settlements—according to the purposes mentioned in our Memorial presented to the Board in the Month of February last has succeeded or not, as also how far our Voyage has already answered the purposes of endeavouring to conciliate the minds of those Barbarians to the

---

[1] Whether C. A. Schloezer was a relation of the famous contemporary German historian, August Ludwig von Schlözer, appears to be unknown. The historian's father and grandfather were Lutheran pastors so it is possible that there is some connection but I have not found any account of the family other than the brief summary in the life by his son; there is no reference to any cousins in that book.

English Nation, for a time at least, till by instilling good principles into their minds, cultivating & watching over the same there may be some more reasonable prospect of a durable good understanding.

An Account of the Voyage of the four Missionaries sent by the Unitas Fratrum to the Esquimaux on the Coast of Labrador, & under the protection of his Britanic Majesty. From the month of May to Novem^R. 1765.

Having received the following Certificates from the R^t. Honble the Lords Commissioners for Trade & Plantations & Governour Palliser we went May the 2^d on board the Lark Captn. Thompson at Spithead. [Only Palliser's proclamation is given here since it is almost identical with that issued by the Lords Commissioners.]

By his Excellency Hugh Pallisser Governor & Commander in Chief in & over the Island of Newfoundland, Coast of Labrador, Islands Anticosta, Madelanes etc. etc.—

'Whereas the Society of the Unitas Fratrum under the protection of his Majesty have from a Pious Zeal for promoting the knowledge of the True God & of the Religion of our blessed Lord & Saviour Jesus Christ among the Heathen, formed a Resolution of establishing a Mission of their Brethren upon the Coast of Labradore, for that purpose have appointed John Hill, Christian Drachart, Jens Haven & Christian Andrew Schloezer to effect this pious purpose & whereas the Lords Commissioners of the Admiralty & the Lords Commissioners of Trade & Plantation have signified to me their entire approbation of an undertaking so commendable in itself, & that promises so great Benefit to the public & are desirous of giving all reasonable Encouragement and Assistance thereto. These are therefore to certify all Persons whom it may concern that the said John Hill, Christian Drachart, Jens Haven & Christian Andrew Schloezer are under his Majesty's Protection, & all Officers Civil & Military, & all other his Majesty's Subjects within my Government are hereby strictly charged & required not to give any interruption or hindrance to the said John Hill, Christ^n Drachart, Jens Haven & Christ^n. Andr^w. Schloezer, but to afford them every aid & friendly Assistance for the success of their pious undertaking for the Benefit of mankind in general & of his Majesty's Subjects in particular.

Given under my Hand & Seal this 30th day of April 1765

By Command of his Excellency   Hugh Pallisser
    John Horsnaill

May 7th   We sailed from Spithead & arrived at Croque the *2^d of June* where we waited without hearing any thing of the Schooner till the

13th July when the *Niger* Frigate came into the Harbour. Sr Thomas Adams came on board the *Lark* to whom B^r Hill was presented by Captn Thompson, whom we can't mention without expressing our gratitude for the kindness he shew'd during the Voyage & our abode on board his Ship while at Croque. Of Sr Thomas we learn'd that the *Hope* Schooner set out from St Laurence the same day with the *Niger*, & he expected her here in Croque every day, but as he must Sail in a day or two for Labrador if she did not come in that time he would take us with him in his Frigate, & leave orders for the Schooner to follow us directly.

15th July According to Sr Thomas Adams's Order we went with our things on board the *Niger*.

16th July We weigh'd Anchor & left Croque. The Breth^n Hill & Drachart din'd with Sr Thomas. At Dinner he propos'd that two of us should stay with him in Pitts' Harbour to wait the coming of the Indians, while the other two went with the Schooner to explore the Coast. B^r Hill told him we could not seperate; the intention of our Expedition would be entirely frustrated thereby as each of us had our proper department, & it was not only expected that we should speak with the Indians but also make proper Draughts of those places we should touch at. Sr Thomas said our making Draughts was needless the Government had employ'd Captn Cook for this purpose, B^r. Hill told him, as he desired it, he would acquaint his Breth^n with it; but was pretty sure they were as much determin'd as he not to seperate.

We sail'd the whole day surrounded with Islands of Ice.

17th July At Noon we saw the Coast of Labrador & saild directly into Chateau-Bay & about 6 in the evening came to an Anchor in Pitt's Harbour.

18th July Two of us went on Shore on Henleys Island where we found evident marks of the Indians being there some time ago. We also found the Ruins of an House which from its construction & several pieces of Red Tyles, evidently appear'd to have been built by Europeans, in one end of this House after removing the Rubbish we found Whale Bone now quite decay'd which if sound would amount to a very large sum, the Shore was covered with the Ribs & other Bones of Whales all which proves that here an extensive Whale Fishery has been carryed on, & that by Europeans. [cf. Banks's diary, p. 49.]

19th July We went on Shore on the main-Land but could find no Traces of the Indians having been there.

22d July Sr Thomas with one of the Fisher Masters went to St Peters Islands, we would gladly have embraced this opportunity of seeing if we could find any signs of the Indians being there, but Sr Thomas put us off till another opportunity. In the evening at 6 o'clock the, by us, long expected Schooner came in Sight; at her entring the Bay she run aground on a sunk Rock & Damag'd her Keel & Cutt-water, however in about an hour they got her afloat again & she anchored with us in Pitts Harbour

23ᵈ July Sʳ Thomas sent for us, & read to us that part of Commodore Pallisser's Orders relative to the Schooner, by these orders she is to proceed to 56 deg. N. to explore the Coast make proper Draughts, & every needful discovery for the future Benefit of Trade & Fishery. That one of the Missionaries who understands the Indian & English Languages may, if he pleases go with her, if not they are all Four to be detained here in Pitts Harbour. We could not help expressing our surprise at this order, but Sʳ Thomas assur'd us he could not recede a little from it, it was as much as his Commission was worth, the Schooner was to Sail in the morning & if we did not directly agree to the Commodore's proposals, she sho'd have orders to sail in the morning & we all Four be detained here. Rather than nothing should be done, we told him two of us would go with the Schooner, provided he certified under his hand the necessity we were under to Seperate which he promissed & accordingly sign'd

In the evening Our two Brethⁿ Haven & Schloezer with heavy Hearts on account of Our being thus forcibly seperated from one another, went on board the Schooner leaving the other two behind in the same affliction.

25 July The *Hope* Schooner Sailed out of Pitts Harbour.

27. July Sʳ Thomas sent for Bʳ Hill & desired to see the paper which he had sign'd previous to his Brethren's going to the Northward certifying his orders to detail two of us here, when he got it in his possession he would not return it saying it was more than he could answer, to sign any such Paper.

Augˢᵗ 8ᵗʰ Commodore Pallisser in the *Guernsey* came into Pitts Harbour.

Augˢᵗ 15ᵗʰ The Governor acquainted us with a large number of Indians living in Newfoundland near Fogo, whom he believed were of the Esquimaux Tribes, & would be glad if we could come to the Speech of them, to know what they were & agree upon terms of accommodation with them. We told him on our return to Sᵗ Johns, if he gave us an opportunity, we would do all we could, he said when we had finished with the Indians whom he expected here, he would send us over to Quirpont to the *Lark* Frigate who had orders to come there, & should take us to the place where the Indians were

Augˢᵗ 17ᵗʰ We heard the agreeable account that the Indians were seen 30 English Miles N.E. from hence. We went out with Sʳ Thomas in his Barge about 8 miles— expecting to meet them, but not seeing them return'd on board.

Augˢᵗ 18ᵗʰ We went early in the morning with Sʳ Thomas to find out, & invite the Indians, in the name of the Governor to come to Pitts Harbour. About 9. Leagˢ off we had the pleasure to see them coming to us in their Kaiaks (Boats) crying out Tous Cammerads, which our Barges Crew repeated. Sr Thomas askd B^r Drachart why he did not with the others cry out Tous Cammerads? He said it was not the manner he chose to use with these people, this method they had learn'd of the French, but he would treat with them in their own way & Language, & beg'd he would desire the Sailors to suffer him to be heard by the Indians, accordingly as soon as the noise subsided, he call'd out to the man in the nearest Kaiak to come to him, which he immediately did, he took him by the hand spoke to him in his own Language & told him, We are your good Friends, he understood him and answered we will also be your good Friends, the Indian calld out to his Countrymen to come near, one of them in a White Jacket came to the Boat & inquired for Jens Inguoak (Bro^r Jens Haven whom our Brethren sent to them last year) & say'd this Jacket which I have on he gave me. Bro^r Drachart ask'd them if they had seen him this summer? They answ^d No! He farther askd them if we should go with them on shore to their Tents? they answ^d Yes! As soon as he set his feet on land, the Old Men came about him took him by the Arms & led him to their Tents accompanied by above 300 Indians, who told him we are your good Friends don't be afraid in the least, we understand you, but from whence do you come & where have you learn'd our speech? He answ^d I am come from the Caralit (Greenlanders) in the East, there I have lived & had a House, Wife, Children & Servants. They conducted him from one Tent to the other, in one of the Tents he said to them, I have words to tell you. As soon as he said this, they led him out to a Green Place & called their people to him. He sat on a piece of Wood & they ranged themselves on the ground about him, while he told them the following: The Caralit in the East among whom I have lived are your good Friends; they not understanding that he meant the Greenlanders, but those Caralit who live contigious to them; with whom they are at enmity; cryed out: the Caralit in the East are bad people, we don't trust them. A young man said we dont fear them let them come! B^r Drachart said hear me, I don't come from the North, I come from over the Great Sea which lies East from here, there are many Caralit who are your good Friends; They say'd: of these people we don't know anything, they may be good People. He sayd further, it is not possible that you should know them, it is so many years since you were seperated, but you were once one people & they by me desire to renew their friendship. The European Brethren have visited your People here in Labrador about 13 years ago. They sayd we have never heard anything of it. He continued, the last year Jens Inguaok visited you. Two men answ^d we know him, where is he? He answer'd he is gone to the Northward to visit your People. They enquired if he would not come here? Bro^r Drachart say'd he expected he would, but I & this Brother are here; we heard of Bro^r J. Inguaok that you are Caralit, & now we see & observe that your speech, manner, Countenance, & Cloathing is exactly like the Caralit in the East. I am come to tell you that these Caralit in the East are acquainted with the Creator of all Things as their Saviour & Redeemer. They repeated each word & struck their hands upon their Breasts, & said to one another be attentive let us hear him, repeat these words again. He repeated the words several time & they say'd to one another what is it he says? A very old Man say'd he means Silla! waved his hand over his head & blew with his mouth. Br Drachart continued: He who made the World & all things therein. He is the Saviour. A young man say'd I don't know this Saviour of whom you speak, who is he? Answr: He is the Creator of all things. Another asked where is he? Bror Drachart waved his hand over his head & blew with his mouth & say'd he is over all in the Silla (Heavens) he became a Man & lived here in this Earth for many years. One of them ask'd him are you a Teacher? He say'd I am, upon which two old men with long white Beards came to him saying, we are also Angikoks (their Teachers) one of them waved his hand over his head blew with his mouth & Repeated as he had heard Br Drachart. 'The Worlds Creator etc.' An old Woman look'd up to Heaven did as the Angikok & repeated the same words.

During this Discourse Sr Thomas, & others of the Ship's Company stood by & everything was as still & orderly as in a Church. Bror Drachart then invited them to come to Pitts Harbour to see the Governor & introduced Sr Thomas to them as an Officer who was their Friend & would on every occasion while they staid here protect & shew them kindness. They sayd they would come but did not appoint a Day. Sr Thomas return'd in his Barge to Pitts Harbour & we went to the Northwd about a league to St Lewis's Bay, where we drop'd anchor for the night.

We were rejoiced at this first interview with the Indians as Bror Drachart found that he could understand & make himself more intelligible to them than he had expected.

Augst 19th We sailed early in the morning for Charles's Bay to the Indians, before we doubled the NE. point which formed the Bay, two of the Indians who were fishing for Cod came to us & accompanied us into the Bay. We could not go on shore having no Boat, but call'd to them & several came off in their Kaiaks and lay along side the Tender, Ten men came on board. Br Drachart ask'd them if they would not go with him to the Governor. They appeared timourous & enquired how Many Ships lay there? Answd 5. They asked him farther if the Kablunets would murder them? He answd No, they are your good Friends, they said it were better you sold us these Guns, which they saw in the Tender, with which we would shoot Deer than that you should keep them to kill men with them. To which Bror Drachart replyed, we also use them to kill Deer, & never against men but in our own defence. He again desired them to go with him to the Governor, they say'd they could not to day they must catch Fish for their Families but another time they would. Br Drachart said the Governor desires very much to see you & has a present to make you. They sayd can we get large Sails, Fyles, &c. He said they should come & see;

198

they laugh'd & said they will kill us. He said NO. we are your good Friends, they answered: We know you wont hurt us, He said I am a Teacher & its certain if you don't hurt me I will do you no harm. They gave him the hand, struck their Breasts & said Good Friend! You are a Teacher, we will hear you; upon which he spent some time in instructing them. About noon Sr Thomas came with his Barge & two Masters of Merchant-Ships. We took this opportunity of getting a Shore; the Men welcome'd us in their usual friendly manner, they assembled round Mr. Drachart, He read them a letter in their Language wrote by one of our Missionaries in Greenland. Sr Thomas was uneasy to find they did not intend to come today as the Governor expected, & was apprehensive they had no intention to come. B^r Drachart told him He had hitherto done what he could, this was a point which he had undertaken to manage & must be left entirely to him or else he would not concern himself in the Affair, he best knew how to manage & treat with these People & if it was left to him would undertake in a day or two to bring them to Pitts-Harbour to the Governor, not all of them with their Wives etc. as he was persuaded they would be averse to trusting them so near the Europeans of whose Morals they had a very bad impression.

Augst 21st   The Governor sent for us & told us he had a present for the Indians to whom we were to present it, & make the peace between them & the English, at the same time wishd we could be able to prevail with some of them to come here to Pitts Harbour; if we could do it no otherwise, he would leave 3 of his men as Hostages with them, till a like number of theirs return'd again. B^r Drachart wo'd not agree to the leaving Hostages; they were not he said used to it, & did not doubt but he should be able to prevail on some of them to come.

We set out for them in the Tender, when we got about ½ way we were met by 20 Kaiaks who on enquiry we found were actually going to the Governor. We return'd with them some of the men came into the Barge to Bro^r Drachart to whom he related: that about 500 years ago your forefathers have lived here on these Islands, & by degrees spread farther northwards along the Coast even to the Eastward in Greenland where many of them remain to this day but cannot on account of the Ice come over to you. The Indians answ^d Now we understand you, you don't mean the Caralit our Neighbours but others who live farther to the Eastward.

As we came near Pitt's Harbour we were met by the Governor, who return'd with us into the Harbour surrounded by the Indian Kaiaks, they were received by the Ships Crew with 3 cheers from the yards, which frightened the Indians & put them to confusion, but Bro^r Drachart spoke with them & propos'd their going rather ashore than to the ships, pointed out a place to them where they presently followed him. He went on shore & called them to him, he formed them in a Circle round the Governor & then read to them the following Articles which the Governor had drawn up for the purpose:

1.) I am glad to see you.

2.) I observe you are suspicious of us & afraid to trust us.

3.) You have reason to be so, I recommend it to you to continue to be on your guard till we are better acquainted; we will do the same.

4.) Our King has heard that some Europeans coming to this Coast have treated some of you Ill & killed some of your people. He is exceeding angry at it.

5.) He has therefore ordered that none of the people who did come here formerly shall ever come again.

6.) He has sent me here to protect you & Mr Drachart to Instruct you.

7.) For he loves you & will not let any Body do you harm.

8.) I observe that you live together as Brethren & Friends as all good people do.

9.) I desire you will observe that we do the same.

10.) And we desire to be on the same footing with you as we become better acquainted.

11.) For the same Great God that made you, made us & all things, and has commanded that we should all Love one another as Brethren, & not hurt each other, then we shall all be happy in this and the next World.

12.) Tell me what Proof you wish to have of our sincerity?

13.) I understand you have your Wives & Children with you.

14.) I make you a present of a good Tent to shelter them from the Weather.

15.) Our People have some things to Truck with you.

16.) If you will let me know what things you want our people shall bring you every thing the next Year to truck for your things.

17.) I will take care that our People take nothing from you but what you chuse to exchange for something else.

I have only three things to desire of you:

1.) That you do not come near our Houses & Ships in the Night.

2.) That in the Day not more than 5. of you come at a time.

3.) That you do not go to our Boats when afishing.
Upon this the Governor asks them many Quest^s the chief of which follows Will you now enter into friendship with us? Will you Trade with us? Shall there be an end to the stealing & killing? Will you keep away from our Ship & Houses in the night? Will no more than five of you come to our Ships in the Day? Will you take care to do our Fishers no harm? Will you come here with your Wives & Children? Will you pitch your Tents some Miles off from the Ship? Will you take Mr Drachart as sent by the King for your Teacher? To every one of these quest^s they answ^d in the Affirmative, took Brother Drachart by the hand & said you are our Teacher.

Upon this the Present was distributed with which they were entirely pleased & upon his Excellencys repeating the quest^n: If they would remain our good friends?

Segullia the Angikok gave him his hand, call'd him Captain Chateau struck him on the Breast, kissd him & said we will remain your good friends. Thus this to us weighty affair was happily concluded & hope that no imprudent conduct from the English for the future may induce the Indians to look upon them otherwise than as their good Friends. The Indians brought Whalebone to the Governor which they would make him a present of, but he declin'd it saying here are Merchⁿ who have goods with whom they might now Trade with their Whalebone. After the Trading was over B^r Drachart had an opportunity of telling them again something of their Creator & Saviour. The Governor desired that we might bring the two Angikoks & two others with us to his Ship, which we did, & during their stay conversed about several things. We gave them an Idea of the English Flag which till now they had an aversion to, & which on that account we never hoisted since their coming to these parts, but now they were reconciled to it & of themselves desired the Commodor that it might be hoisted, which was accordingly done & they sayd, this is a Sign of Friendship, when we see this Flag out at sea we will come out of the Harbours where we are & welcome you. It grew late, B^r Drachart told them they might now go home & acquaint the rest of their People with what they had done, they accordingly set off in their Kaiaks.

The Governor as well as we were entirely pleas'd, & Bro^r Drachart told him: Sir I have now been engaged in a matter which is quite out of my Sphere & find it very difficult to make the Indians understand me as their Ideas are very much confin'd this makes the difficulty to find words to convey the proper meaning of things of which at best they have little conception, I am a Clergyman & my proper call is to preach the Gospel to them, & this I can do with the utmost simplicity. I am however rejoiced that it has succeeded so well.

In the evening the Governor invited us to sup with him & again express'd his satisfaction that we had brought it so far with the Indians & proposed when the Indians came again, to erect a Barrier between them and the Europeans to prevent the latter from taking any undue liberty with them under the pretence of Trade, one of his Officers should always be present to keep order. He immediately gave orders for the Barrier to be erected, & appointed an Officer whom he directed that no European except us two should be allowed to go over the Barrier to the Indians.

Augst 22^d   In the morning the Governor sent for us, having heard a report that the Indians were coming; we went out in a Boat to conduct them in & staid out till 4 o'clock without seeing them, having no provisions & judging too late for them to come this Day we return'd to Pitts Harbour.

Augst 23^d   We went out to visit the Indians & invite them to Trade when we were half way we saw about 26 Kaiaks coming to us. They saluted us & rowed several times round our Boat, on our way back B^r Drachart took 3 of the Indians into our Boat, & ask'd them why they did not as they promissd the Governor bring their wives & Children with them? They said they were afraid to trust their Women among the Sailers. As soon as we came into the Harbour we were met by the Governor, with whom we went to the place appointed for Trade. The Merch^{ts} were there with their goods on their side the Barrier. Bro^r Drachart told the Indians why the Barrier was set up, & shew'd them their side where they could be in perfect security without any ones coming to disturb them. Now said he go & Trade at the Barrier & behave Yourselves like orderly Caralit, which they did to the surprize of every one for 3 hours together. The Governor desired Bro^r Drachart to tell them that they should not trade with the French, but to this they would not assent. He askd them if they wo'd go home tonight? They said it was too late & the Sea too high, they would go out of the Harbour to some of the Islands till morning The Governor with his people & the Merch^{ts} went away, & left us two at our desire alone with the Indians; this opportunity Bro^r Drachart emply'd in preaching the Gospel to them. In about 2 hours the Governor sent a Boat for us & we took leave of the Indians who immediately went into their Kaiaks & paddled out of the Harbour. When we came to the Governor he asked us if we had any hopes that any of these Savages would be converted? B^r Drachardt told him it must be a work of time & had hopes that if we were to live among them by precept & example something real might be effected. We requested the Governor to let us have a Boat in which we could visit the Indians as we had hitherto no proper opportunity to speak with them, but when the Merchⁿ were present & their minds engaged with Trade He immediately gave orders for the Tender to go with us in the morning & stay if we chose it 4 days

Augst. 25th We set out in the Tender with the Commodor's first Lieut^t & two other Officers to the Indians, but as the wind was contrary could not reach farther by night than St Peters Islands where we lay at Anchor.

Augst 26th We set out early for Charles's Bay & came to the Indians, they received us with their accustom'd friendliness took Brother Drachart by the hand & led him to their Tents where he spent several hours in conversing with them, & read a letter to them from one of our Bishops part of which is as follows:

'We Brethren in the Land of the Kablunets have lov'd you for a long time, & longed to visit you & now you see four of us. They this year intend to find out a place where they can dwell among you, & return another year & Build a House' B^r Drachart ask'd them: Shall we come & live with you? they answ^d Yes! Where shall we build our House? they sayd in Kikkertet, you Brethren we will gladly have among us but don't bring any other Kablunets with you. The letter goes on: 'So as you have in your Tents Chief-men, you may also observe in the Ships that we also have Chief-men among us. But in our Land we have also a very great man, George King of Great Brittain his Country is called England, he has also many Countries. He it is who has helped our Brethren with one of his great Ships that they might

202

come to you & visit you. He loves the Innuit, he is like a Father to you, and has given orders to his Subjects, that when they come to your Land they shall Shew you all kindness and do you no harm. Do you also act so towards them. Commit no Hostilities, Steal not & they will not Steal from you, do not kill any of them & they will not kill any of you. When you Trade with the English & become better acquainted with them you will find that they love you & will do you all manner of good; you and your Children will reap the advantage of it. When you learn to know us as well as the Greenlanders know us, then you will join with us in praying for his Majesty King George, that God would give him a long life for he has help'd us that we could come to you. The Creator of all things bless you & give you believing & new hearts. This is wrote to you by your Friend & Brother who truely loves you.

'Johannes Assersoak'

We took a friendly leave of them & went on board the Tender, & anchored 4 leag^s Eastward from them under one of the Cariboo Islands where we staid the night.

Augst 27th   We weigh'd anchor at 2 in the morning & came to the Indians, who brought us to their Tents which are erected on two different Islands. We resolved to visit the furthermost, where we had not yet been & found they were the same Indians, but more cautious in letting us see their Boats which they had drawn up behind the Island than those on the other Island. They even stop'd the Lieut. who was going over the Hill to take a view of their Shallops. Bro^r Drachart employed himself in speaking with them about our Saviour. A Woman brought a New Born Infant to him & desired he would bless it. He laid his hands on its head & recommended it to the care of its Creator & Redeemer. He then went into another Tent & said I have words to tell you from the Governor, there came a great many together, of whom he enquired about some matters which the Governor desired to be informed of: contained in the following:

Memorandum for our Brethren of the Unitas Fratrum Missionarys on the Coast of Labrador.

 After giving the Savages such impressions and Informations as you judge best for making yourselves acceptable & for facilitating the pious & Laudable Object of your Mission you'l please to make the following enquirys for his Majesty's Information & for the Benefit of the Publick: [a shortened version of Palliser's questionnaire and the Eskimos' replies is given on pp. 218–21].

The Indians ask'd B^r Drachart why the Boat was this time furnish'd with more Arms than hitherto? He answ^d why are you so mistrustfull, don't you carry many Darts & Arrows concealed in your Kaiaks? These you don't use to kill Seals with but men. Upon which they were quiet. He then went into a Tent & they wanted to

203

see what he had in his Pockets, he permitted them to search him, which they did effectually & took everything he had in them away, One took away his Hat & went into another Tent with it. Drachart sayd I have no Hat. Upon which they calld out to their People who brought his Hat & all his things to him again. He then askd them where have you your winter Houses your Benches Lamps, Chests & other Household Furniture they sayd in the North. He observ'd they were very poorly furnished here & described to them how how convenient & orderly the Greenlanders were in their Houses. They told him at home in the North theirs were exactly so—He then desired them to tell him what he had related to them of their Creator, they repeated to him several things with which he was entirely satisfied; thus he conversed with them till noon, when we return'd to the Tender, which we had enough to do before we effected as the Sea run prodigious high. We found it impossible to reach the Ship this night as the wind was contrary, we therefore put into Niger-Bay (pl. 91) & anchored for the night.

Aug^st 28th We set sail & arrived in Pitts Harbour. They were concerned about us the weather was so stormy they had placed a Centinal on Castle Hill who made the signal for seeing the Tender which brought the Governor & Sr Thomas in their Barges to meet us & bring us in. The Commodore acquainted us that the Merch^ts would go in the morning to trade with the Indians; The Tender also went to protect & wish'd if we were not too much fatugued [*sic*] we might go in too

Aug^st 29th In the morning at 2 O'clock we set out accompanied by Sr Thomas in his Barge, with 7 or 8 Fishing & Trading Shallops. Our Tender saild so slow that we were soon left behind, but Sr Thomas made a signal to speak with the headmost Shallop, which he sent to take us in, we went on board & soon overtook the Barge into which Sr Thomas took us, leaving orders with the trading Shallops to lye at Anchor between the innermost of S^t. Peters Islands & the Continent while we went to call the Indians to Trade. When we came to them we found they would not let any of the Sailers to go on Shore armed & even searched Sr Thom^s & would have taken a Case of Pocket Pistols from him. They said they wanted to Trade with us as friends, & did not understand how the Sending of so many armed men among them was consistent with the expressions of friendship we made use of. B^r Drachart told them they must always expect to find whenever they met us that we were armed not with a view to do any of our Friends harm, but to protect them & Defend ourselves. He then told them we were come to invite to Trade at S^t. Peters where the Merch^ts waited for them, as we thought it would be more agreable to them to go there than that the Merch^ts should come here. They said they would go with us, but seemed irresolute; when we Set of several Kaiaks accompanied us, but when we were about 100. fath^ms from the Shore Segullia the Angikok call'd them upon which they every one left us, saying they did not know whether they should come to us to-day or not. We however continued our Course & came about 4 o'clock to the Shallops resolving to stay there that night & in the morning go down to the Indians & trade with them at their Tents. This was scarce resolved when we saw several Kaiaks, with Indians they Landed on Truck Island* behaved very friendly & traded freely with us; when they were about to go, we told them we should stay there all night & if they chose it, they might come early in the morning & have further trade. [See pl. 91.]

Aug^st 30th they accordingly came early in the morning & by Sun rise the little Island was like a Fair; they also brought one of their Women's Boats or Skin Battoes with near 20 Women with their Children in it. They behaved extreamly friendly & orderly & both they & the Merch^ts were pleased; they were very much pleased with this place & method of Trade & promised when ever we let them know they would come here & trade with us.

Bro^r Drachart called the Old men together & shewed them a Picture wherein the Commodor's Ship with the Yards man'd, the two Barges accompanied by the Indians, just as it appeared on the Day when we made peace with them was represented.[1] He explain'd this to them & told them the Commodor made them a present of it, that they might take it home with them & shew it to their people & tell them of the league of friendship which we have entered into with their Nation. And when ever they look'd upon this picture they should think on their good Friends the English. All this they understood & accepted of the present with great tokens of satisfaction, they even offer'd a large quaintity of Whalebone in return, but we declined it. Thus we took a friendly leave of these poor people & set off from this place which we called Truck-Island in Sr Thomas's Barge, we found it was impossible to reach Pitt's Harbour this night; we therefore run in between an Island & the Main Land N.E. from Nigers Bay. We went on shore & made a Fire & were not long there when one of the trading Shallops put in for Shelter, & let fall her anchor, but the swell increas'd so much that the anchor came home & she drove directly on the Rocks & had not the Barge been here to assist her she must in a few minutes have beat to pieces. The Barge got her off & tow'd her into smooth water where she lay secure. Soon after our Tender came in with her Boom broke. The Water broke over her so much that the men & everything in her was quite wet thro'. They got her Boom mended & went to Sea again. Which made Sr Thomas determine if possible to get to the Ship, we accordingly put off & tho' the men labour'd with all their strength we found that we could make very little way against the swell which set against us; we saw the Tender almost cover'd with water & forced to put back to the Harbour from whence she set off. We would have done the same but the Cockswain durst not venture to put the Barge about. We kept her head to the swell & streched across S^t. Peters Bay where we found 4 of the trading Shallops at Anchor in a smooth Sea close to the shore. We landed, made a Fire &

---

[1] Perhaps drawn by the artist who executed the chart represented in pl. 40.

dried our wet Cloaths & spent the night under the Shelter of a Hill among Craggy Rocks & Stones.

Aug^st 31st At Day-break we all set off & found the swell pretty near as great as yesterday but the wind less. When we came to cross Bad-Bay a Fog arose so thick that we did not know which way to Steer having no Compass in the Boat; but however luckily found the West point of the Bay & soon got safe into Pitts Harbour & on Board. The Signal of the Barges being in sight brought the Commodor on board the *Niger*, who told us that he intended to Sail from hence to Newfoundland in the morning; & desired to know what he could further do to help our design in speaking with the Indians, we told him we hoped to have the liberty as usual when the Boats went there to be permitted to go with them & when the trading was over have a little time allowed us to converse with them. He said he would give Sr Thomas orders accordingly. He saild from hence the *1st Septem^r*.

Sept. 3^d In the morning there came 4 Kaiaks into the Harbour, we went to meet them & bring them to the Ship while we sent to the Merch^ts to bring their goods to the trading place. Sr Thomas being out of the Ship we requested the 1st Lieu^t to permit us to shew them his Majesty's Picture which hung in the Cabin. B^r Drachart shew'd them the Picture, & said here you see the Picture of our King, He it is who has sent the Governor to you; when you made peace with the Governor at the same time you made peace with this King; it was he who sent you the present which the Governor in his name gave to you. When you are obedient to the Governor, it is the same as if you were obedient to the King whose picture you see here, & when you go to Newfoundland or Northward the King will rejoice when he hears that you behave yourselves well & are obedient orderly Caralit. We then told them to go to the trading place where the Merch^ts waited for them. We went with them, where we abode till evening. They could not return home this night but determined to Sleep on the Island. To day we had the pleasure to see the *Hope* Schooner return from the North.

Septr. 4th This morning the Indians who stayed here last night were dispersed all over the place, but behaved quite friendly. We were sent to collect them together & bring them to the Ship, which we did & told them they should go home to their Tents & we would follow them with the Merch^ts. We told them Bro. Haven & the other Bro^r who went to seek them to the northward were come & shew'd them the Schooner where they were, they askd if they might go there? we said yes. The accordingly went & met them on their way to our Ship. They presently knew B^r Haven, & said this is Johannes Inguoak our Friend. Another said I don't know you personally but have heard a great deal of you in the North & that you are our Friend, upon which they took leave & went to their Tents. There were but 3 of them whom he had seen the last year in Newfoundland.

Sr Thomas called us all 4 together & said now you see I was right in not suffering you all to go to the northward; if you had all gone you would certainly have entirely miss'd seeing the Indians. We told him we could not think so; for, had the Schooner come in proper time & began here & proceeded Northward in our Searching the Coast, we must have found the Indians, been able to take draughts of their places of abode & have had time enough to return with them here for the Governor to see them & the Merch^{ts} to trade with them. And even late as the Schooner came, instead of being sent to Davis's Inlet had we been allowed to begin here & proceed to the northward, we either would have met them in their coming here or found them in their winter Houses. But some circumstances considered it is no wonder that our Voyage to the northward has been of so little effect. In the afternoon we set out for the Indians and came by duskish to Truck Island where we anchored.

Sepr 5th Twelve Kaiaks came with Whalebone to truck with the Merchants. We had orders to persuade them not to go to Newfoundland & assured them they would not be secure of their lives there as they are here; but they sayd they could not avoid going, the wood of which they made their Darts & Arrows grew there & not in their Country and desired as we were their Friends we might not hinder them. We spoke with them concerning their place of abode with a view if possible to find it out We asked them in what time they thought our Ship could Sail to their Winter Houses? They said in 3 days. We learned further from Segullia that where they lived was a large Bay in the middle of which was a large Island & nine smaller ones round it. We told him we intended to try next year if we find it out, & stay there & live with him; this pleased him, & he said: Come and build a House by us but bring no Kablunets with you but such people as you are. He also desired we might bring no Guns with us. We told him, they had their Darts & Arrows. He answ^d but these we'll use only to kill Deer with. We replyed, if you behave yourselves so well as you have done since you came here, you may depend upon it we'll never use our Guns but to killing of Deer. B^r Haven told him when we have finished our House which we intend to build with You, then we will shew you how to Build Boats & repair your Old ones. This pleased them very much & they said we will also help you to build your House & we will live together as friends & Brothers. About 11.o'clock there came in a Battoe near 50 Women & Children; they behaved extreamly well, & gave us hopes that the Gospel would not be preach'd to them in vain. They told us they would repeat to their people at home what they had heard of us here concerning their Creator & desired when we came to live among them we might come to the Winter Houses & tell them more good words of their Creator. Thus we took leave, and they went to their Tents. While we thro' contrary wind kept working with the Tender till 3 o'clock in the morning Sepr. 6th when we got quite fatigued on board the *Niger*.

Sr Thomas sent for us this morning hearing that the Indians were determined to go to Newfoundland, said two of you must go over there & the other two remain here in case the Indians should come back, but rather wish'd we might go of our own accord than compell him to force us, He desired us to consider of it & give him our answer this evening. We told him we would never consent to seperate, but if the Indians went to Quirpont, as he told us Captn Thompson lay there, we would all four go over there & stay with him as long as the Indians stay'd & if he chose it return with them here to Pitts Harbour, when they return'd or proceed with Captn Thompson to find out the Indians in Newfoundland according to the Commodor's desire. He urg'd it for this time no farther.

Septr. 7th　The Merchts went to Truck Island to trade with the Indians & we in the Tender accompanied them. Before we got to the Island we observed a White Flag hoisted on a little Island. We immediately bore in to the Land and actually found the Indians with their Tents on the Island. They recd us very friendly, & the first thing we did was to give them an English Jack which we placed instead of the French one, telling them we never carried a White Flag, but such a one as we now had set up, & desired they might keep this, & whenever we saw it thus hoisted, in whatsoever place they were we should directly know that our good friends were there; & this pleased them & they promised to do it. We found there 15 Tents 4 European Battoes which they had bought or stole of the French 3 Indian ones covered over with skins & about 100 Kaiaks. The rest of the Indians we learn'd were gone home to their Winter Houses, & these waited an opportunity of a fair Wind to Cross over to Newfoundland. We enquired of them about their Dwelling Place they told us as before they lived on Islands in a long Deep Bay at the head of which was a fresh water Lake where they went in summer to hunt Deer & Catch Salmon; they also told us the Names & situation of several Islands whereon they lived, they gave us such a description of the place, that we must conclude it could be no other than what the French call Kessisakou or Esquimaux Bay in 55. degrees Upon enquiring where they got the Iron for their Darts & Arrows? they sayd of Ships which come to them. Questn can these people speak with you? Answr only by signs & the few words we have learned of them; from whence we must conclude they were french. They enquired very earnest about Cap. Galliot if he was in Quirpont? we answd we did not know. Questn are any of your Brethn there who can Speak with us? We answd no & advised as their Friends not to go to Newfoundland, but they said they must go to procure wood for their Darts etc & desired us to intreat the Captain & that he might do them no hurt on their passage. About 6.O'clock a violent Storm arose which drove one of the Trading Shallops on Shore, the Indians assisted us to their utmost to get her off & even went to the middle in the water to shove her off but 'twas all in vain as the Tide was going out, She must remain till the mornings Flood We had no Boat but a small Canoa in which Bro.

Hill determined to go on board the Tender in order to acquaint the Officer with our Situation & concert matters with him for our better security & to prevent any confusion which might arise in these circumstances, the Surgeon [Munkhouse] of the *Niger* insisted on going with him; as soon as they came along side the Tender the little Boat overset with the swell & breaking of the Sea, they luckily laid out of a Sweep which lay over the stern & supported themselves by it, till the Tenders people hauled them on board with Ropes; the Boat was gone adrift & no possibility of getting to or from shore. The Tender came as near the Shore as she durst, & we took all the measures in our power for our security in case the Indians should fall upon the people on the stranded Shallop. It rain'd & blew very hard & they had nothing to eat or Drink. The Indians came to the Shallop & told our Brn. Drachart & Haven that the Boat could not be got off till morning, invited them to come ashore to their Tents and sleep there, which they agreed to. Segullia carried them on his back to Land & conducted them to his Tent, where he took their wet cloaths & dryed them & spread skins for them to sit on just in the Greenland manner. The Tent was crowded with people, they sayd now we see that you are no Kablunets but Innuit & askd if they were afraid? they answ[d] No! we are friends & friends are not afraid of one another. They said, now we see that you are indeed our Friends, you come to us in confidence without arms, we'll do you no hurt. The Indians gave them Fish & Bread which they had got of the Europeans. They had a good deal of conversation with them about the difference between theirs and the Greenland speech. The other Indians went to their Tents & Segullia spread skins for his two Guests to sleep on. In about ½ an hour he began with his two wives to sing & afterwards fell on the Ground, distorting his Limbs & feature in a surprizing manner, foam'd at the mouth & appear'd like a Lunatic roaring quite frantic; He at last stretch'd his hand out to Bro[r] Drachart & said the Spirit is here, I see him! & began to mutter something which they could not understand. He then lay motionless for some time & at last desired the two Brethren might come to him & kiss him, which they did, & he began to come to himself, after having playd these frantic tricks for above an hour. He then arose & sat down & began to sing as at first. When he had done Bro[r] Drachart told him, they would sing something better than what he had sung, upon which the two Brethren sang a Hymn which they listened to with great attention. Segullia desired them to repeat the words the most of which he said he understood. They began then to speak about the place where he lived; he said the water in the Bay in Winter was frozen quite over & he could hardly from his Island see the Sea water where it was free from Ice. The Women he sayd fish for Skulpins (as they also do in Greenland) Early in the year when the Ice breaks, the Whales come into the Bay &c &c. It was during this nights hazardous stay among these people that we got the first true notion of the places where they lived & the other particulars of the most importance which we were enabled after-wards to understand more clearly. They were continually interrupted & calld upon

209

by the Fisher People who were stranded or the Indians, who came with complaints against each other, thus they spent the night and were happy enough to prevent any quarrell between the Europeans & Indians.

Sept 13th   In the morning Segullia sayd to our Brethren now you can tell the Caralit in the East that you have spent the night with us you are the very first Europeans that have ever slept in our Tents & we look upon your confidence in us as a proof of your being indeed our good friends. The Boat that went adrift last night was found this morning not far from the stranded shallop, in which they went on board the Tender. About 6 in the evening by the help of the Indians the Shallop was set afloat. The Indians again enquired about Quirpont & the people there, if we knew them? answ^r no! Do you think we may venture to go there? answ^r no we would by no means advise you to it. We remained here on account of contrary wind all night &c

Septr 14   Set out for Pitt's Harbour where we arrived at 6 o'clock in the evening.

15th   Sr Thomas received advice that the Indians were on Henley's Island among the Fishers; upon this we were sent with the Boat to them & found them scatter'd all over the place in every Hut & Fish stage. We soon collected them & among other things, reminded them of the peace which they made with the Governor. They say'd as long as day & night remains, we will continue your good Friends; & when we come next year we will bring all our Whale bone with us. We also learn'd of them that they had pitched their Tents about $\frac{1}{2}$ a League from here. We then desired them to go to their Tents, where the Captⁿ. could come after dinner & see them. Accordingly after dinner we went with Sr Thomas to their Tents & found that they had disposed of all their Whalebone &c, & were now waiting an opportunity to go over to Quirpont. B^r Drachart had a very good opportunity of telling them something more of the Gospel which they heard with attention.

Sepr 16th   We heard the Indians were among the Fisher people, We went to them & found them Dispersed about the Island as before, there were also 3 Battoes full of Women & Children. One of the Boys belonging to the Frigate stole a Dart out of one of the Indian Kaiaks, which the Women perceived from their Boats & set up a cry which alarmed the Indians. The owner of the Dart seized him & wrung the dart out of his hand, with which he would have killd the Boy if we had not luckily been there and prevented him. He complaind of the Boy & insisted he would have satisfaction, which we assured him he sho'd have when the Captⁿ came on shore. When Sr Thomas came & heard what the Boy had done He ordered him to be tied up in presence of the Indians, as soon as he had received two lashes, Segullia step'd forward held the man's hand & cry'd out it is enough, while another Indian untyed the Boy. By this opportunity B^r Haven told, so the Europeans treat the

210

Thieves, take you warning & don't steal. In the evening they returned to their Tents.

Sept. 10th We went to the Indians & enquired of them how they called the Bay in which they lived? answ^r: Kankerlarsoak & also the name of the great Island which lies in the middle? answ^r Kisseksakkut. This last name confirmed us in the opinion that their dwelling place was the same which the french Chart calls Kisseksakku, upon which we determined to draw a draught of Esquimaux Bay and shew it to the Indians in hopes they may be able to understand it. On our return to the ship Sr Thomas again proposed our going to Quirpont in a shallop to attend the Indians while they stayed there. We told him we could not think of it & were surprized he sho'd propose it to us. He said: it was what we ourselves promiss'd the Govern^r We answ^d 'twas true we had promissed the Governor to go there as he told us the *Lark* had orders to come there to attend the Indians, & receive us on board; but since then she has received counter orders. We did not think it safe to trust ourselves in a Shallop, as we could not answer for the orderly behaviour of the Crew, over whom we had no command, if thro' their imprudence the Indians were provoked, which has happened more than once here, we had the greatest reason to think the french would rather Enflame their Resentment than otherwise & thus thro' one false step Ours & the lives of all the Crew were at stake & the present favourable impression which the Indians, thro' us, have of the English be entirely eradicated, besides our hea[l]th was so much impaird by the fatigues we had hitherto gone thro', that it would be the highest imprudence in us at this time of the year to go so far in an open Shallop & stay there at least 3 or 4 weeks. He said we must answ^r for it before the Governor. After Dinner we went again to the Indians; When we shewed them the Chart they understood it, & directly pointed, each of them, to the place where their respective Houses stood. They told the names of the Islands &^c. They also shewed the place where the Ship that sometimes comes to them Anchored, & even pointed out the different anchoring Places in the Bay; We, as well as Sr Thomas who was present, were entirely convinced that Esquimaux Bay as its called in the french Chart is the place of their abode.

Septr 19th At 8 o'clock in the morning several kaiaks with Indians came along side the *Niger*; we called them on board & shew'd them the Chart, & each of them, as before, pointed to the Island where his House stood; they also informed us, of the Seasons when the Whales & seals come into their Bay & their method of catching them. Some of the Indians went to the Wreck of the French snow [a small vessel]. One of them seeing a Rope hang down attempted to cut it, which the Centry perceiving, put him aside with his musket the Indian directly drew his long Knife, which the other Indians seeing, drew also their knives. The sailers on board the wreck took their arms. one of the Indians pulled up his Jacket & presented his bare Breast to the sailers daring them to kill him. It however luckilly ended without any mischief. B^r Haven got in a Boat & called them to follow him, & conducted them to their Tents.

Septr 20th B^r Drachart being sick thro' fatigue could not accompany B^r Haven, who went with Sr Thomas to the Indians, whom they found in their Boats with all their Baggage at the mouth of the Bay on their way to Newfoundland; they directly askd if the Captn was come to hinder them from going to Quirpont? Brother Haven answ^d they might go where they pleased, we have often advised you not to go there, but if you will go, no one will hinder you, but you must look to the consequence. Sr Thomas desired, he might try if possible to detain them here a little longer, as the french must soon leave Quirpont. This he effected so far, that they agreed to go on shore on the West point of the Bay where they set up their Tents. Sr Thomas set him on shore & he remained several hours alone with them, during which he enquired further about the place where they lived got the names of more Islands &c. He wanting to return the Indians offered to set him ashore on the other side which he accepted & on the way was met by Sr Thomas who took him into his Barge, in wch he return'd to the ship about 3 o'clock. In about an hour He with Sr Thomas went again to the Indians. He enquired where they got the stone of which they made their Lamps & Kettles? they said to the N-ward & described the place so exactly that he could easilly perceive they meant to the N-ward of Davis's Inlet. They further told him they got it with difficulty, as there were Caralit with whom they were not in friendship. About duskish the Captain came & acquainted B^r Haven that one of his officers with some people were gone to Red Bay about 14 leagues to the West, where he expected the Indians would land desiring B^r Haven to acquaint the Indians of it & desire them to do them no harm which he did, the Indians promissed to treat them as friends. B^r Haven told them on their return from Quirpont they might probably come here, where they would find Houses & stages which the Fishers left & intended to use next year, these they should not meddle with or destroy, but behave themselves agreable to the friendship they professed to have for us.

Septr 21st In the morning he went again to the Indians, who were preparing to decamp & go further. He took a very affectionate leave of them & reminded them that they should think on what they had heard of their Creator and Redeemer. He stay'd to see them set off & recommended them to the mercy of God their Saviour. When he returned on board the *Niger* Sr Thomas sent for us & proposed as the Indians were now gone he would send the Shallop with two of us to Croque to the *Lark* to speak with the Indians in Newfoundland & keep the other two with him till the Indians return'd or as long as he stay'd. We told him we were always averse to parting & now more so than ever as B^r Drachart & Hill were both sickly & required our attendance. But if he would give us all Four a proper opportunity to go to Croque to the *Lark* we would venture it; to this he agreed, & we accordingly got ourselves ready & packed up our things & got them in the Tender; when we received an order from Sr Thomas not to go, as Captⁿ Darby wanted the Shallop. We got our things on board again & scarce had them in order before we received another Message from Sr Thomas to pack them up again, as he had prevailed on Capt. Darby to let us have a shallop to carry us to Croque. We again packd up, & got our things on board the shallop, & took leave of our friends in the *Niger*. It raind very hard & the wind high & quite contrary, so that it was with great difficulty we workd thro' the Harbour when we got about 3 parts of the way, our Boom broke & unship'd our Rudder, however kept on our way & with the help of our Oars & sweep got with difficulty into Henlys Harbour where they made our Shallop fast to a Fishing Stage & left us for the night. It blew so hard in the night that we expected every moment she'd brake loose & go adrift, there was no one in the shallop but us Four, we fastened her with all the spare Ropes we could find & waited with impatience for day light.

Septr 22^d   we found that the Shallop had received a great deal of damage by beating in the night against the Stage. The Fishers invited us ashore where we dryd our wett cloaths & warmed ourselves, & found in the unhealthy state some of us were in, that it was impossible we could stand it out to go at this time of the year in an open Shallop 30 leagues to Croque. But Mr. Darby soon determin'd it by acquainting us, tho' he had promiss'd Sr Thomas to let us have the Shallop to go to Croque, he had last night received a letter, by which he must employ his Shallop otherwise, & we wait for another opportunity. We directly wrote to Sr Thomas acquainting him the circumstances begging he might give us a passage to S^t. Johns, which he granted, & we again return'd on board the *Niger*.

Sepr 24th   The Officer who had been at Red Bay of whom we told the Indians & desired they might behave friendly to him & his people, return'd, & told us the Indians came to Red Bay Pitched their Tents on an Island near where he was, some of them came to him, but behaved as they had promised us very friendly.

Sepr 30th   We sailed from Pitts Harbour & came the 4th Octo^r to St. John's where we had the Honour to wait on the Governor, to whom we delivered the two Annexed Charts one of Esquemaux Bay [pl. 41] with the several Indian names of the Islands &c, & their meanings in English. The other a Draught we took of Davis's Inlett. Also as specific an account as we from time to time could get from the Esquemaux in answ^r to divers enquiries, proposed by the Governor & what we ourselves could learn about the Affairs of the Esquemaux.

LONDON Decem^r 5th 1765

C. F. Hill
C. L. Drachardt
Jens Haven
Christ. Andr. Schloezer.

JOURNAL OF THE TWO BRETHREN JENS HAVEN & C. A. SCHLOEZER TO EXPLORE THE COAST OF LABRADOR, IN THE 'HOPE' SCHOONER FROM THE 23D JULY TO THE 3D SEPTEMR 1765.

July 23ᵈ We went on board the *Hope* Schooner Lieutᵗ Chandler [*sic*] Commander.

July 24ᵗʰ Our Captain made a Report to Sʳ Thomas Adams that the Schooner was leaky, & that he could not go to Sea till she was repaired. Sʳ Thomas sent his Carpinter to examine her, after hearing his Report, he gave orders that she should go to Sea directly. But the wind was so strong that it was not practicable.

July 25ᵗʰ We weighed anchor early in the morning & sailed out of Pitts Harbour with a fair Wind.

July 26ᵗʰ We sailed through a Multitude of Ice-Islands both to-day & yesterday.

July 28ᵗʰ We met with a large Field of Ice through which at length we found a passage but were very much incommoded with the small drift Ice, so that we were obliged to lay too in the night.

July 29ᵗʰ We saw Land, but durst not venture too near it on account of the foggy weather. As we judged we were as far Northwards as we had orders to go, we continued to sail off & on, till the weather clear'd.

Augˢᵗ 2ᵈ In the night we were near running on a Rock but came off without receiving any damage. Today at noon we had an observation and found 55.53. As the weather was clear & we yesterday observed an opening in the land, Mʳ Lucas who was sent by the Governor to make the needful observations & Bʳ Haven, went out in the Boat to look for a Bay, or secure anchoring Place. They returned in the evening about 4 o'clock having found a good anchoring place from 12 to 20 fathᵐ with tollerable good shelter. We determined to put in there, & tho' there was little wind yet by the Help of our Oars & Boat we got safe in by 8 o'clock & let go our anchor in 20 fathᵐ. It look'd like a Bay; on each side steep Rocks & Barron Hills on the N.E. side where we lay we found a Valley full of Pine Trees.

Augˢᵗ 3ᵈ Br Haven with one of the Officers went early on shore & found on the NE side, several places where Indian Tents had formerly been erected; they also saw fresh tracks of Europeans. At 9 o'clock the Captain sent some sailers on shore to cut wood & at 10 we went out with Mʳ Lucas to take a more exact view of the Bay. We rowed about a leageᵉ & found that it was no Bay but a passage between the main land and a large Island. We went ashore on the North side of the Island & found it Rocky & Barron except here & there some spruce, with small Birch, Alder, Willow, Aspin & Larch Trees; & small patches of Grass in the Vallies. We then went over to the Continent, & saw plainly in the sandy Beach footsteps of both Indians & Europeans, also of Bears & Foxes. We went up a high Hill in order to have a better view, We [?] directly under a deep Bay the end of which was out of sight. This we took to be Davis's Inlet. With these discoveries we returned on board.

Augst 4th We went out to examine an opening we saw to the S.W. and found it to be a passage between the Main land & three large Islands which opened to the Sea. We rowed thro this Passage keeping the Mainland to the Starboard, when we doubled a point of Land that ran out & formed the Passage, we saw a Broad Bay. We went to [a] pretty large Island that lies before the Mouth of the Bay; & went up a high Hill; it was so foggy that we could command but a very confined Prospect, especially towards the Land. We could observe that the Bay run towards the N.W. we could not see the end of it. All the Islands as well as what we could see of the Continent appeared Rocky & Barren. On our return we saw plenty of Cod playing in the water. We had but one line in the Boat which we baited with salt pork & catchd in a few minutes 24 Cod. We also saw plenty of Kepling, Seals & small Whales. At 4 o'clock we came on board. They sent the Boat directly out to fish, but could not, even in the same place where we found them so plenty, in some hours catch more than 15 Cod.

Augst 5th The Master of the Schooner went out in the Boat in order to discover if the first opening we saw to the N.W. went into Davis's Inlet. He found in several places but two fathm water & many Rocks. He returned; & we resolved in the Morning to sail round the large Island & find the entrance of the Inlet. The Boat went out to fish at the former place & in one hour brought more than 200 Cod on board. They are of a middling size but much thinner than those caught on the Banks of Newfoundland.

Augst 6th We could not sail round the Island as we intended on account of the Fogg. The Master & Bror Haven went out with the Boat in order to find the soundings in the Passage between us & the Sea. They went ashore on an Island in the Mouth of the Passage & found Tent Places & other signs of the Indians being there so fresh, that it could not be above three weeks since they were here. They shot some Fowl and caught a good many Fish. They then went East from the place where we lay on a small Island and found a number of Black Ducks nests, they brought a great many Eggs with them on board. They also saw plenty of scurvy Grass.

Augst 7th It continued Foggy & still more so at Sea so that we could not attempt to enter the Inlet that way. The Captn order'd the anchor up & sent the Boat before to sound & by the help of the flood & a favourable wind got safely thro' the passage to the N.W. we found the Inlet 5 or 6 miles broad, it kept pretty near the same breadth for 3 leagues, its course S.W. by W. it then grows narrower & inclines more to the West. On the south side is low ground for about a mile when it begins

215

to be hilly, the low lands is for the most part covered with wood. The Beach is shelving Rocks which makes it difficult to land with a Boat, there is no proper landing place on the Southside. The north side for 10 miles, is very high rocky Land but farther up its lower with patches of Wood & grass. We also saw in shore wood growing on the Hills as far as the Eye could reach. on this side the Inlet there are many small rocky Islands. The Beach is very full of Rocks & Stones, there are also many small Bays but very difficult to land in them. When we saild about 12 miles up the Inlet, we went on shore, & walk'd several miles. We found several green Valleys & Brooks of water. The wood we saw was mostly of the Fir—or Pine—kind many of them above 5 or 6 fath^m high, there were also Larch Trees near as high & some Willows. All along the Beach lay abundence of Drift-Wood some of the Trees as thick as any we saw growing. Of Deers, Foxes & Bears we saw many Tracks, but of Indians none. Seals, Ducks, Partridge & small Fowl we also saw plenty. About 9 o'clock in the evening the Schooner anchord in 12 fath^m. 16 miles from the entrance of the Inlet. We held our Course on the south side & had mostly 20 or 30 fath^m water, the Fog continued at Sea, but here it was quite clear.

Augst 8th We set sail again early & went about 2 miles further, but finding it grow shallow, let the anchor fall in 4 fath^m, we concluded we must be near the end of the Inlet, the Master & B^r Haven went out in the Boat to find out the end of the Inlet. They discover'd that from the entrance of the Inlet at 20 miles up, the land closed, except a narrow passage about 2 Cables length Broad. This passage opened into a Bay about 3 miles long & 1½ broad. They sounded before the mouth of the Passage in the Inlet & found 2 fath^m. In the Passage they found 6 fath^m. The Bay or Lake is full of shallows & in some places 3 fath^m. On the West side of the Lake is a River about 10 fath^m broad & the stream very rapid, & on the southside are 3 small Brooks. We could not find the least traces of the Indians having been here. Here is plenty of large Timber & abundance of Geese, Ducks & Widgeon. They return'd on board about 8 in the evening.

Augst 9th The wind being contrary we could not get out & spent the day in getting wood & water aboard.

Augst 10th We saw a large Black Bear on shore but could not get within shot of him. At noon it Thundered & Lightened surprizingly after which the wind turn'd quite contrary.

Augst 11th We went under sail with a fair wind & brought too again in a little Bay on the North side of the Inlet, 11 miles nearer the entrance than where we lay before. Our intention was to make all the discoveries we could on this side as we before had done on the south side. Today the Captain went on shore with us, this was the first time he was able to go out of the ship since his leaving Chauteau [*sic*]. We went on a high Hill from whence we could see the Coast to the Northward for a

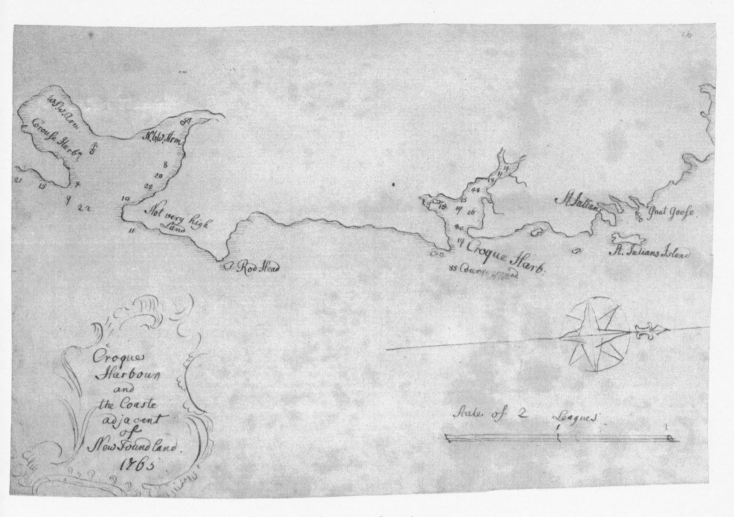

Croque Harbour and the adjacent coast

A rowing boat in Croque Harbour, sketched from the *Lark*

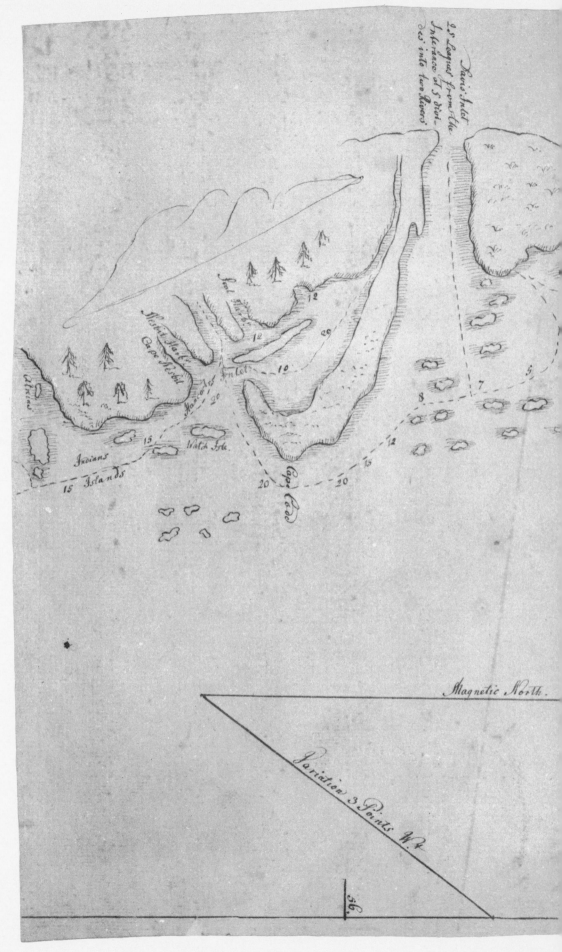

Davis's

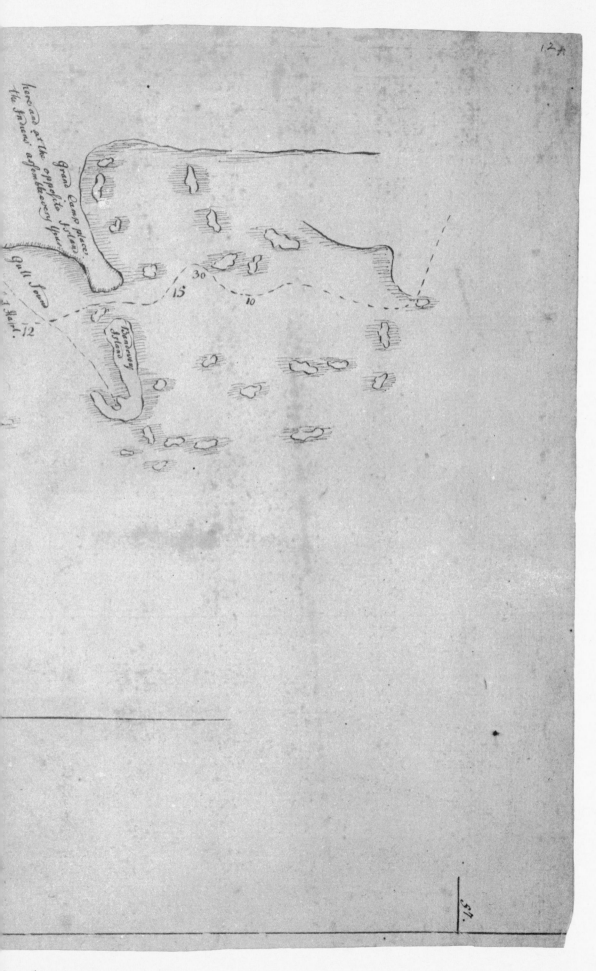

The *Hope* in Comfort Harbour

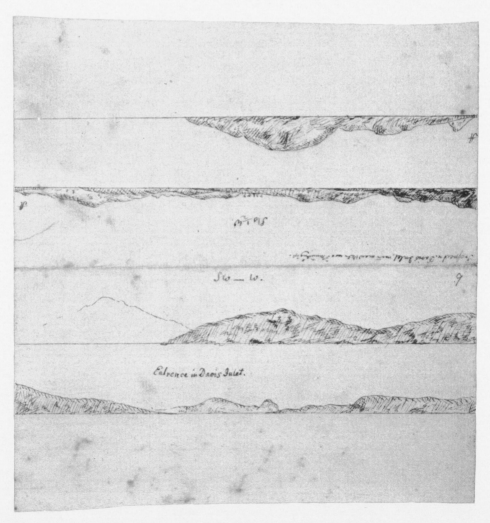

Profiles showing the entrance to Davis's Inlet

great way. We saw North of the Hill at no great distance, two large Bays the first went about 4 miles S.W. into the Land, & the other N.N.W. There were several Islands in the Bays & still more out towards the Sea. We also saw several large Lakes; one directly between the Hill we stood on & the first large Bay. Round this Lake there grew plenty of grass & wood, but farther northward, saw nothing but Rocks & Barren Hills, about 1 o'clock we returned to the Captn & went on board. We desired him to give us an opportunity to examine the Bays we had seen from the Hills as the wind was favourable we weighed anchor & went with the Schooner into the first Bay, & anchored in 15 fath^m. The entrance is 5 or 6 miles broad & we found from 15 to 18 fath^m water. Before the Bay toward the sea lies several large high Islands, by which means you have shelter in the Bay let the wind be in what quarter it will.

Augst 12th.   In the morning we went out with the Boat accompanied by the Captn & other Officers to take a nearer view of the Bay. We row'd along shore & shot two large Deer, of the Moose kind. We went into the 2^d Bay which lies more Northerly, we ascended a high Hill from whence we saw that the supposed Bay was properly a passage between the Continent & a large Island which [lies] on the northside, we rowd more northerly round the Large Island, & went ashore on the most northerly point from whence we saw the shore run NE with high land which hindered us from seeing far or discovering whether the Land we saw were Islands or the mainland. We then returned S.E. to one of the Islands before the Bay which we examined thoroughly. We found here places where Indian Tents had been erected, also a Fox Trap, but it must by the appearance be many years since it was used. We saw on this Island a Hare and round it great numbers of Seals. We then went to a small Island, where we left the Captn at our first going out, on this Island we found several Tent places & a grave with other signs of the Indians having formerly been here. In the evening we returned on board.

Augst 13th   We went under sail in order to go Southward to Nisbits Harbour (where in the year 1752 some of our Brethren built a House). But the wind was contrary, & we met with so many shallows that we were forced to put back & anchored 2 miles South from Davis's Inlet.

Augst 14th   We had a strong wind at N.E. with Fog & Rain which continued till the

Augst 17   When about noon it snowed; soon after the wind abated & we went through the passage to the place where we at first anchored. Here we waited for a wind till the

22^d Augst   when we went out with a N.E. wind hoping soon to reach Nesbit's Harbour, but before we got clear of the Islands the wind failed us, but by the help of the Boat we got free of them & were not long at Sea when the wind freshen'd &

we got quite clear of the Land. We still found a great deal of drift Ice & at a distance to the northward saw large Islands of Ice.

Augst 23d   We had fair wind and came nearer shore, but durst not venture too near with the Schooner as the Coast was unknown. We had but one Boat which the Captn could not venture from the vessell all night, & it was now too late to go on shore & return before night, therefore we must put off again to sea.

Augst 24th   At 9 o'clock we put ship about & made for the shore, but at noon put off again to Sea, as they sayd it was then too late today to do anything. Thus we kept going off & coming to the shore without going near enough to make any further discoveries till the

2d Septemr   when we had an observation & found 52.47. Upon which finding himself so far to the South he determined to go into Pitts Harbour where we arrived the 3d of Septemr.

Pitts Harbour within York—or Chateau   Jens Haven
Bay on the Coast of Labrador   Chr. Andr. Schloezer
Septemr 5th 1765

QUESTIONS proposed from time to time by the Missionaries to the Esquimaux Indians, with their answers:

1,	What do they call themselves?	They call themselves as a People or Nation Caralit, they also by way of eminence in contra-distinction to the Europeans Innuit (the Men) the Europeans they call Kaublunet.
		By this name Caralit they call themselves all along the Coast as far as 72. deg. North they know nothing of the name Esquimaux.
2,	Are they numerous?	There were here this year about 300 & perhaps as many staid at home. By this we'd be understood to mean only those who live South of Davis's Inlet, they tell us of Caralit who live to the northwd of the Inlet & its beyond all dispute that they are to be found in Hudsons Bay, perhaps also in Baffins Bay, & we know certainly they are in Davis's Straits & onwards along the Coast of Greenland to 72 degs.
3,	From whence do they come?	These who come here live at Esquimaux Bay which they call Nueingame & at Mille Isles they call it Kikkertet, their Houses are on the Islands of which their are great numbr at both places.

218

4, What is the nature of the Inland Country?

Inward in the Country are plenty of Trees but near the Shore its Barren, the Isles are also Barren. There are many Fresh Water Lakes.

5, Of the Coast Harbours & Rivers near their Habitations?

Please to look at the annexed Chart. [pl. 41.]

6, On how many places do they live?

These who come here have only the two above mentioned places.

7, Do they know from whence they originally came?

They don't.

8, How long were they in their passage hither?

Twenty days, but they make short stages, one of them say'd if wind & weather favour'd him he could come here in 3 days.

9, Have they seen any Europeans in their passage?

They met one ship with which they traded but whether English or French they don't know.

10, What is the produce of the Country they frequent?

The Sea abounds with Whales, Seals, small Cod, &c &c The Land—with Deer, Foxes, White & Black Bears, Wolves & doubtless other animals. In the fresh water they find plenty of Salmon.

11, What is their employment in the different seasons of the year?

In Winter & early in the spring the men are employed in catching Seals, Whales, Birds &c. In summer they hunt Deer, Fish for Cod & Salmon; they also catch Herrings with a small Hoop Net.
The men make the frames or wood-work of their Womens Boats & their own Kaiaks. The Women sew the skins to cover them with, they also make the Tents & cloaths, & does the Domestic Bussiness.

12, In what manner do they kill the Whales, Seals & Deer &c?

They kill the Whales & Seals with Harpoons which stick fast in the fat; to the end is fastened a leather thong with a Seal skin blown full of wind; this tires the Creature to draw thro' the water, as he comes up they repeat their strokes till the Whale is quite spent. They then put on a dress of skins so boiant that they are from the middle upwards above the water; thus they surround him as he floats & cut & take away as much of the Whale as they think proper.

219

Deer they wound with their Arrows and then hunt them down with their Dogs. Fish they catch with Hooks & Lines as we do.

13,	How do they procure the Weapons they use?	They truck Whalebone &c with the French or English for such things as they [?] the Iron work they form themselves.
14,	Can they preserve their Oil & Fish?	They have both, but only for their own use; the Oil they keep in Seal Skins had they vessells they could procure large quantities. They split the Cod & dry it without salt.
15,	How many generally come here?	Last year there came about 200 & this year 300, the same Indians don't come every year.
16.	How great may the whole number of them be?	We can't learn anything certain with respect to their number.
17.	Do they know of Indians inhabiting the interior part of the Country?	They speak of Caralit who live northward of them besides these they know of no Indians inland or on the Coast.
18.	Do they trade with the Hudson's Bay Company?	These who come here do not; but the Caralit north of Davis's Inlet very likely do.
19.	Have any French ships been on their Coast?	They tell us a ship (we suppose French) frequently comes to Esquimaux Bay & trades with them.
20.	Are their any Europeans among them?	None live among or near them. Our Brethren's attempt in the year 1752 was the first & only one we hear of.
21.	Do they seem fond of the Europeans being with them?	They do not. They are afraid of their irregularities with respect to their Women &c.
22.	On what do they chiefly subsist?	Their chief Food is Cod, fresh & dry they also eat Seals, Whale, Salmon &c. They eat Deer, Foxes & Birds, we have seen them eat Dogs Flesh, all these they boil when they've opportunity to do it if not they eat them raw.
23.	How are they cloathed?	Their cloathing is chiefly Seal or Deer skins. The men wear a Jacket of seal skin close before like a shift it

reaches to the middle of the thigh with a Hood like a Capuchin, they have Breeches of Dog or Bear skin, they also wears [*sic*] Boots the hair side inwards.

The Women dress like the men except the Hood of the Jacket which is so large they carry their Children in it. Their Jacket has also a long flap which hangs down behind. Their Boots are large beyond all proportion in which when they sit they place their child.

24. Have they any ore? We have seen a kind of Marquisite among them which they use as a Flint, beside this, we believe they know of none.

25. What are the most proper things our Merchants should take to them to Barter for their Whalebone, Furr &c?

Files, Rasps, Adzes, Hatches, Saws, Chissells, Gouges, Gimblets, Draw-knives, Large Clasp-Knives, Large Butcher like knives with sharp points, such half round knives as the shoemakers use to cut their upper leathers with, Augars, Spike-nails, & other lesser Nails, Needles square & round pointed Taylers & Womens Thimbles scissars, Hammers, Iron Wire of different thickness Battoes or Shallops, Sail Cloth, Ropes, Cordage, Fish-lines & Hooks, Blocks, Robes & everything thats necessary to rig a large Boat with one sail, small sea chests, Pewter plates, dishes, spoons, ladles, Lead, Large Iron or Brass Kettles, small Potts of [*sic*] Iron saucepans, Course thick milled White Wollen Cloth with one side well raised. Their Women are fond of Beads of different Colours, Rings, Combs (especially small teethed) Brass Medals & Counters. N.B. Strong Liquors they won't as yet taste. Fire armes they would purchase at any Rate. May they never be seduced to like the first; nor our people so imprudent as to trust them with the latter.

10

A note on the ships

THE Progress Books in the Admiralty Library contain details of the building and re-fitting of most ships of the navy.[1] Conditions in ships at the time of Banks's voyages may be more easily imagined if we consider their actual dimensions and try to relate them to the 20,000-ton vessels which are a commonplace today, to the 300,000-ton tankers which have recently come to Ireland from Japan, or to the jumbo jets which are intended to carry 400 passengers across the Atlantic in a few hours.

The *Niger*, a fifth rate 32-gun ship of 679 tons, carried a complement of 220 men. Built at Sheerness, she was launched on 25 September 1759. Her dimensions were: length of gun deck 125 feet; length of keel 103 feet 4 inches; breadth 35 feet 2 inches. In 1760 she captured the *Epreuve*, 14 guns; on 7 March 1779, she was in action with the *Minerva* on the West Indian Station and in 1794 was mentioned on the Glorious First of June. In 1812, she was renamed *The Negro*, and two years later was sold at Portsmouth. (See pl. 25.)

The *Lark*, another 32-gun ship, was built at Rotherhithe in 1761–2. Of 680 tons, she carried a complement of 220 men. The length of her gun deck was 127 feet 2 inches, of her keel 108 feet $0\frac{3}{8}$ inches. Her breadth was 34 feet 5 inches, her depth 12 feet $0\frac{1}{2}$ inch.

The schooner *Hope* was bought at Portsmouth by Lord Colville in 1765. She was a small vessel of 105 tons and carried a complement of 30 men. The length of her keel was 45 feet 5 inches, her breadth 20 feet 2 inches, her depth 8 feet 4 inches. It is possible that she was the small trading vessel of the same name in which the Moravian missionaries sailed to Labrador in 1752. In 1779 she surrendered to an American privateer.

Palliser's flagship, the *Guernsey*, was an older ship, having been built at Blackwall in 1696, and rebuilt at Woolwich in 1717. She was a 50-gun ship of 863 tons, carrying a complement of 350 men. The length of her gun deck was 134 feet, of her keel 100 feet 6 inches; her breadth was 38 feet 8 inches, her depth 15 feet 9 inches. She was converted to a hulk in 1769.

The brig *Grenville* was originally the schooner *Sally*, built in Massachusetts Bay in 1754. On 7 August 1763, she was purchased in Newfoundland by Commodore

[1] I must thank Mr. B. W. Bathe of the Science Museum for kindly drawing my attention to this fact.

Graves, and the following year, in Deptford, her rig was altered to that of a brig. Cook commanded her from 1764 to 1767, and it was in this tiny vessel of 67 tons that he made most of his surveys of the Newfoundland coast.[1] She carried 6 swivel guns and had a complement of 10 men. The length of her gun deck was 54 feet 11 inches, of her keel 43 feet; her breadth was 17 feet $2\frac{1}{2}$ inches, her depth 7 feet 4 inches. In 1775 she was broken up.

The *Endeavour*, in which Cook and Banks were to sail round the world in 1768–71, was considerably larger than the *Grenville* but about half the size of the *Niger*. A ship of 368 tons, she had an overall length of 106 feet. Her greatest breadth was 29 feet 3 inches, her depth 11 feet. Her complement was 84 men. The crew lived on the lower deck, the observing party had special cabins on the poop.

[1] Details of these surveys are given by Skelton and Tooley (1967) in a fully documented publication issued by the Map Collectors' Circle.

11

Notes from the logs of the *Niger*, the *Hope*, the *Guernsey* and the *Grenville*

NOTES FROM THE LOG OF THE *NIGER*, COMMANDED BY SIR THOMAS ADAMS, 1765

2 April	Anchored at Spithead. Arrival of the *Guernsey* on which ship Commodore Palliser had his Broad Pennant.
30 ,,	Sailed for Newfoundland, *Pearl* in company.
3 June	Moored in Great St. Lawrence Harbour (Placentia Bay, Southern Newfoundland). Entry in Master's log: Anchor'd here y^e *Grenville* Brig. Mr. Cook Commander. Employ'd surveying this coast.
14 ,,	The *Guernsey* arrived, with Commodore Palliser.
16 ,,	Sailed hence His Majesty's brig *Granvill*.
8 July	The *Niger* sailed for the north.
13 ,,	Moored in Croque Harbour.
16 ,,	Sailed for Cape de Gratt [Dégrat].
18 ,,	Anchored in Pitt's Harbour, Chateau Bay.
20 ,,	Began to build wharf.
9 August	*Guernsey* arrived.
18 ,,	Our Captain with two missionaries went to look for Indians. Missionaries left with Indians; Captain returned.
21 ,,	Captain brought a party of Indians in two canoes which we saluted with three Cheers.
22 ,,	Moored in Antelope Harbour, Chateau Bay.
29 ,,	Received our shallop from the *Guernsey*.
September	(See Moravian diaries for events this month.)
1 October	Sailed for Bell Isle de Grois.
5 ,,	Anchored at St. John's, *Guernsey* in company.
21 ,,	Anchored here his Majesty's Brigg *Grenville*.

224

TETRAO *canadensis. pedibus hirsutis, rectricibus nigris apice fulvis, lineis duabus alba ad oculos. Linnaeus speimen.*

Pl. V Spruce Grouse, *Canachites canadensis canadensis*
Sydney Parkinson

22	,,	Sent some provisions to the *Guernsey*.
5 November		Sailed for England, with *Guernsey*, *Pearl*, *Spy* and Brigg *Grenville*.

NOTES FROM THE LOG OF THE SCHOONER *HOPE*,
LIEUTENANT JOHN CANDLER, COMMANDER,
JULY-SEPTEMBER, 1765

23 July	Came on board off York Harbour His Majesty's ship *Niger's* Barge Sir Thos. Adams and Capt. Darby. The latter took charge to carry us in When we got within the two outer Heads Capt. Darby went on shore and Sir Thom^s Adams took charge and in comeing in We ran for Shore on a Rock were we remained for one Hour and a Half we carried out our Kedge Anchor to try to heave her off but could not Capt. Darby then came on board with a Shallop and carried out our Best Bow Anchor and hove her off at 9 Anchord in York Harbour with the small Bower Anchor . . . found roading here His Maj^{tys} *Niger*.
26 ,,	[Captain Darby came on board and piloted the *Hope* out of Pitt's Harbour.]
28 ,,	55°.05′ N.
29 ,,	[James Blake, Master's, entry, more dramatic than Candler's.] Saw a field of ice streching the S° W^d farther than we could see from 3/4 Mast head We wase obliged to run through the broken Ice for we could not clear it. 8 F.S. Bro^t to for the weather was so Thick we dare not run for fear of the Ice At 5 a.m. made sail W^r more clear; we have been running through Broken fields of Ice this 5 hours past & still a Grate deal in sight & Several Large Isl^{ds} of Ice.

[The following extracts are mainly limited to those giving the ship's position so that the entries in Schloezer's diary may be followed, approximately, on a map. The drafts made by Lieutenant Lucas, who was with Candler on the *Hope* to help with the survey, have not been traced as yet. There are many particulars about soundings and positions of rocks and islands in the log entries.]

31 July	55°.52′ N.
2 August	55°.56′ N.
3 ,,	Moored in Hancock's Inlet [Gosling equates this with the inlet sheltered by Pownal Is., where Nain now lies]. Sent boat up inlet to look for Indians. [The *Hope* remained here until 7 August.]

7 August		Weighed anchor.
8	,,	Anchored in Davis Inlet. [This lies *55°.57'* N, slightly south of Nain.]
11	,,	Weighed.
12	,,	Moored in Comfort Harbour [see plate g.]
13	,,	Sailing off Cape Cod [see plate g.]
14	,,	Anchored in Hancock Inlet.
18	,,	Went further up inlet and moored.
22	,,	Came to sail.
23	,,	55°.34' N.
24	,,	55°.41' N.
25	,,	55°.45' Cape Endeavour 5 or 6 leagues.
		[They sailed south, sounding and checking positions of islands until Sunday, 1 September.]
1 September		52°.55' N.
2	,,	52°.47' N.
4	,,	Anchored in York Harbour.

NOTES FROM THE LOGS OF THE *NIGER*, 1766

[Only notes of particular interest have been extracted from the original detailed entries.]

12 May		Anchored in St. John's.
12 June		Anchored in Croque Harbour.
19	,,	Sent the Master and the Captain's 8 in the yawl to St. Julian's.
20	,,	Returned from St. Julian's.
21	,,	Petty Officer in a shallop to Fishott Is. Master sailed [no destination].
29	,,	Returned shallop from St. Julian's.
2 July		Longboat back from Conch. The Captain went in barge to St. Julian's.
3	,,	Captain returned.
9	,,	*Grampuss* Sloop with the Master sailed to Northward.
11	,,	Sent longboat to Hare Bay.
14	,,	Returned longboat from Northward.
17	,,	Returned *Grampuss* and Sloop with the Master on board. *Black Joke* came in from Northward.
23	,,	Came in our shallop from the s-ward with the 2nd lieut.
24	,,	Sailed the 2nd lieut. [John Gurling] on a cruise, the *Black Joke* for Hare Bay.

27	,,	Longboat and *Black Joke* both came in from Hare Bay.
28	,,	*Black Joke* sailed on a cruise.
1	August	Sloop returned with the Master. *Black Joke* returned from her cruise.
3	,,	Yawl returned from Hare Bay.
6	,,	2nd Lieut. returned in tender from a cruise, & sailed for Chatteaux Bay.
10	,,	Anchored in Chatteaux Bay in Pitt's Harbour.
12	,,	Came in 2nd lieut. from a cruise.
14	,,	Barge sailed to St. Peter's Is. to look for Indians.
16	,,	Captain sailed to St. Peter's Is. to look for Indians.
20	,,	Sailed Captain to St. Peter's Is. to look for Indians.
21	,,	Returned the Captain from St. Peter's.
25	,,	Sent a petty officer on Henley Island to look for Indians.
26	,,	Returned the petty officer from Henley Is.
27	,,	Schooner sailed to Temple Bay.
28	August	Commodore's schooner returned from Temple Bay. Sent a petty officer to Henley Is.
29	,,	Petty officer still on Henley Is.
30	,,	Petty officer still on Henley Is.
1	September	Petty officer still on Henley Is.
3	,,	Sent petty officer to Henley Is.
6	,,	*Black Joke* sailed to N ward.
7	,,	*Black Joke* anchored in Henley Harbour, but sailed in the afternoon.
9	,,	*Black Joke* came in again and sailed W ward in afternoon.
13	,,	Longboat out fishing.
18	,,	*Black Joke* arrived from W ward.
19	,,	*Black Joke* sailed to examine fishery to the N ward.
20	,,	*Black Joke* returned and sailed again.
23	,,	*Black Joke* returned.
24	,,	Large batteaux in Temple Bay.
1	October	At single anchor.
3	,,	Weighd and came to sail.
4	,,	Moored in Croque Harbour.
5	,,	Delivered the tender to a midshipman of York Fort.
10	,,	Sent a boat out to look for the *Black Joke* which had been wrecked in Lunar Bay.
11	,,	Sailed for St. John's where anchored on 13th.
28	,,	Sailed for Lisbon.
18	November	Anchored in Tagus.

30 December	Weighed anchor.
19 January	Moored in Plymouth Sound.
26 ,,	Moored at Spithead.

Notes from the logbook of Abraham Blundell, Master of the *Niger*. [Only notes that supplement Sir Thomas's log are given.]

25 June	Sloop and shallop with Master and Petty Officer, Surgeon and boats to survey Hare Bay.
26 ,,	Longboat with Captain's mate and boatswain to St. Julian's.
27 ,,	Longboat returned from St. Julian's.
2 July	Longboat returned from Conche. The Captain to St. Julian's.
18 ,,	Sailed *Black Joke* shallop.
14 August	Sir Thos. sailed with the Barge to St. Peter's Islands to look for W./Indians.
15 ,,	Sailed hence the Lieut. and Schooner to W^{so} ward with the surgeon, attended by the yawl and crew to Hare Bay.
27 ,,	Came alongside the Commodore's schooner and delivered the men with their Necessaries which are to remain here the winter. [The *Guernsey* was at St. John's but her log entry for 21 August reads 'Sent the Master & six men in the Shallop in order to carry Lieut. Walters & 17 men to Chateau Bay.']
28 ,,	Master returned from Northward.
3 September	Boatswain etc. employed at Barrier Pt.
4 ,,	Returned the *Black Joke* being forcd back by contrary winds, the yawl breaking adrift from the *Black Joke* in the Gale was Stove in pieces on St. Peter's rocks, nothing saved.
4 October	Anchored in Croque Harbour.
8 ,,	Began to serve brandy, the beer being all expended.
9 ,,	Sent a boat to look for the *Black Joke*. Returned the boat having found nothing of her.
10 ,,	Sent our boat to look for the *Black Joke*. Returned the boat with a batteaux with the officer and people belonging to her, she being driven on shore in St. Lunar Bay, stove to pieces and all her stores lost in the gales of the 2nd instant.
11 ,,	Came to sail.
13 ,,	At 2 p.m. anchored in the Narrows [St. John's]. Came on board the Commodore.
14 ,,	At 2 p.m. anchored in the Narrows His Majesty's Sloops *Favourite* and *Zephyr*. Anchored at midnight in St. John's Harbour. A.M. found riding here his Majesty's ship *Guernsey* Commodore Palliser, with the *Pearl* and *Hope* Schooner.

26	„	Sunday. At 1 p.m. fired 17 Guns per order of the Commodore in honor of the Day.
28	„	Tuesday. Made sail at noon, *Zephyr* in company.
1767.		
26 January		Anchored at Spithead.
31	„	Capt. Andrew Wilkinson to take command of the *Niger* in room of Sir Thomas Adams.

NOTES FROM THE LOG OF THE *GUERNSEY*, OCTOBER 1766

Saturday 25 October		A.M. Drest Ship in dressing several flags were blown away.
Sunday 26	„	P.M. fired 21 guns being the Anniversary of His Majesty's Accession to the Throne. At 6 undrest Ship.
Monday 27	„	A.M. Came in here His Majesty's Brig the *Grenville*.
Tuesday 28	„	Sailed hence the *Niger* and *Zephyr*.

[*Note*. Some discrepancies in dates in the log entries and diaries are due to the fact that nautical time at sea is reckoned from noon, civilian from midnight.]

NOTES FROM THE LOG OF HIS MAJESTY'S BRIGG THE *GRENVILLE*, JAMES COOK, MASTER.

20 April, 1766	Left Deptford.
29 May	Took soundings 4 leagues from St Mary's.
1 June	Moored in a cove on the west side of Bôn Bay. Then to Bay Foche, Cape La Hune and Penguin Islands.
20 „	Moored in Cape Bay.
1 July	Left Cape Bay.
3–9 „	Moored in Fox Island Harbour.
12 „	Moored in a cove between Ramea Isles.
17 „	Moored in harbour west of White Bear Bay.
23 „	Sailed for Burgeo Island.
24 July to 6 August	Anchored in Grandy's Cove between the Burgeo Isles.
9–14 August	Anchored in Connoire Bay.
16–19 „	Moored in Tweeds harbour.
30 August–8 September	Moored in Harbour Le Cou.
10–24 September	Moored in Port aux Basques.
28 September–4 October	Moored at Cod Roy.

6 October		Little Bay, La Poile Bay.
27	,,	At 8 A.M. anchored in St. John's Harbour, found here Commodore Palliser in the *Guernsey*, with the *Niger*, *Favourite* and *Zephyr*.
28	,,	Watering etc.
29	,,	P.M. Sailed hence the *Niger*.

[Cook's log for 11 November 1767, tells how the *Grenville* anchored off the Nore in a gale.]

'All the forepart a hard Storm of Wind with Excessive heavy Squalls & Showers of Rain. At 2 p.m. Took in the Fore I. S. At 4 Anchord above the Nore light (it bearing ESE) in 7 fathm Water with the small Bower & Veerd away to a whole Cable that not bringing her up let go the Best Bower & Veerd away upon both to a whole Cable upon one & a Cable & ½ upon the other was then in 6 fathom water Struck Yards and Topmasts at 6 the Best Bower parted and we traild into shoal water & at seven She Struck very hard got a Spring upon the Small Bower Cable and cut the Cable in order to cast her Head the Southward & get her underweigh but the Spring gave way & She cast to the Northward Directly ashore upon the Shoal called the Knock got the Topsails & Cross Jack Yard down upon Deck & She lay pretty easy untill the flood made when the Gales still continuing she struck very hard and Lay down upon her Larboard bildge. hoisted out the Boats and hove everything over board from off the Decks & Secured all the Hatchways at 12 at Night there being no prospect of the Gale ceasing took all the people away in the Boats the Cutter made the Best of Way to Sheerness for assistance. At 10 a.m. the Wea^r. being mod. came on Board with Proper Assistance from Sheerness Yard in order to get the Vessel off & found She had received Little Damage began lightning her by heaving out Shingle Ballast & pigs of Iron ballast & to lay out Anchor to heave her off.'

12

Admiral Forbes's inscription for Palliser's memorial to Captain Cook

To the memory of Captain James Cook, the ablest and most renowned navigator this or any country hath produced. He raised himself, solely by his merit, from a very obscure birth, to the rank of Post-Captain in the Royal Navy, and was unfortunately killed by the savages of the island of Owhyhee, on the 14th of February, 1779; which island he had not long before discovered, when prosecuting his third voyage round the globe.

He possessed, in an eminent degree, all the qualifications requisite for his profession and great undertakings; together with the amiable and worthy qualities of the best men.

Cool and deliberate in judging: sagacious in determining: active in executing: steady and persevering in enterprising, from vigilance and unremitting caution: unsubdued by labour, difficulties, and disappointments: fertile in expedients: never wanting presence of mind: always possessing himself, and the full use of a sound understanding.

Mild, just, but exact in discipline, he was a father to his people, who were attached to him from affection, and obedient from confidence.

His knowledge, his experience, his sagacity, rendered him so entirely master of his subject, that the greatest obstacles were surmounted, and the most dangerous nagivations became easy, and almost safe under his direction.

He explored the Southern hemisphere to a much higher latitude than had ever been reached, and with fewer accidents than frequently befal those who navigate the coasts of this island.

By his benevolent and unabating attention to the welfare of his ship's company, he discovered and introduced a system for the preservation of the health of seamen in long voyages, which has proved wonderfully efficacious: for in his second voyage round the world, which continued upwards of three years, he lost only one man by distemper, of one hundred and eighteen, of which his company consisted.

The death of this eminent and valuable man was a loss to mankind in general; and particularly to be deplored by every nation that respects useful accomplishments, that honours science, and loves the benevolent and amiable affections of the heart. It is still more to be deplored by this country, which may justly boast of having produced a man hitherto unequalled for nautical talents; and that sorrow is further aggravated by the reflection, that his country was deprived of this ornament by the enmity of a people, from whom, indeed, it might have been dreaded, but from whom it was not deserved. For, actuated always by the most attentive care and tender compassion for the savages in general, this excellent man was ever assiduously endeavouring, by kind treatment, to dissipate their fears and court their friendship; overlooking their thefts and treacheries, and freqeuntly inter-posing, at the hazard of his life, to protect them from the sudden resentment of his own injured people.

The object of his last mission was to discover and ascertain the boundaries of Asia and America, and to penetrate into the Northern Ocean by the North East Cape of Asia.

Traveller! contemplate, admire, revere, and emulate this great master in his profession; whose skill and labours have enlarged natural philosophy; have extended nautical science; and have disclosed the long-concealed and admirable arrangements of the Almighty in the formation of this globe, and, at the same time, the arrogance of mortals, in presuming to account, by their speculations, for the laws by which he was pleased to create it. It is now discovered, beyond all doubt, that the Same Being, who created the universe by his *fiat*, by the same ordained our earth to keep a just poise, without a corresponding Southern continent—and it does so! 'He stretches out the North over the empty place, and hangeth the earth upon nothing.'—Job, xxvi. 7.

If the arduous but exact researches of this extraordinary man have not dis-covered a new world, they have discovered seas unnavigated and unknown before. They have made us acquainted with islands, people, and productions, of which we had no conception. And if he has not been so fortunate as Americus to give his name to a continent, his pretensions to such a distinction remain unrivalled; and he will be revered, while there remains a page of his own modest account of his voyages, and as long as mariners and geographers shall be instructed, by his new map of the Southern hemisphere, to trace the various courses and discoveries he has made.

If public services merit public acknowledgements; if the man who adorned and raised the fame of his country is deserving of honours, then Captain Cook deserves to have a monument raised to his memory, by a generous and grateful nation.

Virtutis uberrimum alimentum et honos.
Val. Maximus, lib. ii. cap. 6.

13

A Selection of Banksian letters and memoranda arranged chronologically

THE following selection has been made in rather an arbitrary fashion; the amount of material available was too large to allow of all the letters referred to in the text being copied again for this section; some additional papers have been incorporated because they have some bearing on the Newfoundland voyage or people connected with it.

The very slender string of dates which connects this material is not intended to be anything but the briefest pointer to a few of the peaks in Banks's life.

No corrections in spelling or in punctuation have been made in these letters and memoranda; the only alteration is that the dates have been transferred to the tops of the letters.

Banks, as stated elsewhere, often wrote on the back of the letters he received the date on which he answered them. Hence, although I have not traced many of his replies their dates are given when possible.

The abbreviations used to denote the chief sources of Banksian MSS are as follows:

D.T.C., the Dawson Turner copies of much of Banks's correspondence; summaries of these are in Warren Dawson (1958); the original copies are in the Botany Library, British Museum (Natural History).

Kew B.C. refers to the volumes of Banks Correspondence in the Library of the Royal Botanic Gardens at Kew.

Add. MS refers to the series known as Additional Manuscripts in the Department of Manuscripts, British Museum.

1757

The opening letter in this series, from Banks's master at Eton, was written after he had been there for one term only. He went to Harrow in April 1752, when he was nine years old; his progress there in Latin and Greek was unsatisfactory and he was moved to Eton in September 1756.

BANKSIAN LETTERS AND MEMORANDA

Edward Young, Master at Eton, to William Banks, Joseph's father.
National Library of Australia, Manuscript Branch, Reference Division, NK 73.

Sir,   February 6th 1757

I have received the Favour of your Letter, and am very glad Master Banks was detained by nothing worse than the Badness of the Roads and weather. I began indeed to be afraid he was kept at home either by his own or your Illness; being well satisfied you would not suffer Him to be absent from School so long without some very substantial Reason. I will take care to explain the Affair to Dr. Barnard and Dr. Dampier according to your desire.

It gives me great Pleasure to find You think Master Banks improved. To be able to construe a Latin Author into English with Readiness and Propriety is undoubtedly no less necessary than to be able to turn an English one into Latin. They ought indeed to go hand in hand together. And I hope we shall by degrees bring Master Banks to a tolerable Perfection in the former; tho' the Point, which I have been hitherto been [*sic*] chiefly labouring, is to improve him in the latter, because of his great Deficiency in that Respect when He came to us. Another Thing which I have been obliged to give particular Attention to for some time past, is the Greek Grammar; in which it is highly necessary for Him to be tolerably perfect at his going into the fourth Form; the Difficulties which usually attend the first Attempts of Boys to parse Greek, being more or less, in proportion to their Perfectness in this Particular. And indeed the Removal into the fourth Form is in all Respects a very critical Time to our young Gentlemen: An intire new Scene of Business, and consequently a difficult one, opens upon them at their first Entrance into it; which if they neglect to give a proper Attention to at first, there is great danger of their being soon confounded and oppressed with the Business, the Difficulties of which are daily encreasing upon them. On the other Hand, a steady Application at this Time, by making them masters of the Groundwork of the Language, and begetting in them likewise an Habit of Attention, and Diligence, is usually attended with good Effects throughout the rest of the School. I should think therefore, it might be of great Use to Master Banks; if, after his Removal into the fourth Form, You would take the Trouble to write to Him, to show the great Necessity there will be for Him to exert particular Diligence at that Time; and I will likewise take all Opportunities of inculcating the same to Him. For You can't but be sensible that there is a great Inattention in Him, and an immoderate Love of Play. (I hope You will excuse my giving You my Opinion of Him so freely, as I cannot think it right to Deceive you in a Point of so much Consequence to his Welfare) which we must endeavour to get the better of in some degree, or it will be a constant Obstacle to his Improvement. This sometimes occasions Quarrels between us; tho' in other respects we agree extremely well together; as I really think Him a very good-tempered and well disposed Boy. Time, I hope, and his own Reflection, as He grows

234

up; together with Proper Care in the Management of Him, will by degrees get the better of those Faults I have mentioned in Him.

> I am
> Sir
> your most obliged and most obedient
> humble Servant
> Ed: Young

Eton

1760

Enrolment at Christ church, Oxford.

1761

Death of father. Mrs. Banks took a house in Paradise Walk, Chelsea, near the Chelsea Physic Garden and only a few minutes from Lindsey House, Cheyne Walk, the headquarters of the Moravians to whom the lease had been given by Sir Hans Sloane ten years earlier. (The grounds of Lindsey House were once part of Sir Thomas More's farm.)

1766

Banks met Pennant. Set sail for Newfoundland and Labrador with his friends Sir Thomas Adams and Constantine Phipps. He was elected F.R.S. on 1 May, after his departure.

JOHN HOPE, Professor of Botany, University of Edinburgh, to JOSEPH BANKS.
   Kew B.C. 1:1

Edinb 17 April 1766

Sir

It being rumoured here that You was going to the Country of the Eskimaux Indians to gratify your taste for natural knowledge Adam Freer a young Gentleman who for some time has distinguished himself in this University by his passion for Botanical knowledge was extreamly desirous of having the honour of visiting that Country under Your Protection & has requested me to mention this to you.

The Young Man is extreamly diligent & indefatigable he is sensible spirited sober & has good & gentle dispositions. I have had the fullest opportunities of knowing him as two years ago being pleased with his Zeal for Botany I gave him an invitation to live in my house wh he has done ever since and has been extreamly serviceable to me in collecting and preparing the indigenous plants and I dare to say if you have no other to relieve you of part of the trouble you would find him very useful.

His father is a Gentleman of the country who has a small Estate & numerous family and at present is not in a situation to defray his expenses on the expedition —he has had an excellent medical education and woud be well qualified to act as Surgeon or assistant Surgeon—it woud make him happy if the offer of his service were acceptable to you, he has not the most distant view to any other gain than that of improving his knowledge of Nature and having the honour of acquiring that under a person so distinguished for his knowledge of Nature and unsatiable desire of knowing more.

I very heartily & sincerely wish you everything good and happy & desirable in so spirited an expedition from wh the Learned world may expect so much and Brittain an acquisi[tion] of many useful trees & pl[ants]

I have the honour of being
wth very great respect
Your most obed Servt
John Hope Professor
of Botany in the University
of Edinburgh—

Joseph Banks to his sister, Sarah Sophia Banks.
Mitchell Library, Public Libraries of New South Wales, Banks Papers, A80⁴, 16:1–3

Chateau Bay
August the 11th 1766

Dear Sister

I receivd yours two days ago with newspapers etc: etc: which I must thank you all for as I can assure you they were the greatest Comfort you can Conceive we all sat round the Fire & hunted out all the Deaths marriages etc: etc: as Eagerly as a schoolboy does Plumbs out of a Pudding

How do you think I have spent my Leisure Time since I have been here Very Musically I can assure you I have Learnt to Play upon a new Instrument as I have Forswore the Flute I have tried my hand upon strings what do you think it is now not a fiddle I can assure you but a Poor innocent Guittar which Lay in the Cabbin on which I can Play Lady Coventries minuet in Infancy etc: with Great success

Pray My Love to Coz Bate & tell her that she & I differ a little in opinion about Stamford races as I had rather be here Than at all the races in Europe not but what I believe she was at Least as happy there as I am here

I hope Mr. Lee has been Very Civil & Given you Nosegays as often as you have been to him if not tell him he shall not have one of my Insects when I come home give my Comp^ts to him also and tell him that if I did not think it might Endanger

Cracking some of Your Ladyships teeth I would let him know by you some of the Hard names of the things I have got

So Miss Frederick is Going to be married to our Countryman a dangerous Experiment I think he Killd his last wife in a hurry I hope he may Keep her alive a little Longer but maybe she intends to Revenge Miss Pit & Kill him I know you women are Sad Husband Killers in your hearts

I do not Know what Else to say I am almost Exhausted thank you however for your ague receipt it has one merit however I think for if it would not Cure an ague I am sure it would kill a horse

We are here in daily Expectation of the Eskimaux Ladies here I wish with all my heart they were Come as I might have sent you a sealskin gown & Petticoat Perfumd with train oil which to them is as Sweet as Lavender water but more of them when I know them better at Present adieu only Believe

me your very affectionate Brother

J Banks

P:S: Pray My Comp^{ts} to all Freinds at Chelsea Especialy our neighbours at the Gardens I mean our Gardening uncle & aunt: adieu

received September ye 30th 1766 [in S. S. Banks's hand]

1767

Banks returned from Lisbon, and reached London on 30 January. He engaged G. D. Ehret to paint some of his Newfoundland plants, and Sydney Parkinson to do the birds and insects; Parkinson apparently executed the wash drawings of fishes the following year. In the late spring Banks and his sister moved from their mother's home in Chelsea to a house in New Burlington Street.

Banks planned to visit Sweden and study with Linnaeus but the plan fell through in spite of the preparations to which Pennant alludes in some of his letters of 1767–8.

THOMAS PENNANT, Zoologist, Historian and Traveller, to JOSEPH BANKS.
    D.T.C. 1:3

Chester 30 Jan. 1767.

Dear Sir

I flatter myself that this will find you safe returned from your voyage, & that you will find no ill consequences to yr health from the dangers & hardships you underwent. I shall be impatient to survey the treasures you bring home; & rejoice that ornithology is to receive such improvements from yr labors, tho' I am not so selfish but must condole with you on the losses you sustain'd in your favourite pursuit. I have not been idle since you left England but have made some progress in the *American Zoology* [published as *Arctic Zoology*] which I shall communicate

237

when we meet. I am to thank you for two obliging Letters, one from Chateau Bay, the other from Lisbon. I am extremely acquainted (by description) with the Bird you saw at the Portuguese Captains: it is the *Anhinga* [Darter] of Margrave;[1] & the *Palamedea cornuta* [Horned Screamer] of Linnaeus's last ed. *Syst. Nat.* [1766: 232]; so extraordinary a bird that I hope you have not omitted procuring a drawing. How should I have revelled amidst that Brasilian aviary! what multitude of singular birds does that southern continent afford of which we know only the parts, and fragments; but those so very eccentric, as makes me wild to be acquainted with the whole.

I have procured for you Regenfuss's shells; & as I quit all thoughts of Botany consign to you several curious works in that science, which I have sent to Mr. White[2]—I hope to have the pleasure of seeing you in less than a month, in the mean time remain, Dear Sir, with the truest regard

> Yours most affec[ly].
> Tho. Pennant

JOHN HOPE to JOSEPH BANKS
    Kew B.C. 1:3

Edinb 14 feb 1767

Sir

I was yesterday honoured wth your obliging Letter it gave me pleasure to hear you was returned in safety . . .

I flatter myself you will favour the Botanical world with an account of what you found at Labrador But if that is not to be the case I pray to be hon[?oured—torn] with a letter on that subject when [torn] Leisure permits and if you can spare a few seeds they woud be most acceptable.

Mr Freer begs his respectful compts to you he woud to be sure have had much pleasure in the jaunt but still a great deal more coud his care have been of service in restoring you to health—I heartily wish you woud favour us with a visit a trip thro our highlands woud I am persuaded afford you much entertainment.

> I have the honour of being Sir
> Your most obed' Serv[t]
> John Hope

[Ans. Mar 16 1767]

[1] Georgius Marcgravius, 1610–44, author of *Historiae rerum naturalium Brasiliae* . . ., 1648.

[2] Benjamin White, a younger brother of Gilbert White of Selborne. Benjamin was a publisher; the first edition of his older brother's famous work *The Natural History of Selborne*, 1789, carries the imprint of his press, Horace's Head, Fleet Street. He seems to have run the press in conjunction with a book shop which was used as a club by Banks and other naturalists; see Banks's letter of 5 May.

BANKSIAN LETTERS AND MEMORANDA

Joseph Banks to Thomas Pennant.
Alexander Turnbull Library, Banks MSS,

(1)

London May yᵉ 5th 1767.

Dear Sr

I hope that if I cannot have the Pleasure on Congratulating you on the recovery of your little People that I shall very soon hear of it as I have so perfect a Confidence in the Security of the Operation they are going through [inoculation against small-pox] I live in daily hopes of hearing they are got well through it

I am ashamd I have not Long before wrote to you to tell you the truth my Idleness is only to be excused by alledging a still greater as a palliative Circumstance which is that I have not yet got your Beaver Colourd to tell you the truth I have been so hurried Ever since you left town by furnishing my house that I have scarcely had time to think of anything Else.

Mr [Gilbert] White Calld upon me today in your name & left some Specimens of Birds one of which *M: Atricapilla* I had not seen the others *M: Trochilus* & *M: montifringilla* are Common I intend tomorrow to Call upon him at Horaces head [see Pennant's letter of 30 January] & hold Ornithological Converse tho I can assure you it does not go on with the spirit it used to do when you was with us

Mazel has not yet sent home your Plates I sent today but he returnd some Excuse I did not Well understand about the paper being spoild Mr Brewer has not usd me well about yours made me pay too much money a shilling a peice for all even the white Bear which you Knew had very little to be done to it but there were but eight of them & I think I will have it out of him if he ever Colours any more for us

I want you of all things to visit a new Branch of Trade I have lately discoverd which I think may be of Service to us the Horners a set of people who live by selling the Horns of all sorts of animals unworkd up to those who work them into Knife Hafts &c the People sell what they call Buffaloes horns every day & must Certainly have many of animals unknown to us

adieu Floreat Res Zoologica says
Your affectionate
J Banks

New Burlington Street

(2)

May 14 1767

Dear Sr

I am Just upon the wing setting out for Dorsetshire have but just time to send my good wishes for the little ones who I make no doubt are by this time Compleatly out of Danger Have you any instructions or any thing I could do for you I mean to be out about a fortnight in which time I shall visit Bristol & the other side of the Channel

I am much obligd to you (for an obligation you are not perhaps at present apprizd of) I have for an acquaintance with Mr White who mentiond your name & promises to Send divers and various discoveries to town Particularly a hawk he has by him which I much suspect is quite new if his description is tolerable he also promises to observe the mouse & the Bat I formerly saw & to send them for our inspection

Instead of remaining Idle as I intended till I should set out for Flint I find I am to be well employd for I must set out for Lincolnshire as soon as I return from my present expedition Where I shall not Fail to Procure your natterjack & any thing Else which I find worthy the observation of a nat Historian

I am ashamd I have not before now sent down your Fossilic plant the reason realy was that I knew I was to send something or other with it but Could not recollect what I have now however so totaly given up all hopes of recollecting it that *Fossilia* is this morning gone alone to St James's Street

The Squirrel is not yet Finishd or should have waited upon you at the same time I have however one peice of good news which is that our Freind Governor V Loten is Fixd in N Burlington Street so we shall with Ease get the Rest of his Drawings

> Adieu I have time for no more than signing
> your affect hble Servant
> Jos Banks

The Colours you wishd to have prepard for your Freind I am ashamd are not yet ready but will be sent very soon

GERARD DE VISME, Merchant and Botanist, to JOSEPH BANKS
Kew B.C. 1:6

Lisbon 2ᵈ June 1767.

I have many acknowledgements to make Dear Sir for the proofs you give me of your memory by your two obliging Letters. We were interested in the voyage of the Niger, & kept a regular account of the winds; I know by experience how happy you must have been to rejoin your friends after so long an absence, & hope the episode of the scene at Lisbon will have its merit in the relation of your voyage. Your acquaintance here have made repeated enquirys after you, Mrs. Hay & her family will soon return to England, Mr. Auriol has made several new discoverys since you left us & now Mrs. Dea and Mrs. May are at Quinta in the neighbour-hood of Marvilla He herborises with them, & gives lectures on Botany, natural history, & what not. Our Venus is still the prettiest creature in the world, but how can you forget D. Anna de Almeyda, who "lets concealement like a worm, i'th bud feed on her damask Cheek" & cannot be joined in wedlock with her Cousin for want

Pl. VI American Goshawk, *Accipiter gentilis atricapillus*
Peter Paillou

of a Dispensation, she has been lately at Quinta as well as the Condeisa de Soure, where we have had some agreeable Partys: we improve there, & I find the advantage of several good hints you gave me in the disposal of the Shrubs etc etc.

The Sun Dial is mighty well executed, & is so great a novelty here that is [*sic*] is the admiration of everyone. I have made a well contrived stand for my Pines, & other Exoticks, on the left of it, against the walls & as that situation is very favourable I have ventured many in the ground, some sunk in pots, which have a very pretty effect; The King, Queen, three Princesses, & Infante D^on Pedro, honoured me lately with an unexpected morning visit. They were all over the grounds, & in the rooms, his majesty will have a Relogio do Sol at Belem, & my care shall be to add J.B. finxit. I am very grateful to the obliging assistance you intend me, in which I have great confidence. it was quite unlucky the Plants detained by Captn Travers (who does not appear yet,) did not come by Captn Richardson, or Hill, who arrived in short passages some weeks ago & are returned again to London. My friend Mr. Jacomb will give punctual intelligence hereafter, & I have desired Tennant to call on you, in order to lend his assistance. This is the season only for exoticks etc in potts, supplied on board with a very little water, the Plants Tennant sent me in Novemb. wer[e p]ackt in two bundles, and you saw . . . [torn] I think arrive, all thrive extreamly we[ll] & are many of them great ornaments. you know my assortment as yet is small & I only am sollicitous to increase it with what has other merits than those of novelty. The views of rural buildings pleased me much, & gives some hints I wanted when any thing of that nature falls in your way pray remember me. I shall also be very glad of some seeds. To encourage my applications you must be kind enough to employ also my services. Van Deck desires much his Compliments to you, he has removed to some very good aparments lately, & will be glad of your assistance. Mr. Perry desires his very particular respects to you, pray assure Mr and Mrs Aufrere of mine & believe me with sincerest regard,

Dear Sir, Your most faithful Servant
Gerard De Visme

We have a Mr. Gordon here, Sgr. to D. Aberdeen, a fine gay young fellow, who knows you, he diverts himself well & is in no immediate hurry for Gibraltar. The Por^tie have a secret expedition carrying on, wch we surmise is to suppress some disturbance in their colonys.

THOMAS PENNANT to JOSEPH BANKS
 Kew B.C. 1:7; D.T.C. 1:8

Downing June 10th 1767

Dear Sir

 I just received y^r favor from the Fens, & fear mine of last week has missed you. I now repeat my request about y^r drawings also the birds you brought from

Newfoundland that I may not be idle this winter. I beg to know when you mean to return, & also y^r address that I may trouble you with a few commissions: any thing I can do for you in the interim please to command. I sincerely wish y^r tour may answer but not being greatly smitten with the charms of Linnaeus, must be doubtful till I hear from you. As to ornithology he is too superficial to be thought of in madrepodology still more deficient. In fossils other judges than myself think him incompetent, his fort is Botany in that perhaps you may edify from instruction . . .

Yours most affect^{ly}.
T. Pennant.

Kew B.C. 1:8

Downing July 3rd 1767

Dear Sir

I have only time to express my regret and my disappointment & to wish you a safe voyage & quick return. I have no very high opinion of Linnaeus's zoologic merits, so do not much lament the impossibility of my attending you but do not forget we are to be fellow travellers next spring. I have much to trouble you with in yr. present journey, which I shall communicate in my next. While in Lincolnshire let me beg you to collect a history of the decoys, & favor me with an acct of the taking of Ruffs.

If you dare trust me with yr drawings in yr absence you will oblige me. They shall be taken great care of.

Adieu
Yours in haste
T. Pennant.

Kew B.C. 1:11; D.T.C. 1:13

July 26th 1767

Happy Dear Banks, to hear you are well. in y^r hurry pray do not forget y^r address, y^r Route etc.

If you call at Copenhagen, visit my worthy friend Mr. Fleischer. I will prepare him for y^r reception . . . I am infinitely obliged to you for giving me the use of y^r drawings, which I will not abuse. I am in vast haste myself: but accept my hearty wishes for the success of y^r journey but warmer wishes for y^r speedy return to

Yours most affec^{ly}
Tho. Pennant

Please to send the drawing of the Penguin to my Sisters—I believe I must see the Penguin again before I publish on it, so beg y^r housekeeper may be acquainted

242

with it. Pray, what is her name, for perhaps in y^r absence I may have some (virtuous) correspondence with the lady.

Kew B.C. 1:12; D.T.C. 1:14

Aug. 4th 1767

Dear Sir

Inclosed are two Letters which I hope will be of use to you. I am extremely glad you take Parkinson with you & doubt not you will gain treasures from the several collections of drawings you will find. in transmitting y^r drawings home please to take this hint, to conceal them in the covers or bindings of books; or the good custom-house officers will charge 1–1–0 for each, charging as pictures: if possible get a drawing of the *Falco rusticola* & *Viverra lutreola*—I defer my ornithology of the European birds *not* found in Great Britain till y^r return in hopes you can augment my list—I will this winter describe all y^r N.-foundland acquisitions, & must beg to be indulged with a fire in y^r library when I am in town . . .

Solander is at y^r Elbow—pray remember me to him. I am obliged to him for a letter which I shall answer next post. Adieu

Yours sincerely
Tho. Pennant

GERARD DE VISME to JOSEPH BANKS
Kew B.C. 1:13

Lisbon the 4th novemb. 1767.

Dear Sir,

I have not had the pleasure of hearing from you lately, perhaps your favourite study may have carried you again to some distant parts, however I cannot part with some little share which you will permitt me to claim in your remembrance, the obliging proofs you gave me thereof at your return to England are some sort of title, there good people call it *Love*, & lay great stress thereon. I wish you had passed the Summer with Us, it has been the most delighfull one I ever enjoyed in Portugal, only five or six sultry days, and an uninterrupted continuation of serene fine weather from the month of April to the present time; we now wish for rain to plow & sow the lands. I will not tell you of the progress I have made at Bemfique where everything thrives à souhait, I am now laying out new walks & providing shade for all the uncultivated ground within my inclosure, where I have made several improvements, & I shall take in some other contiguous fields which are advantageously situated, where my little farm will remove to, & have a communication by means of an Arch over a Rivulet to the Quinta, so that I shall not want for work and amusement. Count Lippe who is very active in putting the troops here on a very good establishment has determined to assemble about 15,000 men in the neighbourhood of Setuval where several military evolutions etc. etc. are to be made, & every body will resort; the Royal Familly will sett out the 15th, I have lately received some fine collections of Plants from Pernambuco in very fine order, & expect others, the Conde de Pavolide who goes Governor there is much my f [large piece torn out] Dr. Luis Pinto de Souza who . . . to the Matto groço, the most distant [terri] . . . tories the Portuguese possess, which are six months voyage from the Marantham, & border on Perou, I can depend on good assistance from Them both, & when I know you are settled I will readily share my little wealth with you. In the mean time give me leave to send you my dear Sir a Hogshead of that choice Calcavellas wch. you tasted at the Quinta, it is old, & requires no Cooperidge, bottle it early in the Spring, and request Mr. Butler to reserve it for your own drink, it will still improve with age, I am with the sincerest regard your most faithfull Servt

Gerard de Visme

My Brother is on his departure from Spain, I hope he will have the pleasure of seeing you in England.

Kew B.C. 1:14

Dec. 12. 1767

I have a thousand acknowledgements to make Dear Sir for the proofs you give of your obliging remembrance; the Plants by Captn Travers arrived in very tollerable orders, all the most valuable ones in potts as fresh as when put on board of the Ship, some few of the others suffered but what occurrences in life do not meet with some disappointments? I had a bed of seedling Renonculas just in readyness to take up, it was in that lucky spot that I placed the American pretty plants and the variegated Hollys, they have thrived there à souhait, & will be in fine order to put out towards the end of next month. Captn Martin of the Bragança who arrived yesterday tells me he has a Parcell of Plants also from you, which I have sent on board for, & I shall find at the Quinta this afternoon, so that I shall have the amusement tomorrow morning to examine, & determine the disposal of them; Several of your friends, the Bristow's, Dea's, Mays etc passed a day at the Quinta last week, we consulted on the choice of a worthy to place in the cobham[1] stile in a nich of Ivy Jasmine, the majority of votes was yours, the Ladies are to give the resemblance, & Auriol asserts he will manage the execution in a manner quite new & masterly; the

---

[1] The Temple of British Worthies was designed by William Kent, c. 1735, for Richard Temple, Lord Cobham, at Stowe. The garden has always been famous for its numerous statues and temples which referred to the family motto 'Templa quam dilecta'—'how delightful are thy temples'. I am indebted to Miss Sandra Raphael for sending me the substance of this note.

truth is that you are a great Patron to Bemfique, and much regretted there, as well as by all your Lisbon acquaintances. We have had a very agreeable cotterie lately with the addition of Mrs Fraser, another Crunetta Sister, Mr. & Mrs. Hobart, etc. but they are now all dispersed, we have also lost Mrs. Hay, whom you will probably see in England. The Venus of Lisbon retains still a crowd of Amorine round about her, & is as beautifull as ever, she passed a day at Bemfique lately, & wishes much to visit England. We have enjoyed a very pleasant summer, temperate, with few sultry days. I have made a discovery under the rising hills opposite the Quinta of a good additional supply of water, wch I shall introduce in a Cascade on the mount and will have a pretty effect, it will enable me to [torn] the whole lower part of the grounds, . . . plant clumps of trees, extend my shrub . . . & have more shady walks, so that I have employment & amusement ready at hand for the approaching Season.

We are much improved in our Theatrical performances, & have a very pretty Burletta at the Rua dos Condes, the Royal Familly go there every Sunday, I have a Box nigh the one of the Condessa de Soure; Da Anna de Almeyda could not possibly reconcile herself to Tongilianus, the match is broke off, & now she smiles on Chearfulness. Do you interest yourself in these distant occurances? your stay here was too much confined by circumstances unavoidable which prevented several little Schemes of amusement & deprived me the pleasure of expressing how sincerely I am

Dear Sir
Your much devoted Servt
Gerard De Visme

P.S. I have inspected the choice collection of Plants by Martin, they are in very tollerable order & but few have suffered.

[Banks wrote on the back of this 'All these answerd Jan 29 1768'.]

ANDREW WILKINSON, Captain of the *Niger* in succession to Sir Thomas Adams, to JOSEPH BANKS
    Kew B.C. *1*:15

London Decem^r the 18th 1767

Sir

As my meeting with the Indians was very uncertain, the Cask of things you left on board of the Niger for Truck with 'em Mr. Palliser took on board the Guernsey to Chatteaux, & I believe he has procurd you some of their dresses etc I'd got a Canoe for you which I sent hom in the Grenville as she came to Deptford, but she Unluckily run on shore [see Cook's log, p. 230] & it was wash'd overboard & lost as I am told tho I have not been able to see Mr. Cook to ask him about it, nor I am afraid shan't as I am going into the Country but if you'll please to send to him he will let you know whether there any hopes of getting it by advertising as I thought off as it was drove ashore on the Essex coast I believe.

I am extremely sorry I have not been able to get you the Fish you gave me the drawing's off I've bro^t. three or four Cappling of both sorts which have sent to your house in a case bottle, the one you sent was broke in coming down in the Chatham Boat the bottle they are in was full but the John's in coming round s[eem] to have taken a fancy to the Liquor tho' the fish was in it. there is likewise two of the Roots of the Flowers you desir'd, & some of the Seeds of the Barren[s] Flower. All your Friends at St. John's & on b^d. the Niger desire to be rembrd to you I was afraid we sho'^{d} have lost Mr. Blundell this voyage he was very ill. Mr. Williams came home in the Guernsey. I dined with him & S^r. Thomas the other day we were wishing for you, I hope you've had a pleasant tour thro' Wales. I set off for [Yo]rkshire tomorrow. I am s[torn out? ailing] fore you come to Town, there [were—torn out] some darts etc. with the Canoe wch I fancy can't be lost. Mr. Cook lives I am told somewhere about mile end but the Vessel I believe is got up to Deptford so that I fancy it will be best to send to enquire on board her. Will any Essence of Spruce be acceptable if it will if you please to send to Doct^r Norton's the Corner of Craven Street he will supply you.

> Your very Obed^t Ser^t
> A. Wilkinson.

THOMAS PENNANT to JOSEPH BANKS
    D.T.C. 1:15

Decr 25th 1767

Dear Sir

Since my last I have formed an account of the migration of British birds; which I wish should undergo your criticism before it visits the press: . . .

> Dear Sir affect^{ly} yours
> Tho. Pennant

As I shall not come very soon to Town I shall be much obliged to you for the loan of y^r Newfoundland Land birds to be sent by the Chester waggon next Wednesday. I will return them soon & safe.

1768

In the summer of this year George Cartwright made his second visit to Newfoundland and decided to become a trader on the Labrador coast and try to improve the conditions of the Eskimos and Indians. Banks was busy planning his equipment and staff for his voyage to the Pacific with Cook. Fabricius, who was to spend so much time later on working on Banks's insect collections, rode from Edinburgh to London and watched the preparations for the voyage, making frequent visits to the *Endeavour*.

THOMAS PENNANT to JOSEPH BANKS
    D.T.C. 1:16

Downing Jan. 15th. 1768

Dear Sir

    I hope this will certainly find you safe arrived in town thro' all the perils of snow & ice; a good pretaste of y^r Lapland Journey.

    I hope to be in Chester in ten days time, when I shall be glad to hear you are well, & to receive the N.foundland Land birds, which I will describe when at Chester & bring up with me

Dear Sir
Yours most affectly
Tho. Pennant

    Kew B.C. 1:20

Chester Feb 20 1768

Dear Sir

    I fear it will be impossible to send up a Shrimp in a condition fit to sit for its picture, I have therefore ordered some to be brought you from the neighbourhood of London.

    As to the *Squilla Littoralis* I cannot get them at present; for I cannot make my people understand what I mean.

    I hope to send the shrimps by means of one Everet of Clare Market[1] whom Mr. Barrington says is the most intelligent fishmonger in all London.

    If Mr. Parkinson's pencil is not employed about things of greater moment, may I take the liberty of desiring he may do the scarcer British Fish that fall in his way: as Fish are the present object.

    I have described all the N.F. land Birds & shall send them back on Monday by the waggon; & am very much obliged to you for the use of them

    I left out the Raven to make room for the box of Br. shells each species is lapp[ed] up in white paper or packed in a pill box with white paper pasted on it, that the names may be written on each that I may adjust the genera the more readily. For the Fish I must call in Dr. Solander to my aid. To whom I beg to be remembered.

---

[1] Clare Market was in the immediate vicinity of the Strand until 1905, but was destroyed when the Aldwych was built.

In the same box is my book of descriptions[1] of yr Birds. When I come up I must compare them with Catesby and Edwards. I think to lodge in Leicester Fields or near it to be midway between my Friends.

Adieu Dr. Sr.
says yours affectly
Tho. Pennant.

SARAH PRIMATT to JOSEPH BANKS
Add. MS 33977, ff. 5–12

Oporto Mar 21st 1768

Sir,

I was favour'd with your Polite address a few days after I had been inform'd by my Friend Mrs Wood of your interview together and the result of it viz: your admission into our Partnership and Correspondence which is a pleasure and advantage I shall value as it deserves by every means in my power of Turning it to your benefit and my own improvement. . . .

Sarah Primatt

[This letter is six pages long, but of little interest save for the reference to Banks becoming a member of the local natural history society, run by a Mrs. Wood; on an additional page there is a list of plants she can send him. She made two copies of this letter both of which are bound in this volume of Add. MSS. There is nothing to show that Banks answered her.]

THOMAS PENNANT to JOSEPH BANKS
Kew B.C. 1:23

Chester April 30th 1768

Dear Sir   I have just time to acquaint you that I will be there to the assignation at Revesby the 10th instant.

As to Tottie I have sent to him to know w[d] he be willing to go as midshipman which I w[d] recommend Excuse my zeal which to serve a friend always overflows. I beg that you w[d] recommend him for the station.

Be so good as to bring your N.F.land journal which I forgot. also List G etc.

I am in much haste here
Most affectly yours
T. Pennant

My service to Lap let him not forget his syst. of shells but I will write to him next week

[1] Untraced.

Kew B.C. 1:26
D.T.C. 1:25

Downing. May 30th 1768

Dear Sir

I take this earliest opportunity of thanking you for the agreeable entertainment I met with at Revesby; & of wishing that you may have found every thing to your mind in respect to your intended voyage.

. . . I am beginning my studies, that are dedicated to the natural history of our Country & a short history of Quadrupeds: the class of native objects I have now in view are the Fish: I therefore must beg you w^d. present my Complim^ts to my late Play-fellow—Master Phipps; & beg he w^d. remember me as to his Cornish friend: I sh^d be even glad to have a correspondency with him; for the fish of that prolific coast are very little known. . . .

I will not detain you longer at present, but after giving my best thanks for all marks of freindship, subscribe myself Dr Sir

Most truely &
affectly yours
Tho. Pennant.

D.T.C. 1:26

Downing June 7th 1768

Dear Sir

Mazel sent me this morning the Proof of the *Anhinga* [see letter of 30th Jan., 1767], so now our twelve plates are done: I must beg you w^d. pay him y^r quota for a Ream of Paper to print the plates off: I shall make my deposite, & write to the Governour for his. . . .

I must beg an Insect Net or two that I may be able to circulate the love of the sport to the very few that are likely to take to it in N. Wales.

You have been so good to promise me such a number of things during y^r absence, that tho' I blush to see the list committed to Paper yet I must do it to help y^r memory.

Y^r N.F.Land journal.
Picture by Gausset.
Drawings, specimen of Mr. Parkinson's skill.
Baster's Op. subseciva.
Insect books, especially those on the Papilionaceous Tribe & spiders.

I beg a line from you soon, that I may hear how y^r preparations go on; & what encouragem^t you have from the acct^s Wallace[1] has brought home. Pray remember me to Doctor Lap, & think me D^r. Sir Most affectly yours

Tho. Pennant.

JAMES DOUGLAS, 14th EARL OF MORTON, P.R.S., Astronomer.
    National Library of Australia, MS Branch, E.A.P., Canberra.
    Hints offered to the consideration of Captain Cooke, Mr. Bankes, Doctor Solander, and the other Gentlemen who go upon the Expedition on Board the Endeavour.

10th August, 1768.

[Extract only]

To exercise the utmost patience and forbearance with respect to the Natives of the Several Lands where the Ship may touch.

To check the petulance of the Sailors, and restrain the wanton use of Fire Arms.

To have it still in view that sheding the blood of those people is a crime of the highest nature :- They are human creatures, the work of the same omnipotent Author, equally under his care with the most polished European; perhaps being less offensive, more entitled to his favor.

They are the natural, and in the strictest sense of the word, the legal possessors of the several Regions they inhabit.

No European Nation has a right to occupy any part of their country, or settle among them without their voluntary consent.

Conquest over people can give no just title; because they could never be the Agressors. They may naturally and justly attempt to repell intruders whom they may apprehend are come to disturb them in the quiet possession of their country, whether that apprehension be well or ill founded.

GILBERT WHITE, naturalist, to THOMAS PENNANT
    Add. MS 35138, ff.19,20

Selborne Octob^r 8; 1768.

. . . I met with a paragraph in the news papers some weeks ago that gave me some odd sensations, a kind of mixture of pleasure & pain at the same time: it was as follows:

'On the sixth day of August Joseph Banks Esqr. accompanyed by Dr. Solander, Mr. Green the Astronomer, etc: set out for Deal in order to embark aboard the Endeavour Captain Cook bound for the South-seas.'

[1] Captain Samuel Wallis in the *Dolphin* sailed round the world 1766–8, and was the European discoverer of Tahiti. The *Dolphin* arrived back in the Thames in May 1768.

When I reflect on the youth & affluence of this enterprizing Gent: I am filled with wonder to see how conspicuously the contempt of dangers, & the love of excelling in his favourite studies stand forth in his character. And yet tho' I admire his resolution, which scorns to stoop to any difficulties, I cannot divest myself of some degree of solicitude for his person. The circumnavigation of the globe is an undertaking that must shock the constitution of a person inured to a sea-faring life from his child-hood: & how much more that of a landman? May we not hope that this strong Impulse, which urges forward this distinguished Naturalist to brave the intemperance of every Climate; may also lead him to the discovery of something highly beneficial to mankind? If he survives, with what delight shall we peruse his Journals, his Fauna, his Flora? . . . if he fails by the way, I shall revere his fortitude, & contempt of pleasures, & indulgences: but shall always regret him, tho' my knowledge of his worth was of late date, & my acquaintance with him but slender.' . . .

Gil. White

1771

The *Endeavour* returned. Banks landed at Deal on 12 July. This year J. R. Forster published his *Catalogue of the Animals of North America* in which Banks's collections from Newfoundland and Labrador were first mentioned, although his name is not given. Forster wrote: 'The Animals which have recently been discovered in *North America,* or overlooked by Mr. Catesby, are distinguished by *N.S.* marking a *New Species*; and by *B.* and *Mus. Bl.* The first authority is from a Collection formed by a Gentleman in his voyage to *Newfoundland*; the second, from a most select and numerous Collection of *American Animals,* belonging to a Lady in Lancashire.' The evidence that '*B*' is Banks is discussed elsewhere (pp. 97, 397). *Mus. Bl.* refers to a collection belonging to Anna Blackburne (1740–93) of Warrington, Lancs. Her father, John Blackburne (1690–1786) of Orford near Warrington, was a considerable botanist and horticulturalist, the second gardener to cultivate pineapples successfully in England; her mother was a relation of Sir Ashton Lever, the founder of the Leverian Museum referred to elsewhere in this book. Anna Blackburne corresponded with Linnaeus, Pennant, Pallas, Latham and other notables of the day. Her brother Ashton Blackburne, a Liverpool merchant, lived in New York and other places in eastern North America; he sent many North American birds to his sister who exchanged specimens with Pallas and other collectors.

GILBERT WHITE to THOMAS PENNANT
    Add. MS 35138:47–48
Number xxxv of White's letters to Pennant was very short in the original published version but Bowdler Sharpe (1900, 1:149–51) gave it in full; it is dated

19th July, 1771, and the paragraph printed below does not appear to have been published elsewhere.

Yesterday I had a letter from town which mentions the safe return of Mr. Banks, & adds that he looks as well as ever he did in his life. So agreeable an event calls for my warmest congratulations. For if we rejoice at the arrival of a friend who has been absent but a few months perhaps in a neighbouring kingdom: how shall we express ourselves when we see one restored as it were from the other world, after having undergone the astonishing hazards & dangers that must attend the circumnavigation of the world itself!！！

I have great reason to regret my disappointment of not meeting you in town: but as we live by hope I trust that I shall be more fortunate an other time.

> With great esteem I remain
> Your obliged, &
> most humble Servant,
> Gil: White.

1772

After the return of the *Endeavour* Banks was busy superintending the arrangement and description of his collections. Owing to a dispute over accommodation (Beaglehole 1962, 2:335 ff.), he did not after all sail on Cook's second voyage round the world, 1772–5, and J. R. Forster, who had first published on Banks's Newfoundland collections, was therefore appointed official naturalist on Cook's ship, the *Resolution*.

On 12 July, Banks and Solander, with a large staff, set out to visit the Hebrides and Iceland, returning by way of the Orkneys.

It was during the following winter that Banks began to advise the King on the development of Kew Gardens.

GERARD DE VISME to JOSEPH BANKS
   Kew B.C. 1:29

Lisbon the 24th. January, 1772.

You will have received my dear Sir some lines from me at the same time your Letter reached my hands a proof that our remembrance of each other was mutual & that there is some simpathy between us. I am impatient to receive some more particulars of your late Tour, & very gratefull for your directions which will be left to send me some Plants of your valuable Collection; many will succeed here better than in any other Climate of Europe, & I am contriving to fence a spot of Ground against the winter rains, which will admitt a pretty assortment of American

Plants, so as to have all the advantages of soil & a free air, by which means I may expect to see them thrive with some luxuriancy; my Quinta will be in great beauty this spring, I wish you could pass some days in it, but I see with more pleasure that you are making every good preparation for a second voyage with two Ships well provided in every respect, as experience will have taught you to supply any omissions; I am extreamly interested for my Country, for your honour & satisfaction, & my own passion for usefull & delightful discoverys that it may prove in every respect a successfull one. I can provide you with Letters to the Governors of any of the Portuguese settlements in case they are acceptable. You request of me some necessarys for the comfort of your Voyage. I have therefore recommended to my friend Mr. Thomas Jacomb, a Lisbon merchant much known in London, by hands of Capt.ⁿ Casey of the Ship Duchess of Manchester Two Portuguese Capotes, made of Irish Camblet, one of them lined with bayze, the other still warmer lined with portuguese manufact. & Cutt of Portuguese Saragossa Cloth, which is warm, pliable, & light, & which you will find very comfortable in a suit of Cloaths for cold weather, tho' as it is spungy it is not good against rain.

Two Pairs of Sheets, made, & marked; of Port.ᵘᵉ Panno de Linho, which is cottony & very snug, especialy at Sea, in your state of Celibacy. I have added a box containing all the Boraxinhos[1] do Maranham which could be collected here; many people have bought them up lately to send to London for the purpose you mention, but a fresh supply will soon come from said Colony. You know they are made from the Gum of a Tree. The cost of the whole is £11.10. wᶜʰ may be paid to my friend Jacomb.

As to Birds they are bought on arrival of Ships from Angola & in the months of May to Aug. for England; in this season all would dye in the way there. I had a great number given me some months ago which I dispersed amongst Ladys; they cost high prices & live but a short time. I would recommend to you to bring over some natives of the new Countrys you explore, with their dresses & utensils, If you have conveniences I foresee the difficultys, the satisfaction of surmounting them will be the greater.

I have thought of making a short trip to England towards May, & shall lament your absence, since I am with a sincere regard, Dear Sir, your much attached Servᵗ⁻

Gerard De Visme

The Rev. William Sheffield to Gilbert White, Dec. 1772.

I have not traced any detailed catalogue of Banks's own collections but Thomas Bell in his edition (1877) of Gilbert White's *Natural History of Selborne* quotes a letter of 2 December 1772 from the Rev. William Sheffield (1742–95) Keeper of

---

[1] Small rubber bottles.

the Ashmolean Museum, to White, describing a visit to Banks: 'My next scene of entertainment was in New Burlington Street at Mr. Banks's. Indeed it was an invitation from this gentleman that carried me to town. It would be absurd to attempt a particular description of what I saw there; it would be attempting to describe within the compass of a letter what can only be done in several folio volumes. His house is a perfect museum; every room contains an inestimable treasure. I passed almost a whole day here in the utmost astonishment, could scarce credit my senses. Had I not been an eyewitness of this immense magazine of curiosities, I could not have thought it possible for him to have made a twentieth part of the collection. I have excited your curiosity; I wish to gratify it; but the field is so vast and my knowledge so superficial that I dare not attempt particulars. I will endeavour to give you a general catalogue of the furniture of three large rooms. First the Armoury; this room contains all the warlike instruments, mechanical instruments and utensils of every kind, made use of by the Indians in the South Seas from Terra del Fuego to the Indian Ocean—such as bows and arrows, darts, spears of various sorts and lengths, some painted with fish, some with human bones, pointed very finely and very sharp, scull-crackers of various forms and sizes, from 1 to 9 feet long, stone hatchets, chisels made of human bones, canoes, paddles, etc. It may be observed here that the Indians in the South Seas were entire strangers to the use of iron before our countrymen and Monsieur Bougainville arrived amongst them; of course these instruments of all sorts are made of wood, stone, and some few of bone. They are equally strangers to the other metals; nor did our adventurers find the natives of this part of the globe possessed of any one species of wealth which could tempt the polite Europeans to cut their throats and rob them. The second room contains the different habits and ornaments of the several Indian nations they discovered, together with the raw materials of which they are manufactured. All the garments of the Otaheite Indians and the adjacent islands are made of the inner bark of the *Morus papyrifera* and of the bread tree *Chitodon altile*; this cloth, if it may be so called, is very light and elegant and has much the appearance of writing paper, but is more soft and pliant; it seems excellently adapted to these climates. Indeed most of these tropical islands, if we can credit our friend's description of them, are terrestrial paradises. The New Zealanders, who live in much higher southern latitudes, are clad in a very different manner. In the winter they wear a kind of mats made of a particular species of *Cyperus* grass. In the summer they generally go naked, except a broad belt about their loins made of the outer fibres of the cocoa nut [this does not grow in New Zealand], very neatly plaited; of these materials they make their fishing lines, both here and in the tropical isles. When they go upon an expedition or pay or receive visits of compliment, the chieftains appear in handsome cloaks ornamented with tufts of white dog's hair; the materials of which these cloaks are made are produced from a species of *Hexandria* plant [*Phormium tenax*] very common in New Zealand, something resembling our hemp, but of a finer harl and much stronger, and when wrought into garments is as soft as silk: if the seeds of this plant thrive with us, as probably they will, this will perhaps be the most useful discovery they made in the whole voyage. But to return to our second room. Here is likewise a large collection of insects, several fine specimens of the bread and other fruits preserved in spirits; together with a compleat *hortus siccus* of all the plants collected in the course of the voyage. The number of plants is about 3000, 110 of which are new genera, and 1300 new species which were never seen or heard of before in Europe. What raptures must they have felt to land upon countries where every thing was new to them! whole forests of nondescript trees clothed with the most beautiful flowers and foliage, and these too inhabited by several curious species of birds equally strangers to them. I could be extravagant upon this topic; but it is time to pay our compliments to the third apartment. This room contains an almost number-less collection of animals; quadrupeds, birds, fish, amphibia, reptiles, insects and vermes, preserved in spirits, most of them new and nondescript. Here I was most in amazement and cannot attempt any particular description. Add to these the choicest collection of drawings in Natural History that perhaps ever enriched any cabinet, public or private:- 987 plants drawn and coloured by Parkinson; and 1300 or 1400 more drawn with each of them a flower, a leaf, and a portion of the stalk, coloured by the same hand; besides a number of other drawings of animals, birds, fish, etc. And what is more extraordinary still, all the new genera and species contained in this vast collection are accurately described, the descriptions fairly transcribed and fit to be put to the press. Thus I have endeavoured to give you an imperfect sketch of what I saw in New Burlington Street; and a very imperfect one it is.'

The man responsible for the arrangement, so much admired, of Banks's collec-tions was Edward Jenner, born in 1749. In 1770 he came from Sodbury, near Bristol, to London to complete his medical studies at St. George's Hospital, and lived with the family of the famous surgeon, John Hunter, for two years. Deeply interested in natural history from the age of nine, he became 'remarkable for the neatness and precision with which he made preparations of anatomy and natural history. His dissections of tender and delicate organs, his success in minute injections, and the taste he displayed in their arrangement, is said to have been almost unrivalled. Mr. Hunter recommended him to Sir Joseph Banks, to prepare and arrange the various specimens brought home by the celebrated circumnavigator, Captain Cook in his first voyage of discovery in 1771' (Pettigrew 1838, vol. 2). He was invited to become the naturalist on Cook's second voyage, but 'fortunately for mankind he preferred the seclusion of a country village', and it was here that his observations on cow pox led him to develop his theory of vaccination. 'Indeed he pressed this subject so much upon his professional brethren, that, at a medical club at Redborough, to which he belonged, he was threatened to be expelled if he persisted in harassing them with a proposition which they then conceived had no foundation but in popular and idle rumour, and which had become so entirely distasteful to them'. His first successful vaccination was made on 14 May 1796.

Pettigrew tells us that Jenner was musical, and played both the violin and the flute. He also amused himself and his friends with his verses, such as the following which he sent with a present of ducks to a lady whose daughter was recovering from an illness:

> I've despatch'd, my dear madam, this scrap of a letter,
> To say that Miss xxxx is very much better;
> A regular doctor no longer she lacks,
> And, therefore, I've sent her a couple of *quacks*.

1773

This was a momentous year for Banks. Just before Christmas, 1772, Cartwright arrived in a ship, which anchored in the Pool of London, with his Eskimo friends and Banks was at last able to talk with these northern people. He introduced them to John Hunter with whom they dined; a portrait of Caubvick, the girl, was painted for Hunter and still hangs in the Royal College of Surgeons.

Banks paid a brief visit to Holland but he was happily in love and probably did not wish to be absent from London for any length of time. His mistress bore him a child at the end of the summer; Fabricius, who had been working on Banks's insect collections that year, wrote him an affectionate letter asking about her and the child.

This summer Phipps sailed north to try to find a north-west passage to the Indies; he carried naturalists on board and had detailed instructions from Banks and John Hunter about the most important things he was to search for: any information that might throw light on the migration of herrings and other fish; the migration of birds breeding in high latitudes; the depredation of shipworms; and they asked him to collect whale foetuses from whalers.

JOSEPH BANKS to CONSTANTINE PHIPPS

Item 2 in the Thordarson collection, University of Wisconsin; 12 ff., 23·5 × 18·5 cm.

Instructions sent out with Captain Phipps on his Northern Voyage (in Banks's hand)

May, 1773

A voyage so short as the intended one is not likely to furnish many objects of Natural history indeed if it was I can have little to say as Mr. Irwin is so well

G. D. Ehret. pinxit 1767.

Dracæna borealis vol. 1. pag. 454.

Pl. VII *Clintonia borealis*
G. D. Ehret

acquainted with the desiderata of Zoology & Mr. Lions with those of Botany.

You will receive with this a cask of double distilld malt spirits a case with glass bottles a ream of drying paper a Tin box for insects with Pinns & Snippers for taking & securing them if any specimen Should be found which is too Large for to be containd in one of the bottles I shall beg the favour of your purcer to supply a Case or Boreca into which it may be put.

Whatever place you may touch at to the Northward of Ferroe must of consequence produce many unknown vegetables it is therefore desireable that Every different kind as far as it is possible to distinguish the least variation may be processd for that purpose the simple method is to take each plant & spreading the leaves a little open with the hand to place it between the leaves of a quire of paper between each plant Two intermediate leaves should be left & fresh quire supplied into which the plants should be removd every three days at least till they are thoroughly dry.

The great but indeed inevitable inconveniences attending this method is the difficulty of drying the Quires out of which plants have been taken in order to render them fit for receiving the plants again in their turn. this I have commonly effected by laying them on the booms or quarter deck with the open side of each Quire to windward & a boy to attend them whose business is to turn each to windward again as soon as the wind has blewn it over which if properly managd it does leaf by leaf. This in dry weather is very sufficient but in wet recourse must be had to the Gally Fire.

Some plants will be dried enough in two or three times changing the most succulent ye will find will probably not require more than ten times if any should I would advise that they are taken out of their sheets & laid on a locker or any place where nothing may be laid upon them for 8 or 10 hours at a time till they are quite dry which they cannot fail to be in two or three days.

All kinds of animals found in the Northern region will be curious if it is possible to bring them home alive a young white bear I should be particularly glad of as I have great reason to suppose that the white bear is an animal differing even generically from the Brown or Black bear.

Of Seels it is more than probable that you will meet with several kinds which have not been taken notice of by naturalists we know indeed but one kind with any degree of precision it varies very much in colour I should therefore advise that if any kind is seen which differs from the common in any other way as properties of its part to each other that the skin compleat & head with the teeth of such animal is procurd I have heard of one kind whose hair is long & shaggy like that of a water dog if any kind is found to be so after they come to maturity I should much wish to see them.

Whales are a kind of animals which naturalists are almost totaly unacquainted with accident might bring you in company with whale fishers if so Foetus's of any

257

species preservd in spirits would be very acceptable as would parts might be preservd in spirits for the doing which Irwin has particular instructions from Hunter.

Birds of the diving kind as Puffins murrs &c must abound where you mean to go & probably new species Lions will easily tell you the few which are known; any such that you may meet with if they should be too large to be preservd whole might still be brought in part by taking off their skins with the heads & feet sticking to them which should be likewise put into spirits.

Observations concerning the species of known birds which you may see especially in their breeding places will be of use as there are several whose migrations we are utterly unacquainted with.

Fish of the High Northern latitudes we know very little of I should therefore advise that a specimen at least of every sort which is not very evidently the same as some one known among us may be put into spirits. how desirable it is to know from whence the immense shoals of Herrings macorals capelings Pilchards shads salmons &c which every year come from the Northward & are seen but to a certain southern point which they never pass derive their origin any observation tending ever so little to illustrate that subject I should receive with great pleasure

The very blubbers &c which in many shapes & sizes from that of my hat to an almost invisible littleness swarm in the polar regions are not insignificant as they seem a necessary branch of all perfect nature does the whale or any other animal use them as food is a question to be answerd a few individuals of as many species as can be procurd will be very acceptable.

Whenever a sounding line or cable is hove in a careful hand attending it is almost sure especially if it has been long overboard to find something adhering to it which may be curious crabs star fish &c are often & once a most curious many headed Polype was taken in this way.

Shells &c may be brought up in the trap for sounding the [price?] of which you know is from fashion very high consequently they are desirable to many people many species of shell are found adhering to sea weed & under stones on the beach There your boats crew may gather them whenever they are left to wait without any more essential employment.

Seaweeds of all kinds may be preservd by merely washing them in fresh water & laying them three or four days to dry after which packd up in canvas bags they can receive no kind of detriment.

Insects will not abound unless the countries you are to visit should be as hot as our wild projector has supposd them to be such as you find Lions well knows how to take & impale with the instruments allotd for that purpose.

Mosses also & all kinds of lichens with which the high latitudes very much abound may be preservd in the same kind of bags in which they may be put while yet a little damp as they are then pliable but when dry become quite brittle.

of plants must be chose such as have if possible flowers & seed pods or fruits upon

258

each plant if that is impossible two of each kind should be taken for each compleat species intended to be brought of all trees shrubbs & plants that are sufficiently large the specimens should be chosen nearly as long as the paper.

so much for my own department I know you will excuse my Blunders so shall venture to swim a little into other peoples.

The large Trunks of Trees which are found floating on the Northern sees seem to afford matter for observations from whence conclusions might be drawn of the utmost consequence towards judging whether or no there is a Passage by the Pole to the other side of the Globe whether the currents realy run from the pole as a center in all directions supplyd again by undercurrents as those must urge who suppose the polar waters heavyer than those nearer the equator on account of their greater saltness or denser on account of their greater degree of cold they are subjected to &c &c it might therefore be satisfactory to know if possible what.

1 What & how many species of trees are thus found floating on the sea.

2 is the bark yet left on any of those found on the North side of Spitzbergen or in more northern latitudes.

3 have they all sufferd material friction against hard substances which may be known by the ends of the branches in what manner they have broken off.

4 have any of them been cut off by the hands of men are they unrooted or broken off by force of winds &c above ground.

5 in what parts of the sea are the greatest quantities of them found

6 why may it be that tho they are in plenty on the North side of Iceland they are very seldom seen on our coast

7 in what parts of the sea do they most abound

8 what quantity are worm eaten & what proportion free from worm

9 is the worm the common ship worm, to what size does it grow, are the shells with which the holes are lind yet unbroken near the mouths of the holes, are any remains of the animals left, or may be in high lat are they still alive & working.

specimens of different grains of woods & different barks also of the works of worms or other insects upon drift wood would be very desireable.

10 are the planks or timbers of ships which have been cast away on this coast ever worm eaten

For the satisfaction of one of my Friends be so good as to weigh certain musquet balls against weights of brass both in air & water & noting down with all convenient accuracy the weights of each on the paper in which it is wrappd up let them be brought home to me with a bottle of the water in which they were weighd carefully corkd up.

God bless you & send you to the Herring Hall or the source of the migration of macerel & thence home to your ever affect but never emulating

J Banks

259

GEORGE CARTWRIGHT, army officer, naturalist and fur trader, to JOSEPH BANKS
Kew B.C. 1:39.

Plymouth, 22d June 1773

Dr Sir

Nothing but the very great confusion of my mind could have made me so long neglect informing you of the fate of my Indian friends.

On my return to this place I had the satisfaction to find Caubvick out of danger, she is now recovering fast, having no other complaint except want of Flesh & Strength, which a good appetite and care will soon restore her to, the Men, as I suspected, did not long survive my departure for Town, they both went off within less than an hour of each other the night after I left them. I last night ventured to tell Caubvick of the death of all the rest, having prepar'd her for it this week past, she was a good deal affected, but not so much as I expected.

If you have any further commands they will reach me before I shall leave this place and you may depend on my executing them to the best of my power If Prints are taken from your drawings of the Indians I beg the favour of you to bespeak me six sets.

My best compliments wait on Miss Banks and Dr. Solander.

I am with many thanks for all your favours Dear Sir,

Your
Most Obedient
Humble Servant

[No address or date of reply]　　　　　Geo. Cartwright.

CONSTANTINE PHIPPS, naval officer and astronomer, to JOSEPH BANKS
MS in grangerised copy of Smith's *Life of Sir Joseph Banks* British Museum
(Natural History)

July 4th, 1773

My dear Banks

I am in 79° 30′ & have not seen a single bit of Ice & have been these three days without any fire and have no one day had a fire all day—I have got you two small Blubbers—a Seal's Bill of Fare out of his Belly containing sundry non-descript: Crabs & other things several Birds stuffed amongst them non descripts particularly a *Larus Rissa*[1] with only 8 Remiges Primores tho' Linnaeus attributes 10 you know to all Birds—a *Larus Niveus*[2] undescribed a Beautiful Bird etc. etc. Remember me to Solander & believe me most sincerely

Yours J. C. Phipps

[1] A kittiwake, *Rissa tridactyla* (L.). Gulls usually have ten primaries but irregularities in their number are not uncommon.

[2] The Ivory Gull, *Pagophila eburnea* (Phipps).

Irvine is well & would probably have said something had he been up it is now 4 OClock in the Morning & the wind fair

God Bless You

Racehorse off Spitsbergen

Lat. 79° 30′ July 4th

JOHANN CHRISTIAN FABRICIUS, entomologist, to JOSEPH BANKS
    Add. MS 8094: 27, 28

10 Nov., 1773.

Dear Sir,
    Here I am happy and merry at Coppenhagen thinking about all the happy houres I spend in Engelland with my friends, and recollecting all the fine things I saw in Your house from the human species down to the little Mosses Dr. Muselius was tired with. Well I hope they are all safe and to know this with certainty would give great pleasure to your friend.
    I would have wrote to You long ago, had I not intended to give You at the same time the news that I had send the plants You wanted out of Mr. Forsk. herbarium, but not finding any occasion I was satisfied with to send them, I write to ask you in what manner You think most proper to get them to Engelland . . .
    My best compliments and wishes in Orchard Street. What has Shee brought You? Well it is all the same if a Boy he will be clever and strong like his father, if a girl, she will be pretty and genteel like her mother. . . . Life well, dear Banks, remember sometimes You have a friend in Coppenhagen, for really if You think their is a man in the world who is more Your friend than I You certainly wrong

Your
most obed. humb. servant
J. C. Fabricius
Professor of Oeconomy

P.S. I will write some few words my dear Sir if well Fabricius tinks I cannot speak yet much english but for all that I have a heart which loves all my husband's english friends. I will tell you master Banks what is better than to runn round the world it is to come to Copenhagen to visit your Fabricius and to see his little wife who estime you if well she never saw you. our friends will be yours and our principle care will be to make your stay agreable. Let me now see you will not disapoient our Wishes and permit me to call myself for ever yours

Cecilie Fabricius

BANKSIAN LETTERS AND MEMORANDA

1775

This year Captain Cook in the *Resolution* returned from his second voyage round the world; a large part of the natural history collections made in the course of the voyage was acquired by Banks who also bought most of Georg Forster's paintings of animals and plants. The sister ship of the *Resolution*, the *Adventure*, commanded by Captain Furneaux, had returned the previous year bringing Omai, a native of Huaheine in the Tahitian group, to London. Banks and his friends had learnt a terrible lesson from the deaths of the Eskimos. It was speedily arranged (apparently at the suggestion of King George), that Omai should be inoculated by Dr. Dimsdale, who inoculated Catherine the Great, the first Russian to be so treated. Omai made a good recovery and in the summer of 1775 he accompanied Banks, Phipps, Lord Sandwich and George Colman, the playwright, to Phipps's home in Yorkshire for a holiday.

Meanwhile in Labrador Cartwright was making notes on natural history and, in between his trapping and fishing, collecting for Banks. He suggested that Banks and Solander should visit him in 1777, and said that he would add to his house if necessary.

An extract from George Colman the Younger's account of his visit to Mulgrave Castle in 1775, first published in *Random Records* in 1830; it begins on p. 157 of the first volume.

'The coach in which we rumbled from York was the ponderous property of Sir. J., and as huge and heavy as a broad-wheeled waggon . . . Its size was by no means too large for its contents . . . the packages of Captain Phipps, who intended to make some stay at Mulgrave, and who was ardent in his professional studies, were laid in like stores for a long voyage; he had boxes and cases cramm'd with nautical lore—books, maps, charts, quadrants, telescopes, etc. etc. Sir Joseph's stowage was still more formidable; unwearied in botanical research, he travell'd with trunks containing voluminous specimens of his *hortus siccus* in whitey-brown paper; and large receptacles for further vegetable materials which he might accumulate in his locomotions. . . . Our progress, under all its cumbrous circumstances, was still further retarded by Sir Joseph's indefatigable botany; we never saw a tree with an unusual branch, or a strange weed, or anything singular in the vegetable world, but a halt was immediately order'd.'

[At Mulgrave Castle]

P. 187. 'In regard to the nature of our daily occupations, they were guided, as I have already observed, by the two principals of our party; and as active enquiry was their ruling passion, the spirit of research predominated over all our amusements. Botany, and the opening of the ancient *tumuli*, of which there were several in the neighbourhood, were our chief objects . . . Sir Joseph Banks, who had a better claim, I imagine, than Dioscorides to the title of "The Prince of Botanists" put the two boys (Augustus Phipps and myself) into active training for the first of these pursuits, by sending us into the woods, early every morning, to gather plants. We could not easily have met with an abler master; and although it was somewhat early for us to turn natural philosophers, the novelty of the thing, and rambling through wild, sylvan tracts of peculiarly romantick beauty, counteracted all notions of studious drudgery, and turned science into a sport.—We were prepared overnight for these morning excursions by Sir Joseph, who could speak like Solomon, "of trees, from the cedar-tree that is in Lebanon, even unto the hyssop that springeth out of the wall". He explained to us the rudiments of the Linnaean system, in a series of nightly lectures, which were very short, clear and familiar; the first of which he illustrated by cutting up a cauliflower, whereby he entertained the adults (Omai excepted) as much as he delighted the younkers. I soon got a Botany mania, which lasted after I return'd to London, not quite as long as a voyage to Botany Bay. . . . I never see a boiled cauliflower, without recollecting the raw specimen, and the dissecting knife, in the hands of Sir Joseph . . . Dislodging the *cineres et ossa* of the ancients, and becoming an antiquarian resurrection man was the gallant Captain's terrestrial hobby, now he had dismounted from his *Racehorse*, which had carried him in his marine hunt after the North Pole; . . . he doated upon a Discovery, (great or small,) as Hotspur did upon Honour . . . it was a kind of field day whenever we open'd a tumulus;—a grand muster of all our party . . . and as the operation which occupied several hours, was effected at some distance from the house, we pitch'd a tent upon the scene of action, under which we dined. . . . We were obliged to cook for ourselves, after our own receipts. Sir Joseph made very palatable stews, in a tin machine which he call'd by a hard name, and which is now very common . . . But at all these anti-grave-digging jollifications, the talents of Omai shone out most conspicuously; and in the culinary preparations, he beat all his competitors. He practised the Otaheitan cuisine' [and Colman goes on to describe a Polynesian earth oven].

SARAH SOPHIA BANKS on JOSEPH BANKS

    Banks Papers, SO 9, Manuscript Branch, Reference Division, National Library of Australia, Canberra.

    Memorandums   13 Feb., 1775

1766. April 7th. Mr. Banks set out from London for Plymouth where he imbarked April 22d for Newfoundland & Labrador, & arrived safe at Lisbon in his way home Nov. 17. 1766.

To the best of my remembrance he arrived at London Jan. 30th 1767.

1767.

Went a little Excursion to Kent beginning Feb^{ry}. 21, & ending March 4th.

1767.

Another to Eastbury Bristol etc. in May & June.

Another began Aug: 13. & ended Jan 29. 1768 to Wales etc.

1768. Aug: 25th. Set Sail from Plimouth (on board the Endeavour Cap^{tn}. Cooke) on a voyage round the World, landed at Deal July 12. 1771.

1772. July 12 Sailed down the River from Gravesend on a voyage to the Western Isles, Iceland, & came from Endinborough by Land: arrived at London Octr. or Novr. 1772.

1773. Feby. 12. Set out from London for Holland returned March 22^{d}. 1773.

Memorandums.

May we ever remember and adore the Gracious Goodness of GOD, in permitting us now to enjoy my Dear Brother in health & safety amongst us again: & may he ever remember & be thankful, & join with us in Praises & Thanksgiving, for the wonderfull known miraculous & numberless unobserved Deliverances he has experienced: & which his gratefull Heart hath told me of, with wonder, & admiration, & gratitude. How often have my Dear Mother & Self contemplated & admired the innumerable & grave dangers he hath escaped; & adored our Gracious GOD, for restoring him to us.

What perilous excapes we all daily hourly experience, need not be said to a thinking mind: but which from their happening so frequently are less regarged [*sic*]: have we not heard anatomists say 'tis wonderfull from the delicate construction of our Bodies, that we do not suffer dislocation whenever we use any the least rough exercise: or almost when we walk. Have we not then the greatest reason to be thankful for the gracious Protection of a mericful GOD, who has not only daily preserv'd us amongst the innumerable dangers that surround us, but hath likewise preserv'd my Dear Brother from the perils, & very great ones, of the Sea; when the Waves had well nigh many times, swallowed him up; & snatched him from the jaws of Death & a Distemper, which carried of a great number of his Ship Mates. Let me conclude this paragraph, with a very sincere wish: that the sense of our Great CREATOR's Goodness, which we have in a particular manner so often experienced; be so lively imprinted on our minds; that we may never cease to think of it, & that it may so influence our Lives & Conversations, that we may as far as our frail nature will permit, do the Will of GOD.

The great importance of a Religious Life v: pages 12 & 13 very justly observes 'What are the most terrible Dangers of the Sea, when compared with those to which the Sinner is continualy exposed'.

Feby. 13. 1775.

This day my Dearest Brother is 32 years of age: (& arrived from Holland) (the last place he was at which took him out to Sea) at London March 22ᵈ. 1773) what very great variety of Scenes he had seen, in the Course of a few years.* May he live

> * He set out from London on his first voyage to Newfoundland, April 7. 1766. Returned to London from Holland (his last voyage) March 22. 1773. Within seven years.

to see many, many happy returns of this day: but, Much above that, May He be Blessed: May He live (as far as our confined and imperfect Nature will permit) a holy, and good, Life: May our Gracious PROTECTOR guide Him wherever He goes, and in whatever He does: May the Rational* Study He takes so much delight in, constantly remind Him of the wonderfull Order, Harmony, Mercy, and Goodness of God in the Creation: and should He ever become a Senator*° May Honour and Honesty be the Rules of his Actions in the small as every other Condition of Life he may experience:

> * Natural History
> *° My Brother has never yet been in Parliament (or attempted it) from a motive highly honest: & Praiseworthy: not thinking it right to undertake so great a trust, without he had determined to give up his time in a proper attendance on the Duties of it.

And finaly, may He be Everlastingly Happy in the World to come: where that we may all meet Him, and enjoy the Blessed State prepared for those** Mortals who (sensible of their great imperfection) rely on the Goodness of GOD; and believe their best, but poor Endeavours, will be accepted at the Throne of Grace, Thro' the Merits & Mercy of our ever Gracious REDEEMER Is the Earnest Prayer of S:S:Banks.

> ** I mean the above Reflexions as regarding those who believe in our Holy Religion: but I both believe & Hope, that those who are not enlightened with the Bright Sunshine of the Gospel, or who differ in points of faith; but who (according to their Faith) use their best Endeavours, far as in their power they can, to do the Will of the SUPREME BEING: will be accepted at the THRONE of GRACE.

GEORGE CARTWRIGHT to JOSEPH BANKS
Add. MS 8094:55

Sandwich Bay

12th Octʳ. 1775

Dear Sir,
    I herewith send you a few Bird skins, Plants, a Frog, and long tailed Mouse, but they are so badly preserv'd I fear they will scarce be worth your acceptance . . . I

shall not be able to procure you any quantity of Flys, as Mr. Williams, for fear I should, took the Instruments and Boxes for them with him. . . . If you have an inclination for another Voyage I think you would be pleas'd with this place & dare say you'd meet with some curiosities, for I've seen many birds that are entirely new to me, some of a beautifull plumage; one day I was surpris'd with the sight of a pair of Doves much the colour & size of Turtle Doves,[1] I kill'd one with a Ball, & preserv'd the skin for you but it was lost while I was gone to Charles Harbour. . . . Next summer I shall be very busy . . . but the summer afterwards, if you and Dr. Solander will faver me with a visit you'll make me happier than I can express: if you will come do not curtail yourself of any necessary part of your retinue, only let me know next sum^r how many your family will consist of, & their qualities, that I may add a room or two to my House if it is not big enough to accomodate you. . . . I've observ'd many kinds of Herbage here that are unknown to me, but had not time to gather or conveniency to cure them having been the whole summer cruising between Charles Harbour & this.

The white Grouse and Hare[2] you'll find in the Bag were kill'd in Spring, the former was just beginning to change colour, the latter was casting her coat, whether they do so in the fall or not I can't tell as this is the first I've seen on the coast. She had five young ones in her, wch is one more than I ever knew a Hare to have before, as many as I've killed.[3] We have great plenty of Rabbits wch are commonly mistaken for Hares here.

Unfortunately three of your large bottles are broke by moving, and all your Paper for Plants is spoil'd by damp, as I was oblig'd to leave your Cases in a bad shed for want of House room. I beg my respectfull compts to Dr. Solander and Mr. J. Hunter. I am Dr Sir with much esteeme

Your most obedient humble servant
Geo. Cartwright.

[1] Cartwright gives further particulars about the doves in his diary for 22 August 1775 and says that they were feeding on the berries of *Empetrum nigrum*. Schorger (1955:260) considers that they were Passenger Pigeons, *Ectopistes migratorius* rather than *Zenaidura macroura*, the Mourning Dove, since those doves live almost exclusively on seeds. Todd (1963:429) thinks they were more probably Mourning Doves, and Derek Goodwin (personal communication) considers that Cartwright's mention of Turtle Doves suggests *Zenaidura* rather than *Ectopistes*.

[2] The white hare was killed on an island between the Seal Islands and the Isle of Ponds, on 11 June 1775, and would have been a Polar Hare *Lepus arcticus*. The Varying Hare *Lepus americanus*, also occurs in Labrador; Cartwright was mistaken in thinking that rabbits lived there as well as hares.

[3] In Hodges's copy of Pennant's *Arctic Zoology*, Cartwright recorded a hare with seven young ones. See p. 82, fn., and Appendix.

BANKSIAN LETTERS AND MEMORANDA

1776

Banks moved into the big house in Soho Square which was to become famous as a meeting place for European scientists and explorers until his death in 1820. Cook left on his third and last voyage round the world.

1777

At the end of the summer Johan Alströmer visited London; he became very friendly with Banks and Solander; Banks gave him much of the duplicate material in his ethnographical collection.

Amongst the notable European scientists and writers who died this year were Voltaire, Haller, Rousseau and Jussieu.

GEORGE CARTWRIGHT to JOSEPH BANKS
> Kew B.C. 1:64

Sandwich Bay 22 Octr. 1777

Dear Sir, I now send you a few trifles which in my opinion are sad rubbish, I most heartily wish you may find them worth your acceptance; but what excuse shall I make you for the damage your case of bottles has met with, it has been so often removed from one place to an other, & the rascals are so careless that they have broken every bottle except one.

As you was so obliging to tell me I need not discharge my bond to you at the expiration of the year unless it was convenient, I must beg leave to make use of that liberty for I never met with so bad a year every thing having failed for these twelve months past. I have wrote to my brother concerning the interest, which I hope he will find means to pay.

With my best compliments to Dr. Solander and Mr. Hunter I remain Dear Sir

> Your
> Much Obliged and
> Very Humble Servant
> Geo. Cartwright   [no address or date of reply]

1778

In 1778 Banks succeeded Sir John Pringle as president of the Royal Society, a post which he held until his death more than forty years later. By virtue of this position he became, the same year, one of the Trustees of the British Museum, attending his first meeting in December 1778, and his last in February 1820.

Linnaeus died on 10 January, 1778.

BANKSIAN LETTERS AND MEMORANDA

George Cartwright to Joseph Banks
  Kew B.C. 1:77

Great Island Isthmuss Bay
14 Septr. 1778

Dr. Sir,

Last year I did myself the pleasure of writing to you, and sent you a box of plants etc, and one of your cases containing some animals in spirits; for want of direct conveyance they went by Capt. Kinloch, in the Countess of Effingham, to Leghorn with orders to forward them from there in case he did not go to England, but he neglected to do so, and upon his return to this place informed me, that he lost the letter along with some others; the box, and case he brought back, and four days after his arrival the Minerva privateer, of twenty guns, belonging to Boston, came in here and took both the ship, and a brig which had arrived from England, together with all my stores, provisions, great part of my household furniture, some of my cloaths, eight hundred quintals of dry fish, and everything they could find, to the amount of upwards of six thousand pounds value, leaving but a small quantity of provisions, together with the remains of my cloathes, and household furniture, and such fish as was not in condition to ship. Not only your case, & box which were in the ship, but your other five cases are gone.

This misfortune happened to me by the villainy of two of my late servants, who left my service this last spring, and served Mr. Pinson at Temple Bay, untill the privateer put in there and served him in the same manner as they have done me when they entered, and piloted the vessel to this place, where thirty two of my people entered, and one of them discovered all my effects. I am now reduced to the utmost distress, and what to do I can not tell. I scarce have it in my power either to quit this coast, or remain the winter upon it; if I do the former must I trust my-self in an open boat one hundred and fifty leagues at the most tempestuous season of the year; if I determine upon the latter, shall run a risk of starving for want of provisions. I've sent two shallops to the southward in quest of supplies, and a vessel to carry my fish to market, having about five hundred and sixty tierces of salmon, and four hundred quintals of codfish left. This is the first year my affairs took a turn in my favor, had this misfortune not happened to me, should have cleared about fifteen hundred pounds; and [indecipherable] were got into such a train, that I should have cleared in all probability, between two and three thousand pr annm. in future; but now I much fear my fortunes are wrecked; and all my schemes frustrated. The Americans behaved with great civility, but they plundered in a most practical manner. The Captain professed himself a man of strict honor, and great humanity, but he proved himself the reverse of both; he refused me a number of trifling necessaries, wch. were of no value to the captors and broke his honor [?] with me in every instance, and he forced away the poor Eskimeaux as slaves, an inhuman action!

My brother John informed me this spring, that with the money with which my relatives furnished me, he had not only purchased the brig, and cargo but had also paid off some of my debts, I hope yours was amongst the number, if not God only knows when I shall be able to discharge it. Believe me, Sir, if no one was concerned in my late misfortune but myself, it would not give me a single moments uneasiness but as it will affect many, I am almost distracted

III 37. I have but one consolation left, and that is but a very poor one indeed, it is, that I have not fallen by my own folly, indolence, or extravagance, but by the villainy of scoundrels, whom I had used more like my children, than servants. Had it but pleased God to have kept enemies clear of me, in two years more I should not only have recovered all my former losses but should have been beforehand with the world. But 'tis time to drop a subject which must be as painfull to you to read, as me to write, therefore, begging my best respects to Dr. Solander, Mr. Hunter and all the rest of my worthy friends of your acquaintance, permit me to subscribe myself Dr. Sir

Your

Much Obliged and

Very sincere

Humble Servant

Geo. Cartwright.

P.S. A little to the northward of this place is a bay, separated from Sandwich Bay by a neck of land of no great breadth, and runs forty, or fifty leagues into the country, having many large rivers emptying into it; this place is called by the Esquimeaux Iboucktoke, and upon an island near the mouth of it was one of their settlements. A planter from Newfoundland went there last year and wintered, and upon the island found an Eskimeau town with all the inhabitants dead, their boats thwarted up, and all their goods left in their houses and tents; amongst other things a suit of laced cloathes and a silver cup known to have belonged to the man Coghlan had in England, and the carpenters tools-boxes, which my Lord Dartmouth and yourself gave the Indians I had were found, from which I conclude that after they left me they reached that place in safety and intended spending the winter there, and that some of the infection of the small pox remaining in Caubvick's cloaths they caught that dreadful distemper and all died of it. Pray communicate this intelligence to the Moravians.

[Banks answered this letter on 9 March 1779, but there appears to be no copy of his reply. There is an entry in Cartwright's diary for 28 March in the same year, stating that his fears of a small pox epidemic amongst the Eskimos have been confirmed by the discovery of a medal amongst their effects, which had just been brought to him. He recognized it as one that had been given to Caubvick's family by one of his brothers in England. The lapse of time between the return of Caubvick to Labrador and the discovery of this tragedy seems rather long.]

BANKSIAN LETTERS AND MEMORANDA

1779–80

Captain Cook was killed in Hawaii on 14 February 1779, but the news did not reach London until 10 January 1780. Joseph Banks married Dorothea Hugessen in March 1779.

João de Loureiro, Portuguese botanist (p. 177), to Joseph Banks
Add. MS 8094:229

Canton 22 January, 1780

Dear Sir,

It is many years, that I have not the pleasure of seeing your amiable Letters. Mr. Hutton, as he told Me, has Likewise received None of Late from You. Perhaps the troubles of War occasioned the Sailing of the Company's Ships Unexpectedly Without your Letters to China. As it May be, I wish You good health, and I pray to God Grant you a true felicity in all your things.

In the past Year I had sent You two Letters: the first by the Ship the Earl of Mansfield, and the next by the Royal George, that sailed from Canton near the Midst of March. On this Last Was inclosed my small Writing *Nova Genera Plantarum*, Which I desired to be printed at London by Your Care, and favour, and by Mr. Perry's, if You be pleased to do so together. At present I send Not another of my Writtings because I think prudent to assay before the good, or ill Success of the former; for it should be of an idle Mind to prosecute a Work, that perhaps Could no[t] obtain the publick allowance. On the Contrary, Could the former Meet Whatsoever good Success among your Friends, I shall no[t] Neglect to send You in the year after the *Flora*, and the *historia Cochinchina*

As My old age and Weakness permit me no more to endeavour to a Long Voyage to England as I Much aspired in Convenient time, at last I do remain at Canton; Where I am treated Very Kindly by the English Gentlemen. Here I Will expect Your Comands for Whatsoever thing You, or Your Friends May desire from this Country: to Which I shall obey With the greatest affection With Which I have the honour to be

> Your most indebted friend, and
> Servant
> John de Loureyro

1781

The first volume of Latham's *General Synopsis of Birds* was published by Benjamin White, brother to Gilbert. This volume included some detailed notes on the birds of prey collected by Banks in Newfoundland and Labrador, taken for the most part from Pennant's MS for the *Arctic Zoology*, referred to, by Latham, as the *American Zoology* or *Am. Zool.*

1782

Banks's very close friend, librarian and scientific colleague, Daniel Solander, died in May after a short illness. Banks's most touching letter about him to Johan Alströmer was printed in Sweden at that time. A translation by Danielsson (1969) is now available. I believe that Banks's deep and lasting grief at Solander's death was the chief reason that decided him finally to abandon the publication of the biological results of the *Endeavour* voyage, on which they had worked so closely together. Banks himself stated 'Everything was written jointly by our combined labour'. Solander was succeeded by Jonas Dryander, 1748–1810.

WILLIAM HENRY PIGOU and JOHN DUNCAN, collectors, to JOSEPH BANKS
     Add MS 33977:148

Sir Joseph Banks Bart: Rio de Janeiro
                                                                    May 31st, 1782

Sir, By the Griffin Cutter now under Dispatch for England, We take the Liberty to inform you that we have delivered to her Commander Lieutenant John Cook, a Box marked with your Address, containing a few specimens of the Plants, Birds, Insects and other Productions of Nature peculiar to this Country; As we are not sufficiently acquainted with the Study of Botany, to attempt a description of the several Plants, We are induced to hope you will be pleased to accept the same without the necessary Information respecting them.

We take the Liberty also to enclose a Letter for Gerard de Visme Esqr of Lisbon signifying our request that he will send to you half the Seeds of the Plants and Fruits of this Country which our Friend Senhor Francisco Xavier Cardosa Caldeira resident here, hath promised to collect at the proper Season, and to transmit them to Mr. de Visme on our Account.

We leave this Place tomorrow on our Voyage to China, where we shall be very happy at all Times to receive your Commands and those of Dr. Solander to whom we request the favor of you to present our best Compliments.

<blockquote>
We are with Respect
     Sir
Your very obedient
humble Servants
Wm Henry Pigou
John Duncan
</blockquote>

271

BANKSIAN LETTERS AND MEMORANDA

JOSEPH BANKS to ROBERT BRUDENELL, later 6th Earl of Cardigan
Kew B.C. 1:119; D.T.C. 2:221

Soho Square,
Novr. 29 82

My Lord

Mr. Masson[1] whom his Majesties Bounty through your Lordship's mediation has renderd Effectualy happy having receivd an invitation from a Gentleman at Lisbon possessed of an ample Botanick Garden to assist in arranging and naming his Plants and being unwilling to remain idle while by prosecuting that business he may have an opportunity of enriching his Majesties botanick garden by exchanges from thence Humbly requests his Majesties permission to undertake the voyage on Condition that if during his absence which he at present intends to continue only a few months his Majesty shall have occasion for his services in any other Line he will on receiving notice thereof instantly return to such place as his Majesties orders shall direct.

[copy in Banks's hand.]

1784

The first volume of Pennant's *Arctic Zoology* appeared this year; Banks's account of the Newfoundland fishery was printed as part of the introduction. The following year the second volume was published with notes on many of the birds collected by Banks in Newfoundland and Labrador, and engravings from some of the paintings by Paillou and Parkinson. The final supplementary volume was published in 1787.

GERARD DE VISME to JOSEPH BANKS
Kew B.C. 1:185

3rd Dec., 1784

I have not had the pleasure of reminding you, Sir, for some time, that you have a friend in Lisbon, allways much attached to you, who recalls often to mind that you saw his plantations at Bemfique in their infant stage, & wishes you would revisit them again to see the effects of vegetation & good culture in this delightfull climate.

I have extended my grounds increased greatly my collection of exoticks, & built an exceeding pretty house with 13 windows in front, very commodious, & elegant. Pillament, who is in a manner fixed here, has painted me two intire rooms, one in marine *scenes*, with all the costume of the Tagus, the other of China. My Italian Saloon for musick is lofty, & well adapted for sound, its dimensions 36. feet by 24.

[1] Francis Masson, 1741–1805, trained at Kew with Aiton. He was the first collector to be sent overseas from the Royal Botanic Gardens.

Pl. VIII *Listera convallarioides*
G. D. Ehret

G. D. Ehret. pinxit
1767

I am now planning a publick Fountain in the Grove opposite my grounds; Her Majesty will grant me a supply of water from the Aqueduct, the overplus will fall from a cascade, already well executed in my largest Tank, & give a good supply to the others; I have made a rustick bridge over the little River, which separates my new acquisition, from the primitive one you was acquainted with, with rock work, Shells, coral, & plants, which has a look of great antiquity.

Masson [see Banks's letter to Brudenell] could not persevere in making a catalogue of my plants; he has worn himself out with fatigue, in roving over wild grounds, & sands, in search of new productions, and did not come near me on his late return from the Island of Madeira, tho' I received by him some seeds from Mr. Murray, the consul there; I expect he will add one to the Martyrs of Botany, wrote by commerson.[1]

I have taken the liberty to offer Lady Banks two boxes of my oranges; they are on board the Lisbon Packet, Capt[n] Hair, to the care of my friend Mr. Jacomb. You will receive also from him 3 Volumes on the natural history of Batavia, published there, which are in the Dutch language, & may perhaps deserve translation. Padre Loureiro [see his letters] visits me sometimes, and continues his work; I encourage him to persevere, before Tarda necessitas letti corripuit gradum,[2] & have given him [. . . torn] istance. I am with constant regard . . . ar Sir, your much attached and humble servant

Gerard de Visme
Lisbon 3th Decem. 1784

[Banks's dates on the back are Jan. 7 and March 17—85.]

1787

Phipps, now Lord Mulgrave, married Ann Elizabeth Cholmeley, a girl of great charm and beauty, only seventeen years old. Fanny Burney, a warm admirer of Phipps, thought their mental endowments too dissimilar for a happy marriage. It was never tested. Lady Mulgrave died in childbirth the following year and Phipps did not recover from her loss. He died four years later.

---

[1] Philibert Commerson, the very able and industrious naturalist who went on Bougainville's voyage round the world, 1766–9, died in 1773 at Mauritius where he had landed on the return journey in order to help his friend Poivre to make a biological survey of the area. His collections were largely neglected; some were stolen by his newly-appointed assistant in Mauritius, Sonnerat, who caused confusion by publishing Commerson's plates and descriptions of South American penguins and other birds in his own *Voyage to New Guinea* (1776) (Lysaght 1952), a country which Sonnerat had, incidentally, never actually visited. How antarctic birds could have reached New Guinea has led to some ingenious ornithological speculation over the years.

[2] 'Before slowly overtaken by inevitable death.'

1788

The first volume now appeared of the thirteenth edition of Linnaeus's *Systema Naturae*, edited by J. F. Gmelin. In this work many of the birds collected by Banks were described and, for the first time, given scientific binomials. Gmelin based his descriptions on those that had already been published in the works of Latham and Pennant, mostly without reference to Banks.

The African Association was founded in this year. Banks was one of its most energetic members.

1789

Aiton's *Hortus Kewensis* was published this year; it contained descriptions of a number of the species brought from Newfoundland and Labrador by Banks, and engravings from five of Ehret's paintings of those plants. Most of the work for the *Hortus* was done by Banks, Solander and Dryander although their names do not appear on the title page. Britten (1912) wrote about the use of Solander's MSS in this publication; our knowledge of Banks's contribution is derived from the letters of the younger Linnaeus (Uggla 1959:90).

From now on Banks was actively engaged in promoting the development of Australia and the knowledge of the Australian flora, culminating in the work of Flinders, Ferdinand Bauer and Robert Brown in the first years of the nineteenth century. No book has yet done justice to Banks's vision in this regard, nor to the care with which he planned Flinders's expedition in 1800, nor to his meticulous work in sending useful plants, including a variety of vines, to the new colony. The volumes of his correspondence concerned with Australia, now in the Mitchell Library in Sydney, are inadequately known and have not yet been calendared. See also Britten 1905.

1790

Cartwright prepared to publish his Labrador journal and asked Banks for advice.

George Cartwright to Joseph Banks
    Kew B.C. 2:4; D.T.C. 7:23–24

Collingham near Newark
24th Jan 1790

Sir Joseph

At the desire of the Duke of Newcastle I am going to publish the Journal of my Voyages to and residences in Labrador. It will be done by subscription, and my proposals will appear in the papers towards the end of this week, or beginning of the next. In the first volumes I shall give a chart of Newfoundland and that of Labrador from Cape Charles to Sandwich Bay. My friends here wish me to give a whole length print of myself in my winter's dress, with my furring accoutriments and I wish to add a print of those Indians whom I brought to England. For those reasons I take the liberty to trouble you with this letter to request of you to inform me, what you think a painter will have for my picture, an engraver for the copper-plate and the expence of paper and working off one thousand prints, quarto size. Also, if you had an engraving done from the picture, which you had taken of the Indians. Though I fear it will be too large, if you had: and if you had not, I think that, the expence of a plate in case you were so kind as to allow me to have one engraved from it, would come to too much money, since I have fixed the price of the three volumes (which it will make) at two guineas the set. His Grace has generously subscribed for twenty five sets.

> I am
> Sir
> Your
> Much Obliged
> humble servant
> Geo. Cartwright.

[No date of reply, but it must have been at once—see next letter.]

Kew B.C. 2:5; D.T.C. 7:25–26

Collingham 27th Jan. 1790

Sir Joseph,

I am greatly obliged to you for your very friendly and polite answer to my letter, which I received today.

I fear you flatter me very much when you tell me you 'expect both entertainment and instruction' from the perusal of my voyages. They may, perhaps, sometimes create a laugh, but instruct, I think, they cannot.

Had I originally entertained the least thought of publishing my journal, I should have taken more pains to have made it worth reading, but I should not have done it now, had I not often been desired so to do, by such of my friends as had perused part of it particularly my good friend the Duke.

I thank you, Sir, for your information respecting the intended engravings but as they will come to so much money, I shall not meddle with them. As to the Charts they will come pretty easy since Faden is already possessed of the plates, which he has engraved from the surveys of Cook, Lane, and others.

The plan which I go upon is as safe as possible, since I shall risk only about twenty pounds for advertisements, handbills, receipts etc, for the particulars of which I beg leave to refer you to Faden, who will be furnished with my handbills in a few days.

And I wish subscriptions to be paid into his hands, in preference to Hochdale or Robinson, since he recieves them gratis and I must pay the others.

Perhaps my observations on the growth of timber and the effects of manures may be of service to s[ome] of my readers.

> Your
> Most faithful
> and obedient servant
> Geo. Cartwright.

[Ans. Jan 29 1790.]

CONSTANTINE PHIPPS, Lord Mulgrave, to JOSEPH BANKS
    D.T.C. 7:169

Oct. 19th, 1790

My dear Sir Joseph,

I found your letter on my arrival in Town last night—I believe the Marine list was so loaded at the end of the last War that there is no probability of its being added to for some time; at least I know that a friend of mine low on the Half pay dispaired of being soon employed—If, however, I find that there is likely to be any addition, I will mention the gentleman (whose name we have not) to Lord Chatham in the way most likely to succeed as our joint wish,—We are still in the same uncertainty as to Peace or War, but the Leviathan is so forward that she will be commissioned in a few days, and I must look only to that, but should we Country Gentlemen have the comfort of honourable Peace I hope to spend much of my time in your Society; we are, I believe, the oldest friends to each other, & I can with great truth assure you that the length has only added to the proofs of the value of such a friendship in my estimation, and I am, with the most sincere Esteem, and attachment,

> Your most affectionate
> friend and servant
> Mulgrave

Whitehall

1791

JOÃO DE LOUREIRO to GERARD DE VISME
    [Translation from Portuguese] Add. MS 8097:412

22nd April, 1791

Sr de Visme.

I have respectfully acknowledged the honour you have paid me in communicating to me the letter of the illustrious Senhor Banks. I am most obliged and grateful to you both thereby. I could wish that I could find in myself more strength to assist this gentleman, not to mention the Royal Society of London, the most celebrated in Europe, and of which he is the most worthy President. In obedience to his command, I am enclosing straightway this paper, in which you will observe the correspondence of my flora with the numbers and names of my manuscript article; and not only of the six plants which you want, but of many others of which the names or numbers have been changed, up to the end of the class Dodecandria. Of the others which remain throughout the flora, I will investigate the correspondence in the same manner as the earlier ones, in order to send them to you if I hear that they can be of any use to you. There are many examples termed 'genera' in the manuscript, for want of better information; and from the literature I have learned since that they were not new nor even genera. Moreover, I admit that I owe this knowledge in great part to the notes which Senhor Banks sent me and which enlightened me so that I was able to correct and change them.

When it was time to collect, as was necessary, the small fruits of my literary work, I find only opposition and trouble in my own country, and this in the name of our own Academy of Lisbon and at the hands of the present Secretary of that body. Eight months ago he published my *Flora Cochinchinensis* against my express wish, as at that time it still needed the *Index Cochinchinensis* which was absolutely necesary. Since then he has put so many obstacles in my way (I do not understand his motive), that only a few days ago was I permitted to receive some copies of my work, printed by the press of the Academy. And the Senhor Secretary is not content with receiving all the expenses of the printing, but also wishes to take half the total production, which greatly exceeds the total of the expenditure. This seems to me unjust and indecent behaviour in a learned society, to take all the profit of a work towards which it has made no contribution.

Moreover, Senhor Banks, patron of letters, has most generously helped me with his notes in the composition of my work, and now promises to assist me further by promoting its sale in London, a procedure which would be very difficult for me to carry out. When you return shortly to your country, perhaps not very pleased to take leave of Portugal, I beg you to lay before Senhor Banks the sentiments of veneration which I profess for his great merits, his science and his benevolence with which he has favoured me and which I hope he will continue to do, and for which I remain most sincerely grateful.

> To Most Estimated
> Snr. de Visme
> Your humble and
> obliged servant

Lisbon   João de Loureiro

[I am indebted to the late Mr. A. C. Townsend for this translation.]

BANKSIAN LETTERS AND MEMORANDA

Joseph Banks to Nicholas Vansittart, Chancellor of the Exchequer

Brabourne Papers: Kent County Archives

Soho Square,
5 July, 1798.

[An extract in a clerk's hand]

I have the honour to enclose to your Grace an Attestation from Colonel von Behm countersigned by the Magistracy of Pernau in Estonia relative to the identity of the Person applying which I thought necessary to procure, & also a Statement of Chevalier de la Garde of the wishes of his Father-in-Law & himself, which will explain the whole of the business & I hope your Grace will allow me to say that I feel so much interest in the success of the son-in-law of the Friend of the British Navigators, that I shall feel infinite gratitude, if your Grace is pleased to honor him with a favorable answer.

> I have the honor to be with due respect & unfeigned regard
> & esteem
>> Your Grace
>> Obt. hble Servt.
>> Jos. Banks.

[See also 1816]

1799

Wilhelmina Sprengel to Joseph Banks

Add. MS 8098:486–7

Halle
4 June 1799.

Sir,

The Liberal kindness with which You, through the friendly Intermediation of Professor Blumenbach, have generously consented to waive the Payment of the Debt of two hundred and fifty Pounds Sterling contracted by my late Father, Dr. John Reinhold Forster, calls for the most grateful acknowledgements from his Widow and Children; and will I hope excuse the Liberty I take of troubling You Sir in all our Names with these few Lines. Give me leave Sir to assure You, that how sensible soever we may be of Sir Joseph Banks generous manner of acting towards the Family of a Man (who with all the great Qualifications of his head and heart still was too often deficient in point of Prudence and cool Discrimination, and through these Defects forfeited the good Opinion, to which his other valuable Qualities and great Learning might else universally have entitled him) I say how sensible soever we may be of this your Kindness, yet nothing in the World could have induced us, to put the known Liberality of your Character to the test, by solliciting the Remission of a Debt so justly due and so long withheld, were it not the ardent desire of making the last Days of an aged and worthy Parent, whose Life has been chequered with numberless Cares and Vicissitudes, easy and chearful during the few years which it may yet please Heaven to bestow on her. With what will accrue from the Sale of my late Father's Library and Collection of Minerals, (the former of which will be purchased by our gracious King) and a small Pension which his Majesty has settled upon my good Mother, we flatter ourselves that She will be enabled to live in a Situation above Want; and her, and our Blessings will daily attend You, for having contributed to this moderate Pittance. Impress'd with the most grateful Sentiments give me Leave Sir to Subscribe myself

Your greatly oblig'd Servant
Wilhelmina Sprengel

[Banks replied on 13 July.]

1810–11

Vandelli, whom Banks met in Lisbon in 1766, asked for his help and visited England. Jonas Dryander, Banks's librarian, died this year. Banks was deeply troubled by his death. Two letters revealing Banks's affection and admiration for him were published by du Rietz in 1964 (p. 57).

DOMENICO VANDELLI, Botanist, to JOSEPH BANKS
Add. MS 8100:86–88 (In Italian with translation attached.)

20 Feb., 1810

Excellency,

I take this means of expressing to your Excell^{cy} my most lively acknowledgements for your powerful protection in obtaining my liberty with permission to proceed to England, by the official despatch of the Minister Plenip^y. in Lisbon to the Governours of that Kingdom, on the 10th of January, who immediately sent a Schooner to this Island with the order- But the wretchedness to which I and my family have been reduced, by a Catastrophy originating with a powerful Enemy, renders it impossible (notwithstanding the Governours have promised to pay the whole of my Salaries and Pensions) for me to proceed to England, which I very anxiously desire to revisit, and to thank my benefactor, and close the career of my unfortunate life, for the greatest part employed in Serving a Prince, from whom I had hoped for a provision for the support of myself and family in a foreign Country, as I can make little or no account of the Patrimonial property which I Have in Modena-

In my unhappy Circumstances I apply to the powerful protection of your Excellency for my assistance being with the most profound respect

Your Excellency's
Most humble and most obliged
Servant

Angra [Azores]   D. Vandelli

    Add MS 8100:84

[This letter is written in Italian with Portuguese phrases and words here and there. I am indebted to Mr. J. H. Price for the literal translation here given of the first part; the rest concerns Vandelli's sufferings and is of no particular interest in the context of this book.]

10.12.1810.

Excellency,

    I have perceived how much your Excellency has interested himself in protecting the two unhappy naturalists, my old friends Broussonet and Correia de Serra, and for the friendship which you showed to me in Lisbon on your return from the Island of Newfoundland; and particularly for the warrant you gave for me to visit in the name of your Excellency Croft, since the many years I interrupted my correspondence; I take the liberty of writing through the medium of Lt. Stewart, commander of the frigate *Lavinia* to recommend myself to the protection of Your Excellency to obtain for me a passport and transport to England: from where I hope it will be possible to obtain compensation to my honour, and for the ruin of my family, and recompense for 47 years service to the public and to the Prince Regent. I was innocent, as the self-same Governors in an obligatory declaration making humble apology to the author of the gazette called *Il Sole*, which cries out against the barbarous procedures of these governors who have banished more than fifty innocent persons. . . .

    Angra Castle   D. Vandelli

JOSEPH BANKS, probably to W. R. HAMILTON, Under-Secretary for Foreign Affairs

    Add. MS 8100:89

(See Warren Dawson, 1958:841)

Soho Square,
May 1st, 1811

My dear Sir,

    allow me to Request of you that you will move Marquis Wellesley [Foreign Secretary] on the subject of my old acquaintance Sig[nr] Dominico Vandelli Lately

42. Joseph Banks.
Henry Edridge

43. Joseph Banks, with a map showing the drainage of the fens in his hand; other maps of the fens in rolls behind him.

Thomas Phillips

Keeper of the Royal Museum and Superintendant of the Royal Exotic Garden at Lisbon. The only man of Science I believe in that Capital who by his Lordship's Kind intervention has been Liberated from the imprisonment he was unjustly doomed to Suffer in the azores and allowed to take Refuge or Rather Sanctuary in this Island.

he is soon Expected to arrive and I am sorry to say that it appears by his Letter to me that he is wholly destitute of Property, his appointments at Lisbon are as we knew intirely at an End he has indeed some paternal Property at Modena but owing to the present disturbed State of Europe he has not for some time been able to Obtain Remittances from thence which he Received at Lisbon.

Well aware of the Liberality and Generosity of the Marquis' Character I can have no doubt of his Intention to assign to this Ancient Philosopher who is Represented to be at least 80 years of age a proper and Competent maintenance such as will give Comfort to the Latter End of a well Spent Life now almost exhausted, what I wish you to Obtain for me is a knowledge of the amount of the Sum that is intended to be applied to the Old man's use, in order that I may be enabled to Look out for some proper house in which he may be boarded and Lodgd with people who will be Kind and Civil to him and these are not Easy to Obtain but which I shall seek for with diligence as soon as I am acquainted with the amount of the offer that it will be in my power to make for the accomodation.

> I am my dear Sir
> with Sincere Esteem and Regard

[Bottom trimmed off but Banks's handwriting unmistakable.]

DOMENICO VANDELLI to JOSEPH BANKS
    Add. MS 33982:15

9th July, 1811

Sir,

I have the Honnour to present to you the Materials of the Petition which I have made to be presented to the Prince Regent of Portugal and also that of My Son, accordingly [*sic*] your Lordship recommendation.

And as I was not Acquainted With the expences of this Country; and it is impossible to get in short time an answer of the Brazils, having been Obliged to leave Portugal So Suddenly and Whithout the proper Means for My Subsistence here My family being not in Circumstances to increase my Debts, and relieve Me, I am obliged Sir, to apply to Your Benevolent Friendship towards Me, and to Accept your Friendly and Generous Offers; being impossible for me to make less than 27. pounds by *Month* for My necessary expenses.

I hope Sir, that you Will be so Good as to excuse Me, and to believe the gratitude and Respectfull Sentiments of high Consideration with which I the honour to

> Your Lordship
> Most Hble Sr and obliged Friend
> Dr. Vandelli

The 9th July 1811
9 Frith Street Soho Sq.

[Vandelli signed this letter but it is not in his writing.]

JOSEPH BANKS to DOMENICO VANDELLI
    Add. MS 33982:16

July 9 1811

Sir,

it was at the desire of Lord Geo Stewart who Represented you as suffering a severe and unmerited imprisonment that I applied for your Release which could not be obtained from your Courts on any terms but those of sending you to England, to this I consented in Remembrance of the Civilities I receivd from you in 1766 when I was at Lisbon but I was not at all aware that you wer to come here wholly unprovided with funds for your maintenance here nor at all supposd that you would bring with you a son as ill provided as yourself I am more sensible than you Can be of the high Prices of all the necessaries of Life. The expences of my own house-hld are now double what they have been and are still upon the increase it is therefore impossible for me to supply you with money at the Rate you have had of £27 a month [see pp. 56–7].

England is full of Emigrants from all different Countries you will find Abundance from your own Country many of Rent and Property at home who are Constreind to Live here at Expences far Short of those you have incurrd hitherto if you will take the advice of these and Conform yourself to the Rate of Expence with which they are Obligd to be Satisfied I will take Care to Find the money for your Support but I think it will be Right for you to send back your Son.

I have deliverd your Petition to Lord Wellesley by whose powerfull influence you have been Released from imprisonment he is well inclind to give it his support and to Recommend it to Ld Strongford at Rio de Janeiro.
[Draft in Banks's hand; on back—'Mr Vandelli July 9 11.']

1814–20

The *Flora Americae Septentrionalis* of Frederick Pursh was published in 1814; it contained many references to Banks's plants from Newfoundland and Labrador.

BANKSIAN LETTERS AND MEMORANDA

Lieutenant Parry's account of his visit to Soho Square in 1817 shows Banks's continuing interest in the problems of the far north.

JOSEPH BANKS to THE RT. HON. N. VANSITTART
Brabourne Papers. Kent County Archives.

Spring Grove
Oct^{er}. 28. 1816.

My dear Sir,

Allow me to implore your attention to a Case in which the honor of the Nation we belong to is in my judgment called in question.

The Complainant is the Daughter of the Colonel Von Behm, who receivd the Ships of Discovery Commanded by Capt Cook at Kampchatka, when in want of many Articles, with markd friendship & attention, & supplied them with every article wanted by them in the most liberal & friendly stile, when a different conduct in him would have placed the whole undertaking in hazard: This conduct was considered by the Admiralty as deserving of a marked attention & was rewarded by a magnificent present of Plate with an appropriate inscription sent as a Public Present to the Colonel.

In consequence of this favorable notice of the British Admiralty, Colonel Von Behm sent his daughter with her Husband the Chev^r de la Garde a man of Family Knight of the Orders of Stanislaus & of Malta & Chamberlain in the Polish Court, but at the same time ruind by the Polish Revolution, to solicit in this country an Asylum in Canada.

The Documents in proof of these allegations are enclosed with this together with a copy of a latter from me [dated 1798] to the Duke of Portland & one from the Duke to General Prescott in which His Grace speaks in hansome terms of the claims of gratitude which Col¹ Von Behm has made on the English Nation.

From the date of my Letter to the Duke to the present time, I do not recollect to have heard from the Parties or to have taken any concern in their Fate, the account they give of it is, that before they had Embarkd for Canada, Gen¹ Prescott returnd home, was waited upon by the Chevalier & receivd by him kindly, in conversation the Chevalier learnd that the Order for a Grant of Land would not enable a Governor to give to an Alien a hereditory Right of Possession & that in Order to obtain this, he must procure a Mandamus under the King's Sign Manual.

This favor was solicited by them for ten Years under various Administrations, but in vain, at last the Duke of Portland placed the Chev^r de la Garde in the Colonial Office as Arabic Interpreter at a Salary of £80 a Year, upon which he his wife & two Children continued to maintain themselves till the present Reform made it expedient to destroy the Office & leave this miserable family wholly destitute.

Their Landlord having found by the Newspapers that their Funds were destroyd seizd their Goods for Rent & they alledge that the four Miserables wanderd about the Streets for two days & a night without being able to procure a Shelter. they are now in a Room in Swallow Street, from whence they urge their Claims for Compassion in all directions.

Further I need not to proceed, that your Compassion is awake to their Sufferings I cannot doubt, nor do I think that you will doubt that the Claims they have upon this Country as having been recommended to us by our benefactor Von Behm have been inadequately compensated, a small Maintenance will support them but in truth I think that your feelings will recommend to you to grant them something more than the Duke of Portland allowed them. My experience has always told me that Whiggs are more profuse in their Jobs to each other & less attentive to the Claims of real distress than Tories are

> beleive my dear Sir
> Your most faithful &
> most hble Servt.
> Jos: Banks

The R^t. Honble N. Vansittart.

Lieutenant William Edward Parry (later Admiral Sir Edward Parry), 1790–1855, Arctic explorer, to his parents, from the original in the Scott Polar Research Institute.

London, Tuesday. Decr. 23^d 1817.

My dearest Parents,

As I am sure that you will be desirous to know the result of my introductions to Sir Joseph Banks, I begin my letter rather earlier than I have hitherto done. I dined very comfortably with Mr. Maxwell yesterday, and of course enjoyed a great deal of pleasant and useful conversation. At $\frac{1}{2}$ past 9 this morning, my Uncle called for me, and we went to Soho Square together. People who know Sir. J. walk into his library without asking any questions, and we were there about a quarter of an hour before ten, which is the breakfast hour. In the mean time, I was introduced to Mr. Brown, his librarian, who is a *walking catalogue* of every book in the world, and of whom I asked several questions. At ten precisely Lady & Mrs Banks [Sarah Sophia] made their appearances, to whom I was introduced in form, and without waiting for Sir J. (who was wheeled in, five minutes after) we sat down to breakfast. Sir J. shook hands with me very cordially, said he was glad to become acquainted with a Son of Dr. Parry's, for whom he entertained the highest respect, and was glad to find I was nominated to serve on the Expedition to the North West. Having breakfasted, *I* wheeled Sir J. into an ante-room which adjoins the library, and, without any previous remark, he opened a map which he had just constructed, and in which the situation is shewn, of that enormous mass of ice which has lately disappeared from the Eastern coast of Greenland. It has been observed, by the Meteorological Journals of several years past (at least 10) that our summers have been decreasing in temperature. Everybody has remarked, in the common vague way, that the seasons have altered lately, and Sir Joseph very confidently attributes this change to a breaking up of the Greenland ices, which are floated down to the more southern parallels of latitude, and impart a very sensible degree of cold to the atmosphere of the countries of Europe during the summer months, He says he has received accounts from Boston that for a year or two past, their crops of maize have not ripened, for which they are at a loss to account. *He* attributes this circumstance to the above cause also. Another very curious fact which he mentioned to me, and the no less curious speculation he has formed upon it, are worthy of remark. The oil of the whales of warm climates is so constituted by nature, that they are suited to a warm temperature, and freeze at a very high degree of the thermometer. That of the Greenland whale, on the other hand, requires a very low temperature to freeze it. Now, Sir. J. has observed that the Greenland oil which he uses in his own lamp will never burn of late, (and *that*, without any great degree of cold) from which he thinks it possible that the constitution of the animal may have been so far changed by a change of temperature in the elements in which he lives, as, by warming his blood &c, to have affected a change in the nature of the oil he produces. The alteration in the temperature of the water he attributes to the clearing away of the mass of ice attached to the shores of Greenland. It is impossible, in the compass of a letter, to repeat to you half of what Sir Joseph Banks said to me upon the subject—much less, to give you any idea of his very affable, communicative manner; he desired that I would come to him as often as I pleased (the oftener the better) and read or take away any books I could find in his library that might be of service to me. He made me take his map with me, and I have it in Mr. Maxwell's office where I am now writing, and where I shall keep it as the safest place. Having obtained a *Carte blanche* from Sir J., I shall of course go to his library without any ceremony, whenever I have occasions: for his invitations are not those of fashionable life, but are given from a real desire to do every-thing which can in the smallest degree tend to the advancement of every branch of science. . . . I am now going to the Hydrographical office, to copy some late information respecting Greenland, transmitted by a clever man of the name of Scoresby, Captn of a Greenland whaler. Even my visits to this office are more advantageous to me than I can express.

Adieu! my dearest Parents . . .

Ever affectionately yours

W.E.Parry.

[My grateful thanks are due to Miss Ann Parry, the great-great-granddaughter of Admiral Parry, for sending me a copy of this letter.]

BANKSIAN LETTERS AND MEMORANDA

JOSEPH BANKS to ROBERT BANKS JENKINSON, 2nd Baron Hawkesbury, 2nd Earl of Liverpool, F.R.S.

[This and the following letter relate to members of the Briscoe family. Peter Briscoe from Revesby was Banks's servant on the Newfoundland voyage and also sailed with him in the *Endeavour*. He appears on the muster roll of the *Niger* as the captain's servant; neither Banks nor Phipps is entered on that muster roll.]

Add. MS 38276:299, 300

Soho Square April 22 1819

My dear Sir

I send with this the memorial your Lordship directed me to obtain from Mr Cross the secretary to our Commission Your Lordship will see by it that we have not incurred any unnecessary expence in Carrying on the Commission I hope and Trust that the assistant we have chosen for the other Commission will be satisfied with a much Smaller Remuneration

I know not how to be sufficiently thankfull to your Lordship for your kindness to my oppressed Protegée Briscoe I shall always Recall it with deep gratitude the favor thus Conferrd upon me.

> I have the honour to be
> with Sincere Esteem and Regard
> Your Lordship's most
> Hble and most Faithfull
> Servt
>   Jos. Banks.

DAVID MACLEAN, Assistant Inspector of Customs, to C. J. BRISCOE

Add. MS 33982:218–219

> East [?] India Office
> Custom House,
> May 31 1820

My dear Sir,

The list of things remaining to be cleared, as transmitted in yours of the 29th instant corresponds exactly with my account . . .

Pray present my dutiful respects to Sir Joseph and say how happy I am to hear of his being better. I remain most humbly yours

> D. Maclean

[Was Briscoe then acting as Banks's secretary?]

BANKSIAN LETTERS AND MEMORANDA

Joseph Banks to an unknown correspondent
  Morgan Library, New York.

Spring Grove
July 21 1819

I feel much indebted to you for your Kind intention of depositing my Picture at Oxford I am not much addicted to the Love of Posthumous Fame but I confess the Idea of being Rememberd by those who in Future Receive intellectual nourishment from the milk of the alma mater by whom I was Fed is an Idea that Renders the natural Fear of Dissolution Less alarming

The Place where you choose to deposit it must Certainly be that chosen by yourself I confess however that my Vanity would receive a Gratification if it could be admitted in to Christ Church Hall Superior to what would accrue from a Place in the Picture Gallery you however ought to chuse it & are able to make a better choice of a Place for it than I can do who have now less [. . . ?] more than half

> Believe me my dear Sir
> Your much obliged & most faithfull Servt
>   Jos Banks

[The name of the addressee is not written on the back of this sheet and the portrait has not been traced.]

19 June 1820

Death of Banks

PART FOUR

Banks's scientific collections
and manuscripts

14

The fate of Banks's specimens

I N spite of Banks's plant collection being damaged by water on the return voyage of the *Niger* much herbarium material remained intact and in a fairly good state of preservation; many of the specimens are still to be seen in the British Museum (Natural History). It was Banks's practice to give duplicate material to other collectors and it is probable that much of this still remains in herbaria in European cities. No systematic search for it has been made and it is hoped that the lists published in this volume will stimulate a search by other botanists for these early Newfoundland specimens in Paris and elsewhere. The existence of material in the British Museum has been noted throughout the systematic lists published later in this volume.

The bird skins have long since disappeared. In the later decades of the eighteenth century very little was known of satisfactory methods of preservation and skins accordingly disintegrated rather rapidly. MS lists of Banks's skin collection are arranged in four series; it appears that a few of his birds from Newfoundland and Labrador were set up and mounted; details are given on p. 401. We know that Banks gave some specimens to Taylor White and it is possible that some went to his friends in France and elsewhere on the continent. If any remain they are more likely to be in Vienna and Leyden than elsewhere; the few skins still intact from Cook's voyages (1768–80) are preserved in the natural history museums of both these cities, where methods of curation were obviously in advance of those favoured in England; only one bird skin from Cook's voyages remains in the British Museum, though two spirit specimens identified recently appear to have been collected on the second or third voyages (Burton, 1969).

Nothing is known of the fate of the fishes so carefully drawn by Parkinson. Although there are historic specimens of this period in the spirit collections at the British Museum and elsewhere, and some skins dried and prepared by Gronovius, 1730–77, are in reasonable condition, it seems probable that the labelling of the specimens from Newfoundland and Labrador was not adequate to ensure their preservation after Banks's death.

Similarly I have not traced any specimens of the insects Banks collected at Croque and Chateau Bay: his few notes in the McGill MS, obviously incomplete, the occasional reference to insects in his diary, and the small number of paintings by Sydney Parkinson are all we have left. It is, however, possible that some of his

291

specimens are among those in the Banksian cabinets in the Entomology Department at the British Museum; many of these lack locality labels but they might be determined by an experienced Newfoundland entomologist.

Of the other invertebrates he collected only one has been found in recent years; this is the bivalve *Chlamys islandicus* (Müller) which Banks recorded (diary 19, n. 34) as a kind of scallop and which is still in the Mollusca collection at the British Museum.

The extent of Banks's private collections from Newfoundland, Labrador, and the countries visited during the voyage of the *Endeavour*, may be gauged from the description given in 1772 by William Sheffield, later to become Keeper of the Ashmolean Museum, in a letter (pp. 253–5) to Gilbert White. The man responsible for the preparation and arrangement of Banks's collections at that time was Edward Jenner, afterwards so famous for his work on vaccination.

15

Banks's plant catalogue: the British Museum MS with supplementary sheets from the McGill MS

BANKS's plant catalogue is a slim leather-bound octavo volume now in the Botany Library, British Museum (Natural History), containing three lists of his collections from Newfoundland and Labrador. The first of these is Banks's holograph MS in which he lists some 250 species, by no means all he collected, arranged according to the system then established by Linnaeus, with very brief notes on habitat and locality. The second list is a fair copy of the first in another hand with a few pencilled additions by Banks. A third list by Banks of twenty-four names completes the volume.

Banks's catalogue was known to James Britten who made a few notes in it concerning Ehret's paintings, and added two species. Fernald made a rough copy of the first list when he visited the British Museum early this century; he examined some of Banks's specimens and made notes on some seventy-five species. He does not seem to have attempted to go through the whole collection, and was perhaps only interested in the plants important to his theories on the origin of the Newfoundland flora. I have used a photostat copy of his MS now in the Gray Herbarium at Harvard.

In 1926 at the International Congress of Plant Sciences at Ithaca, N.Y., Fernald was asked by A. B. Rendle, then Keeper of Botany at the British Museum, whether he would edit Banks's Newfoundland Journal. Three years later he wrote to Rendle offering his assistance in the identification of the plants, but there the matter seems to have rested.

In 1949 Professor Ernest Rouleau spent three months at the British Museum, making a much more careful study of Banks's material. He found and listed 302 of Banks's species. Since then he has given me much help in determining about forty additional species that I have found here and it is quite probable that more will turn up here and elsewhere in due course.

The Linnaean arrangement followed by Banks has been retained in the printed version of his catalogue that follows this note; an account of the great systematist and his classification is given in Stearn's introduction to the facsimile edition (Ray Society, 1957) of Linnaeus's *Species Plantarum* (1753) on which our whole binomial system of plant nomenclature is based. Linnaeus published his first classification of plants in the *Systema Naturae* of 1735, basing it on sexual characters which he set out in dramatic metaphorical form. It had a mixed reception, arousing in some scientists intense criticism and anger, not only because it made a joke of sex in man but also because throughout the history of human thought new ideas of any profundity have always aroused fierce opposition. Linnaeus had indeed the last word: he retaliated by naming insignificant or unpleasant weeds after the most vociferous of his opponents; some of those names still endure.

In 1787 a translation of Linnaeus's text from Reichard's edition (1778) of the *Genera Plantarum* and the *Mantissae Plantarum* was published under the title *Families of Plants* (2 vols.) by the Botanical Society of Lichfield, namely by Erasmus Darwin, with assistance from Banks and other botanists. It also acknowledges the help of 'That great Master of the English tongue Dr. Samuel Johnson, for his advice in the formation of the botanic language.' Much of this was published by Stearn in the Ray Society facsimile (1957). I have taken the Latin text and translation of the Linnaean diagnoses from Stearn's edition and inserted it beneath the names of the classes and orders used by Banks, since the characters on which that system was based have been superseded. When I read through Banks's catalogue I frequently wondered how it was that he had grouped together plants now regarded as only distantly related: the Linnaean diagnoses explain this.

The pages in Banks's catalogue were unnumbered; I have now pencilled in numbers throughout the volume except where pages are blank on both sides. The pagination of the first list runs from 1 to 48; the second list runs from 1a to 16a; the final list is on p. 17a. In order to avoid duplication, list two has not been printed but Banks's few pencil notes in it have been transferred to the first list. They are inset at the end of the appropriate section with the corresponding page number of list two.

Banks inserted a figure after many of the specific names indicating the number of species collected in each genus up to the time of entry. He made the figure one in a curious way so that when Fernald made his copy of the catalogue he frequently transcribed it as three.

In addition to the lists in this catalogue Banks wrote descriptive notes on his plants but unfortunately only five sheets of these notes have been found. They measure $18 \cdot 5 \times 23 \cdot 8$ cm. and are kept in a folder with the zoological MSS in the Blacker-Wood Library at McGill University. These notes relate to five of the twenty-five Linnaean classes under which he arranged his plants from Newfoundland and Labrador; it is possible that if ever the calendaring of the Banksian papers is completed the remaining notes on plants will be found. They were perhaps separated from the rest of the manuscript when it was in the hands of dealers in the 1920s.

Banks used the numbers in his plant catalogue now at the British Museum as a key to the descriptive notes today so far away at McGill (it is ironic that four sheets of the zoological MS should be not at McGill with the bulk of that MS but bound in with Solander MSS at the British Museum). Thus his descriptive notes on *Convallaria bifolia* (now *Maianthemum canadense*), the third species listed under Hexandria in his catalogue, appear in the McGill MS on the page headed Hexandria, against the number 3; no scientific name is quoted in this instance although he sometimes added it.

I have thought it best to print the McGill botanical notes at the end of the plant catalogue; similarly in the case of Banks's notes on mammals which are bound with Solander MSS at the British Museum; in this volume they appear as a supplement to the zoological descriptions comprising the McGill MS.

1 MONANDRIA   2

[Maritus unicus in matrimonio.
Stamen unicum in flore hermaphrodito.
        One male.
One husband in marriage.
One stamen in an hermaphrodite flower.]

1 *Hippuris* 1   in small muddy Pools between Chatteaux and Bad Bay
    1a *Elatine* v. [*Hippuris* has been crossed out].

2 DIANDRIA   3

[Mariti duo in eodem conjugio.
Stamina duo in flore hermaphrodito.
        Two males.
Two husbands in the same marriage.
Two stamens in an hermaphrodite flower.]

1 *Veronica serpyllifolia* 1   St. Johns *Conche* Croque
2 *Circaea lutetiana* 1   shady Places Croque
3 *Pinguicula vulgaris* 1   Bogs & damp Rocks Croque
4 *Utricularia* 1   Bogs Every where about Croque
5 *Valeriana Phu*?   Damp Wood Croque
    1a *Anthoxanthum odoratum* Croque

3 TRIANDRIA

[Mariti tres in eodem conjugio.
Stamina tria in flore hermaphrodito.
Three males.
Three husbands in the same marriage.
Three stamens in an hermaphrodite flower.]

1	*Festuca fluitans* Var: 1	Near high water mark Bad bay
2	*Festuca duriuscula* 2	bogs & grassy places Chatteaux
3	*Poa palustris?* 1	Sandy Places on the Beach in Chatteaux bay
4	*Arundo* 1	Grassy Places Chatteaux
5	*Aira* 1	Grassy Places Chatteaux
6	*Scirpus* 1	Bogs & muddy Pools Chatteaux
7	*Agrostis cappillaris* 1	Croque *Conche* grassy places
8	*Arundo epigejos* 2	Croque *Conche* grassy Places
9	*Poa angustifolia?* 2	grassy places Croque
10	*Aira flexuosa* 2	Grassy Places Croque
11	*Poa* 3	Grassy Places Croque
12	*Hordeum murinum* 1	Grassy Places Croque
13	*Phleum* 1	Grassy Places Croque
14	*Eriophorum polystachion* 1	Bogs Croque
15	*Eriophorum alpinum* 2	Damp Places Croque
16	*Triticum?* 1	Dry woods not too shady Croque
17	*Avena* 1	Near the sea on sunny banks Croque
18	*Poa trivialis* 4	Grassy Places Croque
19	*Schoenus albus* 1	Bogs Croque
20	*Elymus* 1	Sea beach Croque Chatteaux
21	*Poa* 5	Damp Places Croque
22	*Poa* 6	Dry hill sides Croque
23	*Iris* 1	Sea side & Brooks Every where
24	*Eriophorum vaginatum* 3	bogs Croque
25	*Agrostis canina*	Damp Places Chatteaux
26	*Scirpus* 2	Harbour side Chatteaux
27	*Scirpus capitatus?* 3	Boggs
28	*Scirpus* No.4	Near a fresh water Pool
29	*Agrostis* 3	side of the Harbour
30	*Montia fontana?*	near the sea

4 TETRANDRIA

[Mariti quatuor in eodem conjugio.
Stamina quatuor in eodem flore cum fructu.

(Si Stamina 2 proxima breviora sunt, referatur ad Cl. 14.)
Four males
Four husbands in the same marriage.
Four stamens in the same flower with the fruit.
(If the two nearest stamens are shorter, it is referred to Class 14.)]

1	*Plantago loeflingii?* 1	Bogs about Chatteaux
2	*Galium* 1	Shady Places Croque
3	*Plantago maritima* 2	Rocks at High water mark Croque
4	*Cornus sanguinea* 1	Woods Croque
5	*Galium palustre* 2	
6	*Sanguisorba canadensis*	Every where about Croque
7	*Alchemilla vulgaris* 1	under a shady rock St Julians Island
8	*Sagina procumbens* 1	Damp stones cheifly on the sea shore Croque
9	*Cornus canadensis* 2	hill sides Every where
10	*Cornus* 3	near the Edge of the sea in several places Croque

5 PENTANDRIA · 9

[Mariti quinque in eodem conjugio.
Stamina quinque in flore hermaphrodito.
Five males
Five husbands in the same marriage.
Five stamens in an hermaphrodite flower.]

1	*Swertia corniculata*	Grassy Places Croque & Chatteaux
2	*Swertia* 2	Damp bog Chatteaux Damp rock Bellisle
3	*Aralia* 1	shady places Bellisle Hare bay
4	*Pulmonaria maritima* 1:	sea Beach Croque
5	*Primula farinosa* 1	Bogs Croque
6	*Heracleum? spondilium* 1	Croque
7	*Parnassia palustris* 1	Bogs Croque
8	*Drosera longifolia* 1	Bogs Croque
9	*Campanula rotundifolia* 1	Rocks Croque
10	*Azalea procumbens* 1	Dry sandy hillsides
11	*Ribes* 1	shady woods Croque
12	*Ribes uva crispa* 2	Woodsides Croque
13	*Ribes* 3	Woodsides Croque
14	*Diapensia lapponica* 1	Barren & sultry hill tops
15	*Angelica archangelica*	See side

16 *Angelica sylvestris*   see side
17 *Menianthes trifolium*   Bogs
   4a *Ligusticum*
    Ligusticum scoticum
   5a *Pimpinella*
    Pimpinella

6 HEXANDRIA   11

[Mariti sex in eodem conjugio.
Stamina sex in flore hermaphrodito.
(Si ex his Stamina 2 opposita breviora, pertinet ad Cl. 15.)
    Six males
Six husbands in the same marriage.
Six stamens in an hermaphrodite flower.
(If the two opposite stamens are shorter, it belongs to Class 15.)]

1 *Rumex digynus* 1   Bellisle shady Rocks
2 *Juncus* 1   Grassy Places rather Barren
3 *Convallaria bifolia* 1   damp Places Croque St Johns
4 *Uvularia amplexifolia*   Shady Places Croque St Johns
5 *Juncus articulatus* 2   Bogs Croque
6 *Juncus* 3   Bogs Croque
7 *Juncus effusus*   Bogs & near the sea Croque
8 *Anthericum calyculatum*   Bogs Croque
9 *Convallaria stellata*   Bottoms of Dry hills
10 *Juncus* 5   Dry places on the Tops of hills
11 *Juncus* 6:7   Damp Places Whale Island
12 *Rumex*   Sea side
   5a *Convallaria*
    Convallaria
    Convallaria
    Anthericoides

7 HEPTANDRIA   13

[Mariti septem in eodem conjugio.
Stamina septem in flore eodem cum pistillo.
    Seven males
Seven husbands in the same marriage.
Seven stamens in the same flower with the pistil.]

6a *Trientalis* woods St Johns Croque

8 OCTANDRIA   15

[Mariti octo in eodem thalamo cum femina.
Stamina octo in eodem flore cum pistillo.
              Eight males
Eight husbands in the same marriage.
Eight stamens in the same flower with the pistil.]

1	*Epilobium latifolium* 1	Damp rocks Bellisle Hare bay
2	*Vaccinium mucronatum* 1	Shady woods *Bellisle* Croque
3	*Polygonum viviparum* 1	Sea Beach on Rocks Croque
4	*Epilobium* 2	Bogs or dry sunny Banks Croque
5	*Vaccinium myrtillus* 2	Dry Places Croque
6	*Vaccinium* 3	sides of Dryest rocks
7	*Vaccinium uliginosum* 4	High Hills on Dry spotts
8	*Vaccinium oxycoccus*	Bogs
9	*Polygonum aviculare*	Sea side
10	*Epilobium* 3	Damp Rock

[6a Strokes under *Vaccinium* in two places seem to indicate that Banks
had some undetermined material when he made his first list; in
fact he collected seven species, only two of which had been
described. See the systematic list for details.]

9 ENNEANDRIA   17

[Mariti novem in eodem thalamo cum femina.
Stamina novem in flore hermaphrodito.
              Nine males.
Nine husbands in the same marriage.
Nine stamens in an hermaphrodite flower.]
              [No entries.]

10 DECANDRIA   19

[Mariti decem in eodem conjugio.
Stamina decem in flore hermaphrodito.
              Ten males
Ten husbands in the same marriage.
Ten stamens in an hermaphrodite flower.]

1	*Arenaria* 1	Bogs near the sea side where it is washd by the spray in hard weather
2	*Pyrola secunda* 1	shady woods Croque Hare bay

3	*Monotropa uniflora* 1	Shady Woods Conche
4	*Pyrola rotundifolia* 2	Woods Croque
5	*Stellaria graminea* 1	Croque
6	*Saxifraga autumnalis* 1	Bellisle Damp Rock
7	*Saxifraga cotyledon* 2	Damp Rock Bellisle
8	*Kalmia angustifolia* 1	Hillsides about Croque
9	*Pyrola uniflora* 3	Very shady Places Croque
10	*Arbutus uva ursi* 1	Top of a hill Inglie
11	*Cerastium alpinum*	Tops of Barren hills Every where
12	*Lychnis* 1	hillside Conche Bellisle
13	*Cucubalus acaulis*	Tops of hills Every where
14	*Saxifraga oppositifolia* 3	On sides of Rocks Inglie
15	*Arenaria laricifolia*	on dry hill sides scarce
16	*Saxifraga* 4	Clefts of Rocks Inglie
17	*Andromeda* 2	Damp Places & bogs Croque Chatteaux
18	*Kalmia* 2	Dampish places not too wet Croque
19	*Andromeda* 1	Dry hill sides Every where
20	*Andromeda caerulea*	Shady Rocks
21	*Arenaria*	on the Beach within the tides Chatteaux
22	*Saxifraga rivularis*	Rocks & brook sides Chatteaux

6a *Arenaria*
7a *Saxifraga* hirsut.
   Cerastium hirsut.
   Saxifraga tridactyla
   Mitella
8a *Andromeda rubra*

11 DODECANDRIA   21

[Mariti duodecim ad novemdecim in eodem conjugio.
Stamina duodecim ad novemdecim in flore hermaphrodito.
    Twelve males.
Twelve to nineteen husbands in the same marriage.
Twelve stamens to nineteen in an hermaphrodite flower.]
    [No entries]

12 ICOSANDRIA   23

[Mariti viginti communiter, saepe plures.
Stamina (non receptaculo) calycis lateri interno adnata.
    Twenty males.

Generally twenty husbands, often more.
Stamens inserted on the calyx (not on the receptacle)

1	*Potentilla norvegica* 1	grassy Places Croque
2	*Geum urbanum?* 1	woods Croque
3	*Potentilla fruticosa* 2	Bogs about Croque
4	*Potentilla* 3	Dry rocks Croque Conche etc.
5	*Comarum palustre* 1	Dry Places by the sea side & Bogs Croque
6	*Sorbus aucuparia* 1	Woods Croque
7	*Geum rivale* 2	Woods Croque
8	*Rubus arcticus* 1	Bogs not too wet St Julians Island
		Sea Beach Hare Bay
9	*Potentilla anserina* 4	Sea Beach Every where
10	*Potentilla nivea* 5	Dry Bank Conche
11	*Dryas* 1	Dry hill side Inglie
12	*Rubus chamaemorus* 2	Damp grounds Every where
13	*Rubus saxatilis* 3	Shady woods St Johns Croque
14	*Fragaria pratensis*	

8a *Geum grandiflorum*
Mespilus canad.

13 POLYANDRIA 25

[Mariti viginti & ultra in eodem cum femina thalamo.
Stamina receptaculo inserta a 20 ad 1000 in eodem, cum pistillo, flore.
      Many males.
Twenty males or more in the same marriage.
Stamens inserted on the receptacle, from 20 to 1000 in the same flower with the pistil.]

1	*Sarracenia purpurea* 1	Bogs Croque St Johns Hare Bay
2	*Thalictrum minus* 1	Edges of woods Croque
3	*Anemone* 1	Rocks near water Croque Inglie
4	*Thalictrum alpinum* 2	Bogs Croque
5	*Actaea* 1	Shady Places Croque
6	*Ranunculus*	muddy sides of Pools Chatteaux
7	*Ranunculus repens*	Conche

9a *Helleborus trifol.*

14 DIDYNAMIA

[Mariti quatuor, quorum 2 longiores, & 2 breviores.
Stamina quatuor: quorum 2 proxima longiora sunt.
   Two powers.
Four husbands, two taller than the other two.
Four stamens: of which the two nearest are longer.]

1	*Rhinanthus crista galli* 1	Grassy Places Croque Chatteaux
2	*Linnaea borealis* 1	shady Places Croque Chatteaux
3	*Orobanche uniflora* 1	Woods Croque
4	*Galeopsis tetrahit* 1	Croque

9a *Euphrasia*
   Thymus
   Bartsia

15 TETRADYNAMIA

[Mariti sex, quorum 4 longiores in flore hermaphrodito.
Stamina sex: quorum 4 longiora, 2 autem opposita breviora.
   Four powers.
Six husbands, of which four are taller in an hermaphrodite flower.
Six stamens: of which four are longer, and the two opposite ones shorter.]

1	*Thlaspi arvense* 1	Grassy Places Croque Conche
2	*Cardamine pratensis* 2	
3	*Arabis canadensis* 1	hill sides rich soil Inglie
4	*Draba incana*	Barren hills
5	*Cochlearia officinalis*	St Peters Island Chatteaux

16 MONADELPHIA

[Mariti, ut fratres, ex una basi proveniunt.
Stamina filamentis in unum corpus coalita sunt.
   One brotherhood.
Husbands, like brothers, arise from one base.
Stamens are united by their filaments into one body.]

[No entries]

17 DIADELPHIA 33

[Mariti e duplici basi, tamquam e duplici matre, oriuntur.
Stamina filamentis in duo corpora connata sunt.
Two brotherhoods
Husbands arise from two bases, as if from two mothers.
Stamens are united by their filaments into [two] bodies.]

1	*Trifolium repens* 1	grassy Places Croque
2	*Trifolium pratense* 2	grassy Places Croque
3	*Vicia cracca* 1	grassy Places Croque
4	*Astragalus alpinus* 1	Sandy Beach hare bay
5	*Pisum marinum* 1	Sea Beach Every where
6	*Astragalus uralensis*	Dry hill side Inglie

18 POLYADELPHIA 35

[Mariti ex pluribus, quam duabus, matribus orti sunt.
Stamina filamentis in tria, vel plura, corpora coalita.
Many brotherhoods.
Husbands arise from more than two mothers.
Stamens are united by their filaments into three or more bodies.]

[No entries]

19 SYNGENESIA 37

[Mariti genitalibus foedus constituerunt.
Stamina antheris (raro filamentis) in cylindrum coalita.
Confederate males.
Husbands joined together at the top.
Stamens are connected by the anthers forming a cylinder (seldom by the filaments.)]

1	*Achillea millefolium* 1	grassy Places Croque
2	*Lobelia dortmanna*	Rocky Ponds Conche
3	*Jacobaea* 1	Bogs Croque
4	*Erigeron* 1	Rocks in Damp Places Croque
5	*Tussilago* 1	Wood rather Damp Croque
6	*Erigeron philadelphicum*	Rocks by the side of a Brook Croque
7	*Viola palustris*	Whale Island
8	*Aster*	Warm Places

20 GYNANDRIA

[Mariti cum feminis monstrose connati
Stamina pistillis (non receptaculo) insident.
Feminine males.
Husbands and wives growing together.
Stamens are inserted on the pistils (not on the receptacle).]

1	*Ophrys* 1	Shady Damp wood Croque
2	*Orchis* 1	Damp shady Places Croque
3	*Ophrys* 2	by the side of a Rivulet Croque
4	*Ophrys* 3	Bogs Croque
5	*Orchis psycodes* 2	Bogs Croque
6	*Orchis* 3	Bogs Croque
7	*Orchis* 4	Bogs & damp Places Croque
8	*Cyprepedium calceolus* 1	Island Hare Bay
9	*Ophrys* 4	shady woods Croque

21 MONOECIA
41

[Mares habitant cum feminis in eadem domo, sed diverso thalamo.
Flores masculi & feminei in eadem planta sunt.
One house
Husbands live with their wives in the same house, but have different beds.
Male flowers and female flowers are on the same plant.]

1	*Carex* 1	sandy Beach on the side of Chatteaux bay
2	*Carex* 2	Bogs Chatteaux
3	*Sparganium natans* 1	Rocky Ponds Conche Croque
4	*Betula nana* 1	Woods Croque
5	*Myriophyllum spicatum*	Rocky Pools Croque
6	*Carex* 3	Bogs Croque
7	*Carex* 4	Bogs Croque
8	*Carex* 5	Bogs Croque
9	*Carex pulicaris* 6	Bogs Croque
10	*Carex* 7	Bogs Croque
11	*Carex* 8	Bogs Croque
12	*Carex dioica* 9	Bogs Croque
13	*Carex* 10	Bogs Croque
14	*Carex* 11	Bogs Croque

Decandria

1	Arenaria	Bogs near the sea side where it is washd by the spray in hard weather
2	Pyrola Secunda	shady woods Croque Hare bay
3	Monotropa uniflora	shady Woods Conche
4	Pyrola Rotundifolia 2	woods Croque
5	Stellaria Graminea	Croque
6	Saxifraga autumnalis	Bellisle Damp Rock
7	Saxifraga Cotyledon 2	Damp Rock Bellisle
8	Kalmia Angustifolia	Hill sides about Croque
9	Pyrola Uniflora 3	Very shady Places Croque
10	Arbutus Uva Ursi	Tops of a hill Inglie
✗	Cerastium alpinum	Tops of Barren hills Every where
12	Lychnis	hillside Conche Bellisle
13	Cucubalus Acaulis	Tops of hills Every where
14	Saxifraga oppositifolia 3	On Sides of Rocks Inglie
✗	Arenaria Laricifolia	on dry hill sides scarce
16	Saxifraga 4	Clefts of Rocks Inglie
17	Andromeda 2	Damp Places & bogs Croque Chateaux
18	Kalmia 2	Damp ish places not too wet Croque
19	Andromeda	Dry hill sides Every where
20	Andromeda Cærulea	shady Rocks
21	Arenaria	on the Beach within the tides Chateaux
22	Saxifraga Rivularis	Rocks & brook sides Chateaux

44. Page 19 from Banks's catalogue of the plants he collected in Newfoundland and Labrador.

45. *Smilacina trifolia*, one of the plants Banks collected near Kitty Witty pool (now Quidi Vidi) at St. John's.

G. D. Ehret

46. *Habenaria obtusata.*
G. D. Ehret

49. *Potentilla nivea*: Banks's specimens from Conche. The original sheet has been cut and remounted with Banks's note on the locality taken from the top of the original sheet. See Ehret's painting of the species, opposite.

50. *Potentilla nivea.*
G. D. Ehret

Potentilla tridentata vol. 2. pag. 216.

G. D. Ehret. pinxit 1767.

51. *Potentilla tridentata*; this is a drawing of the type specimen which no longer exists. See p. 330.

G. D. Ehret

15	*Carex* 12	Bogs Croque
16	*Betula nigra*	Woods Every where
17	*Carex* 13	Sea Beach Croque
18	*Carex* 14	Bogs Chatteaux
19	*Atriplex hastata*	Sea Side
20	*Empetrum*	Dry Hill Tops [This entry has been deleted]
21	*Salix*	Sea side
22	*Salix*	Riversides
23	*Salix*	
23	[*sic*] *Urtica urens*	Garden

12a *Rhodiola rosea* on rocks near St. Johns
13a *Juniperus*
  Thuya

22 DIOECIA   43

[Mares & feminae habitant in diversis thalamis & domiciliis.
Flores masculi in diversa planta a femineis prognascuntur.
           Two houses.
Husbands and wives have different houses.
Male flowers and female flowers are on different plants.]

1	*Salix repens* 1	Dry hill sides Inglie
2	*Populus balsamifera* 1	Woods Croque Inglie
3	*Salix* 2	High hills Croque
4	*Myrica* 1	Brooksides Croque St Johns Chatteaux
5	*Empetrum*	Dry tops of hills

13a *Empetrum* flore rubro

23 POLYGAMIA   45

[Mariti cum uxoribus & innuptis cohabitant in distinctis thalamis.
Flores hermaphroditi & masculi aut feminei in eadem specie.
           Polygamies.
Husbands live with wives and concubines. [in different houses]
Hermaphrodite flowers, and male ones, or female ones in the same
species.]
       [No entries]

13a *Holcus odoratus*

24 CRYPTOGAMIA

47

[Nuptiae clam celebrantur.
Flores intra fructum vel singulari modo occultati.
Clandestine marriages.
Nuptials are celebrated privately.
Flowers concealed within the fruit, or in some irregular manner.]

1	*Polypodium dryopteris* 1	Damp woods Conche
2	*Sphagnum* 1	Bogs
3	*Osmunda* 1	By a river side Conche
4	*Phascum* 1	Damp Places Croque
5	*Bryum* 1	Dampish Places Croque
6	*Lichen* 1	Rocks Chatteaux
7	*Bryum* 2	Damp Places Croque
8	*Marchantia conica*	Bogs croque
9	*Lichen* 1	Sunny Rock on the tops of hills scarce
10	*Bryum* 3	Dampish Places Croque
11	*Lycopodium selago* 1	on hill sides near springs not common
12	*Lycopodium* 2	Bogs & wet Places Croque
13	*Lichen* 2	on dry rocks Croque
14	*Lichen* 3	Damp Places
15	*Bryum* 4	On dry hills Croque
16	*Bryum* 5	Damp Places Croque
17	*Lichen* 4	Dry rocks
18	*Lycopodium* 3	Dry hills
19	*Bryum* 6	Damp Places Croque
20	*Polytrichum commune* 1	Damp ground
21	*Lichen* 5	tops of the Highest rocks
22	*Lichen lanatus* 6	Trees about Croque
23	*Lichen*	Trees about Croque
24	*Osmunda lunaria*	Whale Island

25	*Lichen* No 7	upon Moss
26	*Polypodium*	Shady Damp Places Chatteaux
27	*Hypnum reflexum*	Bogs
28	*Equisetum*	Pools
29	*Marchantia polymorpha*	
30	*Marchantia*	shady woods
31	*Polypodium*	woods
32	*Polypodium*	woods

14a *Lycopodium dubium*
Lycopodium annotinum
Bryum scoparium
15a *Polytrichum alpinum*

FINAL LIST

17a

Lycopodium complan. 1
    obscurum
    complanat: verum
    annotinum
Andromeda calyculata
Viburnum acerifolium
Lonicera *insulana*
Andromeda *vaccinioides*
Pentandra *Bacciferae*
Gnaphalium plantaginifolium
Empetrum nigrum
Vaccinium *Capill: veneris*

[=Maiden Hair, see Diary 24, n. 53]

Juniperus *Magnus*

Helleborus trifoliatus
Cupressus thujoides
Mespilus canadensis
Asarum Folia
Sisirynchichum
Vaccinium *Erectum*
Rhododendrum Folia
Carex *echinatus*
Juncus stygius
Thalictrum alpinum
Anthericum calyculat:

[The scientific names in this list have not been italicised except where Banks underlined them.]

BOTANICAL SECTION OF THE McGILL MS

The five remaining sheets of Banks's botanical notes were acquired by McGill University together with his notes on birds and insects. When in the hands of the dealer, all the botanical and zoological notes were numbered without regard for scientific content; they have now been re-arranged and re-numbered so that the sequence of botanical notes corresponds to the arrangement of Banks's plant catalogue. All the botanical notes were in Latin; a literal translation is inset below; the current scientific name of each plant is given in square brackets.

TETRANDRIA

95

1 ⎫ Illa Plantaginis species quae in Anglia *P: loeflingii* vocamus Certe Crescit in
3 ⎭ Paludibus Uliginosis circa Chatteaux an vere *P: loeflingii* multum haereo
No. 3 *P. maritima* Vulgatissima est inter Fissuras Rupium Prope mare foliis semicylindricis nonnunquam inventa est in Limo et arena mobili foliis Paulo

Latioribus Postea? in Paludibus uliginosis foliis Latis *Loeflingii* folia non raro tinguntur maculis sanguiniis in hac & altera specie (si non sunt una Eademq. Planta) & non in ulla alia Plantaginis specie quae vidi. *P. loeflingii* in Hispania Crescit in agrorum Limitibus in anglia quidem & in Labrador inventa est in Paludibus Prope mare ubi aestibus altissimis Lotus est

[*Plantago juncoides* Lam. var. *decipiens* (Barnéoud) Fern.]

That species of *Plantago* which in England we call *P. loeflingii* certainly grows in damp marshlands round Chatteaux, although I am in considerable doubt as to whether it really is *P. loeflingii*.

[*Plantago oliganthos* Roem. & Schult. var. *fallax* Fern.]

No. 3 *P. maritima.* This is very common among the rock fissures near the sea, with semi-cylindrical leaves; it is sometimes found in the mud and the shifting sand with leaves a little wider. Again, ? among the damp marshes with broad leaves. The leaves of *loeflingii* are often tinged with red spots in both this and the other species (if they are not one and the same plant), and not in any other species of *Plantago* that I have seen. *P. loeflingii* grows in Spain, at the boundaries of the fields. In England and in Labrador it is found in marshes near the sea where it is washed by the highest tides.

9 *Cornus canadensis* mira quidem abundantia forsmossissima [*sic*] ista Planta obvestit Partes sicciores et Borealis et meridionalis newfoundlandiae Convenit cum *C. suecica* in omnes Partes excepto ramo Laterali qui nunquam vidi quamvis millia istarum Plantarum examinavi

10 *Cornus* Corolla hujus Plantae nigra est haereo tamen an a Praecedenti Differt nunquam enim Specificam Differentiam observare possum quamvis saepissime Plantulam illam inveni semper prope mari nec unquam [?] ab eo distantem semper quoque solus invenitur nec *C. canadensi* mixtus quamvis et *C. canadensi* Aeque mari Propinque non infrequens Prostat.

[*Chamaepericlymenum canadense* (L.) Aschers. & Graebn.]

C. canadensis. This plant clothes in great abundance and beauty the drier parts both of the north and south of Newfoundland. It agrees with *C. suecica* in all parts except in the lateral branch which I have never seen although I have examined thousands of these plants.

[*Chamaepericlymenum suecicum* (L.) Aschers. & Graebn.]

Cornus The corolla of this plant is black; I am, however, in doubt as to whether it differs from the preceding; for I am never able to observe any specific difference, although I have very often found this plant it is always near the sea and never distant from it. Also it always occurs alone and never in association with *C. canadensis* although that species also is not uncommonly near the sea.

2 In solo Pingui Ramosississima Est Et Floribus Conferta in arenoso tamen unica tantum terminalia Corolla nunc quadrifida nunc quinquifida est

[*Lomatogonium rotatum* (L.) Fries]

In a rich soil it has many branches and is dense with flowers; in a sandy soil, however, there is only one terminal corolla, sometimes divided into four, and sometimes into five parts.

3 Radix hujus Plantae non raro Prostat Emptum in officinis anglicis Pro vera sassaparilla Chirurgus primus noster me certum facit quod Possidet omnes Sassaparillae vires sed fortiori gradu et minori dosi medicinam tutam aegroti Praebet.

[*Aralia nudicaulis* L.]

3 The root of this plant is not seldom sold in England as the true sarsaparilla. Our leading physician has informed me that it possesses all the virtues of sarsaparilla but in greater strength, so that it can be given in smaller doses to the sick as a safe medicament.

5 Corolla hujus Plantae mire Colore variat nunc alba nunc Saturate Purpurea quamvis uno eodemque loco Enascuntur

[*Primula laurentiana* Fern. and *P. mistassinica* Michx. forma *leucantha* Fern.]

The corolla of this plant varies remarkably in colour, being sometimes white and sometimes a rich purple, although both grow in one and the same place.

8 Vixunquam vidi Corollam hujus Plantae Explicatam in anglia sub hac vere sole cum congeneri suo *D. rotundifolia* Formosissima explicatur

[*Drosera anglica* Huds.]

I have scarcely ever seen the corolla of this plant unfolded in England, but here, with its congener *D. rotundifolia* it unfolds itself most beautifully.

HEXANDRIA 99

3 In Newfoundland mire Frequens est ista Planta solis quidem Diversissimis [?] et vidi enim inter Sphagnos in Paludibus sterilissimis [?] florens vidi Etiam in apricis aridissimis sed flores optime Profert in solo non nimis humido

[*Maianthemum canadense* Desf.]

This plant is extremely frequent in Newfoundland, and in very different soils, for I have come across it amid the moss in very sterile marshes. I have also seen it flowering in very dry and sun-baked places though it flowers best in a not too damp soil.

DECANDRIA

5 *Stellaria graminea* Primo Aestate hanc Plantam semper inveni sine corolla sed circa medium Julii cum corollas Satis amplas ubique Legitur

[*Stellaria graminea* L.]

In early summer I found this plant always without a corolla but about mid-July it was collected everywhere with a fully-developed corolla.

ICOSANDRIA

5 *Comarum palustre* In Anglia nunquam nisi in Paludibus Uliginosis occurrit circa Croque tamen frequentissima est Prope mare in Locis Sabulosis ubi nunquam nisi Pluviis madefacitur

[*Potentilla palustris* (L.) Scop.]

Comarum palustre in England never occurs other than in wet marshes. About Croque, however, it is most common near the sea in sandy places where it is never wetted except by rain.

16

A systematic list of the plants collected or recorded by Joseph Banks in Newfoundland and Southern Labrador in 1766

THE sequence of families of flowering plants in this list follows the system of Engler & Prantl since that is most generally employed by American botanists, and is used by Fernald in the eighth edition of *Gray's Manual of Botany* (1950). Specific names used by Fernald have been retained except where recent work has shown them to be incorrect.

Algae, thallophytes and bryophytes have been named in accordance with the usage of the British Museum (Natural History), and are listed in alphabetical order under the main groups. Pteridophytes are listed under families according to the first volume of the *Flora Europaea* (1964).

The principal abbreviations are as follows:

Cat. denotes Banks's MS catalogue of his Newfoundland-Labrador collections, reproduced in another part of this volume.

Hb. denotes data on the sheets of Banks's specimens now in the British Museum (Natural History). N. or n. refers to the numbered notes at the end of Banks's diary. The diary numbers refer to Banks's own pagination.

An asterisk shows that Banks's specimens have been located in the British Museum. It is highly probable that a search in other European herbaria will bring to light further specimens collected by him in 1766.

Sol. MSS refers to the twenty-three volumes, plus an index volume, of botanical descriptions prepared by Solander and others for an edition of the *Species Plantarum*; these are in the Botanical Library of the British Museum. Other MS notes which repeat and sometimes add to the information in that set are to be found in three interleaved editions of the *Species Plantarum* from Banks's library, now in the

British Museum (Natural History). The earliest of these is the second edition, 1762–3, bound in six volumes; the second a set of nine volumes edited by J. J. Reichard, 1779–80. These two sets contain many notes by Solander, Dryander and others on the plants collected on Cook's voyages as well as in Newfoundland and elsewhere. The third set, Willdenow's edition of 1797–1810, eighteen volumes, contains many of the notes of the earlier volumes but of course none by Solander who died in 1782. There are various notes by Banks in the twenty-three-volume set of Solander MSS but almost nothing in his hand in his interleaved copies of the works of Linnaeus. It is probable that the sets of the *Species Plantarum* which he took to Newfoundland and on the voyage round the world in the *Endeavour* were heavily annotated by him and that many of his notes were later copied into the interleaved sets by Solander and his clerks when the much-travelled volumes began to wear out.

(Ph.) in brackets after Fernald refers to the photostat copy of his notes on Banks's catalogue, now in the Gray Herbarium at Harvard. For other abbreviations see pp. 113, 233.

SYSTEMATIC LIST OF PLANTS COLLECTED

CRYPTOGAMS OR NON-FLOWERING PLANTS

ALGAE

Ascophyllum nodosum (L.) Le Jolis. Diary 9, 11, n. 11.

Fucus distichus L. Diary 23; n. 49. Banks also collected *Fucus vesiculosus* but this is a species with which he would have been familiar on British coasts whereas *F. distichus* is found chiefly in very exposed areas in the north and west of the British Isles.

Fucus vesiculosus L. Hb.'Newfoundland'. This specimen was recorded by Turner (1809, 2:45).

Halidrys siliquosa (L.) Lyngb. Diary 9, n. 12.

Laminaria longicruris La Pyl. Diary 17, n. 21.

?*Sargassum acinarium* (L.) C. Ag. Diary 11, n. 15.

Sargassum natans (L.) J. Meyen. Taylor (1957:199) records Banks's specimen which is inscribed 'Cast ashore in Newfoundland'. This Caribbean species is brought north by the Gulf Stream and not infrequently cast ashore after storms on exposed coasts from Florida to Southern Massachusetts.

Ulva lactuca L. Diary 23. This is the only *Ulva* species recorded by Taylor from Newfoundland.

THALLOPHYTA

?*Alectoria bicolor* (Ehrh.) Nyl. Diary 18, n. 22. Cat. 47 '22 *Lichen lanatus* about Croque'.

Alectoria fremontii Tuck. Banks's specimen is on a sheet with his Newfoundland specimen of *A. nitidula* (Th. Fr.) Vain.

Alectoria jubata (L.) Ach. em. Mot.

Alectoria nitidula (Th. Fr.) Vain. See *A. fremontii*.

Cetraria hepatizon (Ach.) Vain.

Cetraria nivalis (L.) Ach.

Cladonia sp. Diary, 21, 22.

Cornicularia aculeata (Schreb.) Ach.

?*Ephebe lanata* (L.) Vain. N. 22. Cat. 47 '22 *Lichen lanatus*, trees about Croque'.

Ochrolochea frigida (Swartz) Lynge. Hb.'*Lichen tartareus* Newfoundland'. There are three specimens.

Parmelia sp. This specimen has been sent to the U.S.A. for determination.

Parmelia centrifuga (L.) Ach.

Peltigera aphthosa (L.) Willd.

Sphaerophorus globosus (Huds.) Vain.

Stereocaulon paschale (L.) Hoffm. Diary 18.

?*Usnea hirta* (L.) Weber. Diary 18.

SYSTEMATIC LIST OF PLANTS COLLECTED

BRYOPHYTA

Liverworts

Blepharostoma trichophylla (L.) Dumortier. This is on a sheet with *Mnium punctatum* and *Drepanocladus uncinatus*.

Conocephalum conicum (L.) Underwood. Cat. 47 '8 *Marchantia conica* Bogs Croque'.

Marchantia polymorpha L. Cat. 48 '29 *Marchantia polymorpha*'.

Mosses

Brachythecium reflexum (Stark) Bruch., Schimp. & Gumbel. Cat. 48 '27 *Hypnum reflexum* Bogs'.

Bryum sp. Diary 19, 20, n. 37.

Bryum bicolor Dicks. Diary 18.

Dicranium elongatum Schleich. subsp. *groenlandicum* (Brid.) C. Jens.

Dicranium fuscescens Hedwig. This specimen is on a sheet with a probable Newfoundland specimen of *D. majus* Hedwig, and some *D. scoparium* Hedwig from Cook's second and third voyages.

Drepanocladus fluitans (Dill.) Warnst.

Drepanocladus uncinatus (Hedwig) Warnst. This specimen is on a sheet with *Mnium punctatum* and the hepatic *Blepharostoma trichophylla*.

Mnium hornum Hedwig. Diary 18, 28.

Mnium punctatum Hedwig. This may be the moss Banks referred to as *Mnium aquaticum*, diary 23, 24. It is on a sheet with *Drepanocladus uncinatus*.

?*Polytrichum alpinum* Hedwig. Diary 23, n. 45.

Polytrichum commune Hedwig. Cat. 47 '20 *Polytrichum commune* damp ground'.

Polytrichum strictum Menzies. This moss was named from material 'gathered in the year 1766 on Newfoundland by Sir Joseph Banks Bart. who described it under the foregoing name in a manuscript preserved in his library . . . I found it about twelve years ago near Halifax in Nova Scotia . . . I have been induced to give a new figure of it, from a specimen collected in Nova Scotia'. This note by Menzies (1798:77) shows that although he used Banks's name (Solander MSS 23:5), Banks's specimen cannot be regarded as the type. Menzies's description is not copied from Solander.

PTERIDOPHYTA

LYCOPODIACEAE

Lycopodium annotinum L. Diary 18, n. 23. Hb.'Newfoundland J. B., Labrador Mr. Molesworth'. Cat. 17a, see pp. 294, 307.

Lycopodium clavatum L. Diary 18, n. 23.

Lycopodium complanatum L. Diary 19. Hb.'Newfoundland J. B. Green with anthers'. Cat. 17a.

Lycopodium dendroideum Michx. Diary 18, n. 23. Hb.'*Lycopodium obscurum*. Cat. 17a.

SYSTEMATIC LIST OF PLANTS COLLECTED

Lycopodium sabinifolium ·Willd. var. *sitchense* (Rupr.) Fern. Diary 18, n. 23. Hb.'*Lycopodium alpinum*'.

Lycopodium selago L. Diary 21. Cat. 47 '11 *Lycopodium selago* on hillsides near springs not common'.

SELAGINELLACEAE

Selaginella selaginoides (L.) Link. Hb.'Newfoundland'. One specimen only.

EQUISETACEAE

Equisetum palustre L. Diary 27, n. 61.

Equisetum sylvaticum L. Diary 27, n. 61.

OPHIOGLOSSACEAE

Botrychium lunaria (L.) Swartz. Cat. 47 '24 *Osmunda lunaria* Whale Island'.

OSMUNDACEAE

Osmunda claytoniana L. Hb.'Newfoundland J. B.' Cat. 47 '3 *Osmunda* by a river side Conche'. Solander MSS 22 :60.

THELYPTERIDACEAE

Thelypteris phegopteris (L.) Slosson. Hb.'Newfoundland *Polypodium phegopteris*'.

ATHYRIACEAE

Athyrium distentifolia Tausch. Hb.'*Polypodium cristatum* Newfoundland'.

ASPIDIACEAE

Dryopteris carthusiana (Vill.) H. P. Fuchs. (=*D. spinulosa* pro parte). St. John's. Diary 23, n. 47.

Gymnocarpium dryopteris (L.) Newm. Cat. 47 '*Polypodium dryopteris* Damp woods Conche'.

BLECHNACEAE

Onoclea sensibilis L. Hb. 'Labrador Cape Charles'.

PHANEROGAMS OR FLOWERING PLANTS

TAXACEAE

Taxus canadensis Marsh. Hb.'Newfoundland Croque *Taxus baccifera*'.

PINACEAE

Picea glauca (Moench) Voss. Diary 18.

Picea mariana (Mill.) B.S.P. Diary 18.

Larix laricina (DuRoi) Koch. Diary 20.

Pinus strobus L. Diary 18.

Juniperus communis L. var. *depressa* Pursh. Diary 20, 24. Hb.'St. John's everywhere among the underbrush'. Cat. 13a '*Juniperus*', 17a '*Juniperus magnus*'.

SYSTEMATIC LIST OF PLANTS COLLECTED

Juniperus horizontalis Moench. Diary 20, 24. Hb. 'Damp Grounds about St. John's Between the King's bridge & Kitty witty Pool. *Cupressus Thujoides*'. Cat. 17a *Cupressus Thujoides*'.

SPARGANIACEAE

Sparganium angustifolium Michx. Cat. 41 '3 *Sparganium natans* Rocky Ponds Conche Croque'.

JUNCAGINACEAE

Triglochin maritima L. Hb. 'Croque Fresh bogs distant from the sea'. This specimen was recorded by Rouleau in 1949 (personal communication) but has not been located recently.

GRAMINEAE

Bromus ciliatus L. Hb. 'Chatteaux'. This specimen was recorded in 1949 by Rouleau (personal communication) but has not been located recently.

Festuca rubra L. N. 136. Hb. (1) '*Festuca duriuscula* damp grassy places Labrador Chatteaux Sept[r] 1766'; (2) '*Festuca duriuscula* Newfoundland'. These two sheets are not the same gathering. Cat. 5 '2 *Festuca duriuscula* bogs & grassy places Chatteaux'.

Puccinellia paupercula (Holm) Fern. & Weath. Hb. 'Labrador Chatteaux Near High water mark at Bad bay in a swampy place Sept. 1766'. Cat. 5 '1 *Festuca fluitans* Var: Near high water mark Bad bay'.

Glyceria striata (Lam.) Hitchc. Hb. '*Poa* Newfoundland Croque damp places June 1766'. Cat. 5 '21 *Poa* damp places Croque'.

Poa alpina L. Hb. (1) 'Newfoundland; Croque Dry hillsides June 1766'. (2) 'Newfoundland'. Cat. 5 '22 *Poa* Dry hillsides Croque'.

Poa eminens Presl. Hb. (1) 'Labrador Chatteaux Sandy places on the Beach Sept. 1766 *Poa aquatica*'. (2) 'Newfoundland Croque'. Cat. 5 '3 *Poa palustris?* Sandy Places on the Beach in Chatteaux Bay'.

Poa glauca Vahl. Hb. 'Labrador Chatteaux near the sea *?Poa alpina*'.

Poa nemoralis L. Hb. '*Aira* Labrador Chatteaux Grassy places Sept[r] 1766'. Cat. 5 '5 *Aira* Grassy places Chatteaux'.

Poa pratensis L. Diary 37, n. 94. There are two sheets of specimens; the first is labelled 'Grassy places Croque' and probably corresponds to the catalogue entry '9 *?Poa angustifolia* grassy places Croque'; the second, which is *Poa* cf. *pratensis*, corresponds to the catalogue entry '18 *Poa trivialis* Grassy Places Croque'; '*Poa trivialis*' in Banks's writing is faintly discernible in the bottom right-hand corner.

Hordeum brachyantherum Nevski. Hb. 'Croque Grassy places'. Cat. 5 '12 *Hordeum murinum* Grassy Places Croque'.

Hordeum jubatum L. Hb.(*fide* Fernald ph. 1) 'Sandwich Bay, Capt. Cartwright 1775'. This specimen has not been located recently.

Triticum aestivum L. Fernald's note (ph. 1) on this specimen which has not been located by the writer is 'Glabrous, green, nearly awnless, *T. verum*'. Cat. 5 '16 *Triticum* ? Dry woods not too shady Croque'. This is an introduced Eurasian species.

*Elymus arenarius L. var. *villosus* Mey. Hb.'Newfoundland Croque Labrador Chatteaux Sandy beach'. Cat. 5 '20 *Elymus* Sea beach Croque Chatteaux'.

**Trisetum spicatum* (L.) Richter. Hb.(1) 'Newfoundland Croque sunny banks June 1766, *Aira subspicata*'; (2) Herb. Torner, Croque, Newfoundland'. Törner was one of Banks's librarians and acquired many of his duplicate specimens which he sent to his friends abroad; see also pp. 39, 319.

Avena sp. Cat. 5 '17 *Avena* Near the sea on sunny banks Croque'. This was probably *Avena fatua* L., an introduced European species of waste places, found in Newfoundland and farther south.

**Deschampia flexuosa* (L.) Trin. Hb.'*Aira flexuosa*'. Cat. 5 '10 Aira *flexuosa* Grassy Place Croque'.

**Calamagrostis canadensis* (Michx.) Nutt. Hb.'*Arundo epigejos*'. Cat 5 '8 *Arundo epigejos* Croque *Conche* grassy Places'.

**Calamagrostis labradorica* Kearney. Hb.'Labrador Chatteaux near the sea'. Cat. 5 '4 *Arundo* Grassy Places Chatteaux'.

**Agrostis borealis* Hartm. The herbarium sheet has suffered war damage and the note on locality is missing, but Fernald (ph. 1) stated that Banks had labelled it Croque. An *Agrostis canina* L. recorded by Banks (cat. 5) from Chateau Bay was probably another specimen of *A. borealis* (Polunin 1940:50; H. St. John 1922:64); it has not been located.

**Agrostis geminata* Trin. This war-damaged sheet of specimens was cited by Fernald (ph. 1) as coming from Croque.

**Agrostis hyemalis* (Walt.) B.S.P. Fernald (ph. 1.) equates this with Banks's *A. cappillaris*, see Cat. 5 '7 *A. cappillaris* Croque *Conche* grassy places'. Fernald in his notes, however, wrongly copied the locality, substituting that of a *Scirpus* from Chateau Bay from the preceding entry.

*Agrostis tenuis Sibth. A naturalized European species. Fernald noted that Banks had collected typical material of this *Agrostis* (formerly *A. vulgaris* With.) from Croque and Conche. The remaining war-damaged sheet is marked only 'Newfoundland'. Fernald did not find an *Agrostis* sp. corresponding to Banks's catalogue entry, p. 6, '29 *Agrostis* side of the harbour'.

Phleum alpinum L. Hb.'Croque'. Cat. 5 '13 *Phleum* Grassy places Croque'. Fernald found this specimen which has not been located by Rouleau nor by the writer; war damage throughout this section was extensive.

?*Milium effusum* L. Diary 30. This introduced Eurasian species occurs in Newfoundland but no specimen has been found to confirm Banks's tentative determination of Millet-grass at St. John's.

Anthoxanthum odoratum L. A naturalized European species. Diary 29. Cat. 1a '*Anthoxanthum odoratum* Croque'. Banks's Newfoundland specimen is now missing from the sheet bearing his notes.

***Hierochloe odorata* (L.) Beauv. Hb.'*Holcus odoratus* Newfoundland Croque Damp places near the Sea side July 1766'. Cat. 13a '*Holcus odoratus*'.

CYPERACEAE

**Eleocharis acicularis* (L.) R. & S. Hb.'Newfoundland S. John's. Kitty Witty pool, *Scirpus acicularis*'. Cat. 6 '*Scirpus* No. 4 Near a fresh water Pool'.

**Eleocharis kamtschatica* (C. A. Meyer) Kom. Hb.(1) '*Scirpus palustris* Newfoundland Croque in Bogs'; (2) '*Scirpus palustris* Labrador Chatteaux'. Dr. Svenson kindly determined these specimens for me; the Labrador material is immature and he has queried his determination but he is sure that the Croque material belongs to this species. Fernald (ph. 2) considered that they were typical *E. uniglumis* (Link) Schultes; C. B. Clarke in 1887 determined them as *E. palustris* (L.) R. & S. var. *watsoni* Bab. See also Svenson 1947:61–7; 1957: 524.

**Eleocharis palustris* (L.) R. & S. Hb.'Labrador Chatteaux Bogs & muddy pools Septr 1766 *Scirpus palustris*'. Cat. 5 '6 *Scirpus* Bogs & muddy Pools Chatteaux'.

Scirpus atrocinctus Fern. Rouleau reported (personal communication) seeing Banks's sheet of this species from Newfoundland but there is no other record of it.

**Scirpus cespitosus* L. var. *callosus* Bigel. Diary 29, n. 67. Hb.'Croque'. There is no material from St. John's, although Banks mentioned collecting it there.

**Scirpus hudsonianus* (Michx.) Fern. Diary 23, n. 46. Hb.'*Eriophorum alpinum* Newfoundland St. John's Croque Bogs'. Cat. 5 '15 *Eriophorum alpinum* Damp places Croque'.

Scirpus rubrotinctus Fern. Rouleau (personal communication) reports seeing two Banksian sheets of this species in 1949, one labelled 'Chatteaux Bay, side of the harbour in soft mud', the other 'Croque, side of the harbour near the top'.

**Eriophorum angustifolium* Honckeny. Hb.(1) '*Eriophorum polystachion* Croque Bogs'; (2) 'Labrador, Soc. Un. Frat.'. Cat. 5 '14 *Eriophorum polystachion* Bogs Croque'. Sol. MSS 2:770. *E. polystachion* L. is a nom. ambig.

**Eriophorum spissum* Fern. Hb.'*Eriophorum vaginatum* Newfoundland Croque Boggy places, July 1766'. Cat. 5 '24 *Eriophorum vaginatum* Bogs. Croque'

**Rhynchospora alba* (L.) Vahl. Hb. 'Newfoundland *Shoenus albus*'. Cat. 5 '19 *Schoenus albus* Bogs Croque'.

*Carex angustior Mackenzie. Hb.'Newfoundland *Carex*'.

Carex atratiformis Britton. Diary 29, n. 66. Hb.(1) 'Herb. Rudge, Herb Torner ex *Am. Bor.* Newfoundland' (not Banks's MS); (2) 'Newfoundland'; (3) 'Newfoundland J.B.'. Banks gave one of these sheets to Törner who was for a time his librarian. Törner's collection was purchased by Rudge who described this sedge as *Carex ovata.* After Rudge's death his herbarium came to the British Museum (J. Britten 1917:344). In 1895 N. L. Britton (1895:222) provided a new name, *Carex atratiformis,* to replace *C. ovata* Rudge, invalidated by the earlier homonym *C. ovata* Burm. f. (1768). K. K. Mackenzie (1935: 371–2) states that *Carex atrata* L. occurs in alpine and arctic North America but Raymond (1950) in his study of *Carex* and *Kobresia* from Anticosti Island shows that in eastern North America *C. atrata* is an arctic species found in northern Labrador, and that it is replaced in southern Labrador and Newfoundland by *C. atratiformis.* The sheet of 3 specimens which Banks gave to Törner and which passed to Rudge is thus the type of both *C. ovata* Rudge and *C. atratiformis* Britton. Thus Banks's entry in his diary stating that on 6 June he collected *C. atrata* at St. John's indicates this as the type locality of *C. atratiformis* Britton. Professor Rouleau collected this species at Croque in 1965.

Carex castanea Wahlenb. Hb.(1) 'Herb. Torner Newfoundland, Herb. Rudge' (not Banks's MS); (2) '*Carex nutans* Newfoundland'. Wahlenberg (1803, 24:155) based his description of this *Carex* on material seen in Törner's herbarium. The following year Rudge (1804:98–9) using Törner's material, described the same sedge from Törner's collection (i.e. Banks's) as *C. flexilis* from Newfoundland. Thus Wahlenberg's type became Rudge's. There are five specimens on Törner's sheet; one of them was figured by Rudge. See also *C. atratiformis* for a further note on Törner.

Carex curta Gooden. (=*C. canescens* L. nom. ambig.). Hb.'*Carex spicata*? Newfoundland Croque Bogs'. In addition to the five specimens of *C. curta* on this sheet there is one *C. tenuiflora* Wahlenb.

Carex deflexa Hornem. Hb.'Newfoundland *Carex capillaris*?'.

?*Carex echinata.* Cat. 17a gives merely this name and is the only record of such a species in Banks's Newfoundland MSS. The name *C. echinata* has been applied to several species (L. H. Bailey 1893:422; Mackenzie 1931:105, etc.).

Carex flava L. Hb.'Croque bogs June 1766'.

Carex gynocrates Wormsk. Diary 34, n. 86. Hb.'*Carex dioica* L. Newfoundland'. Cat. 41 '12 *Carex dioica* bogs Croque'.

Carex leptalea Wahlenb. Hb.(1) 'Newfoundland *Carex*'; (2) 'Newfoundland'. Wahlenberg described this species from Törner's material which he cited from *America boreali,* and which was almost certainly collected by Banks; the type locality should be therefore amended to Newfoundland. There are three specimens on the first sheet; another specimen is on a sheet with *Carex angustior.*

Carex leptonervia (Fern.) Fern. Hb.(1 and 2) 'Newfoundland'. There are two specimens on both these sheets but no notes by Banks.

Carex michauxiana Boeckl. Hb.'Bogs about Croque'.

Carex nigra (L.) Reichard. Hb.'Newfoundland *Carex acuta*'. See Fernald 1942: 300–2, for a discussion of the name of this species.

Carex oligosperma Michx. Hb.'*Carex filiformis* Newfoundland'.

Carex palacea Wahlenb. Hb.(1) 'Herb. Torner ex Am. bor. Herb. Rudge' (not Banks's MS); (2) 'Newfoundland *Carex acuta?*' Rudge's specimen is part of Wahlenberg's type collection; since it is only marked Am. Bor. it is not absolutely certain that it was collected by Banks although the existence of Banks's Newfoundland sheet makes it highly probable. Fernald (1942:293), however, states that Professor Alm sent him a photograph of the type from Stockholm in 1934; it is presumably the rest of the material of this species given by Banks to Törner. Fernald, not realizing this, suggests that it came from the Labrador Peninsula and states that Mackenzie mistakenly gives Greenland as the type locality. This is not so. Mackenzie (1935:414) gives Greenland as the type locality of *Carex maritima* O. F. Müll., a synonym, but North America as the type locality for Wahlenberg's species; it should probably be amended to Newfoundland.

Carex pauciflora Lightf. Diary 33, n. 82. Hb.'*Carx* [*sic*] *pauciflora* MS Newfoundland'. Cat. 41 '9 *Carex pulicaris* Bogs Croque'. *C. pulicaris* is a synonym. Sol. MSS 18:665 gives 'Newfoundland, J. Banks', and not Labrador, although he mentions Lightfoot (1777, 2:544) who states that Banks collected this sedge from that country.

Carex rariflora (Wahlenb.) Sm. Hb.'*Carex saxatilis*'.

Carex tenuiflora Wahlenb. Hb.'Newfoundland Croque bogs'. This specimen is on a sheet of *C. curta*.

ERIOCAULACEAE

Eriocaulon septangulare With. Hb.'St. John's Kitty Witty pool Croque in many lakes'.

JUNCACEAE

Juncus balticus Willd. Diary 35, n. 88. Hb.(1) 'Croque bogs near the sea *Juncus effusus*'; (2) 'Labrador Chatteaux Whale Island Bogs near the sea'. Banks's *Juncus effusus* is only just decipherable beneath more recent handwriting. Cat. 11 '7 *Juncus effusus* Bogs & near the sea Croque'.

Juncus brevicaudatus (Engelm.) Fern. Hb.'Boggy places Croque July 1766', '*Juncus articulatus*' (not Banks's MS). Cat. 11 '5 *Juncus articulatus* Bogs Croque'.

Juncus bufonius L. Hb.'Newfoundland'.

Juncus filiformis L. Hb.(1) 'Labrador Chatteaux Whale Island'; (2) 'Labrador Whale Island in Chatteaux bay; Newfoundland J. B.'; (3) 'Labrador Chatteaux Bay near the fort wet places'. Most of the specimens on sheets 1 and 2 have very swollen bases due to insect damage.

Juncus stygius L. Hb.'Bogs about Croque'. Cat. 11 '6 *Juncus* Bogs Croque'.

Juncus trifidus L. Diary 33, n. 81. Hb.'Newfoundland St. John's Dry tops of hills May 1766 Labrador Chatteaux'.

?*Luzula acuminata* Raf. Diary 29, n. 65. No Banksian specimen has been found.

Luzula multiflora (Retz.) Lejeune. Diary 29, n. 64. Hb.'*Juncus campestris* Newfoundland'. This used to be regarded as the variety *multiflora* of *L. campestris*, but has now acquired specific status.

Luzula parviflora (Ehrh.) Desv. n. 104. Hb.'Belisle grassy places rather barren'. Cat. 11 '2 *Juncus* Grassy places rather barren'.

LILIACEAE

Tofieldia glutinosa (Michx.) Pers.=*Triantha glutinosa* (Michx.) Baker. Diary 31. Hb.'*Anthericum calyculatum* Newfoundland Croque damp boggy places. Differt ab europaeo caule glandulose'. Cat. 11 '8 *Anthericum calyculatum* Bogs Croque'. For discussion of this specimen see *Bot. Mag.* 1813, 37:1505; for other notes on the species Gates 1918: 137; Hitchcock 1944: 487–98.

†*Clintonia borealis* (Ait.) Raf. Hb.'*Dracaena borealis* Newfoundland Croque woods & shady places'. The remains of 'Chatteaux' is decipherable on the verso of Ehret's painting, pl. VII, which was reproduced by Aiton (1789, 1:454) when he described this species; the painting is, however, a representation of Banks's specimen and Croque is thus the type locality although it was not cited by Aiton. Aiton made a slip when he stated that this species was introduced by Solander in 1778.

Smilacina stellata (L.) Desf. Diary 31. Hb.'St. John's on a dry tump on the banks of Kitty Witty pool'. Cat. 11 '9 *Convallaria stellata* Bottoms of dry hills'. Banks's footnote in his diary when he found this *Smilacina* refers it to *S. racemosa* but this species has been recorded only twice in south western Newfoundland and he probably realized later that he had made a mistake since he did not enter *S. racemosa* in his catalogue. His specimen is clearly *S. stellata*.

†*Smilacina trifolia* (L.) Desf. Hb.'Croque damp places'. Pl. 45.

Maianthemum canadense Desf. Diary 33. Hb.'*Convallaria bifolia* Croque'. Cat. 11 '3 *Convallaria bifolia* Croque St. John's'. In the McGill MS, p. 99, Banks noted the great variation in the habitats of this species.

Streptopus roseus Michx. Hb.(1) '1 America Sept. Labrador; 2 Newfoundland J. B.'; (2) 'Newfoundland in woods near Croque'. Cat. 11 '4 *Uvularia amplexifolia* Shady Places Croque St. John's'. Banks's catalogue entry makes it possible to refer the four unnumbered specimens on his first sheet to St. John's. There is some variation in these specimens but we have been unable to separate them on the basis of Fernald's key (1950:441). Professor Rouleau is of the opinion that one of the specimens may be *S. amplexifolius* (L.) DC. See also Fernald 1907:106–7; Fassett 1935:88–113.

IRIDACEAE

*Sisyrinchium angustifolium Mill. Hb.'Bogs about the Town of St. John's'. Cat. 17a 'Sisirynchicum' (p. 307).

*Iris hookeri Penny. Hb.'Newfoundland Croque grassy places'. Cat. 5 '23 *Iris* Sea side & Brooks Everywhere'.

ORCHIDACEAE

Cypripedium calceolus L. var. *planipetalum* (Fern.) Vict. & Rousseau. Cat. 39 '8 *Cyprepedium* [*sic*] *calceolus* ? Island Hare Bay'. *C. calceolus* is a Eurasian species and the variety *planipetalum* is the nearest approach to it that occurs in Newfoundland.

*Habenaria dilatata (Pursh) Hook. Hb.'*Orchis acuta* 1. Terra Labrador. Soc. unit. Fratrum 1766. The dark specimen. 2. Newfoundland J. B.' Sol. MSS 18:217 'Locis uliginosis, Julio florens'. Pursh (1814: 588) based his description of this species on both Banks's (i.e. Solander's) MS description of *Orchis acuta*, collected by Colmaster (Kohlmeister, a Danish missionary who sent specimens from Labrador to Banks, Dickson and other European botanists), and on material seen in Dickson's herbarium. Solander based his MS account on Banks's Newfoundland material as well as the Labrador specimen from Kohlmeister; both these specimens are therefore part of the type collection. Nothing is known of the whereabouts of the Dickson specimen. See Schrank 1818:2; Meyer, Ernest 1830:xiv, on Kohlmeister.

*Habenaria hyperborea (L.) R.Br. Hb.'*Orchis* Newfoundland J. B.'

†Habenaria obtusata (Pursh) Richards. Banks's MS description quoted by Pursh (1814:588) is in the interleaved 1762–3 edition of the *Species Plantarum* annotated by Solander, vol. 2, facing p. 1336. Pursh cites material from Hudson's Bay in Herb. Banks. The only record of Banks's having collected this species in Newfoundland is Ehret's painting, pl. 46, annotated 'Newfoundland *Orchis*' by Banks.

*Habenaria psycodes (L.) Spreng. Hb.'Newfoundland J.B.'. Cat. 39 '5 *Orchis psycodes* Bogs Croque'. Sol. MSS 18:223–6, 'Hab. in rudis paludosis prope Croque in Newfoundland'.

*Spiranthes romanzoffiana Cham. Hb.'Bogs above Croque'.

SYSTEMATIC LIST OF PLANTS COLLECTED

†*Listera convallarioides* (Sw.) Nutt. Hb.(1) 'Newfoundland Croque'; (2) 'Newfoundland Croque on the Banks of a small rivulet near the mouth of the Salmon river July 1766'. The first sheet is also marked, but not by Banks, 'Herb, Torner, Herb Rudge'. These two sheets form part of the type collection. It has already been noted (see *Carex atratiformis* p. 319.) that Törner's material was derived from Banks; Swartz (1800:232) described *Epipactis convallarioides* thus: 'Caule bifolio, foliis cordato-subrotundis acutis: labello oblongo apice dilato obtuse bilobo, E. Terra Nova Amer. Sept. Communicato a cl. amico S. Torner'. It follows that the type locality is therefore Banks's 'Salmon' river, but this is not the Salmon river flowing into Hare Bay, but a smaller stream now called the Freshwater River (n. 138) which flows into the head of Croque Harbour. See Ehret's painting, pl. VIII, of Banks's Croque specimen.

Listera cordata (L.) R.Br. Hb.'*Ophrys cordata* Newfoundland Croque damp woods among moss'. Cat. 39, probably '1 *Ophrys* shady damp wood Croque'.

Corallorhiza trifida Chat. Diary 31, n. 75. Hb.'*Ophrys corallorhiza* Newfoundland Croque'.

SALICACEAE

Salix cordifolia Pursh var. *callicarpaea* (Trautv.) Fern. Hb.sheets 1 and 2 are both marked '*Salix depressa* Newfoundland'.

Salix pyrifolia Anderss.

Salix repens unident. Diary 37, n. 95. Cat. 43 '1 *Salix repens* Dry hillsides Inglie'.

?*Salix reticulata* L. var. *semicalva* Fern. Pursh (1814:610) states that he saw specimens of this willow collected from Newfoundland and Labrador in Banks's herbarium but these have not been located.

Salix vestita Pursh. Hb.(1) 'Newfoundland Croque'; (2) 'Labrador Soc. Unit. Frat.'. The four specimens on the second sheet are isotypes. Pursh (1814:610) cited specimens from Labrador 'in Herb. Lambert and Banks'.

Populus balsamifera L. Diary 32, 37. Hb.'*Populus taccamahacca* Inglie'. Cat. 43 '2 *Populus balsamifera* Woods Croque Inglie'.

MYRICACEAE

Myrica gale L. Diary 22. Hb.'Newfoundland St. John's *Myrica Gale* L.' Cat. 43 '4 *Myrica* Brooksides Croque St. John's Chatteaux'.

CORYLACEAE

Betula papyrifera Marsh. Hb.'Newfoundland'; '*Betula nigra*' (not Banks's MS). Cat. 41 '16 *Betula nigra* woods everywhere'.

Betula pumila L. Diary 32. Hb.(1) 'Croque J.B.'; (2) 'Croque'; (3) 'Labrador Chatteaux Bay'. Banks's determinations are indecipherable and later determinations have been written over his lightly pencilled names. Professor Rouleau has kindly determined these sheets for me. See also n. 76a.

Alnus crispa (Ait.) Pursh. Diary 29, n. 68. Hb.'Newfoundland *Betula alnus*'; Solander's MS '*crispa* MS, *Alnus undulata*'. There are two sheets both with the same annotations; a flowering specimen is almost certainly one noted at St. John's in Banks's diary; the second has ripe catkins and I have found no information about its locality. Aiton's description (1789, 3:339) of this species is an exact transcription of Solander's MS (19:45) account of Banks's Newfoundland material, and of a plant in Kew Gardens introduced from Hudson's Bay; a specimen of the latter is still in the herbarium. The Newfoundland and Hudson's Bay sheets together comprise the type material.

URTICACEAE

Urtica urens L. Hb.'Newfoundland *Urtica urens*'. Cat. 41 '*Urtica urens* garden'. This is a widely distributed naturalized species from Eurasia. Banks's remarks about his poultry and his garden plants refer to Phipps's house and garden at Croque.

†*Geocaulon lividum* (Richards.) Fern. Hb.'Croque in apricis'. Ehret's painting (pl. 47) is labelled *Comandra umbellata* and *Nanodea glauca*; the latter is Solander's MS (7:14d) name for Banks's plant.

POLYGONACEAE

Oxyria digyna (L.) Hill. Hb.'Newfoundland Bellisle'. Cat. 11 '1 *Rumex digynus* Bellisle Shady Rocks'.

Rumex fenestratus Greene. Hb.'Croque'. Cat. 11 '12 *Rumex* Seaside'.

Polygonum convolvulus L. Hb. '*Polygonum convolvulus* Croque'. This is a naturalized European species.

Polygonum fowleri B. L. Robinson. Hb.'*Polygonum erectum* Newfoundland Croque near the seaside'.

Polygonum sagittatum L. Hb.'*Polygonum sagittatum* St. John's on the damp sides of Kitty Witty Pool'.

Polygonum aviculare L. Cat. 15 '*Polygonum aviculare* Sea side'. This is a naturalized European species.

Polygonum viviparum L. Hb.'*Polygonum viviparum* Croque near the sea beach'. Cat. 15 '3 *Polygonum viviparum* Sea Beach on Rocks Croque'. I am much indebted to Dr. Peter Raven for determining these *Polygonum* spp. for me.

SYSTEMATIC LIST OF PLANTS COLLECTED

CHENOPODIACEAE

Atriplex glabriuscula Edmonston. Hb.'Newfoundland Croque in arenosis prope mare'.

Chenopodium album L. Hb.'Newfoundland Croque in arenosis prope mare'.

PORTULACACEAE

Montia lamprosperma Cham. Hb.'*Montia* Newfoundland Croque' (2 specimens), 'Labrador Chatteaux' (many specimens).

CARYOPHYLLACEAE

Spergularia canadensis (Pers.) G. Don. Hb.'*Arenaria* Croque'.

Sagina procumbens L. Cat. 7 '8 *Sagina procumbens* L. Damp stones cheifly on the sea shore Croque'.

Honckenya peploides (L.) Ehrh. Hb.(1) 'Newfoundland Croque the Sea Beach No. 1'; (2) 'Terra Labrador No. 2'. Cat. 19? '1 *Arenaria* Bogs near the sea side where it is washd by the spray in hard weather'.

Minuartia groenlandica (Retz.) Ostenf. (=*Arenaria groenlandica* (Retz.) Spreng.) Hb.'Labrador'. See J. McNeill 1962:147.

Minuartia rubella (Wahlenb.) Hiern. (=*Arenaria rubella* (Wahlenb.) Sm.) Diary 38, n. 99. Hb.'*Arenaria saxatilis* Newfoundland Croque etc. dry hillsides'. Cat. 19 '15 *Arenaria laricifolia* on dry hillsides scarce'. This is part of the type collection of *Arenaria juniperina* Pursh; see n. 99.

Stellaria calycantha (Ledeb.) Bong. Hb.(1) 'Newfoundland Islands off the mouth of Hare bay'; (2) 'Newfoundland Hare Bay'.

Stellaria graminea L. Hb.'Croque'. This is another European plant which has become naturalized in North America. Banks noted in the McGill MS, p. 101, that the corollas in this species were defective in early summer. In fact the flowers are variable; they may be fully hermaphrodite, or partially or completely male sterile. In the last case the petals are very small.

Stellaria humifusa Rottb. Hb.'Labrador Chatteaux Salt marsh flats between the fort and Bad Bay, *Arenaria*'. Cat. 19 '21 *Arenaria* on the beach within the tides Chatteaux'.

Cerastium alpinum L. Diary 35, 37. Hb.(1) 'Newfoundland, *Cerastium alpinum*'; (2) 'Croque dry hills among loose stones June 1766, *Cerastium hirtum*'. Cat. 19 '11 *Cerastium alpinum* Tops of Barren hills Everywhere'. Sol. MS 11:245 '*Cerastium hirtum*. Habitat in Terra Labrador'. The Croque specimen is dwarfed and more pubescent than the other. No Labrador specimen has been found. It seems probable that the specimen Banks recorded at Inglie on 20

June corresponds to the sheet marked '*Cerastium alpinum* Newfoundland'. On p. 7a, in the fair copy of his catalogue, he made another entry, '*Cerastium hirsut*', beneath *C. alpinum* but added nothing about locality.

*_Lychnis dioica_ L. Hb. 'Croque'. Cat. 19 '12 *Lychnis* Hillside Conche Bellisle. This is a naturalized Eurasian plant.

*_Silene acaulis_ L. Diary 38. Hb.'Newfoundland Croque, Labrador Chatteaux Near the edge of the Sea on Stony Beaches'.

RANUNCULACEAE

*_Ranunculus flammula_ L. var. *filiformis* (Michx.) Hook. Hb.'*Ranunculus reptans* Newfoundland Conche'. Cat. 25 '7 *Ranunculus repens* Conche'. This specimen was determined by Lyman Benson in 1950.

*_Ranunculus hedereraceus_ L. Diary 30, n. 71. Hb.'Croque, *Ranunculus hederaceus*'. The diary reference is to a bog near St. John's but no specimen other than one from Croque has been found although Lyman Benson (1948:230) states that this species occurs beside Quiddy Viddy Lake.

*_Ranunculus hyperboreus_ Rottb. Hb.'*Ranunculus* Labrador Chatteaux in muddy pools behind the fort'. Cat. 25 '6 *Ranunculus* muddy sides of pools Chatteaux'.

*_Ranunculus pedatifidus_ Smith. Hb.'America Labrador 1763'. This specimen was not of course collected by Banks but it is of special interest since the date shows that he was in touch with someone in Labrador three years before his own visit there.

*_Thalictrum alpinum_ L. Diary 32. Hb.'*Thalictrum alpinum* Croque Bogs'. Cat. 25 '*Thalictrum alpinum* Bogs Croque'.

?*_Thalictrum dioicum_ L. Cat. 25 '2 *Thalictrum minus* Edges of Woods Croque'. It is possible that Banks collected this dioecious species at Croque since it is easily confused with the hermaphrodite species *T. minus* L. found in Europe, boreal Asia and Africa but not in North America. No Banksian specimen of *T. dioicum* has been found but he himself says that his collections at Croque were 'not in a fit state' when the *Niger* left unexpectedly for Chateau Bay.

*_Thalictrum polygamum_ Muhl.46. 'Newfoundland St. Johns'.

*_Thalictrum pubescens_ Pursh. Hb.'Newfoundland St. Johns'. See Bovin 1947:484; 1957:315–18.

†*_Anemone parviflora_ Michx. Diary 38, n. 98. Hb,'*Anemone tenella* MSS Croque Inglie Rocks near the water's edge'. Cat. 25 '3 *Anemone* Rocks near water Croque Inglie'. Sol. MSS 12:633. Ehret's drawing (pl. 48) is a composite representation of three of Banks's specimens. Banks's name *A. tenella* was published in the synonymy of *A. parviflora* by W. J. Hooker (1829:5). *A. tenella* Pursh refers to another species, *A. caroliniana* Walt. A. L. Jussieu (1804:24 pl. 21), examined Michaux's material and published a fuller des-

cription and illustration of Michaux's species under the name of *A. cuneifolia*, which Michaux had written on the herbarium sheet but had discarded in favour of *parviflora* which he published in 1803.

Coptis groenlandica (Oeder) Fern. Diary 22, n. 44. Hb.'*Helleborus trifoliatus* Newfoundland dampish & shady places'. Cat. 9a '*Helleborus trifol.*'; also 17a. This was probably collected at St. John's.

Actaea rubra (Ait.) Willd. Hb.'*Actaea spicata* B Croque shady places in woods'. Cat. 25 '5 *Actaea* shady places Croque'. Banks's specimen is a flowering spray; Aiton's description was based on fruiting material and there appears to be no type specimen extant. There are no descriptions of this species in any of the surviving Solander MSS in the British Museum.

CRUCIFERAE

Draba incana L. var. *incana*. Diary 37, n. 96. Hb.'Croque on a damp rock above the watering place'.

Draba incana L. var. *confusa* (Ehrh.) Lilj. Hb.'Herb. Torner. *Draba incana* J. Banks Labrador on dry hill tops behind the Fort'. Cat. 29 '4 *Draba incana* Barren hills'.

Thlaspi arvense L. Hb.'Croque Conche Grassy places'. Cat. 29 '1 *Thlaspi arvense* grassy Places Croque Conche'. This is a naturalized species from Eurasia.

Cochlearia tridactylites Banks ex DC. Diary 51, n. 110. Hb.'*Cochlearia tridactylites*, 1 Labrador, Chatteaux Whale Island, St. Peters Islands, 2 Labrador, Soc. unit. Fratrum'. Solander MSS 14:67. These specimens are all syntype material.

Brassica rapa L. Hb.(1 and 2) '*Brassica rapa* Newfoundland'. This is a naturalized Eurasian species.

Cardamine pratensis L. Diary 34. Hb.'*Cardamine pratensis* Croque, on a gravelly beach near the sea'. Cat. 29 '2 *Cardamine pratensis*'. A naturalized European species.

Cardamine pratensis L. var. *angustifolia* Hook. Hb.'Croque'.

Arabis alpina L. Diary 37. Hb.'*Arabis alpina* Inglie on hillsides in rich soil'. Cat. 29 '3 *Arabis canadensis* hill sides rich soil Inglie'.

SARRACENIACEAE

Sarracenia purpurea L. Hb.'*Sarracenia purpurea* Croque in Bogs'. Cat. 25 '1 *Sarracenia purpurea* Bogs Croque, St. Johns Hare Bay'.

DROSERACEAE

Drosera anglica Huds. Hb.'Bogs near Croque'. Cat. 9 '8 *Drosera longifolia* Bogs Croque'. *D. longifolia* L. then included *D. anglica*. Banks's note in the McGill

MS, p. 97, on Pentandria 8 (his *Drosera longifolia*) is 'Vixunquam vidi Corollam hujus Plantae explicatam in Anglia sub hac vere sole cum congeneri suo *D: rotundifolia* Formosissima explicatur'. (I have scarcely ever seen the corolla of this plant unfolded in England, under this real sun, with its congener, *D. rotundifolia*, it unfolds itself most beautifully.)

Drosera rotundifolia L. Diary 29, St. John's. Banks apparently collected it at Croque also. See *D. anglica*.

CRASSULACEAE

*Sedum rosea (L.) Scop. Diary 24. Hb.'St. Johns near the mouth of the harbour on the South side near high water mark'. Cat. 12a 'Rhodiola rosea on rocks near St. Johns'.

SAXIFRAGACEAE

*Saxifraga aizoides L. Hb.'Saxifraga autumnalis Belisle on the rocks immediately above high water mark'. Banks's writing on this sheet is faint and someone has written *aizoides* over *autumnalis*. Cat. 19 '6 *Saxifraga autumnalis* Bellisle Damp Rock'. Pursh (1814:312) states that there were specimens of this saxifrage from both Newfoundland and Labrador in Banks's herbarium but the Chateau Bay material has not been located.

*Saxifraga paniculata Miller (=S. aizoon Jacq.) Hb.'Sax. cotyledon Croque on a small island in the mouth of Hare Bay'. Cat. 19 '7 *Saxifraga cotyledon* Damp Rock Bellisle'.

?Saxifraga cernua L. Pursh (1814:312) reported specimens of *S. sibirica* (=S. cernua) from Labrador and Newfoundland in Banks's herbarium, but no corresponding material has been found and there is nothing in the Solander MSS to confirm this.

*Saxifraga cespitosa L. Diary 38. Hb.(1, 2 & 3) 'Saxifraga caespitosa Inglie.' Cat. 19 '16 *Saxifraga* clefts of rock Inglie'.

*Saxifraga cespitosa L. subsp. *cespitosa* [=subsp. *eucaespitosa* Engl. & Irmsch.] Hb.'Sax. groenlandica Newfoundland'. For distribution see Porsild 1957: 105–6, 186.

*Saxifraga oppositifolia L. Diary 38, n. 100. Hb.'Inglie On the rocks near the sides of the harbour. *Saxifraga oppositifolia*'. Cat. 19 '14 *Saxifraga oppositifolia* on sides of rocks Inglie'.

*Saxifraga rivularis L. Hb.'Saxifraga rivularis Labradore Chatteaux on the rocks above bad bay'. Cat. 19 '22 *Saxifraga rivularis* Rocks & brook sides Chatteaux'.

?Saxifraga tricuspidata Rottb. Cat. 7a 'Saxifraga tridactyla'. *S. tridactylites* L. does not occur in North America; its leaves are rather similar to those of *S. tricuspidata* which was described from Greenland by Rottbøll in 1770. It does not appear to have been recorded from Newfoundland but is known from

52. The type specimen of *Rosa blanda* Ait., *Hort. Kew.*, 2: 202 (1789). See p. 331.

53. *Dryas integrifolia*, a charming plant collected by Banks at Inglie.
G. D. Ehret

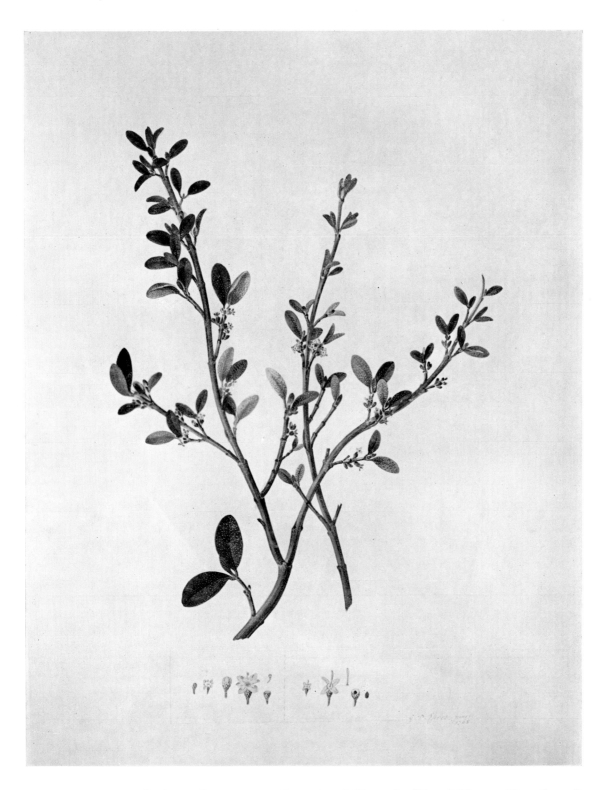

54. *Shepherdia canadensis*. Banks appears to have found this at Inglié and Chateau Bay. One of his specimens is in the Saffron Walden Museum.

G. D. Ehret

57. *Kalmia polifolia*, a common and beautiful plant in Newfoundland.
G. D. Ehret

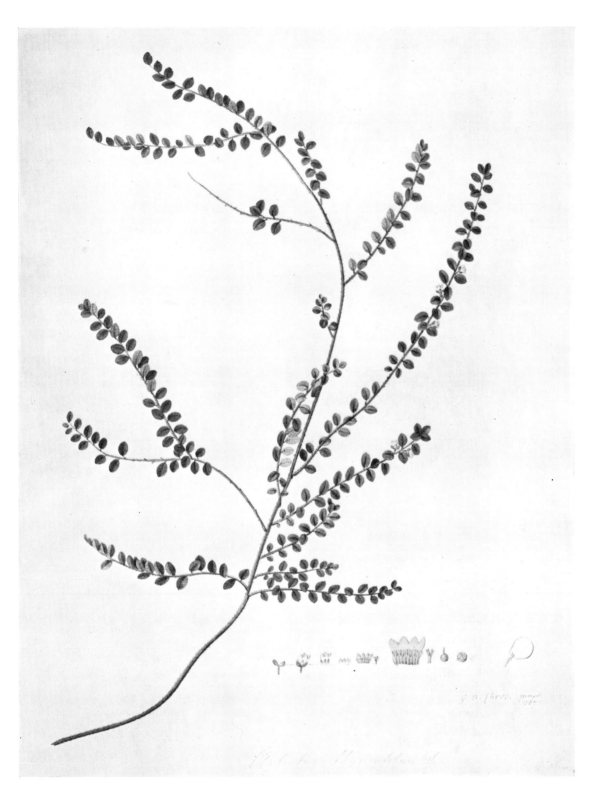

58. *Gaultheria hispidula.*
G. D. Ehret

59. Type specimen of *Solidago macrophylla* Pursh, *Flor. Amer. Sept.*, 542 (1814).
The note on locality is on the back of the herbarium sheet but has been superimposed in this photograph.

northern Labrador and from some alpine regions further south. No Banksian specimen has been found, nor is there any record of Banks's having brought one back from Chateau Bay. It is an unlikely record for any of the localities visited by Banks.

†*Mitella nuda L. Diary 18. Hb.'Newfoundland Croque etc., shady damp places'. Ehret's plate is labelled 'Chatteaux'. It appears that *Tiarella unifolia* Retzius (a synonym of *M. nuda*), described from Newfoundland in 1783, was probably based on material derived from Banks's collections. (Pl. 28.)

*Parnassia parviflora DC. Diary 31. Hb.'Croque Bogs, June 1766'. Cat. 9 '7 *Parnassia palustris* Bogs Croque'. DeCandolle (1824:320) based his description of this species on Banks's material which is therefore the type.

*Ribes glandulosum Grauer. Diary 24, n. 54. Hb.'*Ribes* ['?*prostratum*'. This has been almost erased and '*glandulosum*' written over it] St. Johns woods June 1766'. Solander MSS 6:603. There is a sheet of cultivated material from L'Héritier labelled 'Hort. Paris' which was the basis of his *Ribes prostratum*, probably derived from Banks's collections. For the origin of Grauer's material see n. 54.

*Ribes hirtellum Michx. Diary 35, where Banks referred to these gooseberries as *Ribes* 'grossulariata', i.e. *R. grossularia* L., a species found in Europe and parts of Africa and Asia. Hb.(1 and 2) 'Newfoundland Croque sides of woods June 1766 *Ribes uva crispa*'. 'Uva crispa' has been almost entirely erased but can just be seen beneath '*hirtellum*' on one of the sheets. Cat. 9 '12 *Ribes uva crispa* Woodsides Croque'.

Ribes lacustre Poiret. Diary 35, n. 87. Probably Cat. 9 '13 *Ribes* Woodsides Croque'.

*Ribes triste Pallas. Diary 34. Hb.'*Ribes rubrum* Croque Shady woods June 1766'. Cat. 9 '11 *Ribes* 1 Shady Woods Croque'.

ROSACEAE

*Pyrus decora (Sarg.) Hyland. Hb.'*Sorbus americana* Croque woods'. Cat. 23 '6 *Sorbus aucuparia* Woods Croque'.

*Amelanchier bartramiana (Tausch) Roemer. Diary 29. Hb.'St. Johns Woods *Mespilus canadensis*'. 'Canadensis' has been almost completely erased.

*Fragaria virginiana Duchesne. Diary 30, n. 70. Hb.'*Fragaria pratensis* St. Johns but not at Croque. Grassy places May June 1766'.

*Potentilla anserina L. subsp. *pacifica* (Howell) Rousi. Hb.'Croque Sea beach'. Cat. 23 '9 *Potentilla anserina* Sea Beach Everywhere'. Banks's specimen lacks flowers but the pointed teeth on the leaflets, and the curly hairs on the undersurface, except on the veins where they are straight, indicate that it belongs to this subspecies. See Rousi 1965:104–5.

*_Potentilla crantzii_ (Crantz) G. Beck. This species was collected for Banks by George Cartwright (4 specimens) and by Mr. La Trobe from 'Labrador Okkak the northernmost settlement of the Moravians 1778'. This widely distributed species was originally described by Crantz from European material. Pursh (1814:355) cited Banks's Labrador specimens as _P. opaca_ non. Linn. It appears that they are the first recorded collections from North America.

*_Potentilla fruticosa_ L. Hb.'_Potentilla fruticosa_ Croque boggy places June 1766'. Cat. 23 '3 _Potentilla fruticosa_ Bogs about Croque'.

†*_Potentilla nivea_ L. Diary 38, n. 97 'Hb._Potentilla nivea_ Conche dry hill side 1766'. Cat. 23 '10 _Potentilla nivea_ Dry Bank Coche'. (Pls. 49, 50.)

*_Potentilla norvegica_ L. Diary 37, n. 93. Hb.'_Potentilla_ Croque grassy places June 1766'. Cat. 23 '1 _Potentilla norvegica_ grassy Places Croque'.

*_Potentilla palustris_ (L.) Scop. Hb.'_Comarum palustre_ Croque dry rocky places near the sea side also boggy places'. Cat. 23 '5 _Comarum palustre_ Dry Places by the sea side & Bogs Croque'. Solander MSS 12:215. Banks made a note in the McGill MS, p. 103, on the various habitats of this species in England and Newfoundland.

†*_Potentilla tridentata_ Ait. Hb.'_Potentilla_ Croque Conche etc. Dry rocks etc. June 1766'. Cat. 23 '4 _Potentilla_ Dry rocks Croque Conche etc'. Although Aiton (1789, 2:216, t.9), stated that _Potentilla tridentata_ was introduced from Newfoundland in 1766 by Benjamin Bewick, the engraving accompanying the description was based on a drawing by Ehret, pl. 51, made from a dried specimen brought back earlier (1766–7) by Banks. A specimen exactly corresponding to Ehret's drawing, which can be taken as the type of the species, no longer exists but Banks's two specimens from dry rocks at Croque and Conche evidently form part of the type collection.

†*_Dryas integrifolia_ Vahl. Hb.'Inglie in the mouth of the harbour J.B.' Cat. 23 '11 _Dryas_ Dry hill side Inglie'. This appears to be the type of _Dryas tenella_ Pursh since Pursh (1814:350) cites a specimen in Banks's herbarium and this MS name of _tenella_ appears in the annotated copy of the _Species Plantarum_ (1762, 1, pt. 2, facing p. 717), with a brief description of material from Newfoundland; also in the annotated copy of Reichard's 1779 edition of the _Systema Plantarum_ (2, facing p. 553) with 'J.B.'. after 'Newfoundland'. Pursh however gives the locality as the White Hills of New Hampshire (where this _Dryas_ has never been found), quoting Prof. Peck. This has been discussed by Fernald (1903: 281–3), who suggests that New Hampshire is a slip for Newfoundland, and by Britten (1904:84). Britten is right in stating that Banks did not visit the White Mountains of Newfoundland; Banks's own statement that his specimen was collected from the island at Inglie seems to have been overlooked. The type locality of Pursh's species should therefore be altered but since his name is a synonym of Vahl's _D. integrifolia_ based on material from Greenland it is of minor importance. (Pl. 53.)

Geum macrophyllum Willd. Hb.(1) 'Croque woods June 1766, *Geum*'; (2) '*Geum* Croque woods'; (3) 'America: Labrador 1763'. The third specimen is on a sheet with *Ranunculus pensylvanicus* L.f. Cat. 23 '2 *Geum urbanum* ?Woods Croque'. Banks also catalogued (p. 8a) '*Geum grandiflorum*'; this was perhaps a flourishing specimen of *G. macrophyllum* or a variety of *G. aleppicum*.

Geum rivale L. Hb. (1) 'Croque Woods Jos.Banks 1776', (2) 'Croque woods June 1766 No.1. Coast of Labrador No.2'. Cat. 23 '*Geum rivale* 2 Woods Croque'.

Rubus acaulis Michx. Ns. 76, 92. Hb.'Hare Bay, St. Julian's Island; Labrador (Mr. Molesworth). *Rubus arcticus*'. Cat. 23 '8 *Rubus arcticus* Bogs not too wet St. Julians Island Sea Beach Hare Bay'. Solander MSS 12:139.

Rubus chamaemorus L. Hb.'Newfoundland Labradore Everywhere on bogs'. Cat. 23 '12 *Rubus chamaemorus* Damp ground Everywhere'.

Rubus idaeus L. var. *strigosus* (Michx.) Maxim. Hb.'Croque'.

Rubus pubescens Raf. Diary 29, 32, ns. 63, 76. Hb.'Shady woods Croque St. Johns' Cat. 23 '13 *Rubus saxatilis* Shady woods Croque St. Johns'.

Alchemilla filicaulis Buser. N. 92. Hb.'*Alchemilla vulgaris* Newfoundland'. Cat. 7 '7 *Alchemilla vulgaris* under a shady rock St. Julian's Island'.

Sanguisorba canadensis L. Hb.'*Sanguisorba canadensis* Croque'. Cat. 7 '6 *Sanguisorba canadensis* Everywhere about Croque'.

Rosa blanda Ait. See *Rosa virginiana* Mill.

Rosa nitida Willd. Hb.'America Sept. Newfoundland 1776. Clinch Chirurgus'.

Rosa virginiana Miller. Hb.'Newfoundland near St. Johns'; in another hand '*Rosa blanda*'. This fruiting spray, pl. 52, for the following reasons must be considered as the type specimen of *Rosa blanda* Aiton. Banks, Solander and Dryander prepared the text of the *Hortus Kewensis* published in 1789 under the name of Aiton (Uggla 1959:90). The Solander MSS are in the Botanical Department of the British Museum; the description of *Rosa blanda* (12:83–6) is this: *blanda Rosa* germinibus globosis glabris, caulibus adultis pedunculisque laevibus inermibus. Habitat (α) in Terra nova (J. Banks) & β ad Sinum Hudsonis America septentrionalis. ♄.

α *Caules* adulti laeves, inermes; juniores seu primi aculeis rectis subreflexis tenuibus armati. *Rami* teretes, inermes, rubicundi laeves nitidi. *Folia* pinnata: *Foliola* plerumque septem oblonga, argute & subaequaliter serrata, glabra. *Petioli* glabri, plerumque una alterave spinula instructi. Pedunculi laeves, inermes. *Germen* globosum, laeve. Bacca' globosa', ruberrima', diametro semunculi; erectae.

This Latin description was published in the *Hortus Kewensis* (2:202) with the omission of 'laeves' in the phrase beginning with '*Rami*', the substitution of 'armati' for 'instructi', and the omission of the last two phrases beginning with '*Germen*' and 'Bacca'.

The description of the flowering spray from Hudson's Bay was never

331

published at all; it is on p. 86 of the Solander volume and ends with a note on the flower, 'Petala obcordata, rubra'.

This means that *Rosa blanda* Ait. 1789 is a synonym of *Rosa virginiana* Miller 1768, and that the name *blanda* can no longer be applied to the widely distributed North American species, so familiar under this name to botanists and horticulturists. The confusion in the early literature was considerable, and a note on this and the correct name for the rose commonly known as *blanda*, which is not known from Newfoundland, will appear elsewhere.

There is another Banksian sheet of *Rosa virginiana* consisting of three sprays of Newfoundland material grown from seed. The sheet has been trimmed and Banks's notes cut, but there remains:

'Hort. Dom Bishop 1774
Newfoundland Missa
Hort. Kew 1779
3 Hort. Gordon 1781'

In 1925 Dr. Erlanson determined one of these sprays as *Rosa palustris* Marsh., the others as *R. virginiana*. In 1965 Professor Rouleau confirmed the latter determinations but did not comment on the specimen of *R. palustris*.

*Prunus pensylvanica L. Diary 29. Hb.'St. Johns Woods above the Kings Brewhouse'. The specimen is defective.

LEGUMINOSAE

*Trifolium pratense L. Hb.'Croque' Cat. 33 '2 *Trifolium pratense* grassy Places Croque'. Naturalized from Europe.

*Trifolium repens L. Hb.'*Trifolium repens* Croque'. Cat. 33 '1 *Trifolium repens* grassy Places Croque'. Naturalized from Europe.

*Astragalus alpinus L. Hb.'*Astragalus alpinus* Spec in flower ill spread out'. Cat. 33 '4 *Astragalus alpinus* Sandy Beach Hare bay'.

*Oxytropis johannensis Fern. Hb.'Labrador Mr. Molesworth'.

*Oxytropis terrae-novae Fern. N. 100. Hb.'*Astragalus uralensis* To be laid on the Hudsons Bay specimen'. Cat. 33 '6 *Astragalus uralensis* Dry hill side Inglie'. There is also a Newfoundland sheet of *O. terrae-novae* from the Pallas herbarium. There is nothing to indicate that Banks sent it to the great German naturalist and traveller although they exchanged much material and corresponded for many years. Pallas was two years older than Banks and, like him, had friends and collectors in many countries. The paper carries the watermark 'Hendrik Van Lil', which I have not seen on any of the Banksian sheets.

Vicia cracca L. Cat. 33 '*Vicia cracca* grassy Places Croque'. No Banksian specimen of this naturalized plant has been found but it certainly occurs in Newfoundland (Lindroth:1957:197).

SYSTEMATIC LIST OF PLANTS COLLECTED

Lathyrus japonicus Willd. Hb.'Newfoundland J.B.; Labrador Soc. Un. Frat. Mauve blue flower'. Cat. *33* '*Pisum marinum* Sea Beach Every where'. Solander MSS 15:279.

Lathyrus palustris L. Hb.'Newfoundland'. Sol. MSS 15:293.

EMPETRACEAE

Empetrum nigrum L. Diary 21, 79, n. 38. Hb.(1) '*Empetrum* baccis rubris; Croque dry tops of hills June 1766'; (2) '*Empetrum nigrum* Newfoundland near St. Johns May 1766'. Cat. *43* '5 *Empetrum* Dry tops of hills'; 13a '*Empetrum* flore rubro'. Löve and Löve (1959) show that the European *Empetrum nigrum* L. with unisexual flowers has 2n=26 chromosomes; it occurs only in the southern parts of the boreal distributional area of the genus. The American taxon is a tetraploid with 2n=52 chromosomes, which is found mainly north of *E. nigrum* and in some mountains farther south. They believe that all North American material studied by them belongs to *E. hermaphroditum* (Lange) Hagerup. Banks's plant was dioecious and Professor Rouleau (personal communication) considers that Newfoundland plants are *E. nigrum* L.

AQUIFOLIACEAE

Nemopanthus mucronatus (L.) Baillon. Diary 31, ns. 74, 104. Cat. *15* '2 *Vaccinium mucronatum* Shady woods *Bellisle* Croque'. Trelease is usually regarded as the author of the combination *Nemopanthes mucronata* but he mentions it only as a provisional name under *N. canadensis* (*Trans. Acad. Sci. St. Louis,* 5:349; 1892) which he himself adopted. Article 34 of the *International Code of Botanical Nomenclature* (1966) invalidates a name not accepted by the publishing author and mentioned incidentally or cited as a synonym. The combination *Nemopanthus mucronatus* must accordingly be attributed to Baillon who published it in 1891 (as *Nemopanthes mucronata*) in his *Histoire des Plantes* (11:219–20). The publication dates of the parts of this work are given by M. J. van Steenis and W. T. Stearn (*Flora Malesiana* 1.4:clxviii; 1954). The *Revision of North American Ilicineae and Celastraceae* by Trelease, in which his note on *Nemopanthus canadensis* appears, was published in part 3 of the 5th volume of the *Trans. Acad. Sci. St. Louis*; this volume covers the transactions for the years 1888–91 but was not published until 1892. The date is printed on the cover. The paper was presented in 1889 and is headed *Contributions from the Shaw School of Botany No. 5*. It seems that reprints were issued before the date of publication of the *Transactions*, since Baillon cites Trelease's paper. Rafinesque's generic name *Nemopanthus* (1819) is a conserved name.

No specimen of *Nemopanthus mucronatus* collected by Banks has been found.

333

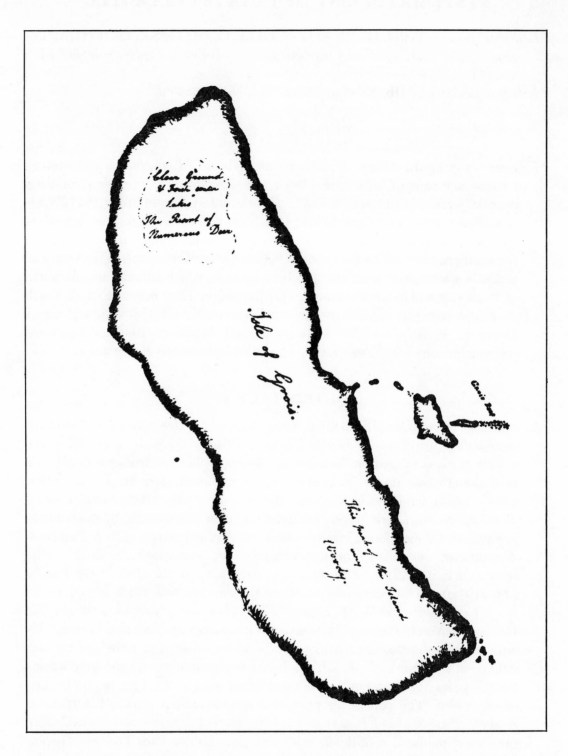

5. Isle of Groais (Grey Island), a detail from The Harbour of Croc, An accurate Survey, by John Willis, Master, H.M.S. *Thalia* May 1808

When he first noted the species in his diary he wrote '*Vaccinium album*' but then crossed out '*album*' and substituted '*mucronatum*', and this was the name he used in his catalogue. I do not know why he underlined some localities in his catalogue, but it seems possible that when he collected material from several localities, especially of shrubs of which he would need only one spray for his herbarium, he underlined the locality whence the selected material came. I am grateful to Professor Rouleau and to Mr. A. W. H. Damman for information on the present distribution of *N. mucronatus* in Newfoundland. It is common in the south but is only occasionally found in the Northern Peninsula, and the most northerly record is of a collection by Fernald in the St. John's Highlands, in the same latitude as Bell Island (Grey Islands). Mr. Damman has searched for it unsuccessfully in the Roddickton area, and Professor Rouleau and I also failed to find it during our brief visit to Croque in 1965. As it is highly localized in the north this is not surprising; apparently since Banks's day no botanist has made any extensive collection on Bell Island which is now rather barren. The neighbouring Groais or Grey Island was well wooded in 1808 (fig. 5) and Bell Island was probably similar in this respect. La Pylaie noted the abundance of willows on the islands when he visited them in 1816 and again a few years later but apparently did little collecting there (1826:530–4).

Vaccinium was a genus used in a wide sense in the eighteenth century but there is little doubt that Banks determined '*Vaccinium mucronatum*' correctly since that species has been underlined and deleted in his interleaved copy (*1*: 499) of the second edition of the *Species Plantarum* (1762–3). In Reichard's edition of the *Systema Plantarum* (1779, 2:166) after the again deleted description of this species Banks has written 'Non hujus generis, ob semina magna 4 vel 5, sed potius *Mespilus*'. Furthermore, on the Linnaean type of *V. mucronatum* Smith has written '*Mespilus*? Sr. J.B.'. In his article on *Vaccinium* in *Rees's Cyclopaedia* (1819) Smith states that *V. mucronatum* is not a *Vaccinium* but makes no statement about its correct systematic position.

VIOLACEAE

*Viola adunca Sm. var. *minor* (Hook.) Fern. (=*V. labradorica* Schrank). Diary 22, n. 43. Hb.'Newfoundland St. Johns; Labrador Williams'. Smith (1817–18) described *Viola adunca* in 1817 from material collected by Menzies in 1790–5; Schrank (1818) based his *V. labradorica* on specimens collected by the Danish missionary Kohlmeister (see under *Habenaria dilatata*). John Williams, who collected for Banks, was surgeon's mate on the *Antelope* in 1770; George Cartwright's brother John was first lieutenant and was probably responsible for Williams's leaving the navy and becoming clerk and surgeon at George's trading post in Labrador.

*_Viola cucullata_ Ait. Diary 22, n. 43. Hb.'Newfoundland'; (Solander's MS). Aiton (i.e. Solander) described this violet from cultivated material derived from the introduction of the species by Samuel Martin in 1772. Banks's specimens were not mentioned in the _Hortus Kewensis_ nor in Solander's MS description (6:631–2).

*_Viola macloskeyi_ Lloyd subsp. _pallens_ (Gingins ex Banks) M. S. Baker. Hb. 'Labrador Williams. Kamschatka Dav. Nelson'. The sheet contains 3 Labrador specimens and four from Kamschatka. Both sets were cited by Gingins in DeCandolle (1824, 1:295) and are hence the type collection. Brainerd (1905: 246) stated that Banks collected the Labrador specimens but they were actually sent to him by John Williams (see _Viola adunca_). Fernald (1949:53) discusses the characters of this violet. Professor Rouleau (personal communication) considers that it should be united with _V. blanda_ Willd. in which case _V. blanda_ would be the correct name. Brainerd (_loc. cit._) discussed this in 1905 and gave reasons for considering the species distinct from each other.

Viola palustris L. There is no Banksian specimen of this violet but it occurs in Labrador and Banks catalogued it (p. 37) from Whale Island.

ELEAGNACEAE

†*_Shepherdia canadensis_ (L.) Nutt. Diary 37. Hb.'Croque'. Ehret's plate 54, '_Hippophae_ Chatteaux'.

ONAGRACEAE

*_Epilobium angustifolium_ L. (=_Chamaenerion angustifolium_ (L.) Scop.) Diary 40. Hb.'_Epilobium angustifolium_ Newfoundland'.

*_Epilobium glandulosum_ Lehm. Hb.'_Epilobium_ Croque'.

*_Epilobium hornemanni_ Reichenb. Hb.'_Epilobium montanum_ Croque'. Cat. 15 '10 _Epilobium_ Damp Rock'. This is the typical habitat of this species.

†*_Epilobium latifolium_ L. Hb.'Nfld Island of Bellisle on damp rocks near the Sea July 1766'. Cat. 15 '1 _Epilobium latifolium_ Damp rock Bellisle'. There is also a sheet with three specimens from the Labrador Moravians which was acquired by Banks from Herb. Dickson. Ehret's plate depicts the Bell Island specimens which have been regarded as the type material of _Chamaenerium halimifolium_ Salisb. This is not correct. Salisbury's description in _The Paradisus Londinensis_ (1805, 1: no. 58) is based on material supplied by the Hon. Charles Greville, but he refers to Banks's having found it on Bell Island. The accompanying plate by W. Hooker (dated 1807) is not taken from Ehret's illustration (pl. 27).

*_Circaea alpina_ L. Hb.'_Circaea alpina_ Croque'. Cat. 3 '2 _Circaea lutetiana_ shady places Croque'.

Tuſſilago palmata vol. 3. pag. 188.

G. D. Ehret
pinxit
1767

Pl. IX *Petasites palmatus*
G. D. Ehret

SYSTEMATIC LIST OF PLANTS COLLECTED

HALORAGACEAE

Myriophyllum alterniflorum DC. Hb.'Newfoundland'. Cat. 41 '5 *Myriophyllum spicatum* Rocky Pools Croque'. *M. spicatum* L. is closely allied to *M. exalbescens* Fern. and differs from *M. alterniflorum* in having much longer leaves as well as in other characters. There is nothing, however, in the Solander MSS to suggest that Banks had any Newfoundland species of the genus other than *M. alterniflorum*.

HIPPURIDACEAE

Hippuris tetraphylla L. Hb.'*Elatine* [erased almost completely] Small muddy pools between Chatteaux and Bad Bay. Sep^tr 1766'. Cat. 2 '1 *Hippuris* in small muddy Pools between Chatteaux and Bad Bay'; the same entry occurs on page 1a but Banks has crossed out '*Hippuris*' and written '*Elatine* v.' beneath it.

ARALIACEAE

Aralia nudicaulis L. Hb.'*Aralia nudicaulis* Newfoundland Hare Bay Bellisle, Shady places'. Cat. 9 '3 *Aralia* shady places Bellisle Hare Bay'. Under Pentandria 3 in the McGill MS (p. 97) Banks noted correctly the medical use of the roots of this species.

UMBELLIFERAE

Ligusticum scothicum L. Hb.'*Ligusticum scoticum* Newfoundland Croque near the sea side'. Cat. 4a (p. 298) '*Ligusticum scoticum*'.

Conioselinum chinense (L.) B.S.P. Hb.'*Ligusticum* Croque'. The *Pimpinella* recorded by Banks on p. 5a (p. 298) of his catalogue may be referable to this species.

Angelica lucida L. (=*Coelopleuron lucidum* (L.) Fern.) Hb.(1) '*Ligusticum* Croque'; (2) '*Angelica archangelica* Newfoundland Croque, Labradore Chatteaux'. Cat. 9 '15 *Angelica archangelica* see [*sic*] side'. I am indebted to Professor Constance for kindly determining these two sheets of specimens for me. Banks's *Angelica sylvestris*, cat. 9, is probably referable to this species.

Heracleum maximum Bartram. Hb.'Newfoundland'. Cat. 9 '6 *Heracleum ? spondilium* Croque'. *H. spondilium* is a naturalized species from Eurasia. *H. maximum* was briefly described by Bartram in 1791.

CORNACEAE

Chamaepericlymenum canadense (L.) Aschers. & Graebn. (=*Cornus canadensis* L.). Hb.'*Cornus canadensis* hill sides Everywhere'. Solander MSS 4:293; McGill MS p. 45.

337

Chamaepericlymenum suecicum (L.) Aschers & Graebn. (=*Cornus suecica* L.). Diary 29. Hb.'*Cornus* St. Johns dry places very near the sea MSS'. Cat. 7 '10 *Cornus* near the Edge of the sea in several places Croque'. Solander MSS 4:289, 'Terra nova J. Banks. in Terra Labrador'. See also McGill MS p. 95.

Thelycrania sericea (L.) Dandy (=*Cornus stolonifera* Michx.). Hb.'Newfoundland Croque'. Cat. 7 '4 *Cornus sanguinea* Woods Croque'.

PYROLACEAE

Moneses uniflora (L.) A.Gray. Hb.(1) 'Croque under a shady rock in the upper side of the harbour of the N [?] Shores'. (2) 'Labrador', Banks's writing is very faint. Cat. 19 '9 *Pyrola uniflora* very shady Places Croque'.

Pyrola asarifolia Michx. Cat. 17a '*Asarum* folia'. No specimen has been found but see n. 137.

Pyrola minor L. Hb.(1) '*Pyrola rotundifolia* Croque Woods'. (2) *Pyrola* Labrador Chatteaux damp grassy places'. Cat. 19 '4 *Pyrola rotundifolia* Woods Croque'.

Pyrola secunda L. Hb.'*Pyrola secunda* Croque Hare Bay'. Cat. 19 '2 *Pyrola secunda* shady woods Croque Hare Bay'.

Monotropa uniflora L. Cat. 19 '*Monotropa uniflora* shady woods Conche'. The section of the British Museum herbarium containing the Pyrolaceae suffered severe war damage and no Banksian specimen of *M. uniflora* has been found; there is no record of any such specimen in any of the Solander MSS.

ERICACEAE

✝*Ledum groenlandicum* Oeder. Hb.'*Ledum latifolium* Newfoundland St. Johns Croque etc.' One of these specimens was painted by Ehret, pl. 55; 'Chatteaux' is written on the drawing. Solander MSS 10:561 '*Ledum latifolium* Habitat in Terra Labrador, Newfoundland Etc.' Oeder described this plant in 1771; in 1788 [1789] (2:308) Jacquin published another account of it under the name *Ledum latifolium*, using cultivated material of unknown origin sent to him from England under that name. We do not know whether it originated from the plants introduced by Bennett (Aiton 1789, 2:64) in 1763, or by Banks in 1767. William Bennett had a nursery garden of some note in Whitechapel and imported many exotic plants (Roberts, *Gardeners' Chronicle* 1918, pt. 2: 245–6); he may have supplied Banks with the material from Labrador dated 1763.

✝*Rhododendron canadense* (L.) Torr. Hb.'Newfoundland Inglie St. Johns etc. on hillsides *Rhodora*'. Cat. 17a '*Rhododendrum folia*'. Aiton (1789, 2:66) records that Banks introduced this species into England in 1767. L'Héritier (1791:141) described this species and published Redouté's drawing of one of Banks's specimens. Ehret had already painted it, pl. 34.

Rhododendron lapponicum (L.) Wahlenb. Hb.[Not Banks's MS] 'America Labrador'. There is a single specimen from Labrador on an old Banksian sheet but the other specimens are marked Herb. Pallas and Herb. Hudson and I am doubtful about its belonging to this series. It is not recorded from Newfoundland or Labrador in the Solander MSS.

Loiseleuria procumbens (L.) Desv. Hb.'*Azalea procumbens* Croque'. Cat. 9 '10 *Azalea procumbens* Dry sandy hillsides'.

Kalmia angustifolia L. Diary 33, n. 80. Hb.'Hillsides Croque'. Cat. 19 '8 *Kalmia angustifolia* Hillsides about Croque'.

✝*Kalmia polifolia* Wangenheim (=*K. glauca* Ait.). Hb.'Croque damp places'. Cat. 19 '18 *Kalmia* Dampish places not too wet Croque'. Ehret's painting was reproduced in the *Hortus Kewensis* (2:64), and the specimen is the type of Aiton's species; the published description is an exact copy of Solander's account (MSS 10:555). Another illustration of this *Kalmia* appeared in the *Botanical Magazine*, pl. 177, 1791–6, but it was not copied from Ehret's plate. Wangenheim's name was published in 1788; he says that this species was first grown in an English garden and then in Holland, but that he based his description on material from Nova Scotia. Banks introduced this *Kalmia* into Kew Gardens in 1767; it was unknown in English gardens before then. (Pl. 57.)

Phyllodoce caerulea (L.) Bab. Cat. 19 '20 *Andromeda caerulea* Shady Rocks'.

Andromeda glaucophylla Link. Diary 30, ns. 69, 136. Cat. 19 '17 *Andromeda* Damp places & bogs, Croque, Chatteaux'. Solander MSS 10:584. Most of the *Andromeda* material in the British Museum was lost during the second world war.

Cassandra calyculata (L.) D.Don. Diary 19, n. 31. Cat. 19? '17 *Andromeda* dry hill sides Every where'. Banks identified *Andromeda calyculata* at St. John's on 15 May but he did not catalogue this species. In their notes both Solander (MSS 10:633–6) and Aiton (1789, 2:70) state that var. *latifolia* occurs in Newfoundland but do not cite this locality for *angustifolia*. It may therefore be assumed that the material from St. John's was var. *latifolia*.

✝*Gaultheria hispidula* (L.) Bigel. Diary 24, n. 53, Hb.'Newfoundland shady places everywhere'. Ehret pl. 58. Solander MSS 9:595 'Newfoundland in umbrosis: J. Banks. *Arbutus thymifolius*'.

Arctostaphylos uva-ursi (L.) Spreng. Diary 37. Cat. 19 '10 *Arbutus uva ursi* Inglie'.

Vaccinium angustifolium Ait. Diary 20. Hb.'Newfoundland, on sides of hills much exposed to sun [3 specimens]; Amer. Sept. Terra Labrador [1 specimen].' These specimens are not the type, since Aiton (1789, 2:11) cites material introduced about 1776 by Benjamin Bewick, and a Bewick specimen dated 1777 is still in the British Museum. It is possible that Banks's *Vaccinium myrtillus* from a 'Dry place, Croque' (Cat. 15) is referable to this species.

Vaccinium cespitosum Michx. Hb.'*Vaccinium incarnatum* Croque rare, Terra Labrador'. Cat. 15? '6 *Vaccinium* sides of dryest rocks'. Solander MSS 9:589.

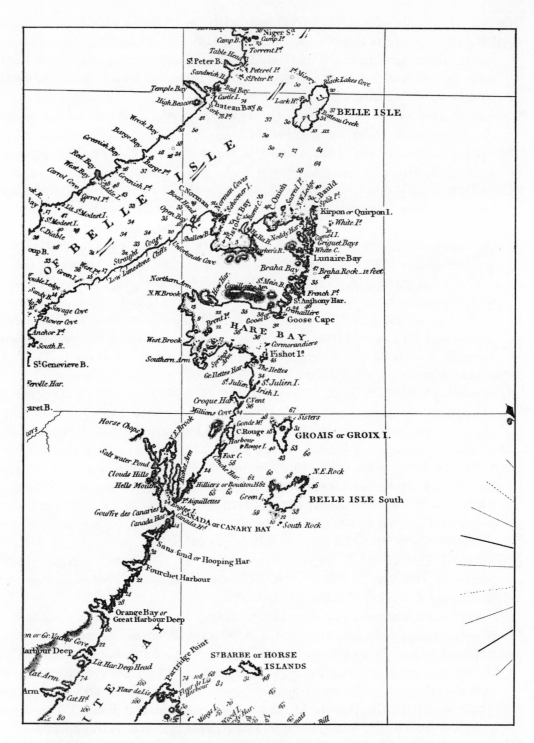

6. Detail from a map of Newfoundland by Findlay and Purdy, 1844, showing The Ilettes, SW of Fishot Island at the southern part of the entrance to Hare Bay

340

†*_Vaccinium macrocarpon_ Ait. Hb.'Newfoundland Bay of Isles'. Banks is probably referring to an island in what is now known as Great Islet Harbour, between St. Julian's Island and Hare Bay, where he collected plants and made notes on the nesting eider ducks. The islands in Great Islet Harbour were called Les Islettes in S. Bellin's chart of 1767, and corrupted to The Illettes in the chart by John Purdy and A. G. Findlay published in 1844 (see fig. 6). The group is often left unnamed in recent maps. Ehret's pl. 36 bears the note 'From a dry specimen brought from Newfoundland St. John's'. Solander's description is missing from vol. 9 of his MSS. Aiton's description was based on material (still in the British Museum) from James Gordon as well as on Ehret's plate so that Banks's specimens are not the type collection. This is a commercial cranberry and Smith in _Rees's Cyclopaedia_ says, 'The best method of having American Cranberries in Europe is by cultivation in an artificial bog with great plenty of water, as first contrived by Sir Joseph Banks'. See also p. 69.

*_Vaccinium oxycoccus_ L. Diary 33. Hb.'_Vaccinium oxycoccus_ Croque Boggy ground'. Cat. 15 '8 _Vaccinium oxycoccus_ Bogs'.

*_Vaccinium uliginosum_ L. Diary 33. Hb.'_Vaccinium uliginosum_ Croque'. Cat. 15 '7 _Vaccinium uliginosum_ High Hills on Dry Spotts'. Solander MSS 9:529 'Habitat in Terra Labrador'. No Labrador specimen has been found in the herbarium.

†*_Vaccinium ovalifolium_ Smith. Hb.'_Vaccinium_ Croque'. There are fruiting and flowering specimens and both were painted by Ehret, pl. 39.

*_Vaccinium vitis-idaea_ L. Hb.'Labrador Mr. Molesworth'. Banks collected seven species of _Vaccinium_ but catalogued only five including '_Vaccinium mucronatum_' which is referable to _Nemopanthus mucronatus_ (L.) Baillon, q.v.

DIAPENSIACEAE

Diapensia lapponica L. Diary 35. Cat. 9 '14 _Diapensia lapponica_ Barren and sultry hill tops'. Banks's Newfoundland specimen has not been located; it is mentioned in R. A. Salisbury's _Paradisus Londinensis_, pl. 104 (1808). There is a La Pylaie specimen in the British Museum labelled 'Terre neuve 1828'.

PRIMULACEAE

*_Primula laurentiana_ Fern. Diary 32, n. 77. Hb.'Bogs near Croque'. Cat. 9 '5 _Primula farinosa_ Bogs Croque'. In the McGill MS, p. 97, Banks made a note on the colour of his _Primula farinosa_ stating that it varied from white to rich purple, both forms occurring together. His specimens were determined by Fernald as _P. laurentiana_ and the white form of _P. mistassinica_ q.v.

*_Primula mistassinica_ Michx. forma _leucantha_ Fern. See notes on _P. laurentiana_.

*_Trientalis borealis_ Raf. Diary 29, n. 62. Hb.'Croque St. Johns Woods & shady places. _Trientalis_'. Cat. 6a '_Trientalis_ Woods St. Johns Croque'.

GENTIANACEAE

✝*Lomatogonium rotatum* (L.) Fries. Hb.(1) '*Swertia* Labrador Chatteaux'; (2) 'Labrador Chatteaux damp Soil *Swertia*'. Cat. 9 '2 *Swertia* Damp bog Chatteaux Damp rock Bellisle'. Ehret's painting, pl. 56, is marked 'Chatteaux'. The translation of Banks's note on this species in the McGill MS, p. 97, is 'In a rich soil it has many branches and is dense with flowers; in a sandy soil, however, there is only one terminal corolla, sometimes divided into four, and sometimes into five parts'. The first sheet consists of tiny plants which are the type material of *Swertia pusilla* Pursh. Pursh stated (1814:101) that the Banksian specimens from Labrador agreed in every respect with the New Hampshire plants but Fernald (1947:153–4) has pointed out that this species has never been recorded from New Hampshire, and added that unfortunately Pursh suffered from dipsomania so that his localities cannot always be regarded as reliable. Cf. the notes on *Dryas integrifolia*, p. 330.

✝*Halenia deflexa* (Sm.) Griseb. Diary 31. Hb.'*Swertia corniculata*? Newfoundland Croque Labrador Chatteaux'. Cat. 9 '1 *Swertia corniculata* Grassy Places Croque & Chatteaux'. Ehret painted a Croque specimen, pl. 35. Smith described this species from notes by Linnaeus on material collected in North America by Kalm. He states that he himself did not examine a specimen.

Menyanthes trifoliata L. var. *minor* Raf. Cat. 9 '17 *Menianthes trifolium* bogs'. No other record of Banks's Newfoundland-Labrador material has been found.

BORAGINACEAE

Mertensia maritima (L.) S. F. Gray. Hb.'*Pulmonaria maritima* Sea beach near Croque; Terra Labrador'. Cat. 9 '4 *Pulmonaria maritima* Sea beach Croque'. Solander MSS 4:629 cites Labrador only.

LABIATAE

Galeopsis tetrahit L. var. *bifida* (Boenn.) Lej. & Court. Hb.'*Galeopsis tetrahit* Croque'. Cat. 27 '4 *Galeopsis tetrahit* Croque'. This is a naturalized Eurasian species.

Satureja calamintha (L.) Scheele. Hb.'*Melissa calamintha* Croque'. This is a naturalized Eurasian species.

?*Thymus pulegioides* L. Cat. 9a '*Thymus*'. This appears to be the only mention of this species in the Banksian MSS. There is an old sheet marked by Banks 'Amer. Sept. *Thymus*'. It is a naturalized European species and has been recorded in Quebec and elsewhere but I have found no other Newfoundland record. Reasons for using the above name are given by N. Roussine (1961) who considers that previous North American records of *T. serpyllum* L. are erroneous, and that *T. pulegioides* is the species commonly found there.

SCROPHULARIACEAE

*Veronica serpyllifolia L. Hb.'*Veronica serpyllifolia* Croque'. Cat. 1 '*Veronica serpyllifolia* St. Johns Conche Croque'. This is another naturalized species from Europe.

*Castilleja septentrionalis Lindl. Hb.'*Bartsia* Newfoundland Croque Shady woods June 1766; Labrador'. Cat. 9a '*Bartsia*'. Solander MSS 13:233–4 gives only Labrador, but there are six specimens from Croque.

*Euphrasia disjuncta Fern. & Wieg. Hb.'*Euphrasia officinalis* Newfoundland'. Cat. 9a '*Euphrasia*'.

*Rhinanthus minor L. (=*Rhinanthus crista-galli* L. *pro parte*). Linnaeus published *Rhinanthus minor* in the second edition of his dissertation on hybrid plants (*Amoenitates Academicae* 1756, 3:54). Hb.'*Rhinanthus crista galli* Newfoundland Croque Labrador Chatteaux dry places'. Cat. 27 '1 *Rhinanthus crista galli* Grassy Places Croque Chatteaux'.

*Pedicularis labradorica Wirsing. There is a Banksian sheet of specimens of this *Pedicularis*; the first series is marked 'America Septentrionalis: Labrador, Soc. Unit. Fratrum'. The second is of the same origin but with 'Okkap', after 'Labrador', and the date 1778. Banks has written *Pedicularis humilis* on the front of the sheet; see also Solander MSS 13:255. Wirsing was a Nuremberg engraver; most of the plates in the *Eclogae Botanicae* of 1778, where he published *Pedicularis labradorica*, were derived from Buc'holz but Wirsing states that this *Pedicularis* is an addition which he has received from Labrador. It may have come from Dr. Trew of Nuremburg, a remarkable character, a doctor, naturalist, and patron of the arts (Stearn 1961:lxxix). It was he who taught Ehret the elements of botany, and helped him to become one of the foremost botanical illustrators of the age. When Ehret moved to London he used to send Trew plants, and also illustrations. He was singularly well placed to do this since he not only worked for Banks but also married Phillip Miller's sister and had therefore a close connection with the Chelsea Physic Garden, of which Miller was curator. It is probable that Ehret was responsible for sending some duplicate material of this *Pedicularis* to Trew; he may even have sent a sketch from which Wirsing made the engraving.

OROBANCHACEAE

*Orobanche terrae-novae Fern. Hb.'*Orobanche uniflora* Newfoundland Croque Very shady woods'. Cat. 27 '3 *Orobanche uniflora* woods Croque'. *O. terrae-novae* is very close to *O. uniflora* L.

SYSTEMATIC LIST OF PLANTS COLLECTED

LENTIBULARIACEAE

Utricularia intermedia Hayne. Hb.'*Utricularia gibba*? Newfoundland'. Cat. 3 '4 *Utricularia* Bogs Every where about Croque'.

Pinguicula vulgaris L. Hb.'Newfoundland J.B.'. Cat. 3 '3 *Pinguicula vulgaris* Bogs & damp Rocks Croque'. Solander MSS 1:683.

PLANTAGINACEAE

Plantago juncoides Lam. var. *decipens* (Barnéoud) Fern. Hb.'Labrador Chatteaux Bogs between Pitts harbour & Bad bay. Sep^tr 1766'. Cat. 7 '1 *Plantago loeflingii*? Bogs about Chatteaux'.

Plantago oliganthos Roem. & Schult. var. *fallax* Fern. Hb.'Croque near the sea at the top of the harbour'. Cat. 7 '3 *Plantago maritima* Rocks at High water mark Croque'. These species of *Plantago* were determined by Fernald (ph. Tetrandria). Banks discussed them in the McGill MS, p. 95; the late Mr. A. C. Townsend translated his notes for me as follows: That species of *Plantago*, which in England we call *P. Loeflingii*, certainly grows in damp marshlands round Chatteaux, although I am in considerable doubt as to whether it really is *P. Loeflingii*. No. 3 *P. maritima*. This is very common among the rock-fissures near the sea, the leaves are semi-cylindrical; it is sometimes found in mud and shifting sand with leaves a little wider, ? again in wet marshes with broad leaves. The leaves of *Loeflingii* are often tinged with red spots in both this and the other species (if they are not one and the same plant), and not in any other species of *Plantago* that I have seen. *P. Loeflingii* grows in Spain, at the boundaries of fields. In England, and in Labrador, it is found in the marshes near the sea, where it is washed by the highest tides.

RUBIACEAE

Galium labradoricum Wieg. Hb.'*Galium palustre* Croque'. Cat. 7 '5 *Galium palustre*'.

Galium triflorum Michx. Hb.'*Galium* Croque Shady places'. Cat. 7 '2 *Galium* Shady Places Croque'.

CAPRIFOLIACEAE

Lonicera villosa (Michx.) Roem. & Schult. Diary 30. This honeysuckle is not mentioned in the Solander MSS and I have found no other record of Banks's specimen from St. John's. Solander (MSS 5:641) records *L. caerulea* L. from Labrador but gives no information about the collector; no Banksian specimen from either Newfoundland or Labrador has been found. See Fernald 1925(1): 1–11 for notes on these species.

Pl. X Rough-legged Hawk, *Buteo lagopus sanctijohannis*
Peter Paillou

Linnaea borealis L. Hb., four gatherings: 'Newfoundland; Croque; Labrador Chatteaux; Labrador Mr. Molesworth'. Cat. 27 '2 *Linnaea borealis* shady Places Croque Chatteaux'.

Viburnum edule (Michx.) Raf. Diary 30. Hb.'*Viburnum acerifolium* woods above the hospital'. Cat. 17a '*Viburnum acerifolium*'.

VALERIANACEAE

Valeriana dioica L. subsp. *sylvatica* (Sol. ex Richards.) F. G. Meyer. Hb.'Croque'. Cat. 3 '5 *Valeriana phu?* Damp wood Croque'. Richardson (1823:730) when publishing the binomial *Valeriana sylvatica* 'MS Herb. Banks', stated that specimens of this plant were brought back from Newfoundland by Banks in 1781, and were preserved in his herbarium under the name given. Richardson made a mistake in the date, confusing a specimen brought back from Fort Albany, Hudson's Bay, by Hutchinson in 1781 with Banks's Croque specimen of 1766. Meyer (1951) selected Richardson's material from the Clearwater River, Alberta ($56\frac{1}{2}°$ N., 110°–111° W.), collected on 10 July 1820, as the lectotype; he pointed out that the oldest North American material in England is the Hudson's Bay specimen collected by Tilden in 1728, now in the Sherardian Herbarium at Oxford. If Banks's plant is maintained as a species distinct from *V. dioica* the correct name will be *V. septentrionalis* Rydb. (1900), the name *V. sylvatica* Solander (1823) being a later homonym of *V. sylvatica* F. W. Schmidt (1795). Solander's description is in his bound MSS, 2:171.

CAMPANULACEAE

Campanula rotundifolia L. Hb.'*C. rotundifolia* Newfoundland'. Cat. 9 '9 *Campanula rotundifolia* Rocks Croque'.

Lobelia dortmanna L. Hb.'Newfoundland'. Cat. 37 '2 *Lobelia dortmanna* Rocky Ponds Conche'.

COMPOSITAE

Solidago macrophylla Pursh. This plant was not actually collected by Banks but he acquired it from Dr. Bewick who grew it from seed sent from Newfoundland. Pursh (1814:542) stated that his description was taken from a Banks MS, presumably from the rather different account by Solander (MSS 17:175–6) of *Aster macrophyllus*, a name which was written over '*Solidago grandiflora*'; Pursh combined the names and pointed out that this species is intermediate between the two genera. His account agrees in essentials with Solander's but is not a copy of it; I have searched in vain for another version which might be closer in style and content. On p. 175 Solander gave the habitat as Newfoundland; on p. 176 he wrote that the specimen came from Dr. Bewick's garden in 1778, and that it was grown from seed from Newfoundland. There is a sheet which corresponds exactly to this account; both Solander's names, '*Aster macrophyllus* (not Aiton)' and '*Solidago grandiflora*' are on the *recto*; the note on the verso is 'Hort Dni. Bewick; semina e Newfoundland missa'. The writing is, I think, Dryander's. It would appear that this material is Pursh's type specimen, see pl. 59.

Asa Gray saw this sheet and identified it as *Solidago thyrsoidea* E. Meyer; the sheet is inscribed and initialled by him but it looks as though he must have forgotten about it since in his 'Studies of *Aster* and *Solidago* in the Older Herbaria' (1882:163–99) he does not mention it, although he identifies (p. 187) *S. macrophylla* Pursh with a sheet of *S. thyrsoidea* Meyer collected by 'Haltgren' or 'Halbgren' in 1779 from Bique Island in the Gulf of St. Lawrence; that sheet is still in the British Museum, with another, even earlier, from Hudson's Bay, 1773. These sheets are both labelled *Solidago pratensis*, an unpublished name from the Solander MSS 17: 219–221, where he described not *Solidago* but *Aster pratensis* from Hudson's Bay; his *S. pratensis*, p. 317, is said to come from China and Japan. Asa Gray saw the Hudson's Bay material too, and determined it as *S. thyrsoidea*.

Fernald (1906:227–8) briefly discusses the history of *S. macrophylla*, and quotes Gray (1882:187); he assumes that the type is not extant and proceeds to describe the variety which now bears his name. Var. *thyrsoidea* is however identical with the original type material and this taxon must therefore bear the name var. *macrophylla*. Consequently a new varietal epithet is needed for the plant with narrower bracts and oblong heads which is characteristic of lowlands and southern regions. Professor Rouleau (personal communication) considers that the apparent differences between the two extremes are due to ecological variants; in the field many intergradient forms occur.

*Solidago multiradiata Ait. Hb.'Labrador 1765'. The description of this species in the *Hortus Kewensis* (1789, 3:218) is copied from Solander's notes (MSS 17:325–6) on the Labrador specimens in Banks's herbarium. These four specimens, dated 1765, are the type specimens, probably acquired by Banks from the Moravian missionary Schloezer (p. 193). The date is too early for them to have been collected by Kohlmeister as Hooker suggested (1829–40, 2:5). The headquarters of the Moravians from 1750 to 1774 were in Cheyne Walk in Chelsea; as noted before, Banks lived nearby in Paradise Walk.

*Solidago purshii Porter = *Solidago humilis* Banks ex Pursh (1814) non Miller (1768). Hb.'Newfoundland J. B. 'Solander's MS notes (17:321) on this species, citing Banks's Newfoundland plant and one from Hudson's Bay, were copied by Pursh (1814:543) who, however, gives only Canada as the habitat, although he states that he saw Banks's specimens. *S. humilis* is untenable (Fernald 1908:88–91; 1949:93–4). Porter (1894:310–11) defined his species, *S. purshii*, merely by citing the synonym *S. humilis* Pursh; Banks's plant was Pursh's type and therefore becomes Porter's. Fernald published a photograph of this plant in 1949 (*loc. cit.*).

*Aster puniceus L. Hb.'*Aster* Newfoundland J.B.'. There are 3 specimens. Banks catalogued only one '*Aster* warm places' on p. 37. Solander MSS 17: 193.

*Aster radula Ait. var. *strictus* (Pursh) Gray. Hb.'Terra nova *Aster nigridus*'. Banks's *A. nigridus* is only just decipherable. Solander (MSS 17:185–6) in his unpublished description of *Aster strictus* gives as habitat 'Terra nova Americae Septentrionalis. J. Banks. prope Croque, prope rivulos'. Pursh (1814:556) uses Solander's name but did not make an exact copy of the MS description; he cited specimens from Labrador, Hudson's Bay and mountains in Pennsylvania, not from Newfoundland.

**Erigeron hyssopifolius* Michx. Hb.'*Aster graminifolius* Newfoundland near Croque J. Banks'. Cat. 37 '4 *Erigeron*, Rocks in damp places Croque'. Solander MSS 17:23. Pursh (1814:545) based his *Aster graminifolius* on Solander's notes on material from Newfoundland and Hudson's Bay but cites only the Hudson's Bay specimens which are therefore to be regarded as the types. Banks's Croque specimens on the same sheet are not type material.

?*Erigeron philadelphicus* L. Diary 35, n. 89. Cat. 37 '6 *Erigeron philadelphicum* Rocks by the side of a Brook Croque'. There is no herbarium material nor is Newfoundland mentioned by Solander (MSS 16:585) who records only Hudson's Bay as the habitat of this species and states (p. 588) that it is very distinct.

**Antennaria neodioica* Greene. Diary 30. Hb.'Nfland upon dry hills above Kitty witty Pond St. Johns'.

**Achillea millefolium* L. Hb.'Croque'. Cat. 37 '1 *Achillea millefolium* grassy Places Croque'. This European species has been naturalized and is widely distributed in North America. It is one of the plants collected by Lindroth (1957:197) from the areas on the south coast of England where the Newfoundland ships used to load their ballast.

*Anthemis cotula L. Hb.'Newfoundland'. This is another naturalized species; it is among those in Lindroth's lists.

**Petastites frigidus* (L.) Fries. Hb.'America septentrionalis: Labrador. 1765. Soc. unit. Frat.'. This writing is not Banks's.

†**Petasites palmatus* (Ait.) A. Gray. Diary 33, n. 79. Hb.'Croque'. Cat. 37 '5 *Tussilago* Wood rather damp Croque'. Solander MSS 16:628. Ehret's painting pl. IX, of Banks's plant which is the type, is marked 'Croque'; it was reproduced by Aiton (1789, 3: facing p. 188). Croque is therefore the type locality. Aiton mentions Labrador as well as Newfoundland as the habitat but

there is no Banksian material of *P. palmatus* from Labrador; Aiton (i.e. Solander) probably made an error in determining the Moravians' specimen of *P. frigidus*, which is not mentioned in the Solander MSS, and assumed that both specimens were *P. palmatus*.

Senecio jacobaea L. Hb. 'Croque'. Cat. 37 '3 *Jacobaea* Bogs Croque'. This European plant has become widely naturalized in maritime regions of eastern North America. Lindroth (1957:197) found it in three of the ballast areas he searched in south west England.

Senecio pauperculus Michx. Hb. 'Croque'. Someone has written '*Senecio strictus*' on this sheet and, below, '*gracilis* Pursh'. Solander (MSS 16:715) in describing *S. strictus* refers to material collected by Bartram; Pursh (1814:529) gives Pennsylvania as the habitat, citing Solander's name *S. strictus*. Banks's Newfoundland specimen is therefore not the type of *S. gracilis* Pursh.

†*Senecio pseudo-arnica* Less. Hb.(1) 'Labrador Bad Bay on the sea beach'; (2) 'Labrador Mr. Williams; Labrador, Soc. Unit. Frat. 1766'. Solander (MSS 17:405) gives the following note: 'Habitat in Terra Labrador, america Septentrionalis, in Hancock's Inlet (55°, 56′ N) et in insulis & in continento. (Soc. Unit. Fratr. 1766)'. Ehret's painting, pl. IV, is marked 'Chatteaux'. Pursh (1814:528) cited Banks's specimen and used Solander's MS name *Arnica maritima*.

The specimen dated 1766 from Hancock's Inlet was probably collected by Schloezer in 1765 (pp. 214–8, 225–6) and handed to Banks in 1766.

Cirsium arvense (L.) Scop. Hb. 'Newfoundland Croque'. This is another naturalized European species which Lindroth has recorded from various sources of ballast in south west England.

Cirsium muticum Michx. Hb. 'Croque'.

Centaurea nigra L. Hb. 'Newfoundland'.

Lactuca biennis (Moench) Fern. Hb. 'Croque'. The specimen is defective.

Prenanthes trifolia (Cass.) Fern. Hb. 'Croque'.

Hieracium canadense Michx. Hb. '*Hieracium kalmii*' [not Banks's MS], 'Newfoundland Croque'. Banks's specimen was determined for me by Dr. C. West, a specialist in this genus. He has compared the Linnaean type of *H. kalmii* with the series of *H. canadense* in the British Museum and considers that they are entirely distinct. See also Lepage (1960:59–107) who has reviewed these two species at considerable length.

17

Banks's zoological manuscripts:
the McGill MS
with supplementary sheets from
the British Museum
(Natural History)

THE McGill MS consists of four series of loose sheets on which Banks wrote his field notes in Newfoundland and Labrador. The paper is smooth laid with chain lines half an inch apart but no watermark. This type of paper was invented by Baskerville of Birmingham in 1760, the smooth surface being obtained by an ironing process. The largest sheets used by Banks were 37 × 23·8 cm in size; these were folded and cut in various ways to make four separate series.

The first and longest series comprises forty-three sheets 11·9 cm high by 18·6 cm wide; Banks's zoological notes are written on the rectos, with information on localities, and sometimes other matters, on the versos. The first sheet differs: on the recto he has written 'Newfoundland Plants and Birds' with 'Chatteaux Sep^tr 14 1766' on the top left-hand corner; this is probably the date of capture of his specimen of *Mergus serrator* described on the verso.

The second series is a sewn booklet of four sheets, the same size as the first but stitched so that the vertical measurement is the greater. This little series contains brief descriptions of birds, written for the most part in English; they are probably rough jottings made by Banks before he seriously set to work on the detailed scientific descriptions forming the first series.

The third series consists of five sheets 23·8 cm high and 37 cm wide which have been folded over to form double sheets, with botanical notes on the first recto of each. It is obvious from the title, and from the fact that the notes relate to only five out of the twenty-five Linnaean classes represented in his catalogue, that most of the botanical descriptive notes are missing. The surviving ones are not printed here as part of this MS, but as a supplement to Banks's plant catalogue in the British Museum, to which they directly refer.

The fourth series consists of only two sheets 23·8 × 18·5 cm on which Banks has written an incomplete list of his spirit collection, i.e. the contents of the keg to which he refers in his diary. Most of the species on the first sheet are numbered according to the system he used throughout his diary and notes (p. 113), i.e. the number of the page in his diary where he noted the collection is followed by a colon with the number of the footnote giving his determination, if any. On the second sheet are double numbers referring to a catalogue and appendix which I have not traced.

The supplement comprises Banks's notes on mammals which are on the same paper as the first series and which clearly once formed a part of this McGill MS. They have however long been separated and are now bound with a series of zoological MSS by Solander in the British Museum (Natural History).

In the first and longest series, most of which is concerned with birds, Banks wrote his notes in a kind of dog Latin; the punctuation is erratic, sometimes absent, sometimes quite misleading. Since his writing is not always easy to read it seemed advisable to provide a fairly literal translation so that others can check my interpretation and determinations. In the following pages each of Banks's descriptions is preceded by the current name of the species, and followed by a translation and notes which have been inset so that they may easily be distinguished. The dates and localities were usually written by Banks not below his descriptions, where I have placed them, but on the verso of the page.

Determinations have in many cases been verified by reference to the bird paintings by Parkinson and Paillou, and to published descriptions by Pennant and Latham. Pennant had the use of Banks's papers and many of his specimens and published notes on them in his *Arctic Zoology* (1784–7). Much of the same material appeared in Latham's *General Synopsis of Birds*, most of which was published 1781–5, with supplementary volumes in 1787 and 1802. Latham often worked from Pennant's notes, but he also had access to Banks's collections.

The numbers to the right of the descriptions refer to the present pagination of the McGill MS which has recently been rearranged in systematic order; those to the left are Banks's own key to the entries in his diary.

None of Banks's Newfoundland bird skins has survived, and all reference to skins in the British Museum relate to subsequent collections.

DESCRIPTIONS IN LATIN OF BIRDS AND INSECTS, WITH NOTES AND TRANSLATIONS

Mergus serrator serrator L.   Red-breasted Merganser.

Aves Anseres

1, 2

Mergus serrator? Crista dependente, capite nigro maculis Ferrugineis Linn: Syst: Nat: 62:3–

Descr: Caput et Crista fusco nigrae Tempera Genae Gula ferrugineae Remiges 1:10 nigrae 11:14 parte interiori albae 15:21 albae Basis nigris supra his tectrices primariae albae sunt Ergo basis remigium 15:21 nigra facit Lineam Transversam nigram . . .

Habitat in Sinubus Circa ostia Fluminum . . .

Pullus antequam Volitat citissime superaquam currit

. . . teaux Sep^tr 14 1766.

> *Mergus serrator*? Drooping crest. Head black with rust-coloured spots. Linn. Syst. Nat. 62.3. Descr. Head and crest brownish black Post-ocular patch, cheeks and throat rust-coloured. Remiges 1:10 black, inner webs of 11:14 white, 15:21 white with black bases. Above these the coverts of the primaries are white so that the black bases of 15–21 make a black transverse bar. Found in bays near the mouths of rivers. The young bird runs along the water very swiftly before flying up. Chatteaux, Sept. 14, 1766.

Bank's notes on this species are not very adequate but his statement that it has a drooping crest and occurs in bays near river mouths shows that he saw the Red-breasted and not the American Common Merganser which prefers fresh water until it freezes, and is much less common in Labrador. Both Pennant (1785:537–8) and Latham (1785:423–5) include Newfoundland in the range of the Red-breasted Merganser. They seldom discriminated between Labrador and Newfoundland when discussing Banks's specimens.

Anas acuta (L.)   Pintail

Aves Anseres

3, 4

Anas 14:15 *Gracilis* Macula Alarum Varia, Dorso nigro-cinereo undulato. maculisq. Lunulatis albidis . . . Descr: Manitudo [*sic*] *A. Boscae*; sed Collum Longissimum; Rostrum Plumbeo nigrum; caput, Collum, Pectus, venter, abdomen sordide albicant; maculis crebrioribus fuscis; dorsum nigrum, cinereo undulatum, maculis Lunulatis albis, in singula Pluma insculptis, sed Plumae illae Longae quae alas Tegunt, nigrae, marginibus albidis; Remiges cinereo fuscae; 1:10 immaculatae, 11:21 albo, nigro, viridiq. variae; supra his Tectricum apices rufae sunt; Tectrices interiores cinereae Plumis nonnullis albidis. Eleganter nigro Punctatis; Pedes Plumbei . . .

Habitat in aquis dulcibus . . .

Chatteaux Sep^tr 1766

Anas 14:15 *gracilis*: Wings spotted; back with blackish-grey vermiculations, and some whitish spots and crescents. Descr: Size of *Anas bosca* [the Mallard] but the neck very long; beak gray-black; head, neck, breast, belly and abdomen dirty whitish, densely spotted with fuscous; black back with ashy-gray vermiculations and white crescentic spots imprinted on each feather, but those long feathers which cover the wings are black with whitish margins; remiges a dusky ashy colour, 1:10 immaculate, 10:21 variegated with white, black and green; above these the tips of the wing coverts are rufous; inner wing coverts are ash-gray, some feathers are whitish, elegantly spotted with black; feet leaden-gray. Lives in fresh water.

Chatteaux, September, 1766.

See Parkinson's pl. 61. Banks's description applies to a young Pintail; the painting is of a very dark young bird and there is nothing to indicate its sex.

Anas carolinensis Gmelin   Green-winged Teal
Aves Anseres

30:31   5, 6

Anas Phascas Fusca, Macula Alarum varia, Puncto minuto albido infra oculos . . .
Descr: Magnitudo *Creciae*, Rostrum nigrum, occiput fuscum; genae, tempora collum, grisea; punctis minutis fuscis; sed punctum album infra oculos, seu potius palpebra inferior tota alba: gula alba; Pectus rufo fuscum, maculis rotundatis nigris; abdomen album, maculis fuscis; tectrices rectricum interiores maculis Linearibus nigris; Dorsum nigrum, Fusco undulatum; Remiges 1:10 fuscae immaculatae, 11:15 Parte anteriori nigrae, apiceq. albae; 16:20 parte anteriori virides, apicibus quoq. albis; 21 parte anteriori Linea nigra; Tectrices remigium superiores primae rufescunt, apicibus . . .

Pedes cinerei . . .

Habitat in aquis dulcibus . . .

Incolis Teal . . .

Chatteaux Sep^tr

60. *Botaurus lentiginosus*, American Bittern.
Peter Paillou

61. *Anas acuta*, Pintail, a young bird.
Sydney Parkinson

ANAS discors, mas

tectricibus alarum cæruleis, remigibus secondariis extus viridibus, fascia frontali alba. Caudal...

62. *Anas discors*, Blue-winged Teal, a female or male in eclipse.
Sydney Parkinson

ANAS discors. (femina)

63. *Anas carolinensis*, Green-winged Teal.
Sydney Parkinson

64. *Histrionicus histrionicus*, Harlequin Duck, male and female.
Sydney Parkinson

ANAS mollissima, mas & femina.

65. *Somateria mollissima borealis*, Northern Common Eider, male and female.
Sydney Parkinson

66. *Somateria spectabilis*, King Eider.
Peter Paillou

69. *Buteo lagopus sanctijohannis*, Rough-legged Hawk, a young bird in the dark phase.
Peter Paillou

70. *Buteo lagopus sanctijohannis*, Rough-legged Hawk; this outline sketch with measurements is on the back of pl. 69.

Peter Paillou

71. *Circus cyaneus hudsonius*, Marsh Hawk.
Peter Paillou

72. *Circus cyaneus hudsonius*, Marsh Hawk; this outline sketch with measurements is on the back of pl. 71.

Peter Paillou

73. *Falco peregrinus anatum*, Peregrine Falcon.
Peter Paillou

FALCO Columbarius femina.

74. *Falco columbarius columbarius*, Pigeon Hawk, young bird.
Sydney Parkinson

75. *Falco columbarius columbarius*, Pigeon Hawk, male.
Sydney Parkinson

30:31

Anas phascas. Dusky with a variegated spot on the wing, a minute whitish spot beneath the eyes.

Descr. Size of *A. crecia* [*Anas crecca crecca* L., the Common Teal], bill black, occiput dusky, cheeks, post-ocular patch and neck grey with minute dusky spots, but a white spot below the eye or, rather, the lower eyelid wholly white; throat white, breast dusky-rufous with round black spots; abdomen white with dusky spots; under tail coverts with black linear spots; back black with dusky vermiculations; remiges 1:10 dusky, immaculate; 11:15 with the anterior part black and the tips white; 16:20 with the anterior part green, the tips also white; 21, anterior part with a black line; the first part of the upper wing coverts becoming rufous at the tips; feet ash-grey. Lives in fresh water. Vernacular name Teal.

Chatteaux, September.

See Parkinson's pl. 63. Banks's description seems to apply to a male in eclipse.

Anas discors (L.)   Blue-winged Teal

Aves Anseres

29:30   7, 8

Anas Caerulescens area alarum magna caerulescente . . .

Descr: Magnitudo *A. Creciae*, Rostrum nigrum; malae, Collum, abdomen, fusco alboque varii; gula alba, pedes fuscae, occiput nigrum, et ut dorsum, sed Margines Pennarum dorsi fuscae sunt; Remiges 1:14 nigrae, 15:21 dimidiato virides; tectrices alarum exteriores albae maculis Basisque nigris; ab his ad scapulum Plumae omnes caerulescunt . . .

Chatteaux Sep^tr 12 1766 . . .

Habitat in aquis dulcibus . . .

Incolis Blew wingd Teal . . .

Chatteanx Sep^tr

    29:30

    Anas caerulescens. A large area of the wing is bluish . . .

    Descr: Size of *A. crecia* [see preceding description]; bill black, cheeks neck and abdomen variegated dusky and white; throat white, feet dusky, occiput black as is the back but the edges of the feathers of the back are dusky; remiges 1:14 black; 15:21 half green; outer wing coverts white, and the bases with black spots; from these to the shoulders all the feathers are bluish.

    Chatteaux, September 12, 1766.

    Lives in fresh water.

    Vernacular name Blew winged Teal.

    Chatteaux, Sept.

    Parkinson's painting, pl. 62, represents either an adult female or a male in eclipse.

353

Histrionicus histrionicus (L.)   Harlequin Duck
                              Aves Anseres
20:21   9, 10
Anas Formosa albo nigro rufoq. varia fascia in sinu oris maculaq. aurium albae
Descr: Magnitudine media *A. Clangulam* Vix aequat Rostrum parvum subrotundum
Plumbeum in sinu oris fascia alba ad oculos extensa Linea nigra Lateribus rufescentibus a fronte ad occipitem ducta est verticem totam tegens tempora genae collum
nigro cinereae sunt exceptae macula aurium rotundata Linea sub eam Dorsum
ducta albo Basis Colli Collari albo circumdatus est Pectus et Dorsum cinereo nigri
macula alba nigro marginata scapulam tegit. Abdomen nigro fuscum sed latera
rufescunt Pedes nigri Rectrices quoque nigricant Remiges.

> 20:21
>
> *Anas formosa.* Banded with variegated black, white and rufous; a white spot
> at the base of the bill, and over the ear.
> Descr: Of medium size, scarcely as large as *A. clangula* [*Bucephala clangula
> clangula* (L.), the Golden Eye]; bill small, rather rounded, leaden-coloured;
> a band of white extends from the base of the bill to the eyes; a black line with
> rufous edges leads from the frons to the occiput covering the entire crown;
> post ocular patch, cheeks and neck are blackish grey save for a round white
> spot over the ears, beneath which a line of the same colour leads to the back;
> the base of the neck is encircled by a white collar. The breast and back are
> ashy black, a white mark edged with black covers the shoulder; the abdomen
> is dusky black with rufous sides; feet black, rectrices also blackish, remiges
> . . . [*unfinished*]

Banks had skins of a pair of these ducks and Paillou painted them, pl. 64.
Linnaeus's description of this species was based on George Edwards's account
of a specimen which he says (1749:99) 'was brought with others, preserved,
from Newfoundland in America; it was lent me by Mr. Holms, of the Tower
of London.'

Somateria mollissima dresseri (Sharpe)   American Common Eider
                              Aves Anseres
                                                                          11, 12
Anas Mollissima Rostro Cylindrico Cera Postice Bifida Rugosa Linn: Syst: Nat:
61:12.
Descript: Mas: Magna Magnitudine *A. Moscatum* Aequans Rostrum Parvum
fuscum Cera fusca rugosa Postice Bifida Pennae ceram circumambientes nigerrimae
Velutinae nucha et occiput cinereae Genae et tempora velutinae albae virido
tinctae sub gula Linea nigra Gula ipsa Collum et dorsi Pars anterior albae Pectus
album ferrugineo tinctum Abdominis et Dorsi partes Posticae nigrae sed ad Latera

uropygii maculae duae rotundae albae remiges nigrae sed tectrices tam Exteriores quam interiores albae Rectrices nigrae . . .

Habitat in mari salso nunquam aquas dulces ingrediens dum foemina Ovis insidet gregarius . . .

descriptio a pelle infarcta

Hare Bay June immensis Catervis.

> *Anas mollissima* Bill cylindrical, cere rugose, bifid posteriorly.
> Linn: Syst: Nat: 61:12.
> Descr: Male: large, equal in size to *A. moschata* [*Cairina moschata* (L.), the Muscovy Duck]; bill small, dusky; cere dusky, rugose, bifid posteriorly, feathers surrounding the cere very black, velvety, nape and occiput ash-grey; cheeks and post-ocular patch are velvety white tinged with green. Under the throat there is a black line, the throat itself, the neck and anterior part of the back are white; the breast white tinged with ferruginous, the abdomen and the lower part of the back are black but there are two round white spots on the sides of the rump. Remiges black but the wing coverts, both upper and lower, are white; rectrices black . . .
> Lives in salt water, never going to fresh, gregarious while the female is on eggs. I describe from a stuffed skin.
> Hare Bay, June, immense flocks.

I am indebted to Dr. Kenneth Parkes for kindly pointing out that I was mistaken in considering that this description of an eider with a black line on the throat applied to the Pacific Common Eider *S. mollissima v-nigra* Gray (Lysaght 1959:267 and see n. 143) since although this character is given by some authors as diagnostic for that subspecies it in fact occurs as a mutation in all the other races of *S. mollissima*, and is not invariably present in the Pacific Eider. Parkinson's plate 65 appears to represent the Northern Common Eider *S.m. borealis* (Brehm) which is abundant in Newfoundland during the non-breeding season but is supposed not to nest there. We have no evidence that the breeding birds were the same as the specimen described by Banks. Austin considers that there is intergrading of the subspecies in Newfoundland-Labrador; Banks wrote nothing to suggest that he saw more than one form.

Oidemia nigra americana Swainson   Common Scoter
Clangula hyemalis (L.)   Long-tailed Duck or Old Squaw

Aves Anseres

25:26   13, 14

Anas Marinus: Nigro Fuscus, Capite rostroq. nigris; Temporibus Gulaq. albidis . . .

Descr: Rostrum Parvum, nigerrimum, ut et Caput supra oculos; sed tempora,

genae, gula, albidae, maculis minutissimis fuscentibus adspersae; Dorsum, remiges, rectrices, et tectrices, nigro fuscae, sed apicibus rectricum macula minuta alba & Rachi Elongato; Pectus et abdomen fuscae undulis albescentibus sed Pars media inter ea sive venter albicat maculis nonnullis fuscentibus Tectrices alarum interiores fuscae apicibus albis Pedes fuscae flavo tinctae . . . Aliae avis Plumae Longae dorsum tengentes flavo tinctae cum Linea minuta alba Prope apicem . . .
Habitat in aquis salsis
Chatteaux

25 :26
Anas marinus. Dusky with black, head and bill black, post-ocular patch and throat whitish . . .
Descr: Bill small, very black as is the head above the eyes; but the post-ocular patch, cheeks and throat are whitish with very small, scattered, dusky spots; back, remiges, rectrices and coverts dusky with black, but the rectrices with a minute white spot at the tip, and with elongated shafts. Breast and abdomen dusky with whitish vermiculations, but the middle part between them, or rather the belly, is whitish with dusky spots. Under wing coverts dusky with white tips; feet dusky tinged with yellow . . . In some birds the back is covered by long feathers tinged with yellow, with a minute white line near the tip . . .
Lives in salt water.
Chatteaux.

Most of Banks's description applies to a moulting juvenile Common Scoter. In the American Museum of Natural History, N.Y., the rectrices of some females are tipped with buff. Banks must have had two species in front of him, in any case, when he made these notes. The birds with long feathers tinged with yellow covering the back are most certainly Long-tailed Duck or Old Squaw, *Clangula hyemalis* (L.). Out of the breeding season Old Squaws and Scoters sometimes occur in the same flock and if Banks shot them at the same time he may have considered them to be different forms of the same species. I am much indebted to Dr. Kenneth Parkes for his help in clearing up these determinations.

Melanitta perspicillata (L.)   Surf Scoter
Aves Anseres
19 :20   15, 16
Anas Salsa Dorso remigibusq. nigris, fronte supra rostrum excurrente . . .
Descrp: Rostrum nigrum, satis magnum, mandibula inferiore apice rubente; Caput nigrum, Plumis supra rostrum Excurrentibus; genae nigro fuscae, macula albida ante et pone oculos; Dorsum, remiges, et rectrices, nigris Gula, Pectus, et

abdomen, fusco cinereae; Pedes et Digiti rubri; membrana nigra; Digiti intimi et Posterioris membrana rubra . . .

Habitat in mare salso nunquam in aquis dulcibus vidi Aliae avis apex rostri Lutescens gula et Pectus Fusci . . .

Chatteaux Septr 13 1766

> 19:20
>
> *Anas salsa* Back and remiges black, frons extended above the bill . . .
>
> Descrp: Bill black, tolerably large, lower mandible with a reddish tip; head black, feathers protruding above the bill; cheeks dusky with some black, a white spot in front of and behind the eyes; back, remiges and rectrices black; throat, breast and abdomen ashy-gray and dusky; feet and toes red, web black, inmost digit and hinder part of web red.
>
> Lives in salt water, I never saw it in fresh. In other birds the tip of the bill was yellowish, the throat and the breast dusky.
>
> Chatteaux, September 13, 1766.

Banks's notes suggest that he was describing a young bird. Paillou painted a female, pl. 67.

Pinguinus impennis (L.)   Great Auk

Aves Anseres

17, 18

Alca Impennis Rostro Compresso-ancipiti sulcato macula Ovata untring. ante oculos Linn: Syst: Nat: 63:2

Descr: Magnitudo Anseris Rostrum Compressum mandibula superiore sulcis 7 una basi proxima & sex prope apicem inferior 8 omnes prope apicem sitae Caput nigrum sed duae maculae albae ovatae ante oculos positae sunt Collum et Dorsum nigriscunt alae minimae columbinae minores (nam nunquam volitat et tanquam ob urinando formatae sunt) nigrae sunt sed pennae Lateri proximae apices albo habent rectrices quoq. minimae nigrae tota avis subtus alba est Pedes nigri rugosi tridactyli . . . Habitat in alto mari rarissimo sinus intrans

Chatteaux Sep^{tr} in Sinum

> *Alca impennis* Bill compressed on both sides, furrowed; with an oval spot in front of the eyes. Linn: Syst: Nat: 63:2.
>
> Descr: Size of a goose; bill compressed, the upper mandible with seven grooves, one near the base and six near the apex; the lower with eight, all near the tip; head black but two white oval spots are placed in front of the eyes; neck and back blackish; wings tiny, less than those of a dove (for it never flies and they are formed for the purpose of diving), black but small areas near the tips have some white; rectrices also very small and black; whole bird white

below; feet black, rugose, tridactyl . . . Lives on the high seas, very rarely comes into bays.
Chatteaux, Sept., in the bay.

I have been unable to find any information about the fate of the skin of this Great Auk; it is not included in the lists of Banks's London collection, neither is it mentioned in the specimens in his keg. It seems probable that it was too oily to remain intact; methods of preparing bird skins were very crude at that date. See also n. 112.

Gavia immer (Brünnich)   Common Loon, or Great Northern Diver
Aves Anseres

19, 20

Colymbus Arcticus Pedibus Palmatis indivisis Gutture Nigro Purpurascenti Linn: Syst: Nat: 68:1
Magnitudine Multum variat Avis quae describo Anserem Aequat Rostrum rectum acutum nigrum marginibus Pallidis Maxilla inferior minor inter superiorem recipitur Caput et Colli Pars superior nigra sed sub gulam Linea Parva alba Collare albo nigroq. varium maximam partem Colli ambit sed nigredo colli Percurrit eum prope pectus Collare alium nigro Purpureum Pectore incumbit Pectus Abdomen et tota avis subtus alba sed Latera nigro alboq. Lineata sunt Tota avis supra nigra maculis rotundatis albis remiges et rectrices nigrae immaculatae Pedes Palmati nigri tibiae compressae Habitat ad Littora maris et in sinubus frequens . . .
Croque Chatteaux

Colymbus arcticus Feet webbed, undivided; throat purplish-black.
Linn: Syst: Nat: 68:1:
Size very variable; the bird which I describe is equal to a goose; bill straight, pointed, black with paler edges, the lower mandible smaller, contained by the upper. Head and upper part of the neck black but under the throat there is a small white line, and a streaked black and white collar surrounds the greater part of the neck but the blackness of the neck crosses it near the breast; another purple and black collar lies on the breast. The breast, abdomen and the whole of the rest of the underparts are white but the sides are streaked with black and white; all the upper parts are black with round white spots but the remiges and rectrices are immaculate black. The feet are webbed and black, the tibiae compressed.
Common on the shore and in bays.
Croque, Chatteaux.

No painting of this loon is now to be seen in the Print Room series of Banks's Newfoundland birds but there is one in the Taylor White collection (*Aves*

15, f. 849) which, though unsigned, appears to be by Paillou. On it Taylor White has written, 'This Bird I had from Mr. Banks and I suppose he brought it from Canada but am not certain'. Banks was always generous with his material and there are many instances of his having given away specimens even of what he must have known were new species of birds, apparently without keeping duplicates for himself.

Gavia stellata (Pontoppidan)   Red-throated Loon or Diver

Aves Anseres

1:2   21, 22

Colymbus Clamitans . . . Capite Colliq. Latera cinerea macula sub Collo Ferrugineo-Rufa . . .

Descr: *C. Arctica* multo minor vix *Anatem Moschatam* magnitudine aequans Caput gula et Latera Colli Cinereae sunt sed dorsum et Basis Colli Albo nigroq. Lineata sub gula macula subrotunda rufo ferruginea Pectus et abdomen niveo-argenteae sed Latera nigra maculis nonnullis albis et infra alas pennae niveae rachidibus albis dorsum remiges rectrices fusco-nigrae. Pedes Palmati dorso concolores Habitat in sinubus et Prope Littora non infrequens . . .

Incolis Whobbie

Obs. Linnaeus Putet hanc esse foeminam *Arctici* fortasse recta sed sono Diversissima est et multo rarior

Chatteaux Sept^r

> *Colymbus clamitans*; Head and sides of the neck ash-gray, a reddish-ferruginous mark on the lower side of the neck.
> Descr: Much smaller than *C. arctica*, scarcely as large as *Anas Moschata* [*Cairina moschata* (L.), the Muscovy Duck]; head, throat, and sides of the neck ash-gray, but the back and base of the neck streaked with black and white; beneath the throat a roundish reddish-rusty mark; the breast and abdomen silvery white but the sides black with a few white spots, and below the wings snow-white feathers with white shafts. The back, remiges and rectrices dusky-black; feet webbed, the same colour as the back. Fairly common in bays and near the shore.
> Vernacular name Whobbie . . . Linnaeus considers that this may be in reality the female of *arcticus* but its cry is very different and it is much rarer.
> Chatteaux, Sept.

Cepphus grylle atlantis (Salomonsen)   Black Guillemot, immature

Aves Anseres

1:2   23, 24

Colymbus Urinator Pedibus palmatis Tridactilis Tectricibus alarum Pone albis apicibus nigris . . .

Descr: Magnitudinis *C. Grylle* Rostrum tenue subulatum nigrum Vertex niger Regio oculorum ut tempora alba punctis minutissimis nigris sed pone oculos Linea Parva nigra Gula et abdomen albae sed Pectus et Latera abdominis punctis seu potius Lineolis minutis nigris adspersa sunt Dorsum nigrum sed supra alas et regione uropigii undulis paucis albis quasi irroratum Remiges nigrae circa basin albae tectrices usq. ad [blank] nigrae sed Pone eum quatuor vel quinq. ordines albae sunt apicibus tantum nigris interiores omnes niveae immaculatae rectrices breves nigri Pedes Tridactili Rufescent.

Incolis Little Diver . . .

Circa medium aut Prope finem Augusti huc veniebant Pauci nunc visae sunt non infrequentes in sinubus et ad Littora maris.

Chatteaux Sep^tr 24 1766

1:2

Colymbus urinator Feet webbed, three-toed, wing coverts white behind with black tips . . .

Descr: Size of *C. grylle*; bill slender, black, awl-shaped; crown black; area round the eyes and post-ocular patch white with very minute black spots but behind the eyes there is a small black line; throat and abdomen white but the breast and sides of the abdomen sparsely covered with spots or rather minute lines of black; back black but above the wings and round the rump a few wavy white lines are sprinkled; remiges black, white about the base; the wing coverts black up to the [blank] but behind are four or five white rows with the tips quite black; all the inner ones are snow white and immaculate. Rectrices short and black. Feet tridactyl, reddish. Vernacular name Little Diver. From the middle to the end of August a few came in and were seen fairly often in the bay and on the shore.

Chatteaux, September 24, 1766

I misidentified this bird in my earlier paper (Lysaght, 1959). Banks had collected a mature guillemot when he first arrived in Newfoundland (see diary 23, n. 48 and his formal description 23:7, no. 6 on p. 91 of this section) and it did not occur to me that he could have mistaken a young guillemot for a grebe. A skin of an immature Black Guillemot here in the British Museum fits his description very well, and the Horned Grebe *Podiceps auritus* (L.) must be eliminated from the list of species ascribed to him.

Larus marinus (L.)   Great Black-backed Gull, young bird.
Aves Anseres

2:3   25, 26

Larus Albidus. Fusco Albidus Totus . . . Tota avis quae describo, Caput, Dorsum, Abdomen, Remiges, Rectrices, albidae; nebula fusca tinctae supra dorsum fuscior;

maculis nonnullis nigrioribus; abdomen tamen et Collum albidiora Canthus oris, et circulus oculorum, albescunt; ut et rostrum; sed apices rostri nigri sunt, usq. ad gibbossitatem mandibulae inferior Pedes quoque albidi; rectrices immaculatae magnitudinis *L: Marini*. . . .

Scolopeto Percussus erat, unicus inter millia *Larum* Piscantium an nova species, an varietas, an Potius Pullus; multum haereo . . .

Chatteaux Sep^{tr}

> 2:3
>
> *Larus albidus*. The whole a whitish dusky colour. The whole bird which I describe,—head, back, abdomen, remiges and rectrices whitish clouded with a dusky colour, the back darker with some blacker spots, the abdomen and neck, however, are a paler whitish colour; the rim of the mouth and the ring round the eyes whitish as is the bill but the tips of the bill are black as far as the swelling on the lower mandible; the feet also whitish; rectrices immaculate; size of *L. marinus*. Killed with a stone, a single example amongst thousands of gulls that were fishing; it may be a new species, a variety or perhaps a young bird; I am stuck for an answer . . .
>
> Chatteaux, Sept.

Pennant called this bird Wagel's Gull (1785:528); he included Newfoundland in its range.

Rissa tridactyla (L.)   Black-legged Kittiwake, young bird
                                                                                27, 28

Larus Parasiticus pullus, an Varietas secunda . . .

Descr: Magnitudinis Primi, sive Columbae minoris; tota avis subtus alba, rostrum nigerrimum; rictus Lutescens; Caput album, sed Pennae circum oculos nigrae ut et maculae duae pone tempora, collum quoq. album; sed semicirculus niger Dorso proximus: Dorsum et remiges cinereo caeruleae; sed 1:4 margine exteriore et apice nigrae; 5:6 prope apicem nigra sed ipsa apice albae; ultima quoq. nigro maculata sunt; remiges secundarii 1:8 Dimidio nigrae sunt, ut et tectrices superiores quae fascia Lata nigra Jungunt remiges primariis et ultimas; uropygium, et rectrices niveae; sed rectricum apicibus [?] nigrae exceptis 1:1 totis albis pedes fusco nigri . . .

Septembris 21 ad nos veniebant cum priore ad *squillas* capiendas

Chatteaux Sep^t:

> *Larus parasiticus* young bird, or a second variety.
>
> Descr: Size of the first or a smallish dove; whole bird white below, bill very black; rictus yellowish; head white but feathers round the eyes black as are two spots behind the postocular patch; neck also white but with a

semicircle of black near the back; back and remiges ashy-blue but 1:4 with the outer edge and tips black, 5:6 black near the tip but the actual tip white; the last also are spotted with black; the secondary remiges 1:8 are half black as are the upper wing coverts and they join on to the first and last remiges in a broad black band; the rump and the rectrices are snow white, but the tips of the rectrices are black except for 1:1 which are quite white. Feet black with brown. On 21st September they appeared with the first, fishing for *Squilla*. Chatteaux, September.

Banks's next account also applies to this species, and there is a further note on p. 90. See Parkinson's pl. 80; Pennant recorded the species from Newfoundland (1785:529).

Rissa tridactyla (L.) Black-legged Kittiwake
29, 30

Larus Tridactyli Pullus sive varietas prima . . .
Descr: Minor, Vix Columbam Parvam magnitudine aequat; Pedes nigerrimi, tridactyli, pollice obsoleto; tota avis infra, Gula, Abdomen, tectrices alarum et Caudae interiores, niveae; rostrum Luteum, gibbo vix notabili; rictus Luteo rubens, ut et Canthus oris; caput album, occiput et colli Pars superior nigro tinctae, [?] pennae nonullae nigrae, oculos circunstant Dorsum et Remiges e cerulea cinereae; Remex Primus margine exteriori et apice niger, secundus apice tantum, tertius et quartus versus apicibus nigrae, sed macula Parva nivea desinentes rectrices nivei . . . Septembris 21 mira quantitate in Chatteax [*sic*] bay veniebant quaesituras *squillarum* parvam speciem. . . . aliae varietatis Rostrum Luteo nigroq. varium . . .
Chatteaux Sep^tr.

Larus tridactylus, a young bird or a first variety. . . .
Descr: Small, scarcely equal in size to a small dove; feet very black, three toed, pollex obsolete; undersurface of the whole bird, throat, abdomen, under coverts of the wings and the tail snow-white. Bill yellow, swelling scarcely obvious, gape red with yellow like the rim of the mouth; head white, occiput and upper part of the neck tinged with black; a few black feathers round the eye; back and remiges bluish gray; first primary with the outer edge and tip black; the tip only of the second primary black, the third and fourth black towards the tip but ending in a small snow-white spot; rectrices snow-white. On 21 September an astonishing number came into Chatteaux Bay chasing a species of small *Squilla*. In another variety the bill was variegated yellow and black. . . Chatteaux, Sept.

For the other descriptions of this species by Banks see his p. 27 above.

Stercorarius sp., A young skua, indeterminable

Aves Anseres

Larus 31, 32

Descr: Magnitudinis *L. Cani*; tota avis subtus cinerea, fusco undulata, sed tectrices interiores caudae fuscae, maculis albis; Pedes fusco Cinerei; Rostrum nigrum, Versus Basin mandibulae inferioris pallidum, nec Canthus oris nec circulus oculorum Coccinei; caput abdomini concolor, sed Paulo fuscior; Dorsum et tectrices alarum superiores, fuscae, marginibus pennarum maculis albis distinctis; remiges fuscae, versus apice nigriores; rectrices quoq. nigrae versus albo maculatae . . . Habitat in mari Decuplo copiosior quam ulla alia *Larum* species: certe Pullus, sed nescio cujus.

Chatteaux Sept^r

Larus

Descr: Size of *L. canus* [Mew or Common Gull]. The whole bird ash-grey beneath with dusky vermiculations, but the under tail coverts are dusky with white spots; feet dusky grey; bill black, the lower mandible paler at the base; no red on the rim of the mouth nor on the ring round the eye. The head the same colour as the abdomen but a little more dusky; back and upper wing coverts dusky, the margins of the feathers with distinct white spots; remiges dusky, rather blacker towards the tips; the rectrices also somewhat spotted with white [?]. Lives in the sea, ten times more numerous than any other species of gull; certainly a young bird but of what kind I know not.

Chatteaux, September.

Three species of skua occur in Newfoundland and Labrador and although we have a painting by Paillou, pl. 79, which probably represents this bird, there is not enough detail to determine the species; it must have been either *Stercorarius parasiticus* (L.) or *S. longicaudis* Vieillot since *S. pomarinus* Temminck is much larger than the Mew Gull.

Buteo lagopus sanctijohannis (Gmelin) Rough-legged Hawk

Aves Accipitres

33, 34

Falco Buteo Cera Pedibusq. Luteis Corpore fusco Abdomine Pallido maculis Fuscis Linn: Syst: Nat: 41:14.

Descr: Tota Avis supra fusca sed Pennae uropigii et tectricum alarum margines ferrugineas habent et albo maculatae sunt Gula et Pectus ferrugineo-albidae sunt immaculatae Abdomen ferrugineo-albidum maculis Longitudinalibus fuscis femora abdomini Concolores sunt sed maculae fuscae obsoletiores sunt Rectricum facies exterior ferrugineo fusca est fasciis plurimis obscurioribus apicibusq. fusco-albidis Palpebra caerulescens maxima.

Habitat in Sylvis.

Chatteaux Sep^tr 20 1766

> *Falco buteo.* Cere and feet yellow, body dusky, abdomen pale with dusky spots. Linn: Syst: Nat: 41:14.
>
> Descr: The whole bird is dusky above but the feathers of the rump and wing coverts have ferruginous margins and are spotted with white. Throat and breast ferruginous whitish, immaculate; abdomen rusty whitish with longitudinal dusky streaks; femora the same colour as the abdomen but the dusky marks are less distinct. Outer aspect of the rectrices rusty brown, with many faint bars of dusky white and tips of the same colour; eyelid large, bluish. Lives in woods.
>
> Chatteaux, Sept. 20, 1766.

> Paillou's paintings, pls. X and 68, represent the type of *sanctijohannis* (Lysaght 1959:270–1). See Systematic List of Birds, pp. 410–1, for full discussion.

Accipiter gentilis atricapillus (Wilson)   American Goshawk

Aves Accipitres

12:13   35, 36

Falco Uncinatus Cera Pedibusq. flavis femoribus albis maculis Rotundatis fuscis . . .

Descr: Magnitudine *F. Milvi* Rostrum nigrum Basi Caerulescens Palpebrae caeruleae Caput et Colli Dorsum nigri Pennarum marginibus Rufo-albidis Dorsum fuscum Rectrices fusci sed apices albae sunt et fasciae quinq. nigricant sed intermediis fascia ultima obsoleta est remiges quoq. fusci fasciis in Pennarum marginibus albis nigro Punctatis tectrices albo marginatae sunt gula Pectus et abdomen albae maculis Longitudinalibus nigris femora quoq. alba sed maculae eorum Rotundatae sunt tectrices alarum interiores albae sunt maculis et fasciis fuscis Pedes lutei unguibus Longissimis nigris facies interna alarum et Caudae multo Pallidior est quam externa Habitat in Sylvis Gallinis nostris infestissimus.

Croque Octr 5 1766

> 12:13
>
> *Falco uncinatus* Cere and feet yellow, femora white with round dusky spots. Descr: Size of *F. milvus* [the European Kite *Milvus milvus milvus* (L.)]; bill black with a bluish base; eyelids blue; head and back of the neck black with the margins of the feathers rufous-whitish; back dusky, rectrices dusky but with white tips and five blackish bands, the last band on the middle feathers is very faint; remiges also dusky with white bars spotted with black on the edges of

the feathers; the coverts are edged with white; throat, breast and abdomen white with longitudinal black spots; femora also white but with rounded spots; under wing coverts white, with dusky spots and bars; feet yellow with very long black claws; inner aspects of wings and tail much paler than the outer. Lives in woods; a great nuisance to our hens.
Croque, Oct. 5, 1766.

The above description is of an immature bird which differs in some respects from that drawn by Paillou, pl. VI. Latham (1781:79) based his account of this Goshawk, which he called the Newfoundland Falcon, on Paillou's painting; Pennant (1785:201) copied Latham's account. In 1789 when Gmelin (p. 274) published a short Latin description of this bird as *Falco novae-terrae* he based it directly on Latham and hence on Paillou's painting which therefore becomes the type of *Falco novae-terrae*; the type locality, according to Banks's note in the McGill MS, is Croque. A short note on Paillou's painting together with a black and white photograph of it was published by the present writer in 1959; owing to a mistaken reading of the localities on the verso of Banks's MS, Chateau Bay was then included in the type locality.

There is a copy of Paillou's painting, probably by him, in the Taylor White collection at McGill, *Aves* 4, f. 393; it differs very slightly from the Print Room plate.

Falco peregrinus anatum (Bonaparte)   Peregrine Falcon
                Aves Accipitres
25:26   37, 38
Falco Vigil Cera Caerulea Pedibus Luteis Remigibus Rectricibusq. fuliginosis Rufo-Albido maculatis . . .
Descr: *F. Palumbario* Affinis sed minor cera Caerulea Rostrum nigrum versus ceram Pallidum nares rotundatae magnae cum puncto in medio Prominente Palpebrae implumes sed Vibrissis instructae caput rufo-albido fuscoq. varium fascia obsoleta rufo-albida ab oculos ad occipite ut in *F. Palumbario* Pone oculos et in sinu oris fasciae nigrae Sed Tempora et Gula rufo-Albidae sunt Pectus et abdomen Rufo-albido Crebris maculis Longitudinalibus nigris anus immaculata tectrices interiores Caudae fasciis Transversis nigris Pedes Lutei Validissimi Digiti Longi subtus tuberculis satis magnis instructi quia saepe in rupibus sedit Dorsum et tectrices alarum fuliginosae marginibus Pennarum Rufis remiges nigricant sed margine interiori maculis sive fasciis rufo-albidis pictae sunt tectrices interiores nigrae maculis in marginibus rufo albidis Rectrices nigrae apicibus albis marginibus maculis rufis duabus intermediis immaculatis
Obs: Et Remigium et Rectricum Pagina interiora Pallidiores et maculae ejus majores quam in exteriore

Habitat in Rupibus Prope mari vigil dum anates ex aquam volitare videt hi vero volitantes simulac Falconem vident alis Clausis Pronos se in aquam Projiciunt Chatteaux Sep^tr 26th 1766

25:26

Falco vigil. Cere blue, feet yellow, remiges and rectrices sooty spotted with rufous-whitish . . .

Descr: Similar to *F. palumbarius* [an old name for the Goshawk *Accipiter gentilis* (L.)] but smaller; cere blue; bill black, pale towards the cere; nostrils round, large, with a prominent opening in the centre; eyelid lacking feathers but provided with bristles; head variegated with reddish-white and dusky, a faint reddish-white stripe leads from the eyes to the occiput as in *F. palumbarius*; behind the eyes and at the corner of the mouth black stripes, but the post-ocular patch and cheek are reddish-whitish; breast and abdomen reddish-dirty-white with crowded black streaks; anus immaculate; under tail coverts with transverse black bars; feet yellow, very stout, toes long, provided with fairly large tubercles beneath, because it often sits on rocks; back and wing coverts sooty with the margins of the feathers rufous; remiges blackish but the inner margins are ornamented with spots or rather bars of a reddish-whitish colour; under wing coverts black with reddish-whitish spots on the edges; rectrices black with white tips and with reddish spots on the margins; the two intermediate ones immaculate.

Chatteaux, Sept. 26, 1766.

The undersides of the remiges and rectrices are paler than the upper, and the spots on them are larger. It lives on rocks near the sea and watches until it sees ducks flying out of the water; the latter as soon as they see the falcon dive with closed wings back into the water.

See the painting by Paillou (pl. 73). The above description applies to a young peregrine.

Surnia ulula caparoch (Müller)   American Hawk Owl
Aves Accipitres

10:11   39, 40

Strix Varius Albo nigroq. varius remige quarta Longiore . . .

Descr: S. *Ululae* minor Rostrum nigrum sed Parte superiori flavescens genae albae semicirculo nigro cinctae occiput nigrum maculis parvis subrotundis Dorsum nigro-fuscum maculis subrotundis albis majoribus remiges et tectrices dorso concolores maculis albis in ambis marginibus rectrices quoq. nigro fuscae fasciis transversis albis Gula macula seu nebula nigra dist incta est Pectus abdomen venter et tectrices

alarum interiores albae fasciis transversis fuscis femorae Luteo tinctae sunt nebulis
fuscis tibiae brevissimae digitos ad ungues Lanatos
Habitat in Sylvis . . .
Croque: chatteaux

10:11
Strix varius Black and white, spotted, fourth primary longer.
Descr: Smaller than *Strix ulula* [but see below]. Bill black but the upper part
yellowish; cheeks white with a semicircle of black round them; occiput black
with small roundish white spots; back blackish-brown with larger roundish
white spots; remiges and tectrices the same colour as the back, with white
spots on both edges; rectrices also dusky black barred with white; throat
marked by a black spot or cloud; breast, abdomen, belly and under wing
coverts white with transverse dusky bars; femora yellow with a dusky tinge;
tibiae very short, toes feathered right to the claws.
Lives in woods.
Croque, Chatteaux.

There is a painting of this owl by Parkinson, pl. II, labelled *Strix funerea*,
obviously in error since the breast is transversely barred. The skin of '*Strix
funerea*' from Labrador noted in the MS lists of Banks's collection was also
barred below, not streaked, according to a note in Latin against this entry
(list 4, no. 9). This probably accounts for the confusion over Pennant's
'Brown Owl' from Newfoundland (1785:236), which is too much of a mixture
to be identified.

Dendrocopus villosus terraenovae (Batchelder)　　　Hairy Woodpecker, female.
Aves Picae

11:12　　　　　　　　　　　　　　　　　　　　　　　　　　　　　41, 42
Picus Varius Albo nigroq. Varius subtus albus occipite nigro Rectricibus Longis.
Descrip: Magnitudinis Praecedentis Rostrum nigrum Setae nares tegentes albae
Caput nigrum sed supra oculos & Tempora nigra Dorsum nigrum Remiges et
earum Tectrices nigrae in ambis marginibus albo maculatae Subtus tota alba
Rectrices Longi Pro ratione avis 1:2 albae totae 3: nigro alboq. dimidiata 4:5
nigrae totae Pedes tetradactili fusci . . .
A Parte Australi Newfoundlandiae autem accepi

11:12
Picus varius. Black and white, spotted, white underparts, occiput black, rectrices
long.

Descr: Size of the preceding [but since these pages were loose when this MS was acquired by McGill we do not know which this was] bill black, white bristles covering the nostrils; head black, but with black [*sic*] above the eyes and post-ocular patch; back black; remiges and wing coverts black spotted with white on both margins; completely white beneath; rectrices long in proportion to the rest of the bird, 1:2 completely white, 3 half black and half white, 4:5 wholly black; feet tetradactyl, dusky. I received this bird from the southern part of Newfoundland.

Banks's note that the back was black shows that he had a typical specimen of the Newfoundland race; in these birds the white dorsal stripe characteristic of the nominate race is usually much reduced or absent. He clearly made a slip in his description when he wrote 'Caput nigrum *sed* supra oculos et tempora nigra'. He must have meant a contrasting adjective after *sed*, and nigra is almost certainly a slip for alba.

Cyanocitta cristata bromia (Oberholser)   Blue Jay
Aves Picae
6:7   43, 44
Corvus Caeruleus supra Caerulea Rectricibus Longis nigro fasciatis exterioribus apicibus albis.
Descr: Rostrum nigrum validum caput Dorsum et tota avis supra caerulea Remiges 1:8 margine exterioris caeruleae immaculatae interiori nigrae reliquae margine exteriori caeruleae nigro fasciatae interiori nigrae sed apices albae Rectrices Longae interiores caeruleae nigro fasciatae exteriores Caeruleae immaculatae sed apicibus albidis tectrices remigium caeruleae nigro fasciatae apicibus albidis Pedes nigri tota avis subtus fusca Excepta fasia [*sic*] Pectoris nigro ad genas excurrens.

6:7
Corvus caeruleus. Sky blue above, rectrices long, banded with black, outer feathers tipped with white.
Descr: Bill black, solid; head, back and all the upper parts blue; remiges 1:8 with the outer edge blue, immaculate, the inner margins black; the remainder with the outer margins blue barred with black, the inner margins black but the tips white. Rectrices long, the inner ones blue, barred with black, the outer ones immaculate but with whitish tips. Wing coverts blue banded with black, with whitish tips. Feet black, the whole bird dusky beneath except for a black band on the breast which runs up to the cheeks.

Pennant gave Newfoundland as a locality where this bird occurs (1785:249) but Latham did not.

Pl. XI Greater Yellowlegs, *Tringa melanoleuca*
Peter Paillou

Perisoreus canadensis (L.)   Gray Jay
                              Aves Picae

11:12   45, 46

Corvus Familiaris Fronte alba rectricibus remigibusq. nigro Plumbeis apicibus Albis.

Magnitudine *C: Infaustum* Paulo superat Rostrum nigrum Basis mandibulae superioris Pennis albis tectum est frons et genae albae occiput nigrum Circulus albidus cingit collum Dorsum et tectrices alarum Plumbei rectrices et remiges Dorso paulo fusciores apicibus parvis albis Pectus et abdomen Cinerea pennis basi nigris tibiae nigrae Digiti Et ungues validi.

Incolis Jay.

Habitat satis frequens inter arbusculos vix unquam Solus Videtur

Croque Chatteaux

11:12

Corvus familiaris. Frons white, rectrices and remiges blackish-gray, tipped with white. In size a little larger than *C. infaustus* [*Perisoreus infaustus* (L.), the Siberian Jay]. Bill black, base of the upper mandible covered with white feathers; frons and cheeks white, occiput black, a whitish collar round the neck; back and wing coverts leaden gray; remiges and rectrices rather more dusky than the back, with small white tips; breast and abdomen ashy gray with black bases to the feathers; tibiae black; strong toes and claws.

Vernacular name Jay.

Is quite common among bushes, hardly ever seen alone.

Croque. Chatteaux.

Pennant noted that this bird occurred in Newfoundland (1785:248).

Megaceryle alcyon alcyon (L.)   Belted Kingfisher, female.
                              Aves Picae
                                                              47, 48

Alcedo Alcyon. Brachyura nigra Abdomine albo pectore ferrugineo Linn: Syst: Nat: 56: 3:

Descr: Rostrum Capite Longius nigrum Validissimum mandibula superiore Paulo Longiore Nares ovatae magnae macula alba ante et infra oculos Caput Cristatum Caeruleo-plumbeum singulae pennae Rachi nigro circulus albus cingit collum dorsum e Plumbeo-Caeruleum ut et uropygium et tectrices alarum Exteriores hae tamen apicibus albis Distinguuntur remiges 1:9: nigrae macula magna alba in margine interiori 10:20 margine exteriori dorso concolores sed interiori nigrae albo punctatae rectrices nigrae albo punctatae Gula alba pectus nigrum tectrices

369

alarum interiores albae fascia ferruginea infra alas Abdomen Album femora sub-
ferruginea tibiae rugosae nigrae Breves Digitus extimus connexus cum intermedio
Habitat ad ostiis rivum rarius.
Croque June 1766.

Alcedo alcyon. Short black tail, abdomen white, breast rust-coloured. Linn:
Syst: Nat: 56:3:
Descr: Bill longer than the head, black, very stout, upper mandible a little
longer, nares oval, large; a white spot in front of and below the eyes; head
with a grayish-blue crest, the shaft of each feather black; a white collar round
the neck; back bluish-greyish as are the rump and the wing coverts, the outermost wing coverts are, however, distinguished by having white tips; remiges
1:9 black with a large white spot on the inner web, 10:20 with the outer
margin the same colour as the back, but the inner margin black spotted with
white; rectrices black spotted with white; throat white, breast black, under
wing coverts white; a rust-coloured band beneath the wings. Abdomen white;
femora somewhat rust-coloured; tibiae corrugated, black, short; outer toe
connected with the middle one.
Occasionally found at the mouth of a stream.
Croque, June 1766.

For notes see diary 33, and n. 83.

Tringa melanoleuca (Gmelin)   Greater Yellowlegs
                                    Aves Grallae

                                                                    49, 50

Scolopax annuens 12:13 Rostro recto Pedibus Lutescentibus.
Descript: Rostrum nigrum, subrecurvatum; gula alba; Caput, Collum & Pectus,
albo nigroq. varii; abdomen, album Dorsum fuscum maculis parvis albidis uropy-
gium, et Cauda, albae; maculis transversis fuscis; femora semi-nuda, tibiae
Longissimae, et Digitis Lutescunt; extimus cum intermedio membrana conjunctus,
ungues nigri.—
Incolis Stone curlew—Habitat in fundis sinum arenosis, Caput continuo motu
annuens:—
Victitat cochleis et insectis marinis—
Chatteaux August 1766

Scolopax annuens 12:13. Bill straight, legs yellowish.
Descr: Bill black, slightly upcurved, throat white; head, neck and breast
variegated white and black; abdomen white, back dusky with small whitish
spots, rump and tail white with transverse dusky streaks; femora half bare,

tibiae very long and yellowish like the digits; outermost joined to the middle one by a web, claws black.

Vernacular name Stone Curlew. Lives in bottoms of sandy bays. Nods the head continuously.

Feeds on snails and marine insects.

Chatteaux, August, 1766.

Luckily we still have Paillou's painting, pl. XI, of what was probably this very specimen. It was described by Pennant (1785:468) and Latham (1785:152); Gmelin (1789:659) based his description of *Scolopax melanoleuca* from Labrador on their accounts when he gave this bird a scientific binomial. The painting may therefore be regarded as the type, and the type locality is accordingly Chateau Bay. Pennant wrote 'Observed in autumn feeding on the sands on the lower part of Chateaux Bay, continually nodding their heads. Are called there Stone Curlews'.

Capella gallinago delicata (Ord.)   Wilson's Common Snipe

Aves Grallae

51, 52

Scolopax Gallinago Rostro Recto apice tuberculato pedibus Fuscis Lineis frontis fuscis Quaternis—Linn: Syst: Nat: 77:11

Descr: Rostrum rectum Longum prope apicem cum post mortem siccum est punctis excavatis adspersum parte anteriori et ubi Punctatum est nigrum sed Versus Basin pallidum vertex nigrum in media parte linea albida distinctum genae albae sed Linea nigra a rostro per oculos Ducta Est Gula Albida ut et collum et Pectus hi tamen maculis sive undulis Fuscis Tincta sunt abdomen album sed Latera Ejus sub ales nigro fasciata Dorsum rufo-albido nigroq. varium est ut et tectrices alarum superiores sed paulo pallidiores sunt. Pennae scapulam tegentes fuscae sunt apicibus albis ut et ut et [*sic*] remiges secundariae primariae fuscae sed prima margine exteriore alba 11:21: apicibus albis tectrices interiores nigro alboq. fasciatae sunt tectrices caudae rufae sunt fasciis sive lineis transversis nigris rectrices 1:2: 1:2 rufae nigro fasciatae reliquae infra apicibus rufis sed linea parva nigra rubedinem percurrit pedes virido plumbei Digitis Longissimus extimus Longitudine tibiae.

Chatteaux Sep^tr

Scolopax gallinago. Bill straight with tubercles at the tip, feet dusky frons with four dusky stripes. Linn: Syst: Nat: 77:11:

Descr: Long straight bill, when dry, after death, the apical region is pitted anteriorly and this part is black, pale at the base. Crown black, marked with a whitish central line; cheeks white but a black line leads from the bill through the eyes. Throat whitish as are the neck and breast but these are marked with

dusky spots and vermiculations. Abdomen white barred with black on the sides beneath the wings. Back marked with rufous, dirty-white and black, as are the upper wing coverts but these are rather paler. Scapulars dusky with white tips, as are the remiges. Secondaries and primaries dusky but the outer margin of the first primary is white: 11:21 tipped with white, inner wing coverts barred with black and white; tail coverts rufous with transverse black bars or lines, rectrices 1:2:1:2 rufous barred with black, the rest below are tipped with rufous but a small black line runs through the ruddy part. Feet greenish grey, outermost digit very long, equal to the tibia.
Chatteaux Sept.

Pennant and Latham do not give Banks's record of this species from Newfoundland and Labrador.

Limosa haemastica (L.)   Hudsonian Godwit
                              Aves Grallae
9:10   53, 54
Scolopax Melanura: Rostro subrecurvato, Longissimo: Pedibus nigris, uropigio albo.—
Descr: Magnitudino *S: Rusticolae*; rostrum Longissimum, nigrum, subrecurvatum, basi tamen maxillae inferioris albidum Caput fuscum, maculis nonullis albidis; Linea Albida a rostro supra oculos: Collum et Pectus, Cinerea: Abdomen, albidum: Dorsum Fuscum, maculis Paucis nigricantibus: Remiges 1:5, fuscae immaculatae; 6:10 Parte superiori dimidio albidae: reliquae Bases habent albos, sed tectrices Partem albam occludunt: Tectrices fuscae, Dorso concolores; Plumae uropigii sive tectrices rectricum, albae sunt apicibus nigris: rectrices ipsae nigrae, exteriores Basi albescentes: omnes apicibus fuscentibus—
Habitat ad Littora Maris.—
Chatteaux Sep^tr

> *Scolopax melanura*: Bill slightly recurved, very long: feet black, rump white.
> Descr: Size of *S. rusticola* [the Woodcock], bill very long, slightly recurved, black, but the base of the lower mandible is whitish. Head dusky with a few whitish spots, a whitish line leading from the bill above the eyes; neck and breast ashy grey, abdomen whitish; back dusky with a few blackish spots; remiges 1:5 dusky, immaculate; 6:10 with half the upper part whitish, the rest have white bases but the wing coverts hide the white part. The wing coverts are dusky and the same colour as the back; the rump, or rather the tail coverts are white with black tips; the rectrices themselves are black, the outer ones with whitish bases, all with brownish tips.
> Lives on the sea shore.
> Chatteaux, Sept.

This is a very interesting record. Townsend and Allen in 1907 (p. 351) stated that the Hudsonian Godwit was then a very rare transient visitor to Labrador. In 1869 Reeks wrote of it (p. 1752), 'Visits Newfoundland in its periodical migrations, but is most common at the fall of the year, when it is generally very fat and much appreciated for the table.' Reeks is regarded as unreliable, but it seems possible that his statement about this wader is in fact correct and that large flocks used formerly to pass through Labrador.

There is a painting, f. 758 in *Aves*, vol. 13 of the Taylor White collection at McGill, which may represent Banks's specimen of the Hudsonian Godwit; although unsigned it resembles other work by Paillou and has a pencil sketch on the verso, a practice he followed when he wished to record measurements. Neither Pennant nor Latham mentions this record of Banks's.

Numenius borealis (Forster)   Eskimo Curlew
                          Aves Grallae

                                                                    55, 56

Scolopax 6:7 Pinguis, Rostro Arcuato; Pectore Subfulvo maculis sagittatis nigris. —Rostrum tenue, nigrum, mandibula superiore paulo Longiore; gula alba, caput collum albi, maculis Linearibus fuscis; Dorsum et tectrices alarum superiores fusci, maculis in marginibus Plumarum albidis; Remiges [?] nigri, fasciis fulvis; Pectus et Latera abdominis fulvi, maculis sagittatis nigris; abdomen fulve albidum; Pedes caerulescentes Remiges fuscae primi secudique [*sic*] rachis niveis; qui mihi quidem videtur multis hujus generis etc Communis:
Habitat in Collibus apricis, victitans Baccis *Empetri* Pinguissima est haec avis, certe maximae hujus Loci deliciae
Incolis Curlew . . . Gregaria.
Chatteaux August 1766.

Scolopax 6:7 Plump. Bill curved. Breast somewhat tawny with sagittate black markings. Bill slender, black, upper mandible rather longer. Throat white, head and neck white with linear dusky streaks. Back and upper wing coverts dusky with whitish spots in the margins of the feathers; remiges [? rectrices] black with tawny barring; breast and sides of the abdomen tawny with sagittate black markings; abdomen tawny white; feet bluish. Remiges dusky, first and second primaries with snow white shafts, which to me at least seems common to many birds of this genus.
Lives on open hills, feeding on the berries of *Empetrum*. This bird is very fat; certainly the greatest delicacy of this place.
Local name Curlew. Gregarious.
Chatteaux August, 1766.

The Eskimo Curlew was one of the most abundant waders in North America. Pennant (1785:461) and Latham (1785:125–6) published notes on it, and the *Arctic Zoology* contains a small engraving taken from Parkinson's painting, pl. III. In the above description Banks used remiges twice; in the first instance it appears to be a *lapsus* for rectrices since he nowhere else mentioned the tail feathers and he later described the primaries as dusky with white shafts. The unbarred primaries are one of the characters that distinguish this species from the Hudsonian Whimbrel which he probably had also. See diary 46, 79, ns. 107, 120 and notes on both species in the Systematic Lists.

Erolia alpina pacifica (Coues)   Red-backed Dunlin
Aves Grallae

4:5   57, 58

Tringa Arenaria: Rostro subulato: Pectore Fuscescenti, maculis nigris: Pedibus Luteo Viridibus:

Descr: Magnitudinis sturni; rostrum subulatum, fuscum, basi subluteum: Gula Alba, Pectus fusco-albidum, maculis Linearibus nigris: Dorsum nigrum, Plumarum marginibus Testaceis, albidisve: remiges fuscae, secundarii sive tectrices primares versus scapulam apicibus albis: aliae Dorso concolores: abdomen album: Pedes sordide Luteo-viridis Rectrices fuscae exteriores albidiores: intermediae Duae reliquis Longiores, fusciores, marginibus testaceis . . .

Habitat in Littoribus arenosis . . .

Aliae avis Pedes et Rostrum nigri toti: remiges 1–6 fuscae, 7:19 Basi albidae, 20 tota alba: rostrum subarcuatum . . .

Chatteaux Septr

Nimium affinis *T. Littoreae* nonnunquam vix major mire magnitudine variat vidi enim magnitudine *Scolopacis Galinaginis* an sexus differentia an varietas tantum nescio.

Tringa arenaria: Bill awl-shaped, breast rather dusky with black spots: feet yellowish-green.

Descr: size of a starling; bill awl-shaped, dusky, tinged with yellow at the base. Throat white, breast dusky-whitish with linear black streaks. Back black, feathers margined with brick-red or dirty white; remiges dusky; secondaries, or rather the primary coverts near the shoulders, with white tips, the rest the same colour as the back; abdomen white; feet dull yellowish-green; rectrices dusky, the outer ones paler, the two central feathers longer and darker than the rest, and with brick-red margins.

Lives on sandy beaches.

Some birds have totally black bills and feet; remiges 1–6 dusky; 7–19 with whitish bases, 20 totally white; bill slightly curved.

Chatteaux, Sept. Extremely close to *T. littorea*, sometimes scarcely larger, but there was marked variation in size for I saw some of the size of *Scolopax gallinago*, but whether this is merely a difference in the sexes, or a variety, I do not know.

Banks's detailed description fits a juvenile Dunlin very well. His final observation possibly applies to mixed flocks of waders in the field.

Having examined series of skins with Dr. Kenneth Parkes I am sure that all of Banks's notes could very well apply to *E. alpina pacifica*, and not to *Erolia melanotos* Vieillot, an exceedingly rare fall transient in Labrador. This latter species should therefore be deleted from Banks's list of species (Lysaght 1959:358). The fact that Banks described the bill of one lot of specimens as awl-shaped, and of another as slightly curved is less important than his emphasis on the brick-red margins of the feathers of the tail and back. These feathers are much brighter in autumn Dunlin than in the Pectoral Sandpiper.

Tringa littorea L. is a synonym of *Philomachus pugnax* (L.), the Ruff, but Banks also employed it as an MS name for *Erolia minutilla* (Viellot), the Least Sandpiper, a bird which he rightly compares in size with a sparrow (p. 61). Here he is probably referring to the sandpiper and not to the larger Ruff.

Arenaria interpres morinella (L.) Ruddy Turnstone
Aves Grallae

59, 60

Tringa Interpres Pedibus Rubris, Corpore nigro albo ferrugineoq. vario Pectore Abdomineq. albo Linn: Syst: Nat: 78:4
Descr: Rostrum nigrum breve Validum caput Fuscum maculis nigricantibus genae et tempora albidiores sed infra et ante fascia parva atra Gula Alba Collum et Pectus albo nigroq. varia abdomen tectrices alarum interiores et Cauda albae pedes Luteo Rubescunt Dorsum abdomini Concolor sed Plumae nigrae Eum tegunt ferrugineo maculatae uropygium nigrum remiges nigrae Basi apiceq. albae exteriores Albidiores rectrices 1:5 nigrae margine interiori albae reliquae basi albescunt remiges Secundarii apice albescunt exceptis 5 primis totis nigris.
Habitat ad Littora maris Gregaria.
Chatteaux Sep^{tr}

Tringa interpres. Feet red, body variegated black, white and ferruginous, breast and abdomen white. Linn: Syst: Nat: 78:4
Descr: Bill black, short, stout; head dusky with blackish spots; cheeks and post-ocular patch whitish but a small black bar below and in front; throat white, neck and breast variegated black and white; abdomen, under coverts of the wings and tail white; feet somewhat yellowish red; back the same colour as

the abdomen but black feathers with ferruginous spots cover it; rump black; remiges black with white tips and bases, the outer ones a paler dirty whitish colour. Rectrices 1:5 black with inner margins white, the rest with whitish bases; secondary remiges with whitish tips, except for the first five which are wholly black.

Lives in flocks on the seashore.

Chatteaux, September.

There is a painting of this bird by Paillou, pl. 76. On another, in the Taylor White collection (*Aves*, 14, f. 781), which is unsigned but appears to be by Paillou, White has written '*Tringa galinula* Mr. Banks'.

Erolia minutilla (Vieillot)   Least Sandpiper or American Stint
                              Aves Grallae

                                                                 61, 62

Tringa littorea Rostro Laevi pedibus fuscis Remigibus fuscis Rachi Primae nivea Linn: Syst: Nat: 78:12

Descr: Magnitudo *Fringillae Domesticae*. Rostrum nigrum Collum Cinereum fusco nebulosum Caput fuscum maculis nigricantibus dorsum nigrum singula pluma macula nigra apiceq. alba uropygium nigrum rectrices fuscae nonalbo undulatae sed exteriores albidiores tectrices inferiores alarum albidae sed nullis Lineis cinereis

Habitat in Paludibus Prope Mari

Chatteaux August

> *Tringa littorea* Bill smooth, feet dusky, remiges dusky, shafts of the first snow-white. Linn: Syst: Nat: 78:12
> Descr: Size of *Fringilla domestica* [House Sparrow, *Passer domesticus* (L.)]. Bill black, neck ash-gray clouded with a dusky colour; head dusky with blackish spots; back black, each feather with a black spot and a white tip; rump black; rectrices dusky with off-white vermiculations, but the outer ones a paler whitish colour; under wing coverts whitish but with no grayish lines at all.
> Lives in marshes near the sea.
> Chatteaux, August.

This is an excellent description of this bird; although the stints in general are not easy to determine, Banks's notes clearly refer to *E. minutilla*. See Parkinson's pl. 77. This drawing was, indirectly, the type of Gmelin's *Tringa novaeterrae* (1788:674) which was based on Latham's description of this bird, taken from this drawing in Banks's collection; it is clear that when Latham saw the drawing there was no specimen available, since he says (1785:181), 'Size uncertain.' Application has been made to the International Commission on Zoological Nomenclature to have Gmelin's name made officially obsolete.

TETRAO Lagopus. Linne.

Pl. XII Allen's Willow Ptarmigan, *Lagopus lagopus alleni*
Sydney Parkinson

Lobipes lobatus (L.)   Northern or Red-necked Phalarope
Aves Grallae

63, 64

Tringa Lobata Rostro subulato apice inflexo Pedibus Virescentibus Lobatis abdomine albido Linn: Syst: Nat: 78:5

Descr: Magnitudine *T. Littoream* aequat vel paulo superat Rostrum nigrum tenuissimum apicibus acutis Caput Parvum frons alba nucha nigra Linea Alba a Fronte supra oculos Tempora nigra Gula Alba Dorsum nigrum Plumarum Marginibus rufis Tectrices alarum Nigrae Apicibus Albidis Pectus Fuscum Venter et abdomen Albae Pedes Plumbei semipalmati Sed Parte Exteriori Lobati . . .

Habitat ad Littora maris sed Rarius

Chatteaux Sep^tr 7th 1766

> *Tringa lobata* Bill awl-shaped, bent at the tip. Feet greenish, lobed. Abdomen whitish. Linn: Syst: Nat: 78:5 . . .
>
> Descr: Equal in size to, or a little larger than *T. littorea* [see notes pp. 58, 61, on Banks's MS name for *Erolia minutilla*]. Bill black, very thin with a sharp tip. Head small, frons white, nape black; a white line from the frons to above the eye; post-ocular patch black; throat white, back black, the feathers margined with rufous. Wing coverts black with whitish tips; breast dusky, belly and abdomen white: feet gray, half-webbed but lobed exteriorly. Lives on the seashore but is uncommon.
>
> Chatteaux, Sep^tr. 7th, 1766.

The bill of these birds is straight but delicate; its bent appearance must have been due to slight damage.

Charadrius semipalmatus (Bonaparte)   Semipalmated Plover
Aves Grallae

65, 66

Charadrias Hiaticula Pectore Nigro fronte nigricante fasciolae albae Vertice fusco pedibus Luteis. Linn: Syst: Nat: 79:2

Descr: Rostrum Croceum apice nigro nonnullis nigrum basi tantum mandibulae inferioris Croceae frons alba Vertex fuscus albo Leviter undulatus regio oculorum albidior genarum fuscior Gula & pars superior Colli albae quae albedo extenditur in Collare album pone collum Dorsum fuscum Cinereo undulatum quae Color Extenditur in Collare fuscum ante pectus abdomen album Remiges fuscae 1:3 margine interiori albescentes 4:14 marginibus exterioribus et interioribus albescentes omnium raches albo nigroq. varii remiges secundarii 1:3 fuscae immaculatae reliquae apicibus albis rectrices fusci exteriores albidiores 6:6 totae fuscae 1:1 totae albae reliquae apicibus albis Pedes Luteo fusci.

377

Habitat ad Littora arenosa Gregaria . . .
Chatteaux Sep[tr] 1766

Charadrias hiaticula Breast black, frons blackish with a white band, crown dusky, feet yellow. Linn: Syst: Nat: 79:2:

Descr: Bill bright yellow, tip black, in some entirely black at the base; lower mandible bright yellow; frons white, crown dusky lightly barred with wavy white lines; area round the eyes whiter, cheeks darker; throat and upper part of neck white, and this whiteness is extended as a white collar behind the neck; back dusky, with ashy gray vermiculations and this colour extends as a dark collar in front of the breast; abdomen white; remiges dusky, 1:3 with a whitish inner edge, 4:14 with the outer and inner margins whitish, all with variegated black and white shafts; secondary remiges 1:3 dusky, immaculate, the remainder with white tips; rectrices dusky, outer ones whiter, 6:6 completely dusky, 1:1 completely white, the rest with white tips; feet a yellowish dusky colour. Lives in flocks on sandy beaches.
Chatteaux Sept., 1766.

This bird is common in Newfoundland and Labrador during the summer, breeding both on the mainland and on the outlying islands. Banks had three or four skins of this species in his collection; the numbers differ in the various lists.

Pluvialis dominica dominica (Müller)   American Golden Plover
Aves Grallae

67, 68

Charadrias Pluvialis Pedibus cinereis corpore nigro viridiq. maculato subtus albido
Linn: Syst: Nat: 79:8

Descr: Rostrum Nigrum frons et malae albidae maculis parvis fuscis Caput et dorsum nigri maculis subrotundis Luteo-fuscis remiges fuscae immaculatae sed versus basin et margine interiori albidae abdomen nonnullis totum albicat sed non raro plumis nigris intermixtis vidi abdomen fere totum nigrum . . .
Habitat in Collibus apricis Gregaria victitans Baccis *Empetri* . . .
Chatteaux Sept[r]:

Charadrias pluvialis Feet ash-gray, body spotted with black and green, whitish beneath. Linn: Syst: Nat: 79:8.

Descr: Bill black, frons and cheeks whitish with small dusky spots; head and back black with rounded dusky-yellow spots; remiges dusky, immaculate but whitish towards the base and inner margin; abdomen completely white in some, but not infrequently with black feathers interspersed; I have seen the abdomen almost entirely black . . .

Lives in flocks on open hills feeding on berries of *Empetrum* . . .
Chatteaux, Sept.

Banks's record (see also diary 46, 79; n. 121) is interesting since this plover
is now an uncommon autumn transient in Newfoundland and Labrador
(Townsend and Allen 1907:358). Pennant (1785:484) says, 'Migrates to
the Labrador Coast, about a week after the Esquimaux Whimbrels, in its way
to New York; but not in such numbers', an observation presumably made on
Banks's authority. There is a detailed discussion of the migration route of this
plover in Todd (1963:293–6).

Crocethia alba (Pallas)   Sanderling

Aves Grallae

2:3   69, 70

Charadrias Tringoides Rostro Longo nigerrimo; pectore abdomineq. albidae; Dorso
albo nigroq. vario . . .
Descr: Magnitudine Vix *C. Hiaticulam* aequat; rostrum *Tringae* Longum, nigerrimum; Tota avis subtus, gula, pectus, abdomen, tectrices alarum, et caudae,
niveae; caput album vertex maculis nigris; circa oculos nebula fusca. Lineaq. fusca
a rostro ad oculos ducta est; colli Pars superior cinerea, maculis minutis fuscis;
Dorsum nigrum, marginibus pennarum maculis albis; remiges 1:4 nigrae; margine
interiori albidae; reliquae Basi et margine exteriore dimidiato albae; tectrices
alarum dorso concolores, sed paulo pallidiores; rectrices fusco albo, sed versus
Basin albidiores; pedes tridactili nigerrimi . . .
Habitant in insulis seal Islands dietis magna Copiae . . .
Chatteaux Septr 21.

> 2:3
>
> *Charadrias tringoides.* Bill long, very black; breast and abdomen whitish; back
> variegated with white and black.
> Descr: Size scarcely equal to *C. Hiaticula* [*Charadrius hiaticula* L., the Ringed
> Plover]; bill as long as that of *Tringa*, very black; the bird entirely white
> below, throat, breast, abdomen, coverts of the wings and tail snow-white.
> Head white with black spots on the crown; a dusky patch round the eyes, and
> a dusky line leads from the bill to the eyes; upper part of the neck ash-gray
> with minute dusky spots; back black, the edges of the feathers spotted with
> white; remiges 1:4 black, the inner edge whitish; the rest with the bases and
> outer margins half white; wing coverts the same colour as the back but rather
> paler; rectrices dusky white but paler towards the base; feet tridactyl, very
> black.
> They live on the Seal Islands where there is plenty of food.
> Chatteaux Septr 21.

379

I am indebted to Dr. Wetmore for determining this species. Pennant (1785: 486) published Banks's note on the abundance of these birds at the Seal Islands. See also Parkinson's pl. 78, on the verso of which Banks wrote '[sp]ecimen . . . foundland gregarious'.

Canachites canadensis (L.)   Spruce Grouse

Aves Gallinae

Tetrao Canadensis? Mas   71, 72

Descr: Rostrum nigrum Pectus nigrum macula magna nivea ad Basin singulae Pennae abdomen quoq. nigrum macula alba ut in Pectore & saepe altera in medio Pennae anus alba femora fusco albidoq. undulata tectrices interiores caudae abdomini concolores Rectrices ipsae nigerrimae apicibus fulvis Dorsum fuscum singula Penna albido undulata Pennae Longae inter Dorsum et alas subrufescunt et raches habent albae Remiges fuscae immaculatae tectrices exteriores dorso concolores sed Paulo fusciores ut et interiores sed apicibus albis Pedes fusci Lanati sed Digiti nudi

Habitat in densis sylvis inter Betulae.

Chatteaux Sept^r

Tetrao canadensis? male.

Descr: Bill black, breast black with a large snow-white spot at the base [*laps. cal.*] of each feather; abdomen also black, with a white spot as in the breast, and often another in the middle of the feather; anus white; femora with dusky and whitish vermiculations; under tail coverts the same colour as the abdomen; rectrices themselves very black with tawny tips; back dusky, each feather with dirty white vermiculations; the long feathers between the back and the wings are somewhat rufous and have white shafts. Remiges dusky, immaculate; upper wing coverts the same colour as the back but rather darker, the under wing coverts are similar but with white tips; feet clothed with dusky feathers but the toes bare.

Lives in dense woods among birches.

Chatteaux, Sept.

Mr. Todd considers (in lit.) that the Spruce Grouse at Chateau Bay and nearby are intermediate forms, nearer to *C. c. canace* (L.) than to *C. c. canadensis*. There is a painting of a pair of these grouse by Sydney Parkinson, pl. V and Banks wrote 'Newfoundland' on the verso. When he wrote the localities on the paintings he seldom discriminated between Newfoundland and Labrador, and here, as in some other cases, he has probably made a mistake, since this species is not known to occur in Newfoundland.

Lagopus mutus rupestris (Gmelin)	Rock Ptarmigan
Lagopus lagopus (L.)	Willow Ptarmigan

Aves Gallinae

Tetrao 73, 74

Tetraonis Lagopi an varietas an nova avis? . . .

Descript: L: *Tetrici* Paulo minor: caput, Collum, Pectus, fusci: Lineis punctisq. nigris et albidis, confertis, nonnullis Leviter flavescentibus: gula albidior est; rostrum breve, nigrum; supra oculos supercilium Latum Laete coccineum remiges omnes albae, sex primae rachidibus nigris, tectrices quoq. albae, sed corpori versus dorso concolores, tectrices interiores omnes albae; Pectoris Pars inferior, abdomen, et tectrices caudae interiores albissimae Sed Latera infra alas sunt dorso concolores, Pedes usq. ad ungulis Lana confertissima albae vestiti sunt; Rectrices nigrae, apicibus albis duabus intermediis totis albis . . .

Per totam aestatem nunquam fuscior est . . .

Alia avis major Erat *T. Tetricem* aequans gula et Pectoris Pars anterior rufescentes Palpebrae Pallidae plumulis nonnullis albis marginatae sub alas Plumae nonullae Luteo nigroq. fasciatae.

Chatteaux Sept^r . . .

Ungues Longiores et Pedes Lana densiore Vestiti

Tetrao. A variety of *Tetrao lagopus*, or a new species?

Descript: Rather smaller than *L. tetrix* [*Lyrurus tetrix* (L.), Black Grouse]; head, neck and breast dusky with black and whitish lines and spots crowded together, some tinged with light yellow; throat a paler whitish colour; bill short, black; above the eyes a broad stripe of bright red; all the remiges white, the shafts of the first six black, wing coverts also white but towards the body they are the same colour as the back; all the under wing coverts are white. The lower part of the breast, abdomen and under tail coverts are very white, but the sides below the wings are the same colour as the back [which Banks forgot to describe]; feet densely covered with white feathers as far as the claws; rectrices black tipped with white, the two central ones wholly white. Throughout the summer it is never darker . . .

Another larger bird was similar to *L. tetrix*, the throat and upper part of the breast rufous, the eyelid pale, a few feathers margined with white, beneath the wings a few feathers barred with yellow and black.

Chatteaux, Sept.

Claws longer, and feet more densely feathered.

The larger birds mentioned at the end of this description of Rock Ptarmigan are probably *Lagopus lagopus albus* (Gmelin), the Willow Ptarmigan. Both appear to have been taken at Chateau Bay. There is a painting by Sydney

381

Parkinson, pl. XII, of Allen's Willow Ptarmigan which must have been taken in Newfoundland since it is confined to that island.

Turdus migratorius nigrideus Aldrich & Nutt American Robin
Aves Passeres

2:3 75, 76

Turdus Ferrugineus. Pectore alisq. subtus ferrugineis: remigibus rectricibusq. omnibus fuscis, immaculatis . . .

Descr: Magnitudinis *T. Iliaci,* cui congener: caput nigrum dorsum cinereo fuscum; ambo nebula viridi flavo tincta: uropygium cinerascens; rectrices nigrae, immaculatae; Palpebrae albae; gula alba, maculis Linearibus nigris; Pectus et abdominis Pars superior Ferruginea, sed Plumarum marginibus Leviter albo tinctis; tectrices interiores caudae albae; remiges fuscae, immaculatae, tectricibus interioribus ferrugineis; Rostrum et Pedes nigri . . .

Incolis Robin . . .

Habitat in Sylvis frequens: circa St. John's Frequentissima . . .

Chatteaux Sept[r]

2:3

Turdus ferrugineus. Breast and undersurface of wings rust-coloured; remiges and rectrices all dusky, immaculate.

Descr: Size of *T. iliacus* [the European Redwing] to which it is related. Head black, back dusky with ashy gray, both tinged with cloudy greenish yellow; rump tending to ashy gray; rectrices black, immaculate; eyebrows white; throat white with black streaks; breast and upper part of the abdomen ferruginous, but the edges of the feathers are faintly tinged with white; lower tail coverts white; remiges dusky, immaculate; under wing coverts rust-coloured; bill and feet black.

Vernacular name Robin.

Common in woods, very abundant about St. John's.

Chatteaux Sept.

Pennant (1785:336) published Banks's note on the abundance of these birds at St. John's. See also diary 18, n. 25. The key number at the top of the above description does not tie up with any known MS; another description of the American Robin is given on p. 87 of this MS.

Hylocichla ustulata clarescens (Burleigh & Peters) Swainson's Thrush
Passeres

No. 14 77, 78

Motacilla Orni

Motacilla supra fusca, remigibus subtus Fascia alba . . .

Descr: Caput, tergum, rectrices, uropygium, remiges Supra Fusci; mandibula superior nigra; inferior Basi Lutea; rictus Lutea; gula et Pectus, albae, maculis triangularibus fuscis; abdomen album; Latera subfuca [*sic*] ut et tectrices alarum inferiores; Remiges 1:3 fuscae, immaculatae; 4:14 versum medium macula alba quasi translucente insignita; tectrices fuscae; Plantae Longae, Ex albido sub-rubentes, digiti fusci, ut et ungues; digitus extimus Basi connexus cum intermedio
. . .

Croque August 34:2

> No. 14
> *Motacilla orni*
> *Motacilla* dusky above, underside of remiges with a white bar.
> Descr: Head, back, rectrices, rump and remiges dusky above; upper mandible black, lower one yellow at the base; gape yellow; throat and breast white with triangular dusky spots; abdomen white, sides rather dusky as are the under wing coverts. Remiges 1:3 dusky, immaculate; 4:14 with a white spot towards the middle, which is remarkable in being almost translucent; feet long, pinkish-whitish, toes and claws dusky; outermost digit connected with the middle one at the base.
> Croque August 34:2.

I should have hesitated to identify this further than *Hylocichla* sp. but Pennant in describing the Little Thrush (1725:338) from Canada, Newfoundland, etc., which is considered to be this thrush, mentions the white eye-ring which is diagnostic. As I have shown elsewhere Banks supplied him with most if not all of his unacknowledged Newfoundland material. Banks's number 34:2 refers to the earlier capture of this bird at Croque, noted on p. 34 of his diary, n. 85.

Loxia leucoptera leucoptera (Gmelin)   White-winged Crossbill
Aves Passeres

1:2   79, 80

Loxia Abietina Rostro forficata Linea alarum duplici alba . . .
Descr: magnitudine *Fringillam domesticam* vix aequat Rostrum nigrum forficatum maxilla superiore Longiore Caput, Pectus Dorsum Uropygium Pallide rubent abdomen Fusco albidum remiges nigrae sed tres posteriores apice albescunt Secundarii 1:8 nigrae immaculatae cetera apicibus albis notantur ut sunt tectrices Cauda forficata nigra tectrices inferiores ejus nigrae marginibus albis Pedes nigri Digiti Validi . . .
Habitat inter Pinetos canorus . . .
Chatteaux Croque

1:2

Loxia abietina Bill forked, double white wing-bar.

Descr: scarcely as large as *Fringilla domestica* [see below]. Bill black, forked, upper mandible longer. Head, breast, back and rump light red; abdomen dusky white. Remiges black but the three posterior ones tipped with white; secondaries 1:8 immaculate black, the rest distinguished by white tips as are the coverts. Tail black, forked, the under tail coverts black margined with white. Feet black, toes stout.

Habitat, sings amongst pine trees.

Chatteaux, Croque.

Passerella iliaca iliaca (Merrem)   Fox Sparrow

Aves Passeres

27:28   81, 82

Fringilla Betulae Rectricibus rufis Pectore albo maculis rufescentibus . . .

Descr: Magnitudine *F. domesticam* aequat vel Paulo superat rostrum Conicum mandibula superiore nigra inferiore Lutescens Caput Rufo-cinereum maculis duabus albis inter Rostrum et oculos tempora rufescunt maculis nonnullis albis Dorsum rufo Cinereum sed rectrices et uropygium rufae sunt remiges nigricant marginibus exterioribus rufis rectricum duae ordines dorso concolores sunt apicibus Pallidis Gula Pectus Et Latera abdominis albae sunt maculis rufis Plurimis abdomen Album Pedes digiti et ungues fusco albidae . . .

Habitat satis frequens in nemoribus non nimis Densis . . .

Croque Octr 7 1766

Fringilla betulae Rectrices reddish, breast white with reddish spots.

Descr: the same size or a little larger than *F. domestica* [*Passer domesticus* (L.), the House Sparrow]. Bill conical, upper mandible black, the lower yellowish. Head reddish gray with two white spots between the bill and the eyes; post-ocular patch reddish with a few white spots. Back gray with red, but rectrices and rump reddish. Remiges blackish, red at the outer edges; both series of rectrices the same colour as the back, with pale tips; throat, breast and sides of abdomen white with many reddish spots, abdomen white. Feet, toes and claws dusky whitish.

Habitat, fairly common in open woodlands.

Croque Oct 7 1766

There is a painting of one of these birds by Sydney Parkinson, (pl. I) labelled *Fringilla betula*. Another finch taken at St. John's on 25 May seems to be one of these Fox Sparrows, except that when Banks wrote his notes on it (pp. 88, 89; 22:6, no. 3) he stated that the rump was white. He may have confused the whitish under tail coverts with the feathers of the rump.

76. *Arenaria interpres morinella*, Ruddy Turnstone.
Peter Paillou

77. *Erolia minutilla*, Least Sandpiper.
Sydney Parkinson

78. *Crocethia alba*, Sanderling.
Sydney Parkinson

PICUS auratus. Linné

81. *Colaptes auratus*, Yellow-shafted Flicker.
Sydney Parkinson

82. *Eremophila alpestris*, Horned Lark, two males.
Peter Paillou

MOTACILLA *petechia*.

Olivacea, subtus flava rubro guttata, pileo rubro. Habitat in America septentrionale. Sxml

83. *Dendroica petechia amnicola*, Newfoundland Yellow Warbler.
Sydney Parkinson

Arhopalus foveicollis (Halleman); syn. *Criocephalus agrestis* Kirby.

Insecta Coleoptera

46:47   83, 84

Cerambyx cymbae Piceus Thorace punctis tribus excavatis Elytris Striatis . . .

Decr: Corpus Angustum Longitudine Pollicis Transversi antenna corpore Paulo breviores caput Elytra Thorax Pedes Picei Elytra striata striis Duabus Elevatis et margine Abdomen Canescens Oculi satis magni nigri . . .

Hujus insectae varietatem vidi Elytris Pedibusque Castaneis Articulis antennarum tibiarumq. albis . . .

Habitat in sinu Chatteaux satis Frequens

46:47

Cerambyx cymbae Pitch black, thorax punctuate with three depressions, elytra striate.

Decr: Body narrow, as long as the width of a thumb, antennae rather shorter than the body; head, elytra, thorax and legs pitch black; elytra striate with two raised ridges and with the margin also raised; abdomen hoary white; eyes fairly large, black. I saw a variety of this insect with chestnut elytra and legs, and with the joints of the antennae and tibiae white . . .

Habitat Chatteaux Bay, fairly common.

I am much obliged to Mr. W. J. Brown and Dr. Howden, Entomological Research Institute, Ottawa, for the identification of this beetle; see also E. G. Linsley (1962:70).

This is a common species that extends to the tree line in Labrador and elsewhere in Canada.

Unidentified beetle

Insecta Coleoptera   85

16:17   Chatteaux

Cerambyx Fasciatus Thorace spinoso Pubescente nigro Elytris testaceis fasciis duabus fuscis . . .

Descr: Thorax et Abdomen nigri pilis raris lanis obsiti Antennae corpore Breviores nigrae Pedes nigri femora et tibiae Longissimae Elytra basi attenuata non conniventia Testacea fasciis duabus fuscis in singula oculi Virido-Caerulei

Habitat in Sinu Chatteaux rarius

Obs: Elytris apice attenuatis ad *Lepturos* accedit.

16:17   Chatteaux

Cerambyx fasciatus Thorax spiny, pubescent and black. Elytra brick red with two brown stripes.

Descr: Thorax and abdomen black covered with wool and a few hairs. Antennae shorter than the body, black; feet black; femora and tibiae very long; elytra narrow at the base, not closing dehiscent brick red with two dusky stripes, greenish-blue eye spots on each.

Habitat, Chatteaux Bay, uncommon.

It resembles *Leptura* in the narrow tip of the elytra.

This beetle has not been identified. The specimens labelled *Cerambyx fasciatus* in the Banks collection at the British Museum belong to an Indian species, now *Pachyteria fasciatus* (Fabr.).

SECTION 2

DESCRIPTIONS IN ENGLISH

The following descriptions of birds are written on two sheets of the same size as those comprising Section One, folded to make a booklet of four leaves, sewn down the middle. Banks left no margins on these pages; the last is blank. Most of the notes are written in English; where he has used Latin, a translation follows in square brackets.

BIRDS

87

Turdus migratorius nigrideus Aldrich & Nutt   American Robin

Mas   Nº: 1. Calld here a robin

18:9: is a bird of the Thrush Kind tho it seems [different] from Linnaeus' *Turdi* in the tongue which instead of being Lacero Emarginato [frayed marginally] is divided at the tip into three by two fine slitts From the Tip of the bill to the End of the Claws he measures $9\frac{1}{2}$ inches his Wings extended $15\frac{1}{2}$ inches his Bill is Yellow But Black upon the tip inside of his mouth Yellow and his Throat white with a few Black spots the upper Part of his head and Both his Cheeks are Black Excepting a White circle Round Each of his Eyes the Pupils of which are Black his Breast sides and the under feathers of his wings are of a lightish Ferrugineous Colour his thighs Brown a little Spotted with white about the Knees his feet and toes of a deep Brown his Rump is White his Tail . . .

88

The outsides of his Wings are Brown his Back dark ash Colour

Another description, in Latin, appears earlier in this MS, p. 75.

See also the diary, p. 18.

Passerculus sandwichensis labradorius Howe   Savannah Sparrow
19:3: No 2.

a Small Bird seems to belong to the Genus of *Fringilla* from the Point of the Bill to the tip of the Claws 5 inches its wings Extended 9 inches the upper Mandible is Black the Lower Flesh Coloured inside of his mouth Flesh Colourd his Throat & Breast are white with Black Spots his Belly & rump white his legs & Toes are Light Brown his Claws a little Darker the under Part of his Tail & wings Light Brown the Top of his head Varies in small Spots with Black white & Brown the Pupils of his Eyes are Black over Each of them is a yellow line his Back is in Colour like the Top of his head his tail which Consists of ten feathers is Brown the two outside feathers being tipd with white

See also n. 30.

?*Passerella iliaca iliaca* (Merrem)   Fox Sparrow
22:6 N°: 3

A bird that seems also to belong to the genus of *Fringilla* his lengh from the tip of his Bill to the End of his feet

89

Six inches his wings Extended 11 inches the upper Mandible is Black his lower white his Throat and breast are White Spoted with Triangular Ferrugineous spots his Sides with Long spots of the same shape tipd with ferrugineous his Rump white his feet, toes & claws of a very light Brown The inside of his wings Light Brown inside of the Tail the same with a ferrugineus Tinge the top of his head ash Colourd with very small Ferrugineus spot [*sic*] the Pupils of his Eyes are Black on the upper side of Each of them is a small white spot his Cheeks Ferrugineous his Back like his head only the spots much Larger the Covert Feathers of his Wings are Ferrugineous the Wings themselves are Brown the Covert Feathers of his Tail are also Ferrugineous His Tail consists of [blank] Feathers the inner Part of which is Brow[n], the outer Ferrugineous

> Banks described this Fox Sparrow earlier under the MS name of *Fringilla betula* (pp. 81, 82 above, pl. I, and see diary 22, n. 42). The under tail coverts, not the feathers of the rump, are whitish, but if the specimen was damaged Banks might have been misled.

Melospiza georgiana ericrypta Oberholser   Swamp Sparrow
22:4 No 4

This also seems to be of the *Fringilla* Genus his lengh is 5½ inches his Breadth 8 his Upper Mandible is Black the Lower

Dusky his Throat is white his breast a little Darker his Belly white again under his wings is dusky with Longish white Spots his feet toes and Claws of a Dusky Flesh Colour his Tail Consisting of ten Feathers ash colourd the top of his head immediately over his Beak is Black above that is a large spot of a deep ferrugineous Colour over his Eyes runs a line of ash Colour his Eyes themselves I had not an opportunity of seeing the Back of his head again is Black his neck dark ash Colour his Back is spotted with Black and Brown the Covert Feathers of his Wings are Black & Ferrugineus as are the innermost Feathers of the wings themselves the Tail Consists of ten Feathers the outside edges of which are of a light Ferrugineous Colour the inside Black

> This bird was taken at St. John's by Captain Williams and given to Banks on 26 May; it is included in his keg list.
> See also diary 22, n. 40.

? *Rissa tridactyla* (L.)   Black-legged Kittiwake
22:5 Nº: 5 Gull
is a Bird of the Gull Kind which differs in some Particulars from the *Larus Canus* [*L. canus* L., Mew or Common Gull]

of which differences only I shall take notice its lengh is 15 inches its Breadth 37 nulla macula alba in medio Nigredines (Excepto Primo) Pedes nigri Palmati Tridactyli cum Pollice obsoleto ut in *L: Tridactylus*
. . . Iris oculorum Potius Caerulea quam cinerea . . .
Lingua Sagittata sed non bifida
   [No white spot in the middle, they are black (except for the first). Feet black, webbed, tridactyl with pollex obsolete as in *L. tridactylus*. Iris of the eyes more blue than ash-grey. Tongue sagittate but not bifid.]

> This very incomplete description probably applies to a young kittiwake.
> See also n. 41, and pp. 27–30 above.

Cepphus grylle atlantis Salomonsen   Black Guillemot
23:7: No 6 Sea Pigeon
Colymbus Grylle Fauna Suecica with some small differences as Tectrices Secundae non totae albae sed Versus Basin nigrae Pennae interiores alarum totae albae oculi nigri Os Palatum Lingua Canthus iris rubri Longitudo unciae 15 Latitudo 21½
   [Secondary coverts not wholly white but black towards the base, inner feathers of the wings totally white; eyes black, mouth, palate, tongue, rim of the mouth and iris red. Length 15 inches, breadth 21½]

> See also pp. 23–24 above; diary 23, n. 48.

Actitis macularia (L.)   Spotted Sandpiper
24:3 Nº: 7 Beach Bird
Tringa Hypoleucos seems to answer in Every thing but the middle feathers of the
tail 4 of Linnaes's Bird were quite

Brown only 2 of this   92

    See diary 24, n. 51.

Pinicola enucleator (L.)   Pine Grosbeak
24:4 Nº: 8
Loxia Enucleator Linnaei answers extreemly well

    See n. 52.

Wilsonia pusilla pusilla (Wilson)   Wilson's Warbler, male
26:2 Nº: 9. Gold Bird.
Motacilla species its Lengh is 4 & $\frac{1}{4}$ inches its breadth 6:$\frac{1}{2}$ its bill rather Flat the
upper mandible is Black Lower Black at the tip but white toward the Base inside
of his mouth white Eyes black his neck throat Breast & Belly of a Beautifull Yellow
his Feet light Brown his Claws somewhat Darker a line of the same yellow is under
his Throat goes over the top of his Bill & eyes the top of his head is Coverd with a
large spot of beautiful Shining Black his Back is green as are the Covert feathers of
his wings & the outer edge of Each of his wing feathers as are those of his tail
except the 2 outermost

Wilsonia pusilla pusilla (Wilson)   Female or young Wilson's Warbler.   93
30:8 [written over 24:3] No 10
Gold Bird Foemina? wants the Black spot upon the head one specimen is Paler
Colourd than the Rest in all other Particulars the same as the Last

    For fuller notes on these warblers see diary 30 and
    ns. 57, 58 and 72.

Dendroica striata (Forster)   Black-polled Warbler, female
30:9: No 11 *Motacilla* species
Breadth 8 inches lengh 4$\frac{1}{2}$ top of his head neck & Back are greenish each feather
having a black spot in the middle the tail is dark each of the outer feathers have a
white spot upon the inside of their Bottoms the upper covert feathers of its wings
are dark with white tips which makes white Bars across the wings the quill feathers

themselves are black with a very narrow greenish line on their outside Edges its Bill is dark its throat tingd with Yellow But Powderd over with Black spots Belly White Legs and Claws flesh colourd

See diary 30, n. 73. Pennant 1785:401

SECTION 3

The third part of the MS, comprising the botanical notes, is printed in this book at the end of Banks's plant catalogue to which it is directly related (see pp. 307–10).

SECTION 4

BANKS'S SPIRIT COLLECTION

Banks's numbering of the following specimens is based on the system he used in the earlier part of this MS except for the eight entries on p. 107 beginning with *Falco Lagopus* Ferrugineous Cat: 1:3:3:. I have found nothing to fit in with these numbers which suggests that there is at least one notebook that has not yet been found. There are, however, paintings or descriptions of these eight birds in various sections of the Newfoundland–Labrador MSS. Since nearly all the material in this list is discussed elsewhere I have simply added after Banks's name the current name of the species or race, and a note on the page where the painting or description is discussed. The digits after each name indicate the number of specimens.

Contents of Keg No. 1 105

Motacilla 1
 Unidentified
19:2: *Gasterosteus aculeatus* 1
 Correct. N. 29.
19:3: Small Bird 11111
 Passerculus sandwichensis (Gmelin). N. 30.
19:7: *Fiber Moscatus* 1
 Ondatra obscurus (Bangs). Diary 19.
Loxia Cardinalis 11
 Richmondena cardinalis (L.). The Cardinal is casual in Nova Scotia and Quebec but I can find no record of it as far north as Newfoundland. Banks may have been given a pair of these birds, since they are commonly caged. See also p. 420.

19:11: Sculpen
   N. 33.

19:12: Sculpen 11
   ? *Myoxocephalus scorpius* (L.). Diary 19.

19:13: Cat Fish 11
   Anarhichas sp. Diary 19.

20:1: *Echinus* 12
   ? *Strongylocentrotus droebachiensis* (O. F. Müller). N. 35.

20:2: *Echinus* 11
   Probably *Echinarachnius parma* (Lamarck). Diary 20, pl. 86a.

20:5: *Fucus* By mistake but seems to be the best way of preserving them.

                             107

18:9: Thrush 1111
   Turdus migratorius nigrideus (Aldrich & Nutt). N. 25, diary 18.

22:4: *Fringilla* Species Capt. Williams 1
   Melospiza georgiana ericrypta Oberholser. N. 40.

22:5: *Lari* 11
   ? *Rissa tridactyla tridactyla* L. N. 41, pl. 80.

22:6: *Fringillae* species 1
   Passerella iliaca iliaca (Merrem). N. 42, pl. I.

   Lusciniam annulans 111
   Unidentified. Gmelin (1789:950) lists various references to *Luscinia*, a genus in which the European Nightingale was sometimes placed, but that bird does not occur in North America. Banks must have collected a bird with a ringing song but there is nothing to show what it was.

24:2: *Murena* 11
   Unidentified. Banks wrote *Blennius gattorugine* against this fish in his diary. N. 50.

24:3: *Tringa Hypoleucos* 1111
   Actitis macularia (L.). N. 51.

24:4: *Loxia enucleator* 1
   Pinicola enucleator (L.). N. 52.

19:1: *Salmonis Species* 1
   Salvelinus fontinalis Mitchill, or *S. alpinus* (L.). N. 28, pl. 87.

26:2: Gold Bird 1
   Wilsonia pusilla pusilla (Wilson). N. 57.

26:3: *Fringilla Species* 1
   ? Not a finch but *Wilsonia pusilla pusilla* Wilson. N. 58.

26:4: *Hirundinis* Species 1
   Hirundo rustica erythrogaster (Boddaert). N. 59.

Parus Palustris 1
> *Parus atricapillus bartletti* (Aldrich & Nutt). N. 24.

Gold Bird Foemina ? 111
> Female or young Wilson's Warbler, *Wilsonia pusilla pusilla* (Wilson).
> P. 93 above; ns. 57, 58.

Falco Lagopus Ferrugineus Cat: 1:3:3:   109
> *Buteo lagopus sanctijohannis* (Gmelin). McGill MS, pp. 33, 34, pls. X,
> 68–70.

Robin or Newfoundland Thrush Cat: 29:29
> *Turdus migratorius nigrideus* Aldrich & Nutt. pp. 75, 76 above.

Lark of St. Julian's Isle Cat: 32:32
> *Eremophila alpestris* (L.). There is a painting, pl. 82, of two male
> Horned Larks by Paillou and this specimen may be one of them. There
> are no MS notes on the painting but Banks had three Labrador skins
> of this species in his London Collection (List 4, 28b, *Alauda alpestris* 3
> [skins] Labrador.

Motacilla Uropygio flavo Cat: 58:58
> This warbler with a yellow rump might have been the Magnolia
> Warbler *Dendroica magnolia* (Wilson), or, more probably, the Myrtle
> Warbler *Dendroica coronata* (L.). There are no sheets in the McGill
> MS with these numbers.

Brown Bittern Cat: 78:78
> *Botaurus lentiginosus* (Rackett), American Bittern. There is a painting
> by Paillou, pl. 60, of this species with Newfoundland written on it by
> Banks. I have found nothing more about it.

Blue wingd teal Cat: 99:99: fig: mal:
> *Anas discors* (L.). McGill MS, pp. 3, 4, pl. 62.

Stink fogel Cat: App: 3
> *Stercorarius* sp. McGill MS, pp. 31, 32, pl. 79.

Ararlia Sarsparilla Cat: App: 16
> *Aralia nudicaulis* L.
> End of McGill MS

SECTION 5

SUPPLEMENT TO THE MCGILL MS

Banks's Descriptions of Mammals
These descriptions were originally part of the series comprising the McGill MS.
Banks wrote them on paper the same size and make as that which he used for his
descriptions of birds in the first part of the McGill MS. I have no idea when the

whole MS was split up; these accounts of mammals were folded and bound in with the smaller zoological slips prepared by Banks and Solander for another edition of the *Systema Naturae*. The following descriptions are in the first volume, entitled *Mammalia*, of the set in the Zoology Library of the British Museum.

Phoca vitulina concolor de Kay

Mammalia Ferae

Phoca vitulina   25

Dentibus Laniariis tectis Linn: Syst: nat: 56:3.

Descr: Pondus lib: 190 Color Dorsi niger rivulis albidis insterstitiis excepto occipite toto nigro Venter Gula malae canae rivulis albis Pinnae vel Pedes et cauda totae nigrae ungues nigerrimi Palatum nigrum mystaces compressae vasi undulatae —Incolis Harbour seal or Dotard Habitat in sinubus frequens unde nomen Dantur quatuor alterae varietates vel species Phocarum in hac mari quae circa medium Hyemem a septentrione huc pervenient

1. *Phoca* Pileo Capitis magno albo. Ellis *Voyage to Hudson's Bay* pag. 134 cum fig Incolis Hooded Seal

2. *Phoca* maxima 500 lib: non raro aequans pile Crispo Longo Incolis Square Phipper Chatteaux Sept. 1766.

3. *Phoca* fusco Albida fascia Lyriforme in dorso Incolis Harp Seal or Honke.
Hab. in Oceano Terram novam alluente J. Banks.

> *Phoca vitulina* Provided with cutting teeth Linn. Syst. Nat. 56:3
> Descr: weight 190 lb.
> Colour of the back black with wavy whitish markings, except for the occiput which is entirely black. Belly, throat and cheeks ash gray with wavy white markings. Fins or feet, and tail quite black. Very black claws. Palate black. Whiskers compressed, v-shaped, undulate, Vernacular name, harbour seal or dotard. Habitat, common in bays whence its name.
>   There are four other varieties or species of *Phoca* in this sea which come here from the north about mid-winter.
> 1. *Phoca* with a large white cap. Vernacular name Hooded Seal.
> 2. *Phoca*, the largest, not infrequently equalling 500 lb., with long crimped hair. Vernacular name Square Phipper. Chatteaux, Sept. 1766.
> 3. *Phoca*, dusky whitish, with a lyre-shaped mark on the back. Vernacular name Harp Seal or Honke.
>   Habitat in the ocean surrounding Newfoundland.

Banks gave other details of these seals on the verso of p. 103 of his diary. See also n. 141.

393

Castor canadensis caecator Bangs 65

Mammalia Glires

Castor Fiber Cauda Ovata Plana *Linn*: *Syst*: 25: 1:—

Descr: Magnitudine *Canis Vulpis* Vel Paulo major Color totius Corporis rufo-fuscus Nitidus sed infra fuscior Caput Parvum acutum Nares pilosi auriculae parvae subrotundae vix Vellere Longiores Collum a corpore Vix distinguendum est Corpus ad femora sensim Latius fit ut a capite ad hos non male figuram Cunei refert a femoribus ad basin Caudae sensim attenuatur et cuneum alterum format Cauda ipsa ovata Plana et horizontalis est Longitudine 8 Latitudine 3 uncias pilos nullos habet sed squamis duris nigris Vestita est et Palmae et Plantae Brevissimae sunt Palmae Pentadactilae Digitis distinctis Plantae quoque Pentadactilae sed Palmatae membrana Lata more anatum et callosae per totam tibiae Longitudinem— Capitur Laqueo inserto in Parte Domus diruto dum reparat

Terra nova J. Banks 1756 [*sic*]

Descr: a Pelle infarcta non ab ipso animali Croque Oct 8 1766

Castor fiber Tail oval, flat. *Linn. Syst. Nat.* 25.1.

Descr: Size about that of *Canis vulpis* [*Vulpes fulva* (L.), Red Fox] or a little larger. Colour of the whole body shining reddish-brown but darker beneath. Head small, pointed, nostrils hairy, ears small, almost rounded, scarcely longer than the fur. Neck scarcely distinguished from the body. The body gradually broadens as far as the thighs, thus from the head to the thighs it is approximately wedge-shaped, from the thighs to the base of the tail it gradually tapers and forms another wedge. The tail itself is oval, flat and horizontal, 8 inches long, 3 inches wide. It lacks hair but is clothed with hard black scales and the fore and hind feet are very short, the forefeet pentadactyl with distinct digits, the hindfeet also pentadactyl but palmate with a broad membrane after the manner of ducks, and callose along the whole length of the tibia.

It is captured by the insertion of a snare in that part of its dwelling which it comes to repair after it has been damaged.

Described from a stuffed skin, not from the animal itself.

Croque Oct. 8, 1766.

Microtus pennsylvanicus terraenovae (Bangs)

Mammalia Glires 72

Mus terrestris Cauda Mediocri subpilosa Palmis subtetradactylis Plantis Penta-dactylis auriculis Vellere brevioribus Linn: Syst: Nat: 26:7: ?—

Descr. Magnitudine *M. Avellanarium* paulo superat caput magnum Genae tumidae mystaces multae Longae aures Magnae Auriculae subrotundae Vix Vellere Longiores dorsum fuscum sive si accurate inspicias fusco nigroq Varium abdomen Cinereo Albidum pilis basi nigris palmae breves tetradactylae sed Pollicis obsoleti unguis

394

ad est plantae seminudae pentadactylae Cauda brevis Vix dimidii Corporis Longi-
tudinem Aequat Pilis raris adspersa Est—Habitat satis frequens in Paludibus et
Sylvis sed frequentissimus in Graminosis juxta mare Hortis nostris infestissimus
Plantas Juxta terram secans

Terra nova J. Banks 1765 [*sic*]

> Tail medium, slightly hairy, forefeet subtetradactyl, hind feet pentadactyl; ears
> shorter than the fur. Linn. *Syst. Nat.* 26 :7 : ?
>
> Description: Slightly larger than *Mus avellanarius*; head large; cheeks swollen,
> many long whiskers, ears large, external ear rather round, barely longer than
> the fur, back dusky, or if carefully examined dusky varied with black; abdomen
> ashy whitish, the base of the hairs black, forefeet short, tetradactyl but with
> the thumb reduced to a claw. Hind feet half bare, pentadactyl. Tail short,
> scarcely equal to half the length of the body, with a few scattered hairs.
> habitat, fairly common in woods and marshes, but very common in grass near
> the sea. A great pest in our garden, cutting off the plants at soil level.
> Newfoundland J. Banks, 1765 [*sic*].

> Pennant (1784:133) gave an abbreviated description of this vole which he
> thought was perhaps a short-tailed field mouse. His account was obviously
> based on Banks's MS. See also the diary, p. 33, n. 78.

Rattus rattus (Linn.)

Mammalia Glires   73

Mus Rattus

Cauda Elongata Subnuda Palmis tetradactylis cum unguiculo pollicari Plantis
Pentadactylis Linn : Syst : Nat : 26 : 9 :

Descr : Major Caput acutum Mystaces multae superiores nigrae inferiores albae
capite Longiores auriculae extantes magnae nudae areaq. parva nuda infra eos sita
est totum animal supra pilis nigris albidis et nonnullis rufescentibus tectum est
infra totum album palmae albae tetradactilae unguiculo Pollicari plantae seminudae
pentadactilae cum Callo per totam tibiam extenso Cauda Longitudine Corporis
nigra squamosa sed pilis raris sparsa ad ejus basin supra anum area parva albida
nuda nec squamosa. Habitat in casis pro horticolos erectos circa finem augusti
primo Visus erat fortasse e navibus Gallicis advena nunc exclusis Pullis abundent.

> Tail long, rather bare; forefeet tetradactyl with thumbnail. Hindfeet penta-
> dactyl. Linn. *Syst. Nat.* 26 :9 :
>
> Description: large, head pointed, many whiskers, upper ones black, lower ones
> white, longer than the head. External ears large, bare, with a small bare patch
> between them. The whole animal covered with black and whitish hairs to-
> gether with a few that are rufous; entirely white below. Forefeet white,

tetradactyl, with a thumbnail; hindfeet partly bare, pentadactyl with a callus extending right along the tibia. Tail as long as the body, black, scaly, with a few scattered hairs. At its base, above the anus, a small whitish area, bare, lacking scales. Habitat in our garden sheds. First seen towards the end of August, perhaps came from French ships. Now are common except for the young.

This was almost certainly the Black Rat *R. rattus* although according to Hall and Kelson (1959:769) the Norway Rat is now more common in northern American ports.

18

A note on J. R. Forster's *Catalogue of the Animals of North America*

Catalogue of the Animals of North America, or Faunula Americana. . . . To which are added Short Directions for Collecting, Preserving, and Transporting all Kinds of Natural History Curiosities. London, 1771.

Reprinted by the Willughby Society in 1882. There are no descriptions in this work. The Willughby reprint contains a preface by Philip Lutley Sclater in which he quotes Pennant's statement that he was responsible for much of the material in Forster's *Catalogue*.

Many of the species attributed to 'Mr.B.' in Forster's *Catalogue* are listed in Banks's Newfoundland MSS which, as recorded earlier in this volume (pp. 40, 95, 246–9), he lent to Pennant. A list of Forster's Newfoundland species brought back by 'Mr.B.' follows. Detailed references are given in the systematic lists.

Gentil Falcon—*Accipiter gentilis atricapillus* (Wilson).

Sacre Falcon—unidentified. Forster gave a detailed description of this bird (1772: 383, 423) but it is unsatisfactory; Hellmayr (1949:296) and Friedmann (1950: 645) both doubt that it applies to the Gyrfalcon *Falco rusticolus obsoletus* Gmelin which was in any case described by Pennant (1795:207, 208) both as the Buzzard and Plain Falcon. Newton's suggestion that it was a Goshawk is not generally accepted. That bird was adequately described as the Gentil Falcon (above) by Pennant, Latham and Gmelin on the basis of Paillou's pl. VI.

Rough-footed Falcon—*Buteo lagopus sanctijohannis* (Gm.), the Rough-legged Hawk. See Paillou's pls. X, 68–70.

Chocolate Falcon—*Buteo lagopus sanctijohannis* (Gm.), a young bird. See the Systematic List for notes on this bird.

Buzzard Falcon—Pennant's Buzzard Falcon (1785:207) and Plain Falcon (1785: 208) are both referable to *Falco rusticolus obsoletus* Gmelin (*Cat. Birds Brit. Mus.*,

397

1874, 1:184), the Gyrfalcon. Pennant gives both Hudson's Bay and Newfoundland as localities for this species, but his records are unsatisfactory.

Brown Owl—Unidentified. Pennant described the Brown Owl from Newfoundland, (1785:236) and referred it to the species now known as *Surnia ulula*. This cannot be correct as the breast of *S. ulula* is barred and that of the Brown Owl was described by him as streaked.

Raven—*Corvus corax* L., the Common Raven. Pennant (1785:245–6) includes Newfoundland in this bird's range. See also p. 418.

Colemouse—*Parus atricapillus bartletti* (Aldrich & Nutt), Black-capped Chickadee. See Systematic List.

House Swallow—*Hirundo rustica erythrogaster* Boddaert, Barn Swallow. Pennant (1785:429) refers to this bird's being seen in Newfoundland 'during summer', and in other parts of America.

Esquimaux Curlew—*Numenius borealis* (Forster). See Banks's diary pp. 46, 47, Parkinson's pl. III, and Pennant (1785:461). Forster's description (1772:411) is based on a specimen from Hudson's Bay.

Nodding Woodcock—*Limnodromus griseus griseus* (Gm.), the Eastern Dowitcher. Pennant (1785:465) and Latham (1785:153) both described young of this species from Chateau Bay as Nodding Snipe, *Scolopax nutans* (Hellmayr & Conover, 1948, pt. 1, no. 3: 143), but there is no drawing or description of it amongst Banks's Newfoundland MSS.

Cinereous Sandpiper—*Calidris canutus rufa* (Wilson), the Knot. Both Pennant (1785:474) and Latham (1785:178) state that these 'Ash-coloured Sandpipers' were 'seen in great numbers on Seal Islands near Chateaux Bay'. As far as I know this species is not mentioned in any Banks MS.

Glossey Sand-piper—Unidentified. I can find no reference to this bird either in Pennant or Latham, and it does not appear to be mentioned in later works of reference.

Great Gull—?*Larus marinus* L., Great Black-backed Gull. There is no 'Great Gull' in the *Arctic Zoology* but Latham describes it (1785:370) referring it to *Larus ichthyaetus* Pallas, the Great Black-headed Gull, which breeds on the inland seas and lakes of south-eastern Russia and central Asia but not on the American continent. Pennant described the adult *L. marinus* (1785:527) but without reference to Newfoundland; his Wagel's Gull from that country and others, (*op. cit.*:528) is a young *L. marinus* (Saunders, H. & Salvin, O. 1896:243); Banks took a young gull of this species at Chateau Bay in September and described it as *Larus albidus* (McGill MS:25–6).

Brown Duck—*Anas rubripes* Brewster [=*Anas fuscescens* Gm.], Black Duck. In 1789 Gmelin described *Anas fuscescens* as follows: 'Alis cinereis: speculo caeruleo, apice albo, caudo obscura. Brown duck, *Arct. Zool.* 2. p. 565. n. 499. Latham Gen. *Syn.* III. 2 p. 486. n. 39. Habitat in insula novae Terrae'.

Latham's description was as follows: Brown Duck *Arct. Zool.* no. 499 'Length sixteen inches. Bill large, thick at the base; colour blueish, with the tip black; nostrils near the end [i.e. the base]; head and neck of a very pale brown; lower part of the last, and breast the same, edged with rust colour; wings cinereous grey; speculum blue tipped with white; tail and legs dusky; inhabits Newfoundland.'

In 1789 Gmelin also described *Anas obscura* (=*A. rubripes*), basing it on the Dusky Duck of Pennant (1785:564) and Latham (1785:545), from New York, omitting the white tips to the speculum, and giving the length as 24 inches. Salvadori (1895:201–2) noted the white-tipped speculum and remarked that Ridgway had classified this duck in the section of those lacking white in the speculum. Nevertheless he failed to realize that Gmelin's *A. fuscescens* was the same bird as his *A. obscura* and regarded it as indeterminable (*op. cit.*: 490). Peter Scott and G. V. T. Matthews consider (*in lit.*) that Latham's description of the Brown Duck clearly applies to *A. rubripes*; Gmelin's name of *A. obscura* was preoccupied (see Hellmayr & Conover 1948:327–9 for references) and since his *A. fuscescens* had so curiously never been determined Brewster's name of *rubripes* (for what he regarded as the subspecies) was adopted.

Since Forster's catalogue was published in 1771 there is no reason to doubt his (i.e. Pennant's) note on the Brown Duck brought back by Banks from Newfoundland; it would indeed be remarkable if Banks had failed to bring back the Black Duck, one of the commonest ducks of that country. If Latham had only stated that the *under* wing was ashy gray it is probable that Gmelin's species would long ago have been determined; it is obvious that this was precisely what Latham meant, since the white tips to the speculum would not have been conspicuous on an ashy gray surface.

Teal—Forster's detailed description (1772:419) makes it clear that this was the Green-Winged Teal *Anas carolinensis* Gm. See Parkinson's plate 29, and McGill MS p. 5–6.

Bony Fishes

Blenny, pustulated—*Macrozoarces americanus* (Bloch & Schneider). See Parkinson's drawing, pl. 88a, and Pennant's description (1787:115) of the Pustulated Blenny from Newfoundland.

Trout—*Salvelinus alpinus* (L.) and *S. fontinalis* Mitchill. See Parkinson's drawing of *S. alpinus*, pl. 87, and ns. 28, 118.

Pike, Under-jaw—*Esox brasiliensis*. This was *Scomberesox saurus* (Walbaum). See Parkinson's drawing, pl. 90a. Pennant (1787:145) wrote 'Taken off Croque Harbour and communicated to me by Sir Joseph Banks.'

Insects without Wings

Crabfish, common—*C. maenas. Cancer irroratus* (Say). Diary 19, n. 32.
Crabfish, spider—*C. araneus. Hyas araneus* (L.). Diary 19.

19

Bird skins from Newfoundland and Labrador in Banks's London collection

THE four MS lists of Banks's collection of bird skins contain the names of thirteen species from Newfoundland and Labrador. These lists are in an unknown hand with an occasional note in Banks's writing. Since they include many birds collected on Cook's voyages round the world they must have been compiled not earlier than 1780 by which time Banks was a very busy man. They are now in the British Museum (Natural History).

The first list is a short one of about thirty species, the second and third contain about 120 and 185 respectively; the lists are similar in arrangement and contain almost identical notes on the species that occur in more than one of them. There is a different arrangement of species in the fourth list, and these may have been mounted and on display. Thus in this series all the species from Newfoundland and Labrador are listed together instead of in systematic order as in the other lists. Labrador is the only locality given for these birds but it is clear that Newfoundland should be included under this heading since there are definite Newfoundland localities from other sources for some of these species. Thus Banks took both *Lanius excubitor* and *Euphagus carolinus* at Croque in mid-June although in these lists Labrador is written against them. In this connection it should be remembered that the bird paintings are labelled Newfoundland but that more detailed localities are inscribed on the drawings of plants, fishes and invertebrates and are probably accurate.

The Labrador Duck *Camptorhynchus labradorium* (Gm.), described briefly in these MS lists, was probably not collected by Banks but sent to him by Cartwright.

Arenaria interpres morinella (L.)
    List 2 No. 106 *morinellus Tringa* L. 2 skins.
    List 3 No. 106 *morinellus Tringa* L.
    List 4 No. 28 *Tringa morinellus* 4 skins Labrador.

Camptorhynchus labradorium (Gmelin).

> List 2 No. 64 *dispar Anas* griseus capite, collo que testaceis linea verticali et collari nigris rostro basi croceo M. et f. 2 skins Labrador fem. grisea remigib. interiorib. albis ut in Mari.
>
> List 3 No. 64. [note precisely the same].
>
> List 4 No. 28h. *Anas* griseus remigibus interioribus albis rostro basi croceo. mas et fem: 2 skins Labrador.

Charadrius semipalmatus Bonaparte.

> List 2 No. 118 *Hiaticula Ch.* L. Labrador 4 skins.
>
> List 4 No. 28a *Charadrius hiaticula* 3 skins [see McGill MS 65].

Eremophila alpestris (L.).

> List 3 No. 143 *alpestris Alauda.*
>
> List 4 No. 28b *Alauda alpestris* 3 skins Labrador.

Erolia fuscicollis (Vieillot).

> List 2 No. 109 *Tringa* rostro pedibusq corpore fusco nigris maculato, uropygio ventreq albis Labrador 1 skin.
>
> List 3 No. 109 [note repeated precisely].
>
> List 4 29g *Tringa* fusca nigro-maculata uropygio ventreque albis.
>
> [The other species listed under 29 have 'American good for nothing' written against them so that the skins were apparently decaying?]

Euphagus carolinus nigrans Burleigh & Peters.

> List 3 No. 148 *unicolor Turdus* corpore toto atro caerulescente Labrador 1 skin.
>
> List 4 No. 28g *Turdus* corpore toto atrocoerulescente [*sic*] Labrador 1 skin.

Lanius excubitor borealis Vieillot.

> List 2 No. 8 *excubitor Lanius* L. Labrador 1 skin.
>
> List 3 No. 8 [note repeated exactly].
>
> List 4 No. 28c *Lanius excubitor* 1 skin Labrador.

Numenius borealis (Forster).

> List 2 No. 101 *maculata Scolopax* rostro arcuato, corpore fusco pallide maculato, ventre ferugineo 2 skins.
>
> List 3 No. 101 [same note].
>
> List 4 No. 43 *Scolopax* rostro incurvato corpore fusco pallide maculata ventre testaceo 2 skins. [then, half crossed out] differet a *Lapponico* rostro incurvata *esquimaux scolopax* Forster? see *Phil: Trans:*

Phalaropus fulicarius (L.).

> List 2 No. 108 *fulicaria Tringa* L. Labrador 1 skin.
>
> List 3 No. 108, [same note].
>
> List 4 No. 30b *Tringa fulicaria* 1 skin.

Pinicola enucleator (L.).

    List 3 No. 156 *Loxia enucleator* fem. Sol. cat.* 131. mas Labrador. 2 skins.

    List 4 No. 28e *Loxia enucleator* 1 skin, Labrador.

Plectrophenax nivalis nivalis (L.).

    List 3 No. 162 *nivalis Emb.* 2 skins, Labrador.

    List 4 No. 28c *Emberiza nivalis* 2 skins, Labrador.

Surnia ulula caparoch (Müller).

    [Since Parkinson's drawing of this owl was labelled *Strix funerea* (see McGill MS 39), the following entries in these lists would seem to apply to *S. ulula*, the breast of which is barred and not streaked, and not to *Aegolius funereus funereus* (L.) which has a streaked breast.]

    List 2 No. 4 *funerea Strix funerea* L. Labrador 1 skin.

    List 3 No. 4 [same note].

    List 4 No. 9 *Strix fuscus* capite pctis minutissimis albis subtus striis transversialib. albis Labrador *funerea* 1 skin. [This entry has a cross through it, perhaps the skin was to be discarded?]

Turdus migratorius nigrideus Aldrich & Nutt.

    List 3 No. 147 *migratorius Turdus* L. Labrador 2 skins. *Sol. cat. 126.

    List 4 No. 28f *Turdus migratorius* 1 skin, Labrador.

[*The reference to 'Sol. cat.' is to a list by Solander of the birds collected and drawn on Cook's third voyage; there is a drawing by William Ellis of one of these robins from the western coast of North America (Lysaght 1959:335); it belongs to another race.]

20

A systematic list of the animals collected or recorded by Banks in 1766

CRUSTACEA

THORACICA

Balanus sp. Newfoundland. Pl. 84a.

Balanus crenatus Bruguière. Solander Zoological MSS, British Museum, Mollusca 2:43 'Habitat in Oceano Atlantico, alluente Newfoundland (Jos. Banks)'. See Ellis & Solander 1786:198, tab. 15, figs. 7, 8.

Mitella coruucopia (Leach), formerly *Pollicipes cornucopia* Leach. Lisbon, pl. 86b.

AMPHIPODA

Hyperia galba (Montagu). N. 17. At sea.

Caprella septentrionalis Kroyer. Newfoundland. Parkinson's wash drawing, pl. 86b, shows a specimen with numerous short setae. These do not exist in material in the British Museum and it is possible that they represent a hydroid growth. Fabricius (1775:419) described Banks's specimen as '*Gammarus linearis* de Terra Nova'.

DECAPODA

Cancer irroratus Say. Diary 19, n. 32.

Homarus americanus (M. Edw.), American Lobster, St. John's. Diary 19.

Hyas araneus (L.), Spider Crab. Diary 19.

INSECTA

ORTHOPTERA

?*Blatella germanica* (L.), Newfoundland. Pl. 84e.

HEMIPTERA

Poecilocapsus lineatus (Fabr.). Diary 18, n. 26. Fabricius described the species from a specimen from 'American boreali in Hirshell's collection'. This may be a reference to William Herschel, the great astronomer, a friend of Banks.

404

SYSTEMATIC LIST OF ANIMALS COLLECTED

'*Cimex atomarius*'. In 1775 Fabricius described *Cimex atomarius* supposedly from one of Banks's Newfoundland specimens. This is however a synonym of *Rhaphigaster nebulosa* Poda 1761, a European species unrecorded from Newfoundland. I am indebted to Dr. China for this information.

NEUROPTERA

Polystoechotes punctatis (Fabr.). Fabricius described this from a specimen in Banks's collection without locality, and gave it the name of *Semblis punctata* (*Syst. Ent.* 1793: 2:73). Parkinson's drawing, pl. 84g, labelled 'Terra nova' probably represents the type. Mrs. Zimsen was unaware of the existence of this painting when she published (1964) her work on the type material of Fabricius. It has not been recorded in Newfoundland since Banks's visit.

COLEOPTERA

?*Carabus maeander* Fisch.-W. Banks's record of *Carabus granulatus*, diary 18, n. 27, probably applies to this species since *C. granulatus*, introduced from Europe into the Maritime Provinces, has not been recorded so far north as St. John's whereas *C. maeander*, which is somewhat, similar occurs there.

Capnodis tenebrionis (L.). 'Lusitania, Portugal'. Pl. 84d.

Arhopalus foveicollis (Halleman) (Syn. *Criocephalus agrestis* Kirby). Chateau Bay. McGill MS 83, 84. Also '*Cerambyx rusticus*' in Solander, Zoological MSS, Coleoptera 2: 169.

'*Cerambyx fasciatus*' described by Banks from Chateau Bay (McGill MS 85, 86) has not been identified, and Dr. Ray Morris tells me that no beetle corresponding to Banks's notes is known to exist in North America. It is possible that it was an imported species taken to Labrador in ballast.

?*Pissodes fraseri* Hopkins. In addition to these beetles, Fabricius in 1775 described *Curculio striatulus* apparently from Banks's Newfoundland specimens. The type which is still in the British Museum (Natural History) is, however, *Pissodes fraseri* Hopkins 1911, a species known only from North Carolina. *C. striatulus* was not mentioned in the literature after 1807. I am indebted to Mr. R. T. Thompson for this information.

HYMENOPTERA

Trichiosoma arcticum (Kirby) (=*crassum* Kirby). Pl. 84h. Newfoundland.

DIPTERA

Bombilius major L. Newfoundland. Pl. 84c.

Hybomitra zonalis (Kirby) or *H. aequetinctus* (Becker). Newfoundland. Pl. 84f. These species are very similar; *H. zonalis* is widespread in Newfoundland, and both have been taken at Goose Bay, Labrador.

SYSTEMATIC LIST OF ANIMALS COLLECTED

MOLLUSCA

Clio limacina Phipps. Newfoundland. Solander, Zoological MSS, Mollusca 1:94.

Chlamys islandicus (O. F. Müller). Diary 19, n. 34.

Mya arenaria L. Solander, Zoological. MSS, Mollusca 2:121. Newfoundland.

Cyrtodaria siliqua (Spengler). Diary 25, n. 56.

ECHINODERMATA

Echinarachnius parma (Lam.) Newfoundland. Diary 20, pl. 86a.

?*Strongylocentrotus droebachiensis* (O. F. Müller). Diary 20, n. 35.

FISHES

ISOSPONDYLI

Mallotus villosus (Müller). Capelin, Newfoundland. Diary 62, 77; n. 114; pl. 29.
Solander Zoological. MSS, Pisces 2:177.

Salvelinus fontinalis Mitchill. Newfoundland. Diary 19, n. 28.

Salvelinus alpinus (L.). Arctic Char, probably taken in Labrador or the Northern
Peninsula, Newfoundland. Diary 19, 78; ns. 28, 118; pl. 87.

APODES

Anguilla rostrata (Lesueur). American Eel. Diary 78, n. 119.

SYNENTOGNATHI

Scomberesox saurus (Walbaum). Skipper or Saury, Croque, Pennant 1787:145.
Pl. 90a.

THORACOSTEI

Gasterosteus aculeatus L. Stickleback, St. John's. Diary 19, n. 29.

ANACANTHINI

Ciliata mustela (L.). Five-bearded Rockling, Plymouth. Diary 3, n. 4; pl. 24b.

Gadus morhua L. Cod, Newfoundland. Diary 62, n. 114; pl. 89b. Solander Zoological MSS, Pisces 1:61.

Urophycis tenuis Mitchill. White Hake. Pl. 88b. Solander Zoological MSS, Pisces
1:86.

PERCOMORPHI

Ammodytes sp. Lance or Sand Eel. Diary 62, n. 114; pl. 89a. Pennant says that
Ammodytes tobianus is common off Newfoundland, a statement probably based
on this drawing and on Banks's notes.

Blennius pholis L. Common Blenny or Shanny, Plymouth. n. 4; pl. 24a. Solander
Zoological. MSS, Pisces 1:79.

Macrozoarces americanus (Bloch & Schneider). Common Eelpout, Newfoundland. Pustulated Blenny of Pennant (1787:115). Pl. 88a. Solander Zoological MSS, Pisces 1:84–5.

Pholis gunnellus L. Butterfish or Gunnel. Pl. 90b. This occurs on both sides of the Atlantic. It is occasionally found on the south coast of Britain but more commonly further north; it is taken from Hudson Strait to Delaware Bay on the east coast of America. See Solander Zoological MSS, Pisces 1:84–5, where he states that Banks found it very commonly feeding with *Cottus quadricornis* on offal under the fish stages on the Newfoundland coast.

SCLEROPAREI

?*Myoxocephalus scorpius* (L.) N. 33. Pennant 1787:118. This may refer to *Cottus quadricornis* L. The descriptions of *Cottus* spp. are missing from the Solander MSS.

HETEROSOMATA

Hippoglossus hippoglossus (L.). Hake. Diary 82.

BIRDS

The following notes summarize very briefly the complicated history of Banks's collection of birds from Newfoundland and Labrador, discussed in detail elsewhere in this volume.

None of Banks's bird skins from this expedition appears to have survived; it is probable that many of them decayed during his absence from home, 1768–71, when he was in the *Endeavour*, though some were mentioned in the MS list of skins in his London collection compiled after Cook's great voyages, probably in the 1780s (p. 401).

While in Newfoundland Banks drew up descriptions of many of the species he collected; after his return to England he lent some of his MSS and specimens to Thomas Pennant who seems to have returned most of the material together with a 'book of descriptions' (p. 248) which has not been traced. Some material not seen by Pennant was given to Taylor White (pp. 413, 415), some was examined by Latham, who had the use of Banks's library and collections (1781:55). Paintings of many of the birds were made by Parkinson, who worked for Banks, and by Paillou, who worked first for Taylor White and then for Pennant.

The first published record of Banks's collections appeared in 1771 in J. R. Forster's *Catalogue of the Animals of North America*, most of which was compiled not by Forster but by Pennant (p. 97).

In 1772 Forster published in the *Philosophical Transactions* a paper on the birds of Hudson's Bay, citing many of the Newfoundland specimens listed in his paper of the previous year. Nine years later, in 1781, the first volume of Latham's *General Synopsis of Birds* appeared; this contained some descriptions based on drawings of Banks's birds, with references to Forster's publications of 1771 and 1772, and to the unpublished *Am. Zool.*, i.e. *American Zoology*, the title first considered for Pennant's *Arctic Zoology* of 1784–7. A comparison of the accounts of the birds from Newfoundland and Labrador in Pennant and Latham shows that both writers had access to each other's MSS and quoted freely from each other; Pennant's work, however, contains more Newfoundland birds than Latham's does. Neither writer published acceptable scientific binomials for the new species discussed in their books but in 1789 many of their descriptions were translated into Latin by Gmelin and published with appropriate binomials in the second part of the first volume of the thirteenth edition of the *Systema Naturae*. Gmelin cited not only their publications but also those that had appeared under Forster's name in 1771 and 1772, as well as many others. In some cases the descriptions cited by Gmelin were based on drawings which are the types of his species. These drawings are therefore of considerable importance and for this reason I have tried to give in the following pages all the major references to Forster, Latham and Pennant. The record has many gaps but I hope that its publication will draw attention to MSS and other material whose importance has hitherto been overlooked, and will thus enable some other worker to make a more complete assessment of Banks's collections in Newfoundland and Labrador.

The sequence of families and species in this list follows that adopted in the *Check-list of North American Birds* of 1957.

GAVIIFORMES

Gaviidae
Gavia immer (Brunnich), Common Loon or Great Northern Diver. Croque and Chateau Bay. McGill MS 19, 20.
Gavia stellata (Pontoppidan), Red-throated Loon. Chateau Bay. McGill MS 21, 22; diary 80.

PROCELLARIIFORMES

Hydrobatidae
Oceanodroma leucorhoa leucorhoa (Vieillot), Leach's Petrel. Diary 63, n. 115.

PELECANIFORMES

Sulidae
Morus bassanus (L.), Gannet. This record depends on the statement of Pennant (1785:582) 'Inhabits the coast of Newfoundland where it breeds'. See also Latham 1785:609. Pennant acknowledged his sources of information on the birds of Labrador and Newfoundland, except as far as Banks was concerned.

84. Insects and barnacles collected by Banks in Newfoundland, Labrador and Lisbon; a composite plate. (*a*) *Balanus* sp. Newfoundland; (*b*) *Mitella cornucopia*, Lisbon; (*c*) *Bombylius major*, Newfoundland; (*d*) *Capnodis tenebrionis*, Portugal; (*e*)? *Blatella germanica*, Newfoundland; (*f*) *Hybomitra zonalis* or *H. aquetinctus*, Newfoundland; (*g*) *Polystoechotes punctatis*, Newfoundland; (*h*) *Trichiosoma arcticum*, Newfoundland (and see next plate).

Sydney Parkinson

85. *Trichiosoma arcticum*, enlarged to show the detail of Parkinson's work.

86. (*a*) *Echinarachnius parma*, perhaps the specimen recorded by Banks at St. John's, on 16 May 1766.
Sydney Parkinson

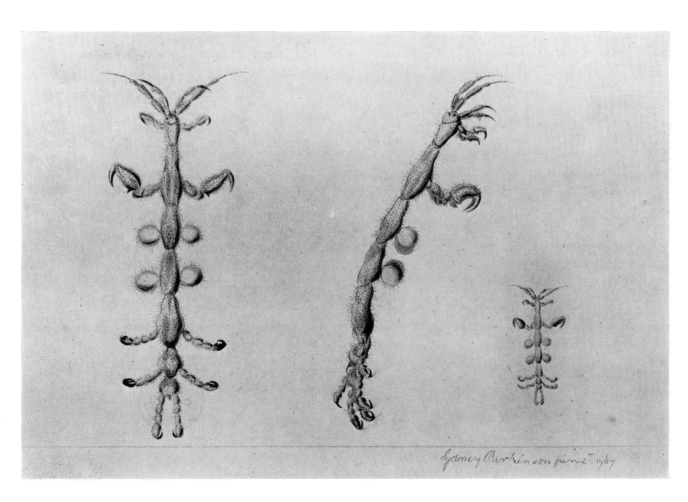

86. (*b*) *Caprella septentrionalis*, Newfoundland.
Sydney Parkinson

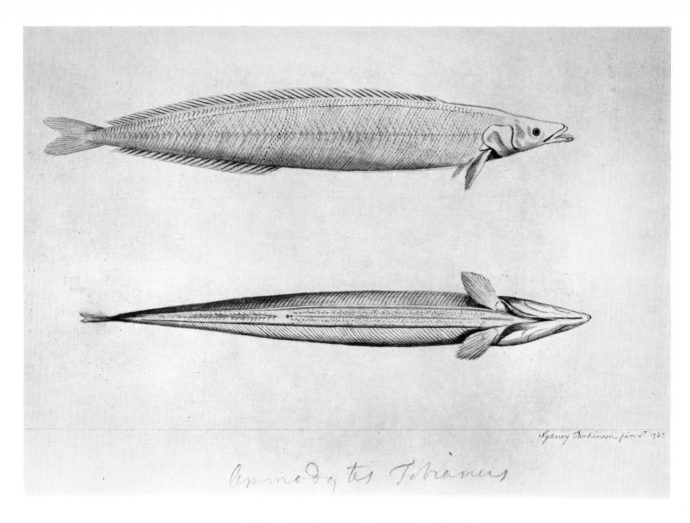

89. (*a*) *Ammodytes* sp., Lance or Sand Eel.
Sydney Parkinson

89. (*b*) *Gadus morhua*, Cod, young fish.
Sydney Parkinson

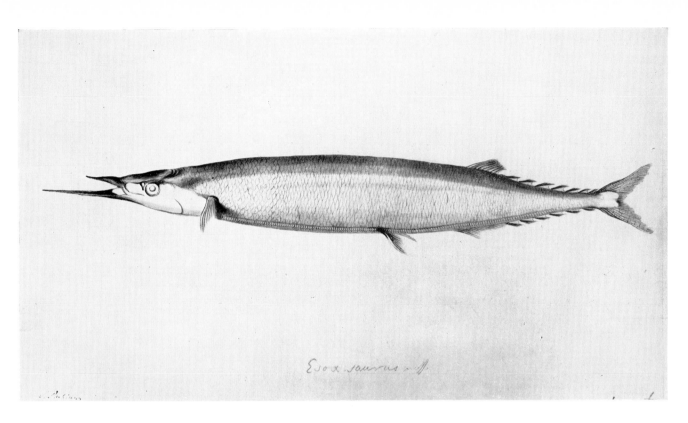

Esox saurus. N.

90. (*a*) *Scomberesox saurus*, Skipper or Saury.
Sydney Parkinson

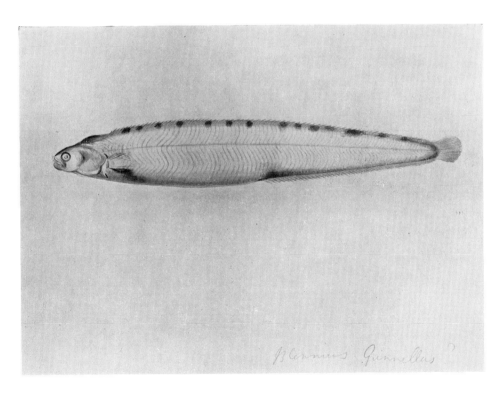

Blennius Gunnellus

90. (*b*) *Pholis gunnellus*, Butterfish or Gunnel.
Sydney Parkinson

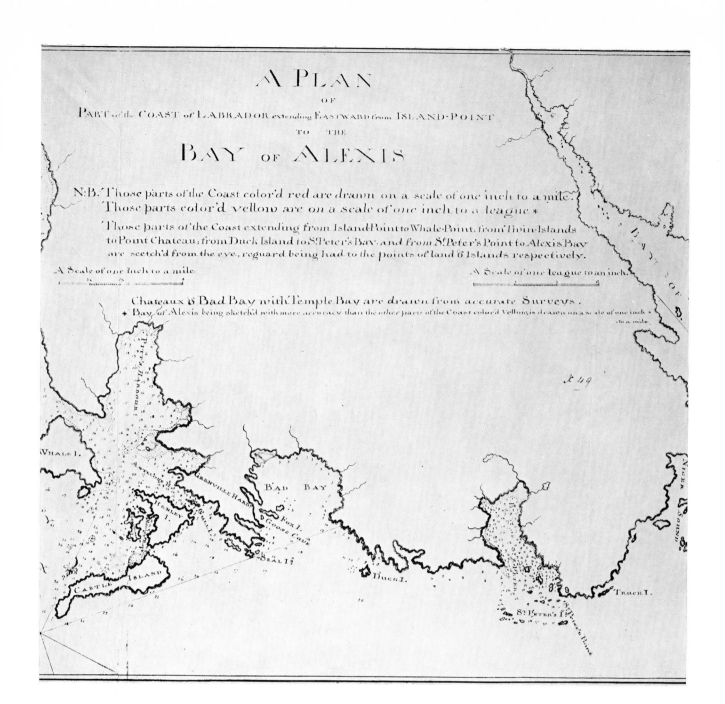

A PLAN

OF

PART of the COAST of LABRADOR extending EASTWARD from ISLAND-POINT

TO THE

BAY OF ALEXIS

N:B: Those parts of the Coast color'd red are drawn on a scale of one inch to a mile.
Those parts color'd yellow are on a scale of one inch to a league *

Those parts of the Coast extending from Island-Point to Whale-Point, from Twin-Islands
to Point Chateau; from Duck Island to S.t Peter's Bay, and from S.t Peter's Point to Alexis Bay
are scetch'd from the eye, reguard being had to the points of land & Islands respectively.

A Scale of one Inch to a mile   A Scale of one league to an inch.

Chateaux & Bad Bay with Temple Bay are drawn from accurate Surveys.
* Bay of Alexis being sketch'd with more accuracy than the other parts of the Coast colour'd Yellow, is drawn on a scale of one inch
to a mile.

91. Detail from a chart by Michael Lane, showing the coastline in the vicinity of Chateau Bay, Labrador; 1765 or after, since Truck Island is named, where the trading with the Eskimos was carried on (p. 205).

SYSTEMATIC LIST OF ANIMALS COLLECTED

CICONIIFORMES
Ardeidae
Botaurus lentiginosus (Rackett), American Bittern. Paillou's painting of this bittern in the Print Room series, pl. 60, is marked by Banks 'Dry specimen brought from Newfoundland'. See also Banks's keg list, McGill MS 109.

ANSERIFORMES
Anatidae
Branta canadensis canadensis (L.), Canada Goose. Chateau Bay. Diary 79.

Anas rubripes Brewster, Black Duck. The first descriptions of this duck were published by Pennant and Latham; Gmelin based both his *Anas obscura* and *A. fuscescens* (1789:541, 534) on their accounts which are discussed in detail in the notes on Forster's *Catalogue of the Animals of North America*, p. 399.

Anas acuta L., Pintail. Chateau Bay. McGill MS 3, 4; Parkinson's pl. 61.

Anas carolinensis Gmelin, Green-winged Teal. Chateau Bay. McGill MS 5, 6; Parkinson's pl. 63. Banks's bird seems to have been part of the type material since Gmelin (1789:533) cites Pennant (1785:569) who cites Forster's paper on the *Animals of Hudson's Bay* (*Phil. Trans.* 1772:419). Forster, in addition to specimens from Hudson's Bay, cites Banks's specimen listed in his earlier *Catalogue of the Animals of North America* (1771:17); as I pointed out earlier (p. 97) Pennant himself wrote this list and included Banks's Newfoundland specimens in it.

Anas discors L. Blue-winged Teal. Chateau Bay. McGill MS 7, 8; Parkinson's pl. 62. Recorded by Pennant (1785:568) as having been collected by Banks.

Clangula hyemalis (L.), Old Squaw or Long-tailed Duck. Chateau Bay. McGill MS 13, 14.

Histrionicus histrionicus (L.), Harlequin Duck. Chateau Bay. McGill MS 9, 10; diary 82; n. 125; Parkinson's pl. 64.

Camptorhynchus labradorium (Gmelin), Labrador Duck. Banks listed a pair of these ducks in his London collection (pp. 401–2). They were described by Latham (1785:497–8) who states categorically 'Inhabits the coast of Labrador; from whence a pair in the collection of Sir Joseph Banks came. That described in the *Arctic Zoology* [1785:559] was sent from Connecticut in New England'. I have elsewhere (p. 99) discussed the possibility that this species was collected not by Banks himself but for him by Cartwright. Fig. 2.

Somateria mollissima borealis (Brehm), Northern Common Eider. Parkinson's pl. 65 shows a female and a fairly typical male bird of this form which does not breed in Newfoundland but is a common winter resident.

Somateria mollissima dresseri (Sharpe), American Common Eider. Croque and Hare Bay. McGill MS 11, 12. Diary 107; Banks states that he saw great numbers of Eider Ducks nesting at Croque and Hare Bay.

Somateria spectabilis (L.), King Eider. Paillou's pl. 66 was marked 'Newfoundland' by Banks.

Melanitta perspicillata (L.), Surf Scoter. Chateau Bay. McGill MS 15, 16. Paillou's painting of a female, pl. 67, has 'Newfoundland' written on it by Banks.

Oidemia nigra americana Swainson, Common Scoter. Chateau Bay. McGill MS 13, 14; Banks's description applies to a moulting juvenile.

Mergus serrator L., Red-breasted Merganser. Chateau Bay. McGill MS 1, 2. Pennant (1785:537–8) and Latham (1785:425) both comment that this Merganser was common in Newfoundland during the summer which suggests that Banks saw it at Croque as well as at Chateau Bay.

FALCONIFORMES

Accipitridae

Accipiter gentilis atricapillus (Wilson), American Goshawk. Croque. McGill MS 35, 36; diary 102; Paillou's pl. VI. Paillou's painting is the type of Gmelin's *Falco novae-terrae*; see the notes in the McGill MS.

Buteo lagopus sanctijohannis (Gmelin), Rough-legged Hawk. Chateau Bay, ? St. John's. McGill MS 33, 34; Paillou's pls. X, 68–70. Although Banks does not mention having taken this hawk at St. John's it is probable that he collected specimens there as well as from Chateau Bay since Latham (1781:77) who cited pls. X and 68, called it the St. John's Falcon; on the other hand a young bird of this form was described as the Placentia Falcon by Latham. Banks certainly did not visit Placentia Bay; his friend Sir Thomas Adams was there in 1765 but there is no record of his having collected for Banks. Latham rightly thought that the Rough-footed Hawk from Newfoundland listed by Forster (1771:9) would probably prove to be identical with either the Placentia or St John's Falcon.

Pennant (1785:200) used Latham's name of St. John's Falcon for Banks's bird and cited Latham's description, but he based his own partly on a specimen in the Blackburne Museum; he illustrated it, however, with an engraving (*t.c.* pl. 9, facing p. 200) from Paillou's painting, pl. 68, of Banks's bird; the lower part of the engraving shows a young Rough-legged Hawk in the dark phase, copied from a painting by Paillou, pl. 69, of another of Banks's specimens. Pennant believed this to be a different species which he named the Chocolate Colored Falcon; he created further confusion by publishing Banks's notes on the habits of a Peregrine in connection with this young bird.

Gmelin's account (1789:273) of *Falco S.Johannis* was based on both Latham and Pennant, and on the published engraving of Paillou's pl. 68 which, therefore, with pl. X, represents Gmelin's type. There are no localities other than Newfoundland on the three paintings of this hawk by Paillou.

410

SYSTEMATIC LIST OF ANIMALS COLLECTED

In Forster's *Catalogue* of 1771 there is a reference (p. 9) to a new species, the Chocolate Falcon collected by 'Mr. B.', i.e., Banks; in his paper in the *Philosophical Transactions* of 1772 (p. 383) he gives this bird the binomial of *Falco spadiceus*.[1] He explains that he had a specimen from Hudson's Bay without data, and that it resembled the 'European Moor Buzzard' but was smaller and lacked the light spots on the head and shoulders; this suggests that he had another young bird in the dark phase, similar to that depicted in pl. 69.

When Latham described the Marsh Hawk, *Circus cyaneus hudsonius* (L.) as the White-rumped Bay Falcon (1781:54) he stated that there was so much variation among buzzards that this was probably only a variety of Forster's *Falco spadiceus*, the Chocolate Falcon, although he noted the white rump and slender yellow legs. He stated that his notes were based on a fine drawing in Banks's collection, said to come from Hudson's Bay (Paillou's drawing of the Marsh Hawk, pls. 71, 72, was marked '—foundland specimen' by Banks). Latham's error about the Marsh Hawk was repeated by Gmelin and the synonymy has remained somewhat confused in later publications.

There are four other paintings of *B. lagopus sanctijohannis* by Paillou in the Taylor White collection at McGill. In *Aves*, 3, f. 372 is a careful copy of Paillou's painting, pl. 69 (f. 107, from the Print Room series); in *Aves* 4, ff. 390, 391 and 392 all represent the same species. There is a note by Taylor White referring to f. 389 which is a painting of a Peregrine Falcon although the notes clearly apply to *B. l. sanctijohannis*; they are as follows:

'*Falco lagopus*. rostro nigro cera flava. pedibus Lanatis. fronto Albo. Corpore fusco. fasciis alarum albis. pedibus flavis. Mas ut Opinor. Habitat in America Septentrionalis.

The Rough Footed Falcon.

From Canada and the Northern parts of America it is supposed to feed on the *Lagopus* and from thence to take its name or perhaps from being feathered to the Toes like the *Lagopus*. This bird and the next which I take to differ in sex only were given to me by Mr. Banks together with the *Lagopus* and many other birds which he brought from Canada and Labrador.'

This reference to Banks is discussed on p. 414 below and in the section on the painters and their paintings; it seems impossible that the 'Mr. Banks' to whom White refers in this context can be Banks's uncle, Hodgkinson Banks; and the single mention of him elsewhere in White's notes at McGill must be a slip for Joseph.

---

[1] When in 1789 Gmelin quoted Forster's *F. spadiceus* he referred it to the *Act. angl.* 62, p. 281 [error for 383]; *Acta Anglica* was the binomial designation used by Linnaeus for the *Philosophical Transactions*, as was explained in his *Critica Botanica* when he reduced his citations of literature to a binomial system anticipating that which he later used for plants and animals. See Stearn's *Bibliography and Natural History*, 1966:7.

Aquila chrysaëtos canadensis (L.), Golden Eagle. Chateau Bay. Diary 91; n. 133.

?*Haliaeëtus leucocephalus alascanus* Townsend, Bald Eagle. Chateau Bay. Banks refers to two species of eagle but took only one. Pennant (1785:194) records *Falco ossifragus* L. in Newfoundland but that is a synonym of *Haliaeëtus albicilla* which does not occur there; according to Peters & Burleigh (1951: 403) records of that eagle are probably due to misidentification, since immature birds are readily confused with those of *H. leucocephalus alascanus* which has been taken in Hare Bay and is said to nest in southern Newfoundland.

Circus cyaneus hudsonius (L.), Marsh Hawk. Paillou's painting of a juvenile bird, pls. 71, 72, was the basis of Latham's account (1781:54–5) of the White-rumped Bay Falcon from 'Hudson's Bay'. Since Latham states that he was describing the bird from the drawing in Banks's possession and since '—found-land— specimen' is written on the verso in Banks's hand, it is clear that Latham's locality is wrong. There is no mention of this painting in the *Arctic Zoology*, nor have I found any reference ot it in the Banksian MSS. A looking-glass copy of this painting is in the Taylor White collection at McGill, *Aves* 4, f. 408.

Falco peregrinus anatum Bonaparte, Peregrine Falcon. Chateau Bay. McGill MS 37, 38; Paillou pl. 73. Neither Pennant nor Latham includes Labrador in the range of this Peregrine.

Falco columbarius columbarius L., Pigeon Hawk. Newfoundland. There are two paintings of this hawk by Parkinson, one of a young bird, the other of a male, pls. 74, 75. Banks wrote on the verso of that of the male, 'bird shot in New-foundland'. Neither Pennant nor Latham seems to have seen Banks's specimens.

GALLIFORMES

Tetraonidae

Canachites canadensis canadensis (L.), Spruce Grouse. Chateau Bay. McGill MS 71, 72; pl. V. Banks described Spruce Grouse from Chateau Bay and although he wrote 'Newfoundland' on the back of Parkinson's painting of a pair of these birds, this is almost certainly a mistake since this species does not occur there. Pennant (1785:307–8) repeated this mistake.

Lagopus lagopus albus (Gmelin), Willow Ptarmigan. Chateau Bay. McGill MS 73, 74; diary 46, 79; n. 123.

Lagopus lagopus alleni Stejneger, Allen's Willow Ptarmigan. Parkinson's pl. XII shows that he had the Newfoundland form of this Ptarmigan in nearly full winter plumage. Pennant (1785:309) records this form.

Lagopus mutus rupestris (Gmelin), Rock Ptarmigan. Chateau Bay. McGill MS 73, 74; diary 46, 79; n. 123.

SYSTEMATIC LIST OF ANIMALS COLLECTED

CHARADRIIFORMES

Charadriidae

Charadrius semipalmatus Bonaparte, Semipalmated Plover. Chateau Bay. McGill MS 65, 66. Banks had three or four skins of this species in his London collection, p. 402.

Pluvialis dominica dominica (Müller), American Golden Plover. Chateau Bay. McGill MS 67, 68; diary 46, 79; Pennant 1785; 483–4.

Arenaria interpres morinella (L.), Ruddy Turnstone. Chateau Bay. McGill MS 59, 60; four skins in Banks's London collection; Paillou's pl. 76. See the McGill MS for a note on a painting of a Turnstone in the Taylor White collection.

Scolopacidae

Capella gallinago delicata (Ord.), Wilson's Common Snipe. Chateau Bay. McGill MS 51, 52.

Numenius phaeopus hudsonicus Latham, Hudsonian Whimbrel. I have not found any painting or description of this Whimbrel among the Banksian MSS in the British Museum, but since Banks states categorically that he saw and ate three distinct species of curlew this would have been one of them; see his diary 79 and note 120. Pennant's statement on the size of the Eskimo Curlew suggests that he also had skins of the Hudsonian Whimbrel which is still common in Newfoundland during the autumn migration. Banks seems indeed to have collected it and to have given Taylor White specimens of both this and the Eskimo Curlew. In the Taylor White collection at McGill University there is an unsigned painting of the Eskimo Curlew (*Aves*, 13, fol. 766) with notes by White on the 'Small Newfoundland Curlew' which apply to the Hudsonian Whimbrel, and on the 'Least Curlew' which apply to the Eskimo Curlew; White was not sure whether the differences were specific or due to sex. His notes on the Whimbrel are these:

Aves Grallae

Phaeopus
Terrae novae

Phaeopus minor

S. rostro arcuato, pedibus Nigriscentibus, femoribus seminudis; parte Superiore corpore fusco. marginibus plumarum palidis & in dorso & superiore parte Alarum Seratis. parte inferiore palida maculis tenuisissimis fuscis notata. habitat in Terra Nova.

The Small Newfoundland Curlew

Its Bill hooked in Length 3 inch the feet dark colloured allmost Black the Thighs are half naked as in most birds of this Species The length of the body from the Extremity from point of the Bill to the Tail is sixteen

413

inches The extent of the Wings when open 2 foot 6 inches length of the legs 6 inch 3 qrs. The Colour of the upper part of the Body Dark brown each feather Edged with a pale or light brown these edges in the feathers which cover the Back are indented like a Saw The belly White [but see Latin description].

This Bird with many others were brought me from North America by my learned friend Hodgkinson Banks Esq.

Since this is the only mention of Hodgkinson Banks in the notes left by Taylor White, since he mentions Newfoundland and Labrador in connection with other species given to him by 'Mr. Banks', and since I have found no suggestion anywhere else that Robert Banks Hodgkinson, Joseph Banks's uncle, ever visited that region, it may be concluded that this Hudsonian Whimbrel and one of the Eskimo Curlews mentioned below were both given to White by Joseph Banks.

Numenius borealis (Forster), Eskimo Curlew. Chateau Bay. McGill MS 55, 56; diary 46, 47, 79; Forster 1771: 9; see also Banks's list of skins in his London collection and Parkinson's pl. III. Pennant (1785:461, pl. 19) published a note on this curlew with a plate engraved from Parkinson's painting; Latham's account was more accurate. There is an unsigned painting of one of these birds given by Banks to Taylor White (see notes on preceding species) with a brief description by White of what he called the Least Curlew:

'Bill in. 2½ upper Mandible Black under mdible partly red. Length from point of the Bill to the tail 15 inch & ½ the distance of the tips of the Wings when open 25 inches. The Wings are longer than the tail the length of the legs from the top of thigh to the end of the Middle toe 6 inch ½

This Bird agrees in Colour with the former except the dark lines drawn from the bill over the Eyes are wanting & the body of this is much less.

I know not whether this differs in Sex only or is a Different Species'.

Actitis macularia (L.), Spotted Sandpiper. St. John's. McGill MS 91, 107; diary 24; n. 51. Pennant's Common Sandpiper (1785 = 474).

Tringa melanoleuca (Gmelin), Greater Yellowlegs. Chateau Bay. McGill MS 49, 50; Paillou's pl. XI. Pennant (1785:468) and Latham (1785:152) called this wader 'Stone Snipe' based on the vernacular name of 'Stone Curlew' quoted by Banks, and give particulars of its occurrence at Chateau Bay. Gmelin (1789:659) cites only Latham and Pennant so that the drawing by Paillou may be taken to represent the type and the type locality is Chateau Bay.

Calidris canutus rufa (Wilson), American Knot. Seal Islands, Chateau Bay. Banks must have described this wader but his MS is missing. Pennant (1785:474) and Latham (1785:178) based some of their notes on the 'Ash colored Sand-piper' (Gmelin's *Tringa cinerea*, 1789:673) on Banks's observations; they both say 'Seen in great numbers on Seal Islands near Chateaux Bay'. Their accounts of the Red Sandpiper (1785:476 and 186; Gmelin 1789:682) also apply to this Knot. See Ridgway (1919:237).

Erolia fuscicollis (Vieillot), White-rumped Sandpiper. This record depends on Banks's entry in his list of skins in the London collection (p. 402), '*Tringa rostro pedibusq corpore fusco nigris maculato, uropygio ventreq albis* Labrador 1 skin.'

This sandpiper is common during the fall migration.

Erolia minutilla (Vieillot), Least Sandpiper. Chateau Bay. McGill MS 61, 62. Parkinson's painting, pl. 77, was indirectly the type of Gmelin's *Tringa novae-terrae* (1789:674); see McGill MS.

Erolia alpina pacifica (Coues), Red-backed Dunlin. Chateau Bay. McGill MS 57, 58, where Banks's notes are discussed in some detail.

Limnodromus griseus griseus (Gmelin), Eastern Dowitcher. Chateau Bay. Gmelin (1789:659) based his name of *Scolopax nutans* (which is preceded by his *S. grisea*) on a young Dowitcher described by both Pennant (1785:465) and Latham (1785:153) as 'Nodding Snipe, Observed in Chateaux Bay, on the coast of Labrador, in September. Are perpetually nodding their heads'. Such a remark must have come from Banks and his specimen is recorded by Forster (1771:14). It is curious that there is no mention of this Dowitcher in the McGill MS, nor a painting. See also Hellmayr & Conover (1948, pt. 1, no. 3:143).

Ereunetes pusillus (L.), Semipalmated Sandpiper. This record depends on Pennant's account of the 'Little Sandpiper' having been found in Newfoundland (1785: 479). Gmelin cited it (1789:681), and there seems no reason to dispute it.

Limosa haemastica (L.), Hudsonian Godwit. Chateau Bay. McGill MS 53, 54. This godwit was not recorded amongst Banks's specimens either by Latham or Pennant.

In the Taylor White collection at McGill there is in *Aves* 13, fol. 758, a painting of the Hudsonian Godwit. It is unsigned but has an outline sketch on the verso; it appears to be by Paillou who has in several instances made an outline sketch on the verso of his paintings of birds of prey. There is no note by Taylor White to show its origin but it is possible that it represents one of the godwits collected in Labrador by Banks.

Crocethia alba (Pallas), Sanderling. Seal Islands, Chateau Bay. McGill MS 69, 70. Latham (1785:197) and Pennant (1785:486) both include the Seal Islands in the range of this wader.

Phalaropodidae

Phalaropus fulicarius (L.), Red Phalarope. Banks had a skin of this phalarope in his London collection (p. 402) but it was not included in the birds described in the McGill MS.

Lobipes lobatus (L.), Northern Phalarope. Chateau Bay. McGill MS 63, 64. Neither of these phalaropes was recorded either by Pennant or Latham.

Stercorariidae

Stercorarius sp., young skua or jaeger. This painting of a young skua by Paillou, pl. 79, probably represents the bird described by Banks from Chateau Bay, McGill MS 31, 32. The species is not determinable from either the painting or Banks's description.

Stercorarius parasiticus (L.), Parasitic Jaeger. Pennant (1785:531) stated that this species inhabited the coast of Newfoundland. Banks saw jaegers hunting gulls relentlessly in Chateau Bay (diary 82) but confused their vernacular name with that of the Harlequin Duck.

Laridae

Larus hyperboreus hyperboreus Gunnerus, Glaucous Gull. This gull is not recorded in any of the Banksian MSS I have seen in Great Britain, but there is an unsigned painting of one, probably by Paillou, in the McGill Library, which was given to Taylor White by Banks. It is a painting of an immature bird, pl. 810 in *Aves* 14, with the following notes by White: '*Larus albus*. Larus albus pennis fuscentibus, pedibus croceis, rostro apice nigro, magnitudine anseres. The Great White Gull. This bird is all White except the Shafts of the Feathers which are of a pale brown The legs and feet Orange coloured the bill pale fresh colour the point Black it is of the size of a Goose. It was brought by Mr. Banks from the Northern part of America'.

Larus marinus L., Great Black-backed Gull. Chateau Bay. McGill MS 25, 26. Banks's description is of a young bird.

?*Larus delawarensis* Ord., Ring-billed Gull. There is no record of this gull in Banks's surviving MSS but Pennant (1785:530) describes the Common Gull *L. canus* as 'frequent on the coast of Newfoundland' which is almost certainly a reference to the Ring-billed Gull. Ridgway (1919:629) considers that the only Labrador specimen of *L. canus* known to him had in fact been misidentified and is a young *L. delawarensis*. Pennant's description of *L. canus* goes thus: 'With a yellow bill: head, neck, tail and all the under side of the body, white: back and coverts of wings light grey: primaries dusky; near their extremities a white spot: legs dull white, tinged with green. Length seventeen inches. Extent three feet. Weight twelve ounces and a half.' There is no mention of the ring on the bill but this is not always conspicuous in preserved material, and otherwise this is a good description of the Ring-billed Gull which is not common in Newfoundland nowadays but breeds on some coastal islands and perhaps in the interior.

Rissa tridactyla tridactyla (L.), Black-legged Kittiwake. St. John's, Chateau Bay. McGill MS 27, 28, 29, 30, 91. Parkinson's pl. 80; this drawing has only recently been identified as one of the Newfoundland series; Parkinson wrote on the recto 'Habitat sub arcto, in Islandia, Christiansoe', and when I first saw this painting I did not realise that he was quoting from Linnaeus (1766: 224); on the back Banks has, however, written 'Newfoundland'. Pennant (1785:529) and Latham (1785:394) recorded this kittiwake from there.

Alcidae

Pinguinus impennis (L.), Great Auk. Chateau Bay. McGill MS 17, 18; diary 54; n. 112; Pennant (1785:509).

Uria aalge aalge (Pontoppidan), Atlantic Common Murre or Northern Guillemot. This record again depends on Pennant's statement that this guillemot is found in Newfoundland (1785:516). Since it is one of the most abundant seabirds in that area it would certainly have been captured by Banks.

Cepphus grylle atlantis Salomonsen, Black Guillemot. St. John's, Chateau Bay. McGill MS 23, 24, 91; diary 23; n. 48.

STRIGIFORMES

Strigidae

?*Bubo virginianus heterocnemis* (Oberholser), Great Horned Owl. Diary 88 and n. 128. This is a doubtful record since Banks had only the claws and a hearsay description.

Surnia ulula caparoch (Müller), Hawk Owl. Croque, Chateau Bay. McGill MS 39, 40; diary 36; n. 90; Parkinson's pl. II. Banks also had a skin, p. 403.

Asio flammeus flammeus (Pontoppidan), Short-eared Owl, Chateau Bay: Pennant (1785:230).

CORACIIFORMES

Alcedinidae

Megaceryle alcyon alcyon (L.), Belted Kingfisher. Croque. McGill MS 47, 48; diary 33, n. 83.

PICIFORMES

Picidae

?*Colaptes auratus* (L.), Yellow-shafted Flicker. Parkinson's painting, pl. 81, of this bird is signed and dated 1768. Banks wrote 'No. 22' on it. Linnaeus based his description of *C. auratus* on birds collected by Catesby and Kalm. Dryander, in his MS catalogue of drawings of animals in Banks's collection, lists this one as having been made from a stuffed skin without locality, which is the same entry he gives for the other drawings of Banks's Newfoundland birds. Since this woodpecker is common in Newfoundland in summer, and also occurs in Chateau Bay it was probably collected by Banks.

SYSTEMATIC LIST OF ANIMALS COLLECTED

Dendrocopos villosus terraenovae (Batchelder), Newfoundland Hairy Woodpecker. Southern Newfoundland. McGill MS 41, 42. Neither Pennant nor Latham records Banks's specimen.

PASSERIFORMES
Alaudidae
Eremophila alpestris (L.), Horned Lark. This painting, pl. 82, by Paillou of two males is inaccurate since no yellow areas are shown on the face or throat, and the downward eyestripe is concurrent with the black chest band; also the rufous patches on either side of the breast appear to extend across it. There are no notes on the painting but Banks had skins of this species from Labrador in his London collection (p. 402).

Hirundinidae
Hirundo rustica erythrogaster Boddaert, Barn Swallow. St. John's. Diary 26; McGill MS 107. Pennant (1785:429) recorded this swallow from Newfoundland.

Corvidae
Perisoreus canadensis (L.), Gray Jay. Croque, Chateau Bay. McGill MS 45, 46. Pennant (1785:248) recorded this jay from Newfoundland, but not from Labrador.

Cyanocitta cristata bromia Oberholser, Blue Jay. No locality. McGill MS 43, 44. Pennant (1785:249) recorded it from Newfoundland.

Corvus corax L., Raven. Pennant's record (1785:245–6) of the raven from Newfoundland is supported by its inclusion in Forster's list, q.v., and by Pennant's letter to Banks, dated 20 Feb., 1768, in which he says that he is returning the Newfoundland birds but 'I left out the Raven to make room for the box of Br. shells'.

Paridae
Parus atricapillus bartletti (Aldrich & Nutt), Black-capped Chickadee. St. John's. This was the first bird recorded by Banks in Newfoundland, see diary 18 and n. 24. This record was the basis of Pennant's statement (1785:424) that a Colemouse had been shot in Newfoundland during the summer. Banks listed it as *Parus palustris* in the McGill MS 107.

Turdidae
Turdus migratorius nigrideus, Aldrich & Nutt, American Robin. St. John's, Chateau Bay. McGill MS 75, 76, 87, Diary 18. Banks had skins of this Robin in his London collection, p. 403. It was recorded by Pennant (1785:336) as being very common in the woods near St. John's.

Hylocichla ustulata clarescens Burleigh & Peters, Swainson's Thrush. Croque. McGill MS 77, 78; diary 34; n. 85; Pennant 1785:338.

SYSTEMATIC LIST OF ANIMALS COLLECTED

Laniidae

Lanius excubitor borealis Vieillot, Great Gray Shrike. Croque. Diary 34; n. 84. There was a skin in Banks's London collection, p. 402.

Parulidae

Dendroica petechia amnicola Batchelder, Newfoundland Yellow Warbler. St. John's. See McGill MS 92–3; diary 26, 30; n. 57; Parkinson's pl. 83. On the verso of this painting of a male Banks has written 'Dry specimen. Newfoundland. Gold Bird. N. 63'. On the recto Parkinson wrote his signature, the date 1767, and the following quotation from Linnaeus (*Systema Naturae* 1766, 1:334): '*Motacilla petechia*. Olivacea, subtus flava rubro guttata, pileo rubra. Habitat in America septentrionali Linn'. Linnaeus is believed to have based his description on the Barbados Golden Warbler, a distinctive form with a dark chestnut forehead and crown; the Newfoundland form lacks the dark cap. The Palm Warbler *Dendroica palmarum hypochrysea* Ridgway, a summer resident in Newfoundland, has a chestnut cap: Banks used 'Gold Bird' for both the Yellow Warbler and Wilson's Warbler; he possibly had a Palm Warbler too.

Pennant (1785:401) discussing '*Motacilla petechia*' says, 'A bird, which I suspect to be the Female, shot in Newfoundland, had the scarlet crown; but the upper part of the body was dusky, edged with pale brown: coverts of the tail white: primaries and tail dusky: breast and belly of a dirty white, and unspotted'.

This bird has not been identified.

?*Dendroica coronata* (L.), Myrtle Warbler. McGill MS 107. Banks's note in the McGill MS 109 '*Motacilla* uropygio flavo Cat 58:58' suggests that he had a Myrtle Warbler; in the Magnolia Warbler *D. magnolia* (Wilson) the underparts are yellow throughout the year, and the yellow rump is less conspicuous than in the Myrtle Warbler, which is much more drab, and in which the yellow rump is accordingly more obvious.

Dendroica striata (Forster), Black-polled Warbler. St. John's. McGill MS 93; diary 30, n. 73. Pennant 1785:401; Latham 1783:460.

Wilsonia pusilla pusilla (Wilson), Wilson's Warbler. St. John's. McGill MS 92, 93; diary 26; ns. 57, 58. Banks's notes on these warblers are confusing; they are discussed in detail in the notes to his diary; the numbering of his specimens, as pointed out earlier usually relates to the pagination of the diary and is a key to the specimens described in the McGill MS.

Icteridae

Euphagus carolinus nigrans Burleigh & Peters, Rusty Blackbird. Croque. Diary 36, n. 91; Banks's list of skins in his London collection, p. 402. Pennant (1785: 340) gave details of birds in both winter and breeding plumage, the latter from Labrador; Latham (1783:46) cited a Labrador specimen from Banks's collection.

Fringillidae

?*Richmondena cardinalis* (L.), Cardinal. Banks records this species in the McGill MS 105. Dr. Leslie Tuck (personal communication) thinks that it is not improbable that this species was taken in Newfoundland, since it is casual in Nova Scotia; it does not seem to have been recorded in Newfoundland except by Banks and by Pennant (1785:349).

Pinicola enucleator (L.), Pine Grosbeak. St. John's. McGill MS 92, 107; diary 24; list of skins in Banks's London collection, p. 403. Pennant 1785:348.

Loxia leucoptera leucoptera Gmelin, White-winged Crossbill. Croque, Chateau Bay. McGill MS 79, 80. Pennant 1785:347.

Passerculus sandwichensis labradorius Howe, Savannah Sparrow. St. John's. Diary 19; McGill MS 88, 105.

?*Spizella arborea arborea* (Wilson), Tree Sparrow. Pennant states (1785:373) that he had seen specimens of this sparrow from Hudson's Bay, Newfoundland and New York.

Zonotrichia albicollis (Gmelin), White-throated Sparrow. Pennant (1785:374) says, 'I have likewise described them from Newfoundland, where they are found during summer: one, which I suppose to be the female, had the yellow spot at the base of the bill very obscure, nor had it the white spot on the chin'.

Passerella iliaca iliaca (Merrem), Fox Sparrow. Croque, St. John's. McGill MS 81, 82, 88, 89, 107; diary 22, n. 42. Parkinson's pl. I. Pennant (1785:375) called this the Ferruginous Sparrow.

Melospiza georgiana ericrypta Oberholser, Swamp Sparrow. St. John's. McGill MS 89, 90, 107; diary 22, n. 40.

Plectrophenax nivalis nivalis (L.), Snow Bunting. This species was listed from Labrador in Banks's London collection, p. 403.

MAMMALS

Banks noted various fur-bearing and other mammals of the region in his diary but here I have listed only those described or discussed by him at some length.

CARNIVORA

Odobenus rosmarus rosmarus (L.), Walrus. Diary 114, n. 145.

Phoca vitulina concolor de Kay, Harbour Seal. Newfoundland seas. McGill MS, Suppt. p. 393. Diary 104, n. 141.

Mustela erminea richardsonii Bonaparte, Weasel. Croque. Diary 102.

SYSTEMATIC LIST OF ANIMALS COLLECTED

RODENTIA

Castor canadensis caecator Bangs, Beaver. Croque. McGill MS, Suppt. p. 394.
Described from a stuffed skin, not the living animal.

Ondatra obscurus Bangs, Musk Rat. St. John's. Diary 19.

Microtus pennsylvanicus terraenovae (Bangs), Vole. Croque, a garden pest. McGill
MS, Suppt. p. 394.

?*Rattus rattus* (L.), Black Rat. Garden sheds, probably Croque. McGill MS,
Suppt. p. 395.

Erethizon dorsatum (L.), Porcupine. Chateau Bay. Diary 92, n. 135.

PART FIVE

References

Appendix 1

Cartwright's annotated copy of Pennant's
Arctic Zoology

Appendix 2

Palliser's notes on Chateau Bay and the
blockhouse there

Index of scientific names

General index

References

T H E following list of books and MSS consists for the most part of works to which reference is made in the text but some others have been included which have been useful although there is no specific mention of them. A detailed list of publications on Labrador is given by Tanner (1944).

Publications from the Royal Botanic Gardens, Kew now have volume numbers printed in Roman instead of bold type. I have followed this usage throughout.

Actuarius, J. 1670. (Ed.) *Aristotelis et Antonii Tilesii Liber de Coloribus*. Trajecti ad Rhenum [Utrecht].

Adams, Percy G. 1962. *Travelers and Travel Liars 1660–1800*. Berkeley and Los Angeles.

— 1965. The case of Swaine versus Drage. An eighteenth-century publishing mystery solved. *Essays in history and literature, presented by Fellows of the Newberry Library to Stanley Pargellis*. Ed. Heinz Bluhm, pp. 157–68.

Aiton, W. 1789. *Hortus Kewensis*. 3 vols. London.

Aiton, W. T. 1810–13. (Ed.) *Hortus Kewensis*, 2nd ed. 5 vols. London.

Albin, E. 1731–8. *A Natural History of Birds* . . . 3 vols. London.

Allen, E. G. 1951. The history of American ornithology before Audubon. *Trans. Amer. Phil. Soc.* N.S. 41 :398–591.

American Ornithologists' Union. 1957. *Check-list of North American Birds*. 5th ed., Baltimore.

Ames, Oakes. 1924. *An Enumeration of the Orchids of the United States and Canada*. Boston.

Anon. 1772. An account of the Ptarmigan, a bird of Hudson's Bay. *Gentleman's Magazine* 42 :74.

— 1792. Biographical memoirs of the late Lord Mulgrave. *Naval Chronicle* 8 : 89–110.

— 1837. [Obituary notice of John Latham.] *The Analyst* 6 :348–51.

Arber, Agnes. 1945. Sir Joseph Banks and botany. *Chronica Botanica* 9 :94–106.

Aristotle, see Actuarius, J.; Smith, J. A. & Ross, W. D.

Austin, O. L. 1932. The birds of Newfoundland and Labrador. *Mem. Nuttall Ornith. Club* 7.

Bachelot de la Pylaie, A. J. M. 1825. Quelques observations sur les productions de l'île de Terre-Neuve, et sur quelques algues de la côte de France appartenant au genre Laminaire. *Ann. Sci. Nat.* (Paris) 4 :174–84.

REFERENCES

— 1826. Sur l'île de Terre-Neuve et quelques îles voisines. *Mem. Soc. Linn. Paris* 4:417–547.

— 1829. *Flore de l'Ile de Terre-Neuve et des Iles St.-Pierre et Miclon.* Paris.

Bailey, L. H. 1893. Notes on *Carex.* xvii. *Bull. Torrey Bot. Club* 20:417–26.

Baillon, H. 1867–95. *Histoire des Plantes.* 13 vols. Paris.

Baker, M. S. 1953. A correction in the status of *Viola macloskeyi* Lloyd. *Madroño* 12:60.

Banks, Joseph. 1766–7. *Journal of a Voyage to Newfoundland & Labrador commencing April ye Seventh & Ending November the 17th 1766.* MS, 2 vols. South Australian Branch, Royal Geographical Society of Australasia, Adelaide.

— 1766. *Newfoundland Plants and Birds.* MS, McGill University Library, Montreal.

— 1766. *Catalogue of Plants collected in Newfoundland and Labrador.* MS, Botany Library, British Museum (Natural History).

— 1767–8. *Journal of an Excursion to Wales . . .* MS, Cambridge University Library.

— n.d. *MS lists in an unknown Hand of the Bird Skins in Banks's Collection from Newfoundland and Labrador, the Voyages of Captain Cook, the Cape of Good Hope, etc.* 4 parts. British Museum (Natural History).

— n.d. *Natural History Drawings by various Artists, namely d'Auvergne, Cleveley, Colnett, Engleheart, Gilpin, Gordon, Greenwood, Metz, Miller, Paillou, Perrin, Rymsdyk, Sowerby et al, in the Collection of Sir Joseph Banks.* Folio vol., 199* B 4, Print Room, British Museum.

— 1768–71 [1962]. *The Endeavour Journal of Joseph Banks.* ed. J. C. Beaglehole. 2 vols. Sydney.

Banks, Sarah Sophia. 1772. *Transcript of Journal of a Voyage to Newfoundland and Labrador etc. by Joseph Banks* q.v., MS, British Museum (Natural History).

Barrington, Daines. 1771–4. A letter addressed to Dr. Maty F.R.S. . . . read 11 March 1773. *Journal Book, Royal Society* 27:400–3.

— 1772. An essay on the periodical appearing and disappearing of certain birds at different times of the year. . . . *Phil. Trans.* 62:265–326.

— 1773. Observations on the *Lagopus*, or Ptarmigan . . . *Phil. Trans.* 63:224–30.

Bartram, Edwin B. 1928. Newfoundland mosses collected by Mr. Bayard Long in 1924–6. *Rhodora* 30:1–12.

Beaglehole, J. C. 1955. (Ed.) *The Journals of Captain James Cook. The Voyage of the Endeavour 1768–1771.* Cambridge.

— 1962. (Ed.) *The Endeavour Journal of Joseph Banks.* 2 vols. Sydney.

Bell, Thomas. 1877. (Ed.) *The Natural History and Antiquities of Selborne . . .*, by Gilbert White. 2 vols. London.

Benson, Lyman. 1948. A treatise on the North American Ranunculi. *Amer. Midland Naturalist* 40 (1):1–261.

REFERENCES

Berkeley, Edmund & D. S. 1963. *John Clayton. Pioneer of North American Botany.* University of North Carolina.

Biggar, H. P. 1924. (Ed.) *The Voyages of Jacques Cartier.* Ottawa.

Birch, Thomas. 1756–7. *History of the Royal Society of London.* 4 vols. London.

Blewitt, Mary. 1957. *Surveys of the Seas.* London.

Blith, Walter, A Lover of Ingenuity. 1649. *The English Improver, or a new Survey of Husbandry . . .* London.

— 1652. *The English Improver Improved.* London.

Blunt, Reginald. 1906. *Paradise Row or a broken Piece of Old Chelsea.* London.

Blunt, Wilfrid & Stearn, W. T. 1950. *The Art of Botanical Illustration.* London.

Boivin, Bernard. 1944. American *Thalictra* and their old world allies. *Rhodora* 46: 337–77, 391–445, 453–487.

— 1957. Etudes Thalictrologiques II *Thalictrum polygamum* Muhlenberg Nomen specificum conservadum. *Bull. Soc. Roy. Bot. Belge* 89:315–18.

Boswell, James. 1960. *Boswell's Life of Johnson.* Everyman ed. 2 vols. London.

Botanical Magazine see *Curtis's Botanical Magazine.*

Botanical Society at Lichfield. 1787. *Families of Plants.* 2 vols. Lichfield.

Bovill, E. W. 1968. The Niger Explored. Oxford.

Brainerd, Ezra. 1905. Notes on New England violets III. *Rhodora* 7:245–8.

Britten, James. 1904. Banks's Newfoundland plants. *J. Bot.* 42:84–6.

— Banks's Newfoundland journal. *Op. cit.*:352.

— 1905. Book-Notes [Record of the sale of Banks's journal] *J. Bot.* 43:248.

— 1905 (2). The Collections of Banks and Solander. *J. Bot.* 43:284–90.

— 1917. Notes from the National Herbarium. IV. Edward Rudge's herbarium. *J. Bot.* 55:344–5.

Britton, N. L. 1895. New or noteworthy North American Phanerogams. IX. *Bull. Torrey Bot. Club.* 22:220–5.

Brougham, H. 1846. *Lives of Men of Letters and Science who flourished in the Time of George III.* 2 vols. London.

Buchheim, Günther. 1965. A bibliographical account of L'Héritier's 'Stirpes novae'. *Huntia* 2:29–58.

Buffon, Count G. L. L. de. [1770] 1771–86. *Histoire Naturelle des Oiseaux.* 10 vols. Paris.

Burney, Frances. 1907. *The Early Diary of Frances Burney 1768–1778.* Ed. A. R. Ellis. 2 vols. Everyman edition, London.

Burton, P. J. K. 1969. Two bird specimens probably from Cook's voyages. *Ibis* 111:388–90.

Cameron, Austin W. 1958. Mammals of the islands in the Gulf of St. Lawrence. *Bull. Nat. Mus. Canada* no. 154, biol. ser. no. 53.

Cameron, H. C. 1962. *Sir Joseph Banks, K.B., P.R.S. The Autocrat of the Philosophers.* London.

427

REFERENCES

Carter, Harold. 1964. *His Majesty's Spanish Flock*. Sydney.

Cartier, Jacques, see Biggar, H. P.

Cartwright, F. D. 1826. *The Life and Correspondence of Major Cartwright*. 2 vols. London.

Cartwright, George. 1792. *A Journal of Transactions and Events, during a Residence of nearly sixteen Years on the Coast of Labrador . . .* 3 vols. Newark.

— 1911. *Captain Cartwright and his Labrador Journal*. Edited by C. W. Townsend [an abridged version with notes on natural history]. Boston.

Catesby, Mark. 1731–43. *Natural History of Carolina, Florida, and the Bahama Islands . . .* 2 vols. London.

— 1754. *Natural History of Carolina, Florida and the Bahama Islands . . .* 2nd ed. revised by George Edwards. 2 vols. London.

— 1763. *Hortus Britannico-Americanus or a . . . curious Collection of Trees and Shrubs . . . adapted to the Soil and Climate of England*. London.

Chambers, J. D. & Mingay, G. E. 1966. *The Agricultural Revolution 1750–1880*. London.

Clayton, John & Gronovius, F. G. 1739, 1743. *Flora Virginica*. Leyden. Second edition, edited by L. T. Gronovius, 1762.

Clokie, Hermia N. 1964. *An Account of the Herbaria of the Department of Botany in the University of Oxford*. Oxford.

Conover, B., see Cory, C. B.

Cook, James, see Beaglehole.

Cormack, W. E. 1824. Account of a journey across the island of Newfoundland. *Edinburgh Phil. J.* 10:156–62.

— 1824 (2). Note sur l'histoire naturelle de Terre-neuve, extrait d'une lettre de M. Cormack. *Ann. Sci. Nat. Paris* 1:156–62.

— 1829. Journey in search of the Red Indians in Newfoundland. *Edinburgh New Phil. J.* 6:318–29.

— 1856. *Narrative of a Journey across the Island of Newfoundland*. St. John's, Newfoundland.

Cornut, J. P. 1635. *Canadarum Plantarum Historia . . .* Paris.

Correll, D. S. 1950. *Native Orchids of North America north of Mexico*. Waltham, Mass.

Cory, C. B., Hellmayr, C. E. & Conover, B. 1918–49. Catalogue of the birds of the Americas and the adjacent islands in the Field Museum of Natural History. *Publ. Field Columbian Mus.*, zool. ser., 13, pts. 1–11.

Crantz, see Cranz.

Cranz, David. 1767. *The History of Greenland . . .* Translated from the High Dutch etc. 2 vols. London.

— 1780. *The Ancient and Modern History of the Brethren*. Translated by Benjamin La Trobe. London.

REFERENCES

— 1820. *History of Greenland with a Sketch of the Mission of the Brethren in Labrador.* 2 vols. London.

Curtis, Roger. 1774. Particulars of the country of Labradore . . . From the papers of Lieutenant Roger Curtis of His Majesty's Sloop the *Otter . . . Phil. Trans.* 64, pt. 1:372–88.

Curtis's Botanical Magazine. 1787–. London.

Cuvier, G. 1821. Eloge historique de Sir Joseph Banks. Lu le 2 avril 1821. From *Memoirs historical and scientific of the Right Honourable Sir Joseph Banks* by George Suttor. Parramatta, 1855.

Dandy, J. E. 1958. *List of British vascular Plants.* London.

Danielsson, Bengt. 1969. The Captain Cook Bicentenary. Reprint from *Ethnos*, 32 pp.

Darwin, Erasmus. 1787. See Botanical Society at Lichfield.

— 1791. *The Botanical Garden.* 2 vols. London.

Davey, J. W. 1905. *The Fall of Torngak or the Moravian Mission on the Coast of Labrador.* London.

Dawson, Warren R. 1958. *The Banks Letters.* London.

De Beer, G. R. 1952. The relations between Fellows of the Royal Society and French men of science when France and Britain were at war. *Notes and Records Roy. Soc.* 9: 244–99.

DeCandolle, Augustin P. 1818–21. *Regni vegetabilis Systema naturale . . .* 2 vols. Paris.

— 1824. *Prodromus Systematis naturalis Regni vegetabilis . . .* Vol. 1, Paris.

Denys, Nicolas. 1672 [1908]. *The Description and Natural History of the Coasts of North America.* Ed. F. W. Ganong. Toronto.

Dobson, Jessie. 1969. *John Hunter.* London and Edinburgh.

Drage, Charles. 1970. *Family Story: The Drages of Hatfield.* London.

Drage, Theodorus Swaine. 1748–9. *An account of a Voyage for the discovery of a North West Passage by Hudson's Streights . . . in the ship California.* London, 2 vols.

— 1768. *The great Probability of a North West Passage . . .* London. [See also Eavenson.]

Du Rietz, Rolf. 1964. More light on Jonas Dryander. *Svenska Linné-Sällsk. Årsskr.* 47:82–3.

— 1965–6. Reviews of work by Adams, P. G. q.v., and others, in *Lychnos*:485–91.

Eames, Edwin J. 1909. Notes upon the flora of Newfoundland. *Rhodora* 11:85–9.

Eavenson, H. N. 1949. *Map Maker and Indian Traders.* Pittsburgh.

— 1950. *Swaine and Drage. A Sequel to Map Maker and Indian Traders.* Pittsburgh.

Edmonds, T. R. 1835. On the mortality of infants in England. *The Lancet* 1:692.

Edwards, George. 1743–51. *A Natural History of Uncommon Birds . . .* 4 pts. London. 2nd ed. 1751–54.

— 1754. See Catesby.

REFERENCES

Ehret, G. D. 1767. *Original Drawings for the Hortus Kewensis*. Fol. British Museum (Natural History).

— 1767 (2). *Original Drawings of some of the Plants collected in Newfoundland and Labrador by Joseph Banks*. Fol. British Museum (Natural History).

Ellis, Annie Raine, see Burney, Frances.

Ellis, Henry. 1748. *A Voyage to Hudson's Bay . . . in 1746 and 1747 . . . with a short Natural History of the Country*. London.

Ellis, John & Solander D. C. 1786. *The Natural History of many curious and uncommon Zoophytes*. London.

Erskine, D. 1954. (Ed.) *Augustus Hervey's Journal*. London.

Fabricius, J. C. 1775. *Systema Entomologiae . . .* Flensburg & Lipsiae [Leipzig].

— 1792–4. *Entomologia systematica emendata et aucta . . .* 4 vols. Hafniae [Copenhagen].

— 1798. *Supplementum Entomologiae systematicae*. Hafniae [Copenhagen].

Fassett, Norman C. 1935. Notes from the herbarium of the University of Wisconsin XIII. A study of *Streptopus*. *Rhodora* 37:88–113.

Faulkner, Thomas, 1829. *An historical and topographical Description of Chelsea and its Environs*, 2 vols. 2nd ed. London.

Fernald, M. L. 1903. Pursh's report of *Dryas* from New Hampshire. *Rhodora* 5: 281–3.

— 1906. An alpine variety of *Solidago macrophylla*. *Rhodora* 8: 227–8.

— 1907. *Streptopus oreopolus* a possible hybrid. *Rhodora* 9: 106–7.

— 1908. Notes on some plants of North-eastern America. *Rhodora* 10:46–55; 84–95.

— 1909. The variations of *Arenaria peploides* in America. *Rhodora* 11: 109–15.

— 1910. Notes on the plants of Wineland the Good. *Rhodora* 12:17–38.

— 1911. A botanical expedition to Newfoundland and southern Labrador. *Rhodora* 13:109–62.

— 1919. *Lomatogonium* the correct name for *Pleurogyne*. *Rhodora* 21: 193–8.

— 1923. *Vaccinium uliginosum* and its var. *alpinum*. *Rhodora* 25: 23–5.

— 1924. Some Senecios of Eastern Quebec and Newfoundland. *Rhodora* 26: 113–22.

— 1925 (1). The American representatives of *Lonicera caerulea*. *Rhodora* 27:1–11.

— 1925 (2). Persistence of plants in unglaciated areas of boreal America. *Mem. Amer. Acad. Arts & Sci.* 15 no. 3:239–342.

— 1926. Two summers of botanizing in Newfoundland. *Rhodora* 28:49–63; 74–87; 89–111; 115–19; 145–55; 161–78; 189–204; 210–225; 234–41.

— 1928 (1). The Eastern American occurrence of *Athyrium alpestre*. *Rhodora* 30: 44–9.

— 1928 (2). *Primula* § *farinosae* in America. *Rhodora* 30:59–77; 85–104.

— 1928 (3). The genus *Oxytropis* in north-eastern America. *Rhodora* 30:137–55.

REFERENCES

— 1942. Critical notes on *Carex. Rhodora* 44:281–331.

— 1943. Notes on *Hieracium. Rhodora* 45:317–25.

— 1944. Overlooked species, transfers and novelties in the flora of Eastern North America. *Rhodora* 46:1–21.

— 1947. Additions to and subtractions from the flora of Virginia. *Rhodora* 49: 85–115; 121–42; 145–59; 175–94.

— 1949. Studies of eastern American plants. No. 5. *Rhodora* 51:43–57; 61–85; 93–104.

— 1950. (Ed.) *Gray's Manual of Botany*. 8th Edition. Harvard.

Fletcher, H. R. 1969. *The Story of the Royal Horticultural Society*. Oxford.

Flora Europaea see Tutin, T. G.

Forster, J. R. 1771. *A Catalogue of the Animals of North America . . .* London.

— 1772. Account of several quadrupeds from Hudson's Bay. *Phil. Trans.* 62: 370–81.

— 1772. An account of the birds sent from Hudson's Bay; with observations relative to their natural history; and Latin descriptions of some of the most uncommon. *Phil. Trans.* 62:382–433.

— 1781. *Indische Zoologie*. Halle.

Frick, G. F. & Stearns, R. P. 1961. *Mark Catesby the colonial Audubon*. Urbana.

Friedmann, H. 1950. Birds of North and Middle America. Pt. 11. Families Cathartidae, Accipitridae . . . *Bull. Smithsonian Inst. U.S. Nat. Mus.* no. 50.

Frobisher, Martin see Stefansson, V.

Galle, J. G. 1894. *Verzeichniss der Elemente der bisher berechneten Cometenbahnen, nebst Anmerkungen und Literatur-Nachweisen . . .* Leipzig.

Ganong, F. W. see Denys, Nicolas.

Gardner, G. 1937. Liste annotée des espèces de pteridophytes, de phanérogames et d'algues récoltées sur la côte du Labrador, à la baie d'Hudson et dans le Manitoba nord, en 1930 et 1933. *Bull. Soc. Bot. France* 84:19–51.

Gates, R. Ruggles. 1918. A systematic study of the North American Melanthaceae from the genetic standpoint. *J. Linn. Soc., (Bot.)* 44:131–72.

Gesner, Conrad 1558. *Historiae Animalium* 3:138. Tiguri [Zurich].

Glass, D. V. & Eversley, D. E. C. 1965. *Population in History*. London.

Gmelin, J. F. see Linnaeus, C. 1787–93; 1796.

Godfrey, W. Earl. 1959. Notes on Newfoundland birds. *Bull. Nat. Mus. Canada* no. 172; Contributions to Zoology:98–111.

Gosling, W. G. 1910. *Labrador, its Discovery, Exploration and Development*. London.

Grauer, Sebastianus. 1784. *Plantarum Minus Cognitarum Decuria*. Kiloniae [Kiel].

Graves, Algernon. 1907. *Society of Artists of Great Britain, 1760–1791*.

Gray, Asa. 1882. Contributions to North American Botany. Studies of *Aster* and *Solidago* in the older herbaria. *Proc. Amer. Acad. Arts & Sci.* 17:163–79.

— 1950. See Fernald, M. L.

REFERENCES

Greenway, J. C. 1958. *Extinct and vanishing Birds of the World*. New York.

Grenfell, W. T. 1909. *Labrador, the Country and the People*. New York.

Gunson, W. N. 1965. Co-operation without paradox: a reply to Dr. Strauss. *Historical Studies Australia and New Zealand* 11: 513–34.

Hall, E. R. & Kelson, K. R. 1959. *The Mammals of North America*. 2 vols. New York.

Hallett, Robin. 1964. *Records of the African Association*, 1788–1831. London.

— 1965. *The Penetration of Africa*. 1. London.

Haven, Jens. 1764. *Account of an interview between Mr. Hans Haven, a Moravian, and the Esquimeaux savages*. MS: transcript by Hugh Palliser. Public Reocrd Office, London; CO 194/16.

Hearne, Samuel. 1795. *A Journey from Prince of Wales's Fort in Hudson's Bay to the Northern Ocean . . . in 1769–72*. London.

Hellmayr, C. E., see Cory, C. B.

Hervey, Augustus, see Erskine, D.

Hervey, John, see Sedgwick, Romney.

Hervey, G. F. & Hems, J. 1948. *The Goldfish*. London.

Hill, J. W. 1952. (Ed.) *The Letters and Papers of the Banks Family of Revesby Abbey*. Hereford.

Hitchcock, A. S. *et. al.* 1937–9. *North American Flora* 17, parts 7, 8: 483–638.

Hitchcock, C. L. 1944. The *Tofieldia glutinosa* complex of western North America. *Amer. Mid. Nat.* 31: 487–98.

Holland, Philemon, see Plinius Secundus.

Holmes, J. 1827. *Historical Sketches of the Missions of the United Brethren . . .* London.

Home, Everard. 1822. *Hunterian Oration*. Reprinted in Cameron, H. C., q.v.

Hooker, W. J. 1829–40. *Flora Boreali-Americana*. 2 vols. London.

Howley, James P. 1915. *The Beothuks or Red Indians*. Cambridge.

Hulton, P. H. 1961. John White's drawings of Eskimos. *The Beaver*, Summer number. Hudson's Bay Co., Winnipeg.

— & Quinn, D. B. 1964. *The American Drawings of John White 1577–1590*. 2 vols. British Museum; University of North Carolina.

Hunt, R. M. 1844. *The Life of Sir Hugh Palliser, Bart . . .* London.

Hustich, I. & Pettersson, B. 1942–3 [1944]. Notes on the vascular plants of the east coast of Newfoundland–Labrador. 1. Preliminary list of plants. *Mem. Soc. Fauna Flora Fennica* 19: 192–200.

— 1943–4 [1945]. Notes on vascular plants of Newfoundland-Labrador. 2. Notes by I. Hustich on the localities where the plant material was collected in 1937. *Mem. Soc. Fauna Flora Fennica* 20: 24–46.

Ingstad, H. 1966. Lund under the Pole Star [trans. N. Walford]. London.

Jacquin, N. J. von. 1786 [1787]–96 *Collectanea Austriaca . . .* 5 vols. [Vienna].

REFERENCES

Jussieu, A. L. 1804. Mémoire sur quelques nouvelles espèces d'anémones. *Ann. Mus. National d'Hist. Nat.* 3:245–50.

Kalm, Peter. 1753–61. *En Resa til Nova America . . .* 3 vols. Stockholm.

Kohlmeister, B. G. & Kmoch, G. 1814. *Journal of a Voyage from Okkak on the Coast of Labrador to Ungava Bay . . .* London.

Lahontan, Baron de, see Lom D'Arce.

La Pylaie, see Bachelot de la Pylaie.

Latham, John. 1781–1802. *A general Synopsis of Birds.* 3 vols [in six], 2 suppts. London.

— 1790, 1801. *Index Ornithologicus.* 2 vols. and suppt. [Date of suppt. 1801 *fide* Sherborn; 1802 *fide* Mullens & Swann.] See also Anon. 1837, and Mathews G.M., 1931.

Latrobe, B. 1774. *A brief Account of the Missions established among the Esquimaux Indians on the Labrador Coast.* London.

Lee, James. 1810. *Introduction to the Science of Botany . . . corrected and enlarged by J. Lee.* London.

Lepage, Ernest. 1960. *Hieracium canadense* et ses alliées en Amérique du nord. *Nat. Canadienne* 87:59–107.

L'Héritier de Brutelle, C. L. 1785–1805 [see Buchheim 1965]. *Stirpes Novae, aut minus cognitae . . .* Paris.

Lichfield, see Botanical Society at.

Lightfoot, J. 1777. *Flora Scotica.* 2 vols. London.

Lindroth, C. H. 1955. The Carabid beetles of Newfoundland. *Opusc. Ent.* Suppl. XII. Lund.

— 1957. *The faunal Connections between Europe and North America.* New York and Stockholm.

Linnaeus, C. 1756. Plantae hybridae. *Amoenitates Academicae* 3:28–62.

— 1758–9. *Systema Naturae.* 10th ed. 2 vols. Holmiae [Stockholm].

— 1762–3. *Species Plantarum.* 2nd ed. Holmiae. [Banks's copy, interleaved, 2 vols. in 6; British Museum (Natural History).]

— 1766–8. *Systema Naturae.* 12th ed. Holmiae. [Banks's copy interleaved, vol. 1 in 6 parts; British Museum (Natural History).]

— 1779–80. *Systema Plantarum.* Ed. J. J. Reichard. Frankfurt. [Banks's copy, interleaved, 4 vols. in 9; British Museum (Natural History).]

— 1788–93. *Systema Naturae.* Ed. J. F. Gmelin. 13th ed. 3 vols. Lipsiae [Leipzig].

— 1796. *Systema Vegetabilium.* Ed. J. F. Gmelin. 2 vols. Lugduni [Lyon].

— 1797–1810. *Species Plantarum.* Ed. C. L. Willdenow. Berolini [Berlin]. Banks's copy, interleaved, 4 vols. in 18 parts; British Museum (Natural History).

— 1957. *Species Plantarum,* Ray Society facsimile edition, see Stearn.

Linsley, E. G. 1962. Cerambycidae of North America. Pt. 2. *Univ. Calif. Publ. Ent.* 19:1–103.

REFERENCES

Lom D'Arce, Louis Armand de, Baron de Lahontan. 1703. *Nouveaux Voyages de M. le Baron de Lahontan dans l'Amérique septentrionale . . .* 2 vols. La Haye.

Loureiro, João de. 1790. *Flora Cochinchinensis . . .* Ulyssipone [Lisbon].

Löve, A. & Löve, D. 1959. Biosystematics of the black Crowberries of America. *Canad. J. Genet. Cytol.* 1:34–8.

Lysaght, A. 1952. Manchots de l'Antarctique en Nouvelle Guinée. *L'Oiseau et R.F.O.* 22:120–4.

— 1959. Some eighteenth-century bird paintings in the library of Sir Joseph Banks (1743–1820). *Bull. Brit. Mus. (Nat. Hist.) Histor. Ser. 1* no. 6:251–372.

— 1964. A grangerized copy of E. Smith's *Life of Sir Joseph Banks. J. Soc. Bibl. Nat. Hist.* 2:206–9

McAtee, W. L. 1950. The North American birds of George Edwards. *J. Soc. Bibl. Nat. Hist.* 2:194–205.

— 1953. North American bird records in the Philosophical Transactions, 1665–1800. *J. Soc. Bibl. Nat. Hist.* 3:56–60.

— 1957. The North American birds of Mark Catesby and Eleazar Albin. *J. Soc. Bibl. Nat. Hist.* 3:133–94.

Mackenzie, K. K. 1931–5. 'Cariceae' in *North American Flora* 18 parts 1–7. New York.

McNeill, J. 1962. Taxonomic studies in the Alsinoideae, 1 & 2. *Notes Roy. Bot. Garden Edin.* 24:79–155; 241–404.

MacPherson, Harold, 1937. *The Book of Newfoundland.* St. John's.

Manville, R. H. 1966. The extinct Sea Mink, with taxonomic notes. *Proc. U.S. Nat. Mus.* 122, no. 3584, 11 pp.

Marcgravius, Georgius. 1648. *Historiae Rerum naturalium Brasiliae . . .* Lugdun. Batavorum & Amstelodami [Leyden & Amsterdam].

Marie-Victorin, Frère. 1935 *Flore Laurentienne.* Montreal.

— 1964. *Flore Laurentienne.* Montreal. 2nd ed. edited by E. Rouleau.

Mathews, G. M. 1931. John Latham (1740–1837): an early English ornithologist. *Ibis* 13th ser., 1:466–75.

Matthiessen, P. 1959. *Wild Life in America.* New York.

Menzies, Archibald. 1798. A new arrangement of the genus *Polytrichum . . . Trans. Linn. Soc.* 4: 63–84.

Merrem, Blasius. 1784–6. *Beyträge zur besondern Geschickte der Vögel.* Gottingen.

— 1786–7. *Avium rar. et minus cognit. Icones et Descript.* Lipsiae [Leipzig; a Latin edition of the *Beyträge*, with scientific binomials].

Meyer, Ernest. 1830. *De Plantis Labradoricis, Libri tres.* Lipsiae [Leipzig].

Meyer, F. G. 1951. *Valeriana* in North America and the West Indies. *Ann. Mo. Bot. Gard.* 38:377–507.

Michaux, A. 1803. *Flora Boreali-Americana . . .* 2 vols. Parisiis et Argentorati [Paris & Strasbourg].

REFERENCES

Miller, Philip. 1768. *Gardeners Dictionary*, 8th ed. London.

Morris, F. & Eames, E. A. 1929. *Our wild Orchids*. New York.

Nansen, Fridtjof. 1911. *In Northern Mists Arctic Exploration in early Times*. 2 vols. London. [Translated by Arthur G. Chater].

Newfoundland Fishery Research Commission. 1932. Annual Report Year 1931. Appendix D. First list of fishes in the Newfoundland fishing area. *Repts. Newfoundland Fish. Res. Com.* 1 no. 4:107–10.

— 1933. Annual Report Year 1932. Appendix D. Second list of fishes in the Newfoundland fishing area. *Repts. Newfoundland Fish Res. Com.* 2, no. 1:125–7.

— 1934. Annual Report 1933. Appendix D. Third list of fishes in the Newfoundland fishing area. *Repts. Newfoundland Fish Res. Com.* 2, no. 2:115–17.

Newton, Alfred. 1893–6. *A Dictionary of Birds*. London.

Packard, Alpheus Spring. 1891. *The Labrador Coast . . .* New York and London.

Paillou, Peter. 1767–8. Unpublished drawings, see Banks, J., and White, Taylor.

Parkinson, Sydney. 1766–8. *Original Drawings of Birds, Fishes*, etc. Vol. 199* B 1. Print Room, British Museum.

— *Drawings of Invertebrates*. Vol. 199 a 8. Print Room, British Museum.

— 1773. *A Journal of a Voyage to the South Seas in His Majesty's Ship the Endeavour*. London.

Pennant, Thomas. 1766. *British Zoology*. London and Chester.

— 1769. *Indian Zoology*. London.

— 1784–7. *Arctic Zoology*. 2 vols. and suppt. London.

— 1790. *Indian Zoology*. 2nd ed. London.

— 1792. *Arctic Zoology*. 2nd ed. 3 vols. London.

— 1792. *Arctic Zoology*. 2nd ed. A set with interleaving, MS notes and copious unpublished marginal and other coloured illustrations, many copied by Mercatti from originals by Sydney Parkinson. McGill University Library.

— 1793. *The Literary Life of the late Thomas Pennant, Esq. by Himself*. London.

Peters, H. S. & Burleigh, T. D. 1951. *The Birds of Newfoundland*. Boston.

Pettigrew, J. J. 1838–40. *Medical Portrait Gallery*. 4 vols. London.

Phipps, J. C. 1774. *A Voyage towards the North Pole, . . .* London.

Plinius Secundus, C. 1634. *The Historie of the World, Commonly called the Natural History of C. Plinius Secundus*. Translated by Philemon Holland. 2 vols. London.

Plischke, Hans. 1960. Insulaner aus der Südsee in Europa am Ende des 18. Jahrhunderts. *Ethnologica* N.F. 2:94–104.

Poiret, J. L. M. 1811. *Encyclopédie Méthodique Botanique*. Suppt. 2. Paris.

Polunin, Nicholas. 1940. Botany of the Canadian Eastern Arctic. Pt. 1 Pteridophyta and Spermatophyta. *Bull. Nat. Mus. Canada*, no. 92:1–408.

— 1959. *Circumpolar Arctic Flora*. Oxford.

Ponsonby, D. A. 1949. *Call a Dog Hervey*. London.

Porsild, M. P. 1935. Stray contributions to the flora of Greenland. XII. On some herbaria from Greenland and Labrador collected by the Moravian brethren. *Medd. om Grønland* 93 : no. 3 :84–94.

— 1957. Illustrated Flora of the Canadian Arctic Archipelago. *Bull. Nat. Mus. Canada* no. 146, 209 pp.

Porter, T. C. 1894. Varieties of *Solidago* and *Aster*. *Bull. Torrey Bot. Club*. 21 :310–11.

Prideaux, John. 1853. *Relics of William Cookworthy*. London.

Prowse, D. W. 1895. *A History of Newfoundland* . . . London.

Pursh, Frederick. 1814. *Flora Americae Septentrionalis*. London.

Rathbun, Mary. 1930. Cancroid crabs of North America. *Bull. U.S. Nat. Mus.* no. 152, 609 pp.

Rauschenberg, R. A. 1968. Daniel Carl Solander . . . *Trans. Amer. Phil. Soc.* 58 :1–68.

Ray, John. 1678. *The Ornithology of Francis Willughby in three Books* . . . London.

Raymond, Marcel. 1950. Les Cypéracées de l'île Anticosti : *Carex* et *Kobresia*. *Canad. J. Res.* C. 28 :406–44.

Reeks, Henry. 1869. Notes on the zoology of Newfoundland. Letter 3, ornithology. Hirundinidae cont. *Zoologist* 2nd. ser. 4 :1741–59.

Rees's Cyclopaedia. [1802]–20. London.

Reichard, J. J. 1779–80, see Linnaeus.

Rendle A. B. 1929. Some early 18th century American collections and their collectors. *Proceedings of the International Congress of Plant Sciences, Ithaca, New York August 16–23, 1926*, 2 :1525–31.

Retzius, A. J. 1779–91. *Observationes Botanicae*. Lipsiae [Leipzig].

Richardson, John. 1823. Botanical appendix to Sir John Franklin's *Narrative of a Journey to the Shores of the Polar Sea in* . . . *1819–22*. London.

Ridgway, R. 1919. Birds of North and Middle America. Pt. 8 [Charadriiformes]. *Bull. U.S. Nat. Mus.* no. 50, 852 pp.

Roberts, W. 1918. A Whitechapel botanical garden. *Gardeners' Chronicle*, ser. 3, no. 53, pt. 2 :245–6.

Robinson, B. L. & Schrenk, H. von. 1896. Notes on the Flora of Newfoundland. *Canad. Record of Science* 7 :1–31.

Rottböll, C. F. 1770. Afhandling om en Deel enten gandske nye eller vel forhen bekiendte, men dog for os rare Planter, som i Island og Grønland . . . *Skrift. Kiøb. Selst.* 10 :393–468.

Rouleau, Ernest. 1949. Enumeratio plantarum vascularum Terrae-Novae. *Contr. Inst. bot. Univ. Montréal* 64 :61–83.

— 1956. Studies on the vascular flora of the province of Newfoundland (Canada). III. A check-list of the vascular plants of the province of Newfoundland (including the French islands of St. Pierre and Miquelon). *Contr. Inst. bot. Univ. Montréal* 69 :41–106.

— 1964. See Marie-Victorin.

REFERENCES

Rousi, Arne. 1965. Biosystematic studies on the species aggregate *Potentilla anserina* L. *Ann. Bot. Fenn.* 2:47–112.

Roussine, N. 1961. Note sur les espèces due genre *Thymus* aux Etats-Unis d'Amérique. *Naturalia Monspeliensia Ser. Bot.* fasc. 13:59–61.

Rudge, E. 1804. Descriptions of some species of *Carex* from North America. *Trans. Linn. Soc.* 7:96–100.

Rydén, Stig. 1963. *The Banks Collection. An Episode in 18th-Century Anglo-Swedish Relations.* Stockholm.

St. John, Harold. 1922. A botanical exploration of the north shore of the Gulf of St. Lawrence including an annotated list of the species of vascular plants. *Canad. Dept. Mines, Victoria Memorial Museum,* Memoir 126:1–117.

Salisbury, R. A. 1805 [1805–8]. *The Paradisus Londinensis.* 2 vols. London.

Salomonsen, Finn. 1939. *Moults and Sequences of Plumages in the Rock Ptarmigan (Lagopus mutus (Montin)).* Copenhagen.

Salvadori, T. 1895. Catalogue of the Chenomorphae, Crypturi, and Ratitae . . . *Cat. Birds. Brit. Mus* 27.

Saunders, Howard, & Salvin, Osbert. 1896. Catalogue of the Gaviae and Tubinares . . . *Cat. Birds Brit. Mus.* 25.

Sawyer, F. C. 1950. Some natural history drawings made during Captain Cook's first voyage round the world. *J. Soc. Bibl. Nat. Hist.* 2:190–3.

Schloezer, C. A. *et al* 1765. *Journal of the Visit of the Moravians to Chateau Bay in the Niger 1765.* Holograph MS, Public Record Office. CO 194/16, ff. 225–39. [Only the rectos are numbered although both sides of each sheet have been used.]

— *Journal of the Voyage of Jens Haven and C. A. Schloezer to Davis Inlet in the Schooner Hope in 1765.* Holograph MS, Public Record Office, CO 194/16, ff. 240–5. [See preceding entry for note on pagination.]

Schorger, A. W. 1955. *The Passenger Pigeon.* Madison.

Von Schrank, R. R. 1818. Aufzählung einiger Pflanzen aus Labrador mit Anmerkungen. *Denkschr. Bot. Ges. Regensb.* 1, pt:1–30.

Sclater, P. L. 1882. (Ed.) *Forster's Animals of Hudson's Bay.* Willughby Society reprint. London. See also Forster, J. R.

— 1882. (Ed.) *Forster's Catalogue of the Animals of North America or Faunula Americana.* Willughby Society reprint. London. See also Forster, J. R.

Scoggan, H. J. 1950. Flora of Bic and the Gaspé Peninsula, Quebec. *Bull. Nat. Mus. Canada* no. 11:1–399.

Seary, E. R. 1959. *Toponymy of the Island of Newfoundland. Check-List no. 1, Maps.* Memorial University of Newfoundland, St. John's.

— 1960. *Toponymy of the Island of Newfoundland. Check-List no. 2, Names. I The Northern Peninsula.* Memorial University of Newfoundland, St. John's.

Sedgwick, Romney. 1931. (Ed.) *Some Materials towards Memoirs of the Reign of King George II by John, Lord Hervey.* London.

REFERENCES

Sharpe, R. Bowdler. 1874. Catalogue of the Accipitres . . . *Cat. Birds Brit. Mus.* 1.

— 1900. (Ed.) *The Natural History & Antiquities of Selborne* . . . by Gilbert White. 2 vols. London.

Shortt, T. M. 1943. Correlation of Bill & Foot Colouring with Age & Season in the Black Duck. *Wilson Bull.* 55 no. 1.

Skelton, R. A. 1954. Captain James Cook as a Hydrographer. *Mariner's Mirror* 40: 91–119.

— 1965. *James Cook Surveyor of Newfoundland.* San Francisco.

—, Marston, T. E. & Painter, G. D. 1965. *The Vinland Map.* Yale.

— & Tooley, R. V. 1967. The marine surveys of James Cook in North America. *Map Collectors' Circle*, no. 37. London.

Smith, Edward. 1911. *The Life of Sir Joseph Banks* . . . London.

Smith, J. A. & Ross, W. D. (Eds.) 1910–52. *The Works of Aristotle.* 12 vols. Oxford.

Smith, J. E. [1802]–20. [Botanical entries in *Rees's Cyclopaedia*, q.v.]

Solander, Daniel C. n.d. *Botanical MSS* 23 vols. and index. Botany Library, British Museum (Natural History).

— n.d. *Zoological MSS* 27 vols. Zoology Library, British Museum (Natural History).

— [MS notes in Banks's interleaved volumes of various works of Linnaeus, q.v.]

Southey, Robert. 1849–51. *Common Place Book.* 4 series. Ed. by J. W. Warter, London.

Stafleu, F. A. 1963. Dates of Botanical Publications 1788–92. *Taxon* 12: 43–87.

Stearn, W. T. 1937. Willdenow's 'Hortus Berolinensis'. *J. Bot.* 75: 233–5.

— 1950. See Blunt W.

— 1954. See van Steenis.

— 1957. An Introduction to the *Species Plantarum* and cognate botanical works of Carl Linnaeus. Pp. 1–176 + XI. [Prefixed to vol. 1, Ray Society facsimile of the *Species Plantarum.*]

— 1960. Humboldt's 'Essai sur la Géographie des Plantes.' *J. Soc. Bibl. Nat. Hist.* 3: 351–7.

— 1961. Botanical gardens and botanical literature in the eighteenth century. *Cat. Botanical Books in Coll. R. M. M. Hunt* 2 pt. 1: XLI–CXL.

— 1966. The use of bibliography in natural history. *Bibliography and Natural History.* Ed. T. R. Buckman. 26 pp. Univ. Kansas.

— 1967. Sibthorp, Smith, the 'Flora Graeca' and the 'Florae Graecae Prodromus'. *Taxon* 16 (3): 168–78.

Stearns, W. A. 1884. *Labrador. A Sketch of its Peoples, its Industries and its Natural History.* Boston.

Stefansson, V. 1938. (Ed.) *The three Voyages of Martin Frobisher in Search of a Passage to Cathay and India . . . From the 1578 text of George Best.* London.

REFERENCES

Stewart, R. E. & Aldrich, J. W. 1956. Distinction of maritime and prairie populations of Blue-winged Teal. *Proc. Biol. Soc. Washington* 69: 29–36.

Stow, J. 1754. (Ed. John Strype) *Survey of the Cities of London and Westminster.* 2 vols. London.

Strauss, W. P. 1963–5. Paradoxical co-operation: Sir Joseph Banks and the London Missionary Society. *Historical Studies Australia and New Zealand* 11: 246–52.

Svenson, H. K. 1947. The group of *Eleocharis palustris* in North America. *Rhodora* 49: 61–7.

— 1957. (Poales) (Cyperaceae) Scirpeae (continuatio). *North American Flora* 18 pt. 9: 505–56.

Swaine, Charles. See Drage, T. S.

Swartz, Olaf. 1800. Orchidernes flagter och arter upställde. *Kongl. Vetens. Acad. nya Handl.* 21: 202–54.

Swenk, Myron H. 1916. The Eskimo Curlew and its disappearance. *Ann. Rep. Smithsonian Inst. for 1915*, pp. 325–30.

Tanner, V. 1944. Outlines of the Geography, life and customs of Newfoundland–Labrador (the eastern part of the Labrador Peninsula). *Acta Geog., Helsinsf.* 8 no. 1. [Republished in 2 vols. by Cambridge University Press, 1947.]

Taylor, W. R. 1957. *Marine Algae of the northeastern Coast of North America.* 2nd ed. revd. Ann Arbor.

Todd, W. E. C. 1963. *Birds of the Labrador Peninsula* . . . Toronto.

Townsend, C. W. 1911. See Cartwright, George.

— & Allen, Glover M. 1907. Birds of Labrador. *Proc. Boston Nat. Hist. Soc.* 33 no. 7: 277–428.

Toynbee, Paget, see Walpole, Horace.

Trelease, William. 1892. Revision of North American Ilicineae and Celastraceae. *Trans. Acad. Sci. St. Louis* 5: 343–57.

Turner, Dawson. 1808–19. *Fuci, sive Plantarum Fucorum Generi* . . . 4 vols. London.

— n.d. *MS copies of Banks's 'Endeavour' diary and his correspondence.* 23 vols. Botany Library, British Museum (Natural History).

Turner, William. 1544. *Avium precipuarum quarum apud Plinium et Aristotelem Mentio est, brevis & succinta Historia.* Coloniae [Cologne].

Tutin, T. G. *et al.* 1964. *Flora Europaea* Vol. 1. Cambridge.

Uggla, A. H. 1958 [1959]. Linné den yngres brev till Abraham Bäck. *Svenska linnésällsk Årsskr* 41: 61–100.

van Steenis, M. J. & Stearn, W. T. 1954. List of works and serials. *Flora Malesiana* 1, pt. 4: clxvi–ccxix.

Wall, C. & Cameron, H. C. 1963. *A History of the Worshipful Society of Apothecaries of London.* I. *1617–1815.* Oxford.

REFERENCES

Waghorne, Arthur C. 1888. *A summary Account of the wild Berries and other edible Fruits of Newfoundland and Labrador*. St. Johns.

— 1890 [1891]–8. The flora of Newfoundland, Labrador, and St. Pierre et Miquelon. *Trans. Nova Scotian Inst. Sci.* 8: 359–73; 9: 83–100; 361–401.

Wahlenberg, Georg. 1803. Inledning til Caricographien. *Vet. Akak. Handl. Stockholm* 24: 138–70.

Walpole, Horace. 1903–1925. *The Letters of Horace Walpole* . . . Ed. Mrs. Paget Toynbee. Oxford.

Wangenheim, F. A. I. von 1788. Beschreibung der Polenblättrigen *Kalmia* . . . *Sch. Gesell. naturh. Fr. Berlin* 8: pt. 2: 129–33.

Waters, J. H. & Ray, C. E. 1961. The former range of the Sea Mink. *J. Mammal.* 42: 380–3.

Weston, Richard. 1650 [err. typogr. '1605']. *A Discours of Husbandrie used in Brabant and Flanders* . . . Ed. S. Hartlib. London.

— 1652. *Op. cit.* 2nd ed. [This edition contains a letter of dedication to Sir Richard Weston's sons, with the date 1645. According to the *Dictionary of National Biography*, Sir Richard's pamphlet was privately circulated in MS but not printed until 1650; Hartlib states in the second edition that he did not know the author's name when he first saw the pamphlet which he edited; hence only Hartlib's name appears in the first edition.]

Weston, Richard. 1775. *The English Flora*. London. (+ suppt. 1780.)

Wheeler, A. C. 1958. The Gronovius fish collection. A catalogue and historical account. *Bull. Brit. Mus. (Nat. Hist.) Histor. Ser.* 1, no. 5: 185–249.

White, Charles. 1773. *A Treatise on the Management of pregnant and lying-in Women*. London.

White, Gilbert. 1789 [1877]. *The Natural History and Antiquities of Selborne* . . . Ed. Thomas Bell. 2 vols. London.

— [1900]. *Op. cit.* Ed. R. Bowdler Sharpe. 2 vols. London.

White, M. H. Towry. 1886. *Memoirs of the House of White of Wallingwells* . . . Edinburgh.

— 1907. Some account of the family of White of Tuxford and Wallingwells. *Trans. Thoroton Soc.* 2: 50–65.

White, Taylor. n.d. [Natural history drawings in folio cases, by Peter Paillou, Charles Collins *et al*; *Aves* cases numbered 1–16, but folio sheets of drawings of birds, continuously numbered from preceding series of mammals, run from 256 to 916; there are sheets of notes from Taylor White in some cases.] McGill University Library, Montreal.

Whiteley, W. H. 1964. The establishment of the Moravian Mission in Labrador and British Policy, 1763–83. *Canad. Hist. Rev.* 45: 29–50.

— 1969. Governor Hugh Palliser and the Newfoundland and Labrador Fishery, 1764–8. *Canad. Hist. Rev.* 50: 141–63.

REFERENCES

Wilkins, G. L. 1955. A catalogue and historical account of the Banks shell collection. *Bull. Brit. Mus. (Nat. Hist.) Histor. Ser.* 1: 69–120.

Willdenow, C. L. 1803–16. *Hortus Berolinensis.* Berolini [Berlin]. See Stearn, W. T., 1937, for dates of publication.

Willson, E. J. 1961. *James Lee and the Vineyard Nursery.* London [Hammersmith Local History Group].

Willughby, F. 1676. *Ornithologia Libri tres: in quibus Aves omnes hactenus cognitae in Methodum Naturis suis convenientem redactae accurate describuntur* . . . London. See also Ray, John.

Wilson, Charles. 1965. *England's Apprenticeship 1603–1763.* London.

Wirsing, A. L. 1778. *Eclogae Botanicae e Dictionario Regni Vegetabilis* . . . Norimbergae [Nuremberg].

Withering, W. 1776. *A Botanical Arrangement of all the Vegetables naturally growing in Great Britain* . . . 2 vols. Birmingham and London.

Wolff, Torben. 1967. *Danish Expeditions of the Seven Seas.* Copenhagen.

Wood, Casey, A. 1931. *An Introduction to the Literature of Vertebrate Zoology* . . . Oxford and London.

Young, Arthur. 1799. *General View of the Agriculture of the County of Lincoln.* London.

Zimsen, Ella. 1964. *The Type material of J. C. Fabricius.* Copenhagen.

Appendix 1

A copy of Pennant's
Arctic Zoology annotated
by George Cartwright

WHEN this book was already in proof Lord Cranbrook showed Mr. Gavin Bridson, Librarian, Linnean Society, his copy of Pennant with annotations believed to be by Cartwright. Mr. Bridson kindly told him of my work on Banks and Cartwright, and Lord Cranbrook then generously lent me the volumes and gave permission for the publication of Cartwright's notes as this appendix. I am indebted to Mr. G. M. Gathorne-Hardy, the previous owner of this copy of the *Arctic Zoology*, for a note on its provenance. It originally belonged to Thomas Hodges, of Hemsted Park, Benenden, Kent, a brother-in-law of Cartwright's. Mr. Gathorne-Hardy's grandfather, the first Lord Cranbrook, purchased the house from a family called Law Hodges; he also bought a number of other books by Pennant, with the Hodges bookplate. Cartwright frequently stayed with the Hodges when he was in England.

Owing to the lateness of this addition, I have been unable to do all the work on it that I should have liked. Roger Curtis, 1746–1816, the subject of an acid comment by Cartwright, was in Labrador in 1773. The chart, published with his account of that country in the *Phil. Trans.* 64:372–88, is an outline chart and although it is not a copy of any of the Moravian maps which I have seen, it is certainly not as good as some of the charts of that coast from the hand of Schloezer. Curtis himself says 'As far as I have been, which is to the latitude of 59° 10′, the draught which I have been able to form is by much the best that has hitherto been made'.

Roger Curtis was created a baronet in 1794. The D.N.B. in reporting his part in the Gambier trial says, 'His whole career shows that his personal courage was so tempered by prudence, as to lead to sympathy with that excess of caution with which Gambier was charged.' Cartwright and Pennant clearly had very different views of Curtis.

APPENDIX 1

Cartwright's annotations

Arctic Zoology, Volume I

Table of Quadrupeds

pp. clxix-xi: Cartwright added these to Pennant's localities:

	Occurrence in New World
Arctic Fox	Labrador, Newfoundland
Grey Fox	Labrador, Newfoundland
Lynx	Labrador
Polar Bear	Newfoundland
Wolverene	Labrador

P. cxciii: Pennant says 'The male Polar Bears rove out at sea, on the floating ice, most of the winter, and till June: the females lie concealed in the wood, or beneath the banks of rivers, till March, when they come abroad with their twin cubs, and bend their course to the sea in search of their consorts'.

Cartwright notes: 'A misinformation. The females rove about all winter as well as the males, and cub on the ice; they have from one to three at a time; their cubs follow them until they breed again, which is every second year.'

P. cxciv: Pennant 'The eastern coast, so admirably described by that honored name, Sir Roger Curtis'.* (Phil Trans. lxiv. 372) is barren past the efforts of cultivation. The surface everywhere uneven, and covered with masses of stone of an amazing size. It is a country of fruitless vallies and frightful mountains, some of an astonishing height: the first watered by a chain of lakes, formed not from springs, but rain and snow, so chilly as to be productive of only a few small trout.** The mountains have here and there a blighted shrub, or a little moss. The vallies are full of crooked stunted trees, Pines, Fir, Birch, and Cdears, or rather a species of Juniper'.

Cartwright notes:[1] *'S^r. R. Curtis was Lieut. of the *Otter* sloop of war when in Labrador, was chiefly in Chateaux Bay and in very few other harbours. He once went to Nain, or Nuninock, the principal settlement of the Moravians, pirated his chart of that coast and invented most of his acct. of that country. There is good soil in many parts and it produces many very large trees. I have measured several which have been nine feet in circumference and carried their substance to a very great height. Numbers of boats and some decked vessels have been built there. Almost all kinds of garden stuff will grow there in very great perfection, but corn, I believe, will not ripen though it grows and ears well and no Pines, but Spruces, Silver Fir, Larch, Birch and Aspin. All grow large'.

**'Pike, Eels and various fresh-water fish are found in the lakes in Labrador. There are springs in that country as the rivers and brooks are never lower in the latter part of the winter than at the end of a dry summer.'

[1] Cartwright's spelling and punctuation have not been altered.

At the bottom of the same page, Pennant commented on the Moravian missionaries: 'They are not actuated by ambition, political views, or avarice'. Cartwright adds: 'These pious people are very attentive to trade, and they have profited much more by their traffic with the Eskimaux, than the latter have done by their preaching'.

On pp. cxcvi–cxcviii, Pennant published Banks's notes on the English fishery in Newfoundland (diary pp. 60–68), without mentioning him by name. Against the description of mud fish (p. 67), Cartwright writes: 'They are split in the same manner as those which are dried, & when shipped are stowed in the hold with fresh salt thrown on them in the same manner as when first salted.' On the following page, where Banks described the straining of the cod livers into 'a vessel set under a hole in the tubs bottom', Cartwright adds, 'They make use of vatts built on purpose'.

On p. 67 of volume one, in his description of the Wolverene, Pennant writes: 'It is a beast of uncommon fierceness, the terror of the Wolf and Bear; the former, which will devour any carrion, will not touch the carcase of this animal, which smells more fetid than that of a Pole cat'. To which Cartwright adds: 'In Spring it has a very strong smell exactly like that of an old He-goat and the flesh tastes in the same manner: but in the winter, when it is in proper season, it has no offensive smell and the flesh is very sweet good eating. It is afraid of a dog, and when attacked by one will run up a tree. I have known them eat through oak tierces to get at salted salmon. It is a great, and I believe the only enemy of the porcupine for I never saw one wch. had not many porcupine quills sticking in its paunch: and I make no doubt but it will kill beavers, but that must be when they go into the woods to cut food, which sometimes they will do to the distance of an hundred yards or more from the pond which they live in.'

On the following page, when Pennant wrote: 'It searches the traps laid for taking other beasts', Cartwright adds: 'Any beast of prey will devour any other beast which he meets with in a trap, but the wolverene, like the bear, has so little suspicion or fear, that he is sure to get into the first trap he meets with. As furriers cut or mark a very long path through the woods and build many small log traps for Martens the Wolverene will haunt those paths and tear the traps down to get at the bait, in which case the furrier sets a steel trap in the path which is sure to catch him, as he follows the furriers track because he has good walking in it. Thirty-two pounds is the greatest weight I ever knew these animals to be of: they are found in Labrador, but not numerous; there are none in Newfoundl^d.'

On p. 71, where Pennant included Labrador in the range of the badger, Cartwright comments, 'I never heard of one in Labrador'. Further down the same page, Pennant quotes Buffon's suggestion that Carcajou is the American name for the badger, not the wolverene. Cartwright writes, 'Carcajou is the Canadian name for the Wolverene.'

Cartwright's annotation on the Varying Hare is of particular interest since he wrote to Banks on 12 October, 1775 (p. 266 of this book) about a hare with five unborn young. In the *Arctic Zoology*, p. 94, he writes: 'I killed one in Labrador with five young ones in her, another with six, and another with seven, and have good reason to believe that they breed two or three times in the summer. They weigh eight pounds and in the autumn are surprisingly fat.'

His longest notes relate to the beaver and are written on the margins of pp. 99 to 105. The first follows Pennant's description of dam-building on which Cartwright comments: 'The whole account is very erronious. The beaver has not more sagacity than other animals. They build themselves an house of sticks and mud, make a dam across the brook and lay up food for winter—many other animals do as much. They make use of no piles or wattling, but lay sticks, stones & mud in a confused heap and beginning under water hollow it out at the same time adding to the outside till the house is large enough to contain the family which generally consists of six or eight beavers, but have been known to amount to sixteen. Many houses being in one pond is owing to no Indians or furriers disturbing a country for several years and great plenty of food growing on its banks'.

On p. 100, where Pennant described the beaver's houses in detail, with particulars of special functions of various apartments and division of labour amongst the inhabitants, Cartwright adds: 'They do make use of stones in building their houses but that is no sign of their sagacity but far otherwise.

A new house has but one apartment, but an old house new built upon will have additional lodgings, but they all serve to sleep in. . . . No opening was ever found to the land for if there was one the water in the other would freeze and not only prevent the beavers getting at their magazine of provisions but also cause them to become an easy prey to their enemies.'

Then again, on p. 101, where Pennant states that there may be as many as four hundred beavers: 'within the precincts of one dam' Cartwright notes: 'No such number was ever found on one piece of water unless it was a very large one with great plenty of food in & about it, for it is surprising how many trees a family of eight will destroy in one year. They will also eat the root of the water-lilly [*sic*] but no fish.'

On p. 102, Pennant referred to an observation on beavers by Andrew Graham who lived for many years at Hudson's Bay, and sent collections of birds and mammals to Daines Barrington and the Royal Society: 'They are said to have a sort of slavish beaver amongst them (analogous to the Drone) which they employ in servile works, and the domestic drudgery'. Cartwright writes: 'Mr. Graham is mistaken; he supposes the Hermit-beaver to be the drone but these are only such as have lost their mates and, like swans not being inclined to pair again, live by themselves.'

Again from Pennant: 'The Indians observe the quantity which the Beavers lay in their magazine at the approach of winter. It is the Almanack of the Savages; who judge from the greater or less stock, of the mildness or severity of the approaching season.' On which Cartwright notes: 'The Savages as well as European furriers judge of the number of the crew, or family of Beavers from the quantity of food, & not of the weather.'

Cartwright is scathing about Pennant's comments on the sagacity of beavers in the selection of places for their dams. 'Beavers have in America variety of lakes and waters in which they might fix their seats; but their sagacity informs them of the precarious tenure of such dwellings, which are liable to be overthrown by every flood. This induces them to undertake their mighty and marvellous labours. They therefore select places where no such inconvenience can be felt.' Cartwright says: 'Their want of sagacity causes them to live in ponds of their own making when they find plenty of food near a place convenient for that purpose, but whenever they are found there they are all of them killed with the greatest ease by cutting the dam or drawing off the water, for they cannot run above one mile in an hour on land. And the same reason often causes them to erect their houses where they are flooded out, or their magazine swept away by a flood, either of which proves equally destructive to them when it happens in the winter time, as the returning frost kills them: for in the first case they are obliged to cut a hole through the top of the house to escape drowning and as the frost always returns before the water subsides they are froze out and die of cold, and in the latter case are starved for want of provisions unless they can find plenty of the roots of water-lilly which never grows in brooks, where I have sometimes seen their houses.' . . . Where there is plenty of food they will always haunt as long as any remain in that part of the country.

. . . They breed in the months of June or July; commonly bring forth by pairs which are male & female & those pair & generally leave their dams [illegible phrase] year, build an house for themselves & breed the next summer; sometimes they will continue with them & breed in the same house. They seldom have more than two, but sometimes have four or six.'

According to Pennant, 'Beavers have, besides man, two enemies; the Otter, and the Wolverene; which watch their appearance, and destroy them. The last is on that account called, in some parts of America, the Beaver-eater. They are very easily overcome; for they make no resistance: and have no security but in flight.' But Cartwright corrects this: 'They have been known to bite the leg of a dog almost off at one stroke: for which reason I cannot think that an Otter can kill an old beaver, but young ones make no resistance.'

On p. 105, Cartwright completes his notes on beavers, after Pennant's statement that the Indians, on the discovery of America, seem to have paid little attention to them. 'The flesh of the Beaver being the most delicious of any which I have ever tasted, and the animal abounding in the northern parts of America and easily killed I must suppose that the Indians did not neglect them; but as their skins are heavy & the fur coarse they probably threw them away. They are now so much sought after, both for food and traffic, that their numbers diminish. The largest I ever saw was forty-five pounds when paunched'.

APPENDIX 1

On page 109, Pennant's account of the porcupine includes the paragraph: 'The size of one, which Sir Joseph Banks brought from Newfoundland, was about that of a Hare, but more compactly made; the back arched; and the whole form resembling that of the Beaver: the tail is six inches long, which, in walking, is carried a little bent upwards. This species inhabits America from Hudson's Bay to Canada, Newfoundland, New England . . . '. Cartwright's marginal note is, 'A mistake, for they were never found in Newfoundland'.

On p. 135, Pennant discussed the migrations of voles in Siberia, much of his information being derived from Pallas, as he says (see also *A Naturalist in Russia, letters from Peter Simon Pallas to Thomas Pennant*, edited by Carol Urness, 1967, pp. 83, 99). Cartwright notes in the margin: 'The Field or Grassmice of Labrador, migrate also, I believe, for at the end of the summer of 1785 few or none were to be found even where they used to be in the greatest plenty, and that winter Foxes and Martens were very scarce. Possibly they might have had an instinctive intimation that there would be several thaws in the winter which would form all the lower part of the snow into ice and kill them. For these mice keep underground in the Summer, but after the snow falls come on the surface, where they collect grass and form a nest like the Dormice and by means of galleries which they work under the snow go out among the grass and seek their food. The Reindeer also, that winter, migrated in great numbers to the Sea coasts.'

There is only one other note of Cartwright's in this volume, on p. 145, where Pennant said that the Eskimos purchase walrus teeth for the tips of their seal-darts from the Indians of Nuckvank; Cartwright adds that those people were 'a tribe of Eskimaux'.

The second volume of the *Arctic Zoology* contains far fewer of Cartwright's notes, and is disappointing in that he adds nothing to Pennant's observations on the Pied, i.e. Labrador Duck, now extinct. Pennant's notes on the Eskimo Curlew were derived from Banks. Cartwright adds (p. 461): 'These birds always make their first appearance on the coast of Labrador between the 28th of July and the 8th of August, and are to be met with in the greatest abundance every where along the sea coast where the ground is clear of timber and provides plenty of heath-berries. At their first coming they are lean, but soon grow very fat. In general they are plentyful till the middle of September, and some few are to be met with as late as the middle of October, but hard gales of wind from the N.W. to the N.E. cause them to migrate sooner. They are never seen on their return to the northward. Some few are double the size of the rest, and not so delicious. I have known a man shoot 150 in a day.'

On p. 468, Cartwright deletes Stone Curlew, which Pennant, quoting Banks, gave as the colloquial name for the Greater Yellowlegs, and inserts 'Aunt Sary: are common in Labrador in the summer time, and in greatest plenty on flat muddy shores.'

On p. 492, Cartwright comments on the Crake in England: 'Breed in great numb-bers in many meadows in England, particularly those on the banks of the river Trent, and when the grass is cut they migrate to Summersetshire.' Cartwright's family home at Marnham, between Lincoln and Tuxford, was on the Trent; I have not traced his connection with Somerset.

His notes on the breeding of the Razor-bill, p. 509: 'These birds breed on rocky islands which lay near the coasts of Newfoundland, where they are called Tinkers. They creep under hollow rocks where they lay one egg on the bare rock, which is bluish white, spotted black and weighs near four ounces'. On the Black Guillemot, p. 516, he adds: 'They do breed in Newfoundland and Labrador in the same manner as the Tinkers do, but lay two eggs. They are there called Sea Pidgeons. They live on fish yet the young ones are very fat and delicious before they leave the nest, and the old birds are always plump and good. The young ones cry like young common Pidgeons.'

On p. 512, Pennant wrote of the Little Auk: 'Is called in Newfoundland, the Ice-bird, being the harbinger of ice.' Cartwright adds 'better known by the name of Bull.'

Pennant had no information on the breeding habits of the Great Black-backed Gull, p. 257. Cartwright adds: 'They breed on small islands on the coasts of Newfoundland & Labrador where they are called Saddlebacks. They build their nests on the eminencies [*sic*] of heath, lay three eggs which are white spotted black, thick at one end and small at the other, and weigh four ounces. They keep a very good look-out, and on sight of a man fly round him at a considerable height making a loud noise which is well known to be a signal of danger by all the beasts and birds in those countries, of course they immediately look to themselves. The young ones are good to eat.'

On Canada Geese, p. 544, he writes: 'These birds breed also in Newfoundland & Labrador. They are a delicious bird, and when fat will come up to fifteen pounds weight. They do not breed till in their third year, and in general weigh twelve pounds.'

Appendix 2

Palliser's notes on the chart of Chateau Bay, reproduced in pl. 30, are given below. The chart shows the final position of the blockhouse built by the marines of the *Niger*; it lies on the point separating Pitt's Harbour from Grenville Harbour.

'This Bay lies N 16° W^d by Compass 8½ Leag^s from Cape De Grat in Newfoundland and N 11¾ W^d 5 Leag^s from the SW: end of Belle Isle, it may be known by two very remarkable Rocks on Castle and Henly (*sic*) Islands, which are flat at top and from the steepness of the Rock all round has much the resemblance of Castle Walls, and likewise by five or Six small Islands to the Eastward but no Islands to the Westward of it which is a even bold Shore. To Sail into it keep Point Grenville either Just open or Just shut with the Point of Henley Island, giving the Shagg Rocks a proper birth, and steer into the Harbour between the Shoal in the Entrance and black Rock, which lies off the Point of Henley Isl^d keeping within half a Cable's length of the Rock, this Passage is recommended only to those who are unacquainted because, the black Rock is a good mark to Sail in by, but as the two Points before mention'd cannot be easily distinguish'd by strangers, they best leave 1/3 of the Bay, on the Starboard Side untill Seal Island is brought behind Henley Island, then Edge over towards Esquimeaux Island, & observe the foregoing Directions.—There is exceedingly good Anchors Ground in all the different Branches of this Harbour, particularly in Pitts Harbour, which must be recommended for Kings Ships, as having the most room & being the most convenient for Wooding and Watering.

The Fisheries here will now soon be very considerable, here being great plenty of Cod, Whale and Seal, & Temple Bay & Pitts Harbour afford plenty of Timber for Building, such as Fur (*sic*), Spruce, Juniper & Birch,—

The two remarkable Rocks above mention'd resembling Castles are not distinguishable at a distance, because of the higher land within them, therefore the best direction for knowing the Bay when at a Distance is as follows.—

All the Land to the Westward of it is high, of a Uniform even figure Sloping away to nothing to the Westward & terminating to the Eastward over this Bay with a conspicuous Nobb from which it is a steep Cliff. This Nobb or hillock is on the West Side of Temple Bay, all the Land about Chateaux, and to the Eastward of it is hilly and uneven with many Islands along shore but no Islands to the Westward of it, Cape Charles makes with a high Hill steep towards the Sea sloping inland, so that when you are to the Westward of Chateaux, Cape Charles will make an Island. The Marks above mention'd for leading up the Bay are not easily distinguish'd by a stranger, because the Shore about Point Grenville makes in several Points, therefore to make it known a beacon is erected on it with a Cross and a cask upon it. Henley Point is easily known by the Black Rock just above Water at a Cables length from it. There is also a beacon upon the low neck of Castle Island, keep that Beacon on with the outer Shag Rock, leads you clear of the middle Rock, between it and the spit of Whale Island, then bring the outer Point of Castle Island a little open with the Point of Whale Island leads up into Pitts Harbour.—'

Palliser's notes on the situation and construction of the blockhouse, the building of which was the reason for the large complement of marines carried in the *Niger* in 1766. The plan referred to is reproduced in pl. 31.

'An Account of the Block House and Stockaded Fort Erected at Pitts Harbour in Labrador, the Object of which is for the Protection and Encouragement of His Majesty's Subjects to carry on the Fisheries on that Coast, for security of their Boats & Fishing Craft and Tackle from being Stolen or distroyed by the Savages of the Country or by Lawless Crews resorting thither from the Colonies. It is Situated on a point of Land on the Northside of Pitts Harbour that forms the Entrance to that Harbour, it has an absolute Command of that Harbour, also of the Adjacent Harbours——likewise Commands the Principal entrance to them all from Chateaux Bay, the ground on which it stands is 25 Feet above high Water Mark, is a long narrow peice of Ground almost a level, and elevated above the swampy Ground (which partly surrounds it) 23 Feet, the Bank in some places has but a very small inclination from a Perpendicular down to the swamp, so that it is like a long narrow Island, and has an Excellent Command over every part it is intended to protect, round the Point at the foot of the Bank immediately under the Fort, any Number of Boats and Craft may be haul'd up and secur'd in the Winter.—

This Block House is an Oblong Square, intirely compos'd of large Timber dove tail'd and well treenail'd together, which renders it exceeding Strong, and is proof against Swivel and Musquet Shot.—it has two Stories and consists of two Rooms on each Floor, the largest on the Ground Fllor is 26 Feet by 16 Feet in the Clear, the other is 18 Feet by 16 Feet, the Upper story on Account of its having a Machicouli defence is 14 Inches under all round, the two largest Rooms are intended for the Garrison, and the two smaller for Officers Appartments.—

There are Windows and Port holes sufficient to receive 20 small Cannon or Swivel Guns, loop holes are also made at proper distances for Wall peices as well as for small arms.—

This Country being Subjected to deep Snows may in some measure render the lower part of the Block House defenceless in Winter, therefore Swivels and Wall Pieces may be fix'd in the upper floor, and on occasion the Cannon likewise may be got up, there being Port Holes for them the same as below.—The floors above and below are laid with 2 Inch Plank—the inside of the House lin'd with 1 Inch Board, the outside batten'd with rough Boards to make it as warm as possible.—between the Jaumbes of the Chimney is a Well of very fine Water, over which is Erected an Oven, adjoining to the Officers Appartments is a Powder Magazine Built with Stone and Arch'd over.

This House will receive 40 Men and on occasion will Admit 60.—

This Block House is Surrounded with a regular Stockaded Fort of four Bastions, the outside of the Square being 150 feet, the faces 42 feet, Flanks 16 Feet and Curtains 64 feet long each.—the Pallisadoes are very strong and 7 Feet high, are just as close together as they well can stand, there is a Banquet all round the inside of the Pallisadoes 4 Feet wide, and 2 Feet: 6 Ins. high, the Saliant Angles of each Bastion are rais'd higher than the Banquet, on which is a Platform, and on each a 3 Pounder mounted, which pointing above the Tops of the Pallisadoes form a Barbet battery, and have an absolute Command of the Place where the Fishing Craft are to be haul'd up, as well as all round the Fort.—there is Stocks for Swivels in each Flank to scouer the Ditch, and in the Curtains for Wall Peices, all which in the Winter may be brought into the House.—

The Ditch on acount of the great difficulty in Digging it, could not be compleated, but it is Mark'd out and Sunk to different Depths all round.—there is a small space left for a foot way across the Ditch immediately opposite the entrance to the Fort, where is hung a strong Barrier Gate,—there is likewise a Covert way, at the extremity of which a row of slanting Pallisadoes pointing outwards is carry'd all round the Fort and Block House, which defence with what has already been mention'd is sufficient to prevent a surprise or the place being taken by a Coup de Main.—

This Block House with this double security is capable of being defended against a great Number of Men except Cannon should be brought against it, and is too formidable to be ever attack'd by the Savages of the Country.—

	References to the Plan of the Harbour	Distance from the Fort	Perpendicular Height above high Water Mark
		Feet	Feet
	Level of the Fort		25
A	Places for hauling up, and securing Boats	400	5
B	Watering Place for Ships		
C	Hill opposite the Fort	4800	620
	Pitts look out	6800	600
	Highest part of Whale Island	6400	303
	D⁰ of Henley Island	5000	223
D	Hill opposite Henley Island	4000	120
E	D⁰ immediately over another place fit for hauling up Boats	3200	74

APPENDIX 2

Abstract of   All the Timber for the House and Picketing was Cut in Temple
the Expence   Bay and Pitts Harbour.—

                Paid for Labour to Men belonging to the Kings Ships   £236:5:0

                D⁰ Contract Artificers   143:3:0

                Cost of Materials carry'd from the Stores at St. John's   70:0:0

The place was pitch'd on & the Work begun the 10th Aug^t & finish'd the 30th
September.—   £449:0:0'

There is another note in a later hand on pl. 30, which is: 'Notes added by Hugh Palliser encl. in Palliser to Shelburne. London 10 Dec., 1766'.

General index

SINCE Joseph Banks is the subject of this book I have made no attempt to index all the page references to him other than those relevant to selected entries. I hope that these, together with the list of contents, will make it relatively simple for readers to find any special facts relating to him. For similar reasons there are relatively few entries under Newfoundland and Labrador. Letters and papers are indexed alphabetically under Letters. The names of persons are for the most part indexed without titles, but when anyone is more widely known under his or her title, e.g. the Duchess of Portland, Lord Sandwich, entries are placed under that title. Names of ships' captains and lieutenants are given with their respective ranks. References to ships are listed separately under Ships, although in some of the sub-headings in other comprehensive entries there are a few additional references to the *Endeavour* and the *Niger*. Most of the references to books and papers are given under the name of the author, but in a few cases where the title of the book or paper is referred to in the text it is indexed separately. References to the *Arctic Zoology* are, however, given under the title since the author, Thomas Pennant, is mentioned in so many other connections. In the case of popular names of plants and animals there is only a minimal amount of cross-referring to the scientific index, since scientists will in any case use that index, and the general reader who wishes to find the scientific name can do so by turning to the appropriate pages of text.

I should like to thank various friends, most of whom are mentioned in the acknowledgements, who have helped me to sort and check the entries, particularly Dr. Shukla Sen Gupta and her husband, Mr. Kalyan Sen Gupta, who undertook the arduous preliminary sorting of the index cards into alphabetical order.

GENERAL INDEX

GENERAL INDEX

Caribou 167, 448; Cartwright's pet calf 82

Caribou Islands 203

Carpik 84

Carter, H. 43

Cartier, J. 165, 182

Cartwright, Catherine, 72, 87; and Caubvick 87

Cartwright, Edmund 72, 73; memorial exhibition 87

Cartwright, F. D. 86

Cartwright, George
acts as chaplain 78, as doctor and midwife 76–7; as nurse 87
Arctic Zoology annotated by 443–9
Banks, Joseph, collects plants and animals for 49, 79, 99, 265, 266, 267, 268, 330, 409
Banks and Solander, suggests visit from 79, 266 and see Letters
barrack-master at Nottingham 79
Baskem, kindness to family of 57
biographical sketch of 71–9
Cook, Captain, comparison with 77, 78
doves observed by 266
education of 73, 75
Eskimos, relations with 83–8; ambitions regarding 84–5; becomes friendly with 85; first fears of 85; first visit to 85; poem about them, 79; teaches them leapfrog 72; reports smallpox among them in Plymouth and Labrador 87, 260, 269; their visit to England with him 49, 86–8, 256
excursion to Scotland 74
gentleman defined by 74
journal, writing of 75, publication of 274–6
Labrador, decision to settle in 84–5, 246
losses at sea and bankruptcy 78–9
Lucas, Lieutenant, partner of 84
Marquis of Granby, aide to 73–4
memorial at Sandwich Bay, Labrador 79
Meteorological records of 73
military service 73–5
naturalist, observations as 9, 82, 170; on colour change 79–82; his pets 82–3; on soils 82; on probable destruction of Great Auks 167–8, of beavers 447
persuades his people to eat rank foxes 77–8
portrait of 78, pl. 22, facing p. 83

Cartwright, George (continued)
religious beliefs 78–9
robbed by privateer 77, 268
sails against smugglers 74; to Newfoundland in the *Guernsey* 41, 74–5
shipwreck, escapes from 78–9
'Truth and the heart' 57, 72, 75

Cartwright, John 41, 65, 72–4, 86, 335; account of the Beothuks 75n, 167; defends American independence, 73; sails against smugglers 74; with Eskimos in London 86; work with Palliser 73

Cartwright, Labrador, named after George and John 79

Casey, Captain 253

Castle Island, Bank's sketch of 28, fig. 3, p. 131

Castle Hedingham 90

Cat fish 121, 391

Catalogue of natural history productions, Bank's note on his 138

Catalogue of the Animals of North America or *Faunula Americana* by J. R. Forster 97, 251, 397–400, 407, 409, 411; Pennant's share of 97, 407

Caterpillar, Black see *Tipula nigra*

Catesby, Mark 37, 45–6, 90, 126, 159, 164, 248, 251

Catherine the Great inoculated against smallpox 262

Caubvick 24, 72, 87, 88, 256, 260, 269; and Catherine Cartwright 87; pl. 21b, facing p. 82

Cauliflower dissected by Banks 263

Causton see Cawsand

Cawsand 116

Centuria II Plantarum by Erik Törner 39n

Chain Rocks, St. John's 151

Chambers, J. D. 105

Chapman Memorial Fund 10

Chappeau Rouge 142

Char, Arctic 28, 169, 406 and see *Salvelinus*, pl. 87, following p. 408

Charity Schools 35

Charles Bay, Moravians and Adams meet Eskimos at 199, 202

Charles River, Cartwright's trading post at 84

Charts by James Cook and his assistants 69–71

GENERAL INDEX

GENERAL INDEX

Index of scientific names

THE arrangement followed in this list is alphabetical with these exceptions: the abbreviations var., sp. and subsp. have been ignored, and no account has been taken of prepositions and conjunctions. In the few cases where the same generic name is used for both plants and animals, e.g. *Mitella* and *Arenaria*, botanical species precede the zoological ones. The species in a single genus are listed consecutively, and any specific epithets similar to the name of the genus follow such a list. In general, no account is taken of upper and lower case initial letters, thus *mustela*, *Ciliata* precedes *Mustela erminea*. Some of Banks's misspellings have been retained but the correct name is also listed in the appropriate place.

Most cross-references are given only in the general index. Names of European species used by Banks for comparison when noting the size of a bird he was describing, have not been indexed save in one or two exceptional cases.

INDEX OF SCIENTIFIC NAMES

INDEX OF SCIENTIFIC NAMES

INDEX OF SCIENTIFIC NAMES

INDEX OF SCIENTIFIC NAMES

INDEX OF SCIENTIFIC NAMES

INDEX OF SCIENTIFIC NAMES

INDEX OF SCIENTIFIC NAMES

Empetrum eamesii Fern. & Wieg. was inadvertently omitted from the list of plants collected by Banks. His herbarium specimen is labelled 'On dry tops of hills, Croque, June 1766'. For a current review of the family Empetraceae see D. M. Moore, J. B. Harborne and Christine A. Williams. 1970. Chemotaxonomy, variation and geographical distribution of the Empetraceae. *Bot. J. Linn. Soc.* 63 : 277.93.